Lecture Notes in Artificial Intelligence   1228

Subseries of Lecture Notes in Computer Science
Edited by J. G. Carbonell and J. Siekmann

Lecture Notes in Computer Science

Edited by G. Goos, J. Hartmanis and J. van Leeuwen

Springer
Berlin
Heidelberg
New York
Barcelona
Budapest
Hong Kong
London
Milan
Paris
Santa Clara
Singapore
Tokyo

Shan-Hwei Nienhuys-Cheng   Ronald de Wolf

Foundations of Inductive Logic Programming

Springer

Series Editors

Jaime G. Carbonell, Carnegie Mellon University, Pittsburgh, PA, USA
Jörg Siekmann, University of Saarland, Saarbrücken, Germany

Authors

Shan-Hwei Nienhuys-Cheng
Ronald de Wolf
Erasmus University of Rotterdam, Department of Computer Science
P.O. Box 1738, 3000 DR Rotterdam, The Netherlands
E-mail: cheng@cs.few.eur.nl

Cataloging-in-Publication Data applied for

Die Deutsche Bibliothek - CIP-Einheitsaufnahme

Nienhuys-Cheng, Shan-Hwei:
Foundations of inductive logic programming / S.-H. Nienhuys-Cheng
; R. de Wolf. - Berlin ; Heidelberg ; New York ; Barcelona ;
Budapest ; Hong Kong ; London ; Milan ; Paris ; Santa Clara ;
Singapore ; Tokyo : Springer, 1997
 (Lecture notes in computer science ; 1228 : Lecture notes in artificial
 intelligence)
 ISBN 3-540-62927-0 kart.

CR Subject Classification (1991): I.2, F.4.1, D.1.6

ISBN 3-540-62927-0 Springer-Verlag Berlin Heidelberg New York

© Springer-Verlag Berlin Heidelberg 1997
Printed in Germany

Typesetting: Camera ready by author
SPIN 10549682   06/3142 – 5 4 3 2 1 0   Printed on acid-free paper

Foreword

One of the most interesting recent developments within the field of automated deduction is *inductive logic programming*, an area that combines logic programming with machine learning. Within a short time this area has grown to an impressive field, rich in spectacular applications and full of techniques calling for new theoretical insights.

This is the first book that provides a systematic introduction to the theoretical foundations of this area. It is a most welcome addition to the literature concerning learning, resolution, and logic programming.

The authors offer in this book a solid, scholarly presentation of the subject. By starting their presentation with a self-contained account of the resolution method and of the foundations of logic programming they enable the reader to place the theory of inductive logic programming in the right historical and mathematical perspective. By presenting in detail the theoretical aspects of all components of inductive logic programming they make it clear that this field has grown into an important area of theoretical computer science.

The presentation given by the authors also allows us to reevaluate the role of some, until now, isolated results in the field of resolution and yields an interesting novel framework that sheds new light on the use of first-order logic in computer science.

I would like to take this opportunity to congratulate the authors on the outcome of their work. I am sure this book will have an impact on the future of inductive logic programming.

March 1997
Krzysztof R. Apt
CWI and University of Amsterdam
The Netherlands

Contents

Contents

About the Book

Inductive logic programming (ILP) is a relatively young branch of machine learning. It is concerned with learning from examples, commonly called *induction*. The possible learning tasks include learning concept descriptions from instances of those concepts, finding regularities among large amounts of data, etc. The feature of ILP that distinguishes it from other branches of machine learning is its use of the framework provided by formal (clausal) logic. On the one hand, the use of logic in knowledge-based systems and problem solving has already been prominent in artificial intelligence (AI) for a long time. On the other hand, machine learning has also been recognized as a key subfield of AI. It seems only natural to combine these two, and to study learning in a logical framework. Hence ILP can be defined as the intersection of machine learning and logic programming.

Although inductive logic programming can be traced back to the work of Plotkin and Reynolds around 1970 and the work of Shapiro in the early 1980s, many researchers have only turned to ILP in the last 5 to 10 years. In these years, the operational side of ILP has been well served: many ILP systems have been implemented and applied quite succesfully to various real-world learning tasks. However, the theoretical side of much work in ILP is sometimes less than optimal. As with many other young fields of research, many of the main concepts and results of ILP are only available in research papers, widely scattered over numerous journals, conference proceedings, and technical reports. As a consequence, concepts are not always uniformly defined, definitions are sometimes imprecise or unclear, and results and proofs are not always correct.

Hence we feel that a unified, rigorous, self-contained book which gives the theoretical basis of ILP is needed. We have written this book to fill that need.

Some existing books on logic could partly serve as a theoretical basis for the logical component of ILP, in particular the book by Chang and Lee [CL73] on theorem proving for general clauses, and the books by Lloyd [Llo87], Doets [Doe94], and Apt [Apt97] on logic programming. However, both Horn clauses and general clauses are sometimes used in ILP, so both should be covered. Existing logic books usually address only one of these, instead of giving a unified treatment of both. Moreover, those books discuss resolution-based theorem proving only in relation to the *refutation completeness*, which is a completeness result for proof by contradiction. Actually, a different completeness result, called the *Subsumption Theorem*, provides a much more "direct" form of completeness than refutation completeness. The Subsumption Theorem gives us a more clear view of the structure of logical implication, which makes it a very powerful and important tool for theoretical analysis in clausal logic in general, and ILP in particular. It is used in many articles on ILP (though not always correctly). Therefore, Part I of the present book, which covers both general clauses and Horn clauses, and includes proofs of several versions of the Subsumption Theorem, is better suited as a basis for the logical component of ILP than existing books. In fact, this first part of the book can be seen as a basis for clausal logic in general.

In Part II of the book, we consider the "learning" component of ILP: induction. This is not discussed in the logic books mentioned above. A number of books related to this learning component have appeared in recent years, but these are generally more oriented towards practice than theory, and typically focus, after a brief general introduction, on one or more particular systems implemented by their authors: [BGS91] focuses on ML-SMART, [DR92] is about CLINT, [MWKE93] is about a series of related systems (particularly MOBAL), [LD94] devotes most attention to LINUS, and [BG96a] is largely devoted to FILP and TRACY. There also exist two collections of ILP papers [Mug92a, DR96]. Though these contain some important papers, they do not provide a unified and self-contained introduction to the field.

Other than earlier books on ILP, the present work neither contains detailed descriptions of existing implemented systems nor case studies of applications. Instead, we intend to explicate here what we regard as the foundations of the field. We give a unified treatment of the main concepts of ILP, illustrated by many examples, and prove the main theoretical results. The book is intended both as a reference book for researchers and as an introduction to ILP from the theoretical perspective. We hope in this work to provide the reader with a sound and sufficiently broad theoretical basis for future research, as well as implementation and application of ILP.

Before giving a quick overview of the book in the following pages, we want to express our gratitude to Krzysztof Apt, who wrote the foreword and gave some very helpful comments concerning the logic programming part of the book. Furthermore, we would like to thank Akihiro Yamamoto and Tamás Horváth, who each read parts of the manuscript and gave many valuable comments. Finally, thanks should go to Springer and its editors Alfred Hofmann and Andrew Ross, for their co-operation and help in publishing this book.

March 1997
Shan-Hwei Nienhuys-Cheng and Ronald de Wolf
Rotterdam
The Netherlands

An Overview of the Book

ILP is concerned with learning a general theory from examples, within a logical framework. Accordingly, its foundations are twofold: one component concerns *logic* (deduction), the other concerns *learning* (induction). This is reflected in the structure of the book. In the first part, Chapters 1–8, we introduce the logical framework that we need. This part is not concerned with induction, so it can be seen as a self-contained introduction to logic programming. The second part of the book, Chapters 9–19, discusses various concepts and techniques that form the fundamentals of learning within logic. Below we give a brief overview of these two parts.

Logic

Chapters 1 and **2** introduce propositional logic and first-order logic. In particular, these chapters define the concepts of a well-formed formula, an interpretation of a language, and logical implication. In ILP, most often we use only a special kind of formula, called a *clause*, and a special kind of interpretation, called a *Herbrand* interpretation. These are introduced in **Chapter 3**.

Then in **Chapters 4–8**, we turn to several ways in which logical implication between clauses can be characterized. We define various proof procedures for this: "unconstrained" resolution (**Chapters 4** and **5**) and linear and input resolution (**Chapter 6**) for general clauses, and SLD-resolution for *Horn* clauses (**Chapter 7**).

For each of these forms of resolution, we prove two completeness results: the Subsumption Theorem and refutation completeness. In the standard literature on resolution, only the latter is given. Though the two results can be proved from each other for the forms of resolution we consider, the Subsumption Theorem is a more direct form of completeness than refutation completeness, and hence sometimes more useful for theoretical analysis.

The first part of the book ends with **Chapter 8**, where we discuss SLDNF-resolution. This is SLD-resolution augmented with a technique for handling negative information. It forms the basis of the logic programming language PROLOG.

Inductive Logic Programming

The introductory **Chapter 9** characterizes ILP by means of two different problem settings. In the *normal* setting, we have to find a theory (a finite set of clauses) that is correct with respect to given example-clauses, taking any given background knowledge into account. In the *nonmonotonic* setting, particularly suited for the task of data mining, the examples are interpretations, and we have to find a theory that conforms to those interpretations. In either setting, we have to *search* for an appropriate theory, using generalization and specialization steps to adjust a theory to fit the examples. If some particular approach mainly uses specialization, it is called a "top-down" approach. If its general direction of search is generalization, it is a "bottom-up" approach.

In **Chapters 10** and **11**, we discuss two early and very influential ideas: Shapiro's framework for model inference, and Muggleton and Buntine's inverse resolution. Except for a few topics in Chapter 10, these chapters serve mainly as illustrations of ILP and as motivation for the study of *generality orders* later on. Hence they are somewhat more informal and sketchy than most of the other chapters.

Chapter 10 introduces the main elements of Shapiro's top-down approach. However, the most important element in his approach, the *refinement operator*, can be defined for different languages and different generality orders. This means that refinement operators can be discussed fully only after we have thoroughly investigated the properties of different orders. Therefore we postpone the discussion of refinement operators to **Chapter 17**, including in **Chapter 10** only a brief introduction.

Inverse resolution, introduced in **Chapter 11**, is one of the most prominent generalization operators used in bottom-up approaches to ILP. It is based on the idea that induction is roughly the dual of deduction. Since resolution is our main tool for deduction, its inverse can be used for induction.

In **Chapter 12** we formulate the top-down dual to inverse resolution, using resolvents to specialize an overly general theory. This is called *unfolding*, which we use to define UDS specialization, a specialization technique based on unfolding, clause deletion and subsumption. We prove that UDS specialization is complete: every specialization problem has a UDS specialization as solution.

Actually, the terms 'specialization' and 'generalization' only make sense within a *generality order*. This is an ordering relation that defines which clauses can be called a generalization (or, dually, a specialization) of which other clauses. Different generality orders are possible, and they can be applied to different languages of clauses.

We investigate the properties of the most important of these orders in **Chapters 13–16**. In **Chapter 13**, we give our main definitions. These concern *least* generalizations and *greatest* specializations of finite sets of clauses, the *lattice* structure of ordered sets of clauses, and upward and downward *covers* of individual clauses. In the same chapter, these concepts are applied to atoms, arguably the simplest interesting language. The generality order for atoms of that chapter is *subsumption*. In **Chapter 14** we extend the subsumption order from atoms to clauses. **Chapter 15** discusses the properties of logical implication as a generality order on clauses. In **Chapter 16**, we will see how we can take background knowledge into account within these generality orders.

As already mentioned, **Chapter 17** examines refinement operators. We investigate both downward and upward refinement operators. The former are designed for specialization, the latter for generalization. **Chapter 18** describes the framework of *probably approximately correct learning*, as well as the ILP results that have been obtained within this framework. Finally, in **Chapter 19** we briefly discuss a number of topics that have been touched on only marginally earlier, such as *language bias, predicate invention, noise handling*, and *implementation*.

In the graph below, we have indicated the dependency relations among the various chapters of our book. An arrow from A to B means that chapter B presupposes concepts, results, or motivation given in chapter A.

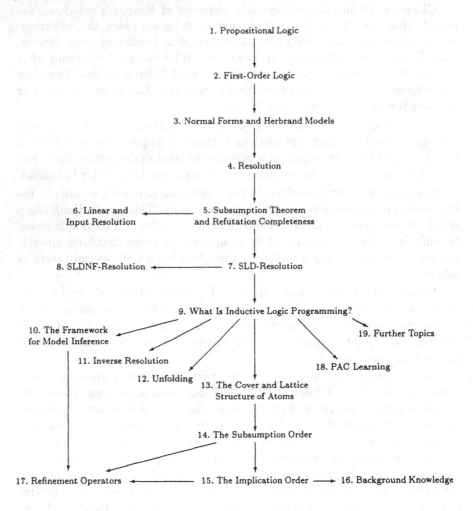

1. Propositional Logic

2. First-Order Logic

3. Normal Forms and Herbrand Models

4. Resolution

6. Linear and Input Resolution   5. Subsumption Theorem and Refutation Completeness

8. SLDNF-Resolution   7. SLD-Resolution

9. What Is Inductive Logic Programming?

10. The Framework for Model Inference

19. Further Topics

11. Inverse Resolution

18. PAC Learning

12. Unfolding

13. The Cover and Lattice Structure of Atoms

14. The Subsumption Order

17. Refinement Operators   15. The Implication Order   16. Background Knowledge

Part I

Logic

Chapter 1

Propositional Logic

1.1 Introduction

Propositional logic is a formalization of some simple forms of reasoning. For example, suppose we know the following sentences (the premises) to be true:

"If I swim, then I will get wet."
"If I take a shower, then I will get wet."

From these sentences, we are justified to conclude:

"If I swim or I take a shower, then I will get wet."

Propositional logic is able to capture the form of this argument. Let P represent "I swim", let Q represent "I take a shower", and let R stand for "I will get wet". Each of these sentences may be either true or false. Then the premises can be rephrased to:

If P, then R.
If Q, then R.

and the conclusion becomes:

If P or Q, then R.

That this is indeed a valid argument (i.e., if the premises are true, the conclusion must also be true), can be explained in propositional logic.

George Boole [Boo58] is usually regarded as the founder of propositional logic, though traces of it can already be found in the stoic philosophers of Greek antiquity. In this chapter we will introduce those parts of propositional logic which are necessary for a thorough understanding of the rest of this work. We discuss propositional logic for two reasons. First, to facilitate the introduction of first-order logic in the next chapter. Propositional logic resembles first-order logic in a number of ways, but is much simpler. It is in fact *embedded* in first-order logic. Accordingly, an introduction to propositional logic will facilitate understanding first-order logic. The second reason for this introduction is the fact that many concepts of the later chapters can be better illustrated by examples using propositional logic, than by examples in first-order logic. If the concepts of propositional logic are sufficient to express something, it is preferable to avoid using the more complex features of first-order logic. Hence we will use propositional logic where possible, avoiding unnecessary complexity.

There are two sides to propositional logic: on the one hand we have *syntax* (or grammar), which specifies which sequences of symbols are considered *well-formed*. On the other hand stands *semantics*, which specifies the relations between those well-formed sequences, and their truth or falsity.

1.2 Syntax

Every formal language has a *syntax*: an exact specification of which sequences of which symbols are allowed (considered *well-formed*), and which are not. Thus syntax starts with a specification of the *alphabet* of the language: the set of symbols from which well-formed sequences are constructed. Here is the definition for the propositional logic.

Definition 1.1 An *alphabet* of the propositional logic consists of the following symbols:

1. A non-empty set of *atoms*: P, Q, etc. These may be subscripted, so P_1, P_2, etc. are also allowed as atoms.
2. The following five *connectives*: $\neg$, $\wedge$, $\vee$, $\rightarrow$, and $\leftrightarrow$.
3. Two *punctuation symbols*: '(' and ')'.   ◇

With every possible set of atoms corresponds a different alphabet, but each alphabet has the same five connectives, and the same two punctuation symbols. Using the symbols from the alphabet, we can form sequences of symbols. The set of well-formed sequences (formulas) is defined as follows.

Definition 1.2 *Well-formed formulas* (usually just called *formulas*) are defined as follows:

1. An atom is a formula.
2. If ϕ is a formula, then $\neg\phi$ is a formula.
3. If ϕ and ψ are formulas, then $(\phi \wedge \psi)$, $(\phi \vee \psi)$, $(\phi \rightarrow \psi)$ and $(\phi \leftrightarrow \psi)$ are formulas.   ◇

The simplest kind of formula is an atom. A formula which is not an atom, for example $\neg P$, or $(P \vee Q)$, is called a *composite* formula.

Example 1.3 The following sequences of symbols are all examples of formulas, assuming that the atoms used here are all in the alphabet:

- P
- $(P \vee R)$
- $(\neg(P \wedge Q) \to (\neg P \vee Q))$
- $(\neg\neg(P \wedge (Q \vee R)) \leftrightarrow (P_1 \to (Q \vee R_2)))$

The following sequences are *not* formulas, since they cannot be "generated" by applying the rules of Definition 1.2:

- (P), the parentheses should be left out.
- $P \vee Q$, this is no formula because, strictly speaking, it should be surrounded by parentheses according to rule no. 2 of Definition 1.2. However, in Section 1.4 we will loosen this restriction somewhat.
- $(P \vee Q \vee R)$ is not a formula, since the placing of parentheses is not in accordance with Definition 1.2 (though see Section 1.4).
- $(P \vee (Q \wedge \to R))$, the sequence '$\wedge \to$' cannot be generated by the three rules in our syntax definition.
- $((P \vee Q) \leftrightarrow \neg\neg P \to Q)$, some parentheses are left out. There are several places where pairs of parentheses can be inserted in this sequence to turn it into a formula. For instance, $((P \vee Q) \leftrightarrow (\neg\neg P \to Q))$, $((P \vee Q) \leftrightarrow \neg(\neg P \to Q))$ and $(((P \vee Q) \leftrightarrow \neg\neg P) \to Q)$ are formulas.

◁

Definition 1.4 The *propositional language* given by an alphabet is the set of all (well-formed) formulas which can be constructed from the symbols of the alphabet. ◇

If alphabet $\mathcal{A}_1$ and alphabet $\mathcal{A}_2$ are different—that is, if the set of atoms belonging to $\mathcal{A}_1$ is different from the set of atoms belonging to $\mathcal{A}_2$—then the propositional language given by $\mathcal{A}_1$ is different from the propositional language given by $\mathcal{A}_2$. Note that a propositional language is always an infinite set, even if the set of atoms in the alphabet contains only one atom.

1.3 Semantics

In the last section, we gave a specification of the concept of a propositional language: the set of (well-formed) formulas which can be constructed from some alphabet. In this section we define the *semantics* of this set. This is where a formula acquires its meaning. A formula can be either true or false, depending on the truth or falsity of the simpler formulas which are its components. For instance, the truth or falsity of $(P \vee Q)$ depends on its components P and Q. Thus we can trace the truth or falsity of some formula all the way back to its smallest elements. These smallest elements are the atoms, which are simply given a value 'true' or 'false' according to some *interpretation*.

1.3.1 Informally

Before giving the formal semantics for the propositional logic, let us explain roughly how the meaning of a formula depends on the simpler formulas and connectives it contains. Since five connectives can be used to construct composite formulas, we can consider five different kinds of composite formulas. Below we will discuss each of these in turn, informally explaining what they mean.

1. First, formulas of the form $\neg\phi$, where ϕ is an arbitrary formula. The connective used here ('$\neg$') is called *negation*. We say the formula $\neg\phi$ is true if the formula ϕ is false, and we say $\neg\phi$ is false if ϕ is true. From this, we see that the connective '$\neg$' can be used to model the way the word 'not' is used in English: "$\neg\phi$ is true if, and only if, ϕ is not true". Thus the formula $\neg\phi$ is pronounced as "not ϕ".

2. Second, formulas of the form $(\phi \wedge \psi)$, where ϕ and ψ are arbitrary formulas. A formula of this form is called a *conjunction*. We say that the formula $(\phi \wedge \psi)$ is true if and only if both components of the formula (i.e., ϕ and ψ) are true. This is similar to the way the word 'and' is used in English: we can say that the sentence "John is 25 years old and John is married" is true if, and only if, the components "John is 25 years old" and "John is married" are both true. Accordingly, $(\phi \wedge \psi)$ is pronounced as "ϕ and ψ".

3. Third, formulas of the form $(\phi \vee \psi)$. A formula of this form is called a *disjunction*. We say that the formula $(\phi \vee \psi)$ is true if and only if at least one of the components of the formula (i.e., ϕ or ψ) is true. This is similar to the way the word 'or' is used in English. Thus $(\phi \wedge \psi)$ is pronounced as "ϕ or ψ". Note that by 'or', we mean 'and/or' here: $(\phi \vee \psi)$ is true if ϕ is true, if ψ is true, or if ϕ and ψ are *both* true.

4. Fourth, formulas of the form $(\phi \rightarrow \psi)$. Such a formula is called an *implication*. By this connective, we want to model the way 'if...then' is used in English. Therefore, $(\phi \rightarrow \psi)$ is pronounced as "if ϕ then ψ", or as "ϕ implies ψ". We model 'if...then' by saying that $(\phi \rightarrow \psi)$ is false just in case ϕ is true and ψ is false (i.e., in English we cannot call "if ϕ is true, then ψ is true" a true sentence if we observe that ϕ is true, but ψ is false), and true otherwise.

   Note that we say $(\phi \rightarrow \psi)$ is true in case ϕ is false, no matter what ψ is. This may seem strange at first: why would "if ϕ, then ψ" be true if ϕ is false? But in fact this way of using the symbol '$\rightarrow$' is not so remote from the way we sometimes use 'if...then' in natural language. Consider for example the case where person A is extremely angry at person B. A might then say for instance to B "If you beg me ten billion times to calm down, I will forgive you". Obviously, the 'if' condition is not true, because B won't beg ten billion times. Yet this 'if...then' sentence certainly makes sense, and it can in a way be said that the sentence is true, independently of the fact whether or not A actually will forgive B.

5. Fifth, formulas of the form $(\phi \leftrightarrow \psi)$. Such a formula is called an *equivalence*. The formula $(\phi \leftrightarrow \psi)$ is similar to the combination of the formulas $(\phi \rightarrow \psi)$ and $(\psi \rightarrow \phi)$. The connective '$\leftrightarrow$' is used to model the English words 'if, and only if'. Thus the formula is pronounced as "ϕ if, and only if, ψ", or as "ϕ is equivalent to ψ". We say $(\phi \leftrightarrow \psi)$ is true if ϕ and ψ are both true, or both false, and $(\phi \leftrightarrow \psi)$ is false otherwise.

Example 1.5 Let L be the propositional language which has $\{P, Q, R\}$ as its set of atoms. Using the concepts defined so far, we can formalize—in terms of the language L—the example given in the introduction to this chapter. Let P represent "I swim", let Q represent "I take a shower", and let R stand for "I will get wet". Then the premises of the example can be represented by:

$(P \rightarrow R)$, or "If I swim, then I will get wet".
$(Q \rightarrow R)$, or "If I take a shower, then I will get wet".

and the conclusion becomes:

$((P \lor Q) \rightarrow R)$, or "If I swim or I take a shower, then I will get wet".

$\triangleleft$

1.3.2 Interpretations

We will now formalize the informal meaning explained in the previous section. A key concept in formal semantics is the *interpretation* of a language. The interpretation defines which atoms of the language are true, and which are false. An interpretation "sets the stage" for determining whether or not some complex formula is true or false. For example, if we use atoms P and Q to denote the sentences "My dog is outside" and "My cat is outside", respectively, then we need to know the truth or falsity of these atoms to be able to determine the truth or falsity of the more complex sentence "My dog is outside and my cat is outside". So knowledge of the truth or falsity of atoms (that is, knowledge of the interpretation), is the first step to determining the truth or falsity of arbitrary complex formulas.

Definition 1.6 Let L be a propositional language. Let $\mathcal{A}$ be the set of atoms of L. Then an *interpretation* of L is a mapping from $\mathcal{A}$ to $\{T, F\}$. T and F are called *truth values*. $\diamond$

An interpretation I can be efficiently expressed as a subset of the atomset $\mathcal{A}$, namely $I = \{A \in \mathcal{A} \mid I(A) = T\}$. So in this representation, I is the set of all atoms in $\mathcal{A}$ that are assigned T by I.

Example 1.7 Let $\mathcal{A}$, the set of all atoms of the language, be $\{P, Q, R\}$. Then an example of an interpretation I is:

$I(P) = T$,
$I(Q) = F$,
$I(R) = T$.

In the "subset representation", $I = \{P, R\}$.
Another possible interpretation I', is the following:

$$I'(P) = T,$$
$$I'(Q) = T,$$
$$I'(R) = F.$$

Which can be represented as $I' = \{P, Q\}$.   ◁

Note that if the set of all atoms contains n atoms, then 2^n different interpretations are possible, since each of the n atoms can be assigned T or F independently of the assignment to the other atoms. Thus in Example 1.7, the set of possible interpretations is $\{\{\}, \{P\}, \{Q\}, \{R\}, \{P, Q\}, \{P, R\}, \{Q, R\}, \{P, Q, R\}\}$, which contains $8 = 2^3$ possible interpretations.

Usually we assume that the language L is fixed. When we give an example, we assume implicitly that the set of atoms of the language is the set of atoms used in the example, unless we state otherwise explicitly. In this case, we will just talk about interpretations, instead of interpretations *of L*.

The truth value of the atoms does not depend on other atoms—an atom is just *defined* to have some truth value by the interpretation I. The truth value of a composite formula, however, depends completely on the connectives and the truth values of the atoms it contains. For instance, the composite formula $(P \vee Q)$ has truth value T under I if, and only if, P and/or Q have truth value T under I. The way that the truth value of a composite formula depends on its components and connectives is laid out in so-called *truth tables*, one for each connective. These truth tables are combined in Table 1.1.

ϕ	ψ	$\neg\phi$	$(\phi \wedge \psi)$	$(\phi \vee \psi)$	$(\phi \rightarrow \psi)$	$(\phi \leftrightarrow \psi)$
T	T	F	T	T	T	T
T	F	F	F	T	F	F
F	T	T	F	T	T	F
F	F	T	F	F	T	T

Table 1.1: The truth table for the five connectives

The truth table should be read row-wise: each row specifies the truth value of a composite formula containing ϕ and ψ (or just ϕ in case of the negation) in regard of the truth values bestowed on ϕ and ψ in the first two columns of that row. Thus if ϕ has truth value T and ψ has truth value F, then we can see from the second row that $(\phi \rightarrow \psi)$ has truth value F.

Example 1.8 Let I be the interpretation $\{P\}$, and let ϕ be the formula $((P \wedge Q) \rightarrow Q)$. Working "bottom-up", we can use the truth table to determine the truth value of ϕ:

1. P has truth value T under I, Q has truth value F.

2. $(P \wedge Q)$ has truth value F.
3. ϕ has truth value T.

◁

Reasoning in the manner of the previous example, we can—given an interpretation I—determine the truth value of any formula, no matter how complex. Instead of the rather unintuitive "truth value", we can also use the following terminology:

Definition 1.9 Let ϕ be a formula, and I an interpretation. ϕ is said to be *true under* I if its truth value under I is T. I is then said to *satisfy* ϕ, or to *make* ϕ *true*.

ϕ is said to be *false under* I if its truth value is F under I. I is then said to *falsify* ϕ, or to *make* ϕ *false*. ◇

1.3.3 Models

The truth value of a formula usually[1] depends on the interpretation; under some interpretations the formula is true, under others it is false. If some formula ϕ is true under a particular interpretation I, then I is called a *model* of ϕ.

Definition 1.10 Let ϕ be a formula, and I an interpretation. I is said to be a *model* of ϕ if I satisfies ϕ. ϕ is then said to *have* I *as a model*. ◇

Example 1.11 Let $\{P, Q, R\}$ be the set of all atoms in the language, and ϕ be the formula $((P \wedge Q) \leftrightarrow (R \rightarrow Q))$. Let I be the interpretation that makes P and R true, and Q false (so $I = \{P, R\}$). We determine whether ϕ is true or false under I as follows:

1. P is true under I, and Q is false under I, so $(P \wedge Q)$ is false under I.
2. R is true under I, Q is false under I, so $(R \rightarrow Q)$ is false under I.
3. $(P \wedge Q)$ and $(R \rightarrow Q)$ are both false under I, so ϕ is true under I.

Since ϕ is true under I, I is a model of ϕ.

Let $I' = \{P\}$. Then $(P \wedge Q)$ is false, and $(R \rightarrow Q)$ is true under I'. Thus ϕ is false under I', and I' is not a model of ϕ. ◁

The definitions sofar only dealt with single formulas. In logic, one often has to deal with *sets* of formulas. The definition of a *model* can easily be generalized to this case.

Definition 1.12 Let Σ be a set of formulas, and I an interpretation. I is said to be a *model* of Σ if I is a model of all formulas $\phi \in \Sigma$. Σ is then said to *have* I *as a model*. ◇

---

[1]The only exceptions are *tautologies* and *contradictions*, see below.

Example 1.13 Let $\Sigma = \{P, (Q \vee R), (Q \to R)\}$, and let $I = \{P, R\}$, $I' = \{P, Q, R\}$, and $I'' = \{P, Q\}$ be interpretations. I and I' satisfy all formulas in Σ, so I and I' are models of Σ. On the other hand, I'' falsifies $(Q \to R)$, so I'' is not a model of Σ.   ◁

A very important concept is the concept of 'logical consequence'. Roughly, some formula ϕ is a logical consequence of some set of formulas, if the truth of all formulas in the set implies the truth of ϕ. This concept is defined as follows.

Definition 1.14 Let Σ be a set of formulas, and ϕ a formula. Then ϕ is said to be a *logical consequence* of Σ (written as $\Sigma \models \phi$), if every model of Σ is a model of ϕ. If $\Sigma \models \phi$, we also sometimes say that Σ *logically implies* (or just *implies*) ϕ. If $\Sigma = \{\psi\}$, this can be written as $\psi \models \phi$.   ◇

Definition 1.15 Let Σ and Γ be sets of formulas. Then Γ is said to be a *logical consequence* of Σ (written as $\Sigma \models \Gamma$), if $\Sigma \models \phi$, for every formula $\phi \in \Gamma$. We also sometimes say Σ (*logically*) *implies* Γ.   ◇

If ϕ is not a logical consequence of Σ, we write $\Sigma \not\models \phi$, and similarly $\Sigma \not\models \Gamma$ if not $\Sigma \models \Gamma$.

Example 1.16 Let P stand for "I am outside", let Q represent "It rains", and let R represent "I will get wet". Suppose we know the following sentences are true:

> "If I am outside and it rains, then I will get wet.", or in formulas:
> $((P \wedge Q) \to R)$.
> "It rains.", or represented as a formula: Q.

From these sentences, we want to conclude:

> "If I am outside, I will get wet.", or the formula $(P \to R)$.

We can prove that this conclusion is correct by proving that $(P \to R)$ is a logical consequence of the set $\Sigma = \{((P \wedge Q) \to R), Q\}$. We will use Table 1.2 for this.

Each row represents a possible interpretation of the atom-set $\{P, Q, R\}$. The only rows which are models of Σ are the first, fifth and sixth row, since these are the only rows in which both $((P \wedge Q) \to R)$ and Q are true (see the underlined truth values). In these three rows $(P \to R)$ is also true, hence every model of Σ is also a model of $(P \to R)$. Therefore $\Sigma \models (P \to R)$, so we have proved that our conclusion is correct.   ◁

Example 1.17 The set $\Sigma = \{(P \wedge Q), (P \to R)\}$ logically implies the set $\Gamma = \{P, Q, R\}$.   ◁

We now have three related concepts, all called 'implication':

P	Q	R	$((P \wedge Q) \to R)$	$(P \to R)$
T	T	T	T	T
T	T	F	F	F
T	F	T	T	T
T	F	F	T	F
F	T	T	T	T
F	T	F	T	T
F	F	T	T	T
F	F	F	T	T

Table 1.2: The truth table for Σ and $(P \to R)$

1. The connective '$\to$': a syntactical symbol called 'if...then' or 'implication'.
2. The concept of 'logical consequence' or '(logical) implication', denoted by '$\models$'.
3. The phrase 'if...then', which is used when stating, for example, propositions or theorems.

In order to avoid confusion, we will here briefly emphasise the differences between these concepts. First, '$\to$'. This is a *syntactical symbol*, appearing *within* formulas. The truth value of the formula $(\phi \to \psi)$ depends on the *particular* interpretation I we happen to be considering: according to the truth table, $(\phi \to \psi)$ is true under I if ϕ is false under I and/or ψ is true under I; $(\phi \to \psi)$ is false otherwise.

Second, the concept of '(logical) implication'. This concept describes a *semantical* relation *between* formulas. It is defined in terms of *all* interpretations: '$\phi \models \psi$' is true if every interpretation that is a model of ϕ, is also a model of ψ.

Third, 'if...then', also sometimes called 'implication'. This describes a relation between *assertions* which are phrased in (more or less) natural language. It is used for instance in proofs of theorems, when we state that some assertion implies another assertion. Sometimes we use the symbols '$\Rightarrow$' or '$\Leftarrow$' for this. If assertion A implies assertion B, we say that B is a *necessary condition* for A (i.e., if A is true, B must necessarily be true), and A is a *sufficient condition* for B (i.e., the truth of B is sufficient to make A true). In case A implies B, *and* B implies A, we write "A iff B", where 'iff' abbreviates 'if, and only if'.

The following Deduction Theorem describes a relation between these notions:

Theorem 1.18 (Deduction Theorem) *Let Σ be a set of formulas, and ϕ and ψ be formulas. Then $\Sigma \cup \{\phi\} \models \psi$ iff $\Sigma \models (\phi \to \psi)$.*

Proof $\Sigma \cup \{\phi\} \models \psi$ iff
All models of $\Sigma \cup \{\phi\}$ are models of ψ iff

All models of Σ are models of $\neg\phi$ or of ψ iff
All models of Σ are models of $(\phi \rightarrow \psi)$ iff
$\Sigma \models (\phi \rightarrow \psi)$.   □

Next we will define the concept of *equivalence* between formulas or sets
of formulas.

Definition 1.19 Two formulas ϕ and ψ are said to be (*logically*) *equivalent*
(denoted by $\phi \Leftrightarrow \psi$), if both $\phi \models \psi$ and $\psi \models \phi$ (so ϕ and ψ have exactly
the same models). Similarly, two sets of formulas Σ and Γ are said to be
(*logically*) *equivalent*, if both $\Sigma \models \Gamma$ and $\Gamma \models \Sigma$.   ◇

Example 1.20 The sets $\Sigma = \{P, \neg Q, (P \vee R)\}$ and $\Gamma = \{(R \vee P), (\neg R \vee \neg Q), P, (P \rightarrow \neg Q)\}$ are equivalent.   ◁

The distinctions between '$\leftrightarrow$', '$\Leftrightarrow$', and 'iff' are analogous to the distinctions
between '$\rightarrow$', '$\models$' and 'if... then' explained above.

Formulas can be divided in the following categories:

Definition 1.21 Let ϕ be a formula. Then:

1. ϕ is called *valid*, or a *tautology*, if every interpretation is a model of ϕ.
   This can be written as $\models \phi$. ϕ is called *invalid* otherwise.
2. ϕ is called *satisfiable*, or *consistent*, if some interpretation is a model of
   ϕ.
3. ϕ is called *inconsistent*, or *unsatisfiable*, or a *contradiction*, if no interpretation is a model of ϕ. In other words, ϕ is inconsistent if it has no
   models.
4. ϕ is called *contingent* if it is satisfiable, but invalid.   ◇

Intuitively, a tautology is "always true" and a contradiction is "always
false". An invalid formula is "not always true" and a satisfiable formula is
"sometimes true". A contingent formula is "sometimes true, and sometimes
false". Note that some formula ϕ is a tautology if, and only if, $\neg\phi$ is a contradiction. Also note that because a contradiction has no models, it logically
implies any formula. The way these definitions subdivide the class of all formulas is graphically illustrated in figure 1.1.

These concepts can be defined similarly for a set Σ of formulas. Σ is a
tautology if every interpretation is a model of Σ, Σ is satisfiable if it has at
least one model, etc.

Example 1.22 Some examples to illustrate Definition 1.21:

- The formula $(P \vee \neg P)$ is a tautology (or a valid formula): every interpretation makes either P or $\neg P$ true, so every interpretation is a model
  of $(P \vee \neg P)$. Even the empty interpretation $I = \{\}$, which makes all
  atoms false, is a model of $(P \vee \neg P)$.

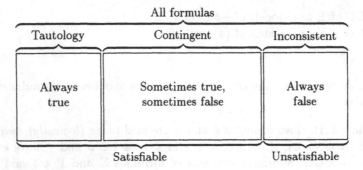

Figure 1.1: The class of tautologies, contingent formulas, etc.

- The formula P is satisfiable, but is invalid (not a tautology), hence a contingent formula.
- The formula $((P \wedge (P \to Q)) \to Q)$ is a tautology (or a valid formula), see Example 1.23.
- The formula $(P \leftrightarrow \neg P)$ is a contradiction (or an unsatisfiable formula).
- The set of formulas $\{P, Q, (\neg P \vee \neg Q)\}$ is a contradiction (an unsatisfiable set of formulas).
- The set $\{P, (Q \wedge R)\}$ is satisfiable, but invalid, hence contingent. The set is true under $I = \{P, Q, R\}$, but false under $I' = \{P, Q\}$.   ◁

Truth tables can be used to prove that some formula is a tautology or a contradiction:

Example 1.23 Let ϕ be the formula $((P \wedge (P \to Q)) \to Q)$. Using a truth table to systematically try out all possible interpretations, we will prove that ϕ is true under all possible interpretations. See Table 1.3.

P	Q	$(P \to Q)$	$(P \wedge (P \to Q))$	$((P \wedge (P \to Q)) \to Q)$
T	T	T	T	T
T	F	F	F	T
F	T	T	F	T
F	F	T	F	T

Table 1.3: The truth table for $((P \wedge (P \to Q)) \to Q)$

Note that the third column is derived from the first two columns, the fourth is derived from the first and the third column, and the last column is derived from the fourth and second columns.

The first two columns contain all possible interpretations of $\{P, Q\}$. The last column shows that ϕ is true under all these interpretations. So every interpretation is a model of ϕ, hence ϕ is a tautology.   ◁

Note the following relation between logical consequence and unsatisfiability:

Proposition 1.24 *Let Σ be a set of formulas and ϕ a formula. Then $\Sigma \models \phi$ iff $\Sigma \cup \{\neg\phi\}$ is unsatisfiable.*

Proof $\Sigma \models \phi$ iff
ϕ is true under all models of Σ iff
$\Sigma \cup \{\neg\phi\}$ has no models iff
$\Sigma \cup \{\neg\phi\}$ is unsatisfiable.   □

Also note the following relation between logical equivalence and tautologies:

Proposition 1.25 *If ϕ and ψ are formulas, then $\phi \Leftrightarrow \psi$ iff $\models (\phi \leftrightarrow \psi)$.*

Proof $\phi \Leftrightarrow \psi$ iff
ϕ and ψ have the same models iff
Every interpretation is a model of ϕ and ψ, or a model of $\neg\phi$ and $\neg\psi$ iff
Every interpretation is a model of $(\phi \leftrightarrow \psi)$ iff
$\models (\phi \leftrightarrow \psi)$.   □

The following assertions will be useful in the rest of the book. The second and third of these are sometimes called *De Morgan's laws*.

Proposition 1.26 *The following assertions hold.*
1. $\phi \Leftrightarrow \neg\neg\phi$
2. $(\neg\phi \vee \neg\psi) \Leftrightarrow \neg(\phi \wedge \psi)$
3. $(\neg\phi \wedge \neg\psi) \Leftrightarrow \neg(\phi \vee \psi)$
4. $((\phi \vee \psi) \wedge \chi) \Leftrightarrow ((\phi \wedge \chi) \vee (\psi \wedge \chi))$
5. $((\phi \wedge \psi) \vee \chi) \Leftrightarrow ((\phi \vee \chi) \wedge (\psi \vee \chi))$
6. $(\phi \rightarrow \psi) \Leftrightarrow (\neg\phi \vee \psi)$
7. $(\phi \leftrightarrow \psi) \Leftrightarrow ((\phi \rightarrow \psi) \wedge (\psi \rightarrow \phi))$

Proof We will only prove the sixth assertion, leaving the other proofs to the reader. This assertion follows from Table 1.4, which shows that $(\phi \rightarrow \psi)$ and $(\neg\phi \vee \psi)$ have exactly the same models.

ϕ	ψ	$(\phi \rightarrow \psi)$	$(\neg\phi \vee \psi)$
T	T	T	T
T	F	F	F
F	T	T	T
F	F	T	T

Table 1.4: The truth table for $(\phi \rightarrow \psi)$ and $(\neg\phi \vee \psi)$

□

1.4 Conventions to Simplify Notation

A complex formula can get overcrowded with parentheses. In this section, we make some simplifying conventions. Strictly speaking, these simplifications are not in accordance with the syntax of Definition 1.2, but since they are unambiguous and will not arouse confusion, no harm will be done.

First, according to Definition 1.2, $(P \vee Q \vee R)$ is not a formula, but $(P \vee (Q \vee R))$ and $((P \vee Q) \vee R)$ are. It can be easily proved that $(P \vee (Q \vee R))$ and $((P \vee Q) \vee R)$ are equivalent. Hence, we will sometimes write $(P \vee Q \vee R)$ instead of $(P \vee (Q \vee R))$ or $((P \vee Q) \vee R)$. Like $(P \vee Q)$, such a formula is called a *disjunction*. Similarly, we will sometimes use $(P_1 \vee P_2 \vee P_3 \vee P_4)$ instead of $(P_1 \vee (P_2 \vee (P_3 \vee P_4)))$. The same conventions can be made regarding the connective '$\wedge$', so we will write $(P \wedge Q \wedge R)$ instead of $(P \wedge (Q \wedge R))$, etc. Such a formula is also called a *conjunction*. Note that a finite set of formulas $\{\phi_1, \ldots, \phi_n\}$ is logically equivalent to the conjunction $(\phi_1 \wedge \ldots \wedge \phi_n)$.

Second, we will often omit the outer parentheses of a formula. So the formula $(P \to Q)$ can also be written as $P \to Q$.

Third, by giving $\vee$ and $\wedge$ precedence over $\to$ and $\leftrightarrow$, we can omit the parentheses around the two components of an implication or equivalence. Combining this with the previous conventions, we can write $P_1 \wedge P_2 \wedge P_3 \to Q$ instead of $((P_1 \wedge (P_2 \wedge P_3)) \to Q)$.

Note that these simplifications still allow no ambiguity. For example, the sequence $P \vee Q \wedge R$ (which might either mean $(P \vee (Q \wedge R))$ or $((P \vee Q) \wedge R)$, which are not equivalent), is not allowed. We will use appropriate parentheses anywhere where confusion or ambiguity might arise.

1.5 Summary

In this chapter we defined propositional logic, a relatively simple system of logic. The *syntax* determined the set of well-formed formulas in a propositional language. Those formulas are well-formed that can be built up from atoms and the connectives we discussed. The *semantics* of propositional logic is based upon the notion of an *interpretation*. An interpretation assigns truth values to the propositional atoms, and extends these truth values to composite formulas using a truth table to handle the connectives. An interpretation is a *model* of a formula if that formula is true under the interpretation. A formula ϕ (*logically*) *implies* a formula ψ, denoted by $\phi \models \psi$, if every model of ϕ is also a model of ψ. Formulas ϕ and ψ are (*logically*) *equivalent*, denoted by $\phi \Leftrightarrow \psi$, if $\phi \models \psi$ and $\psi \models \phi$. Similar concepts were defined for *sets* of formulas.

Chapter 2

First-Order Logic

2.1 Introduction

Propositional logic, as defined in the previous chapter, is a nice little formalism, but not a very strong or expressive one.

Let us try for example to formalize the sentence "John is Peter's father" in propositional logic. Since this sentence cannot be broken up in smaller pieces which could be connected by one of the five connectives, our only option is to use an atom to formalize it. But now let us consider the sentence "Paul is Mary's father". Again, this cannot be broken up into smaller components, and hence must be formalized as another atom. There are obvious similarities between these two sentences: they both mention the same relation (fatherhood). In the first sentence this relation holds between John and Peter; in the second it holds between Paul and Mary. Yet this similarity cannot be expressed in propositional logic, since both sentences can only be denoted by different atoms.

We would like a more expressive system of logic to satisfy the following requirements. Firstly, it should be able to distinguish between "things" (such as 'Paul') and "assertions about things". Secondly, the same "thing" should be denoted everywhere by the same symbol. Thus when formalizing the sentences "Paul is a father" and "Paul is a teacher", the two formalizations should both contain the same symbol denoting 'Paul'. Similarly, a concept or predicate (such as fatherhood) should be denoted by the same symbol everywhere. And thirdly, we would like to be able to use *variables*, which can be used to denote different things. For instance, we want to be able to say "every x who is a child of Mary, is a teacher."

First-order logic is a formalism which satisfies these three requirements. It was initially introduced by Gottlob Frege [Fre79], and further developed by Alfred North Whitehead and Bertrand Russell [WR27]. The semantics of first-order logic was developed by Alfred Tarski [Tar36, Tar56].[1]

Even though first-order logic is much more complex than propositional logic, both are built up along the same lines: first we define what constitutes a well-formed formula (syntax), then we define what a well-formed formula means and how it acquires a truth value (semantics). Syntax is the subject of the next section, semantics of the section after that. Of course, there is much more to first-order logic than just the basic concepts we introduce in this chapter. For a more extensive introduction we refer to [Men87, BJ89].

2.2   Syntax

First-order logic is much more complex than propositional logic. This will be evident from the syntax: whereas in propositional logic we only had formulas, in first-order logic we have two different syntactical categories—*terms* and *formulas*. Intuitively, a term denotes a "thing" which can be talked about (like a number, a human being, etc.), and a formula is an *assertion* about things.

As in propositional logic, we first specify an *alphabet*, the set of all symbols which can be used in forming syntactical structures. Then we define the rules with which well-formed syntactical structures (terms and formulas) can be constructed.

Definition 2.1 An *alphabet* of first-order logic consists of the following symbols:

1. A set of *constants*: $a, b, \ldots$, which may be subscripted.
2. A set of *variables*: $u, v, w, x, y, \ldots$, which may be subscripted.
3. A set of *function symbols*: $f, g, \ldots$, which may be subscripted. Each function symbol has a natural number (its *arity*) assigned to it.
4. A non-empty set of *predicate symbols*: $P, Q, \ldots$, which may be subscripted. Each predicate symbol has a natural number (its *arity*) assigned to it.
5. The following five *connectives*: $\neg$, $\wedge$, $\vee$, $\rightarrow$, and $\leftrightarrow$.
6. Two *quantifiers*: $\exists$ (called the *existential* quantifier) and $\forall$ (called the *universal* quantifier).
7. Three *punctuation symbols*: '(', ')' and ','. $\diamond$

As indicated in this definition, each function symbol has an *arity* assigned to it. By this we mean the number of arguments the function has. This is similar to functions in mathematics. For instance, the mathematical function $f(x, y) = x + 2y$ has two arguments, and is therefore of arity 2. A function

---

[1]As the word "first-order" implies, there are also "higher-order" logics. We will not discuss these here (see [BJ89] for an introduction to second-order logic). Other names sometimes used for first-order logic are *(first-order) predicate logic* or *predicate calculus*.

symbol of arity 1 is called a *unary* function, a function of arity 2 is a *binary* function. In general, a function symbol of arity n is called an *n-ary function symbol*. The arity of a function may be 0, this is similar to for example the constant function 5 in mathematics. Though we mentioned constants as a separate class of symbols in the previous definition, this is not necessary: it is often convenient to view constants as function symbols of arity 0. Thus the set of constants is actually a subclass of the set of function symbols.

Each *predicate* symbol also has an arity assigned to it, which gives its number of arguments. As will be explained in the following section, predicates can be used to denote properties or relations. For example, the relationship "x loves y" could be denoted by a binary predicate symbol. As was the case with function symbols, the predicate symbols of arity 0 play a special role: they can be used in the same way as atoms were used in propositional logic. Since the connectives can also be used in the same way as they were used in propositional logic, first-order logic is in fact a *generalization* of propositional logic. In other words, the structure of propositional logic is *embedded* in the structure of first-order logic.

Definition 2.2 *Terms* are defined as follows:
1. A constant is a term.
2. A variable is a term.
3. If f is an n-ary function symbol and $t_1, t_2, \ldots, t_n$ are terms, then $f(t_1, t_2, \ldots, t_n)$ is a term. $\diamond$

Example 2.3 Suppose we have an alphabet consisting (apart from the connectives, punctuation symbols and quantifiers) of the following:
1. The set of constants is $\{a, b, c\}$.
2. The set of variables is $\{x_1, x_2, y\}$.
3. The set of (non-constant) function symbols is $\{f, g\}$, where f has arity 1, and g has arity 3.
4. The set of predicate symbols is $\{P, Q, R, S\}$, where P has arity 2, Q has arity 1, R has arity 2, and S has arity 0.

Then the following are all examples of terms which can be formed from this alphabet:
- a
- x_2
- $f(c)$
- $f(f(f(x_1)))$
- $g(x_2, x_1, f(f(f(a))))$

The following sequences of formulas are not terms (given this alphabet):
- $f(a, b)$: f has arity 1.
- $P(b, a)$: predicate symbols cannot be used when constructing terms.
- $(a \lor x_2)$: connectives cannot be used when constructing terms. $\triangleleft$

Using terms, we can construct formulas. As in propositional logic, the smallest possible formula is called an *atom*. An atom is constructed by "filling in" the n argument-places of an n-ary predicate symbol with n terms. From atoms, more complex formulas can be constructed using the connectives (similarly to propositional logic), and the quantifiers.

Definition 2.4 *Well-formed formulas* (or just *formulas*) are defined as follows:

1. If P is an n-ary predicate symbol and $t_1, t_2, \ldots, t_n$ are terms, then $P(t_1, t_2, \ldots, t_n)$ is a formula, called an *atom*.
2. If ϕ is a formula, then $\neg\phi$ is a formula.
3. If ϕ and ψ are formulas, then $(\phi \wedge \psi)$, $(\phi \vee \psi)$, $(\phi \to \psi)$ and $(\phi \leftrightarrow \psi)$ are formulas.
4. If ϕ is a formula and x is a variable, then $\exists x\ \phi$ and $\forall x\ \phi$ are formulas.

◇

A formula which is not an atom, for example $(P(a) \vee Q(x, y))$, is called a *composite* formula.

Example 2.5 If we use the same alphabet as in Example 2.3, the following sequences of symbols are all formulas:

- $Q(a)$
- S (remember that S is a 0-ary predicate symbol)
- $P(f(f(x_1)), g(a, c, f(b)))$
- $((R(f(c), f(c)) \to \neg Q(f(c))) \leftrightarrow P(x_2, g(y, y, y)))$
- $\forall x\ Q(x)$
- $\neg\exists x\ Q(x)$
- $(\forall x_1 \exists x_2\ R(x_2, x_1) \wedge \forall y\ Q(a))$
- $\forall x_1 \exists x_2\ (R(x_2, x_1) \wedge \forall y\ Q(a))$
- $\forall x_1\ (\exists x_2\ R(x_2, x_1) \wedge \forall y\ Q(a))$

On the other hand, the following sequences are not formulas:

- $(P(a, b) \vee f(y))$: $f(y)$ is not a formula.
- $P(a)$: P has arity 2.
- $P(a, b) \vee R(a, b)$: this should be surrounded by parentheses according to our present Definition 2.4 (though see Section 2.4 for some simplifying conventions).
- $Q(P(a, b))$: $P(a, b)$ is a formula and not a term, hence it cannot be used to fill the argument place of Q.
- $\forall a\ Q(a)$: a is not a variable, hence cannot be used with the $\forall$-quantifier.

◁

From an alphabet, we can construct an infinite number of formulas. As in propositional logic, the set of all well-formed formulas which can be constructed from some alphabet is called a *language*.

Definition 2.6 The *first-order language* given by an alphabet is the set of all (well-formed) formulas which can be constructed from the symbols of the alphabet. ◇

Strictly speaking, only formulas are in the language L. But sometimes we will speak loosely about the "terms in L", or the "variables in L". Of course, in that case we mean the terms constructable from the alphabet on which L is based.

When we give an example in the rest of this chapter, we will not explicitly specify the alphabet we use. Instead, we assume that all the symbols we use in the example are in the alphabet. Similarly, we assume that the arities of the function and predicate symbols used are as described implicitly in the example. For instance, if we use the formula "$P(x, a)$", we assume that P is a predicate of arity 2 in the alphabet, that x is a variable, and that a is a constant in the alphabet.

We now define some concepts concerning the relation between quantifiers and variables in a formula. We will not need them in this section, but since these are purely syntactical concepts, we define them here.

Definition 2.7 The *scope* of $\forall x$ (respectively $\exists x$) in $\forall x\ \phi$ (resp. $\exists x\ \phi$) is ϕ. ◇

Example 2.8

- The scope of the $\exists$-quantifier in the formula $\exists x\ (P(x, y) \to Q(x))$ is the formula $(P(x, y) \to Q(x))$.
- The scope of the $\exists$-quantifier in the formula $\exists x\ (\forall y\ P(x, y) \land Q(x))$ is the formula $(\forall y\ P(x, y) \land Q(x))$, the scope of the $\forall$-quantifier is the formula $P(x, y)$. ◁

When a formula $\forall x\ \phi$ is constructed, we intend the quantifier $\forall$ to apply to all occurrences of x in ϕ, but not to other occurrences of x or other variables. What this "applying" means is part of the semantics, the subject of the next section. A variable-occurrence within the scope of some quantifier is called *bound*, an occurrence outside of the scope of any quantifier is called *free*. For example, the occurrence of x in $\forall x\ P(x, y)$ is a bound occurrence (since it lies within the scope of the $\forall$-quantifier), the occurrence of y in this same formula is free.

Definition 2.9 A *bound occurrence* of a variable x in a formula is an occurrence of x immediately following a quantifier, or an occurrence of x within the scope of a quantifier that is immediately followed by x. An occurrence of a variable which is not bound, is called *free*. ◇

Example 2.10 Some examples to illustrate the previous definition:

- All occurrences of the variables x and y in the formula $\exists z \ (P(x,y) \to P(z,x))$ are free, the occurrence of z is bound.
- The first occurence of x in $(\forall x \ Q(x) \lor P(x,f(c)))$ is a bound occurrence. The second occurence of x is free, since this second occurrence of x, in $P(x,f(c))$, is not within the scope of the $\forall$-quantifier. ◁

Definition 2.11 A *closed formula* is a formula which does not contain any free occurrences of variables. ◇

Example 2.12 The formula $\neg \exists y \ P(a,y)$ is a closed formula. The formula $\forall x \ (Q(x) \lor P(x,f(c)))$ is a closed formula, but the formula $(\forall x \ Q(x) \lor P(x,f(c)))$ is not, since the occurrence of x in $P(x,f(c))$ is not in the scope of the $\forall$-quantifier in the last formula. ◁

Definition 2.13 A *ground term* (respectively *ground formula*) is a term (resp. formula) which does not contain any variables. ◇

Example 2.14 The term $f(g(a,b))$ is a ground term, $h(a,b,x)$ is not, since it contains the variable x. The formula $P(a,f(g(a,b)))$ is a ground atom, the formula $\forall x \ (Q(a,g(x)) \land P(x,y))$ is not ground. ◁

2.3   Semantics

2.3.1   Informally

In first-order logic, a term refers to a "thing", and a formula is an assertion about things, which may be either true or false. What sort of "things" do the terms refer to? This depends on the way we interpret a first-order language. Part of such an interpretation is a specification of the *domain* that the terms in our language refer to. The domain could for example be the set of natural numbers, a set of blocks, or a set of Dutch people.

A term in the language refers to an object in the domain. The *term assignment* tells us to which domain element each term refers. Thus it tells us what the constants refer to, how to handle function symbols, etc. We visualize the term assignment in Figure 2.1.

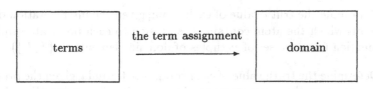

Figure 2.1: The term assignment maps each term to an object in the domain.

When we have interpreted the terms, we can determine the truth value of atoms containing these terms. Remember that an atom is an n-ary predicate symbol whose n argument-places each are "filled" with a term. What we want is to determine the truth value of some atom, given the n-tuple of domain elements to which the n terms in the atom refer.

An example will make this clearer. Suppose we use the set of natural numbers as our domain, so each term in our language refers to a natural number. Suppose also that we have some 3-ary predicate symbol P. We can interpret this predicate symbol as '$+$', as follows: we define the atom $P(t_1, t_2, t_3)$ to be true if the sum of the numbers to which the terms t_1 and t_2 refer, equals the number to which the term t_3 refers, and we define $P(t_1, t_2, t_3)$ to be false otherwise.

Once we have determined to which objects the terms refer, and which atoms are true, we can determine the truth or falsity of the *composite* formulas. Here the connectives are treated in the same way as they were in propositional logic. Thus a formula $(\phi \land \psi)$ is true iff ϕ is true and ψ is true, etc. But, apart from the five connectives, we can also use the two *quantifiers* when constructing a composite formula. The way these quantifiers work can be informally explained as follows:

1. First the existential quantifier $\exists$. Suppose we have some formula $\exists x\ \phi$, where x is a variable which occurs in the formula ϕ (this formula is pronounced as "there exists an x such that ϕ is true"). This formula $\exists x\ \phi$ says that there is *at least one* element in the domain which, when x refers to this element, makes the formula ϕ true. Hence $\exists x\ \phi$ is said to be true iff such an element indeed exists.

2. Second, the universal quantifier $\forall$. Suppose we have some formula $\forall x\ \phi$, where again x is a variable which occurs in the formula ϕ (this is pronounced as "for all x, ϕ is true"). This formula $\forall x\ \phi$ says that *each* element of the domain makes ϕ true, when x refers to this element. Thus we say that $\forall x\ \phi$ is true iff indeed each object in the domain makes ϕ a true formula.

Interpreting a first-order language thus consists of three steps:

1. Determine the domain and the connection between the terms and the domain (i.e., answer the question "to which object refers each term").

2. Determine the truth value of each atom, given the interpretation of the terms which the atom contains (i.e., assign to each predicate symbol a function from the set of n-tuples of domain elements to $\{T, F\}$).

3. Determine the truth value of each composite formula, given the previous two steps in the interpretation. This step involves using the rules for the connectives and the quantifiers.

2.3.2 Interpretations

Part of the semantics of first-order logic is a definition of the relation between the terms in the language, and the domain we talk about. Each term "refers to" (or "denotes") an object from this domain. The *pre-interpretation* is a precise definition of this "referring".

Definition 2.15 A *pre-interpretation* J of a first-order language L consists of the following:

1. A non-empty set D, called the *domain* of the pre-interpretation.
2. Each constant in L is assigned an element of D.
3. Each n-ary function symbol f in L is assigned a mapping J_f from D^n to D. $\diamondsuit$

The domain D may be either finite or infinite. By D^n we mean the set of all n-tuples of domain elements: $D^n = \{(d_1, \ldots, d_n) \mid \text{for every } 1 \leq i \leq n, d_i \in D\}$. So, for instance, if $D = \{2,3\}$, then D^3 contains $2^3 = 8$ elements, such as $(2,2,2), (2,2,3), (2,3,2)$.

We use function symbols to model functions. Suppose for example that we want to model the *mathematical* function which gives the sum of its two arguments. Suppose we use as our domain D the set of natural numbers. We could model this mathematical function by inserting in our language the function symbol g, of arity 2, and assigning in our pre-interpretation the following mapping J_g (from D^2 to D) to g: $J_g(n, m) = n + m$, where '$+$' is the usual mathematical addition function. We see what the phrase "a mapping from D^2 to D" means: two elements of the domain (namely the arguments n and m of J_g) are mapped to one element in the domain (namely the sum $n + m$). It is important not to confuse the function symbol g with the mapping J_g. The function symbol g is a symbol *in* the language, whereas the mapping J_g is not a symbol in the language, but is used to *interpret* the function symbol g to which it is assigned.

Example 2.16 Suppose our alphabet contains only one constant, a, and one function symbol f, of arity 1. We could model the natural numbers (which we take as our domain) as follows: a denotes the number 0, $f(a)$ denotes the number 1, $f(f(a))$ denotes 2, $f(f(f(a)))$ denotes 3, etc. This can be achieved by the following pre-interpretation J:

1. The domain D is the set of natural numbers: $\{0, 1, 2, 3, \ldots\}$.
2. The constant a is assigned the natural number 0.
3. The function symbol f is assigned the following mapping from D to D: $J_f(n) = n + 1$, where '$+$' is the usual addition function.

This gives us for instance the following:

- a refers to the number 0.
- $f(a)$ refers to $J_f(0) = 1$.
- $f(f(a))$ refers to $J_f(J_f(0)) = J_f(1) = 2$. $\triangleleft$

Thus a pre-interpretation "translates" the constants in L to objects in D, and it translates the n-ary function symbols in L to functions from D^n to D. Using a pre-interpretation, we can map each *ground* term to an element in the domain. But, of course, there are also terms which are not ground, that is, terms which contain variables. We want to say something about terms containing variables also. For this we need a separate concept: a variable assignment. The variable assignment tells us to which domain element each variable in the language refers.

Definition 2.17 Let J be a pre-interpretation with domain D of a first-order language L. A *variable assignment* V with respect to L is a mapping from the set of variables in L to the domain D of J.

We use $V(x/d)$ to denote the variable assignment which maps the variable x to $d \in D$, and maps the other variables according to V. ◇

Example 2.18 Let the alphabet and the pre-interpretation J be as described in Example 2.16, and let the alphabet contain also the variables x, y, y_1 and z. Then the following V is a variable assignment with respect to the language L given by the alphabet:

- $V(x) = 5$.
- $V(y) = 0$.
- $V(y_1) = 5$.
- $V(z) = 12$.

◁

Remember that terms are constructed from constants, variables, and function symbols. The variable assignment tells us to which domain element each variable refers. Similarly, the pre-interpretation tells us to which domain element each constant refers, and how to treat function symbols.

We may combine the information we get from a pre-interpretation J and a variable assignment V. Suppose J has as domain the set of natural numbers, and has $J_g(n) = 3 * n$, where '$*$' is the usual mathematical multiplication function. Suppose also that V tells us that the variable x is mapped to the natural number 4. Then we can, from the combination of J and V, figure out that the term $g(x)$ refers to the domain element 12. Such a combination of a pre-interpretation and a variable assignment is called a *term assignment*, since it assigns a domain element to each term in the language.

Definition 2.19 Let J be a pre-interpretation with domain D of a first-order language L, and let V be a variable assignment with respect to L. The *term assignment* with respect to J and V of the terms in L is the following mapping from the set of terms in L to the domain D:

1. Each constant is mapped to an element in D by J.
2. Each variable is mapped to an element in D by V.

3. If $d_1, \ldots, d_n$ are the elements of the domain to which the terms $t_1, \ldots, t_n$ are mapped, respectively, then the term $f(t_1, \ldots, t_n)$ is mapped to $J_f(d_1, \ldots, d_n)$, where J_f is the function from D^n to D assigned to the function symbol f by J. $\diamond$

Example 2.20 Let Z be the term assignment which can be constructed from the pre-interpretation J defined in Example 2.16 and the variable assignment V defined in Example 2.18. Then for instance:

- $Z(f(a)) = 1$.
- $Z(f(f(x))) = 7$.
- $Z(a) = Z(y) = 0$.
- $Z(f(f(f(z)))) = 15$. $\triangleleft$

Once we have a pre-interpretation, we can define an interpretation. An interpretation "translates" each n-ary predicate to a corresponding function from D^n to $\{T, F\}$. That is, to each predicate corresponds a function which assigns either T or F to all possible n-tuples of domain elements.

Definition 2.21 An *interpretation* I of a first-order language L consists of the following:

1. A pre-interpretation J, with some domain D, of L. I is said to be *based on* J.
2. Each n-ary predicate symbol P in L is assigned a mapping I_P from D^n to $\{T, F\}$. $\diamond$

Since a 0-ary predicate symbol has no arguments, its interpretation is simply the assignment of a truth value. Thus 0-ary predicate symbols have the same role as atoms in propositional logic. In this way, propositional logic is embedded in first-order logic.

Example 2.22 Let us continue Examples 2.16, 2.18, and 2.20. Suppose the alphabet contains, apart from a, f and the four variables, one predicate symbol P, of arity 3. We want to model P as '+'. This can be done by the following interpretation I:

1. The pre-interpretation is J as defined in Example 2.16 (thus D is the set of natural numbers).
2. We associate with P the following mapping I_P from D^3 to $\{T, F\}$: $I_P(n_1, n_2, n_3) = T$ if $n_1 + n_2 = n_3$, and $I_P(n_1, n_2, n_3) = F$ otherwise.

Some examples of the way the function I_P works:

- $I_P(1, 2, 3) = T$, since $1 + 2 = 3$.
- $I_P(225, 11, 236) = T$, since $225 + 11 = 236$.
- $I_P(5, 22, 16) = F$, since $5 + 22 \neq 16$.
- $I_P(6, 7, 0) = F$, since $6 + 7 \neq 0$. $\triangleleft$

When we have a pre-interpretation J and a variable assignment V, the term assignment with respect to J and V tells us for each term in the language to which domain element this term refers. Also, when we have an interpretation I (based on J), we can determine the truth value of any atom once we know to which domain elements the terms in the atom refer.

Since any formula is constructed from atoms, connectives, and quantifiers, we can determine the truth value of *any* formula once we know how to handle the connectives and quantifers. How to determine the truth value of any formula, given an interpretation and a variable assignment, is specified in the following definition.

Before giving the definition, we note that special care must be taken in case of quantifiers. Suppose we have the formula $\phi = \forall x\ R(f(x), y)$. The term assignment with respect to J and V assigns a domain element to the variable x, and it also assigns a domain element to the term $f(x)$, so the formula $R(f(x), y)$ can be given a truth value by applying the function I_R to the domain elements assigned to $f(x)$ and y. But the formula ϕ in fact claims that $R(f(x), y)$ is true for *every* assignment to x, not just for the one specific domain element assigned to x *by* V.

We solve this problem by defining that $\forall x\ R(f(x), y)$ has truth value T iff for all elements $d \in D$, $R(f(x), y)$ has truth value T under I and $V(x/d)$. So for ϕ to have truth value T, we require that $R(f(x), y)$ has truth value T for *all* possible assignments to x, keeping I and the rest of V (that is, the assignments to variables other than x) fixed. The $\exists$-quantifier is handled similarly in the next definition. We have inserted some examples in this definition, continuing Example 2.22.

Definition 2.23 Let I be an interpretation, based on the pre-interpretation J with domain D, of the first-order language L, and let V be a variable assignment with respect to L. Let Z be the term assignment with respect to J and V. Then a formula ϕ in L has a *truth value under I and V*, as follows:

1. If ϕ is the atom $P(t_1, \ldots, t_n)$, and d_i is the domain element assigned to t_i by Z ($i = 1, \ldots, n$), then the truth value of ϕ under I and V is $I_P(d_1, \ldots, d_n)$.

   Example (continuing Example 2.22)
   $P(f(a), f(a), f(f(a)))$ has truth value $I_P(1, 1, 2) = T$ under I and V.
   $P(f(x), a, f(f(y)))$ has truth value $I_P(6, 0, 2) = F$ under I and V.

2. If ϕ is a formula of the form $\neg\psi$, $(\psi \wedge \chi)$, $(\psi \vee \chi)$, $(\psi \rightarrow \chi)$ or $(\psi \leftrightarrow \chi)$, then the truth value of ϕ is determined by the truth table for the five connectives, Table 1.1 of the previous chapter (of course, we must determine the truth values of ψ and χ first, before we can apply the truth table to find the truth value of ϕ).

   Example
   $(P(f(x), a, f(f(y)))) \rightarrow P(f(a), f(a), f(f(a))))$ has truth value T under I and V.

3. If ϕ is a formula of the form $\exists x\ \psi$, then ϕ has truth value T under I and V if there exists an element $d \in D$ for which ψ has truth value T under I and $V(x/d)$. Otherwise, ϕ has truth value F under I and V.

Example
$\exists z\ P(z, z, f(a))$ has truth value F under I and V, since there exists no $d \in D$ such that $P(z, z, f(a))$ has truth value T under I and $V(z/d)$ (there is no natural number d such that $d + d = 1$).

4. If ϕ is a formula of the form $\forall x\ \psi$, then ϕ has truth value T under I and V if for all elements $d \in D$, ψ has truth value T under I and $V(x/d)$. Otherwise, ϕ has truth value F under I and V.

Example
$\forall x\ P(x, f(a), f(x))$ has truth value T under I and V, because for all $d \in D$, $P(x, f(a), f(x))$ has truth value T under I and $V(x/d)$ (for all $d \in D$ it is true that $d + 1 = d + 1$).

$\diamondsuit$

Example 2.24 Some more examples, also continuing Example 2.22.

- The truth value of $P(f(a), a, f(a))$ under I and V is T, since we have $I_P(1, 0, 1) = T$ (in other words, $1 + 0 = 1$).
- The truth value of $P(f(f(a)), a, f(y))$ under I and V is F, since $2 + 0 \neq 1$.
- The truth value of the formula $(P(f(a), a, f(a)) \wedge P(f(f(a)), a, f(y)))$ under I and V is F.
- The truth value of $\neg \exists x\ P(f(a), f(a), f(f(f(x))))$ under I and V is T, since there does not exist a natural number x such that $1 + 1 = 3 + x$.
- The truth value of $\forall x \forall y \forall z\ (P(x, y, z) \leftrightarrow P(f(x), y, f(z)))$ under I and V is T.

$\triangleleft$

The truth value under I and V of a *closed* formula does not depend on the variable assignment V we use. This can be seen as follows: in a closed formula, all occurrences of variables are bound occurrences. So all occurrences of variables are within the scope of some quantifier. This means that when we are figuring out what the truth value of some closed formula is, every variable x is handled by the quantifier-rules, which use the variable assignment $V(x/d)$. This in turn means that the assignments made by the particular variable assignment V are irrelevant for the truth value of the closed formula, hence this truth value is determined completely by I.

Example 2.25 Define the interpretation I as follows: let D be a set of human beings, P be a unary predicate symbol which we interpret as "is mortal", and V be a variable assignment which maps x to John $\in D$. Then the closed formula $\phi = \forall x\ P(x)$ has truth value T under I and V, since every element of the domain is human, and hence mortal. Note that it does not matter here that $V(x) =$ John, even though x appears in ϕ. Since the $\forall$-quantifier makes x in ϕ range over the domain as a whole, the particular variable assignment V is irrelevant for the truth value of ϕ. $\triangleleft$

Example 2.26 Let's continue Example 2.22 once more. The closed formula $\forall x \exists y\, P(x, y, f(a))$ has truth value F under I, obtained as follows:

1. $\forall x \exists y\, P(x, y, f(a))$ has truth value T under I and V iff
2. for every $d \in D$, $\exists y\, P(x, y, f(a))$ has truth value T under I and $V(x/d)$ iff
3. for every $d \in D$, there exists a $d' \in D$ such that $P(x, y, f(a))$ has truth value T under I and $V(x/d)(y/d')$ iff
4. for every $d \in D$, there exists a $d' \in D$ such that $I_P(d, d', 1) = T$ iff
5. for every natural number d, there exists a natural number d' such that $I_P(d, d', 1) = T$ iff
6. for every natural number d, there exists a natural number d' such that $d + d' = 1$.

Since the last part of this iff-sequence is false, the closed formula we began with has truth value F under I and V. But while determining this truth value, we have not used the assignments made by V at all. V assigns x the domain element 5, but the truth value of this closed formula does not depend on this particular assignment to x. The formula would have had truth value F even if $V(x)$ were 1,000,000,000. $\triangleleft$

From these examples, we see that V is irrelevant when determining the truth value of some closed formula. In the rest of this work we are only interested in *closed* formulas. Thus we can leave out the variable assignment V, and speak of "truth value under I" instead of "truth value under I and V". Also, when we use the word 'formula' later on, we mean 'closed formula', unless stated otherwise explicitly.

We end this subsection by generalizing the terminology of *true* and *false* to (closed) first-order formulas:

Definition 2.27 Let ϕ be a formula in the first-order language L, and I an interpretation of L. Then ϕ is said to be *true under* I if its truth value under I is T. I is then said to *satisfy* ϕ, or to *make* ϕ *true*.

Similarly, ϕ is said to be *false under* I if its truth value is F under I. I is then said to *falsify* ϕ, or to *make* ϕ *false*. $\diamond$

2.3.3 Models

As in propositional logic, an interpretation which makes some formula true is called a *model* of that formula. The concepts of *logical consequence*, *tautologies*, etc. can also be easily generalized to the case of first-order logic. The following definitions are almost literally the same as in propositional logic, so we will pass over them fairly quickly.

Definition 2.28 Let ϕ be a formula, and I an interpretation. I is said to be a *model* of ϕ if I satisfies ϕ. ϕ is then said to *have* I as a model. ◇

Definition 2.29 Let Σ be a set of formulas, and I an interpretation. I is said to be a *model* of Σ if I is a model of all formulas $\phi \in \Sigma$. Σ is then said to *have* I as a model. ◇

Definition 2.30 Let Σ be a set of formulas, and ϕ a formula. Then ϕ is said to be a *logical consequence* of Σ (written as $\Sigma \models \phi$), if every model of Σ is also a model of ϕ. We also sometimes say Σ *(logically) implies* ϕ. If $\Sigma = \{\psi\}$, this can also be written as $\psi \models \phi$. ◇

Definition 2.31 Let Σ and Γ be sets of formulas. Then Γ is said to be a *logical consequence* of Σ (written as $\Sigma \models \Gamma$), if $\Sigma \models \phi$, for every formula $\phi \in \Gamma$. We also say Σ *(logically) implies* Γ. ◇

Example 2.32 Some examples:

- Let the interpretation I have $D = \{1,2\}$ as domain, P be a binary predicate interpreted as '$\geq$', let a denote 1 and b denote 2. Then I is a model of the formula $\forall x\ P(x,x)$, since $1 \geq 1$ and $2 \geq 2$. On the other hand, I is not a model of the formula $\forall x \exists y\ \neg P(x,y)$, since there is no number n in the domain for which $2 \geq n$ is false.
- The formula $Q(a)$ is a logical consequence of the formula $\forall y\ Q(y)$.
- The set of formulas $\{Q(f(b)), Q(f(f(c)))\}$ is a logical consequence of the set $\{\forall x\ (P(x) \rightarrow Q(f(x))), P(b), P(f(c))\}$. ◁

If ϕ is not a logical consequence of Σ, we write $\Sigma \not\models \phi$, and similarly $\Sigma \not\models \Gamma$ if not $\Sigma \models \Gamma$.

Logical consequence is a very important concept in artificial intelligence. Often, the knowledge of some system (a robot, for instance) can be represented by a set of first-order formulas. We might then say that the system "knows" some sentence, if the formula representing this sentence is a logical consequence of its set of formulas.

In propositional logic, testing whether or not $\Sigma \models \phi$ is easy: the number of possible interpretations that we need to consider, is finite (namely 2^n, where n is the number of atoms occurring in Σ and ϕ), so we can always decide in finite time whether or not ϕ is true in all models of Σ, simply by examining all possible interpretations. This property is called the *decidability* of propositional logic.

Unfortunately, things are not as easy when we let Σ and ϕ consist of *first-order* formulas. Since the number of possible terms is usually infinite, the number of possible interpretations is also usually infinite. Hence we may not be able to find out in finite time whether or not $\Sigma \models \phi$ by checking all possible interpretations. This problem of finding out or proving that $\Sigma \models \phi$

or $\Sigma \not\models \phi$ will be quite prominent in the next chapters. But first we will generalize some other definitions from propositional logic to the first-order case.

Definition 2.33 Two formulas ϕ and ψ are said to be (*logically*) *equivalent* (denoted by $\phi \Leftrightarrow \psi$), if both $\phi \models \psi$ and $\psi \models \phi$ (so ϕ and ψ have exactly the same models). Similarly, two sets of formulas Σ and Γ are said to be (*logically*) *equivalent*, if both $\Sigma \models \Gamma$ and $\Gamma \models \Sigma$. $\Diamond$

Definition 2.34 Let ϕ be a formula. Then:

1. ϕ is called *valid*, or a *tautology*, if every interpretation is a model of ϕ. This can be written as $\models \phi$. ϕ is called *invalid* otherwise.
2. ϕ is called *satisfiable*, or *consistent*, if some interpretation is a model of ϕ.
3. ϕ is called *inconsistent*, or *unsatisfiable*, or a *contradiction*, if no interpretation is a model of ϕ. In other words, ϕ is inconsistent if it has no models.
4. ϕ is called *contingent* if it is satisfiable, but invalid. $\Diamond$

The above definition subdivides the set of all formulas in the same way as in propositional logic. We again illustrate this graphically in figure 2.2.

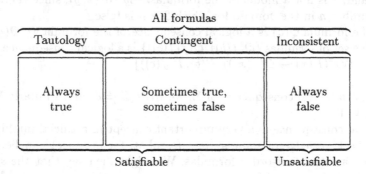

Figure 2.2: The class of tautologies, contingent formulas, etc.

These concepts can be defined similarly for a set Σ of formulas. Σ is a tautology if every interpretation is a model of Σ, Σ is satisfiable if it has at least one model, etc.

Example 2.35 Some examples to illustrate Definition 2.34:

- The formula $(\exists x \, Q(x) \to \neg \forall x \, \neg Q(x))$ is a tautology.
- The set of formulas $\{\forall x \, (P(x) \land Q(x)), \neg P(a)\}$ is unsatisfiable. $\triangleleft$

We now generalize some results from the previous chapter to the case of first-order logic. The proofs are the same as for the propositional case.

Theorem 2.36 (Deduction Theorem) *Let Σ be a set of formulas, and ϕ and ψ be formulas. Then $\Sigma \cup \{\phi\} \models \psi$ iff $\Sigma \models (\phi \rightarrow \psi)$.*

Proposition 2.37 *Let Σ be a set of formulas and ϕ a formula. Then $\Sigma \models \phi$ iff $\Sigma \cup \{\neg\phi\}$ is unsatisfiable.*

Proposition 2.38 *If ϕ and ψ are formulas, then $\phi \Leftrightarrow \psi$ iff $\models (\phi \leftrightarrow \psi)$.*

Before proving the next proposition, we will first illustrate the eighth assertion in that proposition by a more intuitive example.

Example 2.39 Suppose we have a language which contains the predicate P, of arity 2. Suppose we have an interpretation I, with a domain consisting of all human beings currently alive, and a function I_P such that $I_P(h_1, h_2) = T$ iff human being h_1 loves human being h_2. Suppose also that our language contains a constant a, which is mapped by I to the human being John.

Intuitively, the following sentences mean the same thing:

- "John loves everybody."
- "There isn't a human being whom John does not love."

First-order logic confirms this intuition, because we can prove that the following formulas are equivalent:

- $\forall x \ P(a, x)$
- $\neg \exists x \ \neg P(a, x)$ ◁

Example 2.40 We give another example for the same language as in Example 2.39. The two formulas

1. $\forall x \exists y \ P(x, y)$
2. $\exists y \forall x \ P(x, y)$

are not equivalent.

This can informally be illustrated using the interpretation defined in Example 2.39: if we use this interpretation, then the first formula informally means something like "everybody loves someone", and the second formula means "there is someone whom everybody loves". Clearly, the first formula can be true (if for example everbody loves his/her mother) while in the same interpretation the second formula is false (if there does not exist a person whom everybody loves). So these formulas are not equivalent. In fact, $\exists y \forall x \ P(x, y) \models \forall x \exists y \ P(x, y)$, but $\forall x \exists y \ P(x, y) \not\models \exists y \forall x \ P(x, y)$.   ◁

Proposition 2.41 *The following assertions hold.*

1. $\phi \Leftrightarrow \neg\neg\phi$
2. $(\neg\phi \vee \neg\psi) \Leftrightarrow \neg(\phi \wedge \psi)$
3. $(\neg\phi \wedge \neg\psi) \Leftrightarrow \neg(\phi \vee \psi)$
4. $((\phi \vee \psi) \wedge \chi) \Leftrightarrow ((\phi \wedge \chi) \vee (\psi \wedge \chi))$
5. $((\phi \wedge \psi) \vee \chi) \Leftrightarrow ((\phi \vee \chi) \wedge (\psi \vee \chi))$

6. $(\phi \to \psi) \Leftrightarrow (\neg\phi \lor \psi)$
7. $(\phi \leftrightarrow \psi) \Leftrightarrow ((\phi \to \psi) \land (\psi \to \phi))$
8. $\forall x \; \phi \Leftrightarrow \neg \exists x \; \neg\phi$
9. $\exists x \; \phi \Leftrightarrow \neg \forall x \; \neg\phi$

Proof The proofs of the first seven items are the same as the proofs of Proposition 1.26. The proof of the ninth assertion is similar to the proof of the eigth item, which we give below:

$\forall x \; \phi$ is true under some interpretation I iff[2]
$\forall x \; \phi$ is true under I and some variable assignment V iff
for all elements $d \in D$, ϕ is true under I and $V(x/d)$ iff
for all elements $d \in D$, $\neg\phi$ is false under I and $V(x/d)$ iff
there is no element $d \in D$, such that $\neg\phi$ is true under I and $V(x/d)$ iff
$\exists x \; \neg\phi$ is false under I and V iff
$\neg \exists x \; \neg\phi$ is true under I and V iff
$\neg \exists x \; \neg\phi$ is true under I.
Hence $\forall x \; \phi$ and $\neg \exists x \; \neg\phi$ have exactly the same models. □

We end this section by giving a very fundamental result: the Compactness Theorem, which will be needed in later chapters. The proof of this important result lies beyond the scope of our work (see for instance [BJ89] for a proof).

Theorem 2.42 (Compactness) *If Σ is an infinite, unsatisfiable set of formulas, then there exists a finite, unsatisfiable subset of Σ.*

Note the following consequence of this theorem:

Theorem 2.43 *Let Σ be an infinite set of formulas, and ϕ be a formula. If $\Sigma \models \phi$, then there is a finite subset Σ' of Σ, such that $\Sigma' \models \phi$.*

Proof If $\Sigma \models \phi$, then by Proposition 2.37, $\Sigma \cup \{\neg\phi\}$ is unsatisfiable. By the Compactness Theorem, there is a finite unsatisfiable set $\Gamma \subseteq \Sigma \cup \{\neg\phi\}$. Put $\Sigma' = \Gamma \backslash \{\neg\phi\}$. Then $\Sigma' \subseteq \Sigma$, and since $\Sigma' \cup \{\neg\phi\}$ is unsatisfiable, we have $\Sigma' \models \phi$ by Proposition 2.37. □

2.4 Conventions to Simplify Notation

First-order logic faces the same notational problem as propositional logic: huge amounts of parentheses make many complex formulas very hard to read. To avoid this, we will make the same simplifying conventions as we have already made for propositional logic, in Section 1.4 of the previous chapter. So we have for instance the following:

---

[2]Remember that we are only dealing with *closed* formulas.

- Both $(P(a) \lor (\exists x \ Q(x) \lor \forall x \ P(f(x))))$ and $((P(a) \lor \exists x \ Q(x)) \lor \forall x \ P(f(x)))$ will be written as $P(a) \lor \exists x \ Q(x) \lor \forall x \ P(f(x))$.

- $((P(a) \land \exists x \ (Q(x) \lor R(x))) \land (P(f(c)) \land Q(f(b))))$ will be written as $P(a) \land \exists x \ (Q(x) \lor R(x)) \land P(f(c)) \land Q(f(b))$.

- $((\forall x \forall y \ S(x,y) \land P(b)) \rightarrow (Q(a) \lor Q(f(a))))$ is written as $\forall x \forall y \ S(x,y) \land P(b) \rightarrow Q(a) \lor Q(f(a))$.

We will also sometimes abbreviate iterated function symbols in the following manner: $f^2(a)$ denotes $f(f(a))$, $f^3(a)$ denotes $f(f(f(a)))$, etc.

2.5   Summary

This chapter generalized propositional logic to first-order logic, which has a much greater expressive power. It allows us to talk about objects and their properties and relations. The *syntax* of first-order logic has two different categories: terms and formulas. Terms are constructed from constants, variables and function symbols. Atomic formulas are constructed by filling in terms in the argument places of predicate symbols. The set of well-formed formulas in a first-order language can be built up from the atomic formulas, using the five connectives and the universal and existential quantifiers.

The *semantics* of first-order logic consists of a generalization of the notion of an *interpretation* in the propositional logic. An interpretation roughly consists of a domain of objects, an assignment of objects to the terms of the language, and an assignment of truth values to atomic formulas. The truth values of more complex formulas are determined by rules for the connectives (the familiar truth table from propositional logic) and rules for the two quantifiers. A particular interpretation is a *model* of some formula, if that formula is true under the interpretation. A formula ϕ (*logically*) *implies* a formula ψ ($\phi \models \psi$) if every model of ϕ is also a model of ψ. Formulas ϕ and ψ are (*logically*) *equivalent*, denoted by $\phi \Leftrightarrow \psi$, if $\phi \models \psi$ and $\psi \models \phi$. Similar concepts were defined for *sets* of formulas.

Chapter 3

Normal Forms and Herbrand Models

3.1 Introduction

In the previous chapter, we discussed the basic properties of first-order logic. A first-order language consists of formulas, which stand in need of an interpretation. The interpretation defines the domain our language "talks about", it specifies the relation between the terms in the language and the objects in the domain, and it gives each (closed) formula a truth value.

As we have seen, formulas can be built in many different ways. Sometimes formulas which look very differently are in fact logically equivalent. For instance, the formulas $\neg \exists x \, (P(x) \rightarrow Q(x))$ and $\forall y \, (P(y) \wedge \neg Q(y))$ are equivalent, despite their widely differing form.

It would be nice if we had some restricted *normal form*, to which all formulas could in some way be reduced, and in which formulas could be compared. For example, we would like a normal form in which the two formulas above would "look alike". If we had such a normal form, we could for example restrict many proofs to formulas in normal form, since any formula could be put in such a form. In this chapter we will define two special forms: *prenex conjunctive normal form* and *Skolem standard form*.

The prenex conjunctive normal form has the nice property that for any formula, there exists another formula in prenex conjunctive normal form, which is equivalent to the first formula. Skolem standard form does not have this property, but is still very important for inductive logic programming. In the final sections of this chapter, we will discuss the so-called *Herbrand interpretations*, which have the set of ground terms in the language as their domain.

3.2   Prenex Conjunctive Normal Form

In this section we will define a first normal form, the *prenex conjunctive normal form* of a formula. Recall that by 'formula', we mean 'closed formula'. The basic building blocks in the prenex conjunctive normal form are *literals*, which in turn make up *clauses*.

Definition 3.1 A *literal* is an atom or the negation of an atom. A *positive literal* is an atom, a *negative literal* is the negation of an atom.   ◇

Example 3.2 $P(x)$ and $Q(a, y)$ are positive literals, $\neg Q(b, f(c))$ is a negative literal.   ◁

Definition 3.3 A *clause* is a finite disjunction of zero or more literals.   ◇

Example 3.4 The following formulas are clauses:

- $P(a) \vee \neg P(x) \vee Q(x, y)$
- $\neg R(x, a, f(y))$ (this is a "disjunction" of one literal)   ◁

The notion of a first-order language can be restricted to clauses:

Definition 3.5 The *clausal language* $\mathcal{C}$ given by an alphabet, is the set of all clauses which can be constructed from the symbols in the alphabet.   ◇

Clauses are very important, because sets of clauses are commonly used to express theories in inductive logic programming. Note that a clause may be a disjunction of *zero* literals. This is called the *empty clause*, denoted by □. We will explain what we mean by this in the next chapter, for this chapter the empty clause is not relevant.

A formula in prenex conjunctive normal form starts with a sequence of quantifier-variable pairs (called the *prenex* of the formula), followed by a conjunction of clauses (the *matrix* of the formula). For instance, the formula $\exists x\,((P(x) \vee \neg Q(a)) \wedge R(x))$ is in prenex conjunctive normal form.

Definition 3.6 A formula is in *prenex conjunctive normal form* if it has the following form:

$$\underbrace{q_1 x_1 \ldots q_n x_n}_{Prenex}\,\underbrace{(C_1 \wedge \ldots \wedge C_m)}_{Matrix},$$

where each q_i is either $\exists$ or $\forall$, $x_1, \ldots, x_n$ are all the variables occurring in the formula, and each C_j is a clause. The first part of the formula (the sequence of quantifiers with variables) is called the *prenex* of the formula. The second part is called the *matrix* of the formula[1], which we sometimes abbreviate to $M[x_1, \ldots, x_m]$.   ◇

---

[1] This term 'matrix' is just a name we use; it does not have very much in common with the mathematical concept of a matrix.

Example 3.7 These formulas are in prenex conjunctive normal form:

- $\forall x \exists y \ ((P(x) \vee \neg Q(y)) \wedge (\neg R(a, b) \vee \neg P(a)))$
- $\exists x \exists y \exists z \ (S(x, z, y) \wedge P(y))$
- $\forall x \ ((P(a) \vee P(b) \vee P(c)) \wedge \neg P(d) \wedge (Q(x) \vee \neg P(x)))$

These formulas are not in prenex conjunctive normal form:

- $\exists x \neg \exists y \exists z \ (S(z, y, z) \wedge P(x))$
- $\forall x \ (P(x) \rightarrow P(f(x)))$ ◁

In fact, any formula ϕ can be transformed into an equivalent formula ψ, which is in prenex conjunctive normal form. We then say that ψ is a prenex conjunctive normal form of ϕ. As a first, simple example, we will put the formula $\exists x \ P(x) \rightarrow \exists x \ Q(x)$ in prenex conjunctive normal form, taking small steps, each of which preserves equivalence (see Proposition 2.41):

$$\exists x \ P(x) \rightarrow \exists x \ Q(x) \Leftrightarrow$$
$$\neg \exists x \ P(x) \vee \exists x \ Q(x) \Leftrightarrow$$
$$\neg \exists x \ P(x) \vee \exists y \ Q(y) \Leftrightarrow$$
$$\forall x \ \neg P(x) \vee \exists y \ Q(y) \Leftrightarrow$$
$$\forall x \ (\neg P(x) \vee \exists y \ Q(y)) \Leftrightarrow$$
$$\forall x \exists y \ (\neg P(x) \vee Q(y)).$$

The last formula, which is equivalent to the first formula, is in prenex conjunctive normal form. We will now prove the following theorem, which shows that this method of putting a formula in prenex conjunctive normal form always works.

Theorem 3.8 *Let ϕ be a formula. Then there exists a formula ψ in prenex conjunctive normal form, such that ϕ and ψ are equivalent.*

Proof We give a constructive proof, i.e., we describe a procedure to transform ϕ into an equivalent formula ψ, where ψ is in prenex conjunctive normal form. Our procedure consists of five steps. To make the procedure more readily understandable, we will let an example run parallel with the proof: during the proof, we will apply the different steps in the procedure to the formula $\forall x \ (P(x) \rightarrow P(f(x))) \vee \neg \forall x \ (Q(x) \vee R(x, a))$. It is not very difficult to see that each step does what it is supposed to do; we will leave the details of the proof to the reader.

1. Remove all occurrences in ϕ of the connectives $\rightarrow$ and $\leftrightarrow$, using the following operations, which by Proposition 2.41 preserve equivalence:

    1. replace $(\psi \rightarrow \chi)$ by $(\neg \psi \vee \chi)$
    2. replace $(\psi \leftrightarrow \chi)$ by $((\neg \psi \vee \chi) \wedge (\neg \chi \vee \psi))$

    Call the formula thus obtained ϕ_1. Then $\phi \Leftrightarrow \phi_1$.

    Example
    $\forall x \ (P(x) \rightarrow P(f(x))) \vee \neg \forall x \ (Q(x) \vee R(x, a)) \Leftrightarrow$
    $\forall x \ (\neg P(x) \vee P(f(x))) \vee \neg \forall x \ (Q(x) \vee R(x, a))$

2. Rename variables in ϕ_1, such that no two quantifiers are followed by the same variable. Call the formula thus obtained ϕ_2. Then $\phi_1 \Leftrightarrow \phi_2$.

Example

$\forall x \ (\neg P(x) \vee P(f(x))) \vee \neg \forall x \ (Q(x) \vee R(x, a)) \Leftrightarrow$
$\forall x \ (\neg P(x) \vee P(f(x))) \vee \neg \forall y \ (Q(y) \vee R(y, a))$

3. Construct from ϕ_2 an equivalent formula ϕ_3, in which each occurrence of the connective $\neg$ immediately precedes an atom, using the following equivalence-preserving operations:

   1. replace $\neg \forall x \ \psi$ by $\exists x \ \neg \psi$
   2. replace $\neg \exists x \ \psi$ by $\forall x \ \neg \psi$
   3. replace $\neg(\psi \vee \chi)$ by $(\neg \psi \wedge \neg \chi)$
   4. replace $\neg(\psi \wedge \chi)$ by $(\neg \psi \vee \neg \chi)$
   5. replace $\neg \neg \psi$ by ψ

Example

$\forall x \ (\neg P(x) \vee P(f(x))) \vee \neg \forall y \ (Q(y) \vee R(y, a)) \Leftrightarrow$
$\forall x \ (\neg P(x) \vee P(f(x))) \vee \exists y \ \neg(Q(y) \vee R(y, a)) \Leftrightarrow$
$\forall x \ (\neg P(x) \vee P(f(x))) \vee \exists y \ (\neg Q(y) \wedge \neg R(y, a))$

4. Construct from ϕ_3 an equivalent formula ϕ_4, in which all quantifiers are at the front of the formula, using the following equivalence-preserving operations:

   1. replace $\exists x \ \psi \vee \chi$ by $\exists x \ (\psi \vee \chi)$
   2. replace $\psi \vee \exists x \ \chi$ by $\exists x \ (\psi \vee \chi)$
   3. replace $\forall x \ \psi \vee \chi$ by $\forall x \ (\psi \vee \chi)$
   4. replace $\psi \vee \forall x \ \chi$ by $\forall x \ (\psi \vee \chi)$
   5. replace $\exists x \ \psi \wedge \chi$ by $\exists x \ (\psi \wedge \chi)$
   6. replace $\psi \wedge \exists x \ \chi$ by $\exists x \ (\psi \wedge \chi)$
   7. replace $\forall x \ \psi \wedge \chi$ by $\forall x \ (\psi \wedge \chi)$
   8. replace $\psi \wedge \forall x \ \chi$ by $\forall x \ (\psi \wedge \chi)$

   Note that ϕ_4 is of the form $q_1 x_1 \ldots q_n x_n \ \chi$, where χ does not contain any quantifiers. So the first part of the prenex conjunctive normal form (the prenex $q_1 x_1 \ldots q_n x_n$) is already in order.

Example

$\forall x \ (\neg P(x) \vee P(f(x))) \vee \exists y \ (\neg Q(y) \wedge \neg R(y, a)) \Leftrightarrow$
$\forall x \ ((\neg P(x) \vee P(f(x))) \vee \exists y \ (\neg Q(y) \wedge \neg R(y, a))) \Leftrightarrow$
$\forall x \exists y \ ((\neg P(x) \vee P(f(x))) \vee (\neg Q(y) \wedge \neg R(y, a)))$

5. Finally, construct from ϕ_4 an equivalent formula ψ which is in prenex conjunctive normal form. This means that the part of ϕ_4 following the prenex must be transformed into a conjunction of disjunctions of literals. This can be done using the following equivalence-preserving operations:

   1. replace $((\psi \wedge \chi) \vee \xi)$ by $((\psi \vee \xi) \wedge (\chi \vee \xi))$

2. replace $(\psi \vee (\chi \wedge \xi))$ by $((\psi \vee \chi) \wedge (\psi \vee \xi))$

Example

$\forall x \exists y \, ((\neg P(x) \vee P(f(x))) \vee (\neg Q(y) \wedge \neg R(y, a))) \Leftrightarrow$
$\forall x \exists y \, ((\neg P(x) \vee P(f(x)) \vee \neg Q(y)) \wedge (\neg P(x) \vee P(f(x)) \vee \neg R(y, a)))$

The final formula ψ is the desired prenex conjunctive normal form of ϕ. □

The prenex conjunctive normal form of some formula ϕ is not unique. For example, both $\forall x \exists y \forall z \, (P(x, y) \wedge Q(a, z))$ and $\forall x \exists y \, (P(x, y) \wedge Q(a, x))$ are prenex conjunctive normal forms of the formula $\phi = \forall x \exists y \, P(x, y) \wedge \forall x \, Q(a, x)$. When we use the constructive procedure given in the previous proof, we obtain the first of these prenex conjunctive normal forms. However, the second one is also in prenex conjunctive normal form, and can be shown to be equivalent to ϕ.

3.3 Skolem Standard Form

In this section, we will define the *Skolem standard form*, named after the logician Thoralf Skolem. Strictly speaking it is not a normal form, because not every formula is equivalent to a formula in Skolem standard form. Still Skolem standard form, which we will usually just call *standard form*, will turn out to be very useful.

3.3.1 Clauses and Universal Quantification

The Skolem standard form is a conjunction of universally quantified clauses. What do we mean by *universally quantified*? To explain this, note that a clause may contain variables. Since a clause, being a disjunction of literals, does not contain any quantifiers, all occurrences of variables in a clause are *free* occurrences. This means that a clause containing one or more variables is not a closed formula, and hence cannot be given a truth value without a variable assignment. However, we usually take a clause to be preceded by a ∀-quantifier for every variable in the clause. In this way, a clause is treated as a closed formula.

Example 3.9 The following formulas are universally quantified clauses:

- $\forall x \forall y \, (P(x) \vee \neg Q(a, y))$
- $\forall y \forall z \, (\neg Q(g(y, f(z))) \vee \neg P(b))$ ◁

For the general case, we can define universal quantification as follows:

Definition 3.10 Let ϕ be a (not necessarily closed) formula. Let $x_1, \ldots, x_n$ be all distinct variables which occur free in ϕ. Then we use $\forall(\phi)$ to denote the formula $\forall x_1 \ldots \forall x_n \, \phi$. This $\forall(\phi)$ is a *universally quantified* formula. ◇

Intuitively, we can see that the formula $\forall x \ (P(x) \land Q(a, x))$ is logically equivalent to $\forall x \ P(x) \land \forall x \ Q(a, x)$. In particular, if $\forall x \ (P(x) \land Q(a, x))$ is true under some interpretation I, then no matter which domain element is assigned to x, $Q(a, x)$ is true under I. So then $\forall x \ Q(a, x)$ is true under I. Thus it can be shown that $\forall x \ (P(x) \land Q(a, x))$ logically implies $\forall x \ P(x) \land \forall x \ Q(a, x)$. The converse is also easy to see, so these two formulas are indeed equivalent.

In general, if $C_1, \ldots, C_m$ are clauses containing the variables $x_1, \ldots, x_n$, and I is an interpretation with domain D, then

$\forall (C_1 \land C_2 \land \ldots \land C_m)$ is true under I iff
for every $d_1, \ldots, d_n \in D$, $C_1 \land \ldots \land C_m$ is true under I and some $V(x_1/d_1)$
$\ldots (x_n/d_n)$ iff
for every $d_1, \ldots, d_n \in D$, C_1 and $\ldots$ and C_m are true under I and some
$V(x_1/d_1) \ldots (x_n/d_n)$ iff
$\forall (C_1) \land \forall (C_2) \land \ldots \land \forall (C_m)$ is true under I.

Hence: $\forall (C_1 \land C_2 \land \ldots \land C_m) \Leftrightarrow \forall (C_1) \land \forall (C_2) \land \ldots \land \forall (C_m)$. Thus we can write each conjunction of universally quantified clauses as a universally quantified conjunction of clauses, and vice versa.

Something needs to be said about the names of variables in a conjunction of universally quantified clauses, namely that it does not matter whether two or more clauses in the conjunction contain the same variables. Examine for instance the following:

$$\forall x \ (P(x) \lor \neg Q(a, x)) \land \forall x \forall y \ Q(y, x) \Leftrightarrow$$
$$\forall y \ (P(y) \lor \neg Q(a, y)) \land \forall z \forall x \ Q(x, z).$$

Since a conjunction of universally quantified clauses is equivalent to the universally quantified conjunction of these same clauses, we also have:

$$\forall x \forall y \ ((P(x) \lor \neg Q(a, x)) \land Q(y, x)) \Leftrightarrow$$
$$\forall x \forall y \forall z \ ((P(x) \lor \neg Q(a, x)) \land Q(y, z)).$$

From this example, we see that we can rename variables in a clause without regard to the variables occurring in other clauses in the conjunction. Renaming variables in clauses preserves equivalence. Of course, renaming the variables in a clause should not change the meaning of the clause, so we are not allowed to rename $P(x) \lor Q(x, y)$ to $P(z) \lor Q(z, z)$.

3.3.2   Standard Form

In this subsection we will define the Skolem standard form. Every formula can be put in this form, but not every formula has a standard form which is *equivalent* to the original formula. On the other hand, we do have the weaker result that a formula is unsatisfiable iff its standard form is unsatisfiable.

What we want here, is to take a formula ϕ which is in prenex conjunctive normal form, and construct from ϕ a formula which can be written as a conjunction of universally quantified clauses. This new formula will then be called a Skolem standard form of the original formula. Since a conjunction of universally quantified clauses is equivalent to the universally quantified conjunction of these clauses, it does not really matter whether we search for the former or the latter.

Recall what a formula in prenex conjunctive normal form looks like:

$$q_1 x_1 \ldots q_n x_n (C_1 \wedge \ldots \wedge C_m),$$

where each q_i is either $\exists$ or $\forall$, and each C_j is a clause. In fact, without existential quantifiers, a formula in prenex conjunctive normal form would already be a universally quantified conjunction of clauses, and hence could be written as we want it: as a conjunction of universally quantified clauses. So all we have to do, is get rid of the existential quantifiers in the prenex of ϕ. This is done by a process called *Skolemization*.

We will illustrate this process by a small example. Suppose we have the formula $\phi = \forall x \exists y\, Q(x, y)$. We want to construct a "similar" formula without the existential quantifier. Consider the following mathematical proposition: "for every natural number n there exists a natural number m such that $n < m$". We know that if we define the mathematical function $f(n) = n + 1$, then for every natural number n, $n < f(n)$. In other words, we could replace m in the proposition by a function of n. Similarly, we could replace the variable y in ϕ by a unary function symbol having x as argument. So what we do, is take a new function symbol, say f, and add this to the alphabet. Now we replace the variable y by $f(x)$, obtaining $\phi' = \forall x\, Q(x, f(x))$. This new formula ϕ', a *Skolemized form* of ϕ, is a universally quantified conjunction of (in this case only one) clauses.

Definition 3.11 Let $\phi = q_1 x_1 \ldots q_n x_n M[x_1, \ldots, x_m]$ be a formula in prenex conjunctive normal form. Then a *Skolemized form* of ϕ is a formula ϕ' obtained by applying the following procedure to ϕ:

1. Set $\phi' = \phi$.
2. If the prenex of ϕ' contains only universal quantifiers, then stop.
3. Let q_i be the first (from the left) existential quantifier in ϕ'. Let $x_{i_1}, \ldots, x_{i_j}$ be the variables on the left of x_i (that is, those variables from $x_1, \ldots, x_{i-1}$ that have not been deleted).
4. Add a new j-ary function symbol, which we denote here by f, to the alphabet. Replace each occurrence of x_i in the matrix of ϕ' by the term $f(x_{i_1}, \ldots, x_{i_j})$. If there are no universal quantifiers to the left of x_i in ϕ', then replace each occurrence of x_i by a new constant (0-ary function symbol) which is added to the alphabet.
5. Delete $\exists x_i$ from the prenex of ϕ'.
6. Goto step number 2.

The new function symbols and constants which are added to the alphabet are called *Skolem functions* and *Skolem constants*, respectively. $\diamond$

It is important to note that we extend the alphabet in this process: each new Skolem function or constant was not previously in the alphabet.

Example 3.12 Here we describe the steps we take to find a Skolemized form of $\exists x \forall y \forall z \exists u \ (P(x) \land (\neg Q(y, g(a, x)) \lor R(f(u), b, z)))$.

1. We replace each occurrence of x by the new constant c, and remove $\exists x$ from the prenex, to obtain the formula:

   $\forall y \forall z \exists u \ (P(c) \land (\neg Q(y, g(a, c)) \lor R(f(u), b, z)))$.

2. Then we replace each occurrence of u by the new term $h(y, z)$, and remove $\exists u$ from the prenex. We then obtain the following Skolemized form of the original formula:

   $\forall y \forall z \ (P(c) \land (\neg Q(y, g(a, c)) \lor R(f(h(y, z)), b, z)))$.   ◁

Note that a Skolemized form is a universally quantified conjunction of clauses. This can be rewritten as a conjunction of universally quantified clauses. This last form is then called a Skolem standard form.

Definition 3.13 Let ϕ be a formula, let ϕ' be a prenex conjunctive normal form of ϕ, and let $\phi'' = \forall(C_1 \land \ldots \land C_n)$ be a Skolemized form of ϕ'. Define the formula ψ as $\forall(C_1) \land \ldots \land \forall(C_n)$. Then ψ is called a *Skolem standard form* (or just a *standard form*) of ϕ.

We say the standard form ψ is *based on* the prenex conjunctive normal form ϕ'. We also say that ϕ *has* ψ as a standard form.   ◇

Note that in the previous definition, ϕ'' and the standard form ψ are equivalent formulas. Every formula has a prenex conjunctive normal form, every prenex conjunctive normal form has a Skolemized form, and every Skolemized form is equivalent to a conjunction of universally quantified clauses. Thus clearly, every formula has a standard form.

Example 3.14 Below we describe the steps we take to get a standard form of the formula $\phi = \forall x \ (P(x) \to P(f(x))) \lor \neg \forall x \ (Q(x) \lor R(x, a))$.

1. First we construct ϕ', which is a prenex conjunctive normal form of ϕ (see the example in the proof of Theorem 3.8):

   $\forall x \exists y \ ((\neg P(x) \lor P(f(x)) \lor \neg Q(y)) \land (\neg P(x) \lor P(f(x)) \lor \neg R(y, a)))$.

2. Replacing y by $g(x)$ we obtain the following ϕ'', which is a Skolemized form of ϕ', hence a universally quantified conjunction of clauses:

   $\forall x \ ((\neg P(x) \lor P(f(x)) \lor \neg Q(g(x))) \land (\neg P(x) \lor P(f(x)) \lor \neg R(g(x), a)))$.

3. Finally we rewrite ϕ'' into standard form, as a conjunction of universally quantified clauses:

   $\psi = \forall x \ (\neg P(x) \lor P(f(x)) \lor \neg Q(g(x))) \land \forall x \ (\neg P(x) \lor P(f(x)) \lor \neg R(g(x), a))$.   ◁

Example 3.15 Note the difference between the following two cases:

- $\forall x\ P(x, f(x))$ is a standard form of the formula $\forall x \exists y\ P(x, y)$.
- $\forall x\ P(x, a)$ is a standard form of the formula $\exists y \forall x\ P(x, y)$. ◁

A set $\Sigma = \{\phi_1, \ldots, \phi_n\}$ of formulas is equivalent to the formula $(\phi_1 \wedge \ldots \wedge \phi_n)$, so we can define the (Skolem) standard form of the set Σ as the standard from of $(\phi_1 \wedge \ldots \wedge \phi_n)$.

Since the prenex conjunctive normal form of some formula ϕ is not unique, the standard form of this formula is not unique, either. When we replace a variable by a new function symbol, we can choose among different possible function symbols. For example, both $\forall x\ P(a, f(x))$ and $\forall x\ P(a, g(x))$ are standard forms of the formula $\forall x \exists y\ P(a, y)$. The two functions f and g may be interpreted as different functions over the domain. Analogously, in the earlier proposition "for every natural number n there exists a natural number m such that $n < m$", we could replace m by $f(n) = n + 1$, but also by for instance $g(n) = n + 2$.

Example 3.16 In this example we will show that a standard form of some formula need not be equivalent to the original formula. The formula $\psi = P(a)$ is a standard form of the formula $\phi = \exists x\ P(x)$, yet ψ and ϕ are not equivalent. We prove this by the following interpretation I, which is a model of ϕ, but not of ψ.

1. $D = \{1, 2\}$.
2. The constant a is mapped to the number 2.
3. $I_P(1) = T$ and $I_P(2) = F$. ◁

From the previous example we see that putting a formula in standard form does not preserve equivalence: if ψ is a standard form of ϕ, then ϕ and ψ are not necessarily equivalent. However, putting an *unsatisfiable* formula in standard form does preserve unsatisfiablity: the original formula is unsatisfiable iff the standard form is unsatisfiable (equivalently, the original formula has a model iff the standard form has a model). This will be shown in Theorem 3.19. To prove the theorem, we first need the following results.

Proposition 3.17 *Let ϕ be a formula, and let ψ be a standard form of ϕ. Then $\psi \models \phi$.*

Proof Without loss of generality, we assume ϕ is the following prenex conjunctive normal form:

$$q_1 x_1 \ldots q_n x_n\ M[x_1, \ldots, x_n],$$

where we use $M[x_1, \ldots, x_n]$ to denote the matrix of the formula, which contains the variables $x_1, \ldots, x_n$. We also assume (again, without loss of generality) that ψ is based on this prenex conjunctive normal form ϕ.

Let q_r be the first existential quantifier in ϕ. Define ϕ_1 as follows:

$$\forall x_1 \ldots \forall x_{r-1} \, q_{r+1} x_{r+1} \ldots q_n x_n \; M[x_1, .., x_{r-1}, f_r(x_1, \ldots, x_{r-1}), x_{r+1}, .., x_n],$$

where the notation $M[x_1, \ldots, x_{r-1}, f_r(x_1, \ldots, x_{r-1}), x_{r+1}, \ldots, x_n]$ means that each occurrence of x_r in the matrix is replaced by $f_r(x_1, \ldots, x_{r-1})$, f_r being the Skolem function (or Skolem constant if $r = 1$) that has been used to replace x_r when constructing ψ.

We will show that $\phi_1 \models \phi$. Suppose that the interpretation I (with pre-interpretation J and domain D) is a model of ϕ_1. This means that if V is some arbitrary variable assignment, then for all $d_1, \ldots, d_{r-1} \in D$,

$$q_{r+1} x_{r+1} \ldots q_n x_n \; M[x_1, \ldots, x_{r-1}, f_r(x_1, \ldots, x_{r-1}), x_{r+1}, \ldots, x_n]$$

is true under I and $V(x_1/d_1) \ldots (x_{r-1}/d_{r-1})$. Let d_r be the domain element $J_{f_r}(d_1, \ldots, d_{r-1})$. Then

$$q_{r+1} x_{r+1} \ldots q_n x_n \; M[x_1, \ldots, x_{r-1}, x_r, x_{r+1}, \ldots, x_n]$$

is true under I and $V(x_1/d_1) \ldots (x_{r-1}/d_{r-1})(x_r/d_r)$. This means that for all $d_1, \ldots, d_{r-1}$, $\exists x_r \, q_{r+1} x_{r+1} \ldots q_n x_n \; M[x_1, \ldots, x_{r-1}, x_r, x_{r+1}, \ldots, x_n]$ is true under I and $V(x_1/d_1) \ldots (x_{r-1}/d_{r-1})$. And this in turn means that ϕ is true under I, so I is a model of ϕ. Hence $\phi_1 \models \phi$.

Suppose q_s is the first existential quantifier among $q_{r+1}, \ldots, q_n$. From ϕ_1 we can define a new formula ϕ_2, where $q_s x_s$ is removed from the prenex, and each occurrence of x_s in the matrix of ϕ_1 is replaced by another Skolem function f_s, having $x_1, \ldots, x_{r-1}, x_{r+1}, \ldots, x_{s-1}$ as arguments (again, f_s is the Skolem function which has been used to replace x_s when constructing ψ). Then we can prove in the same way as before, that $\phi_2 \models \phi_1$, so $\phi_2 \models \phi$.

In this way, we can continue defining formulas ϕ_i until all existential quantifiers are removed from the prenex (each ϕ_i will contain one existential quantifier less than ϕ_{i-1}). Everytime we will have the result that $\phi_i \models \phi$. So, if ϕ contains k existential quantifiers, then ϕ_k will contain only universal quantifiers, and we will have the result that $\phi_k \models \phi$. But since the Skolem functions used to construct ϕ_k are the same as the Skolem functions used to construct ψ, and since ϕ_k and ψ are based on the same prenex conjunctive normal form ϕ, we see that $\phi_k = \psi$. Hence $\psi \models \phi$. $\qquad\square$

Proposition 3.18 *Let ϕ be a formula, and let ψ be a standard form of ϕ. If ψ is unsatisfiable, then ϕ is unsatisfiable.*

Proof We make the same assumptions (without loss of generality), and we define the same $\phi_1, \ldots, \phi_k$ as in the proof of Proposition 3.17.

We will prove that if ϕ_1 is unsatisfiable, then ϕ is unsatisfiable. So suppose ϕ_1 is unsatisfiable. If ϕ is satisfiable, then there exists an interpretation I (with pre-interpretation J and domain D) such that ϕ is true under I. That is, if V is some arbitrary variable assignment, then for all $d_1, \ldots, d_{r-1} \in D$, there exists a $d_r \in D$ such that

$$q_{r+1}x_{r+1} \ldots q_n x_n \ M[x_1, \ldots, x_{r-1}, x_r, x_{r+1}, \ldots, x_n]$$

is true under I and $V(x_1/d_1) \ldots (x_r/d_r)$.

Now let the interpretation I' (with pre-interpretation J' and domain D) be I, with the addition that $J'_{f_r}(d_1, \ldots, d_{r-1}) = d_r$. Then ϕ_1 is true under I', so ϕ_1 is satisfiable. This is a contradiction, so if ϕ_1 is unsatisfiable then ϕ is also unsatisfiable.

We can also prove in the same way that if ϕ_2 is unsatisfiable, then ϕ_1 is unsatisfiable, so then ϕ is unsatisfiable. And similarly, we can proof that if ϕ_3 is unsatisfiable, then ϕ is unsatisfiable, etc. Finally we have that if ϕ_k is unsatisfiable, then ϕ is unsatisfiable. Since $\phi_k = \psi$, we have the result that if ψ is unsatisfiable, then ϕ is unsatisfiable. $\square$

Now we can prove the theorem:

Theorem 3.19 *Let ϕ be a formula, and let ψ be a standard form of ϕ. Then ϕ is unsatisfiable iff ψ is unsatisfiable.*

Proof

$\Rightarrow$: Suppose ϕ is unsatifiable. If ψ has a model M, then by Proposition 3.17, M is also a model of ϕ. Hence ψ has no models.

$\Leftarrow$: This is Proposition 3.18. $\square$

To end this section, note the following property of clauses:

Proposition 3.20 *A clause C is a tautology iff C contains a complementary pair of literals (i.e., both A and $\neg A$).*

Proof

$\Leftarrow$: This is obvious.

$\Rightarrow$: Suppose $C = L_1 \vee \ldots \vee L_k$ is a tautology, but does not contain A and $\neg A$. Let $x_1, \ldots, x_n$ be all distinct variables in C. Let $D = \{d_1, \ldots, d_n\}$, and V be a variable assignment which assigns d_i to x_i, for every $1 \leq i \leq n$. Because C does not contain a complementary pair, and each x_i is assigned a different d_i, we can define an interpretation I, with domain D, such that every literal L_j in C is false under I and V. But then C is false under I, contradicting that C is a tautology. Hence C must contain a complementary pair. $\square$

3.4 Herbrand Models

In this section, we will describe a special and very interesting class of interpretations, the so-called *Herbrand interpretations*, named after the French logician Jacques Herbrand. Herbrand interpretations are particularly suited for clauses. In the next section, we will prove some interesting propositions concerning Herbrand models. These propositions partly explain why Herbrand models are useful, and why we need them in this work. Another reason why we introduce Herbrand models, is that they provide a very natural semantics for definite programs, which will be discussed in Chapter 7.

We start by defining the *Herbrand universe* (the set of all ground terms in the language), and the *Herbrand base* (the set of all ground atoms in the language).

Definition 3.21 Let L be a first-order language. The *Herbrand universe* U_L for L is the set of all ground terms which can be formed out of the constants and function symbols appearing in L. In case L does not contain any constants, we add one arbitrary constant to the alphabet to be able to form ground terms. $\diamondsuit$

Definition 3.22 Let L be a first-order language. The *Herbrand base* B_L for L is the set of all ground atoms which can be formed out of the predicate symbols in L and the terms in the Herbrand universe U_L. $\diamondsuit$

Often when we give an example, we do not first sum up the alphabet. Instead, we just assume the alphabet consists of all symbols occurring in the formulas we use.

Example 3.23 Consider the set of formulas $\{P(a), Q(a, f(b)), \forall x\ (P(x) \rightarrow Q(x, x))\}$. Let L be the first-order language given by the symbols in this set. Then the Herbrand universe U_L is the infinite set

$$\{a, b, f(a), f(b), f(f(a)), f(f(b)), \ldots\}.$$

The Herbrand base B_L is the infinite set

$$\{P(a), P(b), Q(a, b), P(f(a)), P(f(b)), Q(a, f(a)), Q(a, f(b)), \ldots\}.$$

$\triangleleft$

Like all interpretations, a Herbrand interpretation starts with a pre-interpretation. What is special about Herbrand interpretations, is that we take the set of ground terms (i.e., U_L) as our domain. The mapping from terms to domain elements is such, that each ground term is mapped to the corresponding element in the domain, namely that term itself. So each ground term in the language refers to itself in the domain.

Definition 3.24 Let L be a first-order language. The *Herbrand pre-interpretation* for L is the pre-interpretation consisting of the following:

1. The domain of the pre-interpretation is the Herbrand universe U_L.
2. Constants in L are assigned themselves in U_L.

3. Each n-ary function symbol f in L is assigned the mapping J_f from U_L^n to U_L, defined by $J_f(t_1, \ldots, t_n) = f(t_1, \ldots, t_n)$. ◇

Thus the function J_f maps $t_1, \ldots, t_n$ to the ground term $f(t_1, \ldots, t_n)$ in the Herbrand universe U_L.

Example 3.25 We will give the Herbrand pre-interpretation for the alphabet described in Example 3.23:

1. The domain is U_L, as described in the previous example.
2. The constant a is mapped to $a \in U_L$, b is mapped to $b \in U_L$.
3. The function symbol f is assigned the following mapping J_f from U_L to U_L: $J_f(t) = f(t)$.

So for example, the term $f(f(b))$ is mapped to $f(f(b)) \in U_L$. ◁

Given an alphabet, essentially only one Herbrand pre-interpretation is possible.[2] Based on this Herbrand pre-interpretation, we can define an Herbrand interpretation by assigning to each n-ary predicate symbol P a mapping I_P from U_L^n to $\{T, F\}$. If U_L is an infinite set (as is usually the case), an infinite number of different I_P's are possible, hence an infinite number of Herbrand interpretations can be based on the unique Herbrand pre-interpretation for a given alphabet.

Definition 3.26 Let L be a first-order language and J a Herbrand pre-interpretation. Any interpretation based on J is called a *Herbrand interpretation*. ◇

Since a Herbrand interpretation assigns a mapping I_P from U_L^n to $\{T, F\}$ to each n-ary predicate symbol P, it in fact divides the Herbrand base B_L in two disjoint sets:

1. The set of ground atoms $P(t_1, \ldots, t_n)$ such that $I_P(t_1, \ldots, t_n) = T$, where P is an n-ary predicate symbol.
2. The set of ground atoms $P(t_1, \ldots, t_n)$ such that $I_P(t_1, \ldots, t_n) = F$.

This means that a Herbrand interpretation I is completely specified by the set of all $A \in B_L$ which are true under I. So we can represent any Herbrand interpretation I economically by a subset (which we also call I) of B_L.

Example 3.27 We define the following Herbrand interpretation I of the language L defined in Example 3.23:

1. The pre-interpretation on which I is based, is the pre-interpretation defined in the previous example.

---

[2]The only exception is the case where L does not contain any constants, and we have to add one. Here we could choose different symbols for this new constant (a, or b, or c, etc), so different Herbrand pre-interpretations would be possible in this case.

2. P is assigned the following function from U_L to U_L: $I_P(t) = T$ if $t = a$
   or if $t = f(f(a))$, $I_P(t) = F$ otherwise.
   Q is assigned the following function from U_L^2 to U_L: $I_Q(t_1, t_2) = T$ if
   $t_1 = t_2$, $I_Q(t_1, t_2) = F$ otherwise.

This I can be represented by the following infinite subset of B_L:

$$\{P(a), P(f(f(a))), Q(a, a), Q(b, b), Q(f(a), f(a)), Q(f(b), f(b)), \ldots\}. \qquad \triangleleft$$

As the reader may already suspect, if some formula is true under some
Herbrand interpretation I, then I is called an *Herbrand model* of this formula.

Definition 3.28 Let L be a first-order language, Σ a set of formulas of L,
and I a Herbrand interpretation of L. If I is a model of Σ, it is called a
Herbrand model of Σ. $\diamond$

Example 3.29 Continuing Example 3.23, the following are all Herbrand
interpretations of L:

- $I_1 = \{P(a), P(b), Q(a, b), Q(b, b)\}$.
- $I_2 = \{P(a), Q(a, a), Q(a, f(b))\}$.
- $I_3 = \{P(f(f(a))), P(b), Q(a, a), Q(a, f(b))\}$.
- $I_4 = \{P(a), P(b), Q(a, a), Q(b, b), Q(a, f(b))\}$.

I_2 and I_4 are Herbrand models of $\Sigma = \{P(a), Q(a, f(b)), \forall x\ (P(x) \to Q(x, x))\}$. I_1 and I_3 are not. $\triangleleft$

3.5   Results Concerning Herbrand Models

Now, why do we need Herbrand models? To show the usefulness of Herbrand
models, we need the following proposition.

Proposition 3.30 *Let Σ be a set of clauses in a first-order language L. Then
Σ has a model iff Σ has a Herbrand model.*

Proof
$\Rightarrow$: Suppose Σ has a model M. Then we define the following Herbrand
interpretation I:

1. The pre-interpretation is the Herbrand pre-interpretation of L.
2. Let P be an n-ary predicate symbol occurring in Σ. Then we define
   the function I_P from U_L^n to $\{T, F\}$ as follows: $I_P(t_1, \ldots, t_n) = T$ if
   $P(t_1, \ldots, t_n)$ is true under M, and $I_P(t_1, \ldots, t_n) = F$ otherwise.

It can easily be shown that I is a Herbrand model of Σ.
   $\Leftarrow$: This is obvious (a Herbrand model is a model). $\square$

Note that in the previous proposition, Σ is required to be a set of *clauses*.
The proposition does not hold in the general case of arbitrary non-clausal

formulas. For example, consider the language L given by the symbols in $\Sigma = \{\exists x \ P(x), \neg P(a)\}$. Here Σ has a model, but does not have a Herbrand model. The problem lies in the domain: the Herbrand universe for this set of formulas is the set $\{a\}$, whereas we need a domain of at least two elements to make both formulas in Σ true.

We have already mentioned the importance of the concept of *logical implication* (or logical consequence). Often, we have a set Σ and a formula ϕ, and we want to find out whether $\Sigma \models \phi$ holds. $\Sigma \models \phi$ holds iff each model of Σ is also a model of ϕ. Thus a first idea might be to just check all models of Σ, and see if ϕ is true under these models. But, of course, because of the huge (infinite) number of different ways of defining a model of Σ this approach is intractable. Now a nice thing about Herbrand models is that we can restrict our attention to Herbrand models when trying to prove $\Sigma \models \phi$. This is shown by the following proposition:

Proposition 3.31 *Let Σ be a set of formulas and ϕ a formula. Let S be a standard form of $\Sigma \cup \{\neg\phi\}$. Then $\Sigma \models \phi$ iff S has no Herbrand models.*

Proof $\Sigma \models \phi$ iff (by Proposition 2.37)
$\Sigma \cup \{\neg\phi\}$ is unsatisfiable iff (by Theorem 3.19)
S is unsatisfiable iff
S has no models iff (by Proposition 3.30)
S has no Herbrand models. □

What the previous proposition shows, is that when trying to prove $\Sigma \models \phi$, we only have to consider Herbrand interpretations of a standard form of $\Sigma \cup \{\neg\phi\}$. Though the number of Herbrand interpretations is usually infinite, the task of investigating all Herbrand interpretations is much more tractable than the task of investigating all arbitrary interpretations, since in Herbrand interpretations we restrict ourselves to only one domain: the Herbrand universe U_L.

Example 3.32 Let $\Sigma = \{\forall x \ (P(x) \rightarrow Q(x)), \exists x \ P(x)\}$, and $\phi = \exists x \ Q(x)$. The set of clauses $\{(\neg P(x) \vee Q(x)), P(a), \neg Q(y)\}$ is a standard form of the set $\Sigma \cup \{\neg\phi\}$. Proposition 3.31 implies that $\Sigma \models \phi$ iff S has no Herbrand models. It can be shown that S has no Herbrand models, so $\Sigma \models \phi$. ◁

Example 3.33 Let $\Sigma = \{\exists x \ P(x), \neg P(a)\}$, and $\phi = P(b)$. Then the set of clauses $\{P(c), \neg P(a), \neg P(b)\}$ is a standard form of $\Sigma \cup \{\neg\phi\}$. This standard form has a Herbrand model, namely $I = \{P(c)\}$. Hence it follows that $\Sigma \not\models \phi$.

We have assumed here, in constructing this standard form, that c was not part of the alphabet already (recall that introducing Skolem constants or functions means extending the alphabet). We cannot use b as the new Skolem constant instead of c, since b is already part of the alphabet (it occurs in $P(b)$). For instance, if we took $\{P(b), \neg P(a)\}$ to be a standard form of Σ, then adding $\neg\phi$ would give the set of clauses $\{P(b), \neg P(a), \neg P(b)\}$, which has no Herbrand model. So we would then mistakenly conclude that $\Sigma \models \phi$.

$\lhd$

Finally, it should be noted that though Herbrand interpretations are sufficient for determining the satisfiability of a set of clauses, they are not sufficient for logical implication. For example, suppose we have a language L with only one predicate symbol P, of arity 1, only one constant a, and no function symbols of arity ≥ 1. Then this language has only two Herbrand interpretations: $I_1 = \emptyset$ and $I_2 = \{P(a)\}$. The only Herbrand model of $P(a)$ is I_2, which is also a Herbrand model of $P(x)$. Hence every Herbrand model of $P(a)$ is a Herbrand model of $P(x)$. Still, $P(a) \models P(x)$ does not hold, because we can easily construct a non-Herbrand model of $P(a)$ which is not a model of $P(x)$.

3.6   Summary

This chapter defined two *normal forms* for first-order formulas. Firstly, we discussed prenex conjunctive normal form, in which all quantifiers are at the front of the formula, and the rest of the formula is a conjunction of disjunctions of literals. A disjunction of literals is a *clause*. Sets of clauses will be the vehicle for expressing theories in inductive logic programming. Every formula can be put in prenex conjunctive normal form, and this normal form will be logically equivalent to the original formula. Secondly, we defined (*Skolem*) *standard form*, in which all existential quantifiers are eliminated. A standard form can be written as a set or conjunction of universally quantified clauses. Putting a formula in standard form does not always preserve logical equivalence, but it does preserve satisfiability: the original formula has a model iff the standard form has a model.

Furthermore, we defined the special class of *Herbrand interpretations* and *Herbrand models*, which have the set of ground terms in the language as domain. We showed that a set of clauses has a model iff it has a Herbrand model. This means that in testing unsatisfiability of sets of clauses, we can restrict attention to Herbrand models.

3.A   Alternative Notation for Standard Forms

A standard form is a conjunction of universally quantified clauses. Usually, the universal quantifiers are omitted to simplify notation. Other notational variants are also sometimes used in the ILP-literature for such standard forms. In this appendix, we will discuss most of these different notations.

First, concerning the building blocks of standard forms: clauses. A clause is a finite disjunction of zero or more literals. The following different notations are used in the literature to denote a clause $L_1 \vee \ldots \vee L_n$. We will illustrate each notation on the clause $P(a) \vee \neg Q(x,y) \vee \neg P(x) \vee Q(a, f(x))$.

1. As a universally quantified disjunction of literals.

   Example

   $\forall x \forall y \, (P(a) \vee \neg Q(x,y) \vee \neg P(x) \vee Q(a, f(x)))$

2. As we defined it in the previous section, so as a disjunction of literals, without explicit universal quantifiers.

   Example

   $P(a) \vee \neg Q(x,y) \vee \neg P(x) \vee Q(a, f(x))$

3. As a *set* of literals: $\{L_1, \ldots, L_n\}$.

   Example

   $\{P(a), \neg Q(x,y), \neg P(x), Q(a, f(x))\}$

   Note that both $P(a)$ and $P(a) \vee P(a)$ are represented by the set $\{P(a)\}$. So in case of set-notation, a clause contains a literal only once.

4. As an *implication*. Suppose $L_1 = \neg A_1, \ldots, L_i = \neg A_i$ are all negative literals, and $L_{i+1}, \ldots, L_n$ are all positive literals in the clause. Then the clause is equivalent to the formula $(A_1 \wedge \ldots \wedge A_i) \to (L_{i+1} \vee \ldots \vee L_n)$. If the clause contains only positive literals, the '$\to$' symbol is usually omitted. If there are only negative literals, we can write $(A_1 \wedge \ldots \wedge A_n) \to$.

   For the notation of a clause as an implication there are also several alternatives[3]:

   1. As the formula $(A_1 \wedge \ldots \wedge A_i) \to (L_{i+1} \vee \ldots \vee L_n)$.

      Example

      $(Q(x,y) \wedge P(x)) \to (P(a) \vee Q(a, f(x)))$

   2. Without the parentheses: $A_1 \wedge \ldots \wedge A_i \to L_{i+1} \vee \ldots \vee L_n$.

      Example

      $Q(x,y) \wedge P(x) \to P(a) \vee Q(a, f(x))$

---

[3]To complicate this notational mess even more, the implication $\phi \to \psi$ is often written "the other way around" as $\psi \leftarrow \phi$. We ignore this notation here, but will introduce it in Chapter 7.

3. As $\{A_1, \ldots, A_i\} \rightarrow \{L_{i+1}, \ldots, L_n\}$, where $\{A_1, \ldots, A_i\}$ means $(A_1 \wedge \ldots \wedge A_i)$, and $\{L_{i+1}, \ldots, L_n\}$ means $(L_{i+1} \vee \ldots \vee L_n)$. Note that the commas in the first set mean '$\wedge$', whereas in the second set they mean '$\vee$'.

   Example
   $\{Q(x, y), P(x)\} \rightarrow \{P(a), Q(a, f(x))\}$

4. As the previous case, but without parentheses:
   $A_1, \ldots, A_i \rightarrow L_{i+1}, \ldots, L_n$.

   Example
   $Q(x, y), P(x) \rightarrow P(a), Q(a, f(x))$

Now that we have seen the many different ways of representing a clause, let us see how we can represent a standard form. We will illustrate this by applying each notation to the formula $\forall x \forall y \ (\neg P(a) \vee Q(x, y)) \wedge \forall x \ P(x) \wedge \forall y \ (Q(a, b) \vee \neg P(y))$.

1. As we defined it in the previous section, so as a conjunction of universally quantified clauses.

   Example
   $\forall x \forall y \ (\neg P(a) \vee Q(x, y)) \wedge \forall x \ P(x) \wedge \forall y \ (Q(a, b) \vee \neg P(y))$

2. As a conjunction of clauses, where the universal quantifiers are left implicit for simplicity.

   Example
   $(\neg P(a) \vee Q(x, y)) \wedge P(x) \wedge (Q(a, b) \vee \neg P(y))$

3. As a set of clauses, where the universal quantification is implicit. In principle, this way of representing a standard form as a set of clauses can be combined with any of the clause-representations mentioned above.

   Example (if we represent a clause as a set of literals)
   $\{\{\neg P(a), Q(x, y)\}, \{P(x)\}, \{Q(a, b), \neg P(y)\}\}$

   Example (if we represent a clause as a disjunction of literals)
   $\{(\neg P(a) \vee Q(x, y)), P(x), (Q(a, b) \vee \neg P(y))\}$

Note that that if we do not make clear explicitly which notation we use, sets like $\{P(a), P(b)\}$ are ambiguous: this set may either be the clause $P(a) \vee P(b)$, or a set consisting of the two clauses $P(a)$ and $P(b)$. In this book, it will always be clear from the context whether we mean a set to denote a clause, or a *set* of clauses.

Recall what we said at the end of Subsection 3.3.1: we can rename variables within clauses without regard to the variable names used in other clauses. This means for example that the standard forms represented by the following sets are all equivalent:

$$\{\{\neg P(a), Q(x,y)\}, \{P(x)\}, \{Q(a,b), \neg P(y)\}\}$$
$$\{\{\neg P(a), Q(z,y)\}, \{P(u)\}, \{Q(a,b), \neg P(u)\}\}$$
$$\{\{\neg P(a), Q(y,x_1)\}, \{P(y)\}, \{Q(a,b), \neg P(y)\}\}$$

We hope the reader will not be put off by all these notational variants. In the rest of our work, we will use the notation that seems most appropriate in the context. We will try to be as consistent as possible in our own notational conventions.

In the sequel, we will leave the universal quantification of a clause implicit. So if we have a set $\Sigma = \{C_1, \ldots, C_n\}$ of clauses and a clause C, then we can use $\Sigma \models C$ as an abbreviation of $\forall(C_1) \land \ldots \land \forall(C_n) \models \forall(C)$. Similarly, if C and D are clauses, we use $C \models D$ as an abbreviation of $\forall(C) \models \forall(D)$. For notational convenience, we sometimes use $L \in C$ to denote that a clause C contains a literal L, and $C \subseteq D$ to denote that the set of literals in C is a subset of the set of literals in D.

Chapter 4

Resolution

4.1 Introduction

Logic programming concerns the use of (clausal) logic for representing and solving problems [Kow79].[1] This use is widespread throughout many parts of artificial intelligence. The idea is that some problem or subject of inquiry can be described by a set of formulas, preferably clauses. If this description is sufficiently accurate, then the solution to the problem, or some particular piece of information about the subject of inquiry, is logically implied by the set of formulas. Thus, clearly, finding out which formulas ϕ are logical consequences of some set of formulas Σ is crucial to many areas of artificial intelligence, including inductive logic programming.

Accordingly, we would like to have a procedure, an *algorithm*, which could find out whether or not $\Sigma \models \phi$ is the case. What is an algorithm? We will only give an informal explanantion here, referring to [HU79, CLR90] for the more formal details. Intuitively, an algorithm is a procedure, a specific sequence of operations upon given data. It is used to solve some problem, and should terminate *after a finite number of steps* for the given data. The data (input) given to the algorithm is a particular instance of the problem, and the desired result (output) is a solution to this instance. Consider for instance the problem "is the natural number n prime?" It is well known that there exists an algorithm which can give the right answer for each instance of this problem (i.e., for each particular n).

In general, suppose we have some problem **P**. If there exists an algorithm which can give the right answer to each instance of **P**, then **P** is called *computable*. An example of a computable problem is the problem "give the smallest prime number greater than n". The most straightforward algorithm

---

[1] The term 'logic programming' is often restricted to the use of *Horn* clauses (see Chapter 7). However, in the broad sense in which we take it here, it refers to anything having to do with clauses and resolution.

to solve this problem simply checks whether $n + 1$ is prime; if so, it outputs $n + 1$; if not, it checks whether $n + 2$ is prime, etc. Since there is no greatest prime number, this procedure outputs the right answer after a finite number of steps, for each instance of the problem.

One special class of problems, are the problems where the answer to each instance can only take on the values 'yes' or 'no'. An important example of this, is logical implication: "given a finite set of formulas Σ and a formula ϕ, does $\Sigma \models \phi$ hold?" Clearly, each instance of this problem can only have 'yes' or 'no' as answer. If such a two-valued problem is computable, it is called *decidable*, and an algorithm which solves it is called a *decision procedure*. If not, the problem is called *undecidable*.

For the propositional logic, logical implication is indeed decidable. For suppose we are given Σ and ϕ. Let n be the number of distinct atoms in these formulas. Then the number of interpretations is finite, namely 2^n. Hence there is an algorithm to find out whether $\Sigma \models \phi$ holds: this decision procedure simply checks whether ϕ is true in all models of Σ, and outputs 'yes' if this is the case, and 'no' otherwise.

But what about logical implication in first-order logic? Here we can have infinitely many different domains and hence infinitely many different interpretations, which means that the decision procedure for propositional logic will not work here. In fact, it can be proved that such a decision procedure *does not exist at all* for first-order logic: logical implication for first-order logic is an undecidable problem. This is called *Church's Theorem*. It follows from a result proved independently by Alonzo Church [Chu36] and Alan Turing [Tur36], the proof of which is beyond the scope of this book (see for instance [BJ89]).

Theorem 4.1 (Church) *The problem whether $\Sigma \models \phi$, where Σ is an arbitrary finite set of formulas and ϕ is an arbitrary formula, is undecidable.*

Note carefully that the problem is undecidable for *arbitrary* Σ and ϕ: there is no single algorithm which can always—after a finite number of steps—return the right answer to the problem "is ϕ a logical consequence of Σ?" for *any* Σ and ϕ.

So our problem of deciding $\Sigma \models \phi$ cannot be solved by an algorithm (and hence cannot be solved by a computer). There are, however, procedures which can be of great help here. These are called *proof procedures*. Before explaining what a proof procedure is in the next subsection, we will first make some remarks on the impact of such procedures on the problem of deciding $\Sigma \models \phi$.

There exist procedures which, when given as input arbitrary Σ and ϕ *for which $\Sigma \models \phi$ holds*, can verify in a finite number of steps that indeed $\Sigma \models \phi$.[2] This seems perhaps a bit trivial (what's the point of verifying $\Sigma \models \phi$ when

---

[2]Because of the existence of such procedures, logical implication is sometimes called *semi-decidable*.

you already know this?), but it is not. The point is that such a procedure can be given Σ and ϕ as input for which *you do not know yet* whether $\Sigma \models \phi$. The procedure is then guaranteed to terminate in a finite number of steps and give a correct answer if indeed $\Sigma \models \phi$. If, on the other hand, the input has the property that $\Sigma \not\models \phi$, then the procedure either terminates with the correct answer 'no', or continues forever. This last property of such procedures, that they need not terminate if $\Sigma \not\models \phi$, is very unfortunate. However, it is unavoidable: if the procedure also always terminated with the right answer if $\Sigma \not\models \phi$, it would contradict Church's Theorem. In the next section, we will elaborate a bit on such procedures. After that, we will introduce the *resolution* rule, which forms the basis of some important proof procedures.

4.2 What Is a Proof Procedure?

In the previous section, we have already made some remarks on proof procedures, without really explaining what a such procedure is. We will explain this presently. Roughly, a proof procedure is a way of generating a *proof* that some formula ϕ is a logical consequence of some set of formulas Σ. The formulas in Σ are usually called the *premises* of the proof, and ϕ is called the *conclusion* of the proof.

Usually, such a proof consists of a number of small steps of some special form. In each step, a new formula is "derived" from the premises and previously derived formulas. By 'deriving a formula' we mean constructing a formula from the premises and previously derived formulas, according to some specific rule. For instance, a proof procedure that is often used in mathematics is *modus ponens*. Modus ponens is the rule that allows one to derive the formula ψ from the set of formulas $\{\phi, (\phi \to \psi)\}$. This rule can be schematized as follows. Here the premises are above the line, and the derived formula is shown below the line:

$$\frac{\phi, \ \phi \to \psi}{\psi}$$

We can link several modus ponens steps together to form a proof. For example, suppose we have $\Sigma = \{P(a), (P(a) \to Q(b)), (Q(b) \to \exists x \ R(x))\}$. Taking two modus ponens steps, we can derive the formula $\exists x \ R(x)$ from Σ, as follows:

1. Derive $Q(b)$ from $\{P(a), (P(a) \to Q(b))\}$.
2. Derive $\exists x \ R(x)$ from $\{Q(b), (Q(b) \to \exists x \ R(x))\}$.

The previous sequence of steps constitutes a proof that $\exists x \ R(x)$ can be derived from Σ, using modus ponens. In general, a proof consists of one or more steps, each taken according to the rule (or rules) specified by the proof procedure, where in each step the premises are the original set Σ and previously derived formulas.

Clearly, if we use modus ponens, the conclusion ψ is a logical consequence of the premises: $\{\phi, (\phi \to \psi)\} \models \psi$. This property of modus ponens is called *soundness*. In general, a proof procedure is sound if all formulas ϕ that can be derived from some set Σ, according to this proof procedure, are logical consequences of Σ. In other words, a proof procedure is sound if it allows only logical consequences of the premises to be derived.

For most purposes, soundness is a necessary property of a "good" proof procedure: a proof procedure which provides us with "proofs" of things which do not follow from the premises could be rather misleading.[3] The following scheme represents an example of an unsound proof procedure:

$$\frac{\psi, \ \phi \rightarrow \psi}{\phi}$$

This rule allows us to derive the formula $P(a)$ from the set $\{Q(a), (P(a) \rightarrow Q(a))\}$. But clearly $\{Q(a), (P(a) \rightarrow Q(a))\} \not\models P(a)$, so this rule is not sound.

A second desirable property of proof procedures is *completeness*. A proof procedure is complete if every formula that is a logical consequence of the premises Σ, can be derived by this particular proof procedure. Modus ponens by itself is not complete. For instance, there is no sequence of modus ponens steps which can derive the formula $P(a)$ from the premises $\Sigma = \{P(a) \wedge P(b)\}$, though surely $\Sigma \models P(a)$. To see why this is so, note that we need a formula of the form $(\phi \rightarrow \psi)$ to be able to apply modus ponens. The set Σ does not contain any formulas of this form. An example of a complete proof procedure is represented by the following rule:

$$\frac{\phi}{\psi}$$

This rule allows us to derive any formula from any premise. It is clear that this rule is complete: since we can use this rule to derive any formula from the premises, we can also use it to derive any logical consequence of the premises. Unfortunately, this rule is not sound: it allows us for example to derive the formula $\neg P(a)$ from the premises $\{P(a)\}$. We see that obtaining completeness is easy, but obtaining completeness *and* soundness at the same time is much harder. To summarize: a proof procedure is sound if it can *only* derive logical consequences of the premises, and it is complete if it can derive *all* logical consequences of the premises.

In this and the next chapters we will discuss the derivation rule that is probably the most important principle of *mechanical theorem proving*.[4] This rule is called *resolution*. In this chapter we will define this rule and prove its soundness. In later chapters we will prove several completeness results involving resolution: the *refutation* completeness of resolution itself, and a more direct completeness result (the Subsumption Theorem) which combines resolution with another rule, called *subsumption*. Before we go into resolution,

---

[3]One exception is SLDNF-resolution, the topic of Chapter 8.

[4]If ϕ can be derived from Σ using some derivation rules, then ϕ is called a *theorem* of the combination of Σ and these derivation rules. Hence the name mechanical *theorem proving*.

we will first introduce in the following section some tools that are presupposed by the definition of resolution: *substitution* and *unification*.

4.3 Substitution and Unification

4.3.1 Substitution

In this subsection we will define *substitutions*. A substitution replaces variables by terms. For example, we could replace the variable x by the term $f(a)$ in the clause $P(x) \vee Q(x)$. We then get the new clause $P(f(a)) \vee Q(f(a))$. If we take the clauses to be universally quantified, we may say that this substitution makes the clause "less general". Whereas the first clause "says" that $I_P(d) = T$ or $I_Q(d) = T$ is true for *all d* in the domain, the second clause only claims that $I_P(d)$ or $I_Q(d)$ is true if d is the domain element to which the term $f(a)$ is mapped by the pre-interpretation. Note that the second clause is a logical consequence of the first clause: $P(x) \vee Q(x) \models P(f(a)) \vee Q(f(a))$.

Definition 4.2 A *substitution* θ is a finite set of the form

$$\{x_1/t_1, \ldots, x_n/t_n\}, n \geq 0,$$

where the x_i are distinct variables and the t_i are terms. We say t_i is *substituted for* x_i. x_i/t_i is called a *binding* for x_i. The substitution θ is called a *ground substitution* if every t_i is ground.

The substitution given by the empty set ($n = 0$) is called the *identity substitution*, or the *empty substitution*, and is denoted by ε. The *restriction* of θ to a set of variables V is the substitution $\{x/t \in \theta \mid x \in V\}$. ◇

Example 4.3 $\{y/x, x/g(x, y)\}$ and $\{x/a, y/f(z), z/f(a), x_1/b\}$ are substitutions. The restriction of the latter to $\{x, z\}$ is $\{x/a, z/f(a)\}$. ◁

Definition 4.4 An *expression* is either a term, a literal, or a conjunction or disjunction of literals. A *simple expression* is a term or a literal. ◇

Note that a clause is an expression. A substitution can be applied to an expression, this means that variables in the expression are replaced by terms according to the substitution.

Definition 4.5 Let $\theta = \{x_1/t_1, \ldots, x_n/t_n\}$ be a substitution, and E an expression. Then $E\theta$, the *instance* of E by θ, is the expression obtained from E by simultaneously replacing each occurrence of x_i by t_i, $1 \leq i \leq n$. If $E\theta$ is ground, then $E\theta$ is called a *ground instance*. If θ is a ground substitution and $E\theta$ is ground, then θ is called a ground substitution *for E*.

If $\Sigma = \{E_1, \ldots, E_n\}$ is a finite set of expressions, then $\Sigma\theta$ denotes $\{E_1\theta, \ldots, E_n\theta\}$. ◇

Example 4.6 Let E be the expression $P(y, f(x))$ and let θ be the substitution $\{x/a, y/g(g(x))\}$. The instance of E by θ is $E\theta = P(g(g(x)), f(a))$. Note that x and y are *simultaneously* replaced by their respective terms, meaning that the x in $y/g(g(x))$ is not affected by the substitution x/a. Another substitution is $\sigma = \{x/f(a), y/b\}$. $E\sigma = P(b, f(f(a)))$ is ground, so $E\sigma$ is a ground instance of E, and σ is a ground substitution for E. $\triangleleft$

To understand substitutions, it may help to regard a substitution $\theta = \{x_1/t_1, \ldots, x_n/t_n\}$ as the following mapping from the set of variables in the language to the set of terms in the language:

$$\theta(v) = \begin{cases} t_i & \text{if } v = x_i, \\ v & \text{otherwise.} \end{cases}$$

In this case, ε would represent the identity mapping.

For example, suppose that the set of variables in the language is $\{x, y, z\}$, and $\theta = \{x/a, z/f(z)\}$. Then θ represents the following mapping from $\{x, y, z\}$ to the set of terms in the language:

$$\theta(v) = \begin{cases} a & \text{if } v = x, \\ y & \text{if } v = y, \\ f(z) & \text{if } v = z. \end{cases}$$

Applying θ to an expression E (i.e., determining the instance $E\theta$) then means replacing each v in E by $\theta(v)$, for each variable v occurring in E. For example, if $E = P(x, z, g(y, x))$, then $E\theta$ is obtained by replacing in E each x by a, "replacing" each y by y, and replacing each z by $f(z)$: $E\theta = P(a, f(z), g(y, a))$.

It is always possible to expand a substitution θ such that it works on more variables in the language, by just adding the binding x/x for variables x that θ does not act on. Hence we can always assume without loss of generality that a substitution is defined on any variable in the language. For the previous substitution θ we could add y/y, which yields $\{x/a, y/y, z/f(z)\}$. This way we can make explicit the way in which a substitution works like a mapping, in the usual mathematical sense.

If E is an expression which is not a term (i.e., a literal or a conjunction or disjunction of literals), and θ is a substitution, then the following holds: $E \models E\theta$. For example, $P(x) \vee \neg Q(y) \models P(a) \vee \neg Q(y)$, where we have used the substitution $\{x/a\}$. The proof for this example is easy: suppose I is a model, with domain D, of $P(x) \vee \neg Q(y)$. Then for all $d_1 \in D$, and for all $d_2 \in D$, $I_P(d_1) = T$ or $I_Q(d_2) = F$. Suppose a is mapped to domain element d by I. Then for all $d_2 \in D$, $I_P(d) = T$ or $I_Q(d_2) = F$. Hence I is a model of $P(a) \vee \neg Q(y)$. It is clear that for different E or θ, a similar proof can always be given. Hence always $E \models E\theta$.

We can apply some substitution θ, and then some substitution σ. We then get the *composition* of these two substitutions. Again, regarding substitutions as mappings is helpful in understanding this definition. The composition of the substitutions θ and σ is like the composition of two mappings: first apply θ, and then apply σ. This composition can then itself be regarded as a mapping from the set of variables in the language to the set of terms.

For instance, the composition of $\theta = \{y/f(z)\}$ and $\sigma = \{x/b, y/a, z/a\}$ is $\theta\sigma = \{y/f(a), x/b, z/a\}$. Let us see how this operates on the variable y: $y\theta = f(z)$, and $(y\theta)\sigma = f(z)\sigma = f(a)$. This gives the same result as applying the composition $\theta\sigma$ immediately to y: $y(\theta\sigma) = f(a)$.

Definition 4.7 Let $\theta = \{x_1/s_1, \ldots, x_m/s_m\}$ and $\sigma = \{y_1/t_1, \ldots, y_n/t_n\}$ be substitutions. Consider the sequence of bindings

$$x_1/(s_1\sigma), \ldots, x_m/(s_m\sigma), y_1/t_1, \ldots, y_n/t_n.$$

Delete from this sequence any binding $x_i/(s_i\sigma)$ for which $x_i = (s_i\sigma)$, and any binding y_j/t_j for which $y_j \in \{x_1, \ldots, x_m\}$. The substitution consisting of the bindings in the resulting sequence is called the *composition* of θ and σ, and is denoted by $\theta\sigma$. $\diamond$

Example 4.8 Let $\theta = \{x/f(y), z/u\}$ and $\sigma = \{y/b, u/z\}$. We construct the sequence of bindings $x/(f(y)\sigma), z/(u\sigma), y/b, u/z$, which is $x/f(b), z/z, y/b, u/z$. Deleting the binding z/z, we obtain the sequence $x/f(b), y/b, u/z$, which yields the composition $\theta\sigma = \{x/f(b), y/b, u/z\}$.

Let $\theta = \{x/y\}$ and $\sigma = \{x/a, y/a\}$. We construct the sequence of bindings $x/(y\sigma), x/a, y/a = x/a, x/a, y/a$. After deleting the second occurrence of the binding x/a (though not the first occurrence!) from this sequence, we obtain $\theta\sigma = \{x/a, y/a\}$. $\triangleleft$

Definition 4.9 Let θ and σ be substitutions. We say θ is an *instance* of σ if there exists a substitution γ such that $\sigma\gamma = \theta$. $\diamond$

Example 4.10 The substitution $\theta = \{x/f(b), y/a\}$ is an instance of $\sigma = \{x/f(x), y/a\}$, since $\sigma\{x/b\} = \theta$. $\triangleleft$

We now prove some properties of substitutions (if we regard substitutions as mappings—as explained above—then these properties are obvious consequences of properties of mappings in general).

Proposition 4.11 *Let E be an expression, and let θ, σ and γ be substitutions. Then the following hold:*

1. $\theta = \theta\varepsilon = \varepsilon\theta$.
2. $(E\theta)\sigma = E(\theta\sigma)$.
3. $(\theta\sigma)\gamma = \theta(\sigma\gamma)$.

Proof

1. This is obvious, since ε does not change anything.

2. It is sufficient to prove that the result holds for all variables occurring in
E. Let x be a variable occurring in E. Suppose $\theta = \{x_1/s_1, \ldots, x_m/s_m\}$
and $\sigma = \{y_1/t_1, \ldots, y_n/t_n\}$.

If $x \notin \{x_1, \ldots, x_m\} \cup \{y_1, \ldots, y_n\}$, then $x = (x\theta)\sigma = x(\theta\sigma)$.

If $x = x_i \in \{x_1, \ldots, x_m\}$, then $(x\theta)\sigma = s_i\sigma = x(\theta\sigma)$.

If $x = y_i \in \{y_1, \ldots, y_n\}$, and $x \notin \{x_1, \ldots, x_m\}$, then $(x\theta)\sigma = x\sigma = t_i = x(\theta\sigma)$.

3. Let x be a variable. Then, using the previous part of this proposition,
$x((\theta\sigma)\gamma) = (x(\theta\sigma))\gamma = ((x\theta)\sigma)\gamma = (x\theta)(\sigma\gamma) = x(\theta(\sigma\gamma))$.   □

Since $(E\theta)\sigma = E(\theta\sigma)$, we will usually omit the parentheses, and write
this as $E\theta\sigma$. Though the previous proposition shows that substitutions have
some nice properties, it is not generally true that $\theta\sigma = \sigma\theta$. For example, let
$\theta = \{x/a\}$ and let $\sigma = \{x/b\}$. Then $\theta\sigma = \{x/a\}$, but $\sigma\theta = \{x/b\}$.

Sometimes we need to rename the variables in a formula. The new formula,
which is equivalent to the old one, is called a *variant* of the old formula. We
can obtain such a variant by applying a *renaming substitution*, defined as
follows:

Definition 4.12 Let E be an expression, and let θ be the substitution
$\{x_1/y_1, \ldots, x_n/y_n\}$. We say θ is a *renaming substitution for E* if each x_i
occurs in E, and $y_1, \ldots, y_n$ are distinct variables such that each y_i is either
equal to some x_j in θ, or y_i does not occur in E. $\Diamond$

Example 4.13 Let $E = f(a, x, y, z)$. Then $\theta = \{x/x_1, z/x\}$ is a renaming
substitution for E and $E\theta = f(a, x_1, y, x)$. On the other hand, $\sigma = \{x/y\}$ is
not a renaming substitution for E, because y is not equal to x and y already
occurs in E. $\triangleleft$

Definition 4.14 Let E and F be expressions. We say E and F are *variants*,
or E is a *variant* of F, if there exist renaming substitutions θ and σ such that
$E = F\theta$ and $F = E\sigma$. $\Diamond$

Example 4.15 The clauses $C = P(x) \vee Q(x, y)$ and $D = P(y) \vee Q(y, z)$ are
variants, since $C = D\theta$ for $\theta = \{y/x, z/y\}$, and $D = C\sigma$ for $\sigma = \{x/y, y/z\}$,
where θ is a renaming substitution for C_2, and σ is a renaming substitution
for C_1. $\triangleleft$

Proposition 4.16 *Let E and F be expressions. If there exist substitutions
θ and σ such that $E = F\theta$ and $F = E\sigma$, then E and F are variants.*

Proof We assume without loss of generality that θ only acts on variables in
F, and σ only acts on variables in E. If θ was not a renaming substitution
for F, then we could not have $F\theta\sigma = E\sigma = F$, so θ must be a renaming
substitution for F. Similarly, σ must be a renaming substitution for E, and
E and F are variants.   □

4.3.2 Unification

A *unifier* for the set of expressions $\{E_1, E_2, \ldots, E_n\}$ is a substitution θ such that $E_1\theta = E_2\theta = \ldots = E_n\theta$.

Definition 4.17 Let Σ be a finite set of expressions. A substitution θ is called a *unifier for* Σ if $\Sigma\theta$ is a singleton (a set containing exactly one element). If there exists a unifier for Σ, we say Σ is *unifiable*. $\diamond$

Example 4.18 The substitution $\theta = \{x/a, y/f(a)\}$ is a unifier for the set $\Sigma = \{(P(x) \vee \neg Q(y)), (P(a) \vee \neg Q(f(x)))\}$, since $\Sigma\theta = \{P(a) \vee \neg Q(f(a))\}$.

The set $\{P(a, f(x)), P(a, g(x))\}$ is not unifiable, because $f(x)$ and $g(x)$ are not unifiable. The set $\{P(a, x), P(y, b)\}$ is unifiable, while the set $\{P(a, x), P(x, b)\}$ is not. $\triangleleft$

Definition 4.19 If θ is a unifier for Σ, and if for any unifier σ for Σ there exists substitution γ such that $\sigma = \theta\gamma$, then θ is called a *most general unifier* (abbreviated to *mgu*) for Σ. $\diamond$

Example 4.20 Let Σ be the set $\{R(x, x), R(z, f(y))\}$. Then $\theta = \{x/f(y), z/f(y)\}$ is an mgu for Σ. The substitution $\sigma = \{x/f(a), z/f(a), y/a\}$ is a unifier for Σ, but not an mgu, since there does not exist a substitution γ for which $\sigma\gamma = \theta$. $\triangleleft$

The mgu for some set of expressions is not unique: both $\{x/y\}$ and $\{y/x\}$ are mgu's for the set $\{P(x), P(y)\}$. Note that $\theta = \{x/z, y/z\}$ is not an mgu for this set, since there is no γ such that $\{x/y\} = \theta\gamma$. In particular, $\theta\{z/y\} = \{x/y, z/y\} \neq \{x/y\}$.

Below, we describe an algorithm to find an mgu for a set of expressions.

Definition 4.21 Let Σ be a finite set of simple expressions. The *disagreement set* of Σ is defined as follows. Locate the leftmost symbol position at which not all members of Σ have the same symbol, and extract from each expression in Σ the subexpression beginning at that symbol position. The set of all these expressions is the disagreement set. $\diamond$

Example 4.22 Let Σ be the set

$$\{P(x, y, v), P(x, \underline{f(g(a))}, x), P(x, \underline{f(z)}, f(a))\}.$$

The leftmost symbol position at which not all members of Σ have the same symbol is in this case the second argument place of P. The disagreement set of Σ is thus the set $\{y, f(g(a)), f(z)\}$, the set of all subexpressions at the second argument place of each expression in Σ (the underlined subexpressions). The disagreement set of $\Sigma = \{P(x), Q(a), \neg R(x)\}$ is $\{P(x), Q(a), \neg R(x)\}$. $\triangleleft$

The following algorithm takes as input a set Σ of simple expressions (terms or literals), and attempts to construct an mgu for this set. It can be proved that the algorithm always finds an mgu if one exists, and always reports that Σ is not unifiable if there does not exist an mgu for Σ.

Algorithm 4.1 (Unification Algorithm)
Input: A finite set Σ of simple expressions.
Output: An mgu for Σ (if Σ is unifiable).

1. Set $k = 0$ and $\sigma_0 = \varepsilon$.
2. If $\Sigma\sigma_k$ is a singleton, then stop: σ_k is an mgu for Σ.
   Otherwise, find the disagreement set D_k of $\Sigma\sigma_k$.
3. If there exist x and t in D_k such that x is a variable not occurring in t, then set $\sigma_{k+1} = \sigma_k\{x/t\}$, increment k by 1 and go to step 2.
   Otherwise, report that Σ is not unifiable, and stop.

Example 4.23 We will show how the algorithm works on the set $\Sigma = \{P(x, y, v), P(x, f(g(a)), x), P(x, f(z), f(a))\}$. In each $\Sigma\sigma_k$, we have underlined the members of the disagreement set.

1. $\sigma_0 = \varepsilon$.
   $\Sigma\sigma_0 = \{P(x, \underline{y}, v), P(x, \underline{f(g(a))}, x), P(x, \underline{f(z)}, f(a))\}$.
2. $D_0 = \{y, f(g(a)), f(z)\}$, $\sigma_1 = \{y/f(g(a))\}$.
   $\Sigma\sigma_1 = \{P(x, f(\underline{g(a)}), v), P(x, f(\underline{g(a)}), x), P(x, f(\underline{z}), f(a))\}$.
3. $D_1 = \{g(a), z\}$, $\sigma_2 = \{y/f(g(a)), z/g(a)\}$.
   $\Sigma\sigma_2 = \{P(x, f(g(a)), \underline{v}), P(x, f(g(a)), \underline{x}), P(x, f(g(a)), \underline{f(a)})\}$.
4. $D_2 = \{v, x, f(a)\}$, $\sigma_2 = \{y/f(g(a)), z/g(a), v/x\}$.
   $\Sigma\sigma_3 = \{P(x, f(g(a)), \underline{x}), P(x, f(g(a)), \underline{f(a)})\}$.
5. $D_3 = \{x, f(a)\}$, $\sigma_3 = \{y/f(g(a)), z/g(a), v/f(a), x/f(a)\}$.
   $\Sigma\sigma_4 = \{P(f(a), f(g(a)), f(a))\}$.

$\Sigma\sigma_4$ is a singleton, so σ_4 is an mgu for Σ.   ◁

Example 4.24 Another application of the algorithm, this time to the set $\Sigma = \{Q(a, x), Q(y, f(x))\}$, which is not unifiable.

1. $\sigma_0 = \varepsilon$.
   $\Sigma\sigma_0 = \{Q(\underline{a}, x), Q(\underline{y}, f(x))\}$.
2. $D_0 = \{a, y\}$, $\sigma_1 = \{y/a\}$.
   $\Sigma\sigma_1 = \{Q(a, \underline{x}), Q(a, \underline{f(x)})\}$.
3. $D_1 = \{x, f(x)\}$, and there are no variable x and term t in D_1 such that x does not occur in t, so the algorithm terminates and correctly reports that Σ is not unifiable.   ◁

Note the phrase "*x is a variable not occurring in t*" in the third step of the algorithm. This check if x does not occur in t is called the *occur check*. The occur check is crucial for the performance of the algorithm. For example, without the occur check, the algorithm would not detect that the set $\Sigma = \{x, f(x)\}$ is not unifiable, and would continue forever. We will give the first few steps of the way the algorithm *without the occur check* would handle this Σ:

1. $\sigma_0 = \varepsilon$.
   $\Sigma\sigma_0 = \{\underline{x}, f(x)\}$.
2. $D_0 = \{x, \overline{f(x)}\}$ (note that x occurs in $f(x)$!), $\sigma_1 = \{x/f(x)\}$.
   $\Sigma\sigma_1 = \{f(\underline{x}), f(\overline{f(x)})\}$.
3. $D_1 = \{x, f(x)\}$, $\overline{\sigma_2 = \{x/f(f(x))\}}$.
   $\Sigma\sigma_2 = \{f(f(\underline{x})), f(f(\overline{f(x)}))\}$.

$\vdots$

Clearly, this goes on forever. In each step, the algorithm mistakenly sets $\sigma_k = \sigma_{k-1}\{x/f(x)\}$, since it does not notice that x occurs in $f(x)$.

It can be proved by induction on the number k of steps used, that algorithm 4.1 always terminates, and always finds an mgu if one exists. We will not give the details of the proof here, but refer instead to [Llo87, Theorem 4.3] or [CL73, Theorem 5.2].

Theorem 4.25 (Unification Theorem) *Let Σ be a finite set of simple expressions. If Σ is unifiable, then the Unification Algorithm terminates and gives an mgu for Σ. If Σ is not unifiable, then the Unification Algorithm terminates and reports the fact that Σ is not unifiable.*

For more efficient unification algorithms, see [PW78, MM82]. More on substitutions and (most general) unification may be found in [Ede85, LMM88] and in Chapter 2 of [Apt97].

4.4 An Informal Introduction to Resolution

Now that we know what a proof procedure is, and how to use substitutions to unify sets of simple expressions, we can explain resolution. To avoid stating immediately a large sequence of definitions, we will first informally introduce the resolution principle in this section. Let us start with some examples:

- If we know that
    1. Peter plays chess or Peter plays football.
    2. Peter does not play football.
  then we can conclude that Peter plays chess.
- $\{(P \vee Q), \neg Q\} \models P$ (note that this can be seen as a formal representation of the previous example, where P stands for "Peter plays chess", and Q stands for "Peter plays football").
- $\{(\neg\exists x\ P(x) \vee Q(a)), (Q(b) \vee \exists x\ P(x))\} \models Q(a) \vee Q(b)$
- $\{(P(a) \vee Q(b)), (\neg P(a) \vee (Q(a) \rightarrow R(a,b)))\} \models Q(b) \vee (Q(a) \rightarrow R(a,b))$

Note the resemblance between these examples—they all conform to the following scheme: $\{(\phi \vee \psi), (\neg\phi \vee \chi)\} \models \psi \vee \chi$. This scheme, where ψ and/or χ may be omitted, and the order of the formulas is not important, can be viewed as the following derivation rule:

$$\frac{\phi \vee \psi, \quad \neg\phi \vee \chi}{\psi \vee \chi}$$

The proof procedure based on this rule is called *resolution*. It was introduced in 1965 by J. A. Robinson [Rob65], who proved its refutation completeness (for which see the next chapter).

It can be easily shown that the resolution rule is sound. Suppose both premises are true. Since either ϕ or $\neg\phi$ must be false, at least one of the formulas ψ and χ must be true, for otherwise one of the premises $\phi \vee \psi$ or $\neg\phi \vee \chi$ would be false. Hence the derived formula $\psi \vee \chi$ is true. Thus $\psi \vee \chi$ is a logical consequence of the two premises.

The formulas ϕ and $\neg\phi$ which occur in the two premises are said to form a *complementary pair*. In the scheme above, the formulas of the complementary pair are required to be the leftmost subformulas of the two premises, respectively. But this order within each premise is of course not necessary: the derivation of $R(a) \vee Q(a)$ from $\{(R(a) \vee P(b)), (Q(a) \vee \neg P(b))\}$ is a valid application of resolution, even though the formulas in the complementary pair $(P(b)$ and $\neg P(b))$, are not at the front of their respective premises.

Resolution can be applied to all sorts of formulas, but usually the application of resolution is restricted to *clauses*. That is, the premises and the conclusion of the derivation are required to be clauses (thought to be universally quantified, as usual). The reason for this restriction is that we can prove some important completeness results if we restrict ourselves to clauses. So henceforth, we will only use resolution to derive clauses from clauses. Applying a resolution step to two clauses is easy: the conclusion is just the disjunction of all the literals in the two premise-clauses, except for the complementary pair. For example, $P(a) \vee Q(a)$ can be derived from the premises $P(a) \vee R(b)$ and $\neg R(b) \vee Q(a)$.

One or more applications of this derivation rule (resolution) together form a derivation. As a simple example from propositional logic, let us see how we can derive the clause $P \vee Q$ from the set $\Sigma = \{(P \vee S), (\neg S \vee Q \vee \neg R), R\}$:

1. Derive $P \vee Q \vee \neg R$ from $\{(P \vee S), (\neg S \vee Q \vee \neg R)\}$.
2. Derive $P \vee Q$ from $\{(P \vee Q \vee \neg R), R\}$.

Since resolution is a sound derivation rule, we have found a proof that $\{(P \vee S), (\neg S \vee Q \vee \neg R), R\} \models (P \vee Q)$.

Such a derivation can be represented by a binary tree. For the previous example this tree is pictured in Figure 4.1. The tree should be read top-down: the leaves are clauses from Σ, each node N that is not a leaf is derived (using the resolution-scheme) from the two clauses on the nodes leading to N, and the root of the tree is the conclusion of the derivation.

In the case of first-order logic, we have to make one important addition, namely that we often must use unification to create a complementary pair. For instance, the clauses $C_1 = \neg P(x) \vee \neg R(a)$ and $C_2 = R(y) \vee \neg Q(y)$ do not contain a complementary pair. However, when we apply the mgu $\theta = \{y/a\}$, then $C_1\theta$ and $C_2\theta$ contain the complementary pair $\{\neg R(a), R(a)\}$. So after

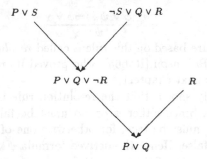

Figure 4.1: The tree for the derivation of $P \vee Q$

applying this substitution, we can use the resolution principle to derive the new clause $R = \neg P(x) \vee \neg Q(a)$ from $C_1\theta$ and $C_2\theta$; see Figure 4.2.

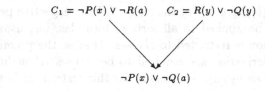

Figure 4.2: Derivation of $\neg P(x) \vee \neg Q(a)$, with mgu $\{y/a\}$

Also in the first-order case, several resolution steps together form a derivation. For instance, we can find a derivation of the clause $R(a)$ from the set $\Sigma = \{(Q(a) \vee P(a)), (\neg Q(x) \vee P(x) \vee R(x)), \neg P(y)\}$; see Figure 4.3.

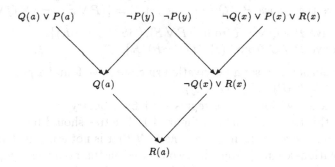

Figure 4.3: Derivation of $R(a)$

One special case of a derivation is a *refutation*, this is a derivation of the *empty clause* $\square$. For instance, there exists a refutation of the set $\{P(a), \neg P(x)\}$, involving one resolution step.

Up till now, we have not explained what the empty clause means. We will explain this presently. A clause C is thought to be universally quantified. Suppose $x_1, \ldots, x_n$ are all the variables appearing in C. Then C is true under some interpretation I, with domain D, if for all $d_1, \ldots, d_n \in D$, *at least one* literal in C is true under I and $V(x_1/d_1) \ldots (x_n/d_n)$ (where V is some arbitrary variable assignment). But the empty clause does not contain any literals which can be true, hence it is false under *any* I. This means that we can consider $\Box$ as a contradiction. Later on in this chapter, we will formally prove the soundness of derivations. This soundness implies that if we have found a refutation (a derivation of the contradiction $\Box$), we have found a proof that Σ is unsatisfiable: every model of Σ is then a model of $\Box$, but $\Box$ has no models, so Σ has no models.

4.5   A Formal Treatment of Resolution

In this section, we will make the informal discussion of the previous section more precise, by providing formal definitions of the concepts used there. Because the syntax of propositional logic is embedded in the syntax of first-order logic, all these definitions apply to propositional logic as well as to first-order logic. Some subtle points that have been swept under the rug in the previous section, will also be explained here.

To be able to apply resolution to clauses, we need two clauses which contain a complementary pair, such as $P(a)$ and $\neg P(a)$. So we start off with the corresponding definition:

Definition 4.26 Let L_1 be a positive literal, and let L_2 be a negative literal. Then L_1 and L_2 form a *complementary pair* if $\neg L_1 = L_2$. $\Diamond$

Here we adopt the convention that the negation of a negative literal $\neg A$ is A. So for instance, if $L = \neg Q(x, y)$, then we use $\neg L$ to denote $Q(x, y)$.

Example 4.27

- $\neg Q(x, y, f(b))$ and $Q(x, y, f(b))$ form a complementary pair.
- The clauses $P(x) \vee Q(a)$ and $R(x, y) \vee \neg Q(a) \vee \neg P(f(a))$ contain the complementary pair $Q(a)$ and $\neg Q(a)$. $\triangleleft$

If we have two clauses containing a complementary pair, we can derive a clause which is called a *binary resolvent* of these two clauses, following the resolution scheme presented in the previous section. The binary resolvent then contains all the literals in the two original clauses, except for the two literals in the complementary pair.

But as we have seen in Figure 4.2, sometimes we first have to apply a substitution to the two original clauses in order to obtain a complementary pair. An important and rather subtle point concerns the names of variables in a clause. Suppose we have $C_1 = P(a) \vee Q(x)$ and $C_2 = \neg P(a) \vee S(x)$. Then by the resolution scheme, we could derive $R = Q(x) \lor S(x)$ from C_1 and C_2. But suppose we rename C_2 to $C_2' = \neg P(a) \lor S(y)$. Then we could derive $R' = Q(x) \lor S(y)$. Clearly, R and R' are not equivalent, in fact $R' \models R$ but $R \not\models R'$. The problem is, of course, that C_1 and C_2 both contain the variable x. Intuitively, this is not "the same variable x". Yet the difference between these two variables x is obliterated when we derive the clause R.

We want our binary resolvents to be as "general" as possible. Thus in the previous example we would prefer R' to R as a binary resolvent. In order to assure that we always get the binary resolvent we want, we make the convention of renaming one (or both, though this is not necessary) of the premises such that they do not have any variables in common. They are then said to be *standardized apart*. This way, we do not accidentally consider a variable x occurring in both of the original clauses to be the "same" variable. Only after the renaming we construct the binary resolvent.

Definition 4.28 Let C_1 and C_2 be clauses. If C_1 and C_2 have no variables in common, then they are said to be *standardized apart*. $\diamond$

Definition 4.29 Let $C_1 = L_1 \lor \ldots \lor L_i \lor \ldots \lor L_m$ and $C_2 = M_1 \lor \ldots \lor M_j \lor \ldots \lor M_n$ be two clauses which are standardized apart. If the substitution θ is an mgu for the set $\{L_i, \neg M_j\}$, then the clause

$$(L_1 \lor \ldots \lor L_{i-1} \lor L_{i+1} \lor \ldots \lor L_m \lor M_1 \lor \ldots \lor M_{j-1} \lor M_{j+1} \lor \ldots \lor M_n)\theta$$

is called a *binary resolvent* of C_1 and C_2. The literals L_i and M_j are said to be the literals *resolved upon*. $\diamond$

If C_1 and C_2 are not standardized apart, we can use a variant C_2' of C_2 such that C_1 and C_2' are standardized apart, and then take a binary resolvent of C_1 and C_2'. For simplicity, this is then also called a binary resolvent of C_1 and C_2 itself.

Note that if L_i and M_j are the literals resolved upon and θ is the mgu used, then $L_i\theta$ and $M_j\theta$ form a complementary pair. We require θ to be a *most general* unifier, instead of an arbitrary unifier. The reason for this is that we want to restrict the number of possible binary resolvents. If we allowed θ to be an arbitrary unifier, the set of binary resolvents of two clauses would often be infinite, which makes the search for a deduction (see Section 5.6) extremely complex.

Example 4.30 Let $C_1 = Q(x) \lor \neg P(x) \lor R(y)$ and $C_2 = P(x) \lor \neg S(y, x)$. C_1 and C_2 are not standardized apart, so we rename C_2 to $C_2' = P(u) \lor \neg S(v, u)$. Let $\theta = \{u/x\}$. Then θ is an mgu for $\{P(x), P(u)\}$. Hence $C = Q(x) \lor R(x) \lor \neg S(v, x)$ is a binary resolvent of C_1 and C_2. $\neg P(x)$ and $P(u)$ are the literals resolved upon here. $\triangleleft$

In the previous definition, the binary resolvent may be the empty clause. This is the case if C_1 and C_2 each consist of exactly one literal. For example, the empty clause $\square$ is a binary resolvent of the clauses $C_1 = P(x)$ and $C_2 = \neg P(a)$. We have already explained in the previous section that $\square$ represents a contradiction.

The previous definition of a binary resolvent is not sufficient: it does not allow us yet to derive all the clauses we want. For instance, we would like to be able to derive the empty clause $\square$ from the clauses $C_1 = P(x) \vee P(y)$ and $C_2 = \neg P(u) \vee \neg P(v)$, since clearly, $\square$ is a clause which is a logical consequence of the clauses C_1 and C_2. However, given only the definition of a binary resolvent, it is not possible to construct a series of binary resolvents from C_1 and C_2 which leads to the empty clause $\square$, because every such resolvent would still contain two literals.

To be able to derive $\square$ from this C_1 and C_2, we need to introduce the notion of a *factor*. A factor of a clause C is obtained by applying a substitution θ to C which unifies one or more literals in C, and then deleting all but one copy of these unified literals. For instance, $\theta = \{y/x\}$ unifies the two literals $P(x)$ and $P(y)$ in C_1. Thus $C_1' = P(x)$ is a factor of C_1, obtained by deleting the second copy of $P(x)$ from $C_1\theta = P(x) \vee P(x)$. Similarly, $C_2' = \neg P(u)$ is a factor of C_2.

Definition 4.31 Let C be a clause, $L_1, \ldots, L_n$ ($n \geq 1$) some unifiable literals from C, and θ an mgu for the set $\{L_1, \ldots, L_n\}$. Then the clause obtained by deleting $L_2\theta, \ldots, L_n\theta$ from $C\theta$ is called a *factor* of C. $\diamond$

Note that every non-empty clause C is a factor of C itself, using the identity substitution ε as mgu for one literal in C. It can easily be shown that if C' is a factor of C, then $C \models C'$. We leave this to the reader.

Example 4.32 Some examples of factors:
- $\neg Q(a) \vee P(f(a))$ is a factor of the clause $\neg Q(a) \vee P(f(a)) \vee P(y)$, using $\{y/f(a)\}$ as an mgu for $\{P(f(a)), P(y)\}$.
- $Q(x) \vee P(x, a)$ is a factor of $Q(x) \vee Q(y) \vee Q(z) \vee P(z, a)$. $\triangleleft$

Factors are important, because they enable us to derive from two clauses C_1 and C_2 clauses which are not binary resolvents of C_1 and C_2. If we allow factors of C_1 and C_2 to be used as intermediate clauses before taking a binary resolvent, we can for instance derive $\square$ from $C_1 = P(x) \vee P(y)$ and $C_2 = \neg P(u) \vee \neg P(v)$, using the factor $P(x)$ of C_1 and the factor $\neg P(u)$ of C_2. When we use factors to find a resolvent, the resulting clause is called a *resolvent*. From the following definition we see that every binary resolvent is a resolvent, but not every resolvent is a *binary* resolvent.

Definition 4.33 Let C_1 and C_2 be two clauses. A *resolvent* C of C_1 and C_2 is a binary resolvent of a factor of C_1 and a factor of C_2, where the literals resolved upon are the literals unified by the respective factors. C_1 and C_2 are called the *parent clauses* of C. $\diamond$

Example 4.34 Some examples:

- $\neg P(a) \vee Q(a, y)$ is a factor of $C_1 = \neg P(x) \vee \neg P(a) \vee Q(x, y)$. So $Q(a, y) \vee R(z)$ is a resolvent of C_1 and $C_2 = R(z) \vee P(a)$. Note that the literal $\neg P(a)$ that was resolved upon, was the literal unified in the factor of C_1.

- $\square$ is a resolvent of $C_1 = Q(x)$ and $C_2 = \neg Q(a) \vee \neg Q(x)$. ◁

A *derivation* of some clause C from some set of clauses Σ is a sequence of clauses, such that each clause is either a member of Σ, or a resolvent of two earlier clauses in the sequence.

Definition 4.35 Let Σ be a set of clauses and C a clause. A *derivation* of C from Σ is a finite sequence of clauses $R_1, \ldots, R_k = C$, such that each R_i is either in Σ, or a resolvent of two clauses in $\{R_1, \ldots, R_{i-1}\}$. If such a derivation exists, we write $\Sigma \vdash_r C$. We then say C can be *derived* from Σ. A derivation of the empty clause $\square$ from Σ is called a *refutation* of Σ. ◇

In the previous section, we have already seen some examples of derivations, in their representation as binary trees. Some more examples:

Example 4.36 We will give a derivation of $\neg P(x)$ from $\Sigma = \{(\neg P(x) \vee \neg R(x) \vee \neg Q(a)), R(y), \neg Q(b), (Q(a) \vee Q(b))\}$. See Figure 4.4.

1. $\neg P(x) \vee \neg R(x) \vee \neg Q(a)$
2. $R(y)$
3. $\neg Q(b)$
4. $Q(a) \vee Q(b)$
5. $\neg P(x) \vee \neg Q(a)$ (from 1 and 2)
6. $Q(a)$ (from 3 and 4)
7. $\neg P(x)$ (from 5 and 6) ◁

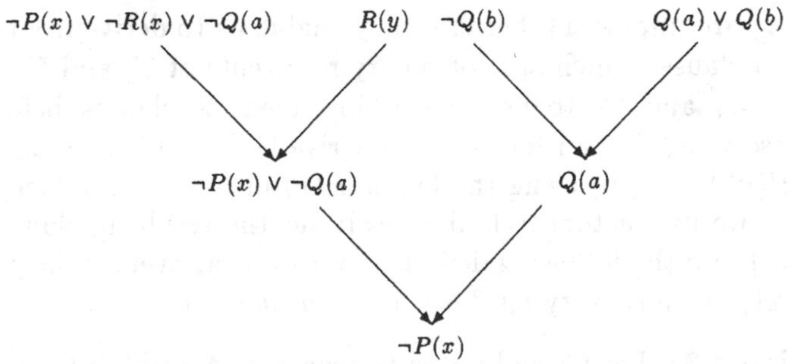

Figure 4.4: The tree for the derivation of $\neg P(x)$ from Σ

Example 4.37 We can prove that the set $\Sigma = \{(P(x) \vee Q(x,y)), \neg P(z),$ $(\neg Q(a,b) \vee P(a) \vee P(b))\}$ is unsatisfiable, by giving a refutation of Σ. See Figure 4.5 for illustration.

1. $P(x) \vee Q(x,y)$
2. $\neg P(z)$
3. $\neg Q(a,b) \vee P(a) \vee P(b)$
4. $Q(x,y)$ (a resolvent of 1 and 2)
5. $P(a) \vee P(b)$ (from 4 and 3)
6. $P(b)$ (from 5 and 2)
7. $\square$ (from 6 and 2) $\triangleleft$

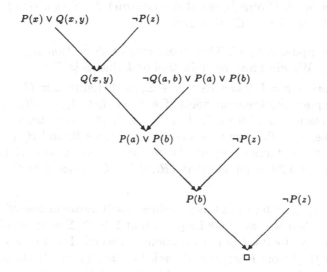

Figure 4.5: The tree for the refutation of Σ

The soundness of resolution is easily proved. First for a single resolution step:

Lemma 4.38 *Let C_1 and C_2 be clauses. If R is a resolvent of C_1 and C_2, then $\{C_1, C_2\} \models R$.*

Proof Without loss of generality, we assume C_1 and C_2 are standardized apart. Suppose R is a binary resolvent of C'_1 (a factor of C_1) and C'_2 (a factor of C_2). Let L_i (a literal in C'_1) and M_j (a literal in C'_2) be the literals resolved upon, and let θ be the mgu for $\{L_i, \neg M_j\}$ that is used to obtain R. Then $C_1 \models C'_1\theta$ and $C_2 \models C'_2\theta$.

Suppose the interpretation I (with domain D) is a model of $\{C_1, C_2\}$. Then I is also a model of $\{C'_1\theta, C'_2\theta\}$. Let $x_1, \ldots, x_n$ be all the variables occurring in $C'_1\theta$ or $C'_2\theta$. Let V be an arbitrary variable assignment. Then for all $d_1 \in D, \ldots, d_n \in D$, if $L_i\theta$ is false under I and

$V(x_1/d_1)\ldots(x_n/d_n)$, at least one of the other literals in $C_1'\theta$ is true under I and $V(x_1/d_1)\ldots(x_n/d_n)$. Similarly, for all $d_1 \in D, \ldots, d_n \in D$, if $M_j\theta$ is false under I and $V(x_1/d_1)\ldots(x_n/d_n)$, at least one of the other literals in $C_2'\theta$ is true under I and $V(x_1/d_1)\ldots(x_n/d_n)$.

R consists of all literals in $C_1'\theta$ and $C_2'\theta$, except for $L_i\theta$ and $M_j\theta$. Since either $L_i\theta$ or $M_j\theta$ (which form a complementary pair) is false under I and $V(x_1/d_1)\ldots(x_n/d_n)$, at least one of the literals in R is true under I and $V(x_1/d_1)\ldots(x_n/d_n)$, so I is a model of R. Hence $\{C_1, C_2\} \models R$. □

The soundness of derivations follows easily from the previous lemma.

Theorem 4.39 (Soundness of derivation) *Let Σ be a set of clauses, and C be a clause. If $\Sigma \vdash_r C$, then $\Sigma \models C$.*

Proof Suppose $\Sigma \vdash_r C$. Then there exists a derivation $R_1, \ldots, R_k = C$ of C from Σ. We will prove by induction on k that $\Sigma \models C$.

1. Suppose $k = 1$. Then $R_1 = C \in \Sigma$, so obviously $\Sigma \models C$.
2. Suppose the theorem holds if $k \leq m$. Let $R_1, \ldots, R_{m+1} = C$ be a derivation of C from Σ. If $R_{m+1} \in \Sigma$ then the theorem is obvious. Otherwise, $R_{m+1} = C$ is a resolvent of some R_i and R_j $(i, j < m + 1)$. By the induction hypothesis, we have $\Sigma \models R_i$ and $\Sigma \models R_j$. From Lemma 4.38, it follows that $\{R_i, R_j\} \models C$. Hence $\Sigma \models C$. □

Note in particular what this soundness result means in case of a refutation. If $\Sigma \vdash_r \Box$, then we have found a proof that $\Sigma \models \Box$: Σ is unsatisfiable.

Resolution by itself is not complete in general. For instance, we cannot derive $P(f(x))$ from $P(x)$, even though $P(x) \models P(f(x))$. In the next chapter, we will examine what needs to be added to resolution to get a complete proof procedure. On the other hand, we will also show that resolution is complete with respect to *unsatisfiable* sets of clauses: Σ is unsatisfiable iff Σ has a refutation.

4.6 Summary

Logic programming is concerned with describing problems as a set of formulas (clauses), and solving those problems by checking which formulas are logically implied by those formulas. According to Church's Theorem, logical implication is *undecidable* for first-order logic: there is no algorithm that can find out whether $\Sigma \models \phi$ holds, for every Σ and ϕ. However, there do exist proof procedures which are both *sound* and *complete*, that is, which can prove all and only logical consequences of a set Σ.

One of the most important proof procedures is based on the *resolution* rule. In essence, this rule derives a *resolvent* $\psi \vee \chi$ from two premises $\phi \vee \psi$ and $\neg \phi \vee \chi$. For first-order clauses, we also need *unification* and *factors* in such a resolution step. Combining several resolution steps, starting from clauses in Σ and ending in a clause C, we get a derivation from Σ, denoted by $\Sigma \vdash_r C$. Derivations are sound: if $\Sigma \vdash_r C$, then $\Sigma \models C$. Completeness results involving resolution will be given in the following chapters. A derivation of the empty clause $\square$ is called a *refutation* of Σ. Since $\square$ is a contradiction, a refutation of Σ is a proof that Σ is unsatisfiable.

Chapter 5

Subsumption Theorem and Refutation Completeness

5.1 Introduction

We start this chapter with an example showing how resolution can be used to formalize some every-day reasoning. After that, we will see what needs to be added to resolution in order to get a complete proof procedure.

Example 5.1 Mary, the school teacher of little John, notices that little John is not in school today. She knows that if someone is not in school then that persoon is either ill, or lazy. She also knows that ill people do not go shopping, but she has seen little John come out of the candy shop today.

We can formalize this as follows: a denotes little John, $P(x)$ means "x is in school today", $Q(x)$ means "x is ill", $R(x)$ means "x is lazy", and $S(x)$ means "x goes shopping". Now we have the following premises:

1. $\neg P(a)$ ("little John is not in school today")
2. $\forall x\ (\neg P(x) \rightarrow (Q(x) \vee R(x)))$ ("people who are not in school are either ill or lazy (or both)")
3. $\forall x\ (Q(x) \rightarrow \neg S(x))$ ("ill people don't go shopping")
4. $S(a)$ ("little John has gone shopping today")

We can write these formulas as the following clauses:

1. $\neg P(a)$
2. $P(x) \vee Q(x) \vee R(x)$
3. $\neg Q(x) \vee \neg S(x)$
4. $S(a)$

We can now prove that little John is lazy, by deriving the clause $R(a)$ ("little John is lazy") from these clauses: see Figure 5.1. ◁

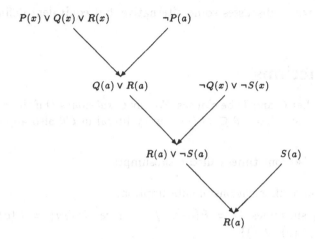

Figure 5.1: The proof that little John is lazy

Derivations are a powerful tool. However, sometimes it is not possible to derive a clause we want to prove, but only something more general. For instance, suppose we want to prove that $R(a) \lor R(b)$ is a logical consequence of the clauses in the previous example, which it clearly is, since $R(a) \models R(a) \lor R(b)$. Even though there is a derivation of $R(a)$ from those clauses, there is no derivation of $R(a) \lor R(b)$. Or take another example: suppose $\Sigma = \{(Q(x) \lor P(a)), \neg P(a)\}$ and $C = Q(b)$. Clearly, $\Sigma \models C$, but using resolution there only exists a derivation of $Q(x)$ from Σ, not of $Q(b)$. We can patch this up by introducing *subsumption*. C subsumes D if there is a substitution θ, such that $C\theta \subseteq D$. Clearly, $R(a)$ subsumes $R(a) \lor R(b)$, and $Q(x)$ subsumes $Q(b)$.

In this chapter we introduce a *deduction* as the combination of a derivation and a subsumption step. We then prove the soundness and completeness of deductions. The main result is the *Subsumption Theorem*. We also prove another completeness result, the *refutation completeness* of resolution for unsatisfiable sets of clauses, and show that these two completeness results are in a sense equivalent: the one can be proved from the other. Refutation completeness was originally proved by Robinson [Rob65]. The Subsumption Theorem was first proved in [Lee67, SCL69], where it was called the 'completeness theorem for consequence finding'. Kowalski [Kow70] first used the name 'Subsumption Theorem'. In ILP, it was rediscovered by Bain and Muggleton [BM92]. The proofs in this chapter are adapted from [NW95, NW96d].

The two completeness results mentioned here only apply to sets of clauses. However, in Section 5.5 we show a way in which logical implication between formulas other than clauses can also be proved by means of resolution. After that, we give a procedure to *find* a proof if one exists. The chapter is followed by an appendix which discusses some alternative, but equivalent definitions of resolution.

5.2 Deductions

Definition 5.2 Let C and D be clauses. We say C *subsumes* D if there exists a substitution θ such that $C\theta \subseteq D$ (i.e., every literal in $C\theta$ also appears in D). $\Diamond$

Subsumption is also sometimes called θ-subsumption.

Example 5.3 Some illustrations of subsumption:

- $C = P(x)$ subsumes $D = P(a) \vee Q(x)$, since $C\{x/a\} = P(a)$, and $\{P(a)\} \subseteq \{P(a), Q(x)\}$.
- $C = P(a) \vee P(a)$ subsumes $D = P(a)$. Also, D subsumes C.
- $C = P(x) \vee \neg Q(a)$ subsumes $D = P(a) \vee \neg P(f(x)) \vee \neg Q(a)$.
- The empty clause $\square$ subsumes any clause, because the empty set is a subset of the set of literals in any clause.
- The only clause which subsumes the empty clause $\square$, is $\square$ itself. $\triangleleft$

We leave it to the reader to prove that if C subsumes D, then $C \models D$. The combination of a derivation and subsumption yields a *deduction*.[1] Note that $\Sigma \models C$ may be true for clauses C which have nothing to do whatsoever with Σ. This is the case with tautologies: $C = Q(x) \vee \neg Q(x) \vee R(y)$ is a tautology, hence $\Sigma \models C$ for any set Σ. We want to define a 'deduction' in such a way that it is complete, so it should also work for tautologies. For this reason, we include the case where C is a tautology in our concept of a deduction.

Definition 5.4 Let Σ be a set of clauses and C a clause. We say there exists a *deduction* of C from Σ, written as $\Sigma \vdash_d C$, if C is a tautology, or if there exists a clause D such that $\Sigma \vdash_r D$ and D subsumes C. If $\Sigma \vdash_d C$, we say C can be *deduced* from Σ. $\Diamond$

Example 5.5 Let $C = \neg P(b) \vee R(y)$ and $\Sigma = \{(\neg P(x) \vee \neg R(x) \vee \neg Q(a)), R(y), \neg Q(b), (Q(a) \vee Q(b))\}$. Figure 4.4 (p. 71) showed that $\Sigma \vdash_r \neg P(x)$. Since $\neg P(x)$ subsumes C, we have $\Sigma \vdash_d C$. $\triangleleft$

The soundness of deductions follows immediately from the soundness of derivations (Theorem 4.39) and the fact that if D subsumes C, then $D \models C$.

Theorem 5.6 (Soundness of deduction) *Let Σ be a set of clauses, and C be a clause. If $\Sigma \vdash_d C$, then $\Sigma \models C$.*

---

[1] It should be noted that our terminology is somewhat non-standard here. For instance, Chang and Lee [CL73] use the term 'deduction' for what we call a derivation.

5.3   The Subsumption Theorem

In this section, we give a proof of our most important completeness result: if $\Sigma \models C$, then $\Sigma \vdash_d C$. In other words: any clause which is a logical consequence of Σ, can be deduced from Σ. Combined with its converse, the soundness of deductions, this is called the *Subsumption Theorem*. We prove this in a number of successive steps in the following subsections. First we prove the result in case both Σ and C are ground, then we prove it in case Σ consists of arbitrary clauses but C is ground, and finally we prove the theorem when neither Σ nor C need be ground.

5.3.1   The Subsumption Theorem for Ground Σ and C

Lemma 5.7 *Let Σ be a set of ground clauses, and C be a ground clause. If $\Sigma \models C$, then $\Sigma \vdash_d C$.*

Proof By Theorem 2.43, we can assume Σ is finite. Assume C is not a tautology. Then we need to find a clause D such that $\Sigma \vdash_r D$ and $D \subseteq C$ (for ground clauses D and C, D subsumes C iff $D \subseteq C$). The proof is by induction on the number of clauses in Σ.

1. Suppose $\Sigma = \{C_1\}$. We will show that $C_1 \subseteq C$. Suppose $C_1 \not\subseteq C$. Then there exists a literal L such that $L \in C_1$ but $L \notin C$. Let I be an interpretation which makes L true, and all literals in C false (such an I exists, since C is not a tautology). Then I is a model of C_1, but not of C. But that contradicts $\Sigma \models C$. So $C_1 \subseteq C$, and $\Sigma \vdash_d C$.

2. (See Figure 5.2 for illustration of this case). Suppose the theorem holds if $|\Sigma| \leq m$. We will prove that this implies that the theorem also holds if $|\Sigma| = m + 1$. Let $\Sigma = \{C_1, \ldots, C_{m+1}\}$, and $\Sigma' = \{C_1, \ldots, C_m\}$. If C_{m+1} subsumes C or $\Sigma' \models C$, then the theorem holds. So assume C_{m+1} does not subsume C and $\Sigma' \not\models C$.

   The idea is to derive, using the induction hypothesis, a number of clauses from which a derivation of a subset of C can be constructed. First note that since $\Sigma' \cup \{C_{m+1}\} \models C$, it follows from Theorem 2.36 that $\Sigma' \models (C_{m+1} \rightarrow C)$, hence $\Sigma' \models C \vee \neg C_{m+1}$.

   Let $L_1, \ldots, L_k$ be all the literals in C_{m+1} which are not in C ($k \geq 1$ since C_{m+1} does not subsume C). Then we can write $C_{m+1} = L_1 \vee \ldots \vee L_k \vee C'$, where $C' \subseteq C$. Since C does not contain L_i ($1 \leq i \leq k$), the clause $C \vee \neg L_i$ is not a tautology. Also, since $\Sigma' \models C \vee \neg C_{m+1}$ and C_{m+1} is ground, we have that $\Sigma' \models C \vee \neg L_i$, for each i. Then by the induction hypothesis there exists for each i a ground clause D_i such that $\Sigma' \vdash_r D_i$ and $D_i \subseteq (C \vee \neg L_i)$.

   We will use C_{m+1} and the derivations from Σ' of these D_i to construct a derivation of a subset of C from Σ. For each i, $\neg L_i \in D_i$, for otherwise we would have $D_i \subseteq C$ and $\Sigma' \models C$. So we can write each D_i as $\neg L_i \vee D'_i$, and $D_i' \subseteq C$ (the case where some D_i contains $\neg L_i$ more than once can be solved by taking a factor of D_i).

Now we can construct a derivation of the ground clause defined as $D = C' \vee D_1' \vee \ldots \vee D_k'$ from Σ, using C_{m+1} and the derivations of $D_1, \ldots, D_k$ from Σ'. See Figure 5.2 for a schematic representation of this derivation. In this tree, the derivations of $D_1, \ldots, D_k$ are indicated by the vertical dots. So we have that $\Sigma \vdash_r D$. Since $C' \subseteq C$, and $D_i' \subseteq C$ for each i, we have that $D \subseteq C$. Hence $\Sigma \vdash_d C$. □

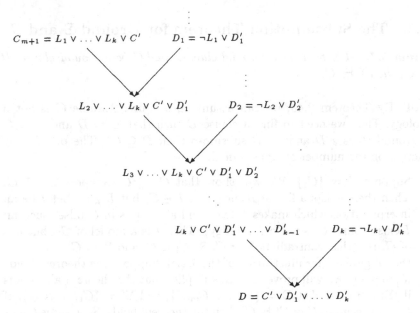

Figure 5.2: The tree for the derivation of D from Σ

5.3.2 The Subsumption Theorem when C is Ground

In this section, we will prove the Subsumption Theorem in case C is ground and Σ is a set of arbitrary clauses. The idea is to "translate" $\Sigma \models C$ to $\Sigma_g \models C$, where Σ_g is a set of ground instances of clauses of Σ. Then by Lemma 5.7 there is a clause D such that $\Sigma_g \vdash_r D$, and D subsumes C. Finally, we "lift" this derivation to a derivation from Σ. The next two results show that logical implication between clauses can be translated to logical implication between ground clauses. The first of these is Herbrand's Theorem.

Theorem 5.8 (Herbrand) *A set of clauses Σ is unsatisfiable iff there exists a finite unsatisfiable set Σ_g of ground instances of clauses from Σ.*

Proof

⇐: Σ_g is a finite set of ground instances of clauses from Σ, so $\Sigma \models \Sigma_g$. Hence if Σ_g is unsatisfiable, then Σ is unsatisfiable.

⇒: Let Σ' be the (possibly infinite) set of all ground instances of clauses from Σ. It is not very difficult to see that a Herbrand interpretation I is a model of a clause C iff I is a model of the set of all ground instances of C. Hence such an I is a model of Σ iff it is a model of Σ'. Now:

> Σ is unsatisfiable iff (by Proposition 3.30)
> Σ has no Herbrand models iff
> Σ' has no Herbrand models iff (by Proposition 3.30)
> Σ' is unsatisfiable.

Finally, by the Compactness Theorem (Theorem 2.42) there is a *finite* unsatisfiable subset Σ_g of Σ'.   □

Theorem 5.9 *Let Σ be a non-empty set of clauses, and C be a ground clause. Then $\Sigma \models C$ iff there exists a finite set Σ_g of ground instances of clauses from Σ, such that $\Sigma_g \models C$.*

Proof

⇐: If Σ_g is a finite set of ground instances of clauses from Σ, then $\Sigma \models \Sigma_g$. Hence if $\Sigma_g \models C$, then $\Sigma \models C$.

⇒: Suppose $\Sigma \models C$. Let $C = L_1 \vee \ldots \vee L_k$ $(k \geq 0)$. Note that since C is ground, $\neg C$ is equivalent to $\neg L_1 \wedge \ldots \wedge \neg L_k$. Then:

> $\Sigma \models C$ iff (by Proposition 2.37)
> $\Sigma \cup \{\neg C\}$ is unsatisfiable iff
> $\Sigma \cup \{\neg L_1, \ldots, \neg L_k\}$ is unsatisfiable iff (by Theorem 5.8)
> there exists a finite unsatisfiable set Σ', consisting of ground instances of clauses from $\Sigma \cup \{\neg L_1, \ldots, \neg L_k\}$.

Since adding clauses to an unsatisfiable set preserves unsatisfiability, we may assume without loss of generality that Σ' contains every $\neg L_i$, $1 \leq i \leq k$. Thus we can write $\Sigma' = \Sigma_g \cup \{\neg L_1, \ldots, \neg L_k\}$, where Σ_g is a finite set of ground instances of clauses from Σ. (Σ_g may be empty if C is a tautology.) Now:

> Σ' is unsatisfiable iff
> $\Sigma_g \cup \{\neg L_1, \ldots, \neg L_k\}$ is unsatisfiable iff
> $\Sigma_g \cup \{\neg(L_1 \vee \ldots \vee L_k)\}$ is unsatisfiable iff (Proposition 2.37)
> $\Sigma_g \models L_1 \vee \ldots \vee L_k$.   □

Example 5.10 Let $\Sigma = \{(P(f(x)) \vee \neg P(x)), P(a)\}$ and $C = P(f(f(a)))$. Then $\Sigma \models C$. Here $\Sigma_g = \{(P(f(f(a))) \vee \neg P(f(a))), (P(f(a)) \vee \neg P(a)), P(a)\}$ is a set of ground instances of clauses of Σ, for which we have $\Sigma_g \models C$.   ◁

The following two lemmas are sufficient to "lift" a derivation, that is, to turn a derivation from instances of certain clauses into a derivation from those clauses themselves.

Lemma 5.11 *Let C_1 and C_2 be two clauses, and C_1' and C_2' instances of C_1 and C_2, respectively. If R' is a resolvent of C_1' and C_2', then there exists a resolvent R of C_1 and C_2, such that R' is an instance of R.*

Proof We assume without loss of generality that C_1 and C_2, and C_1' and C_2' are standardized apart. Let $C_1 = L_1 \vee \ldots \vee L_m$, $C_2 = M_1 \vee \ldots \vee M_n$, $C_1' = C_1 \sigma_1$, and $C_2' = C_2 \sigma_2$. Suppose R' is a resolvent of C_1' and C_2'. Then R' is a binary resolvent of a factor of C_1' and a factor of C_2'. See the figure for illustration.

For notational convenience, we assume without loss of generality that the factor of C_1' is $(L_1 \vee \ldots \vee L_a)\sigma_1\theta_1$, where θ_1 is an mgu for $L_a\sigma_1, \ldots, L_m\sigma_1$. Similarly, the factor of C_2' that is used, is $(M_1 \vee \ldots \vee M_b)\sigma_2\theta_2$, where θ_2 is an mgu for $M_b\sigma_2, \ldots, M_n\sigma_2$. Let $L_i\sigma_1\theta_1$ and $M_j\sigma_2\theta_2$ be the literals resolved upon, with mgu μ. Abbreviate $L_1 \vee \ldots \vee L_{i-1} \vee L_{i+1} \vee \ldots \vee L_a$ to D_1, and $M_1 \vee \ldots \vee M_{j-1} \vee M_{j+1} \vee \ldots \vee M_b$ to D_2. Then $R' = (D_1\sigma_1\theta_1 \vee D_2\sigma_2\theta_2)\mu$. By our assumption of standardizing apart, this can be written as $R' = (D_1 \vee D_2)\sigma_1\theta_1\sigma_2\theta_2\mu$.

Let γ_1 be an mgu for $L_a \vee \ldots \vee L_m$. Then $(L_1 \vee \ldots \vee L_a)\gamma_1$ is a factor of C_1. Note that $\sigma_1\theta_1$ is a unifier for $L_a, \ldots, L_m$. Since γ_1 is an mgu for $L_a, \ldots, L_m$, there exists a substitution δ_1 such that $\sigma_1\theta_1 = \gamma_1\delta_1$. Similarly, $(M_1 \vee \ldots \vee M_b)\gamma_2$ is a factor of C_2, with γ_2 as mgu for $M_b \vee \ldots \vee M_n$, and there is a δ_2 such that $\sigma_2\theta_2 = \gamma_2\delta_2$.

Since $L_i\sigma_1\theta_1$ and $\neg M_j\sigma_2\theta_2$ can be unified (they have μ as mgu) and γ_i is more general than $\sigma_i\theta_i$ $(i = 1, 2)$, $L_i\gamma_1$ and $\neg M_j\gamma_2$ can be unified. Let θ be an mgu for $L_i\gamma_1$ and $\neg M_j\gamma_2$. Define $R = (D_1\gamma_1 \vee D_2\gamma_2)\theta$, which can be written as $R = (D_1 \vee D_2)\gamma_1\gamma_2\theta$. Since R is a binary resolvent of the above-mentioned factors of C_1 and C_2, it is a resolvent of C_1 and C_2.

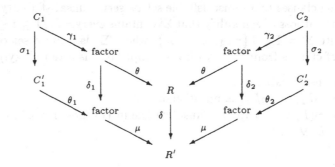

It remains to show that R' is an instance of R. Since $L_i\gamma_1\delta_1\delta_2\mu = L_i\sigma_1\theta_1\delta_2\mu = L_i\sigma_1\theta_1\mu = \neg M_j\sigma_2\theta_2\mu = \neg M_j\gamma_2\delta_2\mu = \neg M_j\gamma_2\delta_1\delta_2\mu$, the substitution $\delta_1\delta_2\mu$ is a unifier for $L_i\gamma_1$ and $\neg M_j\gamma_2$. θ is an mgu for $L_i\gamma_1$ and

$\neg M_j \gamma_2$, so there exists a substitution δ such that $\delta_1 \delta_2 \mu = \theta \delta$. Therefore $R' = (D_1 \lor D_2)\sigma_1\theta_1\sigma_2\theta_2\mu = (D_1 \lor D_2)\gamma_1\delta_1\gamma_2\delta_2\mu = (D_1 \lor D_2)\gamma_1\gamma_2\delta_1\delta_2\mu = (D_1 \lor D_2)\gamma_1\gamma_2\theta\delta = R\delta$. Hence R' is an instance of R.   □

Lemma 5.12 (Derivation lifting) *Let Σ be a set of clauses, and Σ' a set of instances of clauses from Σ. Suppose $R'_1, \ldots, R'_k$ is a derivation of the clause R'_k from Σ'. Then there exists a derivation $R_1, \ldots, R_k$ of the clause R_k from Σ, such that R'_i is an instance of R_i, for each i.*

Proof The proof is by induction on k.

1. Suppose $k = 1$. $R'_1 \in \Sigma'$, so there exists a clause $R_1 \in \Sigma$ such that R'_1 is an instance of R_1.

2. Suppose the lemma holds if $k \leq m$. Let $R'_1, \ldots, R'_m, R'_{m+1}$ be a derivation of R'_{m+1} from Σ'. By the induction hypothesis, there exists a derivation $R_1, \ldots, R_m$ of R_m from Σ, such that R'_i is an instance of R_i for all i, $1 \leq i \leq m$. If $R'_{m+1} \in \Sigma'$, the lemma is obvious. Otherwise, R'_{m+1} is a resolvent of two clauses C'_1 and C'_2 in $\{R'_1, \ldots, R'_m\}$. Then there exist two clauses C_1 and C_2 in $\{R_1, \ldots, R_m\}$ such that C'_1 is an instance of C_1, and C'_2 is an instance of C_2. It follows from Lemma 5.11 that there is a resolvent R_{m+1} of C_1 and C_2, such that R'_{m+1} is an instance of R_{m+1}. Hence the lemma holds for $k = m + 1$.   □

The previous lemmas are sufficient to prove the Subsumption Theorem for the case where C is ground.

Lemma 5.13 *Let Σ be a set of clauses, and C be a ground clause. If $\Sigma \models C$, then $\Sigma \vdash_d C$.*

Proof Assume C is not a tautology. We want to find a clause D such that $\Sigma \vdash_r D$ and D subsumes C. From $\Sigma \models C$ and Theorem 5.9, there exists a finite set Σ_g such that each clause in Σ_g is a ground instance of a clause in Σ, and $\Sigma_g \models C$. Then from Lemma 5.7 there exists a clause D' such that $\Sigma_g \vdash_r D'$, and D' subsumes C. Let $R'_1, \ldots, R'_k = D'$ be a derivation of D' from Σ_g. It follows from Lemma 5.12 that we can lift this to a derivation $R_1, \ldots, R_k$ of R_k from Σ, where D' is an instance of R_k. Let $D = R_k$. Then $\Sigma \vdash_r D$ and D subsumes C (since D' subsumes C).   □

5.3.3   The Subsumption Theorem (General Case)

Finally we prove the Subsumption Theorem for arbitrary Σ and C. Here we need a *Skolem substitution*, which is related to the introduction of Skolem constants that we used in Chapter 3.

Definition 5.14 Let Σ be a set of clauses, and C be a clause. Let $x_1, \ldots, x_n$ be all the variables appearing in C, and $a_1, \ldots, a_n$ be distinct constants not appearing in Σ or C. Then the substitution $\{x_1/a_1, \ldots, x_n/a_n\}$ is called a *Skolem substitution* for C with respect to Σ.

Similarly, if S is a set of clauses, $y_1, \ldots, y_m$ are all the variables appearing in S, and $b_1, \ldots, b_m$ are distinct constants not appearing in Σ or S, then $\{y_1/b_1, \ldots, y_m/b_m\}$ is a *Skolem substitution* for S with respect to Σ. $\diamond$

Example 5.15 Let $\Sigma = \{P(x) \vee \neg Q(y, f(a))\}$ and $C = Q(z, y) \vee P(b)$. Then $\{z/c, y/d\}$ is a Skolem substitution for C with respect to Σ. If $S = \{P(x), Q(x, y)\}$, then $\{x/b, y/c\}$ is a Skolem substitution for S with respect to Σ. $\triangleleft$

The following lemma shows that if we have derived some clause D from Σ which subsumes $C\theta$—where θ is a Skolem substitution for C with respect to Σ—then D also subsumes C. For instance, suppose $D = P(x)$, $C = P(y) \vee Q(z)$ and $\theta = \{y/a, z/b\}$. D subsumes $C\theta$, but since θ replaces each variable by a constant that does not appear in Σ, C or D, D also subsumes C itself.

Lemma 5.16 *Let C and D be clauses. Let $\theta = \{x_1/a_1, \ldots, x_n/a_n\}$ be a Skolem substitution for C with respect to D. If D subsumes $C\theta$, then D also subsumes C.*

Proof Since D subsumes $C\theta$, there exists a substitution σ such that $D\sigma \subseteq C\theta$. Let σ be the substitution $\{y_1/t_1, \ldots, y_m/t_m\}$. Let σ' be the substitution obtained from σ by replacing each a_i by x_i in every t_j. Note that $\sigma = \sigma'\theta$. Since θ only replaces each x_i by a_i ($1 \leq i \leq n$), it follows that $D\sigma' \subseteq C$, so D subsumes C. $\square$

Finally we can prove the general case of the Subsumption Theorem:

Theorem 5.17 (Subsumption Theorem) *Let Σ be a set of clauses, and C be a clause. Then $\Sigma \models C$ iff $\Sigma \vdash_d C$.*

Proof
$\Leftarrow$: By Theorem 5.6.
$\Rightarrow$: Assume C is not a tautology. Let θ be a Skolem substitution for C with respect to Σ. Then $C\theta$ is a ground clause which is not a tautology, and $\Sigma \models C\theta$. So by Lemma 5.13 there is a clause D such that $\Sigma \vdash_r D$ and D subsumes $C\theta$. Since D is derived from Σ, D does not contain any of the constants in θ. Therefore θ is also a Skolem substitution for C with respect to D. Then by Lemma 5.16, D subsumes C. Hence $\Sigma \vdash_d C$. $\square$

5.4   Refutation Completeness

5.4.1   From the Subsumption Theorem to Refutation Completeness

The Subsumption Theorem actually tells us that resolution and subsumption form a complete set of derivation rules for clauses. Though the resolution rule by itself is not complete for clauses in general, it is complete with respect to unsatisfiable sets of clauses. This *refutation completeness* is an easy consequence of the Subsumption Theorem:

Theorem 5.18 (Refutation completeness of resolution) *Let Σ be a set of clauses. Then Σ is unsatisfiable iff $\Sigma \vdash_r \square$.*

Proof
$\Leftarrow$: By Theorem 4.39.
$\Rightarrow$: Suppose Σ is unsatisfiable. Then $\Sigma \models \square$. So by Theorem 5.17 there exists a clause D, such that $\Sigma \vdash_r D$ and D subsumes the empty clause $\square$. But $\square$ is the only clause which subsumes $\square$, so $D = \square$. $\square$

Surprisingly, the Subsumption Theorem hardly ever appears in the standard literature about resolution, which mainly focuses on refutations. We include the Subsumption Theorem here because it is a much more "direct" form of completeness than refutation completeness. Though $\Sigma \models C$ can be proved by giving a refutation of $\Sigma \cup \{\neg C\}$ (see Section 5.5), a direct deduction of C from Σ is much more straightforward. A deduction has the advantage that the relation between the premises in Σ and the conclusion C is easier to see. For this reason, the Subsumption Theorem will be very useful in the proofs of a number of results in the second part of this book.

5.4.2   From Refutation Completeness to the Subsumption Theorem

In the previous subsection, we showed that refutation completeness is a direct consequence of the Subsumption Theorem. Here we will show the converse: that we can obtain the Subsumption Theorem from refutation completeness. This shows that these two results are in a sense equally powerful in case of unconstrained resolution.

To prove the Subsumption Theorem from refutation completeness, we will first show how to turn a refutation of $\Sigma \cup \{\neg L_1, \ldots, \neg L_k\}$ into a deduction of $L_1 \vee \ldots \vee L_k$ from Σ. Thus our proof is constructive. We start with an example. Suppose $\Sigma = \{(P(x) \vee \neg R(f(f(b)))), (R(f(x)) \vee \neg R(x))\}$, and $C = P(x) \vee Q(x) \vee \neg R(b)$. First we note that $\theta = \{x/a\}$ is a Skolem substitution for C with respect to Σ. Now $\neg C\theta \Leftrightarrow \{\neg P(a), \neg Q(a), R(b)\}$. Figure 5.3 shows a refutation of $\Sigma \cup \{\neg P(a), \neg Q(a), R(b)\}$.

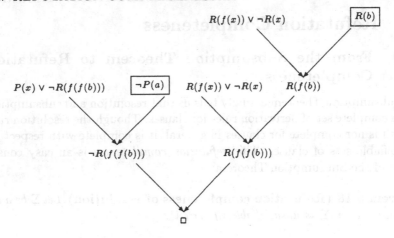

Figure 5.3: A refutation of $\Sigma \cup \{\neg P(a), \neg Q(a), R(b)\}$

Now by omitting the leaves of the refutation tree which come from $\neg C\theta$ (the framed literals) and by making appropriate changes in the tree, we get a derivation of the clause $D = P(x) \vee \neg R(b)$ (Figure 5.4). D subsumes C, so we have turned the refutation of Figure 5.3 into a deduction of C from Σ.

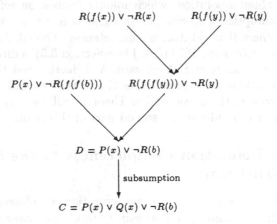

Figure 5.4: A deduction of C from Σ, obtained from the previous figure

This approach also works in the general case. The following lemma does most of the work.

Lemma 5.19 *Let Σ be a set of clauses, and $C = L_1 \vee \ldots \vee L_k$ be a nontautologous ground clause. If $\Sigma \cup \{\neg L_1, \ldots, \neg L_k\} \vdash_r \square$, then $\Sigma \vdash_d C$.*

Proof Suppose $\Sigma \cup \{\neg L_1, \ldots, \neg L_k\} \vdash_r \square$. Then there exists a refutation $R_1, \ldots, R_n = \square$ of $\Sigma \cup \{\neg L_1, \ldots, \neg L_k\}$. Let r be the number of resolvents in this sequence (i.e., $r = n-$ the number of members of $\Sigma \cup \{\neg L_1, \ldots, \neg L_k\}$ in $R_1, \ldots, R_n$). We prove the lemma by induction on r.

1. If $r = 0$, then $R_n = \square \in \Sigma$. Since $\square$ subsumes any C, the lemma holds.

2. Suppose the lemma holds for $r \leq m$. We will prove that this implies that the lemma also holds for $r = m + 1$. Let $R_1, \ldots, R_n = \square$ be a refutation of $\Sigma \cup \{\neg L_1, \ldots, \neg L_k\}$ containing $m + 1$ resolvents. Let R_i be the first resolvent. Then $R_1, \ldots, R_n = \square$ is a refutation of $\Sigma \cup \{R_i\} \cup \{\neg L_1, \ldots, \neg L_k\}$ containing only m resolvents, since R_i is now one of the original premises. Hence by the induction hypothesis, there is a clause D, such that $\Sigma \cup \{R_i\} \vdash_r D$ and D subsumes C.

Suppose R_i is itself a resolvent of two members of Σ. Then we also have $\Sigma \vdash_r D$, so the lemma holds in this case.

R_i cannot be a resolvent of two members of $\{\neg L_1, \ldots, \neg L_k\}$, since this set does not contain a complementary pair (C is not a tautology).

The only remaining case we have to check, is where R_i is a resolvent of $C' \in \Sigma$ and some $\neg L_s$ ($1 \leq s \leq k$). Let $C' = M_1 \vee \ldots \vee M_j \vee \ldots \vee M_h$. Suppose R_i is a binary resolvent of $(M_1 \vee \ldots \vee M_j)\sigma$ (a factor of C', using σ as an mgu for $\{M_j, \ldots, M_h\}$) and $\neg L_s$, with θ as mgu for $M_j \sigma$ and L_s. Then $R_i = (M_1 \vee \ldots \vee M_{j-1})\sigma\theta$ and $C'\sigma\theta = R_i \vee L_s \vee \ldots \vee L_s$ ($h - j + 1$ copies of L_s), since $M_j, \ldots, M_h$ are all unified to L_s by $\sigma\theta$. Now replace each time R_i appears as leaf in the derivation tree of D, by $C'\sigma\theta = R_i \vee L_s \vee \ldots \vee L_s$, and add $L_s \vee \ldots \vee L_s$ to all decendants of such an R_i-leaf. Then we obtain a derivation of $D \vee L_s \vee \ldots \vee L_s$ from $\Sigma \cup \{C'\sigma\theta\}$. Since $C'\sigma\theta$ is an instance of a clause from Σ, we can lift (by Lemma 5.12) this derivation to a derivation from Σ of a clause D', which has $D \vee L_s \vee \ldots \vee L_s$ as an instance. Since D subsumes C and $L_s \in C$, D' also subsumes C. Hence $\Sigma \vdash_d C$. $\square$

Now we can prove the Subsumption Theorem (Theorem 5.17) once more, this time starting from Theorem 5.18.

Theorem 5.17 (Subsumption Theorem) *Let Σ be a set of clauses, and C be a clause. Then $\Sigma \models C$ iff $\Sigma \vdash_d C$.*

Proof

$\Leftarrow$: By Theorem 5.6.

$\Rightarrow$: If C is a tautology, the theorem is obvious. Assume C is not a tautology. Let θ be a Skolem substitution for C with respect to Σ. Suppose $C\theta = L_1 \vee \ldots \vee L_k$. Because C is not a tautology, $C\theta$ is not a tautology. Since $C\theta$ is ground and $\Sigma \models C\theta$, by Proposition 2.37 the set of clauses $\Sigma \cup \{\neg L_1, \ldots, \neg L_k\}$ is unsatisfiable. Then it follows from Theorem 5.18 that $\Sigma \cup \{\neg L_1, \ldots, \neg L_k\} \vdash_r \square$. Therefore by Lemma 5.19, there exists a clause D such that $\Sigma \vdash_r D$, and D subsumes $C\theta$. Finally, from Lemma 5.16, D also subsumes C itself. Hence $\Sigma \vdash_d C$. $\square$

5.5 Proving Non-Clausal Logical Implication

The two previous completeness results, the Subsumption Theorem and refutation completeness, are very important, but they only apply to sets of *clauses*. In general, if we want to prove $\Sigma \models \phi$, Σ need not be a set of clauses, nor does ϕ have to be a clause. For instance, let $\Sigma = \{\forall x \ (P(x) \rightarrow Q(x)), P(a)\}$, and let $\phi = \exists x \ Q(x)$. Clearly $\Sigma \models \phi$, but there is no way that this can be proved by resolution "directly".

There is, however, a trick to avoid this problem. The trick is not to apply resolution to Σ, but to a standard form of $\Sigma \cup \{\neg \phi\}$. A standard form can always be represented by a set of clauses, hence we can apply resolution to it. If $\Sigma \models \phi$, then this standard form of $\Sigma \cup \{\neg \phi\}$ will be unsatisfiable, and the refutation completeness of resolution guarantees us that we can prove this. We then have the following result, which shows that resolution can be used to prove *any* case of logical implication.

Theorem 5.20 *Let Σ be a set of formulas, let ϕ be a formula, and let S be a set of clauses representing a standard form of $\Sigma \cup \{\neg \phi\}$. Then $\Sigma \models \phi$ iff $S \vdash_r \square$.*

Proof $\Sigma \models \phi$ iff (by Proposition 2.37)
$\Sigma \cup \{\neg \phi\}$ is unsatisfiable iff (by Theorem 3.19)
S is unsatisfiable iff (by Theorem 5.18)
$S \vdash_r \square$ $\qquad\qquad\qquad\qquad\qquad\qquad\qquad\qquad\qquad\qquad\qquad\qquad$ $\square$

So to prove a case of non-clausal implication $\Sigma \models \phi$, we use the refutation completeness of resolution. It should be noted that we cannot determine separately a standard form S of Σ and a standard form Γ of ϕ and then use the Subsumption Theorem. For instance, suppose $\Sigma = \{P(a)\}$ and $\phi = \exists x \ P(x)$. Then $S = \{P(a)\}$ is a standard form of Σ, and $\Gamma = \{P(b)\}$ is a standard form of ϕ. We had $\Sigma \models \phi$, but this property is lost in this case when we move to standard forms: $S \not\models \Gamma$, because of the introduction of the new constant b in Γ.

Example 5.21 Let $\Sigma = \{\forall x \ (P(x) \rightarrow Q(x)), P(a)\}$, and let $\phi = \exists y \ Q(y)$. We will prove that $\Sigma \models \phi$. We first obtain a standard form of $\Sigma \cup \{\neg \phi\}$: $S = \{(\neg P(x) \lor Q(x)), P(a), \neg Q(y)\}$. Then we prove by resolution that S is unsatisfiable, by giving a refutation of S. See Figure 5.5. Thus S is unsatisfiable, and we have $\Sigma \models \phi$ from Theorem 5.20. $\qquad\qquad$ $\triangleleft$

5.6 How to Find a Deduction

Suppose we want to find out whether $\Sigma \models C$ holds. By the Subsumption Theorem, this is the case iff there is a deduction of C from Σ. There are

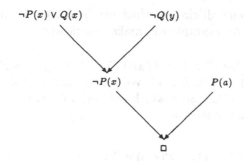

Figure 5.5: The tree for the refutation of S

two kinds of deductions: (1) C is a tautology, and (2) there is a derivation from Σ of a clause D, which subsumes C. Checking the first case is easy: by Proposition 3.20, C is a tautology iff C contains a complementary pair. Unfortunately, checking the second case is much harder. In fact, this is an undecidable problem, even if Σ contains only one clause. This follows from a result proved by Schmidt-Schauss [SS88]:

Theorem 5.22 (Schmidt-Schauss) *The problem whether $C \models D$, where C and D are arbitrary clauses, is undecidable.*

Some related undecidability results are given in Section 7.8.

Since $C \models D$ iff $C \vdash_d D$, the existence of a deduction of D from C is also undecidable. Then clearly, if Σ is a set of clauses and C is a clause, $\Sigma \vdash_d C$ is also undecidable.

This means that the best we can do, is find a procedure that always finds a deduction of C from Σ *if one exists*. Such a procedure is not guaranteed to terminate if a deduction does not exist. The simplest procedure of this kind is based on two observations. Firstly, the set of clauses which can be derived from Σ by a derivation tree of depth n, is finite. And secondly, whether some clause subsumes C is decidable (see Section 14.3). Thus we first check if some clause in Σ subsumes C. If not, we construct the set of clauses which can be derived from Σ by a derivation tree of depth 1, and check if one of these subsumes C. If not, we construct the set of clauses which can be derived from Σ by a derivation tree of depth 2, and see if one of these clauses subsumes C, etc. If $\Sigma \vdash_d C$ and C is not a tautology, then there is a derivation of a clause which subsumes C, and this will eventually be found.

The following procedure, called the *level-saturation method*, implements this idea. It tries to find a derivation from Σ of a clause which subsumes C, by summing up $\Sigma^0, \Sigma^1, \Sigma^2, \ldots$ defined as follows:

$\Sigma^0 = \Sigma$
$\Sigma^{n+1} = \{C \mid C$ is a resolvent of $C_1 \in (\Sigma^0 \cup \Sigma^1 \cup \ldots \cup \Sigma^n)$ and $C_2 \in \Sigma^n\}$

The set Σ^n contains all clauses which can be derived from Σ by a derivation tree of depth n. An example will make this clearer.

Example 5.23 Let $C = P(x,b)$ and $\Sigma = \{(P(x,y) \vee R(z)), (Q(u) \vee \neg R(a)), (\neg Q(b) \vee \neg Q(v))\}$. Then $\Sigma \models C$. We will use the level-saturation method to find a derivation of a clause which subsumes C. See Table 5.1 for the first three sets that are generated.

$$
\begin{array}{lll}
\Sigma^0 : & (1) \quad P(x,y) \vee R(z) & \\
& (2) \quad Q(u) \vee \neg R(a) & \\
& (3) \quad \neg Q(b) \vee \neg Q(v) & \\
\Sigma^1 : & (4) \quad P(x,y) \vee Q(u) & \text{from (1) and (2)} \\
& (5) \quad \neg R(a) \vee \neg Q(v) & \text{from (2) and (3)} \\
& (6) \quad \neg R(a) \vee \neg Q(b) & \text{from (2) and (3)} \\
& (7) \quad \neg R(a) & \text{from (2) and (3)} \\
\Sigma^2 : & (8) \quad P(x,y) \vee \neg Q(v) & \text{from (1) and (5)} \\
& (9) \quad P(x,y) \vee \neg Q(b) & \text{from (1) and (6)} \\
& (10) \quad P(x,y) & \text{from (1) and (7)} \\
& (11) \quad \neg R(a) \vee \neg R(a) & \text{from (2) and (5)} \\
& (12) \quad \neg R(a) \vee \neg R(a) & \text{from (2) and (6)} \\
& (13) \quad \neg Q(b) \vee P(x,y) & \text{from (3) and (4)} \\
& (14) \quad \neg Q(v) \vee P(x,y) & \text{from (3) and (4)} \\
& (15) \quad P(x,y) & \text{from (3) and (4)} \\
& (16) \quad P(x,y) \vee \neg R(a) & \text{from (4) and (5)} \\
& (17) \quad P(x,y) \vee \neg R(a) & \text{from (4) and (6)}
\end{array}
$$

Table 5.1: The sets of resolvents constructed by the level-saturation method

Note that two clauses may have more than one resolvent. For instance, clauses (5), (6) and (7) are all resolvents of (2) and (3). We wanted to find a derivation of a clause which subsumes $C = P(x,b)$. Σ^2 contains such a clause: clause (10) is $P(x,y)$. One such a clause is enough, so there is no need to construct Σ^3, Σ^4, etc.

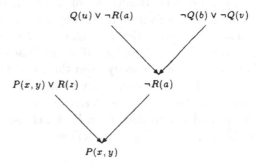

Figure 5.6: The derivation obtained from the level-saturation method

Since $P(x,y) \in \Sigma^2$, there exists a derivation tree of depth 2, representing a derivation of $P(x,y)$ from Σ. The parent clauses of $P(x,y)$ were clauses (1) and (7). (1) is a member of Σ, and (7) has (2) and (3) as parents, which are also in Σ. Hence the derivation of $P(x,y)$ is as pictured in Figure 5.6.   ◁

Note that when looking for a deduction of the empty clause $\square$, we can ignore the subsumption step, since $\square$ is the only clause which subsumes $\square$. Thus it suffices to check whether some Σ^n contains $\square$.

As can be seen from the previous example, the number of clauses in Σ^n rapidly increases, even for small n. This can make the search for a deduction very inefficient. Numerous tricks and procedures have been invented to speed up the search. For instance, all tautologies can be removed from Σ^n, since tautologies are not necessary in a deduction anyhow—if C_n is a tautology and $\{C_1, \ldots, C_n\} \models C$, then also $\{C_1, \ldots, C_{n-1}\} \models C$. Removing the tautologies decreases the number of clauses in Σ^{n+1} and later sets, since we won't have to bother then about resolvents that have one of the tautologies in Σ^n as parent clause. For discussions of what can be done to speed up the search, we refer the interested reader to books such as [CL73, Lov78, GN87], and articles such as [KK71, MR72, Ino92]. In the next chapter, we will give two examples of more efficient procedures, called *linear* resolution and *input* resolution. Here some restrictions are put on the form of derivations. This decreases the number of possible derivations, thus making the search for a derivation more efficient. We will show that the first of these is still complete, while the second is not.

5.7   Summary

A *deduction* combines a derivation and a *subsumption* step. Deduction is sound and complete: the *Subsumption Theorem* states that $\Sigma \models C$ iff $\Sigma \vdash_d C$. This result immediately implies the *refutation completeness*: Σ is unsatisfiable iff $\Sigma \vdash_r \square$. Conversely, we can also prove the Subsumption Theorem starting from the refutation completeness. Furthermore, refutation completeness can also be used to prove non-clausal cases of logical implication. The *level-saturation* method, essentially a way of summing up all possible derivations, can be used to find a deduction if one exists.

5.A   Alternative Definitions of Resolution

It should be noted that the way we have defined resolution here is not the only possible way. Here we will briefly discuss three alternatives which have appeared in the literature. This appendix is somewhat subtle and perhaps confusing; since it is not necessary for an understanding of the rest of this work, the reader may wish to skip it.

Robinson

Firstly, in Robinson's paper [Rob65] which first introduced resolution, a clause is taken to be a *set* of literals (see the Appendix to Chapter 3), and factors are built into the resolution step itself.[2] A *set* M of positive literals from a clause C_1 is (most generally) unified with the atoms in a *set* N of negative literals from a clause C_2, instead of resolving upon a single literal from each parent. If θ is the mgu used, then the resolvent is

$$((C_1 \backslash M) \cup (C_2 \backslash N))\theta.$$

For example, if we consider the clauses $C_1 = \{P(x,y), P(a,a), Q(x)\}$ and $C_2 = \{\neg P(z,z), \neg P(a,z), R(z)\}$, then we can use $M = \{P(x,y), P(a,a)\} \subseteq C_1$, $N = \{\neg P(z,z), \neg P(a,z)\} \subseteq C_2$, and mgu $\{x/a, y/a, z/a\}$, to obtain the resolvent $\{Q(a), R(a)\}$.

Chang and Lee

Secondly, in Chang and Lee's [CL73] a clause is treated as a set of literals (but written down as a disjunction). A binary resolvent of C_1 and C_2, resolved upon literals $L_1 \in C_1$ and $L_2 \in C_2$ with mgu θ, is defined as

$$(C_1\theta - L_1\theta) \cup (C_2\theta - L_2\theta).$$

A resolvent of C_1 and C_2 is defined as a binary resolvent of factors of C_1 and C_2. Since a set of literals contains literals only once, taking a factor is a special case of applying a substitution. There is no need to delete all but one copies of the unified literals, since by definition a set contains literals only once, and hence all but one of the unified literals as it were "disappear automatically" from the clause. For instance, if $C = P(a) \vee P(x) \vee Q(x)$, then the mgu $\theta = \{x/a\}$ yields the factor $C\theta = P(a) \vee Q(a)$.

Note that every [Rob65]-resolvent is also a [CL73]-resolvent: if the sets $M \subseteq C_1$ and $N \subseteq C_2$ are used to construct a [Rob65]-resolvent R of C_1 and C_2, then we can use an mgu σ_1 of M and an mgu σ_2 of N to construct factors $C_1' = C_1\sigma_1$ and $C_2' = C_2\sigma_2$. It is easy to see that R is a [CL73]-resolvent, obtained as a binary resolvent of C_1' and C_2'. Conversely, not every

---

[2]In this work, we have chosen to separate the definitions of a factor and a binary resolvent, since binary resolution without factors is sufficient in case of SLD-resolution for Horn clauses (see Chapter 7).

[CL73]-resolvent is a [Rob65]-resolvent: if $C_1 = \{P(x), P(a), Q(a)\}$ and $C_2 = \{\neg Q(a)\}$, then $\{P(a)\}$ is a [CL73]-resolvent (using the factor $\{P(a), Q(a)\}$ of C_1), while the only [Rob65]-resolvent is $\{P(x), P(a)\}$.

Genesereth and Nilsson

A third alternative is used in Genesereth and Nilsson's [GN87]. There a clause is, again, treated as a set of literals. A binary resolvent of C_1 and C_2, resolved upon literals L_1 and L_2 with mgu θ, is defined as

$$((C_1 - L_1) \cup (C_2 - L_2))\theta.$$

Apart from the set notation, this is the same as our own definition. Clearly, for every binary resolvent R of C_1 and C_2 in our definition, there exists a binary resolvent R' of C_1 and C_2 in the definition of [GN87], such that $R' \subseteq R$. [GN87] define a resolvent of C_1 and C_2 as a binary resolvent of factors of C_1 and C_2. Thus it can be seen that if R is a resolvent of C_1 and C_2 in our definition, then there is a [GN87]-resolvent R' of C_1 and C_2 such that $R' \subseteq R$ (and hence $R' \models R$).

   Note that if R is a [GN87]-resolvent of C_1 and C_2, then there is a [CL73]-resolvent R' of C_1 and C_2 such that $R' \subseteq R$. Some [GN87]-resolvents are not [CL73]-resolvents. For instance, suppose $C_1 = \{P(x, a), P(x, x)\}$ and $C_2 = \{\neg P(a, a)\}$. Then $\{P(a, a)\}$ is a [GN87]-resolvent of C_1 and C_2, while the only [CL73]-resolvent is the empty clause. On the other hand, every [CL73]-resolvent is a [GN87]-resolvent, due to the use of factors.

   Despite the differences between these alternative definitions and our own, our proof of the Subsumption Theorem in this chapter can fairly easily be adjusted to accommodate these alternative definitions. Thus, even though the number of resolution steps required for the deduction of some particular clause may vary between definitions, eventually each definition can deduce exactly the same clauses from a set Σ, namely the logical consequences of Σ.

Chapter 6

Linear and Input Resolution

6.1 Introduction

In the previous two chapters, we defined resolution, and proved deductions to be sound and complete. We also explained how the level-saturation method can find a deduction of C from Σ, if one exists. Essentially, it just tries out all possible derivations—and often the set of all possible derivations is infinite. Searching for a proof is very cumbersome, because in "unconstrained" resolution, any two clauses (both clauses from the original set Σ, and previous resolvents), can be resolved together. This means that in each step, there is a large number of possibilities which all ought to be tried.

This number of possibilities could be reduced by imposing constraints on the derivations that are allowed. Ideally, such a restricted form of resolution significantly reduces the number of possibilities that have to be tried (compared to unconstrained resolution), without sacrificing completeness. That is, we want a restricted form of resolution which is more efficient than unconstrained resolution, but which still allows us to deduce any clause that is a logical consequence of the premises.

Many important restrictions have been developed since the introduction of the resolution principle by Robinson in 1965. The most important of these can be subdivided into two broad classes: forms of *semantic* resolution and forms of *linear* resolution.

Semantic resolution takes particular interpretations and orderings of literals into account. By imposing all sorts of restrictions on the possible derivations, in terms of the chosen interpretation and ordering, semantic resolution is much more efficient than unconstrained resolution. It was introduced by Slagle in [Sla67]. Chapter 6 of [CL73] discusses several forms of semantic resolution, and proves the refutation completeness of those forms. Slagle, Chang, and Lee proved versions of the Subsumption Theorem for semantic resolution in [SCL69].

However, in this book we will not discuss semantic resolution in detail. Instead, we define a simple form of *linear* resolution, and prove its completeness. We prefer linear resolution over semantic resolution here, because it is conceptually simpler and provides a bridge between the unconstrained resolution of the previous chapters, and the SLD-resolution of the next chapter (which is a special case of linear resolution).

Linear resolution is characterized by the linear shape of its derivations. It was independently introduced by Loveland [Lov70] and Luckham [Luc70]. An important further restriction called *SL-resolution* (Linear resolution with a Selection function) was introduced by Kowalski and Kuehner [KK71], and proven to be refutation-complete. Chang and Lee [CL73] discuss OL-resolution (Ordered Linear resolution).[1] Minicozzi and Reiter proved the Subsumption Theorem for linear resolution in [MR72]. More recently, Inoue [Ino92] developed SOL-resolution (Skip-OL-resolution) and proved a version of the Subsumption Theorem for it.

For the sake of transparency, we will discuss a very simple form of linear resolution here. Many features and restrictions could be added on to improve efficiency (see the references given above). We will prove the Subsumption Theorem and refutation completeness for this form of linear resolution. After that, we will define a further restriction of linear resolution called *input* resolution, and show that this is *not* complete for general clauses, not even when the set of premises contains only one clause.

6.2   Linear Resolution

Definition 6.1 Let Σ be a set of clauses and C be a clause. A *linear derivation* of C from Σ is a finite sequence of clauses $R_0, \ldots, R_k = C$, such that $R_0 \in \Sigma$ and each R_i with $1 \leq i \leq k$ is a resolvent of R_{i-1} and a clause $C_i \in \Sigma \cup \{R_0, \ldots, R_{i-2}\}$.

R_0 is called the *top clause*, $R_0, \ldots, R_k$ the *center clauses*, and $C_1, \ldots, C_k$ are called the *side clauses* of this linear derivation. If a linear derivation of C from Σ exists, we write $\Sigma \vdash_{lr} C$.

A linear derivation of $\square$ from Σ is called a *linear refutation* of Σ. $\Diamond$

It is instructive to see how linear resolution fits into the definition of unconstrained resolution. Whereas in unconstrained resolution a clause R_i in the derivation can be a resolvent of any two previous clauses, in linear resolution R_i should be a resolvent of R_{i-1} and a clause from Σ or one of the previous center clauses. This greatly reduces the search space of possible derivations.

---

[1] However, their proof of refutation completeness contains an error. OL-resolution is not refutation-complete, as described on pp. 324–325 of [Ino92].

Linear derivations are characterized by the "linear" shape of their corresponding derivation trees. See Figure 6.1. Such a tree can be turned into a derivation tree for unconstrained resolution by adding the derivations of each side clause C_i which is not in Σ.

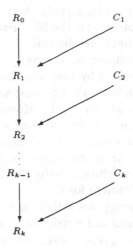

Figure 6.1: The characteristic shape of a linear derivation

Linear deductions are defined as follows:

Definition 6.2 Let Σ be a set of clauses and C a clause. There exists a *linear deduction* of C from Σ, written as $\Sigma \vdash_{ld} C$, if C is a tautology, or if there exists a clause D such that $\Sigma \vdash_{lr} D$ and D subsumes C. $\Diamond$

Example 6.3 We will give a linear deduction of $C = Q(a) \lor R(a)$ from $\Sigma = \{(P(x) \lor \neg Q(x)), (\neg P(x) \lor \neg Q(a)), (\neg P(x) \lor Q(x)), (P(x) \lor Q(x) \lor R(x))\}$. Figure 6.2 shows a linear derivation of $D = R(a)$ from Σ. Note that the underlined side clause C_4 is the center clause R_1. Note also that we sometimes rename side clauses to achieve that the side clauses and the corresponding center clauses are standardized apart. Since D subsumes C, we have a linear deduction of C from Σ. Hence $\Sigma \vdash_{ld} C$. $\lhd$

6.3 Refutation Completeness

A proof of the refutation completeness of linear resolution is given in Theorem 7.2 of [CL73] (but see the note on p. 94). We adapt this proof for our own definitions here, first proving the case for ground clauses, which is then lifted. The proof of the following lifting lemma is similar to Lemma 5.12.

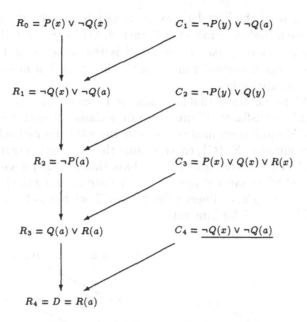

Figure 6.2: A linear derivation of D from Σ

Lemma 6.4 (Linear derivation lifting) *Let Σ be a set of clauses, and Σ' be a set of instances of clauses from Σ. Suppose $R'_0, \ldots, R'_k$ is a linear derivation of the clause R'_k from Σ'. Then there exists a linear derivation $R_0, \ldots, R_k$ of the clause R_k from Σ, such that R'_i is an instance of R_i, for each i.*

The following lemma is the refutation completeness of linear resolution for ground clauses.

Lemma 6.5 *If Σ is an unsatisfiable set of ground clauses, and $C \in \Sigma$ such that $\Sigma\backslash\{C\}$ is satisfiable, then there is a linear refutation of Σ with C as top clause.*

Proof By the Compactness Theorem (Theorem 2.42), we can assume Σ is finite. Let n be the number of distinct ground atoms occurring in literals in clauses in Σ. We prove the lemma by induction on n.

1. If $n = 0$, then $\Sigma = \{\Box\}$. Since $\Sigma\backslash\{C\}$ is satisfiable, $C = \Box$

2. Suppose the lemma holds for $n \leq m$, and suppose $m + 1$ distinct atoms appear in Σ. We distinguish two cases.
   Case 1: Suppose $C = L$, where L is a literal. We first delete all clauses from Σ which contain the literal L (so we also delete C itself from Σ). Then we replace clauses which contain the literal $\neg L$ by clauses constructed by deleting these $\neg L$ (so for example, $L_1 \vee \neg L \vee L_2$ will be replaced by $L_1 \vee L_2$). Call the finite set obtained in this way Γ.

Note that neither the literal L, nor its negation, appears in clauses in Γ. If M were a Herbrand model of Γ, then $M \cup \{L\}$ (i.e., the Herbrand interpretation which makes L true, and is the same as M for other literals) would be a Herbrand model of Σ. Thus since Σ is unsatisfiable, Γ must be unsatisfiable.

Now let Σ' be an unsatisfiable subset of Γ, such that every proper subset of Σ' is satisfiable. Σ' must contain a clause D' obtained from a member of Σ which contained $\neg L$, for otherwise the unsatisfiable set Σ' would be a subset of $\Sigma \backslash \{C\}$, contradicting the assumption that $\Sigma \backslash \{C\}$ is satisfiable. By construction of Σ', we have that $\Sigma' \backslash \{D'\}$ is satisfiable. Furthermore, Σ' contains at most m distinct atoms, so by the induction hypothesis there exists a linear refutation of Σ' with top clause D'. See the left of Figure 6.3 for illustration.

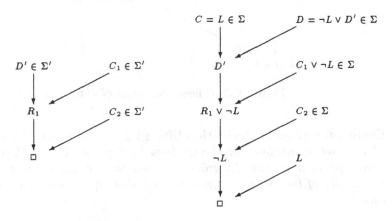

Figure 6.3: Case 1 of the proof

Each side clause in this refutation that is not equal to a previous center clause, is either a member of Σ or is obtained from a member of Σ by means of the deletion of $\neg L$. In the latter kind of side clauses, put back the deleted $\neg L$ literals, and add these $\neg L$ to all later center clauses. Note that afterwards, these center clauses may contain multiple copies of $\neg L$. In particular, the last center clause changes from $\square$ to $\neg L \vee \ldots \vee \neg L$. Since D' is a resolvent of C and $D = \neg L \vee D' \in \Sigma$, we can add C and D as parent clauses on top of the previous top clause D'. That way, we get a linear derivation of $\neg L \vee \ldots \vee \neg L$ from Σ, with top clause C. Finally, the literals in $\neg L \vee \ldots \vee \neg L$ can be resolved away using the top clause $C = L$ as side clause. This yields a linear refutation of Σ with top clause C (see the right of Figure 6.3).

Case 2: Suppose $C = L \vee C'$, where C' is a non-empty clause. C' cannot contain $\neg L$, for otherwise C would be a tautology, contradicting the assumption that Σ is unsatisfiable while $\Sigma \backslash \{C\}$ is satisfiable.

Obtain Σ' from Σ by deleting clauses containing $\neg L$, and by removing the literal L from the remaining clauses. Note that $C' \in \Sigma'$. If M were a Herbrand model of Σ', then $M \cup \{\neg L\}$ is a Herbrand model of Σ. Thus since Σ is unsatisfiable, Σ' is unsatisfiable.

Furthermore, because $\Sigma \backslash \{C\}$ is satisfiable, by Proposition 3.30 there is a Herbrand model M' of $\Sigma \backslash \{C\}$. Since Σ is unsatisfiable, M' is not a model of C. L is a literal in C, hence L must be false under M'. Every clause in $\Sigma' \backslash \{C'\}$ is obtained from a clause in $\Sigma \backslash \{C\}$ by deleting L from it. Since M' is a model of every clause in $\Sigma \backslash \{C\}$ and L is false under M', every clause in $\Sigma' \backslash \{C'\}$ is true under M'. Therefore M' is a model of $\Sigma' \backslash \{C'\}$, which shows that $\Sigma' \backslash \{C'\}$ is satisfiable.

Then by the induction hypothesis, there exists a linear refutation of Σ' with top clause C'. Now similar to case 1, put back previously deleted L literals to the top and side clauses, and to the appropriate center clauses. This gives a linear derivation of $L \vee \ldots \vee L$ from Σ with top clause C.

Note that $\{L\} \cup (\Sigma \backslash \{C\})$ is unsatisfiable, because L is false in any Herbrand model of $\Sigma \backslash \{C\}$, as shown above. On the other hand, $\Sigma \backslash \{C\}$ is satisfiable. Thus by case 1 of this proof, there exists a linear refutation of $\{L\} \cup (\Sigma \backslash \{C\})$ with top clause L. Since L is a factor of $L \vee \ldots \vee L$, we can put our linear derivation of $L \vee \ldots \vee L$ "on top" of this linear refutation of $\{L\} \cup (\Sigma \backslash \{C\})$ with top clause L, thus obtaining a linear refutation of Σ with top clause C. $\square$

Theorem 6.6 (Refutation completeness of linear resolution) *Let Σ be a set of clauses. Then Σ is unsatisfiable iff $\Sigma \vdash_{lr} \square$.*

Proof

$\Leftarrow$: From Theorem 4.39.

$\Rightarrow$: Suppose Σ is unsatisfiable. Then by Theorem 5.8, there is a finite unsatisfiable set Σ_g of ground instances of clauses in Σ'. Let Σ'_g be an unsatisfiable subset of Σ_g, and $C \in \Sigma'_g$ such that $\Sigma'_g \backslash \{C\}$ is satisfiable. From Lemma 6.5, we have $\Sigma'_g \vdash_{lr} \square$. Hence $\Sigma \vdash_{lr} \square$ by Lemma 6.4. $\square$

6.4 The Subsumption Theorem

Starting from refutation completeness, it is now possible to prove also the Subsumption Theorem for linear resolution. Our proof is similar to the one given in [MR72]. We use refutation completeness, and then turn a linear refutation into a linear deduction, using the following lemma:

Lemma 6.7 *Let Σ be a set of clauses, and $C = L_1 \vee \ldots \vee L_k$ be a non-tautologous ground clause. If $\Sigma \cup \{\neg L_1, \ldots, \neg L_k\} \vdash_{lr} \square$, then $\Sigma \vdash_{ld} C$.*

Proof Suppose $\Sigma \cup \{\neg L_1, \ldots, \neg L_k\} \vdash_{lr} \square$. Then there exists a linear refutation $R_0, \ldots, R_n = \square$ of $\Sigma \cup \{\neg L_1, \ldots, \neg L_k\}$. Notice that the top clause and the first side clause in this linear refutation cannot both be members of $\{\neg L_1, \ldots, \neg L_k\}$, because C is not a tautology. Thus we can assume $R_0 \in \Sigma$. It is then possible to prove by induction on n that this linear refutation can be transformed into a linear deduction of C from Σ with top clause R_0:

1. If $n = 0$, then $R_0 = \square$ is a member of Σ. Since $\square$ subsumes any clause C, the result follows.

2. Suppose the lemma holds for $n \leq m$. Let $R_0, \ldots, R_{m+1} = \square$ be a linear refutation of $\Sigma \cup \{\neg L_1, \ldots, \neg L_k\}$. Then $R_1, \ldots, R_{m+1}$ is a linear refutation of $\Sigma \cup \{R_1\} \cup \{\neg L_1, \ldots, \neg L_k\}$. By the induction hypothesis, there is a linear derivation of a clause D from $\Sigma \cup \{R_1\}$, with top clause R_1, such that D subsumes C.

   Suppose R_1 is itself a resolvent of two members of Σ. Then we also have $\Sigma \vdash_{lr} D$, so the lemma holds in this case.

   The only remaining case we have to check, is where R_1 is a resolvent of $R_0 \in \Sigma$ and some $\neg L_s$ ($1 \leq s \leq k$). Let $R_0 = M_1 \vee \ldots \vee M_j \vee \ldots \vee M_h$. Suppose R_1 is a binary resolvent of $(M_1 \vee \ldots \vee M_j)\sigma$ (a factor of R_0, using σ as an mgu for $\{M_j, \ldots, M_h\}$) and $\neg L_s$, with θ as mgu for $M_j\sigma$ and L_s. Then $R_1 = (M_1 \vee \ldots \vee M_{j-1})\sigma\theta$ and $R_0\sigma\theta = R_1 \vee L_s \vee \ldots \vee L_s$ ($h - j + 1$ copies of L_s), since $M_j, \ldots, M_h$ are all unified to L_s by $\sigma\theta$. Now replace each time R_1 appears as leaf (i.e., top or side clause) in the derivation tree of D, by $R_0\sigma\theta = R_1 \vee L_s \vee \ldots \vee L_s$, and add $L_s \vee \ldots \vee L_s$ to all decendants of such an R_1-leaf. This gives a new derivation, in which each resolvent is the corresponding resolvent in the old derivation of D plus some extra copies of L_s. Thus we obtain a linear derivation of $D \vee L_s \vee \ldots \vee L_s$ from $\Sigma \cup \{R_0\sigma\theta\}$. Since $R_0\sigma\theta$ is an instance of a clause from Σ, we can lift (by Lemma 6.4) this derivation to a derivation from Σ of a clause D', which has $D \vee L_s \vee \ldots \vee L_s$ as an instance. Since D subsumes C, D' also subsumes C. Hence $\Sigma \vdash_{ld} C$. $\square$

Theorem 6.8 (Subsumption Theorem for linear resolution) *Let Σ be a set of clauses, and C be a clause. Then $\Sigma \models C$ iff $\Sigma \vdash_{ld} C$.*

Proof

$\Leftarrow$: From Theorem 5.6.

$\Rightarrow$: If C is a tautology, the theorem is obvious. Assume C is not a tautology. Let θ be a Skolem substitution for C with respect to Σ. Let $C\theta$ be the clause $L_1 \vee \ldots \vee L_k$. Since C is not a tautology, $C\theta$ is not a tautology. $C\theta$ is ground and $\Sigma \models C\theta$, so the set of clauses $\Sigma \cup \{\neg L_1, \ldots, \neg L_k\}$ is unsatisfiable by Proposition 2.37. Then it follows from Theorem 6.6 that $\Sigma \cup \{\neg L_1, \ldots, \neg L_k\} \vdash_{lr} \square$. Therefore by Lemma 6.7, there exists a clause D such that $\Sigma \vdash_{lr} D$, and D subsumes $C\theta$. From Lemma 5.16, D also subsumes C itself. Hence $\Sigma \vdash_{ld} C$. $\square$

6.5   The Incompleteness of Input Resolution

Linear resolution is a restriction of unconstrained resolution. Linear resolution itself can be further restricted to *input* resolution, by stipulating that each side clause should be a member of Σ. Input resolution is significant for two reasons. Firstly, SLD-resolution, which we will introduce in the next chapter, is in turn a restricted form of input resolution. And secondly, input resolution is used fairly often in the literature. Contrary to linear resolution, input resolution is not complete, not even when the set of premises Σ contains only one clause. Before we give our counterexample, we will first formally define input resolution:

Definition 6.9 Let Σ be a set of clauses and C be a clause. An *input derivation* of C from Σ is a linear derivation in which each side clause C_i is a member of Σ. The side clauses $C_1, \ldots, C_k$ in an input derivation are also called *input clauses*. If an input derivation of C from Σ exists, we write $\Sigma \vdash_{ir} C$.

An input derivation of $\Box$ from Σ is called an *input refutation* of Σ. $\diamond$

Definition 6.10 Let Σ be a set of clauses and C a clause. There exists an *input deduction* of C from Σ, written as $\Sigma \vdash_{id} C$, if C is a tautology, or if there exists a clause D such that $\Sigma \vdash_{ir} D$ and D subsumes C. $\diamond$

Most examples of the previous chapters were cases of input resolution, and many derivations that are not input derivations can be transformed into input derivations. This might induce us to expect that input resolution is complete. That is, we might expect that the Subsumption Theorem and refutation completeness can be stated in terms of input resolution. However, this is not the case.

Input resolution is not refutation-complete. A simple propositional example suffices to show this. Let $\Sigma = \{(P \vee Q), (P \vee \neg Q), (\neg P \vee Q), (\neg P \vee \neg Q)\}$. Figure 6.4 shows a refutation by unconstrained resolution of Σ. This proves that Σ is unsatisfiable.

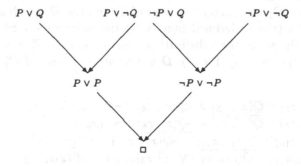

Figure 6.4: An unconstrained refutation of Σ

Unfortunately, there does not exist an *input* refutation of Σ. It is easy to see why this is so. To reach the empty clause $\Box$, the last input clause should contain only one literal, or have a factor containing only one literal. However, each clause in Σ contains two distinct literals. Hence there is no input refutation of Σ, and input resolution is not refutation-complete.

This also implies that the Subsumption Theorem does not hold either for input resolution, since refutation completeness would be a direct consequence of it. We can in fact prove a stronger negative result, namely that the Subsumption Theorem for input resolution is not even true in the simple case where Σ contains only a single clause. In our counterexample we let $\Sigma = \{C\}$, where C is the following clause:

$$C = P(x_1, x_2) \vee Q(x_2, x_3) \vee \neg Q(x_3, x_4) \vee \neg P(x_4, x_1).$$

Figure 6.5 shows that clause D (see below) can be derived from C by unconstrained resolution. This also shows that $C \models D$.

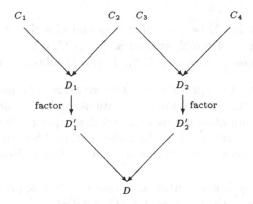

Figure 6.5: The derivation of D from C by unconstrained resolution

Figure 6.5 makes use of the clauses listed below. C_1, C_2, C_3, C_4 are variants of C. D_1 is a binary resolvent of C_1 and C_2, D_2 is a binary resolvent of C_3 and C_4 (the underlined literals are the literals resolved upon). D_1' is a factor of D_1, using the substitution $\{x_5/x_1, x_6/x_2\}$. D_2' is a factor of D_2, using $\{x_{11}/x_{12}, x_{13}/x_9\}$. Finally, D is a binary resolvent of D_1' and D_2'.

$C_1 = P(x_1, x_2) \vee \underline{Q(x_2, x_3)} \vee \neg Q(x_3, x_4) \vee \neg P(x_4, x_1).$
$C_2 = P(x_5, x_6) \vee \underline{\overline{Q(x_6, x_7)}} \vee \neg Q(x_7, x_8) \vee \neg P(x_8, x_5).$
$C_3 = P(x_9, x_{10}) \vee \underline{Q(x_{10}, x_{11})} \vee \neg Q(x_{11}, x_{12}) \vee \neg P(x_{12}, x_9).$
$C_4 = P(x_{13}, x_{14}) \vee \underline{\overline{Q(x_{14}, x_{15})}} \vee \neg Q(x_{15}, x_{16}) \vee \neg P(x_{16}, x_{13}).$
$D_1 = P(x_1, x_2) \vee \neg Q(x_3, x_4) \vee \neg \underline{\overline{P(x_4, x_1)}} \vee P(x_5, x_6) \vee Q(x_6, x_2) \vee \neg Q(x_3, x_5).$

$D_2 = P(x_9, x_{10}) \vee \neg Q(x_{11}, x_{12}) \vee \neg P(x_{12}, x_9) \vee P(x_{13}, x_{14}) \vee Q(x_{14}, x_{10}) \vee$
$\qquad \neg P(x_{11}, x_{13})$.
$D'_1 = P(x_1, x_2) \vee \neg Q(x_3, x_4) \vee \neg P(x_4, x_1) \vee Q(x_2, x_2) \vee \neg P(x_3, x_1)$.
$D'_2 = \overline{P(x_9, x_{10})} \vee \neg Q(x_{12}, x_{12}) \vee \neg P(x_{12}, x_9) \vee P(x_9, x_{14}) \vee Q(x_{14}, x_{10})$.
$D = \neg Q(x_3, x_4) \vee \neg P(x_4, x_1) \vee Q\overline{(x_2, x_2)} \vee \neg P(x_3, x_1) \vee P(x_2, x_{10}) \vee$
$\qquad \neg Q(x_1, x_1) \vee P(x_2, x_{14}) \vee Q(x_{14}, x_{10})$.

Thus D can be derived from C using unconstrained resolution. However, neither D nor a clause which subsumes D can be derived from C using only *input* resolution. We prove this in Proposition 6.12. This shows that input resolution is not complete, not even if Σ contains only one clause.

The following lemma shows that each clause which can be derived from C by input resolution contains an instance of $P(x_1, x_2) \vee \neg P(x_4, x_1)$ or an instance of $Q(x_2, x_3) \vee \neg Q(x_3, x_4)$.

Lemma 6.11 *Let C be as defined above. If $C \vdash_{ir} E$, then E contains an instance of $P(x_1, x_2) \vee \neg P(x_4, x_1)$ or an instance of $Q(x_2, x_3) \vee \neg Q(x_3, x_4)$.*

Proof Let $R_0, \ldots, R_k = E$ be an input derivation of E from C. We prove the lemma by induction on k:

1. $R_0 = C$, so the lemma is obvious if $k = 0$.
2. Suppose the lemma holds for $k \leq n$. Let $R_0, \ldots, R_{n+1} = E$ be an input derivation of E from C. Note that the only factor of C is C itself. Therefore E is a binary resolvent of C and a factor of R_m. Let θ be the mgu used in obtaining this binary resolvent. If $P(x_1, x_2)$ or $\neg P(x_4, x_1)$ is the literal resolved upon in C, then E must contain $(Q(x_2, x_3) \vee \neg Q(x_3, x_4))\theta$. Otherwise $Q(x_2, x_3)$ or $\neg Q(x_3, x_4)$ is the literal resolved upon in C, so then E contains $(P(x_1, x_2) \vee \neg P(x_4, x_1))\theta$. Hence the lemma also holds for $k = n + 1$. $\qquad \square$

Proposition 6.12 *Let C and D be as defined above. Then $C \not\vdash_{id} D$.*

Proof Suppose $C \vdash_{id} D$. Then since D is not a tautology, there exists a clause E such that $C \vdash_{ir} E$ and E subsumes D. From Lemma 6.11 we know that E contains an instance of $P(x_1, x_2) \vee \neg P(x_4, x_1)$ or an instance of $Q(x_2, x_3) \vee \neg Q(x_3, x_4)$. It is easy to see that neither $P(x_1, x_2) \vee \neg P(x_4, x_1)$ nor $Q(x_2, x_3) \vee \neg Q(x_3, x_4)$ subsumes D. But then E does not subsume D, so we have found a contradiction. Hence $C \not\vdash_{id} D$. $\qquad \square$

So we see that input resolution is not complete: $C \models D$, but $C \not\vdash_{id} D$. This is unfortunate, since input resolution is more efficient than unconstrained resolution or linear resolution. However, if we restrict ourselves to *Horn clauses* (clauses containing at most one positive literal), a special case of input resolution called *SLD-resolution* can be shown to be complete. This will be the topic of the next chapter.

6.6 Summary

This chapter defined *linear* resolution and *input* resolution, two important restrictions of unconstrained resolution, which are characterized by the linear shapes of their derivations. We proved the Subsumption Theorem for linear resolution, as well as its refutation completeness. On the other hand, input resolution is not complete, not even when Σ (the set of premises) contains only one clause.

Chapter 7

SLD-Resolution

7.1 Introduction

Thus far, we have concerned ourselves with the set of *all* clauses. However, in practice as well as theory, one often restricts this set. In this chapter, we will discuss an important example of such a restriction, namely the restriction to *Horn* clauses, named after the logician Alfred Horn. These are clauses with at most one positive literal. The set of Horn clauses is indeed a restriction, since formulas such as $P(a) \vee P(b)$ cannot be expressed as Horn clauses.

This loss of expressive power is compensated for by a gain in tractability: due to their restricted form, sets of Horn clauses are easier to handle than sets of general clauses. In particular, deduction based on *SLD-resolution*[1], which is a special case of input resolution, is complete for Horn clauses. One form of this completeness is the Subsumption Theorem for SLD-resolution, a second is its refutation completeness. A third form of completeness is in terms of the *least Herbrand model* of a set of Horn clauses.

SLD-resolution was introduced by Kowalski in [Kow74]. It is simpler than the unconstrained or linear resolution that we need for general clauses. Furthermore, the use of Horn clauses is supported by the wide availability and applicability of the programming language PROLOG, which is built on SLD-resolution and which will be discussed in the next chapter. For these reasons, most applications and much theoretical work in ILP is only concerned with Horn clauses.

In this chapter we will discuss Horn clauses and SLD-resolution, and prove its soundness and completeness. Much of the material in this chapter—particularly in the later sections—is drawn from [Llo87], which is the standard reference for logic programming. However, we also refer to more recent

---

[1] The abbreviation 'SLD' stands for 'SL-resolution for Definite clauses', where 'SL-resolution' abbreviates 'Linear resolution with a Selection function' (see [KK71]). A 'selection function' is similar to the concept of a 'computation rule' that we will introduce in this chapter.

texts [Doe94, Apt97] on logic programming, which correct some subtle errors
in [Llo87]. The completeness results of the later sections were first proved in
[Hil74, Cla79, AE82], and more recent proofs may be found in [Stä90, Bez90].
The definition of SLD-derivation we give here is more general than the one
given in [Llo87], which only focuses on refutations. Our main completeness
result, the Subsumption Theorem for SLD-resolution, is not given in [Llo87],
nor in the other references mentioned above. Furthermore, the proofs of some
of the completeness results we give here are quite different from the ones given
in [Llo87], in that we do make use of fixed-point theory, but use only the basic
definitions of resolution.

7.2   SLD-Resolution

Definition 7.1 A *definite program clause* is a clause containing one positive,
and zero or more negative literals. A *definite goal* is a clause containing only
negative literals. A *Horn clause* is either a definite program clause, or a
definite goal.   ◇

If a definite program clause consists of the positive literal A and the
negative literals $\neg B_1, \ldots \neg B_n$, then such a clause can equivalently be written
as the following implication:

$$(B_1 \wedge \ldots \wedge B_n) \rightarrow A.$$

In most papers and books about logic programming, this is written as:

$$A \leftarrow B_1, \ldots, B_n.$$

A is called the *head* of the clause, $B_1, \ldots, B_n$ is called the *body* of the clause.
It will be convenient to denote the head of a clause C by C^+, and the body
(the conjunction $B_1 \wedge \ldots \wedge B_n$) by C^-. In case of an atom A (that is, if $n = 0$),
we can omit the '$\leftarrow$' symbol. A definite goal can equivalently be written as

$$\leftarrow B_1, \ldots, B_n.$$

The empty clause □ is also considered to be a goal.

In the same way as we have clausal languages, we also have more restricted
Horn languages:

Definition 7.2 The *Horn language* $\mathcal{H}$ given by an alphabet is the set of all
Horn clauses which can be constructed from the symbols in the alphabet. ◇

As our proof procedure for Horn clauses, we use SLD-resolution. This is
input resolution with some restrictions:

1. SLD-resolution is only applied to a set Σ of Horn clauses. The top clause
   can be either a definite program clause or a goal in Σ.
2. All input clauses are definite program clauses from Σ.

3. The literals resolved upon are the head of the input clause, and a *selected atom* in the body of the center clause.
4. No factors are used, so all resolvents are *binary* resolvents.

More formally:

Definition 7.3 Let Σ be a set of Horn clauses, and C be a Horn-clause. An *SLD-derivation* of length k of C from Σ is a finite sequence of Horn clauses $R_0, \ldots, R_k = C$, such that $R_0 \in \Sigma$ and each R_i $(1 \leq i \leq k)$ is a binary resolvent of R_{i-1} and a definite program clause $C_i \in \Sigma$, using the head of C_i and a *selected atom* in the body of R_{i-1} as the literals resolved upon.

R_0 is called the *top clause*, and the C_i are the *input clauses* of this SLD-derivation. If an SLD-derivation of C from Σ exists, we write $\Sigma \vdash_{sr} C$. An SLD-derivation of $\Box$ from Σ is called an *SLD-refutation* of Σ. $\diamond$

Note that either each R_i in an SLD-derivation is a goal, or each R_i is a definite program clause. We will discuss the selected atom in Section 7.6.

Definition 7.4 Let Σ be a set of Horn clauses and C a Horn clause. There exists an *SLD-deduction* of C from Σ, written as $\Sigma \vdash_{sd} C$, if C is a tautology, or if there is a Horn clause D, such that $\Sigma \vdash_{sr} D$ and D subsumes C. $\diamond$

Example 7.5 Consider $\Sigma = \{P(0, x, x), (P(s(x), y, s(z)) \leftarrow P(x, y, z))\}$, a set of clauses which formalizes addition. Let us see how we can prove $C = P(s^2(0), s(0), s^3(0))$ (i.e., $2 + 1 = 3$) from this set by SLD-resolution. Figure 7.1 shows an SLD-derivation of $R_2 = P(s^2(0), y, s^2(y))$ from Σ. The selected atoms are underlined. Since R_2 subsumes C, we have $\Sigma \vdash_{sd} C$. $\triangleleft$

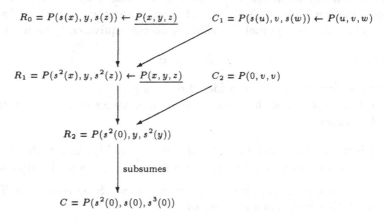

$$R_0 = P(s(x), y, s(z)) \leftarrow \underline{P(x, y, z)} \qquad C_1 = P(s(u), v, s(w)) \leftarrow P(u, v, w)$$

$$R_1 = P(s^2(x), y, s^2(z)) \leftarrow \underline{P(x, y, z)} \qquad C_2 = P(0, v, v)$$

$$R_2 = P(s^2(0), y, s^2(y))$$

subsumes

$$C = P(s^2(0), s(0), s^3(0))$$

Figure 7.1: An SLD-deduction of C from Σ

7.3   Soundness and Completeness

In this section, we are concerned with the soundness and completeness of SLD-resolution. Since SLD-resolution is a special case of unconstrained resolution, the soundness is obvious: if $\Sigma \vdash_{sd} C$, then $\Sigma \models C$. For the completeness of SLD-resolution, we have to do a little more work. The main result here will be the Subsumption Theorem for SLD-resolution, which we prove starting from the refutation completeness.

7.3.1   Refutation Completeness

In this subsection, we will prove that SLD-resolution is refutation-complete: a set of Horn clauses is unsatisfiable iff it has an SLD-refutation. First we establish refutation completeness for ground Horn clauses:

Lemma 7.6 *If Σ is a finite unsatisfiable set of ground Horn clauses, then $\Sigma \vdash_{sr} \Box$.*

Proof Let n be the number of facts (clauses consisting of a single positive literal) in Σ. The proof is by induction on n.

1. If $n = 0$, then $\Box \in \Sigma$, for otherwise the empty set would be a Herbrand model of Σ.

2. Suppose the lemma holds for $0 \leq n \leq m$. Suppose Σ contains $m + 1$ distinct facts. If $\Box \in \Sigma$, the lemma is obvious, so suppose $\Box \notin \Sigma$.
   Let A be a fact in Σ. We first delete all clauses from Σ which have A as head (so we also delete the fact A from Σ). Then we replace clauses which have A in their body by clauses constructed by deleting these atoms A from the body (so for example, $B \leftarrow A, B_1, \ldots, B_k$ will be replaced by $B \leftarrow B_1, \ldots, B_k$). Call the set obtained in this way Σ'.
   If M is a Herbrand model of Σ', then $M \cup \{A\}$ is a Herbrand model of Σ. Thus since Σ is unsatisfiable, Σ' must be unsatisfiable. Σ' only contains m facts, so by the induction hypothesis, there is an SLD-refutation of Σ'. If this refutation only uses clauses from Σ' which were also in Σ, then this is also an SLD-refutation of Σ, so then we are done.
   Otherwise, if C is the top clause or an input clause in this refutation and $C \notin \Sigma$, then C was obtained from some $C' \in \Sigma$ by deleting all atoms A from the body of C'. For all such C, do the following: restore the previously deleted copies of A to the body of C (which turns C into C' again), and add these atoms A to all later resolvents. This way, we can turn the SLD-refutation of Σ' into an SLD-derivation of $\leftarrow A, \ldots, A$ from Σ. See Figure 7.2 for illustration, where we add previously deleted atoms A to the bodies of R_0 and C_2. Since also $A \in \Sigma$, we can construct an SLD-refutation of Σ, using A a number of times as input clause to resolve away all members of the goal $\leftarrow A, \ldots, A$. $\Box$

The proof of the lifting lemma for SLD-resolution is similar to Lemma 5.12.

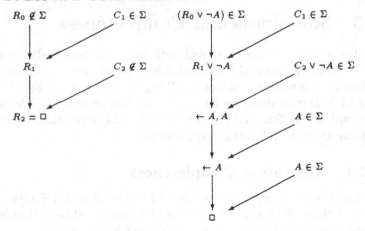

Figure 7.2: The SLD-refutations of Σ' (left) and Σ (right)

Lemma 7.7 (SLD-derivation lifting) *Let Σ be a set of Horn clauses, and Σ' be a set of instances of clauses from Σ. Suppose $R'_0, \ldots, R'_k$ is an SLD-derivation of the clause R'_k from Σ'. Then there exists an SLD-derivation $R_0, \ldots, R_k$ of the clause R_k from Σ, such that R'_i is an instance of R_i, for each i.*

The previous lemmas allow us to prove the refutation completeness of SLD-resolution:

Theorem 7.8 (Refutation completeness of SLD-resolution) *Let Σ be a set of Horn clauses. Then Σ is unsatisfiable iff $\Sigma \vdash_{sr} \Box$.*

Proof
$\Leftarrow$: By Theorem 4.39.
$\Rightarrow$: Suppose Σ is unsatisfiable. By Theorem 5.8, there is a finite unsatisfiable set Σ' of ground instances of clauses from Σ. From Lemma 7.6, we have $\Sigma' \vdash_{sr} \Box$. Using Lemma 7.7, we can lift this to $\Sigma \vdash_{sr} \Box$. $\qquad\Box$

7.3.2 The Subsumption Theorem

Here we will prove the Subsumption Theorem for SLD-resolution. As in the case of linear resolution, we establish this result by translating a refutation to a deduction, using the following lemma:

Lemma 7.9 *Let Σ be a set of Horn clauses, and $C = L_1 \vee \ldots \vee L_k$ be a non-tautologous ground Horn clause. If $\Sigma \cup \{\neg L_1, \ldots, \neg L_k\} \vdash_{sr} \Box$, then $\Sigma \vdash_{sd} C$.*

Proof Suppose $\Sigma \cup \{\neg L_1, \ldots, \neg L_k\} \vdash_{sr} \Box$, that is, there exists an SLD-refutation $R_0, \ldots, R_n = \Box$ of $\Sigma \cup \{\neg L_1, \ldots, \neg L_k\}$. By induction on n:

1. If $n = 0$, then $R_0 = \square \in \Sigma$, so then the lemma is obvious.
2. Suppose the lemma holds for $n \leq m$. Let $R_0, \ldots, R_{m+1} = \square$ be an SLD-refutation of $\Sigma \cup \{\neg L_1, \ldots, \neg L_k\}$. Then $R_1, \ldots, R_{m+1}$ is an SLD-refutation of $\Sigma \cup \{R_1\} \cup \{\neg L_1, \ldots, \neg L_k\}$. By the induction hypothesis, there is an SLD-derivation $R'_1, R'_2, \ldots, R'_l$ from $\Sigma \cup \{R_1\}$, where R'_l subsumes C. Note that R_1 must be a definite goal, so R_1 is either the top clause in this derivation, or not used at all.

   If $R'_1 \neq R_1$, then $R'_1 \in \Sigma$. Moreover, in that case R_1 is used nowhere in the SLD-derivation of R'_l, so then this is an SLD-derivation of R'_l from Σ, and hence $\Sigma \vdash_{sd} C$. In case $R'_1 = R_1$, we distinguish three possibilities:

   1. R_1 is a binary resolvent of a goal $G \in \Sigma$ and a definite clause $C_1 \in \Sigma$. Then $G, R'_1, R'_2, \ldots, R'_l$, with C_1 as first input clause, is an SLD-derivation from Σ. R'_l subsumes C, so then $\Sigma \vdash_{sd} C$.
   2. R_1 is a binary resolvent of a negative literal $\neg L \in \{\neg L_1, \ldots, \neg L_k\}$, and a definite clause $C_1 \in \Sigma$ (note that this means that C is a definite program clause, with L as head). Let θ be the mgu used in this resolution-step, so $C_1\theta = L \vee R_1$. Then $C_1\theta, L \vee R'_2, \ldots, L \vee R'_l$ is an SLD-derivation of $L \vee R'_l$ from $\Sigma \cup \{C_1\theta\}$. (See Figure 7.3 for illustration.) $C_1\theta$ is an instance of a clause in Σ, so by Lemma 7.7, we can find an SLD-derivation from Σ of a clause D, of which $L \vee R'_l$ is an instance. Since R'_l subsumes C and $L \in C$, $L \vee R'_l$ subsumes C, and hence D also subsumes C. Therefore $\Sigma \vdash_{sd} C$.

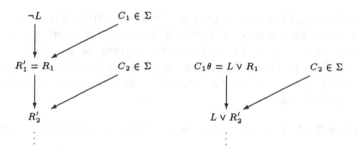

Figure 7.3: Illustration of case 2 of the proof

   3. R_1 is a binary resolvent of a goal $G \in \Sigma$, and a positive literal $L \in \{\neg L_1, \ldots, \neg L_k\}$. Let θ be the mgu used in this resolution step, so $G\theta = \neg L \vee R_1$. Then $G\theta(= \neg L \vee R'_1), \neg L \vee R'_2, \ldots, \neg L \vee R'_l$ is an SLD-derivation of $\neg L \vee R'_l$ from $\Sigma \cup \{G\theta\}$. $G\theta$ is an instance of a clause in Σ, so by Lemma 7.7, we can find an SLD-derivation from Σ of a clause D, of which $\neg L \vee R'_l$ is an instance. Since R'_l subsumes C and $\neg L \in C$, $\neg L \vee R'_l$ subsumes C, and hence D also subsumes C. Therefore $\Sigma \vdash_{sd} C$. $\square$

Now we can prove the Subsumption Theorem for SLD-resolution:

Theorem 7.10 (Subsumption Theorem for SLD-resolution) *Let Σ be a set of Horn clauses, and C be a Horn clause. Then $\Sigma \models C$ iff $\Sigma \vdash_{sd} C$.*

Proof

$\Leftarrow$: By Theorem 5.6.

$\Rightarrow$: If C is a tautology, the theorem is obvious. Assume C is not a tautology. Let θ be a Skolem substitution for C with respect to Σ. Let $C\theta$ be the clause $L_1 \vee \ldots \vee L_k$. Since C is not a tautology, $C\theta$ is not a tautology. $C\theta$ is ground and $\Sigma \models C\theta$, so by Proposition 2.37 the set of clauses $\Sigma \cup \{\neg L_1, \ldots, \neg L_k\}$ is unsatisfiable. Then it follows from Theorem 7.8 that $\Sigma \cup \{\neg L_1, \ldots, \neg L_k\} \vdash_{sr} \square$. Therefore by Lemma 7.9, there exists a clause D such that $\Sigma \vdash_{sr} D$, and D subsumes $C\theta$. From Lemma 5.16, D also subsumes C itself. Hence $\Sigma \vdash_{sd} C$. $\qquad\square$

Note the following special case of this result: if Σ is a set of definite program clauses and A is an atom such that $\Sigma \models A$, then there exists an atom B such that $\Sigma \vdash_{sr} B$ and A is an instance of B.

7.4 Definite Programs and Least Herbrand Models

It should be noted that our definition of SLD-resolution is more general than usual. Usually, for instance in [Llo87], SLD-resolution is only applied to find the logical consequences of sets of definite program clauses, rather than arbitrary sets of Horn clauses. Moreover, only SLD-*refutations* are used for this, not arbitrary derivations. In this and the next sections, we will discuss this more restricted case.

Definition 7.11 A *definite program* is a finite set of definite program clauses. $\qquad\diamond$

We will usually denote definite programs by the symbol Π.

Example 7.12 The set Π consisting of the following clauses is a definite program.

1. $P(0, x, x)$
2. $P(s(x), y, s(z)) \leftarrow P(x, y, z)$
3. $Q(s(0), s(0))$
4. $Q(s(s(0)), s(0))$
5. $Q(s(s(x)), u) \leftarrow Q(x, y), Q(s(x), z), P(y, z, u)$

It formalizes the *Fibonacci numbers*, which are defined as follows: the first and second Fibonacci numbers are both equal to one, while the $(n + 2)$-th number is the sum of the n-th and $(n+1)$-th number. The predicate symbol P denotes addition (i.e., $P(t_1, t_2, t_3)$ means $t_1 + t_2 = t_3$), and the predicate Q denotes the Fibonacci numbers (i.e., $Q(n, m)$ means that the n-th Fibonacci number is m).   ◁

We will use Herbrand models to specify the semantics of definite programs. To define a Herbrand model, we need a Herbrand pre-interpretation. This means that we must first define an alphabet. Usually, we assume the alphabet is implicitly given in the program Π we are dealing with. That is, we use the alphabet which consists of all symbols appearing in Π. If Π does not contain a constant, we add one constant a to the language. We will use U_Π to denote the Herbrand universe for the language given by this alphabet, and B_Π to denote the Herbrand base for this language.

Note that B_Π (the set of all ground atoms which can be constructed from the symbols in Π) is a Herbrand model of every definite clause, while the empty set is a Herbrand model of every definite goal other than □. If Π is a definite program, then B_Π is a Herbrand model of every clause in Π, so every definite program is satisfiable. Usually, some subsets of B_Π are Herbrand models of Π, and some other subsets are not. As the next proposition shows, the intersection of some Herbrand models of Π is itself also a Herbrand model of Π. This does not hold for sets of arbitrary non-Horn clauses. For example, both $\{P(a)\}$ and $\{Q(a)\}$ are Herbrand models of $\Sigma = \{P(a) \lor Q(a)\}$, while their intersection is the empty set, which itself is not a model of Σ.

Proposition 7.13 *Let Π be a definite program. If $\{M_1, M_2, \ldots, M_k, \ldots\}$ is a (possibly infinite) set of Herbrand models of Π, then their intersection $M = \cap_i M_i$ is also a Herbrand model of Π.*

Proof Suppose each of the M_i is a Herbrand model of Π, but $M = \cap_i M_i$ is not. Then there is a ground instance $C\theta$ of a clause $C \in \Pi$ which is false under M. Let $C\theta = A \leftarrow B_1, \ldots, B_n$ $(n \geq 0)$. Then $B_j \in M$ for every $1 \leq j \leq n$, but $A \notin M$. Since $M = \cap_i M_i$, we have $B_j \in M_i$ for every $1 \leq j \leq n$ and $i \geq 1$. But since each M_i is a model of $C\theta$, we must then also have $A \in M_i$, for each $i \geq 1$. But then $A \in M = \cap_i M_i$, which is a contradiction. □

It follows from the previous proposition that the intersection of *all* Herbrand models of Π, which will be called the *least* Herbrand model, is itself also a Herbrand model of Π.

Definition 7.14 Let Π be a definite program. The intersection of all Herbrand models of Π is called the *least Herbrand model* of Π, and is denoted by M_Π.   ◇

Example 7.15 Suppose we have the following definite program Π:

  1. $P(x, z) \leftarrow Q(x, y), P(y, z)$

   2. $P(x, x)$

   3. $Q(a, b)$

Then $M = \{P(a, a), P(b, b), P(a, b), Q(a, b)\}$ is a Herbrand model of Π. Clearly, every other Herbrand model of Π must contain this M, so M is in fact the least Herbrand model M_Π of Π.   ◁

The least Herbrand model of a definite program Π is the model that is "implicit" in the program. The domain of the model is the set of ground terms constructable from the symbols in Π; each ground term in the language denotes the corresponding ground term in the domain; furthermore, exactly those ground atoms which are logical consequences of Π, are true in M_Π:

Theorem 7.16 *If Π is a definite program, then $M_\Pi = \{A \in B_\Pi \mid \Pi \models A\}$.*

Proof Let $A \in B_\Pi$. Then we have:
$\Pi \models A$ iff (by Proposition 2.37)
$\Pi \cup \{\neg A\}$ is unsatisfiable iff
$\Pi \cup \{\neg A\}$ has no models iff (by Proposition 3.30)
$\Pi \cup \{\neg A\}$ has no Herbrand models iff
A is true under all Herbrand models of Π iff
$A \in M_\Pi$.   □

Definition 7.17 Let Π be a definite program. The *success set* of Π is $\{A \in B_\Pi \mid \Pi \cup \{\leftarrow A\} \vdash_{sr} \square\}$.   ◇

Thus the success set of Π consists of those ground atoms A such that $\Pi \cup \{\leftarrow A\}$ has an SLD-refutation. Since $\Pi \cup \{\leftarrow A\} \vdash_{sr} \square$ iff $\Pi \cup \{\leftarrow A\}$ is unsatisfiable iff $\Pi \models A$ iff $\Pi \in M_\Pi$, we have the following completeness result:

Theorem 7.18 (Completeness with respect to M_Π) *Let Π be a definite program. The success set of Π is equal to its least Herbrand model M_Π.*

7.5   Correct Answers and Computed Answers

In this section we will take a slightly different approach towards SLD-resolution than used in the Subsumption Theorem, by considering *correct* and *computed* answers. This approach, which points forward to PROLOG, views SLD-refutations as a means of answering the question "What follows from a definite program?" (hence the term 'answer'). Such questions are answered by examining the substitutions used in SLD-refutations of a set $\Pi \cup \{G\}$, where G is a goal. In the rest of this chapter, when we discuss some SLD-refutation of $\Pi \cup \{G\}$, we assume $G \neq \square$.

Because the actual mgu's used in a refutation are crucial for computed answers, we have to be very precise about the condition of standardizing apart. It is not sufficient here merely to require—as we have done up till now—that the two parent clauses in each resolution step are standardized apart. Example 7.22 below shows what might go wrong if we only use that. Instead, when dealing with correct and computed answers we will require SLD-refutations to satisfy the following stronger condition:

Condition *
In an SLD-refutation of $\Pi \cup \{G\}$, with mgu's $\theta_1, \ldots, \theta_n$ and input clauses $C_1, \ldots, C_n$, no variable in C_i should occur in G or in $C_1, \ldots, C_{i-1}$ or in $\theta_1, \ldots, \theta_{i-1}$.

In other words, C_i neither shares variables with G, nor with earlier mgu's and input clauses. This can easily be achieved by using appropriate variants of clauses in Π as input clauses: given some SLD-refutation which does not satisfy Condition *, we can simply rename some input clauses and make corresponding changes in later mgu's and center clauses to obtain an SLD-refutation which does satisfy Condition *. In the remainder of this chapter, whenever we use a phrase like "let $\mathcal{D}$ be an SLD-refutation", we assume this refutation to satisfy Condition *. Note that Condition * implies that every C_i is standardized apart from each earlier center clause.

With this additional condition in place, we can now define correct and computed answers.

Definition 7.19 Let Π be a definite program, $G = \leftarrow A_1, \ldots, A_k$ a definite goal, and θ be a substitution for variables of G. We say that θ is a *correct answer* for $\Pi \cup \{G\}$ if $\Pi \models \forall((A_1 \wedge \ldots \wedge A_k)\theta)$. $\diamond$

A correct answer for $\Pi \cup \{G\}$ provides a correct answer to the question "What follows from Π?" A correct answer is a semantical notion, which has its proof procedural counterpart in the concept of a *computed answer*, obtained from an SLD-refutation of $\Pi \cup \{G\}$ (satisfying Condition *, as we stated above). Later on in this section, we will show that θ is a correct answer iff θ is (roughly) an instance of a computed answer.[2]

Definition 7.20 Let Π be a definite program, and G a definite goal. Let $\theta_1, \ldots, \theta_n$ be the sequence of mgu's used in some SLD-refutation of $\Pi \cup \{G\}$. A *computed answer* θ for $\Pi \cup \{G\}$ is the restriction of the composition $\theta_1 \ldots \theta_n$ to the variables of G. $\diamond$

Example 7.21 Consider again the following program Π:

1. $P(x, z) \leftarrow Q(x, y), P(y, z)$

---

[2] An important result, the proof of which lies beyond the scope of this book, says that any computable function is computable by a definite program. See [Llo87, Theorem 9.6] or [Doe94, Chapter 7].

  2. $P(x, x)$
  3. $Q(a, b)$

Suppose $G =\leftarrow P(x, b)$. Figure 7.4 shows an SLD-refutation of $\Pi \cup \{G\}$, where the θ_i denote the mgu's used in each step. The selected atoms are underlined. This refutation corresponds to the computed answer $\{x/a\}$, since $\theta_1 \theta_2 \theta_3 = \{v/a, x/a, y/b, z/b, w/b\}$.   ◁

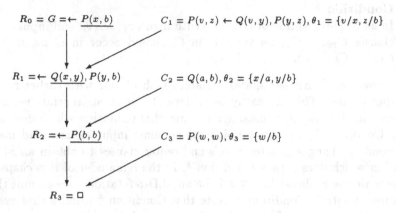

Figure 7.4: An SLD-refutation of $\Pi \cup \{G\}$, with computed answer $\{x/a\}$

Example 7.22 The following example, adapted from Apt and Doets [AD94], shows what can go wrong if we do not impose Condition *. Consider the program Π:

  1. $Q(x', y') \leftarrow Q(y', y')$
  2. $Q(x, x)$

Suppose $G =\leftarrow Q(x, y)$. Since $\Pi \models \forall x \forall y\, Q(x, y)$, the empty substitution ε is a correct answer, and we would like this to be a *computed* answer as well. Figure 7.5 shows an SLD-refutation of $\Pi \cup \{G\}$. The composition of the mgu's in this refutation, restricted to the variables in G, is $\{x/y\}$. Note that in each resolution step, the two parent clauses are standardized apart, so the weak requirement that we used up till now is satisfied. However, G and the second input clause share the variable x, so Condition * is not satisfied. Because of this, we do not get the computer answer ε that we want, but only the weaker answer $\{x/y\}$. On the other hand, if we rename the second input clause to its variant $Q(w, w)$, thus satisfying Condition *, then we do get ε as computed answer. Thus, if we do not impose Condition *, two SLD-refutations with the same center clauses, the same selected atoms in each center clause, and variant input clauses, sometimes yield very different results.   ◁

The problem described in the last example does not matter if we are only interested in the existence of an SLD-derivation or SLD-refutation: as

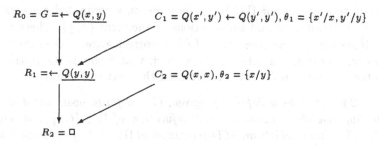

$$R_0 = G = \leftarrow \underline{Q(x,y)} \qquad\qquad C_1 = Q(x',y') \leftarrow Q(y',y'), \theta_1 = \{x'/x, y'/y\}$$

$$R_1 = \leftarrow \underline{Q(y,y)} \qquad\qquad C_2 = Q(x,x), \theta_2 = \{x/y\}$$

$$R_2 = \Box$$

Figure 7.5: The variables x in G and in C_2 interfere

long as the two parent clauses in each resolution step are standardized apart, renaming an input clause to one of its variants gives a resolvent which is a variant of the old resolvent. However, when we are particularly interested in computed answers we really need Condition *.

In the rest of this section, we will show how the correct and computed answers coincide. That is, we will show that θ is a correct answer iff θ equals the restriction of some instance of a computed answer to the variables in G. First we will prove that if θ is a computed answer, then θ (and hence also all instances of θ) is correct. This is another form of soundness.

Theorem 7.23 (Soundness of computed answers) *Let Π be a definite program, and G a definite goal. Then every computed answer for $\Pi \cup \{G\}$ is a correct answer for $\Pi \cup \{G\}$.*

Proof Let $G = \leftarrow A_1, \ldots, A_n$, and $\theta_1, \ldots, \theta_k$ be the sequence of mgu's in an SLD-refutation of length k of $\Pi \cup \{G\}$ with computed answer θ. We will prove by induction on k that $\Pi \models \forall((A_1 \wedge \ldots \wedge A_n)\theta_1 \ldots \theta_k)$, thus showing that θ is a correct answer.

1. If $k = 1$, then $G = \leftarrow A_1$ and there is an atom $B \in \Pi$ such that $B\theta_1 = A_1\theta_1$. Hence $B \models \forall(A_1\theta_1)$.

2. Suppose the result holds for $k \leq m$, and let $\theta_1, \ldots, \theta_{m+1}$ be the sequence of mgu's in an SLD-refutation of length $m+1$ of $\Pi\cup\{G\}$ with computed answer θ. Suppose the first input clause is $C_1 = B \leftarrow B_1, \ldots, B_q$ ($q \geq 0$), and A_s is the selected atom in G. Then the second center clause in the refutation is $\leftarrow (A_1, \ldots, A_{s-1}, B_1, \ldots, B_q, A_{s+1}, \ldots, A_n)\theta_1$. By the induction hypothesis, we have $\Pi \models \forall((A_1 \wedge \ldots \wedge A_{s-1} \wedge B_1 \wedge \ldots \wedge B_q \wedge A_{s+1} \wedge \ldots \wedge A_n)\theta_1 \ldots \theta_{m+1})$. Furthermore, note that $C_1 \cup \forall((B_1 \wedge \ldots \wedge B_q)\theta_1 \ldots \theta_{m+1}) \models B\theta_1 \ldots \theta_{m+1}$, hence also $\Pi \models \forall((A_1 \wedge \ldots \wedge A_{s-1} \wedge B \wedge A_{s+1} \wedge \ldots \wedge A_n)\theta_1 \ldots \theta_{m+1})$. Finally, since $B\theta_1 = A_s\theta_1$, we can replace B by A_s in the previous formula, thus obtaining $\Pi \models \forall((A_1 \wedge \ldots \wedge A_n)\theta_1 \ldots \theta_{m+1})$. □

Not every correct answer is a computed answer. Take for instance $\Pi = \{P(x,a)\}$, $G = \leftarrow P(x,a)$ and $\theta = \{x/a\}$. Then θ is a correct answer but not a computed answer for $\Pi \cup \{G\}$, since the only computed answers are the empty substitution ε and substitutions of the form $\{x/y\}$, where y is a variable. However, we can prove that if θ is a correct answer, then there is a computed answer σ and a substitution γ, such that θ equals the restriction of $\sigma\gamma$ to the variables in G. For this, we need the next two lemmas.

Lemma 7.24 *Let Π be a definite program, G a definite goal, and θ a substitution. Suppose there exists an SLD-refutation of $\Pi \cup \{G\theta\}$ with mgu's $\theta_1, \ldots, \theta_k$. Then there exists an SLD-refutation of $\Pi \cup \{G\}$ of the same length with mgu's $\theta'_1, \ldots, \theta'_k$, such that there is a substitution γ with the property that $G\theta\theta_1 \ldots \theta_k = G\theta'_1 \ldots \theta'_k\gamma$.*

Proof By induction on k:

1. If $k = 1$, then $G\theta =\leftarrow A\theta$, the first input clause is some $C_1 = B \in \Pi$, and θ_1 is an mgu for $A\theta$ and B. We can assume G and C_1 are standardized apart, then $\theta\theta_1$ is a unifier for A and B. Let θ'_1 be an mgu for A and B, then there is a γ such that $\theta\theta_1 = \theta'_1\gamma$. Now $R'_0 = G, R'_1 = \square$, with input clause C_1 and mgu θ'_1, is an SLD-refutation of $\Pi \cup \{G\}$, and we have $G\theta\theta_1 = G\theta'_1\gamma$.

2. Suppose the lemma holds for $k \leq m$. Let $R_0 = G\theta, R_1, \ldots, R_{m+1} = \square$ be an SLD-refutation of $\Pi \cup \{G\theta\}$ with mgu's $\theta_1, \ldots, \theta_{m+1}$, and with C_1 as first input clause (see Figure 7.6 for illustration). Assume G and C_1 are standardized apart. Then θ_1 is an mgu for the selected atom $A_s\theta$ in $G\theta$ and C_1^+, so $\theta\theta_1$ is a unifier for A_s in G and C_1^+. Let θ'_1 be an mgu for these two atoms, then there is a ρ such that $\theta\theta_1 = \theta'_1\rho$. Let $G =\leftarrow A_1, \ldots, A_n$. There is a binary resolvent $R'_1 =\leftarrow (A_1, \ldots, A_{s-1}, C_1^-, A_{s+1}, \ldots, A_n)\theta'_1$ of G and C_1, with mgu θ'_1, such that $R'_1\rho = R_1$. By the induction hypothesis, there is an SLD-refutation $R'_1, \ldots, R'_{m+1} = \square$ of $\Pi \cup \{R'_1\}$ with mgu's $\theta'_2, \ldots, \theta'_{m+1}$, and there is a γ' such that $R'_1\rho\theta_2 \ldots \theta_{m+1} = R'_1\theta'_2 \ldots \theta'_{m+1}\gamma'$. We may assume without loss of generality that the SLD-refutation $R'_0 = G, R'_1, \ldots, R'_{m+1} = \square$ satisfies Condition *. Because $R'_1 =\leftarrow (A_1, \ldots, A_{s-1}, C_1^-, A_{s+1}, \ldots, A_n)\theta'_1$ and $\theta'_1\rho = \theta\theta_1$, we have $(G - \neg A_s)\theta\theta_1 \ldots \theta_{m+1} = (G - \neg A_s)\theta'_1 \ldots \theta'_{m+1}\gamma'$. Let $x_1, \ldots, x_p$ be the variables in $A_s\theta'_1$ that do not occur in R'_1. It follows from Condition * that $\theta'_2, \ldots, \theta'_{m+1}, \gamma'$ do not act on any of these x_i, so $x_i\theta'_2 \ldots \theta'_{m+1}\gamma' = x_i$ for $1 \leq i \leq p$. Define $t_i = x_i\rho\theta_2 \ldots \theta_{m+1}$ and $\gamma = \gamma' \cup \{x_1/t_1, \ldots, x_p/t_p\}$. Now suppose x is a variable in A_s, and y is a variable occurring in $x\theta'_1$. If y occurs in R'_1, then $y\theta'_2 \ldots \theta'_{m+1}\gamma = y\theta'_2 \ldots \theta'_{m+1}\gamma' = y\rho\theta_2 \ldots \theta_{m+1}$. If y does not occur in R'_1, then $y = x_j$ for some $1 \leq j \leq p$, so then $y\theta'_2 \ldots \theta'_{m+1}\gamma = x_j\theta'_2 \ldots \theta'_{m+1}\gamma = x_j\gamma = t_j = x_j\rho\theta_2 \ldots \theta_{m+1} = y\rho\theta_2 \ldots \theta_{m+1}$. Hence $x\theta'_1\theta'_2 \ldots \theta'_{m+1}\gamma = x\theta'_1\rho\theta_2 \ldots \theta_{m+1} = x\theta\theta_1\theta_2 \ldots \theta_{m+1}$. Since this holds for every variable x in A_s, we have $A_s\theta\theta_1 \ldots \theta_{m+1} = A_s\theta'_1 \ldots \theta'_{m+1}\gamma$. Combining the conclusions of the last two paragraphs, it follows that $G\theta\theta_1 \ldots \theta_{m+1} = G\theta'_1 \ldots \theta'_{m+1}\gamma$. $\square$

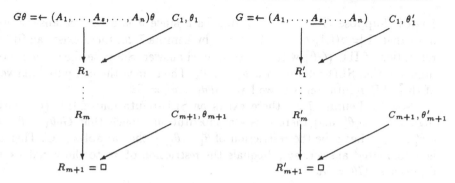

Figure 7.6: The induction step in the lemma

Lemma 7.25 *Let Π be a definite program, and let $G = \leftarrow A_1, \ldots, A_n$ be a definite goal. If $\Pi \models \forall (A_1 \wedge \ldots \wedge A_n)$ then there exists an SLD-refutation of $\Pi \cup \{G\}$ with the empty substitution ε as the computed answer.*

Proof Suppose $\Pi \models \forall (A_1 \wedge \ldots \wedge A_n)$. Let $x_1, \ldots, x_m$ be all distinct variables in G, and let $\theta = \{x_1/a_1, \ldots, x_m/a_m\}$ be a Skolem substitution for G with respect to Π. $(A_1 \wedge \ldots \wedge A_n)\theta$ is ground and we have that $\Pi \models (A_1 \wedge \ldots \wedge A_n)\theta$. Then $\Pi \cup \{G\theta\}$ is unsatisfiable, hence by Theorem 7.8 there exists an SLD-refutation of $\Pi \cup \{G\theta\}$. We may assume this refutation satisfies Condition * (if not, renaming some input clauses will do).

Suppose the sequence of mgu's in this SLD-refutation is $\theta_1, \ldots, \theta_k$. Let $\sigma = \theta_1 \ldots \theta_k$. Then the computed answer for $\Pi \cup \{G\theta\}$ of this SLD-refutation is the restriction of σ to the variables in $G\theta$. Since $G\theta$ contains no variables, it follows that this computed answer is ε. We assume without loss of generality that none of the variables $x_1, \ldots, x_m$ appears in this SLD-refutation. Then replacing each a_i by x_i $(1 \leq i \leq m)$ in this SLD-refutation yields an SLD-refutation of $\Pi \cup \{G\}$ with ε as the computed answer. $\square$

Now we can prove the completeness of computed answers:[3]

Theorem 7.26 (Completeness of computed answers) *Let Π be a definite program, and G be a definite goal. If θ is a correct answer for $\Pi \cup \{G\}$, then there exist a computed answer σ for $\Pi \cup \{G\}$ and a substitution γ, such that θ equals the restriction of $\sigma\gamma$ to the variables in G.*

---

[3]In Theorem 8.6 of [Llo87], it is stated that if θ is a correct answer, then there are a computed answer σ and a substitution γ such that $\theta = \sigma\gamma$. This is not quite correct. Take for instance $\Pi = \{P(f(y, z))\}$, $G = \leftarrow P(x)$. Then $\theta = \{x/f(a, a)\}$ is a correct answer for $\Pi \cup \{G\}$. Since all variants of $P(f(y, z))$ are of the form $P(f(u, v))$, where u and v are distinct variables, every computed answer for $\Pi \cup \{G\}$ is of the form $\sigma = \{x/f(u, v)\}$. However, there is no γ such that $\theta = \sigma\gamma$. In particular, $\sigma\{u/a, v/a\} = \{x/f(a, a), u/a, v/a\} \neq \theta$. This example was reported in [She94]; see also [Apt97, pp. 100–101].

Proof Suppose $G = \leftarrow A_1, \ldots, A_n$. Then since θ is a correct answer, we have that $\Pi \models \forall((A_1 \wedge \ldots \wedge A_n)\theta)$. So by Lemma 7.25, there exists an SLD-refutation of $\Pi \cup \{G\theta\}$ with ε as computed answer. Suppose the sequence of mgu's in this SLD-refutation is $\theta_1, \ldots, \theta_k$. Then since the computed answer of this SLD-refutation is ε, we have $G\theta\theta_1 \ldots \theta_k = G\theta$.

Now by Lemma 7.24, there exists an SLD-refutation of $\Pi \cup \{G\}$ with mgu's $\theta_1', \ldots, \theta_k'$ and there exists a substitution γ such that $G\theta\theta_1 \ldots \theta_k = G\theta_1' \ldots \theta_k'\gamma$. Let σ be the restriction of $\theta_1' \ldots \theta_k'$ to the variables in G. Then σ is a computed answer, and θ equals the restriction of $\sigma\gamma$ to the variables in G, because $G\theta = G\sigma\gamma$. $\qquad\qquad \square$

7.6 Computation Rules

In this section, we will explain the role of the selected atom in an SLD-derivation. This selected atom can be selected by a *computation rule*. The concept of an SLD-refutation can be refined by specifying that the selected atoms in that refutation should be selected according to some particular computation rule $\mathcal{R}$. The refutation is then called a refutation *via* $\mathcal{R}$.

Example 7.27 Consider the program Π:

1. $P(x, z) \leftarrow Q(x, y), P(y, z)$
2. $P(x, x)$
3. $Q(a, b)$

Suppose $G = \leftarrow P(x, b)$. Figure 7.4 showed an SLD-refutation of $\Pi \cup \{G\}$, with computed answer $\{x/a\}$, using a computation rule which always selects the *leftmost* atom in a goal. Now let $\mathcal{R}$ be the computation rule which always selects the *rightmost* atom in a goal. Figure 7.7 shows an SLD-refutation of $\Pi \cup \{G\}$ via $\mathcal{R}$, also with $\{x/a\}$ as computed answer. $\qquad \triangleleft$

A computation rule is often (for instance in [Llo87]) defined as a function from the set of goals to atoms in those goals. For example, the computation rule in the above example always simply selects the rightmost atom in a goal in a derivation, without taking into account the "history" of the derivation (i.e., the earlier steps in the derivation). However, it is sometimes useful to be able to take this history into account. This would enable us for instance to define a kind of "first in, first out" computation rule, which will be useful in the next chapter. Such a rule always selects one of the "oldest" atoms, i.e., one of the atoms in the last goal that have been present in center clauses at least as long as other atoms. For instance, consider a derivation $\mathcal{D}_1$ with only two center clauses $(\leftarrow P, Q)$, $(\leftarrow P, R)$, and input clause $Q \leftarrow R$, and a derivation $\mathcal{D}_2$ with center clauses $(\leftarrow Q, R)$, $(\leftarrow P, R)$, and input clause $Q \leftarrow P$. Both derivations have the same final goal, so if we define a computation rule as a function from goals to atoms, a computation rule has to select the same

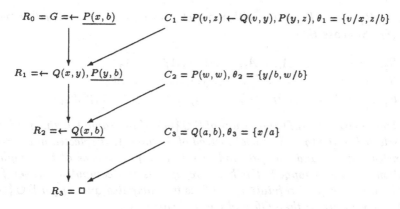

Figure 7.7: An SLD-refutation of $\Pi \cup \{G\}$ via $\mathcal{R}$

atom in the last goal of $\mathcal{D}_1$ and in the last goal of $\mathcal{D}_2$. On the other hand, the "first in, first out" rule would select P in the last goal of $\mathcal{D}_1$ and R in the last goal of $\mathcal{D}_2$.

In order to allow computation rules which take into account the whole derivation, we follow Apt [Apt97] in defining a computation rule as a function which takes as input a derivation (with a non-empty conclusion), and selects an atom in the last goal in this derivation (Apt actually uses the term 'selection rule').

Definition 7.28 Let $\mathcal{S}$ be the set of all SLD-derivations (with an arbitrary definite goal as top clause and arbitrary definite program clauses as input clauses) that end in a non-empty definite goal. A *computation rule* $\mathcal{R}$ is a function from $\mathcal{S}$ to the set of atoms, such that if $\mathcal{D}$ is a derivation in $\mathcal{S}$, then $\mathcal{R}(\mathcal{D})$ is an atom (the *selected atom*) in the last goal of $\mathcal{D}$. ◇

Definition 7.29 Let Π be a definite program, G a definite goal, and $\mathcal{R}$ a computation rule. An *SLD-refutation of* $\Pi \cup \{G\}$ *via* $\mathcal{R}$ is an SLD-refutation of $\Pi \cup \{G\}$, in which the selected atoms are selected by using $\mathcal{R}$. ◇

Definition 7.30 Let Π be a definite program, G a definite goal, and $\mathcal{R}$ a computation rule. An $\mathcal{R}$-*computed answer* for $\Pi \cup \{G\}$ is a computed answer for $\Pi \cup \{G\}$ which is obtained from an SLD-refutation of $\Pi \cup \{G\}$ via $\mathcal{R}$. ◇

Notice that the two SLD-refutations in figures 7.4 and 7.7 yield the same computed answer $\{x/a\}$, even though they use different computation rules. This *independence* of the computation rule holds in general. The proof is based on the following rather elaborate lemma, which shows that it is possible to "switch" the selected atoms between two consecutive center clauses.

Lemma 7.31 (Switching Lemma) *Let Π be a definite program, and G a definite goal. Suppose that $\Pi \cup \{G\}$ has an SLD-refutation $R_0 = G, R_1, \ldots,$*

$R_{q-1}, R_q, R_{q+1}, \ldots, R_k = \square$, *with input clauses* $C_1, \ldots, C_k$ *and with mgu's*
$\theta_1, \ldots, \theta_k$. *Suppose that*

$$R_{q-1} = \leftarrow A_1, \ldots, A_{i-1}, A_i, \ldots, A_{j-1}, A_j, \ldots, A_n$$
$$R_q = \leftarrow (A_1, \ldots, A_{i-1}, C_q^-, \ldots, A_{j-1}, A_j, \ldots, A_n)\theta_q$$
$$R_{q+1} = \leftarrow (A_1, \ldots, A_{i-1}, C_q^-, \ldots, A_{j-1}, C_{q+1}^-, \ldots, A_n)\theta_q\theta_{q+1}$$

Then there exists an SLD-refutation of $\Pi \cup \{G\}$ *of the same length, in which*
A_j *is selected in the* $(q-1)$-*th goal instead of* A_i, *and* A_i *is selected in the* q-*th*
goal instead of A_j, *and the* q-*th and* $(q+1)$-*th input clauses of the original*
refutation are interchanged. Furthermore, if θ *is the computed answer for*
$\Pi \cup \{G\}$ *in the original refutation and* θ' *is the computed answer for* $\Pi \cup \{G\}$
in the new refutation, then $G\theta$ *and* $G\theta'$ *are variants.*

Proof We assume without loss of generality that R_{q-1}, C_q and C_{q+1} are
standardized apart. Since $A_j\theta_q\theta_{q+1} = C_{q+1}^+\theta_{q+1} = C_{q+1}^+\theta_q\theta_{q+1}$, A_j and C_{q+1}^+
can be unified. Let θ_q' be an mgu for A_j and C_{q+1}^+. Since $\theta_q\theta_{q+1}$ is a unifier
for A_j and C_{q+1}^+, there exists a σ such that $\theta_q\theta_{q+1} = \theta_q'\sigma$.

Since $C_q^+\sigma = C_q^+\theta_q'\sigma = C_q^+\theta_q\theta_{q+1} = A_i\theta_q\theta_{q+1} = A_i\theta_q'\sigma$, C_q^+ and $A_i\theta_q'$ can
be unified. Let θ_{q+1}' be an mgu for C_q^+ and $A_i\theta_q'$. We have that σ is a unifier
for C_q^+ and $A_i\theta_q'$, so there exists a σ' such that $\sigma = \theta_{q+1}'\sigma'$. This means that
$\theta_q\theta_{q+1} = \theta_q'\theta_{q+1}'\sigma'$. Now we can select A_j in the $(q-1)$-th goal instead of A_i,
and A_i in the q-th goal instead of A_j, by interchanging the q-th and $(q+1)$-th
input clauses of the original refutation. This gives us the following (the goals
$R_0', \ldots, R_{q-1}'$ in this new refutation are the same as $R_0, \ldots, R_{q-1}$ in the old
refutation):

$$R_{q-1}' = \leftarrow A_1, \ldots, A_{i-1}, A_i, \ldots, A_{j-1}, A_j, \ldots, A_k$$
$$R_q' = \leftarrow (A_1, \ldots, A_{i-1}, A_i, \ldots, A_{j-1}, C_{q+1}^-, \ldots, A_k)\theta_q'$$
$$R_{q+1}' = \leftarrow (A_1, \ldots, A_{i-1}, C_q^-, \ldots, A_{j-1}, C_{q+1}^-, \ldots, A_k)\theta_q'\theta_{q+1}'$$

Now we will show that R_{q+1} and R_{q+1}' are variants. Since $A_i\theta_q'\theta_{q+1}' =
C_q^+\theta_q'\theta_{q+1}'$, and θ_q is an mgu for A_i and C_q^+, there exists a γ such that
$\theta_q'\theta_{q+1}' = \theta_q\gamma$. Also, $A_j\theta_q\gamma = A_j\theta_q'\theta_{q+1}' = C_{q+1}^+\theta_q'\theta_{q+1}' = C_{q+1}^+\theta_q\gamma = C_{q+1}^+\gamma$,
so γ is a unifier for $A_j\theta_q$ and C_{q+1}^+. Since θ_{q+1} is an mgu for $A_j\theta_q$ and C_{q+1}^+,
there exists a substitution σ'' such that $\gamma = \theta_{q+1}\sigma''$.

So $\theta_q'\theta_{q+1}' = \theta_q\theta_{q+1}\sigma''$. We have already shown that $\theta_q\theta_{q+1} = \theta_q'\theta_{q+1}'\sigma'$,
so R_{q+1} and R_{q+1}' are variants. Now the rest of the new refutation after R_{q+1}'
can be the same as the original one, modulo variants. Here we may assume
without loss of generality that the new refutation satisfies Condition *. Hence
if θ is the computed answer for $\Pi \cup \{G\}$ in the original refutation and θ' is
the computed answer for $\Pi \cup \{G\}$ in the new refutation, then $G\theta$ and $G\theta'$
are variants. $\qquad\square$

Theorem 7.32 (Independence of the computation rule) *Let* Π *be a definite program,* G *a definite goal, and* $\mathcal{R}$ *a computation rule. If there is an SLD-refutation of* $\Pi \cup \{G\}$ *with computed answer* θ*, then there is an SLD-refutation of* $\Pi \cup \{G\}$ *via* $\mathcal{R}$ *with computed answer* θ'*, such that* $G\theta$ *and* $G\theta'$ *are variants.*

Proof Let $R_0 = G, R_1, \ldots, R_k$ be an SLD-refutation of $\Pi \cup \{G\}$ with mgu's $\theta_1, \ldots, \theta_k$ and computed answer θ. G itself is an SLD-derivation in $\mathcal{S}$. Suppose $\mathcal{R}(G) = A_s$. If A_s is not the selected atom in G in this refutation, then for some $1 \leq j \leq k$, $A_s\theta_1 \ldots \theta_j$ is the selected atom in R_j. Hence by repeatedly applying the Switching lemma we can move the selection of A_s "upward" in the refutation, obtaining an alternative SLD-refutation $R_0' = G, R_1', \ldots, R_k' = \Box$ of $\Pi \cup \{G\}$, with computed answer σ, such that $G\theta$ and $G\sigma$ are variants, and such that A_s is the selected atom in R_0', in accordance with $\mathcal{R}$.

Repeating this procedure $k-1$ times, we can also bring the selected atoms in later goals in accordance with $\mathcal{R}$, eventually obtaining an SLD-refutation $R_0'' = G, R_1'', \ldots, R_k'' = \Box$ of $\Pi \cup \{G\}$, with computed answer θ', such that $G\theta$ and $G\theta'$ are variants, and such that all selected atoms are selected according to $\mathcal{R}$. $\Box$

This result shows that it does not really matter, in terms of completeness, which computation rule we use. Thus when searching for an SLD-refutation, we only need to consider the derivations via one particular $\mathcal{R}$, which greatly reduces the search space of all possible SLD-derivations. Combining the previous theorem with Theorems 7.8 and 7.26, we also immediately have the following:

Theorem 7.33 *Let* Π *be a definite program,* G *a definite goal, and* $\mathcal{R}$ *a computation rule. Then* $\Pi \cup \{G\}$ *is unsatisfiable iff there exists an SLD-refutation of* $\Pi \cup \{G\}$ *via* $\mathcal{R}$*.*

Theorem 7.34 *Let* Π *be a definite program,* G *a definite goal, and* $\mathcal{R}$ *a computation rule. If* θ *is a correct answer for* $\Pi \cup \{G\}$*, then there exist an* $\mathcal{R}$*-computed answer* σ *for* $\Pi \cup \{G\}$ *and a substitution* γ*, such that* θ *equals the restriction of* $\sigma\gamma$ *to the variables in* G*.*

The latter result is sometimes called the *strong* completeness of SLD-resolution.

7.7   SLD-Trees

The previous sections showed that if θ is a correct answer for $\Pi \cup \{G\}$ and $\mathcal{R}$ is a computation rule, then there exists an SLD-refutation via $\mathcal{R}$ corresponding to a computed answer σ of which θ is (roughly) an instance. But how do we *find* such a refutation? This is done by constructing and searching (parts of) an *SLD-tree*. Such a tree essentially contains all possible SLD-derivations via some computation rule $\mathcal{R}$, thus also all possible SLD-refutations via $\mathcal{R}$. In order to be able to conveniently denote the input clauses used in refutations in this tree, we assign a unique number to each of the clauses in the program Π. Here we also make the convention that SLD-derivations need not be finite: they can go on indefinitely long. We will see an example of such an infinite SLD-derivation later in this section.

Definition 7.35 Let Π be a definite program, and G a definite goal. An *SLD-tree for* $\Pi \cup \{G\}$ is a tree satisfying the following:

1. Each node of the tree is a (possibly empty) definite goal.
2. The root node is G.
3. Let $N = \leftarrow A_1, \ldots, A_s, \ldots, A_k$ $(k \geq 1)$ be a node in the tree, with A_s as selected atom. Then, for each clause C in Π such that A_s and (a variant of) C^+ are unifiable, the node N has exactly one resolvent of G and C, resolved upon B_s, as a child. The edge between the node and the child is labeled with the number of the input clause C. The node has no other children.
4. Nodes which are the empty clause $\Box$ have no children. $\diamond$

Definition 7.36 Let Π be a definite program, G a definite goal, and $\mathcal{R}$ a computation rule. The *SLD-tree for* $\Pi \cup \{G\}$ *via* $\mathcal{R}$ is the SLD-tree for $\Pi \cup \{G\}$ in which the selected atoms are selected by $\mathcal{R}$. $\diamond$

An SLD-tree for $\Pi \cup \{G\}$ may contain three kinds of branches. First, branches which are a path from the root to a leaf having $\Box$ as its goal. Such a branch corresponds to a refutation of $\Pi \cup \{G\}$, and a computed answer for $\Pi \cup \{G\}$ can be obtained from the branch. Since such a refutation is exactly what we are looking for, these branches are called *success branches*.

Second, branches which are a path from the root to some leaf having a non-empty goal. This non-empty goal is a leaf because no further derivation steps are possible from this goal. Thus this branch does not lead us to a refutation. Hence these branches are called *failure branches*.

Third, *infinite branches*. These correpond to infinite SLD-derivations. We cannot get much useful information from such an infinite branch (in fact, infinite branches are nothing but trouble).

Example 7.37 Suppose we have the following program Π:

1. $P(x, z) \leftarrow Q(x, y), P(y, z)$
2. $P(x, x)$
3. $Q(a, b)$

Suppose also that our goal G is $\leftarrow P(x, b)$ (that is, we want to find out for which x the formula $P(x, b)$ is a logical consequence of Π). If we use the computation rule $\mathcal{R}$ which always selects the leftmost atom in a goal, we can

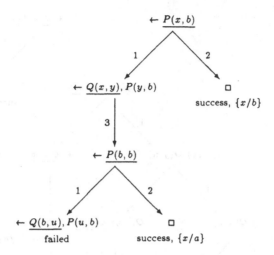

Figure 7.8: An SLD-tree

visualize the SLD-tree for $\Pi \cup \{G\}$ via $\mathcal{R}$ as in Figure 7.8. Here the computed answer for a success branch is shown below the $\square$-leaf in which this branch ends.

The tree contains two success branches: one having the substitution $\{x/a\}$ as its computed answer, and one having $\{x/b\}$ as its computed answer. Note that the success branch with $\{x/a\}$ as computed answer corresponds to the refutation shown in Figure 7.4.   ◁

Changing the computation rule may radically alter the structure of the SLD-tree, as the next example (adapted from [Llo87]) shows.

Example 7.38 Consider the same Π and G as in the previous example, but now with a computation rule $\mathcal{R}'$ which selects the *rightmost* atom in each goal. The SLD-tree for $\Pi \cup \{G\}$ via $\mathcal{R}'$ is shown in Figure 7.9. Like the tree in Figure 7.8, this tree contains two success branches, corresponding to the computed answers $\{x/a\}$ and $\{x/b\}$. However, the change of computation rule from $\mathcal{R}$ to $\mathcal{R}'$ has resulted in the change from a finite to an infinite SLD-tree! Here the leftmost branch corresponds to an infinite SLD-derivation.   ◁

Constructing the SLD-tree for $\Pi \cup \{G\}$ via some $\mathcal{R}$ can be regarded as a refinement of the level-saturation method we described earlier for uncon-strained resolution. Roughly, the n-th level in the SLD-tree (where G is the 0-th level) contains all clauses which can be derived from $\Pi \cup \{G\}$ by an SLD-derivation of length n, in which the selected atoms are selected by $\mathcal{R}$. Since the SLD-tree for $\Pi \cup \{G\}$ via $\mathcal{R}$ thus contains all possible SLD-refutations of $\Pi \cup \{G\}$ via $\mathcal{R}$, our completeness theorems can also be translated to the SLD-tree:

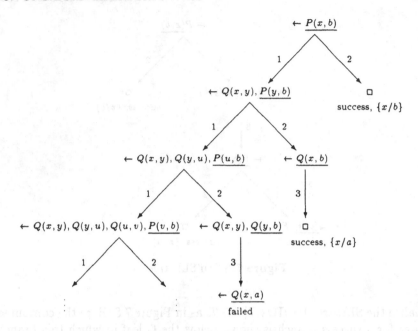

Figure 7.9: An infinite SLD-tree

Theorem 7.39 *Let* Π *be a definite program,* G *a definite goal, and* R *a computation rule. Then* Π ∪ {G} *is unsatisfiable iff the SLD-tree for* Π ∪ {G} *via* R *contains at least one success branch.*

Theorem 7.40 *Let* Π *be a definite program,* G *a definite goal, and* R *a computation rule. If* θ *is a correct answer for* Π ∪ {G}, *then the SLD-tree for* Π ∪ {G} *via* R *contains a success branch corresponding to a computed answer* σ, *such that for some* γ, θ *equals the restriction of* σγ *to the variables in* G.

7.8 Undecidability

In this section we state, without proof, two important undecidability results for Horn clauses. Firstly, implication between two Horn clauses is undecidable (Theorem 4.5 of [MP92]).

Theorem 7.41 (Marcinkowski & Pacholski) *It is undecidable whether a definite program clause that contains at least two negative literals, logically implies another definite program clause.*

Consequently, {C} ⊢$_{sd}$ D is undecidable as well.

The second result, proved in [HW93], states that satisfiability of a set of only 3 Horn clauses is already undecidable.

Theorem 7.42 (Hanschke & Würtz) *It is undecidable whether a set consisting of an atom, a definite program clause with one negative literal, and a definite goal with one negative literal, is satisfiable.*

From Theorem 7.39, we know that $\Pi \cup \{G\}$ is unsatisfiable iff the SLD-tree for $\Pi \cup \{G\}$ via some $\mathcal{R}$ contains at least one success branch (i.e., an SLD-refutation via $\mathcal{R}$). It follows that there is no algorithm for deciding whether such an SLD-tree actually contains a success branch.

7.9 Summary

Horn clauses are clauses with at most one positive literal, *definite program clauses* are clauses with exactly one positive literal, *definite goals* are clauses without positive literals, and a *definite program* is a finite set of definite program clauses. In ILP, attention is often restricted to a language of Horn clauses instead of a full clausal language.

For Horn clauses we can define *SLD-resolution*, a restricted form of input resolution. We proved various different forms of completeness of SLD-resolution: the Subsumption Theorem and the refutation completeness, from which it follows that the *success set* of a definite program equals the unique *least Herbrand model* of that program, and also completeness in terms of *computed answers*. The latter form of completeness is independent of the *computation rule* that is used.

An *SLD-tree* is a tree containing all possible derivations from a program Π and a goal G, via some computation rule. Such a tree contains all computed answers for $\Pi \cup \{G\}$. Implication between two Horn clauses is undecidable, and so is the satisfiability of sets of Horn clauses.

Chapter 8

SLDNF-Resolution

8.1 Introduction

Suppose we are given some definite program Π. If a particular ground atom A is implied by Π, we can say on the basis of Π that A is true. But what about an atom A such that $\Pi \not\models A$? If $\Pi \not\models A$, then A is not a member of the least Herbrand model M_Π, so we cannot conclude on the basis of this program that A is true. On the other hand, there are models of Π which make A true as well, so it seems we cannot conclude that A is false either. Given only this program, we do not know whether A is true or false.

At first sight, it may seem we should treat the truth value of such an atom as unknown. However, there are often quite good reasons to treat such an atom as *false*. For example, consider a definite program Π which describes a time-table for the times of departure of trains from some particular fixed station to various destinations. The program consists of ground atoms such as $To(amsterdam, 12{:}00)$, meaning that the train to Amsterdam will leave at 12 o'clock. Now suppose Π does not contain the atom $To(rotterdam, 12{:}00)$. Then, strictly speaking, the program does not tell us whether or not a train to Rotterdam will depart at 12 o'clock, since $\Pi \not\models To(rotterdam, 12{:}00)$ and $\Pi \not\models \neg To(rotterdam, 12{:}00)$. However, when dealing with a time-table, we naturally assume the table is *complete*: every departure is explicitly stated in the table. This means that in our case we can assume that no train to Rotterdam departs at 12 o'clock, so $To(rotterdam, 12{:}00)$ is taken to be false. And more generally, we can consider as false each instance of $To(x, y)$ that is not implied by the program.

The assumption that a time-table is complete, is an instance of the *Closed World Assumption* (*CWA*), which is often applicable when we are dealing with some piece of knowledge. The CWA, introduced by Reiter [Rei78], is the assumption that the given description of the world of interest is not only *true*, but *complete* as well: it contains all information concerning the world.

In the case of some given definite program Π which purports to describe
this world, this means that we assume that all and only ground atoms that
describes true "facts about the world", are implied by Π.[1] Consequently, for
us the CWA amounts to the following:

1. If A is a ground atom and $\Pi \models A$, then A is taken to be true.
2. If A is a ground atom and $\Pi \not\models A$, then A is taken to be false.

Let us consider how the CWA might be implemented for some given
definite program Π. For the first part, this is conceptually quite simple: if
we want to infer some atom A that is implied by Π, we can find an SLD-
deduction of A from Π (or an SLD-refutation of $\Pi \cup \{\leftarrow A\}$).

Since $\Pi \models A$ iff $\Pi \cup \{\leftarrow A\}$ has an SLD-refutation, the second part of the
CWA can be translated to the following *negation as failure* rule:

> if we *fail* to find an SLD-refutation of $\Pi\cup\{\leftarrow A\}$, we can infer $\neg A$.

The name 'negation as failure' was introduced by Clark [Cla78], who studied
the logical properties of this rule in detail. Note that the above rule is not
sound, in the strict sense of Chapter 4: in the case of the time-table we
inferred $\neg To(rotterdam, 12{:}00)$, even though $\Pi \not\models \neg To(rotterdam, 12{:}00)$.

There exists an SLD-refutation of $\Pi \cup \{\leftarrow A\}$ iff any SLD-tree for $\Pi \cup \{\leftarrow A\}$ contains a success branch. Hence negation as failure can be effected by
searching some particular SLD-tree for $\Pi \cup \{\leftarrow A\}$: we can infer $\neg A$ if we
do not find a success branch in this tree. However, as we have already noted
in Section 7.8, in general it is undecidable whether an SLD-tree actually
contains a success branch, because such a tree may contain branches of infinite
length. Thus the negation as failure rule is rather hard to implement for the
general situation where trees may be infinite. If, on the other hand, we only
consider *finite* trees, we can find out after a finite number of steps whether
a tree contains a success branch or not. For this reason, the application
of negation as failure is usually restricted to finite SLD-trees. An SLD-tree
whose branches are all finite and which contains no success branches is called
finitely failed. Thus 'negation as failure' is restricted to 'negation as *finite*
failure':

> if some SLD-tree for $\Pi\cup\{\leftarrow A\}$ is finitely failed, we can infer $\neg A$.

This derivation rule is actually a *nonmonotonic* rule. A derivation rule is said
to be monotonic if formulas which can be derived from a set Σ of premises
(clauses, in our case) are still derivable if we add new premises to Σ; it is said
to be nonmonotonic otherwise. The proof procedures we have introduced
up till now, unconstrained deduction, linear deduction, input deduction and
SLD-deduction are all monotonic. For example, if $\Pi \vdash_{sd} A$, then $\Pi' \vdash_{sd} A$ for
every $\Pi' \supseteq \Pi$.

On the other hand, negation as finite failure is nonmonotonic. Consider
again the time-table Π. Since $To(rotterdam, 12{:}00) \notin \Pi$, negation as finite

---

[1] Why we restrict attention to *ground* atoms will be explained in Section 8.4.

failure allowed us to derive $\neg To(rotterdam, 12{:}00)$ from Π. But now suppose we extend the time-table to $\Pi' = \Pi \cup \{To(rotterdam, 12{:}00)\}$. Since now $To(rotterdam, 12{:}00)$ is implied by the program, our derivation rule is no longer applicable in this case. Thus $\neg To(rotterdam, 12{:}00)$, which could be derived from Π, can no longer be derived from its superset Π'. The nonmonotonic property of negation as finite failure can also be seen by considering SLD-trees. If we have a finitely failed SLD-tree for $\Pi \cup \{\leftarrow A\}$, we can infer $\neg A$. But if we extend Π to Π', the SLD-tree is extended as well, and if a success branch or an infinite branch is added, the tree is no longer finitely failed.

Let B_Π be the Herbrand base of some program Π. When considering negation as finite failure, we can take B_Π to consist of three disjoint subsets:

1. The set of atoms A that are logically implied by Π. This is the familiar least Herbrand model M_Π.

2. The set of atoms A such that there is a finitely failed SLD-tree for $\Pi \cup \{\leftarrow A\}$. This set is called the *finite failure set*, denoted by F_Π.

3. The remainder: the set of atoms A such that every SLD-tree for $\Pi \cup \{\leftarrow A\}$ is infinite, but contains no success branch.

This division of B_Π is illustratred on the left of Figure 8.1. The inner circle is M_Π, the outward rim is F_Π, and the area between M_Π and F_Π represents the third set.

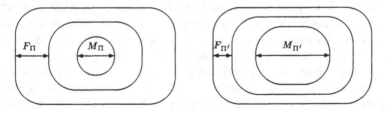

Figure 8.1: The division of B_Π (left) and $B_{\Pi'}$ (right)

Given Π, we can infer the atoms in M_Π using ordinary SLD-resolution, and the negations of the atoms in F_Π using negation as finite failure. However, we can infer neither A nor $\neg A$ if $A \notin M_\Pi$ and $A \notin F_\Pi$.

To illustrate again the nonmonotonicity of negation as failure, suppose some clauses are added to Π, yielding Π'. Suppose this enlarges the least Herbrand model: $M_\Pi \subset M_{\Pi'}$. Assuming the new clauses do not contain new symbols, we have $B_\Pi = B_{\Pi'}$. This means that the union of the second and third sets will have to "shrink" in order to make room for the larger $M_{\Pi'}$, as illustrated on the right of Figure 8.1. In particular, $F_{\Pi'}$ will be a subset of F_Π, and if $A \in F_\Pi \backslash F_{\Pi'}$, then $\neg A$ can no longer be inferred.

Since negation as failure can be used to derive negative literals from a program, it can also be employed to support the use of negative literals in the body of a clause. Consider for instance a murder case. In most judicial systems, one is innocent until proven guilty. This could be formalized by the implication $C = Innocent(x) \leftarrow \neg Guilty(x)$. When we use negation as finite failure, C does not simply express the obvious truth that someone who is not guilty is innocent. It expresses something stronger: if we *cannot prove* that someone is guilty, we take him to be innocent—which is just what we want in a legal context. Implications of this form are often very useful. Since definite program clauses are not sufficiently expressive for such implications, we generalize them to *program* clauses, which do allow both positive and negative literals to appear in their body. A *normal program* is then a finite set of such program clauses. Suppose we have some normal program Π, with $C \in \Pi$, which describes the evidence against some suspect a. If we fail finitely to prove $Guilty(a)$, negation as finite failure allows us to infer $\neg Guilty(a)$. Using clause C, we then conclude $Innocent(a)$.

Actually, the above program clause C is logically equivalent to the non-Horn clause $Innocent(x) \vee Guilty(x)$. However, in order to be able to generalize SLD-resolution to normal programs, normal clauses are given the same structure as definite program clauses (i.e., one atom in the head, and the other literals in the body). Moreover, the choice of which atom to put in the head of a program clause also gives certain predicates a kind of precedence over other predicates. For instance, the program clause $D = Guilty(x) \leftarrow \neg Innocent(x)$ is logically equivalent to C, but negation as finite failure treats these two logically equivalent clauses quite differently, and different conclusions may be drawn from C than from D. C corresponds to the assumption that if we cannot prove someone's guilt, then that person is innocent. Clause D reverses the burden of proof: if we cannot prove someone's innocence, he is taken to be guilty.

In order to derive information from a normal program, we can apply SLD-resolution to program clauses, resolving the heads of input clauses with atoms in the body of a goal. But SLD-resolution by itself is clearly not enough, since it has no means for handling negative literals in a goal. Therefore we combine SLD-resolution with negation as finite failure to handle such negative literals. This combination is called SLDNF-resolution, and will be discussed in later sections of this chapter. In the final section of this chapter we discuss some properties of the programming language PROLOG, which implements SLDNF-resolution.

8.2   Negation as Failure

In Chapter 7 we defined SLD-resolution, which could be used to infer an atom A from Π whenever $\Pi \models A$. In this section we will define negation as (finite) failure for definite programs. As explained above, our main interest is in the set of ground atoms A such that $\Pi \cup \{\leftarrow A\}$ has a finitely failed SLD-tree. For such atoms, we can infer $\neg A$ from Π. In the next section we will extend negation as failure in order to be able to deal with clauses having negated literals in their body.

Definition 8.1 Let Π be a definite program, and G a definite goal. An SLD-tree for $\Pi \cup \{G\}$ is called *finitely failed* if it is finite and contains no success branches. ◇

Definition 8.2 Let Π be a definite program and B_Π be the Herbrand base of Π. The *SLD finite failure set* of Π is $F_\Pi = \{A \in B_\Pi \mid$ there exists a finitely failed SLD-tree for $\Pi \cup \{\leftarrow A\}\}$. ◇

Example 8.3 Consider the definite program Π consisting of the following clauses:

1. $Pet(x) \leftarrow Small(x), Dog(x)$
2. $Pet(x) \leftarrow Cat(x)$
3. $Small(a)$
4. $Spider(a)$

Figure 8.2 shows a finitely failed SLD-tree for $\Pi \cup \{\leftarrow Pet(a)\}$, so $Pet(a)$ is in the SLD finite failure set F_Π of Π. Hence we can infer that a is not a pet, even though $\Pi \not\models \neg Pet(a)$. ◁

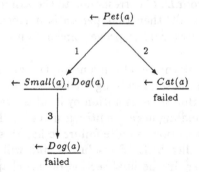

Figure 8.2: A finitely failed SLD-tree for $\Pi \cup \{\leftarrow Pet(a)\}$

In order to show that some ground atom A is in F_Π, we need to find at least one finitely failed SLD-tree for $\Pi \cup \{\leftarrow A\}$. However, it might be that some SLD-trees for $\Pi \cup \{\leftarrow A\}$ are finitely failed, while some others are infinite. For example, suppose Π consists of the clause $P(x) \leftarrow P(f(x)), Q(a)$. Then the SLD-tree for $\Pi \cup \{\leftarrow P(a)\}$ via the computation rule which always selects the rightmost atom in a goal is finitely failed. On the other hand, the computation rule which always selects the leftmost atom in a goal yields an infinite SLD-tree for $\Pi \cup \{\leftarrow P(a)\}$.

Searching all SLD-trees for $\Pi \cup \{\leftarrow A\}$ in order to check whether one of them is finitely failed, is rather cumbersome. Thus we would like to find some restrictions on SLD-trees for $\Pi \cup \{\leftarrow A\}$, such that if one of them is finitely failed, then they all are. This would allow us to restrict attention to one particular SLD-tree. In the remainder of this section, we will show that the following *fairness* restriction on SLD-trees is sufficient for our purposes.

Definition 8.4 Let Π be a definite program, and G be a definite goal. An SLD-derivation from $\Pi \cup \{G\}$ with G as top clause is called *fair* if one of the following holds:

1. The derivation is finite.
2. The derivation is infinite, and for every atom A appearing in some goal in the derivation, (some further instantiated version of) A is the selected atom in a later goal in the derivation.

An SLD-tree for $\Pi \cup \{G\}$ is *fair* if every branch of the tree is a fair SLD-derivation. $\diamond$

Note that a finitely failed SLD-tree is fair.

Given a definite program Π and a definite goal G, a fair SLD-tree for $\Pi \cup \{G\}$ can always be constructed. We might for instance apply a "first in, first out"-computation rule, which in a goal in a derivation always selects one of the atoms that have been present in earlier goals in the derivation at least as long as other atoms. Using such a computation rule ensures that, even in an infinite derivation, each atom eventually gets selected.

The next theorem shows that if A is in the SLD finite failure set of Π, then the SLD-tree via any fair computation rule will be finitely failed.

Theorem 8.5 *Let Π be a definite program and $A \in B_\Pi$. Then $A \in F_\Pi$ iff every fair SLD-tree for $\Pi \cup \{\leftarrow A\}$ is finitely failed.*

Proof

$\Leftarrow$: If every fair SLD-tree for $\Pi \cup \{\leftarrow A\}$ is finitely failed, there is at least one finitely failed SLD-tree for $\Pi \cup \{\leftarrow A\}$, hence $A \in F_\Pi$.

$\Rightarrow$: Suppose $A \in F_\Pi$. Then there is at least one finitely failed SLD-tree $\mathcal{T}$ for $\Pi \cup \{\leftarrow A\}$. Let d be the length of the longest derivation in $\mathcal{T}$. Now suppose there is a fair SLD-tree $\mathcal{T}'$ for $\Pi \cup \{\leftarrow A\}$ that is not finitely failed. Then $\mathcal{T}'$ must contain an infinite fair SLD-derivation $\mathcal{D}$, with goals $G_0(=\leftarrow A), G_1, G_2, \ldots$

Note that since A in $\leftarrow A$ must be selected in the root of $\mathcal{T}$, $\mathcal{T}$ must contain an SLD-derivation starting with G_0, G_1. It need not contain an SLD-derivation starting with G_0, G_1, G_2, because the atom selected in G_1 in $\mathcal{T}$ may be different from the atom selected in G_1 in $\mathcal{D}$ in $\mathcal{T}'$. However, since $\mathcal{D}$ is fair, (an instance of) the atom selected in G_1 in $\mathcal{T}$ must also be selected in some later goal in $\mathcal{D}$ in $\mathcal{T}'$. Thus by applying the Switching Lemma several times to $\mathcal{D}$, we can transform it into another infinite fair SLD-derivation, with goals $G_0(=\leftarrow A), G_1, G'_2, G'_3, G'_4, \ldots$, such that G_0, G_1, G'_2 must be (the first goals in) an SLD-derivation in $\mathcal{T}$.

Repeating this procedure a number of times, we obtain an infinite fair SLD-derivation $H_0(=\leftarrow A), H_1, \ldots, H_d, H_{d+1}, \ldots$, such that $H_0, \ldots, H_{d+1}$ must be (the first goals in) an SLD-derivation (of length $d+1$) in $\mathcal{T}$. But $\mathcal{T}$ only contains SLD-derivations of length $\leq d$. Thus we have a contradiction, which shows that every fair SLD-tree for $\Pi \cup \{\leftarrow A\}$ is finitely failed. $\quad\square$

8.3 SLDNF-Trees for Normal Programs

Suppose Π is a definite program and G a definite goal. In the previous chapter, we have seen that we can construct an SLD-tree for $\Pi \cup \{G\}$, which will contains a success branch iff $\Pi \cup \{G\}$ is unsatisfiable. In the last section, we saw how negation as finite failure can be used to derive negative ground literals from a definite program. Using this, we are now able to generalize our notion of a goal, by allowing negative as well as positive literals in its body.

Definition 8.6 A *normal goal* is of the form $\leftarrow L_1, \ldots, L_n$, $n \geq 0$, where each L_i is a literal. $\qquad\diamond$

When we have a definite program Π and a *normal* goal G, we need to generalize the SLD-tree to an SLDNF-tree. We adapt the definition of SLDNF-trees given by Apt and Doets [AD94, Doe94], which is slightly more general than the definition of [Llo87]. An SLDNF-tree combines SLD-resolution with so-called *subsidiary* trees. Such subsidiary trees are invoked whenever a *negative* ground literal is selected. An example will make this clearer.

Example 8.7 Let us continue Example 8.3. Suppose we have the normal goal $G =\leftarrow \neg Pet(a)$. Figure 8.3 shows an SLDNF-tree for $\Pi \cup \{G\}$. This tree consists of two distinct trees. On the left we have the *main* tree, containing two nodes, with G as root. The fact that a negative ground literal is selected in G leads us to construct a subsidiary tree for $\Pi \cup \{\leftarrow Pet(a)\}$ (on the right of the picture). Since this subsidiary tree is finitely failed, we can infer $\neg Pet(a)$. This in turn allows us to delete $\neg Pet(a)$ from the body of G in the main tree.[2] Thus we end up with the empty clause in the main tree. As in the case of SLD-trees, a branch which ends in the empty clause is called a *success* branch, and an SLDNF-tree whose main tree contains a success branch is called *successful*. $\qquad\triangleleft$

Given a definite program Π and a normal goal G, an SLDNF-tree for $\Pi \cup \{G\}$ is actually a *set* of trees, organized around a main tree, which has

---

[2]Deleting a selected negative literal $\neg Pet(a)$ from the body of a normal goal after having inferred $\neg Pet(a)$ is analogous to deleting a selected atom $P(a)$ from the body of a goal by resolving with an input clause $P(a)$.

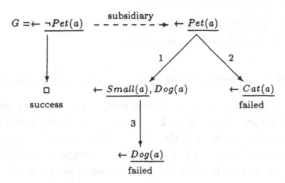

Figure 8.3: A successful SLDNF-tree for $\Pi \cup \{\leftarrow \neg Pet(a)\}$

G as root. This main tree is similar to an SLD-tree. When a positive literal is selected in some goal G' in the main tree, we add the binary resolvents of G' and clauses in Π as children to G', just as in SLD-trees. Additionally, whenever a negative ground literal $\neg A$ in the body of some goal G' in the main tree is selected, a new subsidiary SLDNF-tree for G' is constructed, with $\leftarrow A$ as root. Note that we cannot treat a selected negative literal in the same way as a positive literal, since a negative literal cannot be unified with an atom in the head of a clause in Π. Applying negation as finite failure, we delete $\neg A$ from the body of G' just in case the subsidiary tree for G' finitely fails. If the subsidiary tree is successful, we cannot apply negation as finite failure, so then the node G' is marked *failed*. We should not construct a subsidiary tree in case a *non-ground* negative literal is selected in G'. In fact, if a non-ground negative literal is selected, we cannot continue with G'. This is the problem of *floundering*, which will be dealt with in Section 8.4

When we start with a definite program Π and a normal goal G, the only negative literals in the bodies of goals in the tree stem from G. However, now that we are able to handle negative literals in the initial goal, there is no reason to stop here: we may as well allow the clauses in Π to contain negative literals in their body. In this case, resolving a goal with a clause from the program may introduce new negative literals in the goal. For instance, resolving $\leftarrow P(x)$ with $P(a) \leftarrow \neg Q(a)$ yields the goal $\leftarrow \neg Q(a)$. Such new negative literals can be handled by subsidiary trees, in the same way as we handled negative literals from the original goal G. For example, if $\Pi = \{Innocent(x) \leftarrow \neg Guilty(x)\}$ and $G =\leftarrow Innocent(a)$, then resolving G with the clause in Π yields $G_1 =\leftarrow \neg Guilty(a)$. Since the tree for $\leftarrow Guilty(a)$ will fail immediately, G_1 has the empty clause as only child. Thus we have an SLDNF-refutation of $\Pi \cup \{G\}$, and we may conclude $Innocent(a)$ from Π. On the other hand, if $\Pi' = \{Guilty(x) \leftarrow \neg Innocent(x)\}$, then we cannot find an SLDNF-refutation of $\Pi \cup \{G\}$, and we cannot infer $Innocent(a)$ from Π'. In this case we can infer $Guilty(a)$ from Π'.

In general, we can generalize *definite* program clauses to program clauses:

Definition 8.8 A *program clause* is of the form $A \leftarrow L_1, \ldots, L_n$, $n \geq 0$, where A is an atom and each L_i is a literal.   ◇

Definition 8.9 A *normal program* is a finite set of program clauses.   ◇

Normal programs are also sometimes called *general* programs in the literature. In a program clause $A \leftarrow L_1, \ldots, L_n$, the atom A will be called the *head*, and $L_1, \ldots, L_n$ the *body* of the clause. The head of a program clause C is sometimes denoted by C^+, the body by C^-. If each L_i in a program clause is positive, the program clause is simply a *definite* program clause.

A program clause $C = A \leftarrow L_1, \ldots, L_n$ is the following implication: $\forall((L_1 \wedge \ldots \wedge L_n) \rightarrow A)$. This is logically equivalent to $\forall(\neg L_1 \vee \neg \ldots \vee \neg L_n \vee A)$. For each *negative* literal $L_i = \neg B_i$, we can replace $\neg L_i$ by the logically equivalent positive literal B_i, thus obtaining a disjunction of literals, with possibly more than one positive literal. Hence a non-definite program clause C is actually logically equivalent to a non-Horn clause. Similarly, normal goals may also be logically equivalent to non-Horn clauses, for instance $\leftarrow \neg P(a), \neg P(b)$ is equivalent to $P(a) \vee P(b)$. However, as we noted in the introduction, there is more to SLDNF-resolution than just logical implication and logical equivalence. For example, the two logically equivalent clauses $Innocent(x) \leftarrow \neg Guilty(x)$ and $Guilty(x) \leftarrow \neg Innocent(x)$ are treated quite differently by SLDNF-resolution, as we saw above.

Contrary to definite programs, normal programs need not have a least Herbrand model. Consider the normal program $\Pi = \{Male(peter) \leftarrow \neg Female(peter)\}$. Both $\{Male(peter)\}$ and $\{Female(peter)\}$ are Herbrand models of Π, yet their intersection (the empty set) is not.

Now let us get back to SLDNF-trees. Suppose Π is a normal program and G is a normal goal. Constructing an SLDNF-tree for $\Pi \cup \{G\}$ is similar to the case of the definite program. The main tree starts with G as initial goal. Whenever a positive literal is selected in some goal G', G' has the binary resolvents of G' and clauses in Π as children, as before. Whenever a ground negative literal $\neg A$ is selected in G', we construct a new subsidiary tree with $\leftarrow A$ as root. If this new tree has been completely constructed and turns out to be finitely failed, we add the goal obtained by deleting $\neg A$ from the body of G' as a child to G'. If, on the other hand, the subsidiary tree contains a success branch, the goal G' fails.

Given a normal goal, one important distinction between the cases of a definite program and a normal program should be noted. In the definite case, a subsidiary tree starts with a definite goal $\leftarrow A$, and resolving goals with definite program clauses does not introduce new negative literals in the body of a goal. Hence each node in the subsidiary tree is a definite goal, and the subsidiary tree is an ordinary SLD-tree. However, as we have seen, resolving a goal with a program clause whose body contains negative literals adds those negative literals to the goal. This implies that in the case of a normal program, a subsidiary tree may contain goals in which a ground negative literal is selected, which requires constructing another subsidiary tree. Hence subsidiary trees may need their own subsidiary trees, something which does not occur when we are dealing with a definite program.

The actual definition of an SLDNF-tree will be given below. It is based on the notion of a *pre*-SLDNF-tree. This is a finite set of finite trees, containing a main tree and a number of subsidiary trees. An initial pre-SLDNF-tree only contains a main tree, consisting of the root G. This initial tree can be extended to another pre-SLDNF-tree, which can in turn be extended to a further pre-SLDNF-tree, and so on. Before we give the formal definition, let us first give an example.

Example 8.10 Let $G = \leftarrow P(x)$, and Π be the following normal program:

1. $P(y) \leftarrow Q(y)$
2. $P(y) \leftarrow R(y), \neg S(y)$
3. $Q(y) \leftarrow S(a)$
4. $Q(a)$
5. $R(b)$
6. $S(b) \leftarrow S(a)$
7. $S(b) \leftarrow \neg S(c)$
8. $S(c)$

Figure 8.4 shows the construction of an SLDNF-tree for $\Pi \cup \{G\}$. Here we select the leftmost literal in each goal.

Initially, we start with only G, which is pre-SLDNF-tree **(1)** in the figure. In order to extend it, we select $P(x)$ in G, and the first extension (pre-SLDNF-tree **(2)**) is obtained by adding as children to G the resolvents of G and clauses in Π. On the edges between nodes, we add the mgu and the number of the input clause used. A further extension yields the pre-SLDNF-tree **(3)**. Note that *both* leaves of **(2)** are expanded to get **(3)**. When extending **(3)** to **(4)**, we select the atom $S(a)$ in the leftmost leaf. This atom cannot be unified with the head of any clause in Π, so in extension **(4)**, we mark this leaf as *failed*. Since the second leaf of **(3)** is empty, it is marked *success* in **(4)**. In the rightmost leaf of **(3)** we select the negative ground literal $\neg S(b)$, so we construct a subsidiary tree with $\leftarrow S(b)$ as root in **(4)**. In extension **(5)**, two children are added to this subsidiary tree. A number of further extensions (omitted from the figure) finally yield pre-SLDNF-tree **(6)** in Figure 8.5. Since all leaves in the main tree (as well as in all subsidiary trees) are marked, it is a complete SLDNF-tree. In the extensions that led to this tree, the success of the second subsidiary tree (for $\leftarrow \neg S(c)$) caused the goal $\leftarrow \neg S(c)$ to be marked failed. This in turn made the first subsidiary tree (for $\leftarrow \neg S(b)$) finitely failed, which allowed us to delete $\neg S(b)$ from the goal $\leftarrow \neg S(b)$, leading to a success branch.   ◁

Note that if a subsidiary tree is constructed for some node N, then adding a child to N or marking N as *failed* can only take place *after* further extensions have made the subsidiary tree finitely failed or successful. For instance, tree

(1) $G = \leftarrow P(x)$

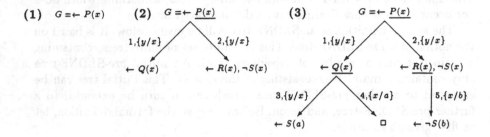

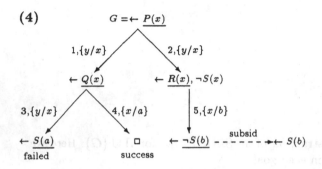

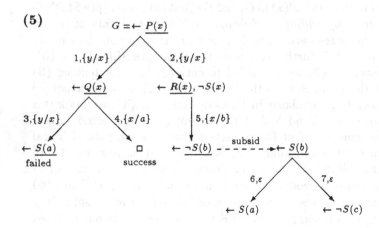

Figure 8.4: A sequence of pre-SLDNF-trees.

(6)

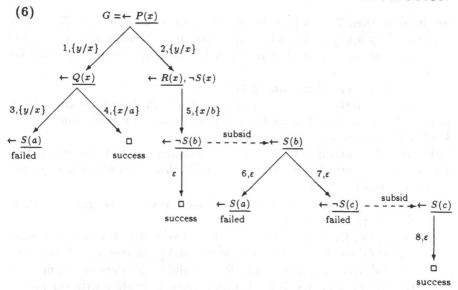

Figure 8.5: A successful SLDNF-tree for $\Pi \cup \{G\}$

(4) is an extension of (3) in Figure 8.4, which adds a subsidiary tree for $\leftarrow \neg S(b)$. That this subsidiary tree is finitely failed only becomes apparent after some further extensions have been constructed, so only after those extensions can we add the empty clause as a child to $\leftarrow \neg S(b)$.

This process of starting with an initial tree and then constructing extensions, is formally defined below.

Definition 8.11 A tree is called *successful* if it contains a leaf marked as *success*, and is called *finitely failed* if it is finite and all its leaves are marked *failed*. ◇

Definition 8.12 Let Π be a normal program and G a normal goal. A *pre-SLDNF-tree* $\mathcal{T}$ for $\Pi \cup \{G\}$ is a finite non-empty set of finite trees, such that one element in $\mathcal{T}$ is called the *main tree*, each node in each tree in $\mathcal{T}$ is a normal goal, and some nodes N in some trees in $\mathcal{T}$ may be assigned a *subsidiary* tree $subsid(N) \in \mathcal{T}$. The leaves in trees in $\mathcal{T}$ may be marked. The possible markings for leaves are *failed*, *success*, and *floundered*.

Such pre-SLDNF-trees are inductively defined as follows:

1. An *initial* pre-SLDNF-tree $\mathcal{T}_0$ for $\Pi \cup \{G\}$ contains only a main tree, which has G as single node.

2. If $\mathcal{T}_n$ is a pre-SLDNF-tree for $\Pi \cup \{G\}$, then any *extension* $\mathcal{T}_{n+1}$ of $\mathcal{T}_n$ is a pre-SLDNF-tree for $\Pi \cup \{G\}$ as well. The extension of a pre-SLDNF-tree is defined below.

Extension of $\mathcal{T}_n$:
Let $\mathcal{T}_n$ be a pre-SLDNF-tree for $\Pi \cup \{G\}$. If all leaves of the main tree of $\mathcal{T}_n$

are marked, then T_n has no extension. Otherwise, an extension T_{n+1} of T_n is obtained by applying the following procedure **Extend** to the main tree of T_n. This recursive procedure may change the main tree, as well as subsidiary trees.

Procedure Extend (extends a tree T):

For each non-marked leaf G' of T, from left to right (the left-right order is induced by the numbers of the input clauses used), do the following:

If $G' = \square$, mark it with *success*.

Otherwise, if no literal in G' has yet been selected (which is the case if thus far no subsidiary tree has been assigned to G'), then select one. If the selected literal L is positive, then:

1. If there is no (variant of) $C \in \Pi$ whose head can be unified with L, then mark G' as *failed*.

2. Otherwise, for every *input clause* $C \in \Pi$ such that R is a binary resolvent of G' and (a variant of) C, with L and (a variant of) C^+ as literals resolved upon and mgu θ, add R as a child to G'. Here we require that the variant of C that is used, neither shares variables with the root of T, nor with other input clauses or mgu's used in the branch leading to G' (this is similar to Condition * of the previous chapter). Mark the edge from G' to R with the mgu θ and the number of the input clause used.

If $L = \neg A$ is negative, then:

1. If A is not ground, then G' is marked as *floundered*, and will have no children.

2. If A is ground and $subsid(G')$ is undefined, then add to the set of trees a new tree, with $\leftarrow A$ as single node, and define $subsid(G')$ to be this newly added tree.

3. If A is ground and $subsid(G')$ is defined and successful, then mark G' as *failed*.

4. If A is ground and $subsid(G')$ is defined and its leaves are all marked *floundered*, then mark G' as *floundered*.

5. If A is ground and $subsid(G')$ is defined and finitely failed, then add $R = G' - \neg L$ (i.e., G' after L has been deleted from its body) as only child to G'. Mark the edge from G' to R with the empty substitution.

6. Otherwise, i.e., if none of the previous four items could be applied, apply the **Extend** procedure to $subsid(G')$. $\diamond$

The *main* tree of a pre-SLDNF-tree T for $\Pi \cup \{G\}$ is the tree in T which has G as root, the other trees in T are the *subsidiary* trees. Though we defined a pre-SLDNF-tree as a *set* of trees, it is often convenient to regard it as a single tree, with two kinds of edges: ordinary edges between nodes, and special edges from a node to the root of its subsidiary tree (in Figure 8.4 and 8.5, these special edges were dashed).

Let us now explain how we can get from a sequence of pre-SLDNF-trees to an actual SLDNF-tree. Starting with an initial pre-SLDNF-tree T_0 containing only G, we can construct a sequence of extensions $\mathcal{T}_0, \mathcal{T}_1, \mathcal{T}_2, \ldots$. Each $\mathcal{T}_{i+1}$ in this sequence has its predecessor $\mathcal{T}_i$ as a subtree. If the sequence reaches some pre-SLDNF-tree $\mathcal{T}_n$ which has no further extension, then this $\mathcal{T}_n$ is an SLDNF-tree for $\Pi \cup \{G\}$. Otherwise, if the sequence is infinite, then the *union* of all pre-SLDNF-trees in the sequence is an SLDNF-tree. This is formally defined as follows:

Definition 8.13 Let Π be a normal program, and G be a normal goal. A set of trees $\mathcal{T}$ is called an *SLDNF-tree* for $\Pi \cup \{G\}$ if there exists a (possibly infinite) sequence $\mathcal{T}_0, \mathcal{T}_1, \ldots, \mathcal{T}_i, \ldots$ of pre-SLDNF-trees, with the following properties:

1. $\mathcal{T}_0$ is the initial pre-SLDNF-tree for $\Pi \cup \{G\}$ (i.e., only a main tree with G as only node).
2. Each $\mathcal{T}_{i+1}$ is an extension of $\mathcal{T}_i$.
3. If the sequence is finite and $\mathcal{T}_n$ is the last pre-SLDNF-tree in the sequence, then $\mathcal{T}_n$ has no extension and $\mathcal{T} = \mathcal{T}_n$.
4. Otherwise, $\mathcal{T}$ is the smallest tree (including subsidiary trees) which has each $\mathcal{T}_i$ as a subtree.

The *main tree* of $\mathcal{T}$ is the tree in $\mathcal{T}$ which has G as root, without its subsidiary trees.

$\mathcal{T}$ is called *successful* (resp. *finitely failed*) if its main tree is successful (resp. finitely failed). We say $\Pi \cup \{G\}$ *succeeds* (resp. *finitely fails*) if there is a successful (resp. finitely failed) SLDNF-tree for $\Pi \cup \{G\}$.   ◇

The SLDNF-tree can be constructed by starting with G, and then constructing an extension of G, an extension of an extension of G, etc. Note that in an infinite sequence of extensions each pre-SLDNF-tree is finite, while the actual SLDNF-tree obtained from this sequence may be infinite. Nevertheless, if the main tree in an infinite SLDNF-tree $\mathcal{T}$ is successful or finitely failed, then we will get to know this after a finite number of extensions (though note that a successful main tree may grow in further extensions, even if it already contains a success branch). Similarly, each success branch in the main tree will be finished after a finite number of extensions.

In an SLDNF-tree, we are particularly interested in the properties of the main tree. Each branch in the main tree represents an SLDNF-derivation, and each SLDNF-derivation of the empty clause is an SLDNF-refutation. The substitutions employed in such a refutation can be used to obtain a computed answer.

Definition 8.14 Let Π be a normal program, and G a normal goal. An *SLDNF-derivation* from $\Pi \cup \{G\}$ is a branch in the main tree of an SLDNF-tree $\mathcal{T}$ for $\Pi \cup \{G\}$, together with the subsidiary trees in $\mathcal{T}$ whose roots can be reached from this branch.

If such an SLDNF-derivation ends with the empty clause in the branch of the main tree, it is called an *SLDNF-refutation* of $\Pi \cup \{G\}$.   ◇

Definition 8.15 Let Π be a normal program, and $G = \leftarrow L_1, \ldots, L_n$ a normal goal. Let $\theta_1, \ldots, \theta_k$ be the sequence of substitutions on the edges of some SLDNF-refutation of $\Pi \cup \{G\}$. A *computed answer* θ for $\Pi \cup \{G\}$ is the restriction of $\theta_1 \ldots \theta_k$ to the variables in G. If θ is a computed answer for $\Pi \cup \{G\}$, we write $\Pi \vdash_{snf} (L_1, \ldots, L_n)\theta$ ◇

Note that the particular mgu's used in the subsidiary trees do not affect the computed answer: the only thing we are interested in, regarding subsidiary trees, is whether they are successful or finitely failed (or neither). Also note the nonmonotonicity: $\{P(a)\} \vdash_{snf} \neg P(b)$, while $\{P(a), P(b)\} \nvdash_{snf} \neg P(b)$.

Example 8.16 For the $\Pi \cup \{G\}$ from Example 8.10, we can extract two computed answers from the main tree: $\theta_1 = \{x/a\}$ and $\theta_2 = \{x/b\}$. Note that $\Pi \models P(x)\theta_1$, while $\Pi \nvDash P(x)\theta_2$. ◁

It is not very difficult to see that SLDNF-derivations generalize SLD-derivations. In particular, if Π is a *definite* program and G is a *definite* goal, then an SLDNF-tree for $\Pi \cup \{G\}$ is simply an SLD-tree for $\Pi \cup \{G\}$. We can also easily generalize the definition of fairness to SLDNF-trees, though we will not need this in the sequel.

We end this section by defining the notion of a computation rule for SLDNF-resolution. In ordinary SLD-resolution, we use a computation rule to select the atom that will be resolved upon in the next resolution step in a derivation. As this may have to do with the history of the derivation, we defined a computation rule as a function that took an SLD-derivation as input, and returned an atom in the last goal of the derivation. Since SLDNF-derivations are defined in terms of SLDNF-trees, and we already need to select literals when constructing an SLDNF-tree, we cannot simply generalize the definition from the previous chapter, taking an SLDNF-derivation as input to the rule. Instead, in SLDNF-resolution a computation rule takes a complete pre-SLDNF-tree $\mathcal{T}$ as input, together with a leaf G in $\mathcal{T}$, and outputs a literal in G.

Definition 8.17 Let $\mathcal{P}$ be the set of all pre-SLDNF-trees, and $\mathcal{G}$ the set of all normal goals. A *computation rule* $\mathcal{R}$ is a function from $\mathcal{P} \times \mathcal{G}$ to the set of literals, such that if $\mathcal{T}$ is a pre-SLDNF-tree and G is a non-empty, non-marked leaf in $\mathcal{T}$, then $\mathcal{R}(\mathcal{T}, G)$ is a literal (the *selected literal*) in the body of G. ◇

A pre-SLDNF-tree, SLDNF-tree, SLDNF-derivation, or -refutation is said to be *via* $\mathcal{R}$, if $\mathcal{R}$ is used for selecting the selected literal in each node. Similarly, we can define an $\mathcal{R}$-computed answer.

8.4 Floundering, and How to Avoid It

Let us now explain *floundering*. Why do we only construct a subsidiary tree if a *ground* negative literal is selected, and mark a node as *floundered* if a non-ground negative literal is selected? Why not select a non-ground literal and construct a finitely failed tree, just as we do for ground negative literals? As the next example shows, dropping the restriction to ground literals may cause unsoundness.

Example 8.18 Let $\Pi = \{(P(f(x)) \leftarrow \neg Q(x)), Q(a)\}$. Then $\Pi \cup \{\leftarrow Q(x)\}$ succeeds, and hence, if we allow a subsidiary tree for $\leftarrow \neg Q(x)$ to be constructed, $\Pi \cup \{\leftarrow \neg Q(x)\}$ finitely fails. Consequently, $\Pi \cup \{\leftarrow P(f(x))\}$ finitely fails as well, so $\Pi \cup \{\leftarrow \neg P(f(x))\}$ succeeds, with computed answer ε. Thus $\Pi \vdash_{snf} \neg P(f(x))$.

On the other hand, $\Pi \cup \{\leftarrow Q(f(a))\}$ finitely fails. Therefore $\Pi \cup \{\leftarrow \neg Q(f(a))\}$ succeeds, and $\Pi \cup \{\leftarrow P(f(a))\}$ succeeds as well. Thus allowing the selection of non-ground negative literals leads to the unsound result that both $\Pi \vdash_{snf} \neg P(f(x))$ and $\Pi \vdash_{snf} P(f(a))$.   ◁

Given this unsoundness, we should avoid the selection of non-ground negative literals as much as possible: we need a computation rule which does not select a non-ground negative literal if other (positive and/or ground) literals can be selected. Such a computation rule is called *safe*.

Definition 8.19 A computation rule is *safe* if it selects a non-ground negative literal in the body of a goal G only if the body of G consists exclusively of non-ground negative literals.   ◇

In other words, a safe computation rule only selects a non-ground negative literal if it has no alternative. For example, if $\mathcal{R}$ is a safe computation rule, then $\mathcal{R}(\mathcal{T}, (\leftarrow Q(x, y), \neg P(x))) = Q(x, y)$ for any pre-SLDNF-tree $\mathcal{T}$. On the other hand, if $G = \leftarrow \neg P(x), \neg R(x)$, then even a safe computation rule can only select a non-ground negative literal. Thus we should avoid goals which only contain non-ground negative literals in their body. Such goals are called *blocked*, and cause floundering:

Definition 8.20 Let Π be a normal program, and G be a normal goal. We say G is *blocked* if its body consists exclusively of non-ground negative literals. $\Pi \cup \{G\}$ *flounders* if some SLDNF-tree for $\Pi \cup \{G\}$ via a safe computation rule $\mathcal{R}$ contains a blocked node.   ◇

Note carefully that being blocked is a property of a goal G, while floundering is a property of $\Pi \cup \{G\}$.

In order to avoid floundering, we might allow only a restricted kind of programs and goals. The definition of allowedness we adopt here, taken from [AB94], is slightly less general, but perhaps more readable than the one given in [Llo87].

Definition 8.21 A normal goal G is *allowed* if every variable that occurs in a negative literal in the body of G also occurs in a positive literal in the body of G. A program clause $C = A \leftarrow C^-$ is *allowed* if the normal goal $\leftarrow \neg A, C^-$ is allowed. A normal program is *allowed* if each of its clauses is allowed.   ◇

Observing that negative literals in the body of a clause are actually positive literals in the clause, the above condition can be restated more simply as follows: a normal clause or goal is allowed if each variable that appears in a positive literal also appears in a negative literal.

Example 8.22 $\leftarrow \neg P(a, x), Q(f(x))$ and $P(a, y) \leftarrow \neg Q(a), P(x, y)$ are allowed. $P(x, y) \leftarrow Q(x, x)$ is not allowed. $\lhd$

Note that a blocked goal is not allowed, while every definite goal is allowed. Furthermore, an atom is allowed iff it is ground, which is rather restrictive. Thus not every definite program is allowed. However, in case of a definite program and a definite goal, we need not worry about allowedness, because floundering will not happen anyway due to the absence of negative literals from the bodies of clauses and goals. In case of normal programs and normal goals, Proposition 8.25 shows that allowedness, together with the use of a safe computation rule, is sufficient to avoid floundering.

Lemma 8.23 *Let G be an allowed normal goal, and C an allowed normal clause. Then any binary resolvent of G and C is allowed.*

Proof We assume G and C are standardized apart, $G = \leftarrow L_1, \ldots, L_n$, $C = A \leftarrow C^-$, and $G' = \leftarrow (L_1, \ldots, L_{s-1}, C^-, L_{s+1}, \ldots, L_n)\theta$ is a binary resolvent of G and C. Note that L_s must be positive. Let x be a variable occurring in a negative literal in the body of G'. Due to the allowedness of C, if x occurs in $C^-\theta$, then x must also occur in a positive literal in $C^-\theta$. Since G is allowed, $G\theta$ is allowed as well. Then if x occurs in a negative $L_i\theta$ and does not occur in any positive $L_j\theta$ $(j \neq s)$ in G', it must occur in $L_s\theta$. $L_s\theta = A\theta$ and every variable in $A\theta$ occurs somewhere in a positive literal in $C^-\theta$, so x must occur in a positive literal in $C^-\theta$. $\Box$

Before proving the next proposition, we first illustrate its second part with an example.

Example 8.24 Suppose $\Pi = \{Q(a), (P(y) \leftarrow \neg R(a), Q(y))\}$ and $G = \leftarrow P(x)$. Both Π and G are allowed. Figure 8.6 shows an SLDNF-refutation of $\Pi \cup \{G\}$. The computed answer is $\{x/a\}$, which is a ground substitution for G. $\lhd$

Proposition 8.25 *Let Π be an allowed normal program, and G an allowed normal goal. Then:*

1. *$\Pi \cup \{G\}$ does not flounder.*
2. *Every computed answer for $\Pi \cup \{G\}$ is a ground substitution for G.*

Proof
1. Let $\mathcal{R}$ be an arbitrary safe computation rule, and $\mathcal{T}$ be an SLDNF-tree for $\Pi \cup \{G\}$ via $\mathcal{R}$. The initial pre-SLDNF-tree from which $\mathcal{T}$ is constructed

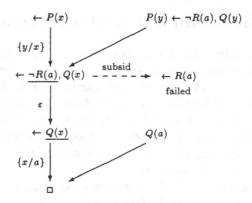

Figure 8.6: An SLDNF-refutation with allowed program and goal

only contains the allowed goal G. Moreover, using Lemma 8.25 it can easily be shown that any further extension adds only allowed goals to the tree. Thus every node in $\mathcal{T}$ is allowed, so not blocked. Hence $\Pi \cup \{G\}$ does not flounder.

2. Let $\theta_1, \ldots, \theta_k$ be the sequence of substitutions on the edges of some SLDNF-refutation of $\Pi \cup \{G\}$. We will show by induction on k that if x is a variable in G, then $x\theta_1 \ldots \theta_k$ is ground.

1. Suppose $k = 1$, then G contains only one literal. If this literal is positive, the result follows immediately from the fact that the only input clause must be an atom A, which is allowed and hence ground. Then $G\theta_1 = A$ will be ground. If the only literal in G is negative, it must be ground because of the allowedness of G, so any substitution will be a ground substitution for G.

2. Suppose the result holds for $k \leq m$, let $\theta_1, \ldots, \theta_{m+1}$ be the sequence of substitutions on the edges of some SLDNF-refutation of $\Pi \cup \{G\}$, x be a variable in G, and G_1 be the next goal.
   If a positive literal L was selected in the body of G, then G_1 is a binary resolvent of G and some input clause $C \in \Pi$, which we assume to be standardized apart. If x occurs in some literal in G other than L, then $x\theta_1$ occurs in G_1. Since $L\theta_1 = C^+\theta_1$, any variable in $L\theta_1$ also occurs in $C^+\theta_1$. Furthermore, since C is allowed, any variable in $C^+\theta_1$ also occurs in $C^-\theta_1$, and hence in G_1. Thus if x occurs in L, then any variable in $x\theta_1$ occurs in G_1. Therefore any variable in $x\theta_1$ occurs in G_1. By the induction hypothesis, for any variable y in G_1, we have that $y\theta_2 \ldots \theta_{m+1}$ is ground. Hence $x\theta_1 \ldots \theta_{m+1}$ is ground as well.
   If a ground negative literal L was selected in the body of G, then G_1 is G without L, so then x occurs in G_1 and $\theta_1 = \varepsilon$. The result follows again from the induction hypothesis.   □

8.5 The Completion of a Normal Program

We have already noticed that negation as (finite) failure is not *sound*: if Π is a definite program and $A \in F_\Pi$ then we can derive $\neg A$ from Π, even though $\Pi \not\models \neg A$. This unsoundness carries over to SLDNF-derivations for normal programs. Still we can prove a form of soundness, by comparing our derivation rules with what is logically implied by the *completion* of a normal program, rather than by the program itself. The completion of a program is intended to make explicit the "negative information" in a program, based on the Closed World Assumption.

How does this work? Let us start with an example. Consider a time-table program Π, consisting of the following:

> $To(amsterdam, 12{:}00)$
> $To(maastricht, 13{:}30)$

This program states that $To(x, y)$ is true if (1) $x = amsterdam$ and $y = 12{:}00$, or (2) $x = maastricht$ and $y = 13{:}30$. Now under the Closed World Assumption, we can assume this is a *complete* description of $To(x, y)$: there are no train departures other than those explicitly mentioned here. In other words: $To(x, y)$ is true if *and only if* (1) or (2) hold. The program itself only states the *if* part, but thanks to the added *only if* part, we can now say that $To(rotterdam, 12{:}00)$ is false.

Suppose we have in our language a predicate symbol '$=$', which captures our intuitive notion of equality. It is written in infix notation, so we write '$t = s$' instead of '$= (t, s)$', and we use $t \neq s$ to denote the negated atom $\neg(t = s)$. Using this predicate, we can make explicit the assumption of completeness, by strengthening Π to the following formula Π':

$$\forall x \forall y \, (To(x, y) \quad \leftrightarrow \quad (((x = amsterdam) \wedge (y = 12{:}00)) \vee$$
$$((x = maastricht) \wedge (y = 13{:}30)))).$$

If the predicate symbol '$=$' correctly formalizes equality, then we have $rotterdam \neq amsterdam$ and $rotterdam \neq maastricht$. Together with Π' this implies $\neg To(rotterdam, 12{:}00)$. Thus the atom $\neg To(rotterdam, 12{:}00)$ is a logical consequence of the completed program.

Before we can define the completion in general, something needs to be said about the predicate symbol '$=$'. In first-order logic, predicates by themselves have no meaning. For instance, without constraints on the interpretation of '$=$', $amsterdam = rotterdam$ might be either true or false, just as $P(a, b)$ is true in some interpretations, and false in others. Similarly, $amsterdam = amsterdam$ might be false, just as $P(a, a)$ may be false. So in order to make '$=$' conform to our intuitions about equality, we need to put some restrictions on its interpretation. This is done by including the following *equality theory* in the completion of the program, which states the properties that '$=$' should have.

Definition 8.26 The *equality theory EQ* for some alphabet consists of the following formulas (called *equality axioms*):

1. $\forall(f(x_1,\ldots,x_n) \neq g(y_1,\ldots,y_m))$, for every pair f,g of distinct function symbols. Here $n,m \geq 0$, so the inequality of distinct constants is included in this case.

2. $\forall(t[x] \neq x)$, where $t[x]$ is any term containing the variable x, but not the same as x.

3. $\forall((x_1 \neq y_1) \vee \ldots \vee (x_n \neq y_n) \rightarrow (f(x_1,\ldots,x_n) \neq f(y_1,\ldots,y_n)))$, for each function symbol f.

4. $\forall(x = x)$.

5. $\forall((x_1 = y_1) \wedge \ldots \wedge (x_n = y_n) \rightarrow (f(x_1,\ldots,x_n) = f(y_1,\ldots,y_n)))$, for each function symbol f.

6. $\forall((x_1 = y_1) \wedge \ldots \wedge (x_n = y_n) \rightarrow (P(x_1,\ldots,x_n) \rightarrow P(y_1,\ldots,y_n)))$, for each predicate symbol P (including '=' itself). $\Diamond$

These axioms are intended to capture syntactical identity in the Herbrand universe (i.e., the set of ground terms). We will later be interested in Herbrand models of the axioms. Note that a term is always equal to itself, by the fourth axiom. If s and t are distinct ground terms, then $EQ \models (s \neq t)$. For example, $EQ \models \forall x \forall y\ (f(x) \neq g(y))$ by the first equality axiom, so $EQ \models (f(a) \neq g(f(a)))$. The equality axioms do not completely specify the equality relation for non-ground terms. For instance, $EQ \not\models \forall(x = f(y))$ and $EQ \not\models \forall(x \neq f(y))$, since $EQ \models (f(a) = f(a))$ and $EQ \models (a \neq f(a))$.

Before formally defining the completion, let us give another example, slightly more complex than the time-table. Suppose we want to write a program describing some university records. Only two kinds of persons are present at this very simple university: professors and students. Everyone is either a student or a professor. There are only two professors, Confucius and Socrates, and everyone else is a student. In a normal program Π, this would look as follows:

$Prof(confucius)$
$Prof(socrates)$
$Student(y) \leftarrow \neg Prof(y)$

However, these clauses do not tell us that if someone (for instance Plato) is a student, then that person is not a professor. To make explicit that a student is not a professor, we need to complete the program.

Let us first consider the clauses with *Prof* in their head. The program itself only states that if $x = confucius$ or $x = socrates$, then $Prof(x)$ is true. Similar to the case of the time-table, we assume this is a *complete* description of the set of professors. Hence we add the *only if*-side to the above statement, obtaining that x is a professor if, *and only if*, $x = confucius$ or $x = socrates$. We can do something similar with the clause having *Student* in its head: the completion states that x is a student if, *and only if*, x is not a professor. Thus the completion of Π makes explicit that Confucius and Socrates are the only professors (and not students), and that everyone else is a student:

$$\forall x \ (Prof(x) \leftrightarrow ((x = confucius) \vee (x = socrates)))$$
$$\forall x \ (Student(x) \leftrightarrow \exists y \ ((x = y) \wedge \neg Prof(y)))$$

The somewhat complex form of the body of the second formula will be explained in a moment. Apart from these two formulas, the completion $comp(\Pi)$ of Π also contains the equality theory.

Note that by the first equality axiom we have $plato \neq confucius$ and $plato \neq socrates$, assuming $plato$ to be a constant in the alphabet. Thus $comp(\Pi) \models \neg Prof(plato)$ by the first formula in the completion, and consequently $comp(\Pi) \models Student(plato)$ by the second formula. Neither $\neg Prof(plato)$ nor $Student(plato)$ are logical consequences of Π itself. Nevertheless, the CWA allows us to infer these two literals, and the completion makes this explicit by logically implying them.

The general way to transform a program into its completion is as follows.

Definition 8.27 Let Π be a normal program, and P be a predicate symbol. Then the *definition of P in Π* is the set of clauses in Π which have P in their head. ◇

Suppose the definition of some m-ary predicate symbol P in Π consists of k program clauses. We want to turn this definition into something of the form

$$\forall x_1 \ldots \forall x_m \ (P(x_1, \ldots, x_m) \leftrightarrow E),$$

where $x_1, \ldots, x_m$ are new variables not appearing in the definition of P, and E is roughly the disjunction of the bodies of the clauses in the definition. The first thing we must do in order to achieve this, is give each of the k clauses in the definition the same head $P(x_1, \ldots, x_m)$. Let

$$C_1 = P(t_1, \ldots, t_m) \leftarrow L_1, \ldots, L_n$$

be the first of the clauses in the definition of P, and suppose the variables in C_1 are $y_1, \ldots, y_d$. The first step in the transformation turns this clause into the clause

$$C_1' = P(x_1, \ldots, x_m) \leftarrow (x_1 = t_1), \ldots, (x_m = t_m), L_1, \ldots, L_n.$$

Let us call *E-Herbrand interpretations* all those Herbrand interpretations which satisfy the equality theory. Since C_1' together with the fourth equality axiom logically implies C_1, any E-Herbrand model of C_1' is also an E-Herbrand model of C_1. Conversely, it is not very difficult to see that any E-Herbrand model of C_1 is also an E-Herbrand model of C_1', using axiom 6. Since C_1 and C_1' have exactly the same E-Herbrand models, we may say that the above transformation from C_1 to C_1' has preserved equivalence with respect to E-Herbrand interpretations.

To motivate the second step that we want to take for the transformation, note that the body of the clause C_1' contains $y_1, \ldots, y_d$, which are universally quantified. This universal quantification may cause problems. Consider for instance $\Pi = \{P \leftarrow Q(y)\}$, where P is a 0-ary predicate symbol meaning that Holland is inhabited, and $Q(y)$ means that y lives in Holland. $P \leftarrow Q(y)$ thus means that if some y lives in Holland, then Holland is inhabited. If we simply added the "only if"-side, we obtain $\forall y\ (P \leftrightarrow Q(y))$. But this implies that if P is true, then $Q(y)$ is true *for every* y. In other words, if Holland is inhabited, then every person lives in Holland. This is clearly too strong, considering that Holland is a rather small country. What we would like to have as a completion, is something like "Holland is inhabited iff there is at least one person y living in Holland." Therefore the second step turns the universal quantifiers for $y_1, \ldots, y_d$ into existential quantifiers in the body of the formula itself:

$$P(x_1, \ldots, x_m) \leftarrow \exists y_1 \ldots \exists y_d\ ((x_1 = t_1) \wedge \ldots \wedge (x_m = t_m) \wedge L_1 \wedge \ldots \wedge L_n),$$

which may be abbreviated to

$$C_1'' = P(x_1, \ldots, x_m) \leftarrow E_1.$$

Note that C_1' and C_1'' are logically equivalent. For instance, $\forall x \forall y\ (P(x) \leftarrow (x = y), Q(y)) \Leftrightarrow \forall x\ (P(x) \leftarrow \exists y\ ((x = y) \wedge Q(y)))$. This implies that C_1, C_1', and C_1'' all have the same E-Herbrand models.

Suppose the above transformation is made for each of the k clauses in the definition of P, so we have

$$P(x_1, \ldots, x_m) \leftarrow E_1.$$

$$\vdots$$

$$P(x_1, \ldots, x_m) \leftarrow E_k.$$

Together these k formulas imply

$$\forall x_1 \ldots \forall x_m\ (P(x_1, \ldots, x_m) \leftarrow (E_1 \vee \ldots \vee E_k)).$$

The *completed definition* of the predicate symbol P is the closed formula

$$\forall x_1 \ldots \forall x_m\ (P(x_1, \ldots, x_m) \leftrightarrow (E_1 \vee \ldots \vee E_k)).$$

In case Q is an m-ary predicate symbol in Π that does not occur in the head of a clause in Π, we take every instance of Q to be false. So in this case the completed definition of Q is $\forall x_1 \ldots \forall x_m\ \neg Q(x_1, \ldots, x_m)$.

The completed definition of some predicate is not itself a set of clauses, nor can it always be transformed into an equivalent set of clauses, due to the presence of existential quantifiers. For instance, if $\Pi = \{P \leftarrow Q(y)\}$, then the completed definition of P is $P \leftrightarrow \exists y\ Q(y)$, which cannot be transformed to an equivalent set of clauses.

The completion of a normal program combines the completed definitions with the equality theory:

Definition 8.28 Let Π be a normal program. The *completion of* Π, denoted by $comp(\Pi)$, is the set of the completed definitions of the predicate symbols in Π, together with the equality theory. $\diamond$

The completion of a program is sometimes unsatisfiable. Consider $\Pi = \{P(a) \leftarrow \neg P(a)\}$, which itself is satisfiable, since it has $\{P(a)\}$ as a model. However, $comp(\Pi)$ combines $\forall x \ (P(x) \leftrightarrow ((x = a) \wedge \neg P(a)))$ with the equality theory, which is unsatisfiable. It is not very difficult to show that if Π is a definite program, then $comp(\Pi)$ is satisfiable. For restrictions on (non-definite) normal programs which ensure a satisfiable completion, we refer to [Llo87, AB94] and the references therein.

Note the following relation between a program and its completion:

Proposition 8.29 *If Π is a normal program, then $comp(\Pi) \models \Pi$.*

Proof Let $C = P(t_1, \ldots, t_m) \leftarrow L_1, \ldots, L_n \in \Pi$, and

$$D = \forall x_1 \ldots \forall x_m \ (P(x_1, \ldots, x_m) \leftrightarrow (E_1 \vee \ldots \vee E_k))$$

be the completed definition of P. Suppose E_i was obtained from C:

$$E_i = \exists y_1 \ldots \exists y_d \ ((x_1 = t_1) \wedge \ldots \wedge (x_m = t_m) \wedge L_1 \wedge \ldots \wedge L_n).$$

D implies $\forall x_1 \ldots \forall x_m \ (P(x_1, \ldots, x_m) \leftarrow E_i)$, which is equivalent to the clause

$$P(x_1, \ldots, x_m) \leftarrow (x_1 = t_1), \ldots, (x_m = t_m), L_1, \ldots, L_n.$$

This clause has the following instance (substituting t_j for x_j):

$$P(t_1, \ldots, t_m) \leftarrow (t_1 = t_1), \ldots, (t_m = t_m), L_1, \ldots, L_n.$$

This instance, together with the 4th equality axiom, implies C. Hence $comp(\Pi) \models C$. $\square$

It follows from this proposition that if L is a literal and $\Pi \models \forall(L)$, then $comp(\Pi) \models \forall(L)$.

It should be noted that the completion, though motivated by and based upon the Closed World Assumption, is actually weaker than the CWA. Consider the definite program $\Pi = \{P(y) \leftarrow P(f(y))\}$. Then $\Pi \not\models P(a)$, so the CWA would justify inferring $\neg P(a)$. Nevertheless, $comp(\Pi) = \{\forall x \ (P(x) \leftrightarrow ((x = y) \wedge P(f(y))))\} \cup EQ$ does not imply $\neg P(a)$, because an interpretation that satisfies the equality axioms and makes true $P(f^n(a))$ for every $n \geq 0$ would be a model of $comp(\Pi)$ but not of $\neg P(a)$. Thus the completion makes explicit only part of the CWA, just as negation as *finite* failure is only a partial implementation of "full" negation as failure.

As mentioned at the beginning of this section, in order to be able to prove soundness results we should compare SLDNF-derivations with what is implied by the completion, not with what is implied by the program itself. Thus we define the notion of a *correct* answer, the semantical counterpart to the *computed* answer, as follows:

Definition 8.30 Let Π be a normal program, $G =\leftarrow L_1, \ldots, L_k$ a normal goal, and θ be a substitution for variables of G. We say that θ is a *correct answer* for $comp(\Pi) \cup \{G\}$ if $comp(\Pi) \models \forall((L_1 \wedge \ldots \wedge L_k)\theta)$. $\diamondsuit$

To end this section, let us compare the previous definition with the definition of a correct answer for *definite* programs, given in the last chapter. Suppose Π is a definite program and G a definite goal. It follows from Proposition 8.29 that a correct answer for $\Pi \cup \{G\}$ in the old sense is also a correct answer for $comp(\Pi) \cup \{G\}$ in the sense of this chapter. It can be shown that the converse holds as well (see Proposition 14.5 of [Llo87]). So in the definite case, θ is a correct answer for $\Pi \cup \{G\}$ iff it is a correct answer for $comp(\Pi) \cup \{G\}$.

8.6   Soundness with Respect to the Completion

In this section we prove two important soundness results: the first for finitely failed SLDNF-trees, the second for successful ones. Suppose Π is a normal program, and $G =\leftarrow L_1, \ldots, L_n$ a normal goal. Firstly, if $comp(\Pi) \cup \{G\}$ has a finitely failed SLDNF-tree, then $comp(\Pi) \models \forall(\neg(L_1 \wedge \ldots \wedge L_n))$, which is the same as $comp(\Pi) \models \forall(G)$. Secondly, if some success branch in an SLDNF-tree for $comp(\Pi) \cup \{G\}$ yields a computed answer θ, then this is also a *correct* answer: $comp(\Pi) \models \forall((L_1 \wedge \ldots \wedge L_n)\theta)$.

The basis of the proof is the next lemma. Rather than including the very technical proof of this lemma (Lemma 15.3 of [Llo87]; a similar result is given in Section 5.7 of [Apt90]), we illustrate it with an example.

Lemma 8.31 *Let Π be a normal program, G a normal goal, and L_s a positive literal in the body of G.*

1. *If there is no (variant of) $C \in \Pi$ whose head can be unified with L_s, then $comp(\Pi) \models G$.*
2. *If the set $\{G_1, \ldots, G_r\}$ of all binary resolvents of G and clauses in Π (resolved upon L_s) is non-empty, then $comp(\Pi) \models G \leftrightarrow G_1 \wedge \ldots \wedge G_r$.*

Example 8.32 Let $\Pi = \{P(a), (P(f^2(y)) \leftarrow P(y))\}$. Then $comp(\Pi) = \{\forall x \, (P(x) \leftrightarrow ((x = a) \vee \exists y \, ((x = f^2(y)) \wedge P(y))))\} \cup EQ$.

Let $G =\leftarrow P(f(a))$. Since $P(f(a))$ cannot be unified with any atom in the head of a clause in Π, there are no resolvents from G and Π. Thus $\Pi \cup \{G\}$ finitely fails, and we infer $\neg P(f(a))$. This is sound with respect to the completion, since $comp(\Pi) \models \neg P(f(a))$.

If $G =\leftarrow P(f^2(a))$, then the only resolvent of G and clauses in Π is $G_1 =\leftarrow P(a)$. Now it easy to see that through substituting $f^2(a)$ for x in the formula in the completion, we have $comp(\Pi) \models P(f^2(a)) \leftrightarrow P(a)$, hence also $comp(\Pi) \models \neg P(f^2(a)) \leftrightarrow \neg P(a)$. $\triangleleft$

Theorem 8.33 (Soundness of negation as finite failure)   *Let Π be a normal program, and G a normal goal. If $\Pi \cup \{G\}$ has a finitely failed SLDNF-tree, then $comp(\Pi) \models G$.*

Proof Let $G = \leftarrow L_1, \ldots, L_n$, and $\mathcal{T}$ be a finitely failed SLDNF-tree for $\Pi \cup \{G\}$. Then G must be non-empty. The main tree of $\mathcal{T}$ is finitely failed, so there exists a finite number $k \geq 1$, such that this main tree is complete after k extensions of the initial tree G. The proof is by induction on k.

1. If $k = 1$, then $G = \leftarrow L_1$. L_1 cannot be negative, since constructing a subsidiary tree (which must first finitely fail or become successful before the main tree can be further extended) would involve at least two more extensions. Hence L_1 is an atom, and there is no (variant of) $C \in \Pi$ whose head can be unified with L_1. Then $comp(\Pi) \models G$ by the first part of Lemma 8.31.

2. Suppose the theorem holds for $k \leq m$, the main tree of $\mathcal{T}$ is complete after $m+1$ extensions, and L_s is selected in G in the initial pre-SLDNF-tree.

   1. Suppose L_s is positive. Let $G_1, \ldots, G_r$ $(r \geq 1)$ be the children of G in the main tree of $\mathcal{T}$. For each $1 \leq i \leq r$, the subtree initiating in G_i is itself a finitely failed SLDNF-tree, so by the induction hypothesis we have that $comp(\Pi) \models G_i$. Then $comp(\Pi) \models G_1 \wedge \ldots \wedge G_r$, and $comp(\Pi) \models G$ from Lemma 8.31, part 2.

   2. If $L_s = \neg A$ is negative, then A is ground. Because the main tree of $\mathcal{T}$ is finitely failed, the subsidiary SLDNF-tree $subsid(G)$ for $\Pi \cup \{\leftarrow A\}$ is either successful or finitely failed.

      Case 1. First suppose $subsid(G)$ is successful. Then this subsidiary tree contains a success branch (i.e., an SLDNF-refutation of $\Pi \cup \{\leftarrow A\}$). Let the length of this success branch be l. Now it can be proved by induction on l that $comp(\Pi) \cup \{\leftarrow A\} \models \Box$, using (1) the soundness of resolution steps, and (2) the fact that each subsidiary tree used on this success branch must be finitely failed after m or less extensions (so the induction hypothesis can be applied). Therefore $comp(\Pi) \cup \{\leftarrow A\}$ is unsatisfiable, and $comp(\Pi) \models A$ by Proposition 2.37. Then also $comp(\Pi) \models \neg L_s$, and since $\neg L_s \in G$ (i.e., $L_s \in G^-$), it follows that $comp(\Pi) \models G$.

      Case 2. Now suppose $subsid(G)$ is finitely failed. Then the only child of G is $G' = \leftarrow L_1, \ldots, L_{s-1}, L_{s+1}, \ldots, L_n$, and the tree with this G' as root is finitely failed after m or less extensions. Hence by the induction hypothesis we have $comp(\Pi) \models G'$. Since $G' \subset G$, the result follows. $\Box$

In particular, if A is a ground atom and $\Pi \cup \{\leftarrow A\}$ has a finitely failed SLDNF-tree, then $comp(\Pi) \models \neg A$. Using this result, we can prove the soundness of answers computed by SLDNF-refutations in the next theorem.

Example 8.34 In Example 8.16 we noted that the SLDNF-tree of Example 8.10 contained two computed answers, $\theta_1 = \{x/a\}$ and $\theta_2 = \{x/b\}$, and that $\Pi \models P(x)\theta_1$ but $\Pi \not\models P(x)\theta_2$. Thus computed answers are not sound with respect to the program Π itself. On the other hand, the next theorem guarantees us the soundness of computed answers with respect to the completion: we have $comp(\Pi) \models P(x)\theta_1$ as well as $comp(\Pi) \models P(x)\theta_2$.   ◁

Theorem 8.35 (Soundness of SLDNF-resolution) *Let Π be a normal program, and G a normal goal. Then every computed answer for $\Pi \cup \{G\}$ is a correct answer for $comp(\Pi) \cup \{G\}$.*

Proof Suppose $G = \leftarrow L_1, \ldots, L_n$, and $G_0 = G, G_1, \ldots, G_k = \square$ be the main branch of an SLDNF-refutation of $\Pi \cup \{G\}$ with computed answer θ. Let $\theta_1, \ldots, \theta_k$ be the substitutions used. We will prove by induction on k that $comp(\Pi) \models \forall((L_1 \wedge \ldots \wedge L_n)\theta_1 \ldots \theta_k)$, thus showing that θ is a correct answer for $comp(\Pi) \cup \{G\}$.

1. If $k = 1$, then $G = \leftarrow L_1$.
    1. If L_1 is positive, then there is an atom $B \in \Pi$ such that $B\theta_1 = L_1\theta_1$. Hence $B \models \forall(L_1\theta_1)$. Now $comp(\Pi) \models B$ by Proposition 8.29, and the result follows.
    2. If $L_1 = \neg A$ is negative, then A is ground, and there is a finitely failed SLDNF-tree for $\Pi \cup \{\leftarrow A\}$. The computer answer is just ε here. By Theorem 8.33 we have $comp(\Pi) \models \leftarrow A$. Since $\leftarrow A \Leftrightarrow \neg A$ and $\neg A = L_1$, we have $comp(\Pi) \models L_1$, so ε is a correct answer.
2. Suppose the result holds for $k \leq m$, and let $G_0 = G, G_1, \ldots, G_{m+1} = \square$ be the main branch of an SLDNF-refutation of $\Pi \cup \{G\}$ with substitutions $\theta_1, \ldots, \theta_{m+1}$ and computed answer θ. Let L_s be the selected literal in G.
    1. Suppose L_s is positive, and the first input clause is $C = B \leftarrow C^-$. Then the second goal in the refutation is $G_1 = \leftarrow (L_1, \ldots, L_{s-1}, C^-, L_{s+1}, \ldots, L_n)\theta_1$. By the induction hypothesis we have $comp(\Pi) \models \forall((L_1 \wedge \ldots \wedge L_{s-1} \wedge C^- \wedge L_{s+1} \wedge \ldots \wedge L_n)\theta_1 \ldots \theta_{m+1})$. Furthermore, note that $C \cup \forall(C^-\theta_1 \ldots \theta_{m+1}) \models B\theta_1 \ldots \theta_{m+1}$. Then we have $comp(\Pi) \cup \forall(C^-\theta_1 \ldots \theta_{m+1}) \models B\theta_1 \ldots \theta_{m+1}$, since $comp(\Pi) \models C$ by Proposition 8.29. Therefore also $comp(\Pi) \models \forall((L_1 \wedge \ldots \wedge L_{s-1} \wedge B \wedge L_{s+1} \wedge \ldots \wedge L_n)\theta_1 \ldots \theta_{m+1})$. Finally, since $B\theta_1 = L_s\theta_1$, we can replace B by L_s in the previous formula, thus obtaining $comp(\Pi) \models \forall((L_1 \wedge \ldots \wedge L_n)\theta_1 \ldots \theta_{m+1})$.
    2. If $L_s = \neg A$ is negative, then A is ground and there is a finitely failed SLDNF-tree for $\Pi \cup \{\leftarrow A\}$. We have $comp(\Pi) \models L_s$ by Theorem 8.33. Combining this with $comp(\Pi) \models \forall((L_1 \wedge \ldots \wedge L_{s-1} \wedge L_{s+1} \wedge \ldots \wedge L_n)\theta_1 \ldots \theta_{m+1})$ (induction hypothesis), the result follows.   □

8.7 Completeness

In this section we will devote some attention to the completeness and incompleteness of SLDNF-resolution. First, consider a definite program Π and a definite goal G. At the end of Section 8.5, we mentioned that a substitution θ is a correct answer for $\Pi \cup \{G\}$ iff it is a correct answer for $comp(\Pi) \cup \{G\}$, so the set of correct answers remains the same when we consider the completion of Π. Since, furthermore, an SLDNF-tree for $\Pi \cup \{G\}$ is simply an SLD-tree for $\Pi \cup \{G\}$, the set of *computed* answers remains the same as well. Hence, for definite Π and G, the completeness of computed answers for SLDNF-resolution follows from the completeness of computed answers for SLD-resolution (Theorem 7.26 of the last chapter).

Computed answers stem from trees with success branches. What about trees without success branches? We would like these to be finitely failed, so we won't get stuck in infinite branches. The next result says that if $comp(\Pi) \models G$, then every *fair* SLD-tree for $\Pi \cup \{G\}$ is indeed finitely failed. In particular, if A is a ground atom and $comp(\Pi) \models \neg A$, then every fair SLD-tree for $\Pi \cup \{\leftarrow A\}$ will be finitely failed, hence $A \in F_\Pi$. We will not prove this result here, which is originally due to Jaffar, Lassez, and Lloyd [JLL83] (for a proof, see [Llo87, Theorem 16.1] or [Apt90, Theorem 5.30]).[3]

Theorem 8.36 (Completeness of negation as finite failure) *Let Π be a definite program, and G a definite goal. If $comp(\Pi) \models G$, then every fair SLD-tree for $\Pi \cup \{G\}$ is finitely failed.*

The previous result on negation as failure for definite programs, as well as the results on SLD-resolution of the previous chapter, are quite strong. Unfortunately, equally strong results are missing for SLDNF-resolution for normal programs. In fact, SLDNF-resolution is not complete, not even in case of a definite programs combined with a normal goal. For example, let $\Pi = \{Q(a, b)\}$ and $G = \leftarrow \neg Q(x, a)$ (note that G is not allowed according to Definition 8.21). Then $comp(\Pi) \models \neg Q(b, a)$, so $\{x/b\}$ is a correct answer for $\Pi \cup \{G\}$. However, no SLDNF-tree for $\Pi \cup \{G\}$ contains a success branch, since $\neg Q(x, a)$ cannot be selected due to floundering.

Thus in order to obtain completeness results, we have to put some constraints on the programs and goals we use. Theorem 16.3 of [Llo87] gives a completeness result for so-called allowed *hierarchical* normal programs and allowed normal goals. A normal program Π is hierarchical if there is an assignment of natural numbers to each of the predicates in Π, such that for every $C \in \Pi$, the number assigned to the predicate in C^+ is greater than the numbers assigned to the predicates in C^-. Unfortunately, the restriction to hierarchical programs rules out any recursion: for instance, a program containing $P(f(x)) \leftarrow P(x)$ is not hierarchical.

---

[3] For a different completeness result for SLDNF-resolution, see Theorem 8.52 of [Doe94]. This result employs a 3-valued semantics, where the possible truth values are 'true', 'false', and 'undefined', rather than only 'true' and 'false'.

8.8 Prolog

The use of normal programs as a means for knowledge representation and computation has been implemented in several practical programming languages. In this section, we will briefly give an overview of the best-known of these languages, the language PROLOG (short for Programming in logic). PROLOG was introduced in the early 1970s by Colmerauer and his co-workers, and its subsequent development influenced, and was itself influenced by, the development of logic programming. Many ILP systems are implemented in PROLOG, and many examples in the ILP literature are given in terms of PROLOG. We will here mainly discuss some of the logical aspects of PROLOG. For a more extensive introduction to PROLOG as a practical programming language, we refer to [CM87, Bra90, SS94, Apt97].

8.8.1 Syntax

In PROLOG, names of predicates are strings of symbols starting with a lower case letter. Names of variables start with an upper case letter or an underscore, and names of constants and function symbols start with a lower case letter. We will here denote PROLOG clauses and terms in a `typewriter`-style font. The implication sign '←' of a Horn clause is in most PROLOG-systems written as ':-', and a negative literal $\neg A$ in the body of a program clause is usually written as **not** `A`.

An important feature of PROLOG is its ability to handle *lists* of terms. Lists can be implemented using a special binary function symbol '·' and a special constant *nil* (which denotes the empty list), so they can be incorporated within first-order logic without any additional concepts. The first element of the list is placed at the first argument place of the '·'-function, the remainder of the list is put at the second place. For instance, the list `[a,b,c]` can be represented by the term $·(a, ·(b, ·(c, nil)))$. The empty list `[]` is represented by *nil*. `[X|L]` denotes a list with `X` as first element, and list `L` as remainder, and `[X,Y|L]` is a list which has `X` as first element, and `Y` as second element, followed by the list `L`.

Example 8.37 The familiar operations on lists can easily be formalized in PROLOG.[4] For instance, the following program describes when object `X` is a member of the list at the second argument place:

1. `member(X,[X|L])`
2. `member(X,[Y|L]) :- member(X,L)`

Appending two lists `L1` and `L2` to get a third list `L3` can be done by the following program:

1. `append([],L2,L2)`

---

[4]ILP systems are often tested by making them learn definitions of these list-operations from a few examples.

2. append([X|L1],L2,[X|L3]) :- append(L1,L2,L3)   ◁

PROLOG also provides operators like +, *, etc., for doing relatively simple arithmetic, such as addition, multiplication, etc. Here '+' is a binary function symbol, written in infix notation. To assign some value to a variable in the body of a clause, the operator is is used. Comparison of values is done by operators like =:=, >, >=, etc. '>' is a binary predicate symbol, again written in infix-notation. For a more complete overview over these operators, and also for the operators for reading, writing, etc., we refer the reader again to [CM87, Bra90, SS94, Apt97].

Example 8.38 Consider the following recursive algorithm for computing the greatest common divisor (gcd) d of two positive integers x and y:

1. If $x = y$, then $d = x$.
2. If $x < y$, then d is the gcd of x and $y - x$.
   Otherwise, d is the gcd of $x - y$ and y.

This algorithm can be translated into PROLOG using operators for subtraction and comparison, as follows:

1. gcd(X,X,X)
2. gcd(X,Y,D) :- X<Y, Y1 is Y-X, gcd(X,Y1,D)
3. gcd(X,Y,D) :- X>Y, X1 is X-Y, gcd(X1,Y,D)   ◁

8.8.2 Prolog and SLDNF-Trees

There are two sides to each PROLOG program: a declarative side and a procedural side. The declarative side concerns the content of a normal program (*what* the program says), while the procedural side concerns *how* PROLOG extracts this content from the program. One of the ideas behind PROLOG is that a programmer only needs to worry about the declarative side. He can restrict himself to describing the problem he wants to solve, without bothering *how* it will be solved: the procedural side is left to the system.

Let us assume some normal program Π is given to a PROLOG system. The procedural side is invoked when a question is posed to the system. Questions (often called *queries*) are put to a PROLOG system in the form of a conjunction of literals $L_1, \ldots, L_n$. This question can be seen as the question "for which substitutions θ is $\forall((L_1 \land \ldots \land L_n)\theta)$ a logical consequence of the completion of the program?", or in other words: "what are the correct answers for $\Pi \cup \{\leftarrow L_1, \ldots, L_n\}$?"

PROLOG answers this question by constructing computed answers, which are the counterpart of the correct answers. It does this by searching an SLDNF-tree for $\Pi \cup \{\leftarrow L_1, \ldots, L_n\}$, using the computation rule which always selects the leftmost literal in a goal. The system searches this tree in a *depth-first* fashion, printing out every computed answer it finds in the main tree.

This depth-first search can be described by the following recursive procedure, which is initially called with $G = \leftarrow L_1, \ldots, L_n$.

Search(G):
If $G = \square$, construct the computed answer for this leaf.
If the leftmost literal L in G is positive, then
> Construct the resolvents $G_1, \ldots, G_n$ of G and clauses in Π.
> Search(G_1).
> ...
> Search(G_n).

If $L = \neg A$ is negative, then Search($\leftarrow A$). (Note that if this call to Search returns, then the SLDNF-tree for $\leftarrow A$ is finite.) If this call to Search found no success branches, then Search($G - \neg L$).

Though the way PROLOG works can more or less be equated with the search of SLDNF-trees, a number of difficulties arise as a consequence of some subtle differences between PROLOG and "proper" SLDNF-trees.

Firstly, as can be seen from the Search procedure described above, PROLOG ignores floundering. When a negative literal $\neg A$ is selected, PROLOG does not distinguish between ground and non-ground literals. In both cases, the system tries to construct a finitely failed SLDNF-tree for $\Pi \cup \{\leftarrow A\}$. This may lead to the unsoundness exhibited in Example 8.18. Moreover, PROLOG's computation rule is not safe: it always selects the leftmost literal in a goal, even when this literal is negative and non-ground, and other positive or ground negative literals are available in the goal.

Secondly, a PROLOG program is an ordered *list* of clauses, not a *set* of clauses. Combined with the depth-first search, completeness now depends on the order of clauses in the program:

Example 8.39 Consider the infinite SLDNF-tree (actually, just an SLD-tree) that PROLOG would have to search given a goal :- p(X) and a program Π consisting of

1. p(a)
2. p(f(X)) :- p(X)

The SLD-tree for $\Pi \cup \{G\}$ is shown on the left of Figure 8.7. PROLOG's depth-first search will not terminate due to the presence of an infinite branch, but the system will eventually find and print out each computed answer.

However, now suppose we would reverse the order of clauses in Π: 1 becomes 2, and 2 becomes 1:

1. p(f(X)) :- p(X)
2. p(a)

This gives the SLD-tree shown on the right of Figure 8.7. Now PROLOG's depth-first search will find no computed answer at all because it gets stuck in the leftmost branch, which stretches downward without end.   ◁

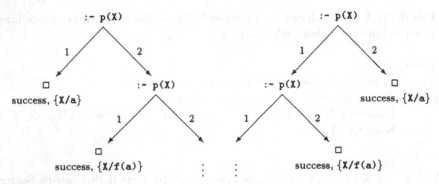

Figure 8.7: The effect of reversing the order of clauses in Π

The most important distinction between PROLOG and SLDNF-trees is the use of the *cut* operator, which is the topic of the next subsection.

8.8.3 The Cut Operator

The cut operator is incorporated in PROLOG for reasons of efficiency. By inserting this operator—usually denoted by a '!'-symbol—in the body of some clauses in the program, the programmer can control the search. The effect of the cut operator is that certain parts of the SLDNF-tree are pruned from the tree and hence will not be searched.

How does this work? Consider the Search procedure described on p. 156. Suppose G is resolved with $C_1, \ldots, C_n \in \Pi$, yielding, respectively, the new normal goals $G_1, \ldots, G_n$. Moreover, suppose C_i contains the cut operator ! as an atom (with arity 0) in its body[5], then G_i contains this cut as well. Now if this cut becomes the leftmost literal in a goal at some moment during the call of Search(G_i), then it is selected, and resolved away immediately—we may assume any program contains ! as a "hidden" atomic clause. However, after this call to Search(G_i) returns, the calls to Search(G_{i+1}), ..., Search(G_n) are not executed. In this way, the cut operator prunes the subtrees which have, respectively, $G_{i+1}, \ldots, G_n$ as root: these subtrees are not searched, and any computed answer in them is ignored. If the cut was not selected at some moment during the call of Search(G_i), the calls to Search(G_{i+1}),... are made as if G_i did not contain a cut.

Example 8.40 Suppose we want to compute the sign function:
$$f(x) = \begin{cases} -1, & \text{if } x < 0; \\ 0, & \text{if } x = 0; \\ 1, & \text{if } x > 0. \end{cases}$$

---

[5]Though it is convenient to describe ! as an atom, the cut does not have any logical significance: it is only used to control the search through the SLDNF-tree. As argued in [Llo87], it does not affect the semantics of the program. If we view the cut as "always true", then for instance A :- B,C ⇔ A :- B,!,C.

This function can be formalized by the following PROLOG program Π, the first two clauses of which contain a cut:

1. `sign(X,-1) :- X<0,!`
2. `sign(X,0) :- X=0,!`
3. `sign(X,1) :- X>0`

Suppose $G =$ `:- sign(-2,Y)`. The tree for $\Pi \cup \{G\}$ is shown in Figure 8.8. PROLOG evaluates the atom `-2<0` as true when selected, and `-2=0` and `-2>0` as false. The root G contains three children, one for each of the clauses in Π. The first input clause adds a cut operator to the body of the leftmost child. Since this cut is selected after two steps on the leftmost branch, the subtrees initiating in the other two children of G are not searched. Thus the framed part of the tree is discarded.

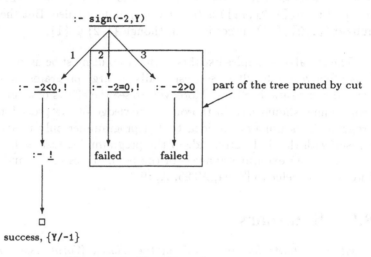

Figure 8.8: The effect of a cut

In this case, the pruning is beneficial: since `Y` in `sign` can have only one value, it is no use to search the other two subtrees, given that the value of `Y` has already been found in the leftmost subtree. Note that if the goal had been `sign(0,Y)`, then the leftmost branch would have immediately led to failure, hence `!` would not be selected in the leftmost branch. In this case, the cut in the center branch would be selected, leading to the discarding of only the rightmost subtree.   ◁

In the previous example, the pruned parts of the tree did not contain any success branches. However, if these pruned parts contained success branches, then the computed answers corresponding to these branches would not be found. This leads to a form of incompleteness. Moreover, when combined with negation as finite failure, use of the cut may even cause unsoundness, as the next example (adapted from [Llo87]) shows:

Example 8.41 Suppose we want to write a program for the subset-relation. Here sets are represented as lists, and `subset(L1,L2)` should succeed just in case there is no X which is a member of L1 but not of L2. Let Π consist of the following clauses:

1. `subset(L1,L2) :- not p(L1,L2)`
2. `p(L1,L2) :- member(X,L1), not member(X,L2)`
3. `member(X,[X|L]) :- !`
4. `member(X,[Y|L]) :- member(X,L)`

At first sight, it seems a good idea to use a cut in the first clause of the definition of `member`, because if this clause applies (i.e., if its head can be unified with the selected atom in some goal), we already know X is a member of the list at the second argument place, so the second clause of the definition will not be needed. However, because of this cut, PROLOG's SLDNF-tree for the goal `:- p([1,2],[1])` is (incorrectly) finitely failed. But then the query `subset([1,2],[1])` succeeds, even though $\{1,2\} \not\subseteq \{1\}$. ◁

The moral of examples like this, is that the cut must be used very carefully. It is often very difficult to see, especially in large programs, whether it will have any undesirable effects. Moreover, to see the effects of a cut, a PROLOG-programmer should have a thorough knowledge of the procedural side of a program. This impairs the idea that a programmer only needs to concern himself with the declarative side of the programming task at hand.

For a more extensive analysis of the peculiarities of cut and negation in PROLOG, we refer to [SS94, AT95, Apt97].

8.9 Summary

Negation as finite failure, based on the *Closed World Assumption*, is the derivation rule which states that if $\Pi \cup \{\leftarrow A\}$ finitely fails, then we can derive the ground atom $\neg A$ from Π. The possibility of deriving negative literals from a definite program allowed us to generalize definite program clauses to *program clauses*, which may contain negative literals in their body. A *normal program* is a finite set of program clauses.

Combining SLD-resolution and negation as finite failure yields *SLDNF-resolution*, which handles negative literals in a goal by negation as finite failure. Negation as failure should only be applied to *ground* negative literals (i.e., no *floundering*), in order to avoid unsoundness. We proved the soundness of SLDNF-resolution in terms of the *completion* of normal programs, and stated a completeness result. Finally, we discussed the language PROLOG and some of its difficulties, in particular the potentially adverse effects of the cut operator.

Part II

Inductive Logic Programming

Part II

Inductive Logic Programming

Chapter 9

What Is Inductive Logic Programming?

9.1 Introduction

Learning a general theory from specific examples, commonly called *induction*, has been a topic of inquiry for centuries. It is often seen as a main source of scientific knowledge. Suppose we are given a large number of patient's records from a hospital, consisting of properties of each patient, including symptoms and diseases. We want to find some general rules, concerning which symptoms indicate which diseases. The hospital's records provide *examples* from which we can find clues as to what those rules are. Consider measles, a virus disease. If every patient in the hospital who has a fever and has red spots suffers from measles, we could infer the general rule

    1. "If someone has a fever and red spots, he or she has measles."

Moreover, if each patient with measles also has red spots, we can infer

    2. "If someone has measles, he or she will get red spots."

These inferences are cases of induction. Note that these rules not only tell us something about the people in the hospital's records, but are in fact about *everyone*. Accordingly, they have predictive power: they can be used to make predictions about future patients with the same symptoms.

Usually when we want to learn something, we do not start from scratch: most often we already have some *background knowledge* relevant to the learning task. For instance, in the hospital records we might find that patients suffer from measles if they are infected by virus a or by virus b, and patients not infected by a or b are not bothered by measles. Now suppose the background knowledge tells us that both a and b belong to a virus family c, which consists of viruses with a similar structure. In this case, we may induce the rule

3. "If someone is infected by a virus x from family c, he or she has measles"

assuming, of course, that this rule is not contradicted by other patients in the records. If we had ignored this background knowledge, it would have been sensible to induce the following two much weaker rules:

4. "If someone is infected by virus a, he or she has measles."
5. "If someone is infected by virus b, he or she has measles."

Rule 3, together with the background knowledge, implies rules 4 and 5, and has more predictive power than 4 and 5 taken together.

The study of induction can be approached from many angles. It used to be mainly an issue for philosophy of science (see Section 9.5), but is nowadays also often studied in relation to computer algorithms, within the field of artificial intelligence (AI, see [RN95] for a general introduction). As Marvin Minsky, one of the founders of AI, wrote: "Artificial Intelligence is the science of making machines do things that would require intelligence if done by man" [Min68, p. v]. Given this view, the study of induction is indeed part of AI, since learning from examples certainly requires intelligence if done by man.

The branch of AI which studies learning is called *machine learning*. Some of the main approaches in machine learning are learning in *neural networks*, *decision trees*, *genetic algorithms*, and finally *logic*. The latter approach is nowadays called inductive logic programming (ILP). Stephen Muggleton, when introducing the name inductive logic programming, defined this field as the intersection of machine learning and logic programming. Thus ILP studies learning from examples, within the framework provided by clausal logic. Here the examples and background knowledge are given as clauses, and the theory that is to be induced from these, is also to consist of clauses. Using logic has some important advantages over other approaches used in machine learning:

- Logic in general, and first-order logic in particular, is a very well developed mathematical field, providing ILP with a large stock of well understood concepts, techniques, and results.

- Logic provides a uniform and very expressive means of representation: the background knowledge and the examples, as well as the induced theory, can all be represented as formulas in a clausal language. In particular, due to this uniform representation, the use of background knowledge fits very naturally within a logical approach towards machine learning. Theory and background knowledge are of the same form, they just derive from different sources: theory comes from inductive learning, while background knowledge is provided by the user of the system.

- Knowledge represented as rules and facts over certain predicates comes much closer to natural language than any of the other approaches in machine learning. Hence the set of clauses that an ILP system induces is often much easier to interpret for us humans than, for instance, a neural network.

In the next section, we will define the normal problem setting of induction in the precise terms of clausal logic, and introduce some terminology. In Sections 9.3 and 9.4 we discuss some alternatives to this setting. We end the chapter by giving a brief survey of the history of induction in general, and ILP in particular.

9.2 The Normal Problem Setting for ILP

Inductive logic programming concerns learning a general theory from given examples of the predicates that we want to learn, possibly taking background knowledge into account. We can distinguish between two kinds of examples: positive examples, which are true, and negative examples, which are false. Usually, the positive and negative examples are given as sets E^+ and E^-, respectively, of *ground atoms*. However, ground *clauses* are also sometimes used as examples, for instance in a *least generalization* approach. In fact, there is no theoretical reason against using non-ground clauses as examples, though this is rather unusual.

In ILP, both background knowledge and the induced theory are represented as finite sets of clauses. In the ordinary setting, after the learning is done, the theory together with the background knowledge should imply all given positive examples in E^+ (*completeness*), and should not contradict the given negative examples in E^- (*consistency*). Completeness and consistency together form *correctness*.

Before going into the formal definitions, let us look at a simple example. Suppose $E^+ = \{P(0), P(s^4(0)), P(s^8(0))\}$, $E^- = \{P(s(0)), P(s^3(0))\}$, and the background knowledge is empty. Then a program containing the following clauses

1. $P(s^2(x)) \leftarrow P(x)$
2. $P(0)$

will imply all positive examples (completeness) and no negative ones (consistency), and hence is correct.

If we consider only definite programs as theories, it suffices for consistency to require that no negative examples are implied. However, this need not be the case if we allow arbitrary clauses. For instance, let $\Sigma = \{P(a) \vee P(b)\}$ and $E^- = \{P(a), P(b)\}$. Then Σ does not imply any of the negative examples, yet it still contradicts the negative examples: E^- tells us that $P(a)$ and $P(b)$ are both false, so the clause $P(a) \vee P(b)$ from Σ cannot be true. In other words, the set $\{(P(a) \vee P(b)), \neg P(a), \neg P(b)\}$ is unsatisfiable. In order to rule out cases like this, we have to complicate the definition of consistency a bit, requiring that Σ, together with the *negations* of the negative examples, is consistent (satisfiable). This is formally defined below.

Definition 9.1 A *theory* is a finite set of clauses. $\diamond$

Definition 9.2 If $\Sigma = \{C_1, C_2, \ldots\}$ is a (possibly infinite) set of clauses, then we use $\overline{\Sigma}$ to denote $\{\neg C_1, \neg C_2, \ldots\}$. $\diamond$

Definition 9.3 Let Σ be a theory, and E^+ and E^- be sets of clauses. Σ is *complete* with respect to E^+, if $\Sigma \models E^+$. Σ is *consistent* with respect to E^-, if $\Sigma \cup \overline{E^-}$ is satisfiable. Σ is *correct* with respect to E^+ and E^-, if Σ is complete with respect to E^+ and consistent with respect to E^-.[1] $\diamond$

Example 9.4 Suppose we are given $E^+ = \{P(0), P(s^4(0)), P(s^8(0))\}$, and $E^- = \{P(s^2(0)), P(s^3(0))\}$. Then a theory Σ that consists of

1. $P(s^2(x)) \leftarrow P(x)$
2. $P(0)$

is complete with respect to E^+, because it implies every positive example. On the other hand, we have $\Sigma \models P(s^2(0))$. Hence $\Sigma \cup \overline{E^-}$ is unsatisfiable, which means that Σ is not consistent with respect to E^-. $\triangleleft$

Note the following property of consistency:

Proposition 9.5 *Let Σ be a theory, and $E^- = \{e_1, e_2, \ldots\}$ be a set of clauses. Then Σ is not consistent with respect to E^- iff there are $i_1, \ldots, i_n$ such that $\Sigma \models e_{i_1} \vee \ldots \vee e_{i_n}$.[2]*

Proof Σ is not consistent with respect to $E^- = \{e_1, e_2, \ldots\}$ iff
$\Sigma \cup \{\neg e_1, \neg e_2, \ldots\}$ is unsatisfiable iff (using Theorem 2.42)
there are $i_1, \ldots, i_n$ such that $\Sigma \cup \{\neg e_{i_1}, \ldots, \neg e_{i_n}\}$ is unsatisfiable iff
there are $i_1, \ldots, i_n$ such that $\Sigma \cup \{\neg(e_{i_1} \vee \ldots \vee e_{i_n})\}$ is unsatisfiable iff (by
Proposition 2.37) there are $i_1, \ldots, i_n$ such that $\Sigma \models e_{i_1} \vee \ldots \vee e_{i_n}$. $\square$

By the previous proposition it is *necessary* for the consistency of Σ with respect to E^- that Σ does not imply one of the clauses in E^-. As we saw above, in the general case of arbitrary clauses this is not *sufficient* for consistency:

---

[1] If we are working with normal programs as theories and background knowledge, these definitions may be changed somewhat to take into account the *completion* of the program. If Π is a normal program, we can say Π is *complete* with respect to E^+ if $comp(\Pi) \models E^+$, and *consistent* with respect to E^- if $comp(\Pi) \cup \overline{E^-}$ is satisfiable.

[2] Note that $e_{i_1} \vee \ldots \vee e_{i_n}$ need not be a clause, for instance if $e_1 = \forall x\, P(x)$ and $e_2 = \forall y\, Q(y)$. However, if the $e_{i_1}, \ldots, e_{i_n}$ are standardized apart (in particular, if each e_{i_j} is ground), then $e_{i_1} \vee \ldots \vee e_{i_n}$ is logically equivalent to the clause consisting of all literals in the e_{i_j}'s. For instance, $\forall x\, P(x) \vee \forall y\, Q(y)$ is equivalent to the clause $P(x) \vee Q(y)$.

$\Sigma = \{P(a) \lor P(b)\}$ is not consistent with respect to $E^- = \{P(a), P(b)\}$, even though $\Sigma \not\models P(a)$ and $\Sigma \not\models P(b)$. However, in the quite common case where the possible theories are restricted to definite programs and the examples to ground atoms, it is sufficient:

Proposition 9.6 *Let Π be a definite program, and E^- be a set of ground atoms. Then Π is consistent with respect to E^- iff $\Pi \not\models e$, for every $e \in E^-$.*

Proof Π is consistent with respect to $E^- = \{e_1, e_2, \ldots\}$ iff
$\Pi \cup \{\neg e_1, \neg e_2, \ldots\}$ is satisfiable iff (by Proposition 3.30)
$\Pi \cup \{\neg e_1, \neg e_2, \ldots\}$ has a Herbrand model iff
M_Π does not contain any $e \in E^-$ iff (by Theorem 7.16)
$\Pi \not\models e$, for every $e \in E^-$. □

Several deviations from correctness are the following:

Definition 9.7 Let Σ be a theory, and E^+ and E^- be sets of clauses. Σ is *too strong* with respect to E^-, if Σ is not consistent with respect to E^-. Σ is *too weak* with respect to E^+, if Σ is not complete with respect to E^+.

Σ is *overly general* with respect to E^+ and E^-, if Σ is complete with respect to E^+ but not consistent with respect to E^-. Σ is *overly specific* with respect to E^+ and E^-, if Σ is consistent with respect to E^- but not complete with respect to E^+. ◇

Note that Σ is correct iff it is neither too strong nor too weak.

Example 9.8 Suppose we are given $E^+ = \{P(s(0)), P(s^3(0)), P(s^5(0)), P(s^7(0))\}$, and $E^- = \{P(0), P(s^2(0)), P(s^4(0))\}$. Then a theory Σ

1. $P(s^2(x)) \leftarrow P(x)$
2. $P(s(0))$

is correct with respect to E^+ and E^-. Note that Σ can be viewed as characterizing the odd numbers.

$\Sigma' = \{P(s^2(x))\}$ is both too strong with respect to E^- *and* too weak with respect to E^+. It is too strong because it implies some negative examples, and it is too weak because it does not imply the positive example $P(s(0))$.

$\Sigma'' = \{P(s(x))\}$ is overly general with respect to E^+ and E^-. ◁

Now the learning problem for ILP can be formally defined:

Inductive Logic Programming: Normal problem setting

> **Given:** A finite set of clauses $\mathcal{B}$ (*background knowledge*), and sets of clauses E^+ and E^- (positive and negative *examples*).
> **Find:** A theory Σ, such that $\Sigma \cup \mathcal{B}$ is correct with respect to E^+ and E^-.

Apart from being called the *normal* setting, this setting also sometimes goes under the name of *explanatory* setting, since the theory should, in a sense, be an *explanation* of the examples. As we have emphasized above, E^+ and E^- are most often restricted to ground *atoms*. We may sometimes be learning from scratch. In this case, no background knowledge is present, and $\mathcal{B}$ (the empty set) can be dropped from the problem setting.

Note that a solution Σ does not always exist. The first reason for this is rather trivial: $\mathcal{B} \cup E^+$ may be inconsistent with respect to the negative examples, for instance if $P(a)$ is both a positive and a negative example at the same time. To solve this, we have to require that $\mathcal{B} \cup E^+$ is consistent with respect to E^-.

The second reason for the non-existence of a solution is more profound. Note that our problem setting allows *infinite* sets of examples. One instance of this is Shapiro's setting for model inference, the topic of the next chapter. Here the examples are given in an *enumeration*, which may be infinite. Allowing an infinite number of examples implies, roughly, that there are "more" possible sets of examples than there are theories. Hence a correct theory does not always exist, even when the examples can only be ground atoms and background knowledge is not used, as proved in the next theorem.

The proof of this theorem employs two different "kinds of infinity". The first kind concerns sets containing the same number of elements as the set of *natural* numbers. Such sets are called *enumerably infinite*, or *denumerable*. The second kind of infinite set is called *uncountable*. An example of an uncountable set is the set of *real* numbers. It is well known that the *power set* of an enumerably infinite set S (the set of all subsets of S) is uncountable, and that the latter is "larger" than the former. A more extensive introduction into these matters can be found in many mathematics books, for instance [BJ89].

Theorem 9.9 *There exist sets E^+ and E^- of ground atoms, such that there is no theory which is correct with respect to E^+ and E^-.*

Proof Consider a clausal language $\mathcal{C}$ containing (possibly among others) a function symbol of arity ≥ 1 and a constant a. Let $\mathcal{A}$ be the set of ground atoms in $\mathcal{C}$. If $\Sigma \subseteq \mathcal{C}$ is a theory, let $\mathcal{A}_\Sigma = \{A \in \mathcal{A} \mid \Sigma \models A\}$.

The number of clauses in $\mathcal{C}$ is enumerably infinite. Then because a theory is a finite set of clauses, the number of theories is also enumerably infinite. Thus the number of different $\mathcal{A}_\Sigma$'s induced by all possible theories, is also only enumerably infinite.

The power set of $\mathcal{A}$ is uncountable. Since an uncountable set is much larger than an enumerably infinite one, there must be a set $E^+ \subseteq \mathcal{A}$, such that there is no finite Σ for which $\mathcal{A}_\Sigma = E^+$. Define $E^- = \mathcal{A} \backslash E^+$. Note that for every theory Σ, we have $E^+ \not\subseteq \mathcal{A}_\Sigma$ or $\mathcal{A}_\Sigma \not\subseteq E^+$. If $E^+ \not\subseteq \mathcal{A}_\Sigma$, then Σ is not correct with respect to E^+. On the other hand, if $\mathcal{A}_\Sigma \not\subseteq E^+$, then there is a ground atom A such that $A \in \mathcal{A}_\Sigma$ but $A \notin E^+$, hence $A \in E^-$ and Σ is not consistent with respect to E^-. Therefore a theory Σ is correct with respect to E^+ and E^- only if $\mathcal{A}_\Sigma = E^+$. Hence there is no such correct Σ. $\square$

If E^+ is finite, then $\Sigma = E^+$ will be a correct theory, but a rather uninteresting one. In this case, we would not have learned anything beyond the given examples: the induced theory has no predictive power. To avoid this, we can put some constraints on the theory. For instance, we might demand that Σ contains less clauses than the number of given positive examples. In that case, $\Sigma = E^+$ is ruled out. Since constraints like these mainly depend on the particular application at hand, we will not devote much attention to them.

In any case, if one or more correct theories do exist, then they are "hidden" somewhere in the set of clauses in the language we use. Accordingly, finding a satisfactory theory means that we have to *search* among the permitted clauses: learning is searching for a correct theory [Mit82]. Hence the set of clauses that may be included in the theory is called the *search space*.

The two basic steps in the search for a correct theory are *specialization* and *generalization*. If the current theory together with the background knowledge contradicts the negative examples, it is too strong. Accordingly, it needs to be weakened. That is, we need to find a more specific theory, such that the new theory and the background knowledge are consistent with respect to the negative examples. This is called specialization. On the other hand, if the current theory together with the background knowledge does not imply all positive examples, we need to strengthen the theory: we need to find a more general theory such that all positive examples are implied. This is generalization. Note that a theory may be both too strong and too weak at the same time, witness Σ' in Example 9.8. In this case, both specialization *and* generalization are called for. In general, finding a correct theory amounts to repeatedly adjusting the theory to the examples by means of specialization and generalization steps. Whether a particular theory is too weak or too strong, can be tested using one of the proof procedures we introduced in the previous chapters.

In general, most ILP systems conform roughly to the following scheme:

Input: $\mathcal{B}$, E^+ and E^-.
Output: A theory Σ, such that $\Sigma \cup \mathcal{B}$ is correct with respect to E^+ and E^-.

Start with some initial (possibly empty[3]) theory Σ.
Repeat

    1. If $\Sigma \cup \mathcal{B}$ is too strong, specialize Σ.
    2. If $\Sigma \cup \mathcal{B}$ is too weak, generalize Σ.

until $\Sigma \cup \mathcal{B}$ is correct with respect to E^+ and E^-.
Output Σ.

---

[3] If we start with a non-empty theory Σ, the learning task is sometimes called *theory revision*.

Thus the main operations an ILP system should perform, are specialization and generalization. The following chapters can be considered as an investigation into the properties of a number of different approaches towards specialization and generalization. Each of these can be used when searching for a correct theory.

Flanking the repeat-until-correct cycle of the search for a correct theory, often a learner starts with an initial *pre-processing* phase and ends with a *post-processing* phase. In the pre-processing phase, we may for instance try to detect and eliminate errors in the given examples (*noise*, see Section 19.5 for more on this). The post-processing phase is mainly used to "clean up" the learned theory Σ, for instance by successively removing redundant clauses C for which $\Sigma \cup \mathcal{B} \Leftrightarrow (\Sigma \backslash \{C\}) \cup \mathcal{B}$, or by restructuring Σ in order to improve its comprehensibility or efficiency.

We will now introduce some terminology often used in ILP:

Top-down and bottom-up
One useful distinction among ILP systems concerns the direction in which a system searches. First, there is the *top-down* approach, which starts with a Σ such that $\Sigma \cup \mathcal{B}$ is overly general, and specializes this. Secondly, there is the *bottom-up* approach which starts with a Σ such that $\Sigma \cup \mathcal{B}$ is overly specific, and generalizes this. Admittedly, a top-down system may sometimes locally adapt itself to the examples by a generalization step. Such a generalization step may be needed to correct a (large) earlier specialization step, which made the theory too weak. After the correction, the system continues its general top-down search. Analogously, a bottom-up system may sometimes make a specialization step. Nevertheless, a system can usually be classified in a natural way as top-down or bottom-up, depending on the general direction of its search.

Example 9.10 Consider the sets E^+ and E^- of Example 9.8. Assume the background knowledge is empty. A top-down approach may take the following steps to reach a correct theory.

1. Start with $\Sigma = \{P(x)\}$.
2. This is clearly overly general, since it implies all negative examples. Specialize it to $\Sigma = \{P(s(x)), P(0)\}$.
3. Σ is still too general, for instance, it implies $P(0) \in E^-$. Specialize it to $\Sigma = \{P(s^2(x)), P(s(0))\}$.
4. Now Σ no longer implies $P(0)$, but it is still overly general. When we specialize further to $\Sigma = \{(P(s^2(x)) \leftarrow P(x)), P(s(0))\}$, we end up with a theory that is correct with respect to E^+ and E^-.   ◁

Single- and multiple-predicate learning
We can also distinguish between *single-predicate learning* and *multiple-predicate learning*. In the former case, all given examples are instances of

only one predicate P, and the aim of the learning task is to find a set of clauses which implies $P(x_1, \ldots, x_n)$ just for those tuples $\langle x_1, \ldots, x_n \rangle$ whose denotation "belongs" to the concept denoted by P. In other words, the set of clauses should "recognize" the instances of P. Though all examples have the same predicate P, other predicate symbols (pre-defined in the background knowledge) may be used to construct a correct theory.

In multiple-predicate learning, the examples are instances of more than one predicate. Note that multiple-predicate learning cannot always be split into several single-predicate problems, because the different predicates in a multiple-predicate learning task may be related.

Batch learning and incremental learning
The distinction between *batch learning* and *incremental learning* concerns the way the examples are given. In batch learning, we are given all examples E^+ and E^- right at the outset. This has the advantage that errors in the given examples (noise) can be measured and dealt with by applying statistical techniques to the set of all examples.

On the other hand, in incremental learning the examples are given one by one, and the system each time adjusts its theory to the examples given so far, before obtaining the next example.

Interactive and non-interactive
Interactive systems can interact with their user in order to obtain some additional information. For instance, they can ask the user whether some particular ground atom is true or not. In this way, an interactive system generates some of its own examples during the search. A non-interactive system does not have the possibility to interact with the user.

Bias
Bias concerns anything which constrains the search for theories [UM82]. Following [NRA+96], we will distinguish three kinds of bias: *language* bias, *search* bias, and *validation* bias.

Language bias has to do with constraints on the clauses in the search space. These may for instance be a restriction to Horn clauses, to clauses without function symbols, to clauses with at most n literals, etc. The more restrictions we put on clauses, the smaller the search space, and hence the faster a system will finish its search. On the other hand, restrictions on the permitted clauses may cause many good theories to be overlooked. For example, we may restrict the search space to clauses of at most 5 literals, but if all correct theories contain clauses of 6 or more literals, no solution will be found. Thus there is in general a *trade-off* between the efficiency of an ILP system, and the quality of the theory it comes up with.

One important issue concerning language bias is the capability of a system to introduce new predicates when needed. A restriction of the language to the predicates already in use in the background theory and the examples may sometimes be too strict. In that case *predicate invention* (the automatic introduction of new useful predicates) is called for. For example, if we are learning about family relations, and neither the examples nor the background knowledge contain a predicate for *parenthood*, it would be nice if the system could introduce such a useful predicate itself. Some more on language restrictions and predicate invention may be found in Sections 19.2 and 19.3, respectively.

Search bias has to do with the way a system searches its space of permitted clauses. One extreme is exhaustive search, which searches the search space completely. However, usually exhaustive search would take far too much time, so the search has to be guided by certain *heuristics*. These indicate which parts of the space are searched, and which are ignored. Again, this may cause the system to overlook some good theories, so here we see another trade-off between efficiency and the quality of the final theory.

If a system has found that a correct theory is not available using its present language and search bias, it can try again using a more general language and/or a more thorough search procedure. This is called a *bias shift*.

Finally, *validation* bias concerns the stopping criterion of the learner: when should we stop the search? One obvious criterion would be to stop as soon as we have found a correct theory. However, it may be worthwhile to search a little further. For instance, if we have found a correct theory containing 100 clauses, but we have reason to believe that there also exist correct theories with only 10 clauses, we may not be satisfied with the first correct theory. On the other hand, it may sometimes also be worthwhile to stop the search when the theory is not yet quite correct—for instance, when a few positive examples are not implied and/or a few negative negative examples *are* implied. This has to do with noise handling, for which see Section 19.5.

9.3   The Nonmonotonic Problem Setting

The normal problem setting that we introduced above is used in some form or other by the majority of ILP researchers. However, in recent years a family of other problem settings has appeared. These settings have in common that the induced theory should no longer *imply* the positive examples, but should be a set of general relations that are *true* for the examples. Examples are Helft's *nonmonotonic* setting for induction [Hel89, DD94, Dže95b], Flach's *weak* confirmation [Fla92] and *confirmatory* induction [Fla94, Fla95]. These settings are well suited for the problem of *data mining* or *knowledge discovery*: given a large amount of data, find "interesting" regularities among the data.

We will describe a simple variant of the nonmonotonic setting, which we adapt from [Dže95b]. Here the examples are not clauses, but *Herbrand interpretations*. Given is a set $\mathcal{I}^+$ of Herbrand interpretations which are positive examples, and a set $\mathcal{I}^-$ of Herbrand interpretations which are negative examples. The aim of the learning task is simply to find a set of clauses that is true under every positive example, and false under every negative one. Each of those interpretation may be seen as a kind of "description" of a situation, and the induced theory expresses regularities that hold in the positive examples and not in the negative ones.

Inductive Logic Programming: Nonmonotonic problem setting

> **Given:** Two sets $\mathcal{I}^+$ and $\mathcal{I}^-$ of Herbrand interpretations (positive and negative *examples*).
> **Find:** A theory Σ which is true under each $I \in \mathcal{I}^+$ and false under each $I \in \mathcal{I}^-$.

Quite often, only positive examples are used. As a further requirement to this setting, we may demand that if $C \in \Sigma$ is one of the induced clauses, then it should be "most general" in the sense that any clause more general than C is false under at least one of the positive examples. There is one major problem with this setting, namely that we cannot handle *infinite* Herbrand interpretations very well as examples. A possible solution for this is to restrict attention to languages with only a finite number of constants, and no function symbols of arity ≥ 1. In this case, the Herbrand base will be finite, and each Herbrand interpretation will be a finite set of ground atoms.

In the following chapters, we will usually assume we are working in the normal problem setting. However, in both the normal and the nonmonotonic settings the main activity of a learning system is a *search* for appropriate clauses, and specialization or generalization of clausal theories are the main operations in this search. This means that the techniques of the next chapters are applicable within the nonmonotonic setting as well.

9.4 Abduction

One further setting has to be mentioned, because it has strong links with induction. This is the setting for *abduction*, which was first introduced by the philosopher Charles Sanders Peirce [Pei58]. The logical form of abduction is roughly the same as for induction [KKT93, DK96], and indeed the distinctions between induction and abduction are somewhat blurry. Both proceed from given examples and some background knowledge, and the aim is to find a theory that, together with the background knowledge, "explains" the examples. However, the theory that abduction produces should be a *particular fact*, which together with the background knowledge explains the examples. This is different from induction, which should produce a *general theory*.

As an informal example, suppose you are Robinson Crusoe on his island, and you see a strange human footprint in the sand. Since you know that human footprints are produced by human beings, and the footprint is not your own, you can conclude on the basis of your background knowledge that someone else has visited your island. The hypothesis that someone else has visited the island explains the presence of the footprint (the example). Inferring this particular explanation is a case of abduction.

9.5   A Brief History of the Field

Like most other scientific disciplines, the study of induction started out as a part of philosophy. Philosophers particularly focused on the role induction plays in the empirical sciences. For instance, the Greek philosopher Aristotle characterized science roughly as deduction from first principles, which were to be obtained by induction from experience [Ari60].[4]

After the Middle Ages, the philosopher Francis Bacon [Bac94] again stressed the importance of induction (in the modern sense) from experience as the main scientific activity. In later centuries, induction was taken up by many philosophers. David Hume [Hum56, Hum61] formulated what is nowadays called the problem of induction, or Hume's problem: how can induction from a finite number of cases result in knowledge about the infinity of cases to which an induced general rule applies? What justifies inferring a general rule (or "law of nature") from a finite number of cases? Surprisingly, Hume's answer was that there is *no* such justification. In his view, it is simply a psychological fact about humans beings that when we observe some particular pattern recur in different cases (without observing counterexamples to the pattern), we tend to expect this pattern to appear in all similar cases. In Hume's view, this inductive expectation is a *habit*, analogous to the habit of a dog who runs to the door after hearing his master call, expecting to be let out. Later philosphers such as John Stuart Mill [Mil58] tried to answer Hume's problem by stating conditions under which an inductive inference is justified. Other philosophers who made important comments on induction were Stanley Jevons [Jev74] and Charles Sanders Peirce [Pei58].

In our century, induction was mainly taken up by philosophers and mathematicians who were also involved in the development and application of formal logic. Their treatment of induction was often in terms of the probability or the "degree of confirmation" that a particular theory or hypothesis receives from available empirical data. Some of the main contributors are Bertrand Russell [Rus80, Rus48], Rudolf Carnap [Car52, Car50], Carl Hempel [Hem45a, Hem45b, Hem66], Hans Reichenbach [Rei49], and Nelson Goodman [Goo83]. Particularly in Goodman's work, an increasing number of unexpected conceptual problems appeared for induction.

In the 1950s and 1960s, induction was sworn off by philosophers of science such as Karl Popper [Pop59]. However, in roughly those same years it was recognized in the rapidly expanding field of artificial intelligence that the knowledge an AI system needs to perform its tasks, should not all be handcoded into the system beforehand. Instead, it is much more efficient to provide the system with a relatively small amount of knowledge, and with the ability to adapt itself to the situations it encounters—to *learn* from its experience. Thus the study of induction switched from philosophy to artificial intelligence.

---

[4]Though it should be noted that Aristotle's concept of induction was rather different from the modern one, involving the "seeing" of the "essential forms" of examples.

In AI, many different approaches towards inductive learning exist, for instance using neural networks or genetic algorithms. Two approaches which pre-date ILP and which greatly influenced its development, are *attribute-value learning* and *inductive inference*. In attribute-value learning, an example is an object whose attributes have certain values. For example, an example 'flipper' might be described by "color = grey, length = 3m, swims = yes, mammal = yes, species = dolphin", and the goal of the induction might be to find rules that describe when an object belongs to a certain class (for instance the class of dolphins). A prime example of attribute-value learning is J. R. Quinlan's work on the induction of decision trees for classifying given examples [Qui86, Qui93].

While attribute-value learning is a very experimental and application-oriented area, the field of inductive inference is much more abstract and theoretical in nature. The issue here is in which cases an unknown target set can be identified after reading only a finite number of examples for this set. Gold's fundamental paper [Gol67] may be regarded as its birth; an overview of results can be found in [AS83]. Most work in inductive inference has dealt with learning formal languages and automata, though it has also been applied to clausal logic [ASY92].

In the last 10 or so years, inductive logic programming has grown to become one of the most prominent approaches in machine learning, particularly among European researchers. ILP may be seen as lying somewhere in between attribute-value learning and inductive inference. It is more theoretical in nature than attribute-value learning, and its representational formalism (clausal logic) has greater expressive power than the attribute-value framework. On the other hand, ILP is more practical and more concerned with considerations of efficiency and applicability than inductive inference.[5]

Claude Sammut [Sam93] starts his article on the (ancient) history of ILP with the work of Bruner, Goodnow, and Austin [BGA56] in cognitive psychology. They analyzed the way human beings learn concepts from positive and negative instances (examples) of that concept. In the early 1960s, Ranan Banerji [Ban64] used first-order logic as a representational tool for such concept learning.

Around 1970, Gordon Plotkin [Plo70, Plo71a, Plo71b] was probably the first to formalize induction in terms of *clausal* logic. His idea was to generalize given ground clauses (positive examples) by computing their *least generalization*. This generalization could be relative to background knowledge consisting of ground literals. Plotkin's work, which is related to that of John Reynolds [Rey70], is still quite prominent within ILP. Clauses are still used by virtually everyone for expressing theory, examples and background knowledge, and Plotkin's use of *subsumption* as a notion of generality is also widespread. During the 1970s, Plotkin's work was continued by Steven

---

[5]We can also discern traces of the influence of philosophy of science in ILP. For example, Plotkin's work was influenced by Hempel, and Shapiro's by Popper. See also [Fla94].

Vere [Ver75, Ver77], while Brian Cohen's incremental system CONFUCIUS was inspired by Banerji.

In the early 1980s, Sammut's MARVIN [Sam81, SB86] was a direct descendant of CONFUCIUS. MARVIN is an interactive concept learner, which employs both generalization and specialization. At around the same time, Ehud Shapiro [Sha81b, Sha81a] defined his setting for *model inference*, and contructed his model inference algorithm. This is a top-down algorithm aimed at finding *complete axiomatizations* of given enumerations of examples. Shapiro's work was greatly influenced by work in the field of inductive inference. His framework contains many seminal ideas, in particular the use of the *Backtracing Algorithm* for finding false clauses in the theory, and the concept of a *refinement operator*, used for specializing a theory. Shapiro implemented his algorithm, though only for Horn clauses, in his model inference system MIS. He later incorporated this work in his PhD thesis [Sha83], as part of a system for debugging definite programs.

Then in the second half of the 1980s—no doubt partly as a consequence of the growing popularity of logic programming and PROLOG—research concerning machine learning within a clausal framework increased rapidly. Wray Buntine [Bun86, Bun88] generalized subsumption, in order to overcome some of its limitations. Stephen Muggleton built his system DUCE [Mug87], aimed at generalizing given *propositional* clauses. It became clear that DUCE's generalization operators could be seen as inversions of resolution steps. Thus in [MB88] Muggleton, together with Buntine, introduced *inverse resolution*. They implemented inverse resolution, both as an operator for making generalization steps and as a tool for predicate invention in CIGOL. In the next years, inverse resolution drew a lot of attention and sparked off much new research.

Some early alternatives to inverse resolution were implemented in FOIL, LINUS, and GOLEM. FOIL is based on a downward refinement operator guided by information-based search heuristics, in which Quinlan upgraded his earlier work on decision trees to Horn clauses. LINUS was developed by Nada Lavrač and Sašo Džeroski. It solves ILP problems by transforming them to an attribute-value representation, and then applying one of several possible attribute-value learners to learn a general theory from this simpler representation. Muggleton and Feng's GOLEM was in a way a return to Plotkin: it is based on Plotkin's relative least generalization, though with additional restrictions for the sake of efficiency. These systems, as well as others, are described in some more detail in Section 19.6, at the end of this book.

In 1990, Stephen Muggleton introduced the name inductive logic programming, and defined this field as the intersection of machine learning and logic programming [Mug90, Mug91a]. In the next year he organized, together with Pavel Brazdil, the first International Workshop on Inductive Logic Programming, bringing together a number of researchers involved in learning from examples in a clausal framework. Since 1991 these international work-

shops have been repeated every year, establishing ILP as a flourishing field
of inquiry. Literally dozens of systems have been implemented since, and
have been applied quite successfully in various fields. Among the more theoretical topics, formal learnability theory, predicate invention, data mining
in the nonmonotonic setting, handling real numbers, and handling of noisy
examples have gained an increasing amount of attention in recent years.

9.6 Summary

Induction (learning from examples) used to be mainly a subject for philosophy, but is nowadays also studied within machine learning, a branch of artificial intelligence. *Inductive logic programming* is the intersection of machine
learning and logic programming. Accordingly, ILP is concerned with learning
from examples within a framework of formal—usually clausal—logic.

In the *normal* problem setting, we have a finite set of clauses $\mathcal{B}$ (*background knowledge*), and sets E^+ and E^- of positive and negative *examples*.
A finite set of clauses is called a *theory*. A theory Σ is *complete* if Σ implies
all positive examples, and *consistent* if Σ does not contradict the negative examples. Σ is *correct* if it is both complete and consistent; *too strong* if it is not
consistent; *too weak* if it is not complete; *overly general* if it is complete but
not consistent; and *overly specific* if it is consistent but not complete. In the
normal problem setting, our aim is to find a theory Σ, such that $\Sigma \cup \mathcal{B}$ is correct with respect to E^+ and E^-. To find such a Σ, we have to *search* through
the set of clauses. The two main operations in the search are *specialization*
(weakening the theory) and *generalization* (strengthening the theory).

In the alternative, *nonmonotonic* problem setting, each example is a Herbrand interpretation. We are given a set $\mathcal{I}^+$ of positive examples and a set
$\mathcal{I}^-$ of negative examples. Our aim now is to find a theory which is true under
every positive example and false under every negative one. Search by means
of specialization and generalization is the main activity in this setting as well.

Chapter 10

The Framework for Model Inference

10.1 Introduction

One of the most prominent problems in ILP is the *model inference problem*, introduced by Ehud Shapiro in his seminal paper [Sha81b]. Some parts of his framework, particularly *admissibility* and the *Backtracing Algorithm*, will be discussed extensively in this chapter. Other parts will be described in less detail, either because they are mainly of historical interest, or because they serve as a motivation for more formal analysis in later chapters (see particularly the discussion of refinement operators in Chapter 17).

The model inference problem is concerned with characterizing certain concepts in some domain. Given a domain, a concept is a particular relation that holds between some elements in the domain. Such a relation can be expressed in two ways: either by giving all instances of the relation explicitly, or by giving the rules which characterize those instances. The former is usually called the *extension* of a relation, the latter the *intension*.

Expressing a relation in these two ways is similar to expressing a set in two ways. For example, consider the domain $D = \{0, 1, 2, 3, 4\}$. The relation $R = \{(0, 1), (1, 2), (2, 3), (3, 4)\}$ can also be expressed as $R = \{(x, y) \in D \times D \mid y = x + 1\}$. In the first representation, the set of all 4 instances of the relation R is given explicitly, while in the second representation we only give the rule $y = x + 1$ which characterizes R. Particularly in a large domain, where we have relations with many instances, the second representation is much more compact and useful than the first.

The model inference problem is the problem of discovering the characterizing rules for certain concepts from given instances of those concepts, in the context of logic. Suppose we have a first-order language with a binary predicate symbol P, successor function s, and constant 0. Translating the previous relation R to this language, the instances of the concept are represented by the ground atoms $P(0, s(0))$, $P(s(0), s^2(0))$, $P(s^2(0), s^3(0))$, and $P(s^3(0), s^4(0))$. Making the link with the normal problem setting of the previous chapter, these instances are *positive examples* for the concept. As *negative* examples, we have for instance $P(s^2(0), s^1(0))$, $P(s^3(0), s^5(0))$, which are not in the concept. Given these examples, we could use $\{P(x, s(x))\}$ as a set of rules which characterizes the concept R in the domain $\{0, 1, 2, 3, 4\}$, thereby solving this particular model inference problem.

10.2 Formalizing the Problem

In this section we will formalize the model inference problem. It will turn out to be a special case of the normal problem setting for ILP that we defined in the last chapter. The characterizing rules will be formalized as a "complete axiomatization". To find such an axiomatization, we will need an *enumeration* or an *oracle* to obtain the truth values of the examples.

10.2.1 Enumerations and the Oracle

Let us consider a clausal language $\mathcal{C}$ with finitely many constants, function and predicate symbols. We distinguish two subsets of $\mathcal{C}$, namely $\mathcal{C}_o$ and $\mathcal{C}_h$, such that $\mathcal{C}_o \subseteq \mathcal{C}_h \subseteq \mathcal{C}$. $\mathcal{C}_o$, the *observational language*, is the language in which the positive and negative examples are formulated. Usually, this will be the set of ground atoms or the set of ground literals. $\mathcal{C}_h$, the *hypothesis language*, is the language we use to formulate our theory. For technical reasons, we assume the empty clause $\square$ is a member of $\mathcal{C}_h$.

As we explained informally above, we want to learn the rules in $\mathcal{C}_h$ that characterize concepts, each of which is represented by a set of ground atoms. More precisely, suppose we have some domain D, and several concepts over this domain. Also suppose $\mathcal{C}$ contains a predicate symbol for each of the concepts over the domain. If we can pair up each element in the domain with a ground term in the language, then we can represent each concept by giving all its instances as ground atoms in the language. Doing this for each of the concepts, we obtain a (possibly infinite) *Herbrand interpretation* I of the language, in which each concept is represented by its instances as ground atoms. Our task is to learn the characterizing rules from this interpretation.

All information about I that is available for our learning task is given by examples from $\mathcal{C}_o$. Since it would be rather hard to swallow the complete set of examples from $\mathcal{C}_o$ at once, it is assumed that the examples are given one by one, as a sequence of facts. This is called an *enumeration* of $\mathcal{C}_o$.

Definition 10.1 Let $\mathcal{C}$ be a clausal language, $\mathcal{C}_o \subseteq \mathcal{C}$, and I a Herbrand interpretation. If $\alpha \in \mathcal{C}_o$ and V is the truth value of α under I, then the pair (α, V) is called a *fact of I*. If $V = T$, then α is called a *positive example of I*. If $V = F$, α is a *negative example of I*. $\diamond$

Definition 10.2 Let C be a clausal language, $C_o \subseteq C$, and I a Herbrand interpretation. An *enumeration of C_o under I* is a sequence $F_1, F_2, \ldots$ of facts of I, such that each $\alpha \in C_o$ occurs in at least one fact $F_i = (\alpha, V)$. $\diamond$

Note that in Shapiro's sense of the word, every fact in the enumeration constitutes an 'example', not just the ones that a learner has already seen. Thus an enumeration contains all there is to know about C_o. A device like this should be given as input to an algorithm for solving model inference problems, for without sufficient knowledge of C_o the algorithm would not always be able to find adequate theories.

Another device that is useful in model inference is an *oracle*, which answers questions about the concepts in the domain. For any formula $\alpha \in C_o$, it can return α's truth value under I. Thus the oracle has to have "knowledge" about the part of the interpretation I that pertains to C_o. Two justifications for assuming an oracle can be given:

1. Compare model inference with the work of a scientist. The scientist may not know the general rules that characterize the concepts over his domain of inquiry, but he can obtain knowledge about certain specific, observable instances of those concepts by doing experiments. Posing a question to an oracle in model inference is similar to doing an experiment in science, which is like "posing a question to nature".

2. When learning, a student may have a teacher who can answer questions on particular instances of the concepts. It need not be the case here that the student only learns what the teacher already knows. We only assume the teacher has sufficient knowledge of the instances of the concepts. The teacher may know all about the particular instances of the concepts, and yet be pleasantly surprised by the characterizing rules that a smart student comes up with. Translating this analogy to model inference, the oracle acts as the teacher, while the learning algorithm is the student.

If we assume the set C_o can be summed up, then an enumeration can be constructed from an oracle, and vice versa. Suppose we have an oracle. Then we can obtain an enumeration of C_o under I by just enumerating the formulas in C_o one by one, adding on their truth values which can be obtained by posing questions to the oracle.

Conversely, if we have an enumeration of facts, we can construct an oracle, as follows. Suppose the question "is α true under I" is put to the oracle, where $\alpha \in C_o$. We can just sum up all the facts in the enumeration until we come to (α, V). V is then the answer to the question posed to the oracle. So we need not give both an enumeration *and* an oracle as input to a model inference algorithm: the one can be constructed from the other.

10.2.2   Complete Axiomatizations and Admissibility

Given an enumeration and/or an oracle for I, we want to find a theory containing a finite number of rules that characterize the concepts represented in I. We will now define what constitutes a "good" theory: a finite subset of C_h is a good theory if it is both true under I, and implies exactly those formulas from the observational language C_o that are true under I. Such a theory is called a C_o-complete axiomatization of I; the model inference problem is the problem of finding such an axiomatization.

Definition 10.3 Let C be a clausal language, $C_o \subseteq C$, and I a Herbrand interpretation. Then we use C_o^I to denote the true members of C_o: $C_o^I = \{\alpha \in C_o \mid \alpha$ is true under $I\}$. $\diamond$

Definition 10.4 Let C be a clausal language, $C_o \subseteq C_h \subseteq C$, and I a Herbrand interpretation. A theory $\Sigma \subseteq C_h$ is called a C_o-complete axiomatization of I if Σ is true under I, and $\Sigma \models C_o^I$. $\diamond$

A theory Σ which implies all positive and no negative examples may still be false under I. For instance, suppose $C_h = \{P(x), P(a), P(b), P(c), \Box\}$, $C_o = \{P(a), P(b)\}$, and $I = \{P(a), P(b)\}$. Then the only information the examples can give us, is that $P(a)$ and $P(b)$ are true under I. We do not consider $P(c)$ as an example, since $P(c) \notin C_o$. In the light of these two examples from C_o, $\Sigma = \{P(x)\}$ would be a correct theory. Nevertheless, $P(x)$ is false under I because $P(c)$ is false under I. The problem here is that C_o is not "rich" enough, compared to C_h. Knowing all there is to know about C_o is not enough in this case to know whether clauses in Σ are true under I. Clearly this situation is undesirable. To solve it, we lay down an *admissibility* requirement for the relation between C_o and C_h:

Definition 10.5 Let C_o and C_h be sets of clauses, such that $C_o \subseteq C_h$. We say the pair (C_o, C_h) is *admissible*, if for every Herbrand interpretation I and every satisfiable theory $\Sigma \subseteq C_h$, $\{\alpha \in C_o \mid \Sigma \models \alpha\} = C_o^I$ implies that Σ is true under I. $\diamond$

The pair (C_o, C_h) is admissible if a satisfiable theory which implies all positive and no negative examples, is also *true*. In other words, if a clause in the theory is false under I, then this can be detected from the examples; any false but satisfiable theory should be refutable by facts. Note that if $C_o = C_h$, then the pair (C_o, C_h) is surely admissible. As we have seen, letting $C_o = \{P(a), P(b)\}$ and $C_h = \{P(x), P(a), P(b), P(c), \Box\}$, the pair (C_o, C_h) is *not* admissible. The following theorems provide two important admissible pairs.

Theorem 10.6 *Let C be a clausal language, C_o the set of ground atoms in C, and C_h the set of Horn clauses in C. Then the pair (C_o, C_h) is admissible.*

Proof Let I be a Herbrand interpretation, and $\Sigma \subseteq \mathcal{C}_h$ a satisfiable theory such that $\{\alpha \in \mathcal{C}_o \mid \Sigma \models \alpha\} = \mathcal{C}_o^I$. We have to prove that Σ is true under I. Suppose Σ is not true under I. Then there exists a Horn clause $C \in \Sigma$ which is false under I. Since I is a Herbrand interpretation, there is a ground instance C' of C which is false under I. C' is either a definite program clause, or a definite goal.

Suppose $C' = A \leftarrow B_1, \ldots, B_n$ $(n \geq 0)$. Then A is false under I, and each B_i is true under I. So $A \notin \mathcal{C}_o^I$, while $B_i \in \mathcal{C}_o^I$ for every i. Then because $\{\alpha \in \mathcal{C}_o \mid \Sigma \models \alpha\} = \mathcal{C}_o^I$, we have $\Sigma \models B_i$ for every i. However, since also $\Sigma \models C'$ and $C' \cup \{B_1, \ldots, B_n\} \models A$, we must have that $\Sigma \models A$. Then $A \in \mathcal{C}_o^I$, which contradicts the assumption that $A \notin \mathcal{C}_o^I$. Therefore Σ must be true under I.

Suppose $C' = \leftarrow B_1, \ldots, B_n$. C' is false under I, so every B_i is true under I, hence $B_i \in \mathcal{C}_o^I$, for every $1 \leq i \leq n$. Then also $\Sigma \models B_i$, for every i. $B_1 \wedge \ldots \wedge B_n$ and $\neg C'$ are logically equivalent, hence $\Sigma \models \neg C'$. But on the other hand $C \in \Sigma$, so also $\Sigma \models C'$. This contradicts the satisfiability of Σ. Thus Σ must be true under I. $\square$

It is important to note that the definition of 'admissible' only states a requirement for *satisfiable* theories Σ. Suppose we let $\mathcal{C}_h$ be the set of Horn clauses, and $\mathcal{C}_o$ the set of ground atoms. Recall that we assume $\square \in \mathcal{C}_h$. Now let $\Sigma = \{\square\}$, and I be a Herbrand interpretation which makes all ground atoms in the language—hence every formula in $\mathcal{C}_o$—true. Then $\{\alpha \in \mathcal{C}_o \mid \Sigma \models \alpha\} = \mathcal{C}_o = \mathcal{C}_o^I$, but nevertheless Σ is not true under I, because $\square \in \Sigma$. So the requirement of admissibility says nothing about unsatisfiable sets such as $\{\square\}$ or $\{P(x), \leftarrow P(x)\}$.

The previous theorem tells us that (ground atoms, Horn clauses) is admissible. However, if we extend the hypothesis language to the set of general clauses, the pair (ground atoms, general clauses) is not admissible. A propositional example suffices to show this. Suppose the language contains the atoms P, Q, and R, and $\mathcal{C}_o = \{P, Q, R\}$. Let $I = \{R\}$ and $\Sigma = \{R, (P \vee Q)\}$. Then $\{\alpha \in \mathcal{C}_o \mid \Sigma \models \alpha\} = \{R\} = \mathcal{C}_o^I$. $\Sigma \not\models P$ and $\Sigma \not\models Q$. Nevertheless, Σ is false under I, because $P \vee Q$ is false under I. So in this case $\mathcal{C}_o$ is not sufficiently expressive to detect the falsity of Σ.

This means that if we want to use the set of general clauses as hypothesis language, we must make the observational language more expressive than the set of ground atoms. The following theorem tells us that using the set of ground *literals* as observational language will do.

Theorem 10.7 *Let $\mathcal{C}$ be a clausal language, $\mathcal{C}_o$ the set of ground literals in $\mathcal{C}$, and $\mathcal{C}_h$ the set of clauses in $\mathcal{C}$. Then the pair $(\mathcal{C}_o, \mathcal{C}_h)$ is admissible.*

Proof Let I be a Herbrand interpretation, and $\Sigma \subseteq \mathcal{C}_h$ a satisfiable theory such that $\{\alpha \in \mathcal{C}_o \mid \Sigma \models \alpha\} = \mathcal{C}_o^I$. We have to prove that Σ is true under I. Suppose Σ is not true under I. Then there exists a clause $C \in \Sigma$ which is false under I. Since I is a Herbrand interpretation, there is a ground instance C' of C which is false under I.

Suppose $C' = A_1, \ldots, A_k \leftarrow B_1, \ldots, B_n$. Then each A_i is false under I, each B_j is true. This means that for every i, $\neg A_i \in C_o^I$, and for every j, $B_j \in C_o^I$. Thus $\Sigma \models \neg A_i$, for each i, and $\Sigma \models B_j$, for each j. This means that $\Sigma \models \neg C'$. But since also $\Sigma \models C'$, that would contradict the consistency of Σ. Hence Σ must be true under I. □

When we use the admissible pair C_h = clauses and C_o = ground literals, then we should make sure that our theory Σ not only implies all atoms which are true under I, but also all true negative literals. Thus in the example before the theorem, $\Sigma = \{R, \leftarrow P, \leftarrow Q\}$ would be a C_o-complete axiomatization of $I = \{R\}$ (though a rather trivial one).

Let us briefly consider the definition of a correct theory that we gave in Chapter 9. Σ is correct with respect to a set of positive examples E^+ and a set of negative examples E^-, if $\Sigma \models E^+$ (completeness) and $\Sigma \cup \overline{E^-}$ is satisfiable (consistency). In the setting of the present chapter, we have $E^+ = C_o^I$ and $E^- = C_o \backslash C_o^I$. Note that if Σ is a C_o-complete axiomatization of I, then it is correct with respect to E^+ and E^-: we have that $\Sigma \models E^+$, and $\Sigma \cup \overline{E^-}$ is satisfiable, because it has I as a model. Recall from the previous chapter that it is not sufficient for consistency to have that $\Sigma \not\models e$ for all $e \in E^-$. For instance, suppose C_h is a clausal language, C_o is the set of ground atoms in C_h, and $E^- = C_o \backslash C_o^I = \{P(a), P(b)\}$. Then a theory $\Sigma = \{P(a) \vee P(b)\}$ does not imply any member of E^-, yet still Σ is not consistent with respect to E^-, hence false under I, and not a C_o-complete axiomatization of I. This corresponds to the fact that the pair (ground atoms, general clauses) is not admissible.

10.2.3   Formal Statement of the Problem

Using the concepts we have introduced so far, the model inference problem can now be stated more precisely:

> **Given**: A clausal language C, an observational language C_o, and a hypothesis language C_h, such that $C_o \subseteq C_h \subseteq C$ and the pair (C_o, C_h) is admissible. In addition there is an enumeration and/or an oracle for the clauses in C_o under some Herbrand interpretation I of C.
>
> **Find**: A C_o-complete axiomatization of I.

Clearly, this problem is a special case of the normal problem setting of the last chapter. In that setting, the examples were given as sets E^+ and E^-. In the present setting for model inference, those examples are given as an enumeration and/or an oracle. Note that the background knowledge B of the general setting is not mentioned in the present setting. Shapiro himself did not use background knowledge, but it can be included quite easily in the model inference problem, and also in the Model Inference Algorithm which we will see later on in this chapter.

Example 10.8 This example of a model inference problem in the field of elementary arithmetic was given by Shapiro. It has the set of natural numbers as domain, and deals with the concepts of addition and multiplication. The domain is the set of natural numbers, formalized as the ground terms 0, $s(0)$, $s^2(0)$, $s^3(0)$, etc. The language C contains the 3-ary predicates *Plus* and *Times*, and I is the obvious intended interpretation of these two predicates. C_o is the set of ground atoms, and C_h is the set of definite program clauses in C. The enumeration of I might start as follows:

$(Plus(s(0), 0, s(0)), T)$
$(Plus(s^2(0), s^3(0), s^5(0)), T)$
$(Times(0, 0, s(0)), F)$
$(Times(s^2(0), s^2(0), s^4(0)), T)$
$(Plus(0, s(0), s^2(0)), F)$
...

Our aim in solving this model inference problem is to find, after reading a limited number of examples, a theory which implies $Plus(t_1, t_2, t_3)$ iff $t_1 + t_2 = t_3$, and implies $Times(t_1, t_2, t_3)$ iff iff $t_1 * t_2 = t_3$. Such a theory might for instance be a set Σ consisting of the following Horn clauses:

1. $Plus(x, 0, x)$
2. $Plus(x, s(y), s(z)) \leftarrow Plus(x, y, z)$
3. $Times(x, 0, 0)$
4. $Times(x, s(y), z) \leftarrow Times(x, y, w), Plus(w, x, z)$

The reader may wish to verify that indeed $\Sigma \models Plus(t_1, t_2, t_3)$ just in case $t_1 + t_2 = t_3$, and $\Sigma \models Times(t_1, t_2, t_3)$ just in case $t_1 * t_2 = t_3$. Hence this is a C_o-complete axiomatization of I. Or in other words, these clauses are the rules that characterize the concepts *Plus* and *Times*. ◁

Our hope is that we can construct methods or algorithms which are able to find a C_o-complete axiomatization after reading only a limited number of examples. Shapiro takes the following general incremental top-down approach towards solving model inference problems:

1. Start with a very general theory. It should imply anything.
2. Read a new example from the enumeration.
3. Repeat the following:
   If the theory is too strong (w.r.t. the examples read so far), weaken it.
   If the theory is too weak, strengthen it.
   until the theory is correct with respect to the examples read so far.
4. Goto step 2.

Several questions are raised by this approach:

- If the theory is too strong, which clauses should be weakened, and how?
- If the theory is too weak, how can it be made stronger?
- How do we know when we are finished? Or in other words: when should we stop repeating steps 2–4?

These questions will be addressed in the next sections.

10.3   Finding a False Clause by Backtracing

In this section, we will discuss the question of how to weaken a theory which is too strong. If the hypothesis language and the observational language are admissible, then a theory Σ is too strong just in case it implies a negative example, i.e., a member of C_o that is false under I. Now if all the clauses in the theory were true under I, Σ would not imply a false formula. Hence if the theory is too strong, at least one of the clauses in Σ is false under I. Clearly, if we have a false clause in Σ, then deleting this clause from Σ is an obvious way to weaken the theory as a whole.

So it would be very convenient if we had an algorithm which could find a false clause in a too strong theory. Shapiro gives such an algorithm in [Sha81b], called the *Backtracing Algorithm*. The algorithm uses an oracle extensively. It is assumed here that C_o contains the set of ground atoms, so the oracle "knows" the truth value under I of each ground atom. In Shapiro's original formulation, the algorithm is only applied to refutations. We generalize it here to arbitrary deductions. The algorithm works by inspecting a deduction of a negative example. If C_h is the set of general clauses, then this deduction could be an unconstrained or a linear deduction. If C_h contains only Horn clauses, we only need to investigate SLD-deductions. Note that if the languages C_o and C_h become less expressive, then we can also settle for a less powerful proof procedure. For instance, if C_o is the set of ground atoms and C_h is the set of atoms, then subsumption by itself is already a complete proof procedure. In this case, an atom in Σ should be deleted iff it subsumes a negative example.

Suppose $\Sigma \models C$, where C is a clause which is false under I. Then there exists a derivation from Σ of a clause D which subsumes C. Since C is false and D subsumes C, D itself is also false under I. The Backtracing Algorithm takes as input a tree representing a derivation of such a clause D which is false under I. For convenience, we assume that the tree is such that if C_1 is the left parent and C_2 the right parent of some clause in the tree, then the literal resolved upon in C_1 is negative, and the literal resolved upon in C_2 is positive. Clearly, we can do this without loss of generality.

We will now explain how the algorithm searches through the tree. Let us first suppose all clauses in the derivation are ground, and $N_0 = D_1 \vee D_2$ is the root of the tree, with parent clauses $C_1 = \neg A \vee D_1$ and $C_2 = A \vee D_2$. Since the root N_0 is false under I, at least one of its parent clauses is false under I. Because N_0 is false, both D_1 and D_2 are false. If A is true, then the left parent C_1 is false, since it is the disjunction of $\neg A$ and D_1, which are both false. On the other hand, if A is false, then the right parent C_2 is false. Since the truth value of A can be obtained from the oracle, we can find a false parent clause of N_0. Let us call this parent N_1. By the same method, we can find a false parent N_2 of N_1, etc. This way we can work our way upward in the tree, tracing back the false clauses that led to the derivation of the false root N_0. Eventually, we reach a false leaf of the derivation tree: this is a clause in Σ which is false under I.

Example 10.9 We give an example from propositional logic to show the idea behind the algorithm. Let $\Sigma = \{(R \leftarrow P, Q), (P \leftarrow Q), Q\}$, and $I = \{P, Q\}$. Figure 10.1 shows a derivation of the clause R from Σ. However, since R is false under I, at least one of the leaves of the tree must be false under I. We will now systematically trace back the false clauses, starting from the root (the upward arrows show the path along which we proceed):

1. $N_0 = R$. N_0 has $R \leftarrow P$ and P as parent clauses. One of them must be false under I. We already know R is false. $\neg P$ and P are the literals resolved upon, so we ask the oracle about the truth value of P. The oracle answers that P is true. Hence the algorithm selects the false left parent as N_1.

2. $N_1 = R \leftarrow P$. We ask the oracle about the truth value of Q. It is true, so the left parent is chosen as N_2.

3. $N_2 = R \leftarrow P, Q$. This is a leaf of the tree, hence we have found that N_2 is a member of Σ which is false under I.   ◁

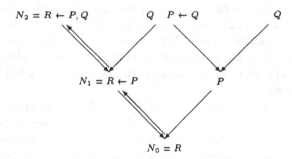

Figure 10.1: Backtracing the derivation of the false clause R

In case of first-order logic, the situation is more complex. Since the oracle only answers questions about *ground* atoms, we have to apply some ground substitution to the atom that is resolved upon before we can give it to the oracle. Suppose we have a non-ground N_0, with parents $C_1 = \neg A_1 \lor D_1$ and $C_2 = A_2 \lor D_2$. For convenience, let us momentarily ignore the use of factors. Since N_0 is false under I, there is a false ground instance $D_1' \lor D_2'$ of N_0, and ground instances $\neg A \vee D_1'$ of C_1 and $A \vee D_2'$ of C_2, where $\neg A$ and A are instances of the respective literals in C_1 and C_2 that were resolved upon in deriving N_0. See Figure 10.2.

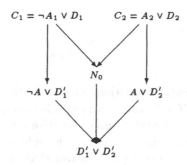

Figure 10.2: Backtracing of non-ground clauses, using ground instances

Now we can apply the same method as before: if the oracle tells us that A is true, then $\neg A \vee D_1'$ is false. This is an instance of C_1, so we can take $N_1 = C_1$ as a false parent of N_0. Otherwise, $A \vee D_2'$ is a false ground instance of C_2, so then C_2 is selected as N_1. In the same way, we can find a false parent N_2 of N_1, etc.

Before giving an example for the first-order logic, we first formally present the Backtracing Algorithm. The algorithm takes a tree $\mathcal{T}$ as input, representing a derivation from Σ of a clause that is false under I, and returns a false leaf of $\mathcal{T}$ (i.e., a false clause from Σ). This algorithm works for unconstrained resolution, for input resolution, and for SLD-resolution. In the latter case, we can ignore the factors, so then $\sigma_1 = \sigma_2 = \varepsilon$.

Algorithm 10.1 (Backtracing Algorithm)
Input: A derivation $\mathcal{T}$ of a clause which is false under I.
Output: A leaf N_k of $\mathcal{T}$ and a ground substitution θ_k for N_k (i.e., $N_k \theta_k$ is ground), such that $N_k \theta_k$ is false under I.

1. Set $k = 0$, N_0 is the root of $\mathcal{T}$, and θ_0 is a ground substitution for N_0 such that $N_0 \theta_0$ is false under I (if $N_0 = \square$, then set $\theta_0 = \varepsilon$).
2. While N_k is not a leaf of $\mathcal{T}$
    1. Let C_1 be the left and C_2 the right parent clause of N_k. Let $\neg A_1 \vee D_1$ and $A_2 \vee D_2$ be the factors of C_1 and C_2 that are used here, and σ_1, σ_2 be the substitutions used in obtaining these factors, respectively. Let $\neg A_1$ and A_2 be the literals resolved upon, with mgu θ. See the figure below for illustration.
    2. Let θ' be a substitution such that $P_{k+1} = A_2 \theta \theta_k \theta'$ is ground.
    3. If $Oracle(P_{k+1}) = T$ then set $N_{k+1} = C_1$ and $\theta_{k+1} = \sigma_1 \theta \theta_k \theta'$ else set $N_{k+1} = C_2$ and $\theta_{k+1} = \sigma_2 \theta \theta_k \theta'$.
    4. Set k to $k + 1$.

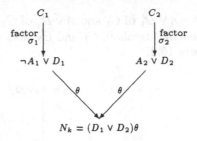

$$N_k = (D_1 \lor D_2)\theta$$

If $\mathcal{T}$ represents a *linear* derivation, a small modification of the algorithm is called for. Namely, if we come to a false side clause which equals a previous center clause, N_{k+1} should become this false center clause where it first appears as resolvent, not the side clause. The side clause is a leaf of $\mathcal{T}$, but we are only interested in finding false leaves that are members of $\mathcal{T}$, hence we cannot terminate the algorithm when we reach such a side clause that equals a previous center clause. Since the side clause may be a *variant* of the corresponding center clause, it is sometimes necessary to rename some of the variables in θ_{k+1}, such that they apply to the variables in the center clause N_{k+1}.

Example 10.10 We will illustrate the algorithm on the refutation tree $\mathcal{T}$ shown in Figure 10.3, which is also given in [Sha81b]. Here the domain is the set of natural numbers, denoted by $0, s(0), s^2(0), \ldots$ as usual. The language contains only one binary predicate $\leq$ (written in infix notation), and the interpretation I makes $t_1 \leq t_2$ true iff the number denoted by t_1 is smaller than or equal to the number denoted by t_2. Let Σ consist of the following:

1. $\leftarrow s(z) \leq 0$ ("no successor is less than or equal to 0")
2. $s(x) \leq y \leftarrow x \leq y$ ("if $x \leq y$, then $x + 1 \leq y$")
3. $0 \leq w$ ("every natural number is greater than or equal to 0")

$\mathcal{T}$ shows an SLD-refutation of Σ. Let us see how the algorithm would work through this tree:

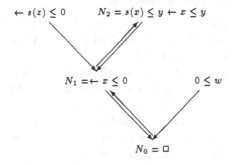

Figure 10.3: Backtracing the refutation of Σ

1. $k = 0$, $N_0 = \square$, $\theta_0 = \varepsilon$.

2. We are dealing with SLD-resolution here, so we can ignore σ_1 and σ_2 (no factors are used here). N_0 has two parent clauses. The literals resolved upon are $\neg(x \leq 0)$ in the left parent, and $0 \leq w$ in the right parent. The mgu is $\theta = \{x/0, w/0\}$. Since $(0 \leq w)\theta\theta_0$ is already ground, $\theta' = \varepsilon$ in this step, and $P_1 = 0 \leq 0$. $Oracle(P_1) = T$, so the algorithm selects the left parent: $N_1 = \leftarrow x \leq 0$. Set $\theta_1 = \theta\theta_0\theta' = \{x/0, w/0\}$, and $k = 1$.

3. N_1 has two parents. The literal resolved upon in the left parent is $\neg(s(z) \leq 0)$, on the right it is $s(x) \leq y$, and the mgu is $\theta = \{z/x, y/0\}$. $(s(x) \leq y)\theta\theta_1 = s(0) \leq 0$ is already ground, so $\theta' = \varepsilon$ again, and $P_2 = s(0) \leq 0$. $Oracle(P_2) = F$, so the algorithm selects the right parent: $N_2 = s(x) \leq y \leftarrow x \leq y$. Set $\theta_2 = \theta\theta_1\theta' = \{x/0, y/0, z/0, w/0\}$, and $k = 2$.

4. N_2 is a leaf of $\mathcal{T}$, so the algorithm terminates.

$\lhd$

We now prove that the algorithm indeed works: if $\mathcal{T}$ represents a derivation of a false clause, then the algorithm finds a false leaf N_k of $\mathcal{T}$, that is, a false clause from Σ.

Theorem 10.11 (Correctness of the Backtracing Algorithm)
Let Σ be a set of clauses, I a Herbrand interpretation, and $\mathcal{T}$ a tree representing a derivation from Σ of a clause which is false under I. Then Algorithm 10.1 with $\mathcal{T}$ as input returns a leaf N_k of $\mathcal{T}$, and a ground substitution θ_k for N_k, such that $N_k\theta_k$ is false under I.

Proof In order to avoid notational overload, we ignore the substitutions σ_1 and σ_2 in this proof. However, the idea should be clear, and the factors can easily be incorporated in the proof. Let k be the number of ground atoms tested by the oracle. We prove the theorem by induction on k.

1. Suppose $k = 0$. Then $\mathcal{T}$ contains only the false root N_0, hence $N_0 \in \Sigma$. The while-loop of the algorithm is never entered. The first step of the algorithm sets θ_0 to a ground substitution such that $N_0\theta_0$ is false under I.

2. Suppose the theorem holds for $k \leq n$. Let $P_1, \ldots, P_{n+1}$ be the ground atoms tested by the oracle during the process. By the induction hypothesis, we can assume the algorithm has "traced back" from N_0 to N_n, and $N_n\theta_n$ is ground and false under I, where N_n is a node in $\mathcal{T}$ having the leaves C_1 and C_2 as parents. See the figure for illustration.

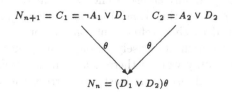

Let θ' be such that $P_{n+1} = A_2\theta\theta_n\theta'$ is ground. We only prove the situation where $Oracle(P_{n+1}) = T$. If P_{n+1} is false, the proof is similar. If P_{n+1} is true, then $N_{n+1} = C_1$ and $\theta_{n+1} = \theta\theta_n\theta'$. We need to prove that θ_{n+1} is a ground substitution for N_{n+1}, and $N_{n+1}\theta_{n+1}$ is false under I.

Firstly, since $N_n\theta_n$ is ground and false under I, and $N_n\theta_n = (D_1 \vee D_2)\theta\theta_n = (D_1 \vee D_2)\theta\theta_n\theta' = (D_1 \vee D_2)\theta_{n+1}$, $D_1\theta_{n+1}$ is ground and false under I. Secondly, $A_1\theta_{n+1} = A_1\theta\theta_n\theta' = A_2\theta\theta_n\theta' = P_{n+1}$ is ground and true under I, so $\neg A_1\theta_{n+1}$ is ground and false under I. Then $N_{n+1}\theta_{n+1} = \neg A_1\theta_{n+1} \vee D_1\theta_{n+1}$ is ground and false under I. $\square$

10.4 Introduction to Refinement Operators

The previous section has shown a way to weaken a theory which is too strong: find a false member of the theory Σ by the Backtracing Algorithm, and delete this clause from the theory. However, deleting a clause might make the theory in turn too weak. A way to strengthen the theory again, is to add weaker versions of previously deleted clauses. For instance, suppose the clause $P(x)$ is false under I, and has been deleted from Σ. It might be that $P(f(x))$, which is a "refinement" of $P(x)$, is true under I. Thus the theory might be strengthened by adding $P(f(x))$ to it.

A systematic way to find refinements of clauses, is by using a *refinement operator*. Because a full discussion of refinement operators presupposes the results of Chapters 13 through 16, we postpone the full treatment of refinement operators to Chapter 17. In this section we will only give a brief introduction.

There are two kinds of refinement operators: upward and downward ones. An upward refinement operator computes a set of generalizations of a given clause, a downward refinement operator computes a set of specializations. What constitutes a 'specialization' or 'generalization' of a clause, is determined by a *generality order* on clauses. Such an order on clauses can for example be denoted by $\succeq$. Then we can say that C is a generalization of D (dually: C is a specialization of D), if $C \succeq D$ holds. Many different generality orders are possible, some of the most important are subsumption and logical implication. In each of these orders, the empty clause $\square$ is the most general clause.

We assume $\mathcal{C}_h$ is ordered by such a generality order $\succeq$. Shapiro's top-down approach only employs a *downward* refinement operator ρ, so $\rho(C)$ is a set of specializations of a given clause C. We start with $\Sigma = \{\square\}$. This is clearly too strong, since it implies any clause. Hence we want to find specializations of $\square$. We use the set $\rho(\square)$ for this. If $\rho(\square)$ is still too strong, its false members can in turn be replaced by their refinements, and so on.

This allows us to search stepwise through the generality order. This stepwise approach will only work if there is a path (a number of refinement steps) from $\square$ to every clause in at least one correct theory. For instance, suppose $\Sigma = \{D_2, D_3, D_4\}$ is a correct theory. Let the refinement operator ρ be such, that $\rho(\square) = \{C_1, C_2\}$, $\rho(C_1) = \{C_3, C_4\}$, $\rho(C_2) = \{D_3, D_4\}$, $\rho(C_3) = \{D_1\}$, and $\rho(C_4) = \{D_2, D_3\}$. Starting from $\square$, we can reach Σ by considering $\rho(\square)$, $\rho(C_1)$, $\rho(C_2)$, $\rho(C_4)$. See Figure 10.4.

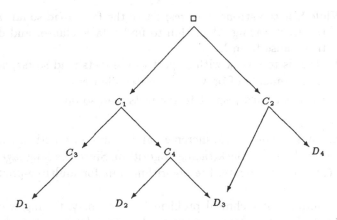

Figure 10.4: Paths through the refinement operator ρ

10.5   The Model Inference Algorithm

Recall that at the end of Subsection 10.2.3, we mentioned three questions with respect to model inference. The first two questions have been dealt with in the previous sections. A short summary:

- If the theory is too strong, it contains at least one clause which is false under the Herbrand interpretation I. This clause can be found by the Backtracing Algorithm, and the theory can be weakened by deleting the false clause

- If the theory is too weak, it can be made stronger by adding refinements of a previously deleted clause to the theory. The refinements of the deleted clause are obtained by applying a refinement operator to it.

Using the tools developed in the previous sections, an outline for an algorithm for solving model inference problems can now be given. Shapiro implemented this algorithm for Horn clauses, in his Model Inference System MIS.

Algorithm 10.2 (Outline of a Model Inference Algorithm)

Set Σ to $\{\Box\}$.
Repeat forever[1]:

> Read the next fact from the enumeration
>
> Repeat
>
> > While Σ is too strong with respect to the facts read so far, apply the Backtracing Algorithm to find a false clause, and delete this clause from Σ.
> >
> > While Σ is too weak with respect to the facts read so far, add to Σ refinements of previously deleted clauses.
>
> until Σ is correct with respect to the facts read so far.

This algorithm is top-down and incremental. It is also interactive, because of the use of an oracle in the Backtracing Algorithm. Since the language may contain more than one predicate, the algorithm is fit for multiple-predicate learning.

There is an important technical problem here. Namely, testing whether the current theory Σ is too strong or too weak means determining whether $\Sigma \models \alpha$ holds for certain α. This is usually undecidable (see Theorem 7.41), because we do not know in advance how many resolution steps we need to deduce α. Hence a procedure that should test if $\Sigma \models \alpha$ is the case need not terminate, and hence is not an algorithm. Shapiro used an idea called *h-easiness* to deal with this problem, which he adapted from [BB75]. Here h is some computable function that assigns a natural number to each formula in $\mathcal{C}_o$. A theory Σ is *h-easy* if, for every C such that $\Sigma \models C$ and $C \in \mathcal{C}_o$, we have that C can be deduced from Σ using at most $h(C)$ resolution steps. Thus h-easiness bounds the maximal number of proof-steps that have to be taken to deduce C, which makes implication decidable (given h). An interpretation I is h-easy if an h-easy $\mathcal{C}_o$-complete axiomatization of I exists. Shapiro then restricts the allowed interpretations I (from which the examples come) to the h-easy ones, where h is some fixed function provided by the user of his system. We will not go further into h-easiness.

Another problem is when to stop reading facts. This was the third and last question that we listed in Subsection 10.2.3. When do you know that Σ is a $\mathcal{C}_o$-complete axiomatization of I? First of all, it should be noted that such a $\mathcal{C}_o$-complete axiomatization need not exist at all. This is a consequence of Theorem 9.9. So in this case, the algorithm will never reach a final theory. But even when we are dealing with an I for which a $\mathcal{C}_o$-complete axiomatization does exist, for an infinite $\mathcal{C}_o$ there is no way of knowing whether you have found it. The reason for this is that you cannot determine if your current theory is correct for all examples in the enumeration that have not been read so far.

---

[1] Of course, if the enumeration is finite, we can stop once all facts have been read.

What the algorithm *can* do, is output its theory-so-far after each time it has digested a new fact. Once it has found a Σ which is a C_o-complete axiomatization of I, it will never change its theory anymore, and output the same Σ after each new fact. If the algorithm eventually finds a C_o-complete axiomatization of I (though without being aware of this), the algorithm is said to have *identified I in the limit*, in accordance with Gold's paradigm [Gol67]. In general, this is the best a model inference algorithm can do.

Example 10.12 Let C be a language that contains only one predicate symbol, P, one constant 0, and one function symbol s. C_h is the set of all definite program clauses with at most one negative literal, plus the empty clause. Thus apart from $\Box$, C_h contains only atoms and clauses of the form $A \leftarrow B$, where A and B are atoms. Let C_o be the set of ground atoms. Since C_h is in this case a subset of the set of Horn clauses, it follows from Theorem 10.6 that the pair (C_o, C_h) is admissible. Suppose we are given the following enumeration of I, which makes $P(t)$ true iff t denotes an even number:

$(P(0), T)$
$(P(s(0)), F)$
$(P(s^2(0)), T)$
$(P(s^3(0)), F)$
$(P(s^4(0)), T)$
. . .

We want to find a C_o-complete axiomatization of I—or in other words, an axiomatization of the set of even numbers—using the following refinement operator:

$$\rho(C) = \begin{cases} \{P(x)\} & \text{if } C = \Box; \\ \{P(s^{n+1}(x)), (P(s^n(x)) \leftarrow P(x)), \\ P(s^n(0))\} & \text{if } C = P(s^n(x)); \\ \emptyset & \text{otherwise.} \end{cases}$$

The algorithm takes the following steps:

1. Set Σ to $\{\Box\}$.
2. Read $(P(0), T)$.
3. Σ is neither too strong nor too weak for the facts read so far.
4. Read $(P(s(0)), F)$.
5. Σ is too strong, since the false example $P(s(0))$ can be deduced from it. The false clause $\Box$ is deleted, so now $\Sigma = \emptyset$.
6. Σ is now too weak, because the positive example $P(0)$ cannot be deduced from it. Add $\rho(\Box) = \{P(x)\}$ to Σ.
7. Σ is now too strong. Delete the false clause $P(x)$. $\Sigma = \emptyset$ again.
8. Σ is too weak. Add $\rho(P(x)) = \{P(s(x)), (P(x) \leftarrow P(x)), P(0)\}$ to Σ.
9. Σ is too strong. Delete the false clause $P(s(x))$ and the superfluous tautology $P(x) \leftarrow P(x)$. Then $\Sigma = \{P(0)\}$ is neither too strong nor too weak with respect to the facts read so far.

10. Read $(P(s^2(0)), T)$.
11. Σ is too weak. Add $\rho(P(s(x))) = \{P(s^2(x)), (P(s(x)) \leftarrow P(x)), P(s(0))\}$ to Σ.
12. Σ is too strong. Delete $P(s(x)) \leftarrow P(x)$ and $P(s(0))$. Then $\Sigma = \{P(s^2(x)), P(0)\}$ is neither too strong nor too weak.
13. Read $(P(s^3(0)), F)$.
14. Σ is too strong. Delete $P(s^2(x))$.
15. $\Sigma = \{P(0)\}$ is too weak. Add $\rho(P(s^2(x))) = \{P(s^3(x)), (P(s^2(x)) \leftarrow P(x)), P(s^2(0))\}$.
16. Σ is too strong. Delete $P(s^3(x))$.
17. $\Sigma = \{P(0), P(s^2(0)), (P(s^2(x)) \leftarrow P(x))\}$, this is correct for all the facts in the enumeration. So the theory will not change hereafter when we continue to read new facts.

The final theory Σ is a $\mathcal{C}_o$-complete axiomatization of I. Note that $P(s^2(0))$ is superfluous, because it is implied by the other two clauses in Σ. Also, the specific refinement operator ρ that we use here, need not work for certain other Herbrand interpretations I of $\mathcal{C}_h$, in other words, it need not be *complete*. The completeness of refinement operators will be treated in Chapter 17. $\lhd$

10.6 Summary

The model inference is concerned with finding clausal rules that characterize certain concepts represented in a Herbrand interpretation. The problem can be stated as follows:

> **Given**: A clausal language $\mathcal{C}$, an observational language $\mathcal{C}_o$, and a hypothesis language $\mathcal{C}_h$, such that $\mathcal{C}_o \subseteq \mathcal{C}_h \subseteq \mathcal{C}$ and the pair $(\mathcal{C}_o, \mathcal{C}_h)$ is admissible. In addition there is an enumeration and/or an oracle for the clauses in $\mathcal{C}_o$ under some Herbrand interpretation I of $\mathcal{C}$.
>
> **Find**: A $\mathcal{C}_o$-complete axiomatization of I (a true theory which implies all true members of $\mathcal{C}_o$).

Shapiro's Model Inference Algorithm takes a top-down approach towards solving model inference problems. It starts with the most general theory $\Sigma = \{\Box\}$, and succesively reads new examples from the enumeration. If after reading an example the theory is too strong, it is weakened by deleting false clauses from it. These false clauses can be found by the *Backtracing Algorithm*. If the theory is too weak, it is strengthened by the addition of specializations of previously deleted clauses. These specializations are constructed by a downward *refinement operator*, which will be dealt with extensively in Chapter 17.

Chapter 11

Inverse Resolution

11.1 Introduction

Induction can be seen as the inverse of deduction. Deduction moves from the general rules to the special case, while induction intends to find the general rules from special cases (examples). As we have seen in previous chapters, one of our main tools for deduction is resolution. This led Muggleton and Buntine [MB88] to introduce *inverse resolution* as a tool for induction. Their paper was followed by a wave of interest and research into the properties of inverse resolution [Wir89, HS91, Mug91b, Mug92b, Mug92c, RP89, RP90, Rou92, NF91, Ide93c, Ide92, Ide93b, Ide93a, LN92, SADB92, Tay93, SA93, BG93]. Inverting resolution is nowadays still a prominent generalization operator for bottom-up approaches to ILP.

In this chapter, we will give the main ideas behind inverse resolution. It is an interesting idea which has been very influential. However, we feel the theoretical foundation of this idea needs much more investigation. Moreover, in the application of inverse resolution, many indeterminacies arise: many different choices of literals, clauses and substitutions lay open. Accordingly, inverse resolution generates a very large search space of possibilities.[1] Therefore we will here only give the intuition behind it. Though the chapter serves as a motivation for some concepts introduced later on, the contents of this chapter are not required for an understanding of the later chapters.

In their article, Muggleton and Buntine described two operators based on inverting resolution steps: the V- and the W-operator. Given C_1 and R, the V-operator finds C_2 such that R is an instance of a resolvent of C_1 and C_2. Thus the V-operator generalizes $\{C_1, R\}$ to $\{C_1, C_2\}$. The W-operator combines two V-operators, and generalizes $\{R_1, R_2\}$ to $\{C_1, C_2, C_3\}$, such that R_1 is an instance of a resolvent of C_1 and C_2, and R_2 is an instance of

---

[1] *Unfolding*, the dual to inverse resolution which we introduce in the next chapter, seems to have relatively less indeterminacy, and hence may be more useful.

a resolvent of C_2 and C_3. In addition, the W-operator is able to invent new predicates. Using V- and W-operators, Muggleton and Buntine implemented an interactive bottom-up system called CIGOL (the name is the inverse of 'logic').

11.2   The V-Operator

Suppose we have a language containing the predicates *Swims*, *Animal* and *Fish*. Suppose we are learning from examples, and our theory sofar is a definite program Π, which as yet only contains the following clauses:

> *Animal*(*sharky*)
> *Swims*(*sharky*)

Here *sharky* is a constant.

Suppose we get a new positive example *Fish*(*sharky*). This example is not implied by Π, so we should adjust our theory. The adjusted theory ought to imply the example *Fish*(*sharky*). This means that a proper way to adjust the theory, is to add clauses that are needed for an SLD-deduction of *Fish*(*sharky*). Usually when we apply SLD-resolution, we have a set of Horn clauses, and we want to see what can be deduced from it. This case is just the opposite: we already know what we want to deduce—namely the clause *Fish*(*sharky*)—and we want to find clauses from which this can be deduced.

Since the only thing we know about the SLD-derivation that we want to construct is its conclusion *Fish*(*sharky*), we start with the bottom of the derivation: the final resolvent should be *Fish*(*sharky*) (see Figure 11.1). We now want to find two parent clauses which have *Fish*(*sharky*) as a resolvent. Or rather, we want to find two clauses that have a resolvent of which *Fish*(*sharky*) is an instance, which is sufficient for our purposes. This approach yields an instance of an SLD-derivation, where the unifiers are not always *most general*. When we lift this to an SLD-derivation (i.e., when we make the unifiers mgu's), we obtain a derivation of a clause of which *Fish*(*sharky*) is an instance. Thus we want to find a center clause and an input clause, which have a resolvent of which *Fish*(*sharky*) is an instance. Clearly, a huge number of possible choices for these two clauses lays open. Let us say we use *Swims*(*sharky*), which is already in Π, as input clause. Then there are several possibilities for the other parent, the center clause. Here we adopt the least general possibility, which is *Fish*(*sharky*) ← *Swims*(*sharky*). Then *Fish*(*sharky*) is a resolvent of these two parent clauses.

We might stop here, and add *Fish*(*sharky*) ← *Swims*(*sharky*) to Π. But suppose we choose to invert another resolution step. We now want to find two parent clauses for *Fish*(*sharky*) ← *Swims*(*sharky*). We decide to use *Animal*(*sharky*) as input clause. Again, there are several possibilities for the other parent clause. Let us say we choose *Fish*(*x*) ← *Animal*(*x*), *Swims*(*x*).

In the intended interpretation, this clause states that swimming animals are fish.[2] Adding this clause to Π, we get Π′:

> $Animal(sharky)$
> $Swims(sharky)$
> $Fish(x) \leftarrow Animal(x), Swims(x)$

Figure 11.1 shows the derivation we have inverted. Thus inverting—more precisely: constructing in a bottom-up fashion—the derivation yields a candidate which can be added to our theory in such a way that the new positive example is implied by the theory.

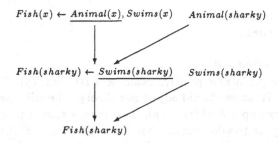

Figure 11.1: Inverting this SLD-derivation yields a clause for the theory

A nice feature of inverse resolution is that the clauses of the "old" (too weak) theory can be used in inverting the derivation. In the previous simple example, we could use the two atoms in Π as input clauses in the derivation. Furthermore, if we had some background knowledge $\mathcal{B}$ at our disposal, we could also use clauses from $\mathcal{B}$ as input clauses. This allows an interesting interplay between the old theory and the background knowledge on the one hand, and the newly induced clauses on the other. However, it should be noted that using clauses from the original Π or $\mathcal{B}$ as input clauses is fairly arbitrary. It artificially restricts the range of choices for one of the parent clauses. It may seem that we ought to try all possible C_1, C_2 such that R is an instance of a resolvent of C_1 and C_2, rather than only considering $C_1 \in \Pi$ or $C_1 \in \mathcal{B}$. However, to reduce the number of possibilities, we assume that C_1 (the input clause) is part of the old Π or in $\mathcal{B}$, and we only consider finding possible C_2's.

The resolution rule takes two parent clauses, and derives a resolvent. Inverse resolution essentially faces the following "inverse" problem: given a clause R and a parent clause C_1, find a second parent clause C_2 such that R is an instance of a resolvent of C_1 and C_2. A *V-operator* is an algorithm

---

[2]Of course, this is biologically incorrect: a whale is a swimming animal, but not a fish. Hence if *moby* denotes some particular whale, then the system will have to adjust its theory after it has seen the positive examples $Animal(moby)$ and $Swims(moby)$, and the negative example $Fish(moby)$.

which can find solutions for this problem. The name of the operator derives from the V-shape of resolution steps. Usually, many alternatives for C_2 are possible, and we should perhaps try out different possibilities. Note that to invert a resolution step for arbitary clauses, we should also have a mechanism to invert *factors*, something which is ignored in [MB88]. For simplicity, we will restrict our discussion in this chapter to definite program clauses, for which factors are not needed. Hence we are here only concerned with finding C_2 such that R is an instance of a *binary* resolvent of C_1 and C_2. In the remainder of this chapter, we will abbreviate 'binary resolvent' to 'resolvent'.

Let two Horn clauses $C_1 = L_1 \vee C'_1$ and R be given. We assume here for notational convenience that L_1 is the leftmost literal in C_1, this is of course not necessary. Our V-operator should find $C_2 = L_2 \vee C'_2$, such that R is an instance of a resolvent of C_1 and C_2. We assume C_1 and C_2 are standardized apart, and L_1 and L_2 are the literals resolved upon. Thus we want to find $C_2 = L_2 \vee C'_2$, such that for some θ which unifies L_1 and $\neg L_2$, $R = C'_1 \theta \vee C'_2 \theta$.[3] Since C_1 and C_2 are standardized apart, the unifier θ can be divided in two disjoint substitutions, namely $\theta = \theta_1 \cup \theta_2$, where θ_1 only acts on variables in C_1, and θ_2 only acts on variables in C_2, and $L_1 \theta_1 = \neg L_2 \theta_2$. Using separate θ_1 and θ_2 rather than a single substitution θ facilitates independent manipulation of C'_1 and C'_2. Let μ be an mgu for L_1 and $\neg L_2$. Then $R' = C'_1 \mu \vee C'_2 \mu$ is a resolvent of C_1 and C_2. Since $\theta_1 \cup \theta_2$ is a unifier for L_1 and $\neg L_2$, there is a γ such that $\mu \gamma = \theta_1 \cup \theta_2$. Thus $R = R' \gamma$, which shows that R is an instance of a resolvent of C_1 and C_2. This analysis gives Figure 11.2.

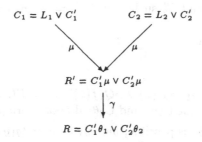

Figure 11.2: The setting for the V-operator

The simplest situation is where $C_1 = L_1$, so where C'_1 is empty. Then for a given θ_1, any C_2 and θ_2 with $C_2 \theta_2 = \neg L_1 \theta_1 \vee R$ will do. Since $\neg L_1 \theta_1 \vee R$ is an instance of any of these possible C_2's, it is clear that $C_2 = \neg L_1 \theta_1 \vee R$ is the "minimal" of all possible C_2's, for a fixed θ_1.

Example 11.1 Suppose $C_1 = P(x, f(x))$ and $R = P(y, f^2(y))$. We want to find the minimal generalization as described above, for $\theta_1 = \{x/f(y)\}$.

---

[3]If some $L = \neg A$ is a negative literal, we use $\neg L$ to denote the atom A.

Here $L_1 = P(x, f(x))$, so the minimal C_2 is $\neg L_1 \theta_1 \vee R = \neg P(f(y), f^2(y)) \vee P(y, f^2(y)) = P(y, f^2(y)) \leftarrow P(f(y), f^2(y))$. ◁

Usually the situation is not as simple, and C_1 will contain more than one literal. How can we find an adequate C_2 in this case? Let us first assume $C_1'\theta_1$ and $C_2'\theta_2$ do not overlap. That is, $C_1'\theta_1$ and $C_2'\theta_2$ have no literals in common. Clearly, if we assume the setting of Figure 11.2, then R can be split into two parts: $C_1'\theta_1$ derives from C_1, and $C_2'\theta_2$ derives from C_2. We have to find a θ_1 such that $C_1'\theta_1 \subseteq R$. Once we know $C_1'\theta_1$, we also know $C_2'\theta_2$, because this is the remaining part of R: $C_2'\theta_2 = R - C_1'\theta_1$.

However, C_2' itself, L_2 and θ_2 are still unknown, and allow many different choices. Any choice for L_2 and C_2' will do, as long as it satisfies $L_1\theta_1 = \neg L_2\theta_2$ and $C_2'\theta_2 = R - C_1'\theta_1$, for some θ_2. In this case, choosing $L_2 = \neg L_1\theta_1$ and $C_2' = R - C_1'\theta_1$ yields the minimal choice for C_2. That is, since $C_2\theta_2 = \neg L_1\theta_1 \vee (R - C_1'\theta_1)$, the clause $\neg L_1\theta_1 \vee (R - C_1'\theta_1)$ is an instance of each of the possible C_2. Thus choosing this clause itself as C_2 (i.e., $\theta_2 = \varepsilon$), is the minimal choice.

The non-deterministic algorithm[4] given below, incorporates this analysis, and constructs all possible C_2's.

Algorithm 11.1 (V-operator)
Input: Horn clauses $C_1 = L_1 \vee C_1'$ and R, where $C_1'\theta_1 \subseteq R$ for some θ_1.
Output: A Horn clause C_2, such that R is an instance of a resolvent of C_1 and C_2.

1. Choose a substitution θ_1 such that $C_1'\theta_1 \subseteq R$.
2. Choose an L_2 and C_2' such that $L_1\theta_1 = \neg L_2\theta_2$ and $C_2'\theta_2 = R - C_1'\theta_1$, for some θ_2.
3. Let $C_2 = L_2 \vee C_2'$.

Example 11.2 Let $C_1 = P(x) \vee \neg Q(f(x))$, $L_1 = P(x)$, and $R = Q(g(y)) \vee \neg Q(f(g(y)))$. We assume $C_1\theta_1$ and $C_2\theta_2$ do not overlap.

1. Here only one θ_1 is possible, namely $\theta_1 = \{x/g(y)\}$.
2. L_2 and C_2' should be such that, for some θ_2, $L_1\theta_1 = P(g(y)) = \neg L_2\theta_2$ and $R - C_1'\theta_1 = Q(g(y)) = C_2'\theta_2$. Figure 11.3 shows all possible $C_2 = L_2 \vee C_2'$ (unique up to renaming of variables) of two literals, from top to bottom in decreasing order of generality. $C_2 = \neg L_1\theta_1 \vee (R - C_1'\theta_1) = \neg P(g(y)) \vee Q(g(y))$ is the minimal choice.

Note that for some C_2, R itself is not a resolvent of C_1 and C_2. For instance, if we let $C_2 = \neg P(z) \vee Q(y)$, then the resolvent of C_1 and C_2 is $\neg Q(f(z)) \vee Q(y)$, of which R is an instance. ◁

---

[4] The algorithm is 'non-deterministic' because its output is not determined by its input. For instance in step 1, the algorithm has to choose one among many different possible θ_1's, which all satisfy $C_1'\theta_1 \subseteq R$.

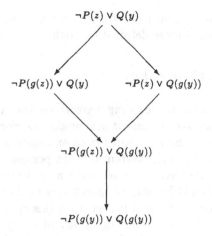

$$\neg P(z) \vee Q(y)$$

$$\neg P(g(z)) \vee Q(y) \qquad \neg P(z) \vee Q(g(y))$$

$$\neg P(g(z)) \vee Q(g(y))$$

$$\neg P(g(y)) \vee Q(g(y))$$

Figure 11.3: The possible C_2

Thus far we have assumed that $C_1'\theta_1$ and $C_2'\theta_2$ do not overlap. But now consider $R = P(a) \leftarrow Q(a)$, $C_1 = P(a) \leftarrow Q(a), R(a)$ and $C_2 = R(x) \leftarrow Q(x)$. Then $R' = P(a) \leftarrow Q(a), Q(a)$ is a resolvent of C_1 and C_2. C_1 and C_2 both contribute a literal $Q(a)$ to the body of R'. The V-operator given above is able to find C_2 from C_1 and R'. Since the only difference between R and R' is the extra copy of $Q(a)$ in the body of R', and an example will usually be given without duplicated literals (i.e., in the form of R rather than R'), we would like the V-operator to be able to find C_2 from C_1 and R as well. However, since $C_1\theta_1$ and $C_2\theta_2$ overlap in the literal $Q(a)$ in the body of R, the V-operator is not capable of doing this. Given C_1 and R as input, it can only find $R(x)$ and $R(a)$ as C_2. Thus we sometimes have to duplicate some literals in R before applying the V-operator, in order to be able to find the desired parent clauses. In this example, we have to duplicate $Q(a)$—in other words, change R into R'—to be able to find C_2 using the V-operator. In general, which literals in R we should duplicate depends on the application. We will not go into details here.

Our goal in inverse resolution is to construct a derivation of a positive example A (usually a ground atom) which hitherto was not implied by the theory. Using the algorithm for the V-operator, we can invert one resolution step, for given C_1 and R. By repeatedly applying the V-operator, we are able to invert any SLD-derivation. However, there are many indeterminacies here, which make an unrestricted search through all possible invertible derivations very inefficient. Within the V-operator itself, many different choices for θ_1, L_2 and C_2' are possible. And even before we can use the V-operator, we have to decide which clause from the old theory or the background knowledge to use as C_1, and which literals to duplicate in R. Thus the total number of possibilities may become very large sometimes, which can make application of inverse resolution very inefficient. We will not go into those issues here, which would require much more detailed research.

11.3 The W-Operator

One of the problems inductive learning algorithms have to face, is the fact that it is sometimes necessary to *invent new predicates*. For instance, suppose we want our algorithm to induce clauses from examples about family life. It would be very unfortunate if the system did not possess a predicate for the concept of 'parent'. If we have not given such a predicate to the system in advance, the system should be able to invent this predicate for itself. If we examine the V-operator carefully, it is clear that this operator cannot invent new predicates: all predicates appearing in any of the possible C_2 that we might construct already appear in C_1 or R. However, by putting two V-settings side-by-side, we get a W-shape. The *W-operator*, which is based on this new setting, is indeed able to invent new predicates.

We will first give an example which shows the idea behind the W-operator. Suppose we have two Horn clauses $R_1 = Grandfather(x, y) \leftarrow Father(x, z), Father(z, y)$ and $R_2 = Grandfather(a, b) \leftarrow Father(a, c), Mother(c, b)$, and suppose we want to generalize these clauses. The W-operator constructs clauses C_1, C_2, C_3, such that R_1 is an instance of a resolvent of C_1 and C_2, and R_2 is an instance of a resolvent of C_2 and C_3. Thus the W-operator generalizes $\{R_1, R_2\}$ to $\{C_1, C_2, C_3\}$. In Figure 11.4, we give possible C_1, C_2, C_3 which can serve this purpose.

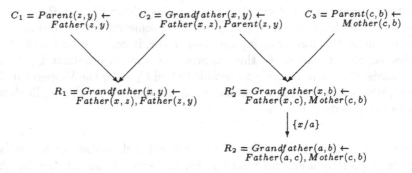

Figure 11.4: Generalization of $\{R_1, R_2\}$ to $\{C_1, C_2, C_3\}$ by the W-operator

The important point to notice about Figure 11.4 is that the predicate *Parent*, which appears in C_1, C_2 and C_3, did not appear in the clauses R_1 and R_2 we started with. Thus in generalizing $\{R_1, R_2\}$ to $\{C_1, C_2, C_3\}$, the W-operator has itself introduced a new predicate. The invention of this new predicate is quite useful, since it allows us to write out the definition of a 'Grandfather' in a very succint way in C_2: x is the grandfather of y, if x

is the father of some z, and z is a parent of y.[5] Note that any predicate name may be assigned the role of *Parent* here, including "old" names such as *Grandfather* or *Mother*, since this predicate is resolved away in the two resolution steps anyway.

The general setting for the W-operator is pictured in Figure 11.5. Given R_1 and R_2, the W-operator constructs C_1, C_2, C_3, with the property that R_1 is an instance of a resolvent of C_1 and C_2, and R_2 is an instance of a resolvent of C_2 and C_3. What we want to find, are $C_1 = L_1 \vee C_1'$, $C_2 = L_2 \vee C_2'$, $C_3 = L_3 \vee C_3'$, θ_1, θ_2, σ_1 and σ_2, such that $L_1\theta_1 = \neg L_2\theta_2$, $L_2\sigma_1 = \neg L_3\sigma_2$, $R_1 = C_1'\theta_1 \vee C_2'\theta_2$ and $R_2 = C_2'\sigma_1 \vee C_3'\sigma_2$. Thus L_1 and L_2 are resolved upon in deriving R_1', while L_2 and L_3 are resolved upon in deriving R_2'. μ is an mgu for L_1 and $\neg L_2$, and ν is an mgu for $\neg L_2$ and L_3. Hence L_1 and L_3 must either be both positive, or both negative. Note that L_1, L_2, L_3 do not appear in R_1 and R_2, which gives the opportunity for inventing a new predicate.

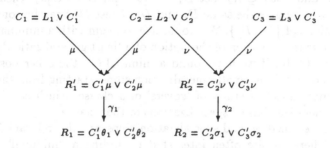

Figure 11.5: The setting for the W-operator

We will here only sketch the idea behind the construction of C_1, C_2 and C_3.

1. Given R_1 and R_2, we first try to find a C_2' such that $C_2'\theta_2 \subseteq R_1$ and $C_2'\sigma_1 \subseteq R_2$, for some θ_2 and σ_1. If such a C_2' cannot be found—which means, intuitively, that R_1 and R_2 have "nothing in common"—we should let C_2' be empty.

2. If we have chosen an appropriate C_2', we can complete C_2 by choosing also L_2. In principle, any L_2 will do.

3. Once we have decided which clause to take as C_2, then a C_1 and C_3 can be found independently. C_1 can be constructed by the V-operator from C_2 and R_1, and C_3 can be constructed by the V-operator from C_2 and R_2.

Consider Figure 11.4 again. Given R_1 and R_2, how did we find C_1, C_2 and C_3? First we note that $(Grandfather(x, y) \vee \neg Father(x, z))\varepsilon \subseteq R_1$,

---

[5]The fact that we have named the new predicate *Parent*, is only intended to serve *our* intuition. Of course, the W-operator itself does not "know" that this new predicate denotes the concept of 'parent'. As far as the W-operator is concerned, the new predicate—and also the old predicates *Grandfather*, *Father*, and *Mother*, might have any name.

and $(Grandfather(x, y) \vee \neg Father(x, z))\{x/a, y/b, z/c\} \subseteq R_2$. Hence $C_2' = Grandfather(x, y) \vee \neg Father(x, z)$ is an appropriate choice.

Secondly, we have to choose L_2. Let us say we take $L_2 = \neg Parent(z, y)$. This gives $C_2 = Grandfather(x, y) \leftarrow Father(x, z), Parent(z, y)$.

Thirdly, the V-operator can find $C_1 = Parent(z, y) \leftarrow Father(z, y)$ from C_2 and R_1. Similarly, it can construct the clause $C_3 = Parent(c, b) \leftarrow Mother(c, b)$ from C_2 and R_2. Thus the W-operator generalizes $\{R_1, R_2\}$ to $\{C_1, C_2, C_3\}$.

11.4 Motivation for Studying Generality Orders

Let us consider the W-operator. We want to find C_2', θ_2 and σ_1 such that $C_2'\theta_2 \subseteq R_1$ and $C_2'\sigma_1 \subseteq R_2$. Let $D_1 = C_2'\theta_2$ and $D_2 = C_2'\sigma_1$. Clearly, many different C_2''s can give the same D_1 and D_2. These C_2''s can be considered as generalizations of $\{D_1, D_2\}$. We would like to begin with a minimal C_2'. This motivates our investigation of the notion of a 'least generalization' of clauses in Chapters 13–16. If we have found a minimal C_2', the other possible C_2''s can be found by taking small generalization steps, starting from the minimal C_2'. This motivates our study of 'covers' of a clause, which can be seen as minimal generalizations or specializations of that clause.

Small generalization and specialization steps are also relevant for the V-operator. There we are often interested in finding a "minimal" C_2, as in Figure 11.3, where $\neg P(g(y)) \vee Q(g(y))$ is the minimal choice. The other C_2's can then be found by taking small generalization steps starting from the minimal C_2.

Similarly, such small steps are also crucial for Shapiro's downward refinement operator. If his refinement operator takes too large specialization steps, it may skip over the right clauses. On the other hand, if it takes steps which are too small, it may take too long before the operator reaches an appropriate clause, or it may even never get there. Again, there is a relation with covers.

To be able to speak about relations of generality between clauses, the set of clauses must somehow be structured by some *generality order*. The arguments given above motivate our study of generality orders, least generalizations, covers, etc. in Chapters 13–16.

11.5 Summary

Since induction can be seen as the inverse of deduction, and resolution is our main tool for deduction, using *inverse resolution* for induction seems a sensible idea. Muggleton and Buntine introduced two operators for this. The V-operator generalizes two given clauses $\{C_1, R\}$ to $\{C_1, C_2\}$, such that R is an instance of a resolvent of C_1 and C_2. The W-operator combines two

V-operators: it generalizes two given clauses $\{R_1, R_2\}$ to $\{C_1, C_2, C_3\}$, such that R_1 is an instance of a resolvent of C_1 and C_2, and R_2 is an instance of a resolvent of C_2 and C_3. In addition, the W-operator is also able to invent new predicates.

Chapter 12

Unfolding

12.1 Introduction

In an ILP problem, it is sometimes the case that we initially start with a theory that is overly general: it is complete, but not consistent. The problem of finding a correct theory then becomes the problem of *specializing* the initial theory to a correct one. In this chapter we will investigate how such specialization can be done using *unfolding*, which can be viewed as the dual of inverse resolution.[1] While inverse resolution is a generalization operator based on constructing a parent clause from a resolvent and another parent clause, unfolding is a specialization operator which constructs resolvents from given parent clauses. As in the previous chapter on inverse resolution, we will restrict attention to definite program clauses, so the theories should be definite programs. Furthermore, we will also assume that the given examples E^+ and E^- consist of ground atoms (ground instances of one or more predicates).

Let us first formally define the *specialization problem*:

> **Given**: A definite program Π and two disjoint sets of ground atoms E^+ and E^-, such that Π is overly general with respect to E^+ and E^-, and suppose there exists a definite program Π' such that $\Pi \models \Pi'$ and Π' is correct with respect to E^+ and E^-.
> **Find**: One such a Π'.

Clearly, this is a special case of the normal problem setting of Chapter 9. We need to presuppose the existence of a correct specialization Π' of Π, because a correct program does not always exist, as proved in Theorem 9.9. Hence trying to solve a specialization problem only makes sense when a correct specialization exists. Note that background knowledge can be included in Π, so we will not mention background knowledge separately in this chapter.

---

[1] Apart from program specialization, unfolding can also be used for program *transformation*, which aims at improving programs, for instance by making them more efficient or readable. For this, see [PP94], and the references therein.

A natural way to specialize Π is, first, to replace a clause in Π by all its resolvents upon some body-atom in this clause. Constructing these resolvents is called unfolding. The new program obtained in this way after unfolding a clause in Π, is clearly implied by Π. The function of the replaced clause is taken over by the set of resolvents produced by unfolding. We can then, secondly, delete some new clauses from the program that have to do with the negative examples, thus specializing the program. Hopefully, after repeating these two steps a number of times, we can get rid of all negative examples. This method was introduced in [BI94].

For simplicity, let all examples be ground instances of $P(x_1, \ldots, x_n)$, for some predicate P. The motivation for the method described above is the fact that it can be used to prune negative examples from the SLD-tree for $\Pi \cup \{\leftarrow P(x_1, \ldots, x_n)\}$. We will illustrate this by an example.

Consider the program Π, consisting of the following clauses:

$$C_1 = P(x, y) \leftarrow Q(x, y)$$
$$C_2 = Q(b, b) \leftarrow Q(a, a)$$
$$C_3 = Q(a, a)$$

and $E^+ = \{P(b, b)\}$, $E^- = \{P(a, a)\}$. The SLD-tree for $\Pi \cup \{\leftarrow P(x, y)\}$ is shown on the left of Figure 12.1. The success branches corresponding to positive examples are marked with a '+', for negative examples with a '−'.

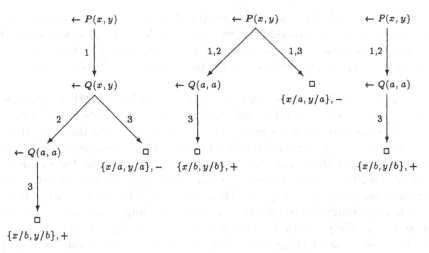

Figure 12.1: The SLD-trees for Π, Π', and Π''

$P(a, a)$ is a negative example, so we would like to remove this by weakening the program. This could be done by deleting C_1 or C_3 from Π. However, this would also make the positive example $P(b, b)$ no longer derivable, thus rendering the program too weak. Another way to specialize is, first, to unfold

C_1 upon $Q(x, y)$. The following $C_{1,2}$ and $C_{1,3}$ are the two clauses produced by unfolding C_1.

$C_{1,2} = P(b, b) \leftarrow Q(a, a)$ (resolvent of C_1 and C_2)
$C_{1,3} = P(a, a)$ (resolvent of C_1 and C_3)

Now we replace the unfolded clause C_1 by its resolvents $C_{1,2}$ and $C_{1,3}$. This results in $\Pi' = \{C_2, C_3, C_{1,2}, C_{1,3}\}$. The SLD-tree for $\Pi' \cup \{\leftarrow P(x, y)\}$ is shown in the middle of Figure 12.1. In this tree, the negative example is directly connected to the root, via the branch that uses $C_{1,3}$. Now the negative example can be pruned from the tree by deleting $C_{1,3}$ from Π', which does not affect the positive example. Then we obtain $\Pi'' = \{C_2, C_3, C_{1,2}\}$, which is correct with respect to E^+ and E^-. The SLD-tree for $\Pi'' \cup \{\leftarrow P(x, y)\}$ is simply the tree for Π', after the rightmost branch has been pruned (right of Figure 12.1).

The idea behind this method is the following:

1. Unfolding removes some internal nodes from the SLD-tree, for instance, the internal node $\leftarrow Q(x, y)$ in the tree on the left of Figure 12.1. This tends to separate the positive from the negative examples, and also brings them closer to the root of the tree.
2. If a negative example hangs directly from the root, and its input clause C is not used elsewhere in the tree for a positive example, then the program can be specialized by deleting C.

In other words: unfolding can transform the SLD-tree in such a way that negative examples can be pruned by deleting clauses from the program, without also pruning positive examples. Thus the use of unfolding as a specialization tool can be motivated by looking at SLD-trees, and the SLD-refutations those trees contain.

It can be seen from some examples that we give later on, that unfolding and clause deletion by itself is not sufficient for a complete specialization method—some specialization problems cannot be solved in this way. However, if we look at program specialization through the perspective of SLD-derivations rather than refutation, then we can see from the Subsumption Theorem for SLD-resolution that *subsumption* is what we need to make our specialization technique complete. Thus we define UDS specialization here, which is a specialization technique based on **U**nfolding, clause **D**eletion, and **S**ubsumption. We prove that UDS specialization is complete: every specialization problem has a UDS specialization as a solution. This chapter is mainly based on [NW96a].

12.2 Unfolding

In this section we will define unfolding, in the next section we will use it to solve specialization problems.

Definition 12.1 Let Π be a definite program, $C = A \leftarrow B_1, \ldots, B_n$ a definite program clause in Π, and B_i the i-th atom in the body of C. Let $\{C_1, \ldots, C_m\}$ be the set of clauses in Π whose head can be unified with B_i.

Then *unfolding* C *upon* B_i *in* Π means constructing the set $U_{C,i} = \{D_1, \ldots, D_m\}$, where each D_j is the resolvent of C_j and C, using B_i and the head of C_j as the literals resolved upon. $\diamond$

Example 12.2 Let Π consist of the following clauses:

$$
\begin{aligned}
C_1 &= P(f(x)) \leftarrow P(x), Q(x) \\
C_2 &= Q(x) \leftarrow R(x, a) \\
C_3 &= P(f(a)) \\
C_4 &= Q(b)
\end{aligned}
$$

Suppose we want to unfold C_1 upon $Q(x)$ in the program Π. $\{C_2, C_4\}$ is the set of clauses in Π whose head can be unified with $Q(x)$, so $U_{C_1,2} = \{(P(f(x)) \leftarrow P(x), R(x, a)), (P(f(b)) \leftarrow P(b))\}$. $\lhd$

Note that $U_{C,i}$ may be the empty set. This is the case if there is no program clause whose head unifies with the i-th atom in the body of C. Note also that an atom cannot be unfolded, since it has no body-atoms.

Using the set $U_{C,i}$, we can construct a new program from Π in two ways. The first way, used in [BI94], *replaces* C by $U_{C,i}$, thus obtaining the program $(\Pi \backslash \{C\}) \cup U_{C,i}$. This is how unfolding was originally considered by Komorowski [Kom82] and formally studied by Tamaki and Sato [TS84]. The second way to obtain a new program *adds* $U_{C,i}$ to Π, without deleting the unfolded clause C from the program.

Definition 12.3 Let Π be a definite program, and $U_{C,i}$ the set of clauses constructed by unfolding C upon B_i in Π. Then $\Pi_{u1,C,i} = (\Pi \backslash \{C\}) \cup U_{C,i}$ is called the *type 1 program* resulting from unfolding C upon B_i in Π.

$\Pi_{u2,C,i} = \Pi \cup U_{C,i}$ is called the *type 2 program* resulting from unfolding C upon B_i in Π. $\diamond$

We will show that constructing the type 1 program preserves the least Herbrand model, while constructing the type 2 program preserves logical equivalence, which is stronger.

Proposition 12.4 *Let Π be a definite program, G a definite goal, and $\Pi_{u1,C,i}$ the type 1 program resulting from unfolding C upon B_i in Π. Then $\Pi \cup \{G\} \vdash_{sr} \square$ iff $\Pi_{u1,C,i} \cup \{G\} \vdash_{sr} \square$.*

Proof

$\Leftarrow$: Suppose $\Pi_{u1,C,i} \cup \{G\} \vdash_{sr} \square$. Then by the soundness of resolution, $\Pi_{u1,C,i} \cup \{G\}$ is unsatisfiable. It is easy to see that $\Pi \models \Pi_{u1,C,i}$. Hence $\Pi \cup \{G\}$ is unsatisfiable, and by Theorem 7.8 we have $\Pi \cup \{G\} \vdash_{sr} \square$.

$\Rightarrow$: Suppose $\Pi \cup \{G\} \vdash_{sr} \square$, and suppose C (the unfolded clause), is $A \leftarrow B_1, \ldots, B_i, \ldots, B_n$, which we abbreviate to $A \leftarrow \overline{B_1}, B_i, \overline{B_2}$, where $\overline{B_1} = B_1, \ldots, B_{i-1}$ and $\overline{B_2} = B_{i+1}, \ldots, B_n$, and B_i is the atom unfolded upon. If there is an SLD-refutation of $\Pi \cup \{G\}$ in which C isn't used as an input clause, then this is also an SLD-refutation of $\Pi_{u1,C,i} \cup \{G\}$. But suppose C is used as input clause in all SLD-refutations of $\Pi \cup \{G\}$. We will prove that from such a refutation, a refutation of $\Pi_{u1,C,i} \cup \{G\}$ can be constructed.

Suppose we have a refutation of $\Pi \cup \{G\}$ with goals $G_0, \ldots, G_n$ and input clauses $C_1, \ldots, C_n$, which uses C at least once as input clause. By the independence of the computation rule (Theorem 7.32), we can assume that for any j, if C is the input clause in the step leading from G_{j-1} to G_j, then the instance of B_i that is inserted in G_j by C, is the selected atom in G_j.

Suppose the j-th input clause is C. We picture this part of the refutation on the left of Figure 12.2. For this picture, we make the following notational conventions:

- G_{j-1}, the $(j-1)$-th goal, is the goal $\leftarrow A_1, \ldots, A_k, \ldots, A_m$, which we abbreviate to $\leftarrow \overline{A_1}, A_k, \overline{A_2}$.
- The input clause used in the $(j+1)$-th step is $C_{j+1} = A' \leftarrow \overline{B'}$, where $\overline{B'}$ is an abbreviation of $B'_1, \ldots, B'_r$.
- θ_j is an mgu for A_k and A (used in the j-th resolution step).
- θ_{j+1} is an mgu for $B_i\theta_j$ and A' (used in the $(j+1)$-th resolution step).

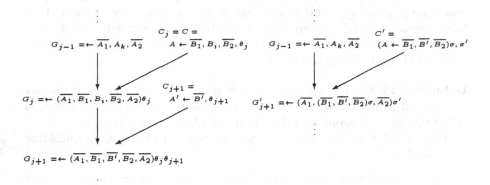

Figure 12.2: Using input clause C' instead of C_j and C_{j+1}

Since the $(j+1)$-th step of the tree on the left of Figure 12.2 shows that B_i and A' can be unified (say, with mgu σ), the clause $C' = (A \leftarrow \overline{B_1}, \overline{B'}, \overline{B_2})\sigma$ (the result of resolving C with $C_{j+1} = A' \leftarrow \overline{B'}$) must be in $U_{C,i}$. We assume without loss of generality that $G_{j-1}, C_j = C, C_{j+1}$, and C' are standardized apart.

What we want is to construct a tree which, instead of using C in the j-th step, uses C'. For this, we will show that G_{j+1} is a variant of the goal G'_{j+1}, which can be derived from G_{j-1} and C'. Then we can replace the j-th step (which uses C) and the $(j+1)$-th step by one single step which does not need C anymore, but instead uses C'. See the right of the figure.

Because θ_{j+1} is an mgu for A' and $B_i\theta_j$ and $A'\theta_j = A'$ (due to the standardizing apart), $\theta_j\theta_{j+1}$ is a unifier for A' and B_i. Since σ is an mgu for A' and B_i, there exists a substitution γ such that $\sigma\gamma = \theta_j\theta_{j+1}$. $A\sigma\gamma = A\theta_j\theta_{j+1} = A_k\theta_j\theta_{j+1} = A_k\sigma\gamma = A_k\gamma$, so γ is a unifier for $A\sigma$ and A_k. This shows that $A\sigma$ and A_k can be unified. Let σ' be an mgu for $A\sigma$ and A_k. Let $G'_{j+1} =\leftarrow (\overline{A_1}, (\overline{B_1}, \overline{B'}, \overline{B_2})\sigma, \overline{A_2})\sigma'$ be the goal derived from G_{j-1} and C'. We will show that G_{j+1} and G'_{j+1} are variants.

1. We have already shown that γ is a unifier for $A\sigma$ and A_k. Furthermore, σ' is an mgu for $A\sigma$ and A_k, so there exists a substitution δ such that $\sigma'\delta = \gamma$. Now $G_{j+1} =\leftarrow (\overline{A_1}, \overline{B_1}, \overline{B'}, \overline{B_2}, \overline{A_2})\theta_j\theta_{j+1} =\leftarrow (\overline{A_1}, \overline{B_1}, \overline{B'}, \overline{B_2}, \overline{A_2})\sigma\gamma =\leftarrow (\overline{A_1}, \overline{B_1}, \overline{B'}, \overline{B_2}, \overline{A_2})\sigma\sigma'\delta =\leftarrow (\overline{A_1}, (\overline{B_1}, \overline{B'}, \overline{B_2})\sigma, \overline{A_2})\sigma'\delta = G'_{j+1}\delta$.

2. σ' is an mgu for A_k and $A\sigma$, and $A_k\sigma = A_k$ (because of the standardizing apart), so $\sigma\sigma'$ is a unifier for A_k and A. Furthermore, θ_j is an mgu for A_k and A, so there exists a substitution γ' such that $\theta_j\gamma' = \sigma\sigma'$.

   $A'\gamma' = A'\theta_j\gamma' = A'\sigma\sigma' = B_i\sigma\sigma' = B_i\theta_j\gamma'$, so γ' is a unifier for A' and $B_i\theta_j$. θ_{j+1} is an mgu for A' and $B_i\theta_j$, so there exists a substitution δ' such that $\theta_{j+1}\delta' = \gamma'$. Now $G'_{j+1} =\leftarrow (\overline{A_1}, (\overline{B_1}, \overline{B'}, \overline{B_2})\sigma, \overline{A_2})\sigma' =\leftarrow (\overline{A_1}, \overline{B_1}, \overline{B'}, \overline{B_2}, \overline{A_2})\sigma\sigma' =\leftarrow (\overline{A_1}, \overline{B_1}, \overline{B'}, \overline{B_2}, \overline{A_2})\theta_j\gamma' =\leftarrow (\overline{A_1}, \overline{B_1}, \overline{B'}, \overline{B_2}, \overline{A_2})\theta_j\theta_{j+1}\delta' = G_{j+1}\delta'$.

We have shown that $G_{j+1} = G'_{j+1}\delta$ and $G'_{j+1} = G_{j+1}\delta'$, so by Proposition 4.16, G_{j+1} and G'_{j+1} are variants.

Since G_{j+1} and G'_{j+1} are variants, we have shown that the two resolution steps leading from G_{j-1} to G_{j+1} can be replaced by a single resolution step, which uses C' as input clause. In the same way, we can eliminate all other uses of C as input clause in the rest of the tree, by constructing a refutation which uses some clause in $U_{C,i}$ to replace a usage of C, each time replacing two resolution steps by one single resolution step. Finally we get an SLD-refutation of $\Pi \cup U_{C,i} \cup \{G\}$ which doesn't use C at all. This means that we have in fact found an SLD-refutation of $\Pi_{u1,C,i} \cup \{G\}$. $\square$

A direct consequence of the proof given above is the following:

Corollary 12.5 *Let Π be a definite program, G a definite goal, and $\Pi_{u1,C,i}$ the type 1 program resulting from unfolding C upon B_i in Π. Suppose there exists an SLD-refutation of length n of $\Pi \cup \{G\}$, which uses C r times as input clause. Then there exists an SLD-refutation of length $n - r$ of $\Pi_{u1,C,i} \cup \{G\}$.*

Intuitively, this corollary shows that unfolding makes refutations shorter. So unfolding has the potential of improving the efficiency of an SLD-based theorem prover. Especially unfolding often-used clauses is worthwhile, since then the value r mentioned in the corollary is highest. On the other hand, unfolding usually increases the number of clauses. So what we see here is an interesting trade-off between the number of clauses and the average length of a refutation: unfolding usually decreases the average length of a refutation, but also usually increases the number of clauses in the program.

We now proceed to prove that constructing the type 1 program preserves the least Herbrand model M_Π of the program. This is also proved in [TS84], though differently from our proof.

Theorem 12.6 *Let Π be a definite program, $C \in \Pi$, and $\Pi_{u1,C,i}$ the type 1 program resulting from unfolding C upon B_i in Π. Then $M_\Pi = M_{\Pi_{u1,C,i}}$.*

Proof Let A be some ground atom. Then:
$A \in M_\Pi$ iff (by Theorem 7.16)
$\Pi \models A$ iff (by Proposition 2.37)
$\Pi \cup \{\leftarrow A\}$ is unsatisfiable iff (by Theorem 7.8)
$\Pi \cup \{\leftarrow A\} \vdash_{sr} \Box$ iff (by Proposition 12.4)
$\Pi_{u1,C,i} \cup \{\leftarrow A\} \vdash_{sr} \Box$ iff (by Theorem 7.8)
$\Pi_{u1,C,i} \cup \{\leftarrow A\}$ is unsatisfiable iff (by Proposition 2.37)
$\Pi_{u1,C,i} \models A$ iff (by Theorem 7.16)
$A \in M_{\Pi_{u1,C,i}}$.
Hence $M_\Pi = M_{\Pi_{u1,C,i}}$. $\Box$

Thus constructing the type 1 program preserves the least Herbrand model. However, it does not preserve logical equivalence. Take for instance $\Pi = \{C = P(f(x)) \leftarrow P(x)\}$. Then $\Pi_{u1,C,1} = \{P(f^2(x)) \leftarrow P(x)\}$. Now $M_\Pi = M_{\Pi_{u1,C,1}} = \emptyset$, but $\Pi \not\Leftrightarrow \Pi_{u1,C,1}$ since $\Pi_{u1,C,1} \not\models \Pi$. Note that this means that a specialization of Π need not be a specialization of $\Pi_{u1,C,i}$. This is actually one of the reasons for the fact that type 1 unfolding and clause deletion cannot solve all specialization problems (see Section 12.3).

On the other hand, constructing the type 2 program *does* preserve logical equivalence. Since $\Pi \subseteq \Pi_{u2,C,i}$ we have $\Pi_{u2,C,i} \models \Pi$; and because $\Pi_{u2,C,i} \backslash \Pi$ is a set of resolvents of clauses in Π, we also have $\Pi \models \Pi_{u2,C,i}$.

Proposition 12.7 *Let Π be a definite program, $C \in \Pi$, and $\Pi_{u2,C,i}$ the type 2 program resulting from unfolding C upon B_i in Π. Then $\Pi \Leftrightarrow \Pi_{u2,C,i}$.*

12.3 UDS Specialization

As the example in the introduction to this chapter showed, the combination of constructing the type 1 program and clause deletion can be used to specialize overly general definite programs. This combination is not complete: it cannot solve all specialization problems. Consider $\Pi = \{(P(f(x)) \leftarrow$

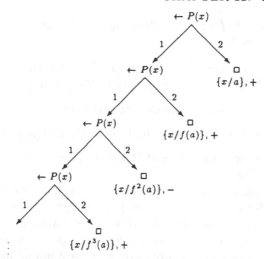

Figure 12.3: The SLD-tree of $\Pi \cup \{\leftarrow P(x)\}$

$P(x)), P(a)\}$. Then $M_\Pi = \{P(a), P(f(a)), P(f^2(a)), P(f^3(a)) \ldots\}$. Let $E^+ = M_\Pi \setminus \{P(f^2(a))\}$ and $E^- = \{P(f^2(a))\}$. See Figure 12.3.

Let $\Pi_1 = \Pi$. The only clause which can be unfolded is $P(f(x)) \leftarrow P(x)$. Unfolding this results in the following type 1 program:

$$\Pi_2 = \{(P(f^2(x)) \leftarrow P(x)), P(f(a)), P(a)\}.$$

Then unfolding $P(f^2(x)) \leftarrow P(x)$ gives

$$\Pi_3 = \{(P(f^4(x)) \leftarrow P(x)), P(f^3(a)), P(f^2(a)), P(f(a)), P(a)\}.$$

Notice that $M_{\Pi_1} = M_{\Pi_2} = M_{\Pi_3}$, but unfolding has nevertheless weakened the program: $\Pi_1 \models \Pi_2 \models \Pi_3$, but $\Pi_2 \not\models \Pi_1$ and $\Pi_3 \not\models \Pi_2$. In Π_3, $P(f^4(x)) \leftarrow P(x)$ can be unfolded, etc. It is not difficult to see that in general, any program which can be constructed from Π by type 1 unfolding and clause deletion, is a subset of

$$\{P(f^{2^n}(x)) \leftarrow P(x)), P(f^{2^n-1}(a)), P(f^{2^n-2}(a)), \ldots, P(f(a)), P(a)\},$$

for some n. To specialize this program such that $P(f^2(a))$ is no longer derivable, we must in any case remove $P(f^2(a))$. However, this would also prune some of the positive examples (such as $P(f^{2^n+2}(a))$) from the program via the clause $P(f^{2^n}(x)) \leftarrow P(x)$. Thus type 1 unfolding and clause deletion are not sufficient for this particular specialization problem.

But suppose we use the type 2 program instead of the type 1 program. That is, suppose we do not immediately delete the unfolded clause from the program. In this case, we *can* find a correct specialization with respect to the examples given above, as follows. We start with $\Pi'_1 = \Pi$, and unfold $P(f(x)) \leftarrow P(x)$ without removing the unfolded clause. This gives Π'_2:

$$\Pi'_2 = \{(P(f^2(x)) \leftarrow P(x)), (P(f(x)) \leftarrow P(x)), P(f(a)), P(a)\}.$$

Now we unfold $P(f^2(x)) \leftarrow P(x)$, again without removing the unfolded clause. This gives Π'_3:

$\Pi'_3 = \{(P(f^4(x)) \leftarrow P(x)), (P(f^3(x)) \leftarrow P(x)), (P(f^2(x)) \leftarrow P(x)), (P(f(x)) \leftarrow P(x)), P(f^3(a)), P(f^2(a)), P(f(a)), P(a)\}.$

If we delete some clauses from Π'_3, we obtain Π'':

$\Pi'' = \{(P(f^4(x)) \leftarrow P(x)), (P(f^3(x)) \leftarrow P(x)), P(f(a)), P(a)\}.$

This is a correct specialization of Π with respect to E^+ and E^-: $\Pi'' \models E^+$, and $\Pi'' \not\models P(f^2(a))$.

Yet the combination of type 2 unfolding and clause deletion is still not sufficient. Consider $\Pi = \{P(x)\}$, $E^+ = \{P(f(a)), P(f^2(a))\}$ and $E^- = \{P(a)\}$. $\Pi' = \{P(f(x))\}$ is a solution for this specialization problem. But since Π contains only a single atom, no unfolding can take place here. Thus the only two programs which can be obtained by type 2 unfolding and clause deletion, are Π itself and the empty set, neither of which is correct. In order to solve this specialization problem, we have to allow the possibility of taking a *subsumption step*. In general, we can define UDS specialization (**U**nfolding, clause **D**eletion, **S**ubsumption) as follows:

Definition 12.8 Let Π and Π' be definite programs. We say Π' is a *UDS specialization* of Π, if there exists a sequence $\Pi_1 = \Pi, \Pi_2, \ldots, \Pi_n = \Pi'$ ($n \geq 1$) of definite programs, such that for each $j = 1, \ldots, n-1$, one of the following holds:

1. $\Pi_{j+1} = \Pi_{j u 2, C, i}$.
2. $\Pi_{j+1} = \Pi_j \backslash \{C\}$ for some $C \in \Pi_j$.
3. $\Pi_{j+1} = \Pi_j \cup \{C\}$ for a C that is subsumed by a clause in Π_j. $\diamond$

UDS specialization is indeed complete: any specialization problem has a UDS specialization as solution. For the proof of completeness, we use the Subsumption Theorem for SLD-resolution (Theorem 7.10).

Theorem 12.9 *Let Π and Π' be definite programs, such that Π' contains no tautologies. Then $\Pi \models \Pi'$ iff Π' is a UDS specialization of Π.*

Proof

$\Leftarrow$: By the soundness of resolution and subsumption.

$\Rightarrow$: Suppose $\Pi \models \Pi'$. Then for every $C \in \Pi'$, we have $\Pi \models C$. Let C be some particular clause in Π' that is not in Π. Then by the Subsumption Theorem for SLD-resolution, there exists an SLD-derivation from Π of a clause D which subsumes C, as shown in Figure 12.4.

Since R_1 is a resolvent of R_0 and C_1 (upon the selected atom B_i in R_0), if we unfold R_0 in Π upon B_i we get the program $\Pi_{u2,R_0,i}$ which contains R_1. Now when we unfold R_1 in $\Pi_{u2,R_0,i}$, we get a program which contains R_2, etc. Thus after n applications of (type 2) unfolding, we can produce a

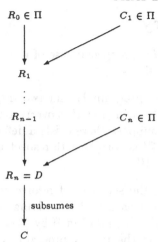

Figure 12.4: An SLD-deduction of C from Π

UDS specialization (a superset of Π) containing the clause $R_n = D$. Since D subsumes C, we can add C to the program, by the third item in the definition of UDS specialization.

If we do this for every $C \in \Pi'$ that is not in Π, we get a program Π'' which contains every clause in Π'. Since Π'' is obtained from Π by a finite number of applications of unfolding and subsumption, Π'' is a UDS specialization of Π. Now delete from Π'' all those clauses that are not in Π'. Then we obtain Π' as a UDS specialization of Π. Thus if $\Pi \models \Pi'$, then Π' is a UDS specialization of Π. $\square$

Now suppose we have Π, Π', E^+ and E^-, such that $\Pi \models \Pi'$ and Π' is correct with respect to E^+ and E^-. We can assume Π' contains no tautologies. Then it follows from the previous theorem that Π' is a UDS specialization of Π. This shows that UDS specialization is complete:

Corollary 12.10 (Completeness of UDS specialization) *Every specialization problem with Π as initial program has a UDS specialization of Π as solution.*

Efficiency

Note that if we want to unfold some particular clause C, we actually only need to consider the resolvents of C and clauses from the original Π. This is clear from Figure 12.4, because in order to produce R_{i+1}, we only need to resolve R_i with C_{i+1}, which is a member of the original Π. In other words, we only need to add a subset of $U_{C,i}$ to the program. We might define $U'_{C,i}$ as the set of resolvents upon B_i of C and clauses from the original Π, and then use $\Pi_{j+1} = \Pi_j \cup U'_{C,i}$ instead of $\Pi_{j+1} = \Pi_{j_{u2,C,i}} = \Pi_j \cup U_{C,i}$. This reduces the number of clauses that unfolding produces, and hence improves efficiency.

12.4 Summary

The *specialization problem*, a special case of the normal problem setting for ILP, can be stated as follows:

> **Given**: A definite program Π and two disjoint sets of ground atoms E^+ and E^-, such that Π is overly general with respect to E^+ and E^-, and suppose there exists a definite program Π' such that $\Pi \models \Pi'$ and Π' is correct with respect to E^+ and E^-.
> **Find**: One such a Π'.

Unfolding, constructing the set $U_{C,i}$ of resolvents of a clause $C \in \Pi$ with clauses in Π, can be used as a tool for solving such problems. The type 1 program is obtained by replacing C in Π by $U_{C,i}$, while the type 2 program is $\Pi \cup U_{C,i}$. Constructing the type 1 program preserves the least Herband model, while the type 2 program preserves logical equivalence with the original program.

A UDS specialization of Π is a definite program obtained from Π by a finite number of applications of unfolding (type 2), clause deletion, and subsumption. UDS specialization is a complete specialization method: every specialization problem with Π as initial program has a UDS specialization of Π as solution.

Chapter 13

The Lattice and Cover Structure of Atoms

13.1 Introduction

As we have explained earlier, the normal problem of inductive logic programming is to find a correct theory, a set of clauses which implies all given positive examples and which is consistent with respect to the given negative examples. Usually, it is not immediately obvious which set of clauses we should pick as our theory. Rather, we will have to *search* among the permitted clauses for a set of clauses with the right properties. If a positive example is not implied by the theory, we should search for a more general theory. On the other hand, if the theory is not consistent with respect to the negative examples, we should search for a more specific theory—for instance, by replacing a clause in the theory by more specific clauses—such that the theory becomes consistent. Thus, as mentioned before, the two most important operations in ILP are generalization and specialization. Repeated application of such generalization and specialization steps may finally yield a correct theory.

To systematically facilitate this search, it would be very handy if the set of clauses that has to be searched, is somehow structured. In this and the following chapters, we will structure the set of clauses by imposing a *generality order* upon it. That is, we will describe several alternatives for what it means for some clause to be more general than another clause. Since generalization (or dually, specialization) can proceed along the lines of such a generality order, using such an order can direct the search for a correct theory.

In this chapter we will be concerned with ordering what is urguably the simplest set of clauses, namely the set of atoms. It is based on the work of John Reynolds [Rey70] and Gordon Plotkin [Plo70]. In particular, we will here discuss *covers*, *least generalizations*, and *greatest specializations* of atoms. Covers form the basis of most refinement operators, for instance those defined by Shapiro [Sha81b], Laird [Lai88], and Van der Laag and Nienhuys-Cheng [LN93]. Least generalizations can be used to generalize given finite sets of examples.[1]

13.2 Quasi-Ordered Sets

All generality orders which we will define, are so-called *quasi-orders*. We first introduce quasi-orders in a very abstract way, as a relation with certain properties. In later sections, we will apply this concept to the set of atoms.

A relation R is defined on a set G, and can be seen as a subset of $G \times G$, the set of all ordered pairs of elements from G. If the pair $(a, b) \in R \subseteq G \times G$, then we write aRb. For example, if G is the set of clauses and $\models$ denotes the usual 'logical implication' relation, then this relation is the set of all pairs (C, D) of clauses where $C \models D$. So then we can write $(P(x), P(a)) \in \models$, or equivalently $P(x) \models P(a)$.

Definition 13.1 Let R be a relation on a set G.

1. R is *reflexive* if for all $x \in G$, xRx holds.
2. R is *symmetric* if for all $x, y \in G$, xRy implies that also yRx.
3. R is *transitive* if for all $x, y, z \in G$, xRy and yRz implies xRz.
4. R is *antisymmetric* if for all $x, y \in G$, xRy and yRx implies $x = y$.

$\diamond$

Definition 13.2 Let R be a relation on a set G.

1. R is called a *quasi-order on G*, if R is reflexive and transitive. The pair $\langle G, R \rangle$ is then called a *quasi-ordered set*.
2. R is called a *partial order on G*, if R is reflexive, transitive and antisymmetric. The pair $\langle G, R \rangle$ is then called a *partially ordered set*.
3. R is called an *equivalence relation on G*, if R is reflexive, symmetric and transitive. $\diamond$

A well known result from mathematics is the fact that an equivalence relation on G partitions G into disjoint equivalence classes. Note that a partial order is also a quasi-order. We will usually denote quasi-orders or partial orders by $\geq$ or $\succeq$, rather than by R.

Example 13.3 Let $G = \mathbf{R} \times \mathbf{R}$ be the set of all ordered pairs of real numbers, which can be seen as representing the plane. We can define a relation $\geq$ on G, as follows: $(a, b) \geq (c, d)$ iff $\sqrt{a^2 + b^2} \geq \sqrt{c^2 + d^2}$. That is, $(a, b) \geq (c, d)$ iff the euclidean distance in the plane from the origin $(0, 0)$ to (a, b) is greater than or equal to the distance from $(0, 0)$ to (c, d).

---

[1]There is also a relation between least generalizations and inverse resolution, see [Mug92b].

For any $(a, b) \in G$, we have $(a, b) \geq (a, b)$, so $\geq$ is reflexive. Also, if $(a, b) \geq (c, d)$ and $(c, d) \geq (e, f)$, then $(a, b) \geq (e, f)$, which shows that $\geq$ is also a transitive relation, hence $\langle G, \geq \rangle$ is a quasi-order.

We can define an equivalence relation $\approx$ on G, by defining $(a, b) \approx (c, d)$ iff $(a, b) \geq (c, d)$ and $(c, d) \geq (a, b)$. Then the equivalence class $[(a, b)]$ of (a, b), which is the set $\{(c, d) \in G \mid (a, b) \approx (c, d)\}$, is the set of all points in the plane with equal distance to the origin as (a, b). That is, $[(a, b)]$ is the circle in the plane with the origin as centre, and $\sqrt{a^2 + b^2}$ as radius. ◁

If $\langle G, \geq \rangle$ is a quasi-ordered set, then we will write $x > y$ iff both $x \geq y$ and $y \not\geq x$. If both $x \not\geq y$ and $y \not\geq x$, we say that x and y are *incomparable* in this quasi-order.

We will now show how, given a quasi-order $\geq$ on some set G, we can turn this into a partial order $\hat{\geq}$ on the set of equivalence classes of G. First we define the following equivalence relation $\approx$ on G: for all $x, y \in G$, we write $x \approx y$ iff $x \geq y$ and $y \geq x$. This relation $\approx$ is an equivalence relation, because:

1. $x \approx x$ for all $x \in G$ ($\approx$ is reflexive).
2. If $x \approx y$, then $x \geq y$ and $y \geq x$, so then $y \approx x$ ($\approx$ is symmetric).
3. Suppose $x \approx y$ and $y \approx z$, then $x \geq y$, $y \geq x$, $y \geq z$ and $z \geq y$. Hence, by the transitivity of $\geq$, we know $x \approx z$ ($\approx$ is transitive).

Thus we can say that x and y are *equivalent* if $x \approx y$. Now let $[x]$ be the equivalence class of $x \in G$. That is, $[x] = \{y \mid x \approx y\}$. The equivalence relation $\approx$ partitions the set G into a number of disjoint equivalence classes. Next we construct a relation $\hat{\geq}$ on the set of these equivalence classes, by defining $[x]\hat{\geq}[y]$ if $x \geq y$. This can be shown to be well-defined: if $x \approx x'$ and $y \approx y'$ then we have $x \geq y$ iff $x' \geq y'$, so it does not matter whether we use $x \geq y$ or $x' \geq y'$ to define $[x] = [x']\hat{\geq}[y] = [y']$. It is easy to see that the relation $\hat{\geq}$ forms a partial order. For instance antisymmetry: if $[x]\hat{\geq}[y]$ and $[y]\hat{\geq}[x]$, then $x \geq y$ and $y \geq x$, so $x \approx y$ and hence $[x] = [y]$.

Thus we can use a *quasi*-order $\geq$ on G to define a *partial* order $\hat{\geq}$ on the set of the equivalence classes of G, via the equivalence relation $\approx$. This partial order is said to be *induced* by the quasi-order on which it is based.

We now turn to defining upper and lower bounds on quasi-ordered sets.

Definition 13.4 Let $\langle G, \geq \rangle$ be a quasi-ordered set, and $S \subseteq G$. An element $x \in G$ is called an *upper bound of* S if $x \geq y$ for all $y \in S$. An upper bound x of S is called a *least upper bound* (*lub*) *of* S, if $z \geq x$ for all upper bounds z of S.

Dually, an element $x \in G$ is called a *lower bound of* S if $y \geq x$ for all $y \in S$. A lower bound x of S is called a *greatest lower bound* (*glb*) *of* S, if $x \geq z$ for all lower bounds z of S. ◇

Example 13.5 Consider $\langle \mathbf{R}, \geq \rangle$, the set of real numbers quasi-ordered by the usual 'greater than or equal to' relation, and let S be the open interval

$(0,1) \subseteq \mathbf{R}$. Then any $x \in \mathbf{R}$ with $x \geq 1$ is an upper bound of S, and $1 \in \mathbf{R}$ is the least upper bound. Also, any $x \leq 0$ is a lower bound of S, and 0 is the greatest lower bound. $\lhd$

Notice that if x and y are both lub's of some set $S \subseteq G$, then $y \geq x$ and $x \geq y$, so then $x \approx y$. This means that all lub's of S are equivalent. Dually, if x and y are glb's of some S, then also $x \approx y$.

Example 13.6 In a quasi-ordered set, a subset need not have a lub or glb. Consider $\langle \mathbf{Q}, \geq \rangle$, where $\mathbf{Q}$ is the set of rational numbers, and $S = \{q \in \mathbf{Q} \mid q^2 < 2\} \subset \mathbf{Q}$. Since $\sqrt{2} \notin \mathbf{Q}$, S has no lub in $\mathbf{Q}$. Also, $-\sqrt{2} \notin \mathbf{Q}$, which implies that S has no glb either. $\lhd$

Example 13.7 Let $G = \{a, b, c, d\}$, and let $\geq$ be defined as $c \geq a$, $c \geq b$, $d \geq a$ and $d \geq b$. Then since c and d are incomparable, the set $\{a, b\}$ has no lub in this quasi-order. See Figure 13.1. $\lhd$

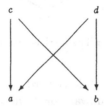

Figure 13.1: $\{a, b\}$ has no lub here

Definition 13.8 Let $\langle G, \geq \rangle$ be a quasi-ordered set. If for every $x, y \in G$, a lub of $\{x, y\}$ and a glb of $\{x, y\}$ exist, then $\langle G, \geq \rangle$ is called a *lattice*. $\diamond$

In mathematics, the concept of a lattice is often defined on a partial order, rather than on a quasi-order. The previous definition is more convenient for us, because in ILP we usually have to do with a quasi-order on clauses, even when we are interested in properties of equivalence classes of clauses. But anyhow, if we have a lattice on a quasi-order, we also have a lattice on the partial order on the equivalence classes induced by the quasi-order.

If some $x, y \in G$ have more than one lub, we let $x \sqcup y$ denote an arbitrary lub. Since all lub's are equivalent under $\approx$, for any given x, y, one $x \sqcup y$ is then equivalent to all other lub's of $\{x, y\}$. Moreover, if $x \approx x'$ and $y \approx y'$, then $x \sqcup y \approx x' \sqcup y'$. It is easy to see that in a lattice $\langle G, \geq \rangle$, any finite non-empty set $S \subseteq G$ has a lub. For if $S = \{x_1, \ldots, x_n\}$, then $((\ldots((x_1 \sqcup x_2) \sqcup x_3) \ldots) \sqcup x_n)$ is a lub of S. Since $(x \sqcup y) \sqcup z \approx x \sqcup (y \sqcup z)$, we may use $x_1 \sqcup x_2 \sqcup \ldots \sqcup x_n$ to denote an arbitrary lub of S.

Analogously, we let $x \sqcap y$ denote an arbitrary glb.

Example 13.9 Let G be the power set of $\{a, b, c\}$, i.e., G is the set of all subsets of $\{a, b, c\}$, and let $\supseteq$ be the usual superset relation between sets. It is easy to see that $\langle G, \supseteq \rangle$ is a partially ordered set. In fact, $\langle G, \supseteq \rangle$ is a lattice. To see this, it is sufficient to note that for all $x, y \in G$, $x \sqcup y = x \cup y$, and $x \sqcap y = x \cap y$, so the lub and glb of any two elements exist. The lattice $\langle G, \supseteq \rangle$ is pictured in Figure 13.2. ◁

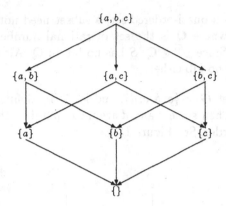

Figure 13.2: The lattice-structure of $\langle G, \supseteq \rangle$

Now we define upward and downward *covers*, which can be seen as the smallest possible non-trivial upward or downward steps in the quasi-order.

Definition 13.10 Let $\langle G, \geq \rangle$ be a quasi-ordered set, and let $x, y \in G$. If $x > y$ and there is no $z \in G$ such that $x > z > y$, then x is an *upward cover* of y, and y is a *downward cover* of x. ◇

Example 13.11 In the previous example, the set $\{a, b\} \in G$ has one upward cover, namely $\{a, b, c\}$, and two different downward covers, namely $\{a\}$ and $\{b\}$. ◁

As we have seen, a set in a quasi-order need not have a lub or glb. We can weaken the requirement of a *least* upper bound (resp. *greatest* lower bound) somewhat, by considering some *minimal* upper bounds (resp. *maximal* lower bounds). Consider Example 13.7. There the set $S = \{a, b\}$ has no lub. However, there is no element "between" c and $\{a, b\}$, nor is there an element between d and $\{a, b\}$. Thus c and d are minimal upper bounds of S.

Definition 13.12 Let $\langle G, \geq \rangle$ be a quasi-ordered set, and let $S \subseteq G$. If $x \in G$ is an upper bound of S, and if for any upper bound $y \in G$ of S we have that $x \geq y$ implies $x \approx y$, then x is called a *minimal upper bound (mub) of* S.

Dually, if $x \in G$ is a lower bound of S, and if for any lower bound $y \in G$ of S we have that $y \geq x$ implies $x \approx y$, then x is called a *maximal lower bound (mlb) of* S. ◇

The differences and similarities between the concepts of an upward cover, a least upper bound, and a minimal upper bound are important in ILP, and are sometimes confused. These differences are similar in the "downward" case.

The main difference between an upward cover on the one hand, and a lub or a mub on the other, is that a lub or a mub is "above" a *subset* of G, whereas an upward cover is "above" a *single element* in G. This difference does not disappear in case the subset contains only a single element. That is, if $S = \{y\}$, then any lub and any mub of S is equivalent to y, whereas an upward cover of y must always be some other element, not equivalent to y.

The main difference between a lub and a mub is that a lub of a set S (if such a lub exists) is unique up to equivalence. On the other hand, a set S may have more than one distinct, incomparable mub's. a lub is a "smallest" upper bound of S, while x is a mub if there are no "smaller" upper bounds than x. If a lub of S exists, it is also a mub of S, and any other mub of S will be equivalent to the lub.

We have already seen that a set need not have a lub or glb. Neither need it have a mub or an mlb, nor upward or downward covers. For instance, let G be the infinite set $\{y, x_1, x_2, x_3, \ldots\}$, and let $\geq$ be a quasi-order on G, defined as $x_1 > x_2 > \ldots > x_n > x_{n+1} > \ldots > y$. Then there is no upward cover of y: for every x_n, there always is an x_{n+1} such that $x_n > x_{n+1} > y$. This is a situation where y has no *complete* set of upward covers.

Definition 13.13 Let $\langle G, \geq \rangle$ be a quasi-ordered set, $y \in G$, S_u a set of upward covers of y in G, and S_d a set of downward covers of y in G. We say S_u is *complete for* y, if for all $z \in G$, $z > y$ implies there is an $x \in S_u$ such that $z \geq x > y$. If there exists a finite set of upward covers of y which is complete for y, we say y *has a finite complete set of upward covers.*

Similarly, S_d is *complete for* y, if for all $z \in G$, $y > z$ implies there is an $x \in S_d$ such that $y > x \geq z$. If there exists a finite set of downward covers of y which is complete for y, we say y *has a finite complete set of downward covers.*   ◇

Note that a complete set of upward covers for y need not contain *all* upward covers of y. However, in order to be complete, it should contain at least one element from each equivalence class of upward covers. On the other hand, even the set of *all* upward covers of y need not be complete for y. Witness the example given before the last definition: here the set of all upward covers of y is empty, but obviously not complete.

An analogous definition can be given for sets of mub's and mlb's:

Definition 13.14 Let $\langle G, \geq \rangle$ be a quasi-ordered set, $S \subseteq G$, S_u a set of mub's of S, and S_d a set of mlb's of S. We say S_u is *complete for* S, if for all upper bounds $z \in G$ of S, there is an $x \in S_u$ such that $z \geq x$. If there exists a finite set of mub's of S which is complete for S, we say S *has a finite complete set of mub's.*

Similarly, S_d is *complete for* S, if for all lower bounds $z \in G$ of S, there is an $x \in S_d$ such that $x \geq z$. If there exists a finite set of mlb's of S which is complete for S, we say S *has a finite complete set of mlb's.* $\diamond$

13.3 Quasi-Ordered Sets of Clauses

All particular quasi-orders we will be interested in in this work, are quasi-orders on sets of *clauses*. The most important quasi-orders we will discuss, are the subsumption order and the implication order. The terminology in the previous sections mostly follows mathematical conventions, but the ILP community has its own terminology regarding quasi-orders on sets of clauses, which is not always uniformly defined. Let $\mathcal{C}$ be a set of clauses, $S \subseteq \mathcal{C}$, and $\geq$ a quasi-order on $\mathcal{C}$. Then we use the following definitions in ILP:

- If $C, D \in \mathcal{C}$ and $C \geq D$, then C is called a *generalization* of D (or C is *more general than* D), and D is a *specialization* of C (or D is *more specific than* C).
- *Covers* are used as defined in the last section.
- An upper bound $C \in \mathcal{C}$ of S is called a *generalization* of S.
- A lub $C \in \mathcal{C}$ of S is called a *least generalization* (LG) of S.
- A mub $C \in \mathcal{C}$ of S is called a *minimal generalization* (MG) of S.
- A lower bound $C \in \mathcal{C}$ of S is called a *specialization* of S.
- A glb $C \in \mathcal{C}$ of S is called a *greatest specialization* (GS) of S.
- An mlb $C \in \mathcal{C}$ of S is called a *maximal specialization* (MS) of S.

The idea behind this is that generalization corresponds to an "upward" step in the quasi-ordered set, while specialization corresponds to a "downward" step. Upward and downward covers generalize or specialize individual clauses to other individual clauses; least or minimal generalizations generalize a set of clauses to an individual clause; and greatest or maximal specializations specialize a set of clauses to an individual clause.[2]

Generality orders are usually defined in a way that is correlated with logical implication. For example, the quasi-order *subsumption*, the topic of this and the next chapter, is consistent with logical implication: if C subsumes D, then $C \models D$.

13.4 Atoms as a Quasi-Ordered Set

In this section, we assume a language with a finite, non-empty set of predicate symbols, a finite set of function symbols and a finite, non-empty set of constants. We will consider the set $\mathcal{A}$ of all atoms in this language. In this chapter, we assume $\mathcal{A}$ includes the special elements $\top$ (the *top element*) and

---

[2]Some work has also been done on minimally generalizing or specializing sets of clauses to other sets of clauses, though we will not discuss this work here. See [AISO94] for generalization and [Wro93] for specialization.

⊥ (the *bottom element*). Atoms of the ordinary form $P(t_1, \ldots, t_n)$ will be referred to as *conventional atoms*. We will here show how $\mathcal{A}$ can be seen as a lattice.

Definition 13.15 We define a quasi-order $\succeq$ on the set $\mathcal{A}$ of all atoms in some language as follows. If $A, B \in \mathcal{A}$, then:

- $\top \succeq A$, for every $A \in \mathcal{A}$.
- $A \succeq \bot$, for every $A \in \mathcal{A}$.
- $A \succeq B$, if A, B are conventional atoms and there is a substitution θ, such that $A\theta = B$, so A subsumes B.   ◇

Right from the very first applications of the subsumption relation in ILP, there has been some controversy about the symbol used for denoting this relation: Plotkin [Plo70] used '$\leq$', while Reynolds [Rey70] used '$\geq$'. We use '$\succeq$' here, similar to Reynolds' '$\geq$', because we feel it serves the intuition to view A as somehow "greater" or "stronger" than B, if $A \succeq B$ holds.

Notice that if the empty clause □ is added to the set of atoms, □ can be used as the top element $\top$, since it subsumes any atom. Actually, in computational logic the symbols '$\top$' and '$\bot$' are often used to denote "true" and "false", respectively. Common usage in ILP is just the reverse: now $\top = $ □ denotes a clause which is always false.

As we explained earlier, A and B are defined equivalent (written as $A \approx B$) if $A \succeq B$ and $B \succeq A$. Using this equivalence relation we have the following lemma, which shows that the equivalence class of some atom A is exactly the set of variants of A.

Lemma 13.16 *Let $A, B \in \mathcal{A}$. Then $A \approx B$ iff one of the following holds:*

- *$A = B = \top$ or $A = B = \bot$.*
- *A and B are conventional atoms which are variants.*

Proof
⇒: Suppose $A \approx B$. If $A = \top$, then by Definition 13.15 also $B = \top$. Similarly for $A = \bot$. If A and B are both conventional, then there are substitutions θ and σ such that $A\theta = B$ and $B\sigma = A$. Hence by Proposition 4.16, A and B are variants.
⇐: Follows immediately from the definition of $\succeq$.   □

The $\succeq$-relation orders the set of atoms according to subsumption. One might think that ordering them according to logical implication would be more natural. As the following lemma shows, the $\succeq$-relation does in fact also order the atoms according to implication, because with respect to conventional atoms, implication and subsumption come to the same.

Lemma 13.17 *For conventional atoms A and B, $A \models B$ iff $A \succeq B$.*

Proof

$\Rightarrow$: A cannot be resolved with itself and B is not a tautology, hence it follows from the Subsumption Theorem (Theorem 5.17) that $A \succeq B$.

$\Leftarrow$: If $A \succeq B$, then A subsumes B, hence $A \models B$. $\qquad\square$

13.4.1 Greatest Specializations

We now proceed to show that $\langle \mathcal{A}, \succeq \rangle$ is a lattice. In order to do this, we have to establish that for any $A, B \in \mathcal{A}$, both an LG (lub) $A \sqcup B$ and a GS (glb) $A \sqcap B$ exist. We start with the GS.

Theorem 13.18 *Let $\mathcal{A}$ be the set of atoms. Then for all $A, B \in \mathcal{A}$, a greatest specialization $A \sqcap B$ exists.*

Proof By the remark following Definition 13.8, we can assume A and B are standardized apart. We divide the proof in the following cases:

- If $A = \bot$ or $B = \bot$, then $A \sqcap B = \bot$. If $A = \top$, then $A \sqcap B = B$ and if $B = \top$, then $A \sqcap B = A$.
- Suppose A and B are conventional atoms which are not unifiable. Since A and B are not unifiable, there is no conventional atom C such that $A \succeq C$ and $B \succeq C$. Hence $A \sqcap B = \bot$.
- Suppose A and B are unifiable conventional atoms. Then there is an mgu θ for $\{A, B\}$. We will show $A \sqcap B = A\theta = B\theta$.
  Let $C \in \mathcal{A}$ such that $A \succeq C$ and $B \succeq C$, then we need to show $A\theta \succeq C$. If $C = \bot$, this is obvious. If C is conventional, then there are substitutions σ_1 and σ_2 such that $A\sigma_1 = C = B\sigma_2$. Here we can assume σ_1 only acts on variables in A, and σ_2 only acts on variables in B. Let $\sigma = \sigma_1 \cup \sigma_2$. Notice that σ is a unifier for $\{A, B\}$. Since θ is an mgu for $\{A, B\}$, there is a γ such that $\theta\gamma = \sigma$. Now $A\theta\gamma = A\sigma = A\sigma_1 = C$, so $A\theta \succeq C$. $\qquad\square$

Example 13.19 Let $A = P(x, f(y), a)$ and $B = P(u, f(a), v)$. The substitution $\{u/x, y/a, v/a\}$ is an mgu for A and B. Therefore $A \sqcap B = A\theta = B\theta = P(x, f(a), a)$. Notice that all variants of $P(x, f(a), a)$ are also GSs of A and B. Thus A and B have more than one GS, but they are all equivalent. $\qquad\triangleleft$

13.4.2 Least Generalizations

If A and B are conventional, then $A \sqcap B$ can be constructed by applying the Unification Algorithm to variants of A and B which are standardized apart. To construct an LG $A \sqcup B$ of A and B, we need to do more or less the opposite. Rather than finding a most general instance, as the Unification Algorithm does, we now need to find a least generalization. Since doing this is more or less the opposite of unification, the algorithm which constructs an LG of A and B is called the *Anti-Unification Algorithm*. It is given in different forms both in [Rey70] and in [Plo70]. We adapt Reynolds' algorithm and his correctness proof here.

This algorithm uses *term occurrences*. Suppose we have the atom $A = P(f(g(y), x), g(y))$. We can identify a term occurrence with its position in the atom. The first term $f(g(y), x)$ has position $\langle 1 \rangle$ in A, the first occurrence of $g(y)$ has position $\langle 1, 1 \rangle$ (the first position within the term that has position $\langle 1 \rangle$ in A), the occurrence of x has position $\langle 1, 2 \rangle$, and the rightmost occurrence of $g(y)$ in A has position $\langle 2 \rangle$ in A.

Definition 13.20 Let $A = P(t_1, \ldots, t_n)$ be a conventional atom. Then t_i has *position* $\langle i \rangle$ in A. If the term $f(s_1, \ldots, s_m)$ has position $\langle p_1, \ldots, p_k \rangle$ in A, then s_j within this term has position $\langle p_1, \ldots, p_k, j \rangle$ in A.

If some term t has position p in A, then the pair (t, p) is called a *term occurrence* in A.   ◇

Positions are also sometimes called *places* by others. Now the two occurrences of $g(y)$ in $A = P(f(g(y), x), g(y))$ can be written as $(g(y), \langle 1, 1 \rangle)$ and $(g(y), \langle 2 \rangle)$. Notice that the fact that the first occurrence of $g(y)$ in A is to the left of the second occurrence of $g(y)$, corresponds to the fact that the position $\langle 1, 1 \rangle$ comes before $\langle 2 \rangle$ in a lexicographical ordering of positions. Suppose $B = P(f(h(a), y), b)$. We can say that the first position where A and B differ, is $\langle 1, 1 \rangle$. A has $g(y)$ at position $\langle 1, 1 \rangle$, B has $h(a)$ at $\langle 1, 1 \rangle$.

Now we can give the Anti-Unification Algorithm, which can be used to find $A \sqcup B$ for conventional atoms A and B. If A and B do not have the same predicate symbol, then their LG is $\top$. So for the following algorithm, we assume A and B have the same predicate symbol.

Algorithm 13.1 (Anti-Unification Algorithm)
Input: Conventional atoms A, B, with the same predicate symbol.
Output: $A \sqcup B$.

1. Set $A' = A$, $B' = B$, $\theta = \varepsilon$, $\sigma = \varepsilon$, and $i = 0$.
   Let $z_1, z_2, \ldots$ be a sequence of variables not appearing in A or B.
2. If $A' = B'$, then output A' and stop.
3. Let p be the leftmost symbol position where A' and B' differ. Let s and t be the terms occurring at this position in A' and B', respectively.
4. If, for some j with $1 \leq j \leq i$, $z_j\theta = s$ and $z_j\sigma = t$, then replace s at position p in A' by z_j, replace t at position p in B' by z_j, and goto 2.
5. Otherwise set i to $i + 1$, replace s at position p in A' by z_i, and replace t at position p in B' by z_i. Set θ to $\theta \cup \{z_i/s\}$, σ to $\sigma \cup \{z_i/t\}$, and goto 2.

Example 13.21 Let $A = P(f(g(x), a), g(x))$ and $B = P(f(h(y), x), h(y))$. We can use Algorithm 13.1 to find $A \sqcup B$, as follows:

1. $A' = P(f(g(x), a), g(x))$, $B' = P(f(h(y), x), h(y))$, $\theta = \varepsilon$, $\sigma = \varepsilon$, and $i = 0$.

   $p = \langle 1, 1 \rangle$ is the leftmost symbol position where A' and B' differ, $s = g(x)$ and $t = h(y)$. Set $i = 1$, and replace s and t at position $\langle 1, 1 \rangle$ by z_1.

2. $A' = P(f(z_1, a), g(x))$, $B' = P(f(z_1, x), h(y))$, $\theta = \{z_1/g(x)\}$, $\sigma = \{z_1/h(y)\}$, and $i = 1$.

   $p = \langle 1, 2 \rangle$ is the leftmost symbol position where A' and B' differ, $s = a$ and $t = x$. Set $i = 2$, and replace s and t at position $\langle 1, 2 \rangle$ by z_2.

3. $A' = P(f(z_1, z_2), g(x))$, $B' = P(f(z_1, z_2), h(y))$, $\theta = \{z_1/g(x), z_2/a\}$, $\sigma = \{z_1/h(y), z_2/x\}$, and $i = 2$.

   $p = \langle 2 \rangle$ is the leftmost symbol position where A' and B' differ, $s = g(x)$ and $t = h(y)$. Note that $z_1 \theta = s$ and $z_1 \sigma = t$, so s and t at position $\langle 2 \rangle$ are replaced by z_1.

4. Now $A' = P(f(z_1, z_2), z_1) = B'$, so the algorithm stops and returns $A' = A \sqcup B$.

$\triangleleft$

Note that if two atoms $A = P(s_1, \ldots, s_n)$ and $B = P(t_1, \ldots, t_n)$ are generalized to $A \sqcup B = P(r_1, \ldots, r_n)$ by Algorithm 13.1, and if $s_i = s_j$ and $t_i = t_j$, then $r_i = r_j$. For instance, if $A = P(a, f(a, x), a)$ and $B = P(x, f(x, y), x)$, then $A \sqcup B = P(z_1, f(z_1, z_2), z_1)$, in which the terms at the first and third argument place are equal.

We will now prove that the Anti-Unification Algorithm does what it is supposed to do. The truth of the next lemma is easy to see:

Lemma 13.22 *After each iteration of the Anti-Unification Algorithm, there are terms $s_1, \ldots, s_i$ and $t_1, \ldots, t_i$ such that:*

1. *$\theta = \{z_1/s_1, \ldots, z_i/s_i\}$ and $\sigma = \{z_1/t_1, \ldots, z_i/t_i\}$.*
2. *$A'\theta = A$ and $B'\sigma = B$.*
3. *For every $1 \leq j \leq i$, s_j and t_j differ in their first symbol.*
4. *There are no $1 \leq j, k \leq i$ such that $j \neq k$, $s_j = s_k$ and $t_j = t_k$.*

Proposition 13.23 *Let A and B be two atoms with the same predicate symbol. Then the Anti-Unification Algorithm with A and B as input returns $A \sqcup B$.*

Proof It is easy to see that the algorithm terminates after a finite number of steps, for any A, B. Let C be the atom that the algorithm returns, and let $\theta = \{z_1/s_1, \ldots, z_i/s_i\}$ and $\sigma = \{z_1/t_1, \ldots, z_i/t_i\}$ be the final values of θ and σ in the computation of C (so C equals the final values of A' and B' in the execution of the algorithm). Then $C\theta = A$ and $C\sigma = B$ by Lemma 13.22, part 2. Suppose D is an atom such that $D \succeq A$ and $D \succeq B$. In order to show that $C = A \sqcup B$, we have to prove $D \succeq C$.

Let $E = C \sqcap D$, which exists by Theorem 13.18. Then $C \succeq E$ and $D \succeq E$. Since E is a GS of $\{C, D\}$ and $C \succeq A$ and $D \succeq A$, we must have $E \succeq A$. Similarly $E \succeq B$. Thus there are substitutions γ, μ, ν, such that $C\gamma = E$,

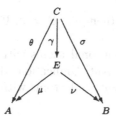

Figure 13.3: Illustration of the proof

$A = E\mu = C\gamma\mu$, and $B = E\nu = C\gamma\nu$. Then $C\theta = A = C\gamma\mu$ and $C\sigma = B = C\gamma\nu$ (see Figure 13.3 for illustration). Hence if x is a variable occurring in C, then $x\theta = x\gamma\mu$ and $x\sigma = x\gamma\nu$.

We will now show that C and $E = C\gamma$ are variants, by showing that γ is a renaming substitution for C. Suppose it is not. Then γ maps some variable x in C to a term that is not a variable, or γ unifies two distinct variables x, y in C.

Suppose x is a variable in C, such that $x\gamma = t$, where t is a term that is not a variable. If x is not one of the z_j's, then $x\gamma\mu = x\theta = x$, contradicting the assumption that $x\gamma = t$ is not a variable. But on the other hand, if x equals some z_j, then $t\mu = x\gamma\mu = x\theta = s_j$ and $t\nu = x\gamma\nu = x\sigma = t_j$. Then s_j and t_j would both start with the first symbol of t, contradicting Lemma 13.22, part 3. So this case leads to a contradiction.

Suppose x, y are distinct variables in C such that γ unifies x and y. (1) If neither x nor y is one of the z_j's, then $x\gamma\mu = x\theta = x \neq y = y\theta = y\gamma\mu$, contradicting $x\gamma = y\gamma$. (2) If x equals some z_j and y does not, then $x\gamma\mu = x\theta = s_j$ and $x\gamma\nu = x\sigma = t_j$, so $x\gamma\mu \neq x\gamma\nu$ by Lemma 13.22, part 3. But $y\gamma\mu = y\theta = y = y\sigma = y\gamma\nu$, contradicting $x\gamma = y\gamma$. (3) Similarly for the case where y equals some z_j and x does not. (4) If $x = z_j$ and $y = z_k$, then $j \neq k$, since $x \neq y$. Furthermore, $s_j = x\theta = x\gamma\mu = y\gamma\mu = y\theta = s_k$ and $t_j = x\sigma = x\gamma\nu = y\gamma\nu = y\sigma = t_k$. But this contradicts Lemma 13.22, part 4. So the assumption that γ unifies two variables in C also leads to a contradiction.

Thus γ is a renaming substitution for C, and hence C and E are variants. Finally, since $D \succeq E$, we have $D \succeq C$.   □

Using this proposition, we can now establish the existence of a least generalization $A \sqcup B$ of any $A, B \in \mathcal{A}$. Notice that $A \sqcup B$ is the only (up to equivalence) minimal generalization of $\{A, B\}$ in $\mathcal{A}$, and $A \sqcap B$ is the only maximal specialization of $\{A, B\}$ in $\mathcal{A}$.

Theorem 13.24 *Let $\mathcal{A}$ be the set of atoms. Then for all $A, B \in \mathcal{A}$, a least generalization $A \sqcup B$ exists.*

Proof We divide the proof in the following cases:

- If $A = \top$ or $B = \top$, then $A \sqcup B = \top$. If $A = \bot$, then $A \sqcup B = B$. If $B = \bot$, then $A \sqcup B = A$.
- If A and B are conventional atoms with the same predicate symbol, $A \sqcup B$ is given by the Anti-Unification Algorithm.
- If A and B are conventional atoms with different predicate symbols, then $A \sqcup B = \top$. $\qquad\qquad\qquad\qquad\qquad\qquad\qquad\qquad\qquad$ □

Example 13.25 Let $A = P(a, x, f(x))$ and $B = P(y, f(b), f(f(b)))$. Then $A \sqcap B = P(a, f(b), f(f(b)))$ is obtained from the Unification Algorithm. On the other hand, $A \sqcup B = P(z_1, z_2, f(z_2))$ can be obtained by applying the Anti-Unification Algorithm to A and B. See Figure 13.4. $\qquad\qquad$ ◁

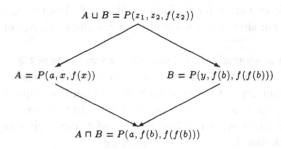

$$A \sqcup B = P(z_1, z_2, f(z_2))$$

$$A = P(a, x, f(x)) \qquad\qquad B = P(y, f(b), f(f(b)))$$

$$A \sqcap B = P(a, f(b), f(f(b)))$$

Figure 13.4: An LG and a GS of atoms A and B

Now that we have established the existence of an LG and GS of any $A, B \in \mathcal{A}$, we have shown that the set of atoms ordered by subsumption, is a lattice.

Theorem 13.26 *Let $\mathcal{A}$ be the set of atoms. Then $\langle \mathcal{A}, \succeq \rangle$ is a lattice.*

Notice that the partial order on the equivalence classes (the sets of variants) of $\mathcal{A}$ induced by $\succeq$, also forms a lattice. In this lattice, the lub and glb of $[x]$ and $[y]$ are $[x \sqcup y]$ and $[x \sqcap y]$. Other than in the quasi-order, the lub and glb are unique here.

The result that $\langle \mathcal{A}, \succeq \rangle$ is a lattice shows that the set of atoms is well-structured. The more structured a set is, the better it is suited to be searched for candidates to include in a theory. This search usually procedes by small upward steps (generalization) or downward steps (specialization) in the lattice. If we want to generalize or specialize a *set* of atoms to a single atom, we can use a least generalization or greatest specialization of this set. On the other hand, we may also want to generalize or specialize an individual atom to another individual atom. The next section discusses covers, which are the smallest non-trivial steps between individual atoms that we can take in the $\mathcal{A}$-lattice.

13.5 Covers

In this section we will discuss the different sorts of covers of atoms. Since B
is a downward cover of A iff A is an upward cover of B, we will first restrict
attention to downward covers. Afterwards, we extend our results to upward
covers.

13.5.1 Downward Covers

The next example gives the first type of downward covers.

Example 13.27 Suppose $A = P(x, z)$. We can prove that $B = P(x, f(y))$ is
a downward cover of A. On the other hand $B' = P(x, f(x))$ is not a downward
cover of A, since we have $A \succ B \succ B'$.   ◁

Lemma 13.28 (Downward cover type 1) *Let A be a conventional atom,
f an n-ary function symbol, z a variable in A, and $x_1, \ldots, x_n$ distinct variables not appearing in A. Let $\theta = \{z/f(x_1, \ldots, x_n)\}$. Then $B = A\theta$ is a
downward cover of A.*

Proof It is clear that A and B are not variants, so $A \succ B$. Suppose there
is a C such that $A \succ C \succ B$. Then there are σ, μ such that $A\sigma = C$ and
$C\mu = B$, hence $A\sigma\mu = B = A\theta$. Here σ only acts on variables in A, and μ
only acts on variables in C.

Let (x, p) be a term occurrence in A, where x is a variable. Suppose $x \neq z$,
then $x\theta = x$, so (x, p) must also be a term occurrence in B. Hence $x\sigma$ must be
a variable, for otherwise $(x\sigma\mu, p)$ in B would contain a constant or a function.
Thus σ must map all variables other than z to variables. Furthermore, σ
cannot unify two distinct variables in A, for then θ would also have to unify
these two variables, which is not the case.

If $z\sigma$ is also a variable, then σ would map all variables to variables, and
since σ cannot unify distinct variables, it would map all distinct variables
in A to distinct variables. But then σ would be a renaming substitution for
A, contradicting $A \succ C$. Hence σ must map z to some term containing a
function symbol.

Now the only way we can have $A\sigma\mu = B$, is if $z\sigma = f(y_1, \ldots, y_n)$ for
distinct y_i not appearing in A, and no variable in A is mapped to some y_i
by σ. But then $A\sigma$ and B would be variants, contradicting $A\sigma = C \succ B$.
Therefore such a C does not exist, and B is a downward cover of A.   □

The next lemma gives another type of cover, which can be obtained by
substituting a constant for a variable in A. Since a constant can be seen as a
function symbol of arity 0, this type of cover can be seen as a subtype of the
previous type. Thus we do not need to prove the next lemma.

Lemma 13.29 (Downward cover type 2) *Let A be a conventional atom, z a variable in A, and let a be a constant. Let $\theta = \{z/a\}$. Then $B = A\theta$ is a downward cover of A.*

Example 13.30 $P(a, z, f(a))$, $P(x, a, f(a))$ and $P(x, b, f(a))$ are downward covers of type 2 of $A = P(x, z, f(a))$.   ◁

Example 13.31 The third type of cover of downward atoms can be obtained by unifying two variables in A. So if $A = P(x, y, f(z))$, then $P(x, x, f(z))$, $P(x, y, f(x))$ and $P(x, y, f(y))$ are downward covers of type 3 of A.   ◁

Lemma 13.32 (Downward cover type 3) *Let A be a conventional atom, and x, z two distinct variables in A. Let $\theta = \{z/x\}$. Then $B = A\theta$ is a downward cover of A.*

Proof It is clear that $A \succ B$. Suppose there is a C such that $A \succ C \succ B$. Then there are σ, μ such that $A\sigma = C$ and $C\mu = B$, hence $A\sigma\mu = B = A\theta$. Here σ only acts on variables in A, and μ only on variables in C. Note that σ and μ can only map variables to variables, since otherwise $A\sigma\mu = B$ would contain more occurrences of functions or constants than A, contradicting $A\theta = B$, since θ does not add any occurrences of function symbols to A.

If σ does not unify any variables in A, then A and C would be variants, contradicting $A \succ C$. If σ unifies any other variables than z and x, then we could not have $A\sigma\mu = B$. Hence σ must unify z and x, and cannot unify any other variables. But then $A\sigma$ and B would be variants, contradicting $A\sigma = C \succ B$. Therefore such a C does not exist, and B is a downward cover of A.   □

In Corollary 13.40, we will show that every downward cover of an atom A is a variant of one of the three types of downward covers we discussed above. Thus a variant of each downward cover can be obtained by applying one of the following *elementary* substitutions:

Definition 13.33 Let C be a clause. An *elementary substitution for C* is one of the following:

- $\{z/f(x_1, \ldots, x_n)\}$, where z is a variable occurring in C, and $x_1, \ldots, x_n$ do not appear in C.
- $\{z/a\}$, where z is a variable occurring in C.
- $\{z/x\}$, where z and x are distinct variables occurring in C.   ◇

It is easy to see that if $A = \top$, then the set of downward covers of A is exactly the set of *most general* atoms, defined as follows:

Definition 13.34 Let P be an n-ary predicate symbol, and $x_1, \ldots, x_n$ distinct variables. Then $P(x_1, \ldots, x_n)$ is a *most general* atom.   ◇

Lemma 13.35 *Every most general atom is a downward cover of* $\top$.

Example 13.36 $P(x)$, $P(y)$ and $Q(x,y)$ are downward covers of $\top$.   ◁

Every most general atom is a downward cover of $\top$, and the three types mentioned above together form all downward covers of a conventional atom A. Since it is clear that $\bot$ does not have any specializations, it does not have any downward covers. So now we have completely specified all downward covers in the set $\mathcal{A}$ of atoms.

13.5.2 Upward Covers

Dually, B is an upward cover of A iff A is a downward cover of B. Thus the upward covers of some conventional atom A are also of three types, which can be constructed by inverting the three elementary substitutions:

- *Type 1:* Let $t = f(x_1, \ldots, x_n)$ occur in A, where all x_i are distinct, and each occurrence of x_i in A is within an occurrence of t. Then replacing all occurrences of t in A by some new variable z not in A yields an upward cover of A.
- *Type 2:* Replacing some occurrences of a constant a by a new variable z gives another upward cover of A.
- *Type 3:* Replacing some (but not all) occurrences of a variable x by a new variable z also yields an upward cover of A.

The next lemma is obvious:

Lemma 13.37 *Every ground atom is an upward cover of* $\bot$.

Note that if we have a finite number of predicate symbols in the language, then the set of downward covers of $\top$ (i.e., the set of all most general atoms), is finite up to variants. On the other hand, if the language contains a function symbol of arity 1 or more, then the set of upward covers of $\bot$ is infinite. For instance, the ground atoms $P(a), P(f(a)), P(f^2(a)), \ldots$ are all upward covers of $\bot$.

Since the top element $\top$ has no generalizations, we have hereby exhausted all upward covers within the set of atoms.

13.6 Finite Chains of Downward Covers

In this section, we will show that given two atoms A and B such that $A \succ B$, there is a finite sequence of downward covers from A to a variant of B. This means that if we want to get from A to B, we only need to consider downward covers of A, downward covers of downward covers of A, etc. First we give an example:

Example 13.38 Let $A = P(x, y)$ and $B = P(f(g(z), g(z)), a)$. Letting $\theta = \{x/f(g(z), g(z)), y/a\}$, we have $A\theta = B$. By decomposing θ into elementary substitutions, we can find the following chain of downward covers from A to a variant of B:

1. Let $A_0 = A$.
2. Let $\sigma_0 = \{x/f(z_1, z_2)\}$ and $A_1 = A_0\sigma_0 = P(f(z_1, z_2), y)$.
3. Let $\sigma_1 = \{z_1/g(z_3)\}$ and $A_2 = A_1\sigma_1 = P(f(g(z_3), z_2), y)$.
4. Let $\sigma_2 = \{z_2/g(z_4)\}$ and $A_3 = A_2\sigma_2 = P(f(g(z_3), g(z_4)), y)$.
5. Let $\sigma_3 = \{y/a\}$ and $A_4 = A_3\sigma_3 = P(f(g(z_3), g(z_4)), a)$.
6. Let $\sigma_4 = \{z_3/z_4\}$ and $A_5 = A_4\sigma_4 = P(f(g(z_4), g(z_4)), a)$.

Thus we have constructed the chain $A_0 = A \succ A_1 \succ A_2 \succ A_3 \succ A_4 \succ A_5 \approx B$, where each A_{i+1} is a downward cover of A_i. The composition $\sigma_0\sigma_1\sigma_2\sigma_3\sigma_4$, restricted to the variables in A, equals θ. ◁

Note that it is not always possible to get from A to B itself using only elementary substitutions. For instance, we cannot get from $A = P(x)$ to $B = P(f(x))$. But we can get to $B' = P(f(y))$, which is a variant of B. Given $A \succ B$, the following algorithm is able to find a finite chain of downward covers from A to a variant of B.

Algorithm 13.2 (Finite Downward Cover Chain Algorithm)
Input: Conventional atoms A, B, such that $A \succ B$.
Output: A finite chain $A = A_0 \succ A_1 \succ \ldots \succ A_{n-1} \succ A_n \approx B$, where each A_{i+1} is a downward cover of A_i.

1. Set $A_0 = A$ and $i = 0$, let θ_0 be such that $A\theta_0 = B$.
2. If no term in θ_i contains a function or a constant, then goto 3.
   If $x/f(t_1, \ldots, t_n)$ is a binding in θ_i ($n \geq 0$), then choose new distinct variables $z_1, \ldots, z_n$.
   Set $A_{i+1} = A_i\{x/f(z_1, \ldots, z_n)\}$.
   Set $\theta_{i+1} = (\theta_i \setminus \{x/f(t_1, \ldots, t_n)\}) \cup \{z_1/t_1, \ldots, z_n/t_n\}$.
   Set i to $i + 1$ and goto 2.
3. If there are distinct variables x, y in A_i, such that $x\theta_i = y\theta_i$, then:
   Set $A_{i+1} = A_i\{x/y\}$.
   Set $\theta_{i+1} = \theta_i \setminus \{x/x\theta_i\}$.
   Set i to $i + 1$ and goto 3.
   Otherwise (if such x, y do not exist), set $n = i$ and stop.

Intuitively, step 2 of the algorithm first instantiates the appropriate variables to functions and constants, and afterwards step 3 unifies appropriate variables to obtain a variant of B. The next lemma shows the Finite Downward Cover Chain Algorithm to be correct.

Lemma 13.39 Let A and B be conventional atoms such that $A \succ B$. Then there is an $n > 0$ such that Algorithm 13.2 with A and B as input terminates. The chain $A = A_0 \succ A_1 \succ \ldots \succ A_{n-1} \succ A_n$ constructed by the algorithm has the properties that each A_{i+1} is a downward cover of A_i, and $A_n \approx B$.

Proof Step 2 of the algorithm cannot be repeated indefinitely long, since θ_{i+1} contains one occurrence of a function symbol less than θ_i after one application of this step. Similarly, step 3 cannot be repeated without end, since θ_{i+1} acts on fewer distinct variables than θ_i after this step. This shows that the algorithm must terminate, for some $i = n > 0$.

It is clear from the algorithm that A_{i+1} is a downward cover (of one of the three types) of A_i. It remains to show that $A_n \approx B$. For this, we prove the invariant $A_i\theta_i = B$, by induction on i. From this invariant, we know the sequence of covers has the following structure:

$$A = A_0 \to A_1 \to \cdots \to A_i \overset{\theta_i}{\to} B.$$

1. $A_0\theta_0 = B$, from the first line of the algorithm.
2. Suppose $A_i\theta_i = B$.
   If step 2 of the algorithm is applied, then:
   $A_{i+1} = A_i\{x/f(z_1,\ldots,z_n)\}$, A_{i+1} is a type 1 or 2 (if $n = 0$) downward cover of A_i,
   $\theta_{i+1} = (\theta_i\backslash\{x/f(t_1,\ldots,t_n)\}) \cup \{z_1/t_1,\ldots,z_n/t_n\}$.
   Now we have $B = A_i\theta_i = A_i\{x/f(z_1,\ldots,z_n)\}\theta_{i+1} = A_{i+1}\theta_{i+1}$.
   If step 3 of the algorithm is applied, then:
   $A_{i+1} = A_i\{x/y\}$, A_{i+1} is a type 3 downward cover of A_i,
   $\theta_{i+1} = \theta_i\backslash\{x/x\theta_i\}$.
   Now $B = A_i\theta_i = A_i\{x/y\}\theta_{i+1} = A_{i+1}\theta_{i+1}$.

Since step 2 of the algorithm was no longer applicable to θ_n (otherwise the algorithm would not have terminated with $i = n$), θ_n cannot map variables to terms containing functions or constants. Also, since step 3 was not applicable to θ_n, θ_n does not unify any variables in A_n. This means that θ_n is a renaming substitution for A_n. Now from the invariant, we know $A_n \approx A_n\theta_n = B$. □

In other words, if $A \succ B$, then there is a sequence $\sigma_1,\ldots,\sigma_n$ of elementary substitutions such that $B \approx A\sigma_1\ldots\sigma_n$. Note that the atoms in the chain constructed above, are all downward covers of one of the three types defined above. Thus if B is a downward cover of A, there is a downward cover A_1 of one of the three types, such that $A = A_0 \succ A_1 \approx B$.

Corollary 13.40 *Every downward cover of a conventional atom A is a variant of a downward cover of A of one of the three types defined above.*

Theorem 13.41 *Let A and B be atoms such that $A \succ B$. Then there is a finite chain $A = A_0 \succ A_1 \succ \ldots \succ A_{n-1} \succ A_n \approx B$, where $n \geq 1$ and each A_{i+1} is a downward cover of A_i.*

Proof We distinguish the following four cases:

- A and B are conventional: this case is Lemma 13.39.
- $A = \top$ and B is conventional: suppose B has predicate P, of arity n. Then $A_1 = P(x_1,\ldots,x_n)$ is a downward cover of A, and $A_1 \succeq B$. If

$A_1 \approx B$, we are done. Otherwise, by the previous case there is a finite downward cover chain from A_1 to B.

- A is conventional and $B = \bot$: if A is ground, B is a downward cover of A. Otherwise, let B' be a ground instance of A (since we assumed our language has a non-empty set of constants, such a ground instance always exists). By the first case of the proof, there is a finite downward cover chain from A to B'. B is a downward cover of B', hence there is a finite downward cover chain from A to B.

- $A = \top$ and $B = \bot$: let $A' = P(x_1, \ldots, x_n)$ be a most general atom, and B' a ground instance of A'. By the first case, there is a finite downward cover chain from A' to B'. A' is a downward cover of A and B is a downward cover of B', hence the result follows. □

It follows from the previous theorem that if $A \succ B$, then there is a downward cover C of A, such that $A \succ C \succeq B$. This shows as a corollary that the set of downward covers of a conventional atom is complete for that atom.

Given that the language contains a finite number of function symbols, the set of non-equivalent (non-variant) type 1 downward covers of a conventional atom is finite. Also, if the number of constants is finite, the number of type 2 covers is finite. Since the set of non-equivalent type 3 covers is also finite, it is possible to construct a finite complete set of downward covers of any conventional atom. Furthermore, since we assume a language with only finitely many predicate symbols, the number of non-equivalent most general atoms is also finite, so the set of non-equivalent downward covers of $\top$ is finite. The set of downward covers of $\bot$ is of course empty, and the empty set is a finite complete set of downward covers of $\bot$. This gives the following corollary:

Corollary 13.42 *Every atom has a finite complete set of downward covers.*

13.7 Finite Chains of Upward Covers

Algorithm 13.2 is given $A \succ B$, and starts from A, working downward to a variant of B. We might want to reverse the algorithm, to start from B instead of A, conducting an upward search towards a variant of A. We will not go into details here, but just give some examples to indicate the differences with the downward algorithm.

Example 13.43 Let $A = P(f(x, y), z)$ and $B = P(f(g(v), g(v)), b)$. The following is one possible chain of upward covers from B to a variant of A:

1. $B_0 = B = P(f(g(v), g(v)), b)$.
2. $B_1 = P(f(g(v), g(z_1)), b)$.
3. $B_2 = P(f(z_2, g(z_1)), b)$.
4. $B_3 = P(f(z_2, z_3), b)$.

5. $B_4 = P(f(z_2, z_3), z_4) \approx A$.

Note that while Algorithm 13.2 first instantiates variables to functions and constants, and then unifies some variables, in this example we do the reverse: first the step from B_0 to B_1 "undoes" the unification of v and z_1, and then the steps from B_1 to B_4 "undo" some instantiations of variables.   ◁

If we want to describe this reversed algorithm in a way symmetrical to Algorithm 13.2, then we should use *inverse substitutions*, instead of the substitutions $\theta_0, \ldots, \theta_n$ used in Algorithm 13.2. However, like the inverse of a function, the inverse of a substitution need not be a function itself, because a substitution may map occurrences of distinct variables to the same term. In order to be able to invert substitutions, we need positions of term occurrences again.

For example, let $A = P(x, y)$ and $B = P(g(b), g(b))$. Letting $\theta = \{x/g(b), y/g(b)\}$, we have $A\theta = B$. If we want to establish an inverse substitution θ^{-1} from B to A, we need to map the first occurrence of $g(b)$ in B to the variable x, but the second occurrence to y. Thus, whereas a substitution is a function from variables to terms, an inverse substitution such as θ^{-1} cannot be a function from terms to variables.

However, since every term occurrence in B has a unique position, θ^{-1} can be regarded as a function from term *occurrences* to variables. Thus we can write $\theta^{-1} = \{(g(b)/x, \langle 1 \rangle), (g(b)/y, \langle 2 \rangle)\}$, denoting that $g(b)$ at position $\langle 1 \rangle$ should be mapped to x, and $g(b)$ at position $\langle 2 \rangle$ should be mapped to y. Using this notation, we have $B\theta^{-1} = A$.

Notice that this notation can also be used to describe the application of the ordinary substitution θ to A. Then $\theta = \{(x/g(b), \langle 1 \rangle), (y/g(b), \langle 2 \rangle)\}$. See [NF91] for a more detailed discussion of inverse substitutions.

Example 13.44 Let $A = P(f(x, y), z)$ and $B = P(f(g(v), g(v)), b)$ again, as in Example 13.43. Then $A\theta = B$, where $\theta = \{x/g(v), y/g(v), z/b\}$, and $B\theta^{-1} = A$, where $\theta^{-1} = \{(g(v)/x, \langle 1, 1 \rangle), (g(v)/y, \langle 1, 2 \rangle), (b/z, \langle 2 \rangle)\}$. Now the following steps give us the chain of upward covers:

1. $B_0 = B = P(f(g(v), g(v)), b)$.
2. $B_1 = B_0\sigma_0 = P(f(g(v), g(z_1)), b)$, for $\sigma_0 = \{(v/z_1, \langle 1, 2, 1 \rangle)\}$.
3. $B_2 = B_1\sigma_1 = P(f(z_2, g(z_1)), b)$, for $\sigma_1 = \{(g(v)/z_2, \langle 1, 1 \rangle)\}$.
4. $B_3 = B_2\sigma_2 = P(f(z_2, z_3), b)$, for $\sigma_2 = \{(g(z_1)/z_3, \langle 1, 2 \rangle)\}$.
5. $B_4 = B_3\sigma_3 = P(f(z_2, z_3), z_4) \approx A$, for $\sigma_3 = \{(b/z_4, \langle 2 \rangle)\}$.   ◁

As we have seen on p. 234, there are three standard types of upward covers. If we work out the details of the inverse of the Finite Downward Cover Chain Algorithm, the following results immediately follow, analogous to the downward case:

Corollary 13.45 *Every upward cover of a conventional atom A is a variant of an upward cover of A of one of the three standard types.*

Theorem 13.46 *Let A and B be atoms such that $A \succ B$. Then there is a finite chain $A \approx B_n \succ B_{n-1} \succ \ldots \succ B_1 \succ B_0 = B$, where $n \geq 1$ and each B_{i+1} is an upward cover of B_i.*

One asymmetry of the downward and upward cases concerns the upward covers of $\bot$. We have shown that every atom, including $\top$ and $\bot$, has a finite complete set of *downward* covers. However, in case of a language without constants but with at least one function symbol of arity ≥ 1, the bottom element $\bot$ has no upward covers at all, let alone a finite complete set of upward covers. In case of a language with at least one constant and at least one function symbol of arity ≥ 1, there are an infinite number of conventional ground atoms, each of which is an upward cover of $\bot$. Together these ground atoms comprise a complete set of upward covers of $\bot$, but again $\bot$ has no *finite* complete set of upward covers in this case. However, each conventional atom does have a finite complete set of upward covers. The top element $\top$ does not have any upward covers at all, but it has the empty set as a finite complete set of upward covers, since no element lies "above" $\top$.

Corollary 13.47 *Every atom other than $\bot$ has a finite complete set of upward covers.*

Example 13.48 Let $A = P(x, f(y), a)$, and suppose the language contains no other function symbols than f, and two constants a and b. The set of non-equivalent downward covers of A consists of the following:

1. *Type 1:* $P(f(z), f(y), a)$, $P(x, f(f(z)), a)$.
2. *Type 2:* $P(a, f(y), a)$, $P(b, f(y), a)$, $P(x, f(a), a)$, $P(x, f(b), a)$.
3. *Type 3:* $P(x, f(x), a)$.

The set of non-equivalent upward covers of A consists of:

1. *Type 1:* $P(x, z, a)$.
2. *Type 2:* $P(x, f(y), z)$.
3. *Type 3:* none. ◁

Why do we consider upward and downward covers separately?

The reader may wonder why we take all this trouble about inverse substitutions to find chains of upward covers. As we have seen before, if $A_0 = A \succ A_1 \succ \ldots \succ A_n \approx B$ is a chain of downward covers from A to B, then this chain in opposite order is also a chain of upward covers from (a variant of) B to A. So, why bother with two different ways (one downward, one upward) of constructing such a chain?

The reason for this is the general direction of search in an application. In top-down search, we want to find some unknown specialization B of A. Then we should use substitutions to try and find a chain of downward covers starting from A, as in Algorithm 13.2. Since such finite chains always exist for atoms, we can restrict attention to downward covers of A, downward covers of downward covers of A, etc. On the other hand, in bottom-up search we want to find some unknown generalization A of B. In that case, we should use inverse substitutions to find a chain of upward covers from B to A, as in Example 13.44.

13.8 Size

The generality relation $\succeq$ on atoms was defined by substitution. Is there a quantitative way to express the complexity of an atom, which coincides with the generality relation $\succeq$? For instance, $A = P(x, y) \succ P(f(x), f(y)) = B$, which coincides with the fact that B contains more occurrences of symbols than A. On the other hand $A = P(x, y) \succ P(x, x) = C$, which coincides with the fact that A contains more distinct variables than C. Roughly, we would expect that a more general atom contains fewer symbols, but more distinct variables than a more specific atom. Based on this intuition, we can define the following *size* to measure the complexity of an atom. This measure was introduced by Reynolds in [Rey70], where it was used to prove Theorems 13.41 and 13.46. We proved these results directly, but *size* is still an interesting measure for expressing the complexity of atoms.

Definition 13.49 The *size* of an atom is defined as follows:

- $size(\top) = 0$.
- $size(\bot) = \infty$.
- if A is a conventional atom, then
  $size(A) =$ the number of symbol occurrences in A
  $-$ the number of distinct variables in A. $\diamond$

By 'symbol occurrences', we mean occurrences of predicates symbols, function symbols, constants, and variables.

Example 13.50 The atom $A = P(x, g(x, y))$ contains 5 symbol occurrences: P, x, g, x, and y. It contains two distinct variables, so $size(A) = 5 - 2 = 3$. Similarly, $size(P(x, y)) = 3 - 2 = 1$ and $size(Q(x, f(x), g(a, f(a)))) = 8 - 1 = 7$. $\triangleleft$

Note that if $A \approx B$, then $size(A) = size(B)$. The converse does not hold. For instance, $A = P(a, x)$ and $B = P(x, a)$ have the same size, but are not variants of each other.

Lemma 13.51 *Let A and B be atoms. If B is a downward cover of A, then $size(A) < size(B)$.*

Proof We distinguish the following cases:

- $A = \top$. Then $size(A) = 0$, and B must be a most general atom $P(x_1, \ldots, x_n)$. Hence $size(B) = (n+1) - n = 1 > 0 = size(A)$.

- A is ground and $B = \bot$. Then $size(A) < \infty = size(B)$.
- A is conventional and B is a type 1 or type 2 cover.
  $B = A\theta$, where $\theta = \{z/f(x_1, \ldots, x_n)\}$ and $x_1, \ldots, x_n$ are new distinct variables ($n = 0$ in case of a type 2 cover). For every occurrence of z in A, there are $n + 1$ new symbol occurrences, namely $f, x_1, \ldots, x_n$, in B. Let k be the number of occurrences of z in A. Then $k \geq 1$ and $size(B) =$ (number of symbol occurrences in $A - k + k * (n + 1)$) − (number of distinct variables in $A - 1 + n) = size(A) + n * k - n + 1 > size(A)$.
- A is conventional and B is a type 3 cover.
  $B = A\theta$, where $\theta = \{z/x\}$. A and B contain the same number of symbol occurrences, but B contains one distinct variable less than A. Hence $size(B) = size(A) + 1$. $\qquad\qquad\square$

The *size*-complexity coincides with the $\succeq$ order in the following way:

Proposition 13.52 *Let A and B be atoms. If $A \succ B$, then $size(A) < size(B)$.*

Proof By Theorem 13.41, there is a finite chain $A = A_0 \succ A_1 \succ \ldots \succ A_{n-1} \succ A_n \approx B$, where $n \geq 1$ and each A_{i+1} is a downward cover of A_i. Using the previous lemma, we have $size(A) < size(A_1) < \ldots < size(A_{n-1}) < size(A_n) = size(B)$ (the final equality holds because variants have equal size). $\qquad\qquad\square$

The converse of this result does not hold. For example, if we put $A = P(a, b)$ and $B = P(a, f(b))$, then $size(A) = 3 < 4 = size(B)$, but $A \not\succ B$.

13.9 Summary

In this chapter, we started by defining the notions of a *quasi-order*, a *partial order*, and an *equivalence relation*. Some important concepts defined for quasi-ordered sets, are the *least upper bound* (in ILP terminology: least generalization) and the *greatest lower bound* (greatest specialization) of a finite subset of the ordered set. These notions may be relaxed to *minimal upper bound* (minimal generalization) and *maximal lower bound* (maximal specialization), respectively. A *lattice* is a quasi-ordered set in which any two elements have a least upper bound and a greatest lower bound. Downward and upward *covers* of an element in the quasi-ordered set can be seen as the maximal non-trivial specializations and the minimal non-trivial generalizations of that element, according to this order.

We used these concepts in an analysis of the set of atoms quasi-ordered by subsumption. Here $\mathcal{A}$ denotes the set of all conventional atoms in a language, with additional top and bottom elements $\top, \bot$. The outcome of this analysis can be summed up in the following points:

- Every finite set of atoms has a greatest specialization (obtainable from the Unification Algorithm) and a least generalization (obtainable from the Anti-Unification Algorithm). Thus $\langle \mathcal{A}, \succeq \rangle$ is a lattice.
- Every conventional atom has a finite complete set of upward and downward covers. The downward covers of a conventional atom A are obtained by applying each of the three kinds of elementary substitutions to it, the upward covers are obtained by inverting those substitutions. The downward covers of $\top$ are the most general atoms. The upward covers of $\bot$ are the ground atoms.
- If $A \succ B$, then there is a finite chain of downward covers from A to a variant of B, and a finite chain of upward covers from B to a variant of A.

The chapter ended by defining *size*, which is a measure for the complexity of atoms. This measure is consistent with $\succeq$. That is, if $A \succ B$, then $size(A) < size(B)$.

Chapter 14

The Subsumption Order

14.1 Introduction

We have met with the subsumption relation a few times before in this book, for example in the subsumption theorems and in the generality order on atoms of the previous chapter. We will extend the subsumption order on atoms in two different ways to an order on clauses. The first is a rather strict generality order, called the *atomic* order. We introduce this mainly as a tool for studying the second extension, the subsumption order on clauses.

We show here that clausal languages and Horn languages are lattices under subsumption: each finite set of clauses has a least generalization (LGS) and a greatest specialization (GSS) under subsumption. On the other hand, the positive results on finite complete sets of covers of atoms do not carry over to arbitrary clauses. We prove that some clauses do not have finite complete sets of downward or upward covers. This chapter is mainly based on the articles [Plo70, NLT93, LN93, LN94a, NW96b].

14.2 Clauses Considered as Atoms

In this section, we will show how clauses can be treated as single atoms. For this, we will introduce a very strict order on clauses, the *atomic order* $\succeq_a$. It provides a bridge between the $\succeq$-order on atoms of the previous chapter, and the subsumption order on clauses we will discuss in the next sections. The subsumption order for clauses and the existence of least generalizations therein can be introduced without this intermediate order $\succeq_a$, as for instance Plotkin does in [Plo70]. However, we feel that the $\succeq_a$-order is useful for understanding subsumption, hence we discuss it here.

Definition 14.1 Let $C = L_1 \vee \ldots \vee L_n$ and $D = M_1 \vee \ldots \vee M_m$ be clauses. If $n = m$ and for every $i = 1, \ldots, n$, L_i and M_i have the same sign and predicate symbol, we say C and D are *compatible*. If not, they are *incompatible*.

C is an *atomic generalization* of D, denoted by $C \succeq_a D$, if C and D are compatible and there exists a substitution θ, such that $L_i\theta = M_i$ for every $i = 1, \ldots, n$. $\diamond$

Example 14.2 $P(a) \vee Q(x) \succeq_a P(a) \vee Q(a)$, but $P(a) \vee Q(x) \not\succeq_a Q(a) \vee P(a)$ and $P(a) \not\succeq_a P(a) \vee P(a)$. $\triangleleft$

If $C \succeq_a D$, then C and D must be compatible, so incompatible clauses are incomparable in this order. For atoms A and B, $A \succeq B$ iff $A \succeq_a B$, so the $\succeq_a$-order is an extension of the $\succeq$-order on atoms of the previous chapter. We will prove in this section that any two clauses C and D have a least generalization in the set of clauses ordered by $\succeq_a$, which we will denote by $LGA(C, D)$. Since for atoms A and B the two orders $\succeq_a$ and $\succeq$ coincide, it follows that $LGA(A, B) = A \sqcup B$, where $A \sqcup B$ is an LG of $\{A, B\}$ under $\succeq$, as defined in the previous chapter.

The reason why the $\succeq_a$-relation is called the *atomic* order, is that clauses are compared as single atoms in this quasi-order. Let $C = P(a) \vee Q(y, f(x)) \vee \neg P(x)$. C can be viewed as an atom $A = \vee(P(a), Q(y, f(x)), \neg P(x))$, where $\vee$ now acts as a 3-ary predicate symbol, and P, Q, and $\neg P$ are treated as function symbols of arities 1, 2, and 1, respectively. Since we have already established the existence of a least generalization of two atoms, the existence of a least generalization of two compatible clauses in $\langle \mathcal{C}, \succeq_a \rangle$ follows easily, by considering such atomic representations:

Theorem 14.3 Let $\mathcal{C}$ be a clausal language, and $C = L_1 \vee \ldots \vee L_n$ and $D = M_1 \vee \ldots \vee M_n$ two compatible clauses in $\mathcal{C}$. Then there is an $LGA(C, D) = N_1 \vee \ldots \vee N_n$. Moreover, for any $1 \leq k \leq n$, if $C' = L_1 \vee \ldots \vee L_k$ and $D' = M_1 \vee \ldots \vee M_k$, then $LGA(C', D') = N_1 \vee \ldots \vee N_k$.

Proof Let $A = \vee(L_1, \ldots, L_n)$ and $B = \vee(M_1, \ldots, M_n)$ be the atomic representations of C and D, respectively. Let $\vee(N_1, \ldots, N_n)$ be the LGS of A and B obtained from Algorithm 13.1 (the Anti-Unification Algorithm). Then it is easy to see that $E = N_1 \vee \ldots \vee N_n$ is an $LGA(C, D)$.

For the second part of the theorem, let $C' = L_1 \vee \ldots \vee L_k$ and $D' = M_1 \vee \ldots \vee M_k$, and let A' and B' be the atomic representations of C' and D', respectively. Let $LGS(A', B')$ denote the atom obtained by applying Algorithm 13.1 to A' and B', and let E' be the clause represented by this atom. Then E' is an $LGA(C', D')$.

Now note how the algorithm operates. The algorithm works from left to right, and when it anti-unifies the terms at some position of the two atoms, it does not take the terms to the right of this position into account. Moreover, the result of anti-unifying the terms at this position is not changed anymore when the algorithm continues with the terms to the right of the position. This means that the k arguments in the atom $LGS(A', B')$ are exactly the first k arguments in $LGS(A, B)$, since the k arguments of A' and B' are exactly the first k arguments in A and B, respectively. This in turn implies that E' equals the first k literals of E. □

Example 14.4 Let

$$C = P(x, g(x)) \vee \neg P(a, b) \vee Q(x, g(f(x)))$$
$$D = P(x, g(y)) \vee \neg P(a, x) \vee Q(y, g(y))$$

The atomic representations of these two clauses are, respectively:

$$A = \vee(P(x, g(x)), \neg P(a, b), Q(x, g(f(x))))$$
$$B = \vee(P(x, g(y)), \neg P(a, x), Q(y, g(y)))$$

Algorithm 13.1 yields $LGA(A, B) = \vee(P(x, g(z_1)), \neg P(a, z_2), Q(z_1, g(z_3)))$, so we have that $E = P(x, g(z_1)) \vee \neg P(a, z_2) \vee Q(z_1, g(z_3))$ is an $LGA(C, D)$.

Note that $P(x, g(z_1)) \vee \neg P(a, z_2)$ (the disjunction of the first two literals of E) is an LGA of $P(x, g(x)) \vee \neg P(a, b)$ and $P(x, g(y)) \vee \neg P(a, x)$ (the disjunction of the first two literals of C and D, respectively). ◁

As we have seen, an LGA of C and D can be obtained by turning to atomic representation and then applying the Anti-Unification Algorithm. Similarly we could obtain a greatest specialization from the Unification Algorithm, which shows that if C is a clausal language including artificial top and bottom elements ⊤ and ⊥, then $\langle C, \succeq_a \rangle$ is a lattice. We will not discuss this any further, since we have mainly introduced the $\succeq_a$-order as a tool for the study of the more important subsumption order.

It follows from the remark following Example 13.21 in the last chapter that if the terms at the i-th and j-th argument place of an atom A are equal, and if the terms at the i-th and j-th argument place in an atom B are equal, then the terms at the i-th and j-th argument place of $LGA(A, B)$ are equal. This extends to the LGA of compatible clauses C and D. For instance, if $C = P(a) \vee Q(a, x) \vee P(a)$ and $D = P(x) \vee Q(x, y) \vee P(x)$, then $LGA(C, D) = P(z_1) \vee Q(z_1, z_2) \vee P(z_1)$, where the first and third literal are equal. Thus we have the following lemma, which will be used in the proof of Theorem 14.27:

Lemma 14.5 Let $C = L_1 \vee \ldots \vee L_n$ and $D = M_1 \vee \ldots \vee M_n$ be compatible clauses, with $LGA(C, D) = N_1 \vee \ldots \vee N_n$. If for some $1 \leq i, j \leq n$ we have $L_i = L_j$ and $M_i = M_j$, then $N_i = N_j$.

14.3 Subsumption

The general subsumption order on clauses is defined as follows:

Definition 14.6 Let C and D be clauses. We say C *subsumes* D, denoted by $C \succeq D$, if there exists a substitution θ such that $C\theta \subseteq D$ (i.e., every literal in $C\theta$ is also a literal in D). C *properly subsumes* D, denoted by $C \succ D$, if $C \succeq D$ and $D \not\succeq C$. Furthermore, C and D are *subsume-equivalent*, denoted by $C \sim D$, if $C \succeq D$ and $D \succeq C$.   ◇

Clearly, the subsumption relation on clauses is reflexive and transitive. Thus it imposes a quasi-order on the set of clauses. Note that if $C \succeq_a D$, then $C \succeq D$, but not necessarily the other way around.

We will now informally show that it is decidable whether a clause C subsumes a clause D. If $C \succeq D$, then there is a substitution θ which maps each $L_i \in C$ to some $M_j \in D$. If C contains n literals, and D contains m literals, then there are m^n ways in which the literals in C can be paired up with literals in D. Then we can decide $C \succeq D$ by checking whether for at least one of those m^n ways of pairing the n literals in C to some of the m literals in D, there is a θ such that $L_i\theta = M_j$, for each (L_i, M_j) in the pairing. If so, there is a θ such that $C\theta \subseteq D$, and hence $C \succeq D$. If not, then there is no such θ, and $C \not\succeq D$.[1]

A clause is always subsume-equivalent with a clause that does not contain literals more than once. So for example $P(x) \lor Q(a) \lor P(x)$ is obviously subsume-equivalent with $P(x) \lor Q(a)$. Similarly, the order of literals in a clause does not matter much. For instance, $P(a) \lor P(b) \sim P(b) \lor P(a)$. It will often be convenient to ignore duplicate literals and the order of literals in a clause, which are not important for the properties we are interested in. For us, the only thing that really matters in a clause, is which distinct literals it contains. This amounts to treating a clause as a *set* of literals, instead of a disjunction of literals. For convenience, we will also adopt this representation from now on. Thus we may use the set $\{P(a), Q(x)\}$ to represent the clauses $Q(x) \lor P(a)$, $P(a) \lor Q(x) \lor P(a)$, $Q(x) \lor P(a) \lor Q(x)$, etc. For most parts of this book, the distinction between on the one hand *ordered* notation, which does not ignore the order and duplication of literals, and set notation of clauses on the other, is just a matter of convenience. The only part where the distinction is crucial is Section 14.7, where we take the step from the atomic order to the subsumption order, using ordered notation for the former and set notation for the latter.

Two atoms are subsume-equivalent iff they are variants. This is not true for clauses in general. For instance, $C = \{P(x, x)\} \sim \{P(x, x), P(x, y)\} = D$, since $C \subseteq D$ and $D\{y/x\} \subseteq C$, yet C and D are not variants. In fact, the subsume-equivalence class of this C contains an infinite number of clauses which are not variants. For example, for each n, the clause $D_n = \{P(x, x), P(x, x_1), P(x_1, x_2), \ldots, P(x_{n-1}, x_n)\}$ is subsume-equivalent

---

[1] Though subsumption is decidable, actually deciding it is rather expensive: subsumption is an NP-complete problem [GJ79, p. 264]. Kietz and Lübbe [KL94] describe some special cases where subsumption is more efficiently decidable.

with $C = \{P(x, x)\}$. Often, we are interested in properties of arbitrary members of these subsume-equivalence classes. In this case, we can use one particular member of an equivalence class to represent that class, for instance a *reduced* member of that equivalence class, as we will discuss in the next section.

14.4 Reduction

A reduced clause is in a way a "smallest" member of its equivalence class. For instance, the smallest members of the equivalence class of $\{P(x, x)\}$ are $\{P(x, x)\}$ and its variants, which are reduced. Reducing a clause makes the clause more tractable. $\{P(x, x)\}$ is often easier to handle than other members of its subsume-equivalence class, such as $\{P(x, x), P(x, x_1), P(x_1, x_2)\}$.

Definition 14.7 A clause C is said to be *reduced* if there is no proper subset D of C $(D \subset C)$ such that $C \sim D$. A reduced clause D such that $C \sim D$ and $D \subseteq C$ is called a *reduction of* C. $\diamond$

Example 14.8 $C = \{P(x, y), P(y, x)\}$ is reduced. $D = \{P(x, x), P(x, y), P(y, x)\}$ is not reduced, since $D' = \{P(x, x)\}$ is a proper subset of D and $D \sim D'$. D' is a reduction of D. $\triangleleft$

A clause C is reduced if there is no substitution θ such that $C\theta$ is a proper subset of C. Although for $C \sim C'$ and $D \sim D'$ we have that $C \succeq D$ iff $C' \succeq D'$, subsume-equivalent clauses need not behave the same with respect to other operations. Firstly, applying the same substitution θ to two subsume-equivalent clauses may yield two clauses which are no longer subsume-equivalent:

Example 14.9 Let $C = \{P(x, y), P(z, u)\}$ and $D = \{P(x, y)\}$, then $C \sim D$. Let $\theta = \{y/f(x), z/f(x), u/x\}$. Then $C\theta = \{P(x, f(x)), P(f(x), x)\}$ and $D\theta = \{P(x, f(x))\}$, which are no longer equivalent. $\triangleleft$

A second perhaps surprising property, is the fact that a subset of a reduced clause need not be reduced itself:

Example 14.10 Let $C = \{\neg Q(x, a), \neg Q(y, a)\}$ and $D = \{P(x, y), \neg Q(x, a), \neg Q(y, a)\}$. Then D is reduced. However, C is a subset of D which is not reduced, since $C\{x/y\}$ is a proper subset of C. $\triangleleft$

Subsume-equivalent clauses need not be variants, but *reduced* subsume-equivalent clauses, such as for example $C = \{P(x, y), P(y, x)\}$ and $D = \{P(z, x), P(x, z)\}$, are variants:

Proposition 14.11 *Let C and D be reduced clauses. If $C \sim D$, then C and D are variants.*

Proof Since $C \sim D$, there are θ and σ such that $C\theta \subseteq D$ and $D\sigma \subseteq C$. Since C and D are reduced, we must have $C\theta\sigma = C$ and $D\sigma\theta = C$. If θ maps some x in C to a term containing a function symbol or constant, then we would not have $C\theta\sigma = C$, so θ (and likewise σ) can only map variables to variables. If θ unifies two or more variables in C, then the total number of variables in $C\theta\sigma(= C)$ would be less than the number of variables in C, which is impossible. Hence θ, and similarly σ, must be a renaming substitution, which shows that C and D are variants. $\qquad\square$

In [Plo70], Plotkin gave an algorithm to compute a reduction of a clause. The following lemma is the basis of his algorithm:

Lemma 14.12 *Let C be a clause. If for some θ, $C\theta \subseteq C$, then there is a reduced clause $D \subseteq C\theta$ such that $C \sim D$.*

Proof Let $C_1 = C\theta$. Clearly $C \sim C_1$. If C_1 is reduced, then let $D = C_1$, and we are done. Otherwise, there is a substitution θ_1 such that $C_2 = C_1\theta_1 \subset C_1$. So C_2 is a proper subset of C_1 which is subsume-equivalent to C_1. Since $C_1 \sim C$, we also have $C_2 \sim C$, in fact $C\theta\theta_1 = C_2 \subset C$. If C_2 is still not reduced, we can go on defining $C_3 = C_2\theta_2 \subset C_2$, etc. Since C only contains a finite number of literals, this cannot go on indefinitely. Hence we must arrive at a $D = C_n$ such that D is reduced and $C \sim D$. $\qquad\square$

Algorithm 14.1 (Reduction Algorithm)
Input: A clause C.
Output: A reduction D of C.

1. Set $D = C$.
2. Find a literal $L \in D$ and a substitution θ such that $D\theta \subseteq D\backslash\{L\}$. If this is impossible, then return D and stop.
3. Set D to $D\theta$ and goto 2.

The previous algorithm gives Plotkin's approach to computing reductions of clauses. A somewhat more sophisticated approach is given in [GF93].

We will now describe an alternative approach, which uses the basic relation between a clause and its reduction expressed in Lemma 14.15. First we give an example.

Example 14.13 Let $C = \{P(x,x), P(x,x_1), P(z,y)\}$. Let $\theta = \{x_1/x, z/x, y/x\}$, then $D = C\theta = \{P(x,x)\} \subseteq C$ is reduced. Notice that θ does not act on any variables in D.

Now let $C = \{Q(y, f(x)), P(x), Q(y, f(z)), Q(a, f(x))\}$, $\theta = \{y/a, z/x\}$, then $D = C\theta = \{P(x), Q(a, f(x))\} \subseteq C$ is reduced. Notice again that θ does not act on any variables in D. $\qquad\triangleleft$

The previous examples suggest that a reduction of C may be obtained by mapping some literals to a subset D of C, without affecting D. This turns out to be true in general.

Lemma 14.14 *Let C be a clause and θ a substitution. If $C\theta = C$, then there is a $k \geq 1$, such that $L\theta^k = L$ for every $L \in C$.*

Proof First note that θ is injective: for all $L_1, L_2 \in C$, if $L_1 \neq L_2$, then $L_1\theta \neq L_2\theta$, for otherwise $|C\theta| < |C|$. Hence if $L_1\theta = L_2\theta$, then $L_1 = L_2$. For each $L \in C$, consider the following infinite sequence

$$L, L\theta, L\theta^2, L\theta^3, \ldots$$

Since $C\theta = C$, each literal in this sequence is a member of C. C contains only a finite number of literals, so for some $i < j$ we must have $L\theta^i = L\theta^j$. Then from the injectivity, also $L = L\theta^{j-i}$. For this L, define $n(L) = j - i$. Notice that $L = L\theta^m$ if m is a multiple of $n(L)$. Let k be the least common multiple of all $n(L)$. Then $L\theta^k = L$ for every $L \in C$. □

Lemma 14.15 *Let C and D be clauses. If D is a reduction of C, then there is a substitution θ such that $C\theta = D$ and $L\theta = L$ for every $L \in D$.*

Proof Suppose D is a reduction of C, then there is a σ such that $C\sigma \subseteq D$. Then also $D\sigma \subseteq C\sigma \subseteq D$, since $D \subseteq C$. If $D\sigma \neq D$, then D would not be reduced, hence $D\sigma = C\sigma = D$. By the previous lemma, there is a $k \geq 1$ such that $L\sigma^k = L$ for every $L \in D$. Now define $\theta = \sigma^k$. Then since $C\sigma = D$ and $D\sigma = D$, we have $C\theta = D$. □

Thus an alternative for Plotkin's approach is to take a proper subset D of C, and see if all other literals in C can be mapped onto D by some θ which does not affect the variables in D. If such a D cannot be found, C is reduced. If D can be found but is still not reduced, then we can take a proper subset of D again, etc. Eventually, we will reach D which is reduced.

14.5 Inverse Reduction

Plotkin's reduction algorithm finds a reduction D of C. In this section we develop an algorithm which does the inverse: given a reduced clause D, the algorithm constructs (possibly non-reduced) members C of the subsume-equivalence class of D. This will be useful in the chapter on refinement operators. Since the subsume-equivalence class of D is infinite, we have to limit the scope of the algorithm. This is done by restricting the number of literals in C.

Given a reduced clause D, we know from Lemma 14.15 that for every non-reduced C such that $D \subset C$ and $D \sim C$, we can find a θ such that

$C\theta = D$, and θ only acts on variables not appearing in D. Thus C can be reduced by mapping $E = C \backslash D$ to literals in D. In the inverse direction, we can find C by adding a set E to D, such that $E\theta \subseteq D$, where θ does not act on variables in D. This is the idea used in the algorithm. If D is a reduced clause and m is some positive integer, then our algorithm finds a variant of every non-reduced C with m or less literals in the subsume-equivalence class of D.

Algorithm 14.2 (Inverse Reduction Algorithm)
Input: A reduced clause D and an integer m.
Output: Variants of every C such that $D \sim C$ and $|C| \le m$.

1. $l = 0$.
2. If $|D| \le m$, then output D.
3. While $l < (m - |D|)$ do
   1. Set l to $l + 1$.
   2. For every sequence $L_1, \ldots, L_l$ such that each $L_i \in D$, but the L_i's are not necessarily distinct:
      Find every (up to variants) set $E = \{M_1, \ldots, M_l\}$ such that (1) every M_i contains at least one new variable not in D, and (2) if $x_1, \ldots, x_n$ are all those new variables, then there is a $\theta = \{x_1/t_1, \ldots, x_n/t_n\}$, such that $M_i\theta = L_i$ for $i = 1, \ldots, l$.
      For every such E, output $D \cup E$.

Example 14.16 Let $D = \{P(x, x)\}$. For $m = 2$, literals M_1 that can be added to D are $P(x, y), P(y, x), P(y, y)$, or $P(y, z)$. For $m = 3$, some of the possible M_1's and M_2's and corresponding θ's are:

M_1	M_2	θ
$P(x, y)$	$P(y, z)$	$\{y/x, z/x\}$
$P(x, y)$	$P(x, z)$	$\{y/x, z/x\}$
$P(x, y)$	$P(z, w)$	$\{y/x, z/x, w/x\}$
$P(x, y)$	$P(y, x)$	$\{y/x\}$
$P(y, y)$	$P(z, z)$	$\{y/x, z/x\}$

$\lhd$

The algorithm does not find every non-reduced equivalent clause with m or less literals, but it does find a variant of every such clause. For instance, given $D = P(x) \leftarrow Q(x, x)$, it finds $P(x) \leftarrow Q(x, x), Q(x, y)$, but not $P(z) \leftarrow Q(z, z), Q(z, u)$.

14.6 Greatest Specializations

We will now investigate the lattice-structure of a clausal language C ordered by the subsumption relation $\succeq$. In this section we will prove that every finite set S of clauses has a *greatest specialization under subsumption* (GSS), in the next section we show that it also has a *least generalization under subsumption* (LGS). This holds both for clausal languages C, and for Horn languages $\mathcal{H}$. It is straightforward to show that the GSS of some finite set S of clauses in C is simply the union of all clauses in S after they are standardized apart:

Theorem 14.17 (Existence of GSS in C) *Let C be a clausal language. Then for every finite non-empty $S \subseteq C$, there exists a GSS of S in C.*

Proof Suppose $S = \{D_1, \ldots, D_n\} \subseteq C$. Without loss of generality, we assume the clauses in S are standardized apart. Let $D = D_1 \cup \ldots \cup D_n$, then $D_i \succeq D$, for every $1 \leq i \leq n$. Now let $C \in C$ be such that $D_i \succeq C$, for every $1 \leq i \leq n$. Then for every $1 \leq i \leq n$, there is a θ_i such that $D_i\theta_i \subseteq C$, and θ_i only acts on variables in D_i. If we let $\theta = \theta_1 \cup \ldots \cup \theta_n$, then $D\theta = D_1\theta_1 \cup \ldots \cup D_n\theta_n \subseteq C$. Hence $D \succeq C$, so D is a GSS of S in C. $\square$

Proving the existence of a GSS of every finite set of Horn clauses in $\mathcal{H}$ requires a little more work, but here also the result is positive. For example, $D = P(a) \leftarrow P(f(a)), Q(y)$ is a GSS of $D_1 = P(x) \leftarrow P(f(x))$ and $D_2 = P(a) \leftarrow Q(y)$. Note that D can be obtained by applying $\sigma = \{x/a\}$ (the mgu for the heads of D_1 and D_2) to $D_1 \cup D_2$, the GSS of D_1 and D_2 in C. This idea will be used in the following proof. Here we assume $\mathcal{H}$ contains an artificial bottom element $\bot$, such that $C \succeq \bot$ for every $C \in \mathcal{H}$, and $\bot \not\succeq C$ for every $C \neq \bot$. Note that $\bot$ is not subsume-equivalent with other tautologies. Two tautologies need not be subsume-equivalent either.

Theorem 14.18 (Existence of GSS in $\mathcal{H}$) *Let $\mathcal{H}$ be a Horn language, with an additional bottom element $\bot \in \mathcal{H}$. Then for every finite non-empty $S \subseteq \mathcal{H}$, there exists a GSS of S in $\mathcal{H}$.*

Proof Suppose $S = \{D_1, \ldots, D_n\} \subseteq \mathcal{H}$. Without loss of generality we assume the clauses in S are standardized apart, $D_1, \ldots, D_k$ are the definite program clauses in S, and $D_{k+1}, \ldots, D_n$ are the definite goals in S. If $k = 0$ (i.e., if S only contains goals), then it is easy to show that $D_1 \cup \ldots \cup D_n$ is a GSS of S in $\mathcal{H}$. If $k \geq 1$ and the set $\{D_1^+, \ldots, D_k^+\}$ (the set of heads of clauses in S), is not unifiable, then $\bot$ is a GSS of S in $\mathcal{H}$. Otherwise, let σ be an mgu for $\{D_1^+, \ldots, D_k^+\}$, and let $D = D_1\sigma \cup \ldots \cup D_n\sigma$ (note that actually $D_i\sigma = D_i$ for $k+1 \leq i \leq n$, since the clauses in S are standardized apart). Since D has exactly one literal in its head, it is a definite program clause. Furthermore, we have $D_i \succeq D$ for every $1 \leq i \leq n$, since $D_i\sigma \subseteq D$.

To show that D is a GSS of S in $\mathcal{H}$, suppose $C \in \mathcal{H}$ is some clause such that $D_i \succeq C$ for every $1 \leq i \leq n$. For every $1 \leq i \leq n$, let θ_i be such that

$D_i\theta_i \subseteq C$, and θ_i only acts on variables in D_i. Let $\theta = \theta_1 \cup \ldots \cup \theta_n$. For every $1 \le i \le k$, $D_i^+\theta = D_i^+\theta_i = C^+$, so θ is a unifier for $\{D_1^+, \ldots, D_k^+\}$. But σ is an mgu for this set, so there is a γ such that $\theta = \sigma\gamma$. Now $D\gamma = D_1\sigma\gamma \cup \ldots \cup D_n\sigma\gamma = D_1\theta \cup \ldots \cup D_n\theta = D_1\theta_1 \cup \ldots \cup D_n\theta_n \subseteq C$. Hence $D \succeq C$, so D is a GSS of S in $\mathcal{H}$. See Figure 14.1 for illustration of the case where $n = 2$. $\square$

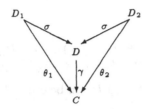

Figure 14.1: D is a GSS of D_1 and D_2

14.7 Least Generalizations

The previous section easily established the existence of the greatest specialization under subsumption. In this section we want to prove the existence of the least generalization, which will be a little harder. We start with an example of least generalization under subsumption.

Example 14.19 Suppose we are given the following two ground clauses as positive examples:

$Tiger(a) \leftarrow Mammal(a), Striped(a), Orange(a)$
$Tiger(b) \leftarrow Mammal(b), Striped(b), Yellow(b)$

These two clauses can be generalized to the following clause, which is their LGS:

$Tiger(x) \leftarrow Mammal(x), Striped(x)$
                                                                                        $\triangleleft$

Plotkin was the first to establish the result that any finite set of clauses has an LGS. We will here give a proof which differs somewhat from Plotkin's, using the $\succeq_a$-order. We use the LGA as a bridge to find the LGS.

Definition 14.20 Let C and D be clauses. A *selection* of C and D is a pair of compatible literals (L, M), such that $L \in C$, $M \in D$. $\diamond$

Example 14.21 $C = \{P(x), P(y), \neg P(a)\}$ and $D = \{Q(b), P(a), \neg P(b)\}$ have three selections: $(P(x), P(a))$, $(P(y), P(a))$, and $(\neg P(a), \neg P(b))$. $\triangleleft$

Given two clauses C and D, there is only a finite number of selections. Suppose C and D have a total of n selections. Then we can order these in a sequence

$$(L_1, M_1), (L_2, M_2), \ldots, (L_n, M_n),$$

and construct two compatible ordered clauses $C' = L_1 \vee \ldots \vee L_n$ and $D' = M_1 \vee \ldots \vee M_n$. We will show that an LGA of C' and D' is also an LGS of C and D.

Example 14.22 Let

$C = \{L_1, L_2, L_3\}$, for $L_1 = P(f(a), f(x))$, $L_2 = P(f(x), g(a))$, $L_3 = Q(a)$.
$D = \{M_1, M_2\}$, for $M_1 = P(f(b), x))$, $M_2 = P(y, g(b))$.

The set of all selections of C and D can be ordered in the following sequence:

$$S = (L_1, M_1), (L_1, M_2), (L_2, M_1), (L_2, M_2).$$

From this sequence we can construct the following clauses:

$C' = L_1 \vee L_1 \vee L_2 \vee L_2$.
$D' = M_1 \vee M_2 \vee M_1 \vee M_2$.

Note that the order and duplication of literals is not ignored in the atomic order. The clauses C' and D' are compatible, and have the following LGA:

$$E' = P(f(z_1), z_2) \vee P(z_3, z_4) \vee P(f(z_5), z_6) \vee P(z_7, g(z_1)).$$

This LGA can be shown to be also an LGS of C and D. That is, if we turn to set notation we have $E = \{P(f(z_1), z_2), P(z_3, z_4), P(f(z_5), z_6), P(z_7, g(z_1))\}$, which can be reduced to $\{P(f(z_1), z_2), P(z_7, g(z_1))\}$. This is an LGS of C and D. Note that the predicate Q does not appear in the LGA or LGS. ◁

We will now prove that the approach of the previous example always yields an LGS of C and D.

Definition 14.23 Let C and D be clauses, and $S = (L_1, M_1), \ldots, (L_n, M_n)$ a sequence of (not necessarily all) selections of C and D. Then we let $C_S = L_1 \vee \ldots \vee L_n$, $D_S = M_1 \vee \ldots \vee M_n$, and we use $LGA(C_S, D_S)$ to denote the least generalization of $\{C_S, D_S\}$ under $\succeq_a$. ◇

From the last example, it can easily be seen that if S' is a sequence of selections obtained by reordering a sequence S, or by adding or deleting duplicate selections to S, then the $LGA(C_S, D_S)$ obtained from S, and the $LGA(C_{S'}, D_{S'})$ obtained from S' will be subsume-equivalent. Thus we have the following lemma:

Lemma 14.24 *Let C and D be clauses, and S and S' be sequences of (not necessarily all) selections of C and D, such that S and S' contain exactly the same selections. Then $LGA(C_S, D_S) \sim LGA(C_{S'}, D_{S'})$.*

Furthermore, we also have the following lemmas:

Lemma 14.25 *Let C and D be clauses, and S and S' be sequences of (not necessarily all) selections of C and D, such that every selection in S' also occurs in S. Then $LGA(C_{S'}, D_{S'}) \succeq LGA(C_S, D_S)$.*

Proof Let T' be obtained by deleting all duplicate selections from S', and T be a permutation of S such that T' is a prefix of T. So for some $m \leq n$, we have

$$C_{T'} = L_1 \vee \ldots \vee L_m, \qquad D_{T'} = M_1 \vee \ldots \vee M_m.$$
$$C_T = L_1 \vee \ldots \vee L_m \vee \ldots \vee L_n, \qquad D_T = M_1 \vee \ldots \vee M_m \vee \ldots \vee M_n.$$

Let $LGA(C_T, D_T) = N_1 \vee \ldots \vee N_m \vee \ldots \vee N_n$. Then it follows from Theorem 14.3 that $LGA(C_{T'}, D_{T'}) = N_1 \vee \ldots \vee N_m$, so $LGA(C_{T'}, D_{T'}) \succeq LGA(C_T, D_T)$, because $(N_1 \vee \ldots \vee N_m)\varepsilon \subseteq N_1 \vee \ldots \vee N_m \vee \ldots \vee N_n$. The selections occuring in S are the same as those in T, and the selections in S' are the same as those in T', so by the previous lemma we have $LGA(C_S, D_S) \sim LGA(C_T, D_T)$ and $LGA(C_{S'}, D_{S'}) \sim LGA(C_{T'}, D_{T'})$. Hence $LGA(C_{S'}, D_{S'}) \succeq LGA(C_S, D_S)$. □

Lemma 14.26 *Let C and D be clauses, and S a sequence of (not necessarily all) selections of C and D. Then $LGA(C_S, D_S) \succeq C$ and $LGA(C_S, D_S) \succeq D$.*

Proof Let $E = LGA(C_S, D_S)$. Then $E \succeq_a C_S$, so $E \succeq C_S$. But $C_S \succeq C$, since the literals in C_S form a subset of C. Hence $E \succeq C$, by the transitivity of $\succeq$. Similarly $E \succeq D$. □

Now we are able to establish the existence of a least generalization under subsumption:

Theorem 14.27 (Existence of LGS in $\mathcal{C}$) *Let $\mathcal{C}$ be a clausal language. Let $C, D \in \mathcal{C}$ be clauses, and S be a sequence of all selections of C and D. Then an $LGA(C_S, D_S)$ is an LGS of $\{C, D\}$.*

Proof Let $E = LGA(C_S, D_S)$. By Lemma 14.26, $E \succeq C$ and $E \succeq D$. Let $F = \{N_1, \ldots, N_m\}$ be a clause such that $F \succeq C$ and $F \succeq D$. In order to establish that E is an LGS of $\{C, D\}$, we need to prove $F \succeq E$.

Since $F \succeq C$ and $F \succeq D$, there are θ_1 and θ_2, and $L_1, \ldots, L_m \in C$ and $M_1, \ldots, M_m \in D$, such that $N_i\theta_1 = L_i$ and $N_i\theta_2 = M_i$, for every $1 \leq i \leq m$. Then $S' = (L_1, M_1), \ldots, (L_m, M_m)$ is a sequence of selections of C and D. Let $C_{S'} = L_1 \vee \ldots \vee L_m$, $D_{S'} = M_1 \vee \ldots \vee M_m$, let $G = K_1 \vee \ldots \vee K_m$ be an $LGA(C_{S'}, D_{S'})$, and σ_1 and σ_2 be such that $G\sigma_1 = C_{S'}$ and $G\sigma_2 = D_{S'}$. Since $(N_1 \vee \ldots \vee N_m)\theta_1 = C_{S'}$ and $(N_1 \vee \ldots \vee N_m)\theta_2 = C_{D'}$, there must be a γ such that $(N_1 \vee \ldots \vee N_m)\gamma = K_1 \vee \ldots \vee K_m$. Thus we have the situation given in Figure 14.2.

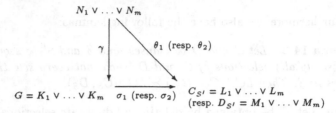

Figure 14.2: Illustration of the proof

$(N_1 \vee \ldots \vee N_m)\gamma = G$, so we have $F \succeq G$. Since every selection in S' also occurs in S, we have $G \succeq E$ from Lemma 14.25. Hence $F \succeq E$. □

Thus the LGS of any two clauses exists, and can be computed by the method explained in Example 14.22. This method is made explicit in the following algorithm:

Algorithm 14.3 (LGS Algorithm)
Input: Two clauses C and D.
Output: An LGS of $\{C, D\}$.

1. Let $(L_1, M_1), \ldots, (L_n, M_n)$ be a sequence of all selections of C and D.
2. Obtain $LGS(\vee(L_1, \ldots, L_n), \vee(M_1, \ldots, M_n)) = \vee(N_1, \ldots, N_n)$ from the Anti-Unification Algorithm.
3. Return $\{N_1, \ldots, N_n\}$.

The LGS of any finite set of clauses can be computed by repeatedly applying this algorithm. Notice that if two clauses C and D have no selections—for instance, when they have no predicates in common—then their LGS is the empty clause □. Thus □ can play the role of top element here, which means that we do not need to add an artificial top element $\top$ to the language $\mathcal{C}$.

Note that if all literals in C and D have the same sign and predicate symbol, then C and D have $|C| \cdot |D|$ selections. Accordingly, the LGS of C and D that can be obtained from these selections may also contain $|C| \cdot |D|$ distinct literals. Thus the number of literals in an LGS may increase quite rapidly.

Since we have now proved the existence of a GSS and LGS of every two clauses, it follows that a clausal language ordered by subsumption has a lattice-structure (we do not need an artificial bottom element $\perp$ for this).

Corollary 14.28 Let $\mathcal{C}$ be a clausal language. Then $\langle \mathcal{C}, \succeq \rangle$ is a lattice.

Since there is at most one selection possible from the heads of a set of Horn clauses, the LGS of a set of Horn clauses has at most one positive literal, and hence is itself also a Horn clause. Therefore $\langle \mathcal{H}, \succeq \rangle$ is a lattice. Here we need the bottom element $\perp$ to guarantee the existence of a GSS of two definite program clauses with different predicate symbols in their head.

Corollary 14.29 *Let $\mathcal{H}$ be a Horn language, with an additional bottom element $\perp \in \mathcal{H}$. Then $\langle \mathcal{H}, \succeq \rangle$ is a lattice.*

14.8 Covers in the Subsume Order

The least generalization and the greatest specialization respectively concern generalizing or specializing a *set* of clauses to a single clause. In this section we will turn to generalizing and specializing single clauses, by investigating covers of clauses in the subsumption order.

Here we will show that there exist clauses which have no complete set of upward covers in the subsumption order. In fact, there are clauses which have no upward covers at all. Dually, for the downward cover we will give a clause which has no finite complete set of downward covers. Whether all clauses have a (sometimes infinite) complete set of downward covers remains an open question.

14.8.1 Upward Covers

In this section we will prove that the clause $C = \{P(x_1, x_1)\}$ has no upward covers. For this we use an infinite chain of clauses $C_2 \succ C_3 \succ \ldots \succ C_n \succ C_{n+1} \succ \ldots \succ C$, defined as:

$$C_n = \{P(x_i, x_j) \mid i \neq j \text{ and } 1 \leq i, j \leq n\}, n \geq 2.$$

So, for instance:

$$C_2 = \{P(x_1, x_2), P(x_2, x_1)\}$$
$$C_3 = \{P(x_1, x_2), P(x_2, x_1), P(x_1, x_3), P(x_3, x_1), P(x_2, x_3), P(x_3, x_2)\}$$
$$\ldots$$

Concerning these clauses, we can prove the following:

Lemma 14.30 *For all $n \geq 2$, C_n is reduced.*

Proof Suppose that for some $n \geq 2$, C_n is not reduced. Then there is a substitution θ such that $C_n\theta \subset C_n$. Thus there are two literals $P(x_i, x_j) \neq P(x_k, x_m)$ in C_n, which are both mapped by θ to the same literal $P(x_s, x_t) \in C_n$. Since $x_i \neq x_k$ or $x_j \neq x_m$, $P(x_i, x_k)$ or $P(x_j, x_m)$ is in C_n. But then $P(x_i, x_k)\theta = P(x_s, x_s)$ or $P(x_j, x_m)\theta = P(x_t, x_t)$ is in $C_n\theta$ and hence also in C_n. This is impossible. $\square$

Furthermore, each C_n properly subsumes C_{n+1} and C:

Lemma 14.31 $C_2 \succ C_3 \succ \ldots \succ C_n \succ \ldots \succ C$.

Proof First we prove that $C_n \succ C$, for every $n \geq 2$. Since $C_n\{x_2/x_1, \ldots, x_n/x_1\} = C$, we have $C_n \succeq C$. On the other hand, if $C \succeq C_n$, then C_n would contain an instance of $P(x_1, x_1)$, which is impossible, so $C \not\succeq C_n$.

Secondly we show that for every $n \geq 2$, $C_n \succ C_{n+1}$. Since $C_n \subset C_{n+1}$, we have $C_n \succeq C_{n+1}$. On the other hand, C_n is a proper subset of C_{n+1} and by the previous lemma C_{n+1} is reduced, so $C_{n+1} \not\succeq C_n$. □

Using these properties of the clauses $C_2, C_3, \ldots$, we can now establish that C has no upward cover in the subsumption order.

Proposition 14.32 *Let $\mathcal{C}$ be a clausal language containing a binary predicate symbol P. Then $C = \{P(x_1, x_1)\}$ has no upward cover in $\langle \mathcal{C}, \succeq \rangle$.*

Proof Suppose some clause $D \in \mathcal{C}$ is an upward cover of C. Then $D \succ C$, so there is a θ such that $D\theta \subseteq C$. If D contains negative literals, or another predicate than P, or a function symbol or constant, then $D\theta$ would contain these too, which is impossible since $D\theta \subseteq C$. Also, D cannot contain a literal of the form $P(x, x)$, for then we would have $C \sim D$.

Hence D can only contain literals of the form $P(x, y)$, where $x \neq y$. Let n be the number of distinct variables in D. Then there is a variant D' of D, such that $D' \subseteq C_n$, hence $D \succeq C_n$. But then $D \succeq C_n \succ C_{n+1} \succ C$, which contradicts the assumption that D is an upward cover of C. Therefore such an upward cover D does not exist. □

From this result, we know that C has no complete set of upward covers.

14.8.2 Downward Covers

Now we turn to downward covers. It is not known whether a clause always has a complete set of downward covers. However, we can show that there is a clause C which has no *finite* complete set of downward covers. So if this particular C does have a complete set of downward covers, this set must be infinite. This result is sufficient to prove in Chapter 17 the negative result that an *ideal downward refinement operator* does not exist for the subsumption order. We use the following clauses (where all x_i and y_j are distinct):

$$C = \{P(x_1, x_2), P(x_2, x_1)\}$$
$$D_n = \{P(y_1, y_2), P(y_2, y_3), \ldots, P(y_{n-1}, y_n), P(y_n, y_1)\}, n \geq 2$$
$$C_n = C \cup D_n, n \geq 3$$

We will show that this C has no finite complete set of downward covers, using a similar technique as in the previous subsection. The clauses D_n have a special form, called a *cycle*:

Definition 14.33 Let C be a clause. A *cycle* of length $n \geq 2$ in C is a set of literals in C which can be arranged in a sequence of the form

$$P(y_1, y_2), P(y_2, y_3), \ldots, P(y_{n-1}, y_n), P(y_n, y_1),$$

where $y_1, \ldots, y_n$ are distinct variables. A clause of the form $P(y_1, y_1)$ is called a cycle of length 1.   ◇

Notice that a cycle can begin with any variable: $P(y_2, y_3), P(y_3, y_4), \ldots,$ $P(y_n, y_1), P(y_1, y_2)$ is also a cycle. The following results give properties of the clauses C, D_n and C_n listed above.

Lemma 14.34 *For all $n \geq 2$, if θ is a substitution which only maps variables to variables, and which unifies at least two variables in D_n, then $D_n\theta$ contains a cycle of length less than n.*

Proof Let i and j be such that $1 \leq i < j \leq n$, $y_i\theta = y_j\theta$, and there are no k, m such that $i \leq k < m < j$, and $y_k\theta = y_m\theta$. Then $y_i\theta, y_{i+1}\theta, \ldots, y_{j-1}\theta$ are distinct variables, and $P(y_i, y_{i+1})\theta, P(y_{i+1}, y_{i+2})\theta, \ldots, P(y_{j-1}, y_j)\theta$ is a cycle of length $j - i < n$, which is contained in $D_n\theta$.   □

Lemma 14.35 *For all $n \geq 2$, D_n is reduced.*

Proof Suppose that for some $n \geq 2$, D_n is not reduced. Then there is a substitution θ such that $D_n\theta$ is a proper subset of D_n. This θ can only map variables to variables, and must unify at least two variables. Then by the previous lemma, $D_n\theta$ contains a cycle of length less than n. But then D_n must also contain this cycle, which is impossible.   □

Lemma 14.36 *If $n = m \cdot k$ for some $k > 1$, then $D_n \succ D_m$.*

Proof Let $y_1, \ldots, y_m$ be the m variables in D_m, and $x_1, \ldots, x_n$ be the n variables in D_n. Define θ in the following way: if for some $p \geq 0$ and $1 \leq j \leq m$ we have $i = m \cdot p + j$, then $x_i\theta = y_j$. Then $P(x_n, x_1)\theta = P(y_m, y_1)$, and in general $D_n\theta = D_m$, hence $D_n \succeq D_m$.

On the other hand, if for some σ, $D_m\sigma \subseteq D_n$, then this σ can only map variables to variables, and must unify at least two variables in D_m, because no variant of D_m is a subset of D_n. Then by Lemma 14.34 $D_m\sigma$, and hence also D_n, must contain a cycle of length less than m. This is impossible, so $D_m \not\succeq D_n$.   □

Lemma 14.37 *For any $n = 3^k$ ($k \geq 1$), we have that C_n is reduced.*

Proof Let $n = 3^k$, for some $k \geq 1$. Suppose $C_n = C \cup D_n$ is not reduced, then there is a θ such that $C_n\theta$ is a proper subset of C_n. Since C and D_n are reduced, θ must map a literal in C to a literal in D_n, or vice versa. The former is impossible, since $\{P(y_i, y_{i+1}), P(y_{i+1}, y_i)\} \not\subseteq D_n$.

Now suppose θ maps some literal in D_n to a literal in C. Without loss of generality, we assume $P(y_1, y_2)\theta = P(x_1, x_2)$. Then $y_2\theta = x_2$, so $P(y_2, y_3)$ must also be mapped to a literal in C, for otherwise $P(y_2, y_3)\theta = P(x_2, t) \notin C_n$. But then $y_3\theta = x_1$, so $P(y_3, y_4)$ must also be mapped to a literal in C, etc. Hence if θ maps some literal in D_n to a literal in C, it should map *every* literal in D_n to a literal in C. That is, in this case we have $D_n\theta \subseteq C$.

Now $D_n\theta \subseteq C$ can only hold when n is even, for otherwise we would have that $P(y_n, y_1)$ would be mapped by θ to $P(x_1, x_1)$, which is not in $D_n\theta$. But n cannot be even, since 3^k is odd. $\quad\Box$

Lemma 14.38 *For any $n = 3^k$ $(k \geq 1)$, we have that $C \succ C_n$.*

Proof Since $C \subset C_n$, we have $C \succeq C_n$. On the other hand, C_n is reduced and C is a proper subset of C_n, so $C_n \not\succeq C$. $\quad\Box$

Now we let

$$E_k = C_n, \text{ where } n = 3^k, k \geq 1.$$

It follows from Lemma 14.36 that $D_{3^{k+1}} \succ D_{3^k}$, hence $E_{k+1} = C_{3^{k+1}} \succ C_{3^k} = E_k$, for every $k \geq 1$. Then we have a chain $C \succ \ldots \succ E_{k+1} \succ E_k \succ \ldots \succ E_2 \succ E_1$. To prove that C has no finite complete set of downward covers, we now need to show that there is no downward cover of C "between" C and this E_k-chain.

Lemma 14.39 *There is no downward cover E of C, such that $E \succeq E_k$, for every $k \geq 1$.*

Proof Suppose such an E does exist. Consider a k such that E_k contains more distinct variables than E. Since $C \succ E \succeq E_k$, E must contain a cycle of length 2, as image of C. Let $E\theta \subseteq E_k$, then $E\theta$ contains a cycle of length 2 in E_k. This cycle must be C. That implies $E\theta = C \cup D'_k$, where D'_k is a subset of the cycle D_k.

Since E_k contains more variables than E, we know there is a variable in E_k which is not in $E\theta$. Without loss of generality we can assume y_1 is such a variable. This means that $P(y_1, y_2)$ and $P(y_n, y_1)$ are not in D'_k. Now define σ as $y_i\sigma = x_1$ if i is odd, and $y_i\sigma = x_2$ if i is even. Then $E\theta\sigma = C$. But then we have $E \succeq C$, which contradicts the assumption that E is a downward cover of C. $\quad\Box$

Proposition 14.40 *Let $\mathcal{C}$ be a clausal language containing a binary predicate symbol P. Then $C = \{P(x_1, x_2), P(x_2, x_1)\}$ has no finite complete set of downward covers in $\langle \mathcal{C}, \succeq \rangle$.*

Proof Suppose C does have a finite complete set $S = \{F_1, \ldots, F_m\}$ of downward covers. Consider the E_k-chain mentioned above. Since S is complete, for every E_i there is an F_j such that $C \succ F_j \succeq E_i$. There are infinitely many E_i, and only finitely many F_j. Thus there must be a particular F_j and an infinite set $T = \{E_{i_1}, \ldots, E_{i_n}, \ldots\}$, such that $F_j \succeq E_{i_n}$, for every $E_{i_n} \in T$. Now for every E_k ($k \geq 1$), we can find an $E_{i_n} \in T$ such that $E_{i_n} \succeq E_k$. But then $F_j \succeq E_k$ for every $k \geq 1$, which contradicts the previous lemma. $\qquad\square$

The negative results of this section imply that the existence of finite chains of upward or downward covers cannot be generalized from the subsumption order on atoms to the subsumption order on general clauses.

These results can be extended to the case where $\mathcal{C}$ only contains unary predicate symbols and a binary function symbol f. For then we can replace every $P(x, y)$ by $Q(f(x, y))$ in C, D_n, C_n, and E_k, and repeat the same argument as above to show that $\{Q(f(x_1, x_2)), Q(f(x_2, x_1))\}$ has no finite complete set of downward covers in $\langle \mathcal{C}, \succeq \rangle$. The same holds for the negative result on upward covers.

Moreover, the negative results of this section also hold when we restrict to *Horn* clauses. We can transform the clauses and chains we used into definite goals, by turning all positive literals into negative literals. The above proofs are not affected by this change. Furthermore, when we add some ground atom A as head to each of those goals, we obtain definite program clauses for which the negative results also hold. Thus $A \leftarrow P(x_1, x_1)$ has no upward covers in $\langle \mathcal{H}, \succeq \rangle$, and $A \leftarrow P(x_1, x_2), P(x_2, x_1)$ has no finite complete set of downward covers in $\langle \mathcal{H}, \succeq \rangle$.

14.9 A Complexity Measure for Clauses

If a language contains at least one function symbol of arity ≥ 1, the set of atoms in this language is infinite, even if we identify variants. Thus to limit the search space, we need a complexity measure, for instance *size* as defined by Reynolds (see the last chapter). By bounding the size of atoms to some number, the search space becomes finite and thus can be searched completely.

The set of clauses in a language with at least one predicate symbol of arity ≥ 1 is of course also infinite, and in this case even the subsume-equivalence class of a clause contains an infinite number of clauses which are not variants. So also in this case, we need a complexity measure to restrict the search space of clauses to a finite set.

14.9.1 *Size* as Defined by Reynolds

As we have seen earlier, Reynolds [Rey70] defined the size of an atom A in the following way:

$size(A)$ = the number of symbol occurrences in A
$-$ the number of distinct variables in A.

Shapiro adapted this definition in his work on model inference [Sha81b]. However, some questions arise with respect to this measure which Shapiro did not observe, and which renders his refinement operator ρ_0, used for searching a clausal language ordered by subsumption, incomplete [LN93, Nib93]. We will not discuss his refinement operator, but only mention some of the difficulties which appear in the application of *size* to clauses.

In the simple case of atoms A and B, we have shown that if $A\theta = B$, then $size(A) \leq size(B)$. Furthermore, if also $B\sigma = A$, then we have $size(A) = size(B)$. Hence if $A\theta = B$ and $size(A) < size(B)$, then $A \succ B$. Thus we can use *size* to help determine whether A properly subsumes B.

However, when applied to clauses, *size* no longer indicates whether some clause C properly subsumes a clause D. For example, let

$$C_1 = \{P(x,y), P(y,x)\}, \; C_2 = \{P(x,x)\}, \; C_3 = \{P(a,a)\}$$

Then $C_1 \succeq C_2$ and $C_2 \succeq C_3$. But on the other hand, $size(C_1) = 6 - 2 = 4$, $size(C_2) = 3 - 1 = 2$, and $size(C_3) = 3 - 0 = 3$. There appears to be no coherent relation between subsumption among clauses, and the respective *sizes* of those clauses. A second difficulty is that subsume-equivalent clauses need not have the same size. For example, $D = \{P(a,a), P(x,x)\} \sim C_3$, but D has size $6 - 1 = 5$.

14.9.2   A New Complexity Measure

To a certain extent, Reynolds's *size* of an atom reflects the complexity of an atom. But it is only a number which does not really tell us very much about the internal structure of the atom. When applied to clauses, it becomes even less informative.

The reason why *size* does not work for clauses, is that the size of a clause is influenced by the number of literals in the clauses. If a clause C subsumes a clause D, then C may still have larger *size* than D just because C contains more literals. On the other hand, if $C \subseteq D$, then $size(C) \leq size(D)$. The number of literals in a clause C is an important structural property of C. Accordingly, it should be taken into account by a complexity measure on clauses, independently of the *sizes* of the particular literals in C.

This induces a new complexity measure *newsize* of a clause C, as a pair of two different coordinates: the first coordinate is the *size* of the biggest literal in C, while the second coordinate is the number of literals in C. Thus we define:

Definition 14.41 Let C be a clause. Then

$$newsize(C) = (maxsize(C), |C|),$$

where $maxsize(C)$ is the maximum of $\{size(L) \mid L \in C\}$, and $|C|$ is the number of literals in C.   ◇

Note that this definition ignores the negation connective: both $\{P(a)\}$ and $\{\neg P(a)\}$ have $newsize$ $(2,1)$.

Example 14.42 Let $C = \{\neg P(a,x), Q(f(y)), P(f(x), f(a))\}$. Here we have $size(\neg P(a,x)) = 2$, $size(Q(f(y))) = 2$, and $size(P(f(x), f(a))) = 4$, so $maxsize(C) = 4$, and $newsize(C) = (4,3)$.   ◁

It is easy to show that if $C \succeq D$, then $maxsize(C) \leq maxsize(D)$. Hence if $C \sim D$, then $maxsize(C) = maxsize(D)$. However, other than in the case of $size$ applied to atoms, a clause C may properly subsume D while still $maxsize(C) = maxsize(D)$. For example, let $C = \{P(x), Q(y)\}$ and $D = \{P(z), Q(z)\}$. Then $C \succ D$, but $maxsize(C) = 1 = maxsize(D)$.

It is often important to limit the number of clauses in the search space. Our new complexity measure $newsize$ can be used to achieve this. That is, given numbers k and m, the set of clauses bounded by a $newsize$ of (k, m) is finite when we identify variants.

Definition 14.43 Let C be a clause, and (k, m) be a pair of natural numbers. We say C is $bounded$ by (k, m) if $maxsize(C) \leq k$ and $|C| \leq m$.   ◇

Proposition 14.44 *Let $\mathcal{C}$ be a clausal language with finitely many constants, function and predicate symbols. Then for given $k, m > 0$, the set $\{C \in \mathcal{C} \mid C$ is bounded by $(k, m)\}$ is finite up to variants.*

We will only sketch the idea behind this. Let $\mathcal{C}$ be a clausal language with finitely many constants, function and predicate symbols, and suppose we are given (k, m). It is not very difficult to see that the set of atoms with $size \leq k$ is finite up to variants. Let v be the maximum of the set $\{n \mid$ there is an atom $A \in \mathcal{C}$ with $size \leq k$ that contains n distinct variables$\}$. Because a clause bounded by (k, m) can contain at most m distinct literals, each of which can contain at most v distinct variables, a clause bounded by (k, m) can contain at most mv distinct variables. Let us fix distinct variables $x_1, \ldots, x_{mv}$. Now let $\mathcal{K}$ be the finite set of all atoms of $size \leq k$ that can be constructed from the predicate symbols, function symbols and constants in $\mathcal{C}$, and variables $x_1, \ldots, x_{mv}$. Since each clause that is bounded by (k, m) must be (a variant of) a subset of $\mathcal{K}$, there are only finitely many such clauses, up to variants.

14.10   Summary

This chapter discussed the *subsumption* order on a clausal language, which is used very often in ILP. We first defined the *atomic* order $\succeq_a$, which treats clauses as atoms. It can be used as a bridge between the subsumption order for atoms and the subsumption order for clauses. Subsumption between clauses is a decidable relation. Equivalence classes under subsumption can be represented by a single *reduced* clause. Reduction can be undone by inverse reduction. The main properties of the subsumption order are the following:

- Every finite set of clauses has a least generalization (LGS) and greatest specialization (GSS) under subsumption in $\mathcal{C}$. Hence $\langle \mathcal{C}, \succeq \rangle$ is a lattice.
- Every finite set of Horn clauses has a least generalization (LGS) and greatest specialization (GSS) under subsumption in $\mathcal{H}$. Hence $\langle \mathcal{H}, \succeq \rangle$ is a lattice.
- Some clauses, such as $\{P(x_1, x_1)\}$, have no upward covers.
  Some clauses, such as $\{P(x_1, x_2), P(x_2, x_1)\}$, have no finite complete set of downward covers.

Finally, since *size* is not very well-suited as a complexity measure on clauses, we defined *newsize*.

Chapter 15

The Implication Order

15.1 Introduction

Subsumption is the generality order that is used most often in ILP. It is used much more than logical implication.[1] The reasons for this are mainly practical: subsumption is more tractable and more efficiently implementable than implication. For instance, subsumption between clauses is decidable (Section 14.3), while implication is not (Section 7.8). However, a clause C which implies another clause D, need not subsume this D. For instance, take

$$C = P(f(x)) \leftarrow P(x)$$
$$D = P(f^2(x)) \leftarrow P(x)$$

Then $C \models D$, but $C \not\preceq D$. Subsumption is too weak in this case. A further sign of this weakness is the fact that two tautologies need not be subsume-equivalent, even though they are logically equivalent.

For the construction of least generalizations, subsumption is again not fully satisfactory. For example, if S consists of the clauses $D_1 = P(f^2(a)) \leftarrow P(a)$ and $D_2 = P(f(b)) \leftarrow P(b)$, then the LGS of S is $P(f(y)) \leftarrow P(x)$. On the other hand, the clause $P(f(x)) \leftarrow P(x)$ seems more appropriate as a least generalization of S, since it implies D_1 and D_2, and is implied by the LGS. However, it does not subsume D_1. Even for clauses without function symbols, the subsumption order may still be unsatisfactory. Consider $D_1 = P(x, y, z) \leftarrow P(y, z, x)$ and $D_2 = P(x, y, z) \leftarrow P(z, x, y)$. The clause D_1 is a resolvent of D_2 with D_2, and D_2 is a resolvent of D_1 with D_1, so D_1 and D_2 are logically equivalent. This means that D_1 is a least generalization under implication (LGI) of the set $\{D_1, D_2\}$. Yet the LGS of these two clauses is $P(x, y, z) \leftarrow P(u, v, w)$, which is clearly an over-generalization. As these examples also show, the subsumption order is particularly unsatisfactory if

---

[1]It is easy to see that logical implication is reflexive and transitive, and hence a quasi-order on clauses.

we consider *recursive* clauses: clauses where the same predicate symbol occurs both in a positive and a negative literal. Thus it is desirable to make the step from the subsumption order to the more powerful implication order.

A further advantage of the implication order is that one can easily compare a *set* of clauses (a theory) with another theory or clause. For example, if $\Sigma = \{(P \leftarrow Q), (Q \leftarrow R)\}$ and $C = P \leftarrow R$, then we have $\Sigma \models C$. On the other hand, subsumption cannot be used here to compare the generality of Σ and C, because neither member of Σ subsumes C.

In this chapter we discuss some of the properties of the implication order. Firstly, we show that if S is a finite set of clauses containing at least one non-tautologous function-free clause (apart from this clause, S may contain a finite number of arbitrary other clauses, including clauses which contain function symbols), then there exists a computable least generalization (LGI) of S under implication. Secondly, every finite set of clauses has a greatest specialization (GSI) under implication. These results are drawn from [NW96b]. The proof of the LGI result makes use of the Subsumption Theorem, of some ideas from [Ide93a, Ide95] concerning a restricted form of implication called *T-implication*, and of an important lemma due to Gottlob [Got87].

This LGI result does not solve the general question concerning the existence of LGIs, but it does provide a positive answer for a large class of cases. These cases may be of great practical significance, since the presence of only one non-tautologous function-free clause in a finite S already guarantees the existence and computability of an LGI of S, no matter what other clauses S additionally contains. Particularly in implementations, the language is often required to be function-free, as can for instance be seen from the systems we survey in Section 19.6.

The third property of the implication order that we discuss concerns *covers*. Here the negative results from the subsumption order carry over to the implication order. This result stems from [LN94b].

15.2   Least Generalizations

The question whether every finite set of clauses has a least generalization under implication (LGI), has been devoted quite a lot of attention. For Horn clauses, this question has already been answered negatively. The following example is taken from [MD94].

Let $D_1 = P(f^2(x)) \leftarrow P(x)$, $D_2 = P(f^3(x)) \leftarrow P(x)$, $C_1 = P(f(x)) \leftarrow P(x)$, and $C_2 = P(f^2(y)) \leftarrow P(x)$. Then we have both $C_1 \models \{D_1, D_2\}$ and $C_2 \models \{D_1, D_2\}$. It is not very difficult to see that a Horn clause which is more specific than either C_1 or C_2, cannot imply both D_1 and D_2. For C_1: no resolvent of C_1 with itself implies D_2, and no clause that is properly subsumed by C_1 still implies D_1 and D_2. Hence, by the Subsumption Theorem, there is no proper specialization of C_1 that implies D_1 and D_2. For C_2: every resolvent of C_2 with itself is a variant of C_2, and no clause that is properly subsumed by C_2 still implies D_1 and D_2. Thus C_1 and C_2 are both minimal generalizations under implication (MGIs) of $\{D_1, D_2\}$. Since C_1 and C_2 are themselves incomparable under implication, there is no LGI of $\{D_1, D_2\}$ in $\mathcal{H}$. Whether any two Horn clauses have a finite complete set of MGIs in $\mathcal{H}$, is at present an open question.

However, the fact that there is no LGI of $\{D_1, D_2\}$ in $\mathcal{H}$, does not mean that D_1 and D_2 have no LGI in $\mathcal{C}$, since a Horn language is a more restricted space than a clausal language. In fact, it is shown in [MP94b] that $C = P(f(x)) \vee P(f^2(y)) \vee \neg P(x)$ is an LGI of D_1 and D_2 in $\mathcal{C}$. For this reason, it may be worthwhile for the LGI to consider a clausal language instead of only Horn clauses.

In the next subsection, we show that any finite set of clauses which contains at least one non-tautologous function-free clause, has an LGI in $\mathcal{C}$. An immediate corollary of this result is the existence of an LGI of any finite set of function-free clauses. In our usage of the word, a 'function-free' clause may contain constants, even though constants are sometimes seen as function symbols of arity 0.

Definition 15.1 A clause is *function-free* if it does not contain function symbols of arity 1 or more. A set of clauses is *function-free* if all its members are function-free. ◇

15.2.1 A Sufficient Condition for the Existence of an LGI

In this subsection, we show that any finite set S of clauses containing at least one non-tautologous function-free clause, has an LGI in $\mathcal{C}$. We start with some lemmas, the first of which was originally proved by Gottlob in [Got87]. It is in fact an immediate corollary of the Subsumption Theorem:

Lemma 15.2 (Gottlob) *Let C and D be non-tautologous clauses, C^{pos} and C^{neg} be the sets of positive and negative literals in C, respectively, and D^{pos} and D^{neg} be the sets of positive and negative literals in D. If $C \models D$, then $C^{pos} \succeq D^{pos}$ and $C^{neg} \succeq D^{neg}$.*

Proof Suppose $C \models D$. Then since $C^{pos} \models C$, we have $C^{pos} \models D$. C^{pos} contains only positive literals, so it cannot be resolved with itself. Then it follows from Theorem 5.17 that $C^{pos} \succeq D$. But then C^{pos} must subsume the positive literals in D, hence $C^{pos} \succeq D^{pos}$. Similarly $C^{neg} \succeq D^{neg}$. □

An important consequence of this lemma concerns the *depth* of clauses, defined as follows:

Definition 15.3 Let t be a term. If t is a variable or constant, then the *depth* of t is 1. If $t = f(t_1, \ldots, t_n)$, $n \geq 1$, then the depth of t is 1 plus the

depth of the t_i with largest depth. The *depth* of a clause C is the depth of
the term with largest depth in C.   ◇

Note that a clause is function-free iff it has depth 1.

Example 15.4 The term $t = f(a, x)$ has depth 2. The clause $C = P(f(x)) \leftarrow$
$P(g(f(x), a))$ has depth 3, since $g(f(x), a)$ has depth 3.   ◁

It follows from Gottlob's lemma that if $C \models D$, then the depth of C is
smaller than or equal to the depth of D—otherwise the positive part of C
could not subsume the positive part of D, or the negative part of C could not
subsume the negative part of D. For instance, take $D = P(x, f(x, g(y))) \leftarrow$
$P(g(a), b)$, which has depth 3. Then a clause C containing a term $f(x, g^2(y))$
(depth 4) cannot imply D.

Lemma 15.5 *Let Σ be a set of clauses, C be a clause, and σ be a Skolem
substitution for C with respect to Σ. Then $\Sigma \models C$ iff $\Sigma \models C\sigma$.*

Proof

$\Rightarrow$: Obvious.

$\Leftarrow$: Suppose C is not a tautology, and let $\sigma = \{x_1/a_1, \ldots, x_n/a_n\}$. If
$\Sigma \models C\sigma$, it follows from the Subsumption Theorem (Theorem 5.17) that
there is a D such that $\Sigma \vdash_r D$, and $D \succeq C\sigma$. All constants in D also appear
in clauses in Σ, so σ is a Skolem substitution for C with respect to D. Then
by Lemma 5.16 we have $D \succeq C$, hence $\Sigma \models C$.   □

The proof in this section can be divided in two steps. First, we use the Subsumption Theorem to adapt Theorem 5.9. That is, if $C \models D$, C is function-
free and σ is a Skolem substitution for D with respect to C, then we can
effectively determine which ground instances of C are needed for a deduction
of $D\sigma$. Secondly, we can then use the finiteness of the number of these ground
instances to establish the existence of an LGI.

Definition 15.6 Let C be a clause, $x_1, \ldots, x_n$ all distinct variables in C, and
T a set of terms. Then the *instance set* of C with respect to T is $\mathcal{I}(C, T) =$
$\{C\theta \mid \theta = \{x_1/t_1, \ldots, x_n/t_n\}$, where $t_i \in T$, for every $1 \leq i \leq n\}$. If $\Sigma =$
$\{C_1, \ldots, C_k\}$ is a set of clauses, then the *instance set* of Σ with respect to T
is $\mathcal{I}(\Sigma, T) = \mathcal{I}(C_1, T) \cup \ldots \cup \mathcal{I}(C_k, T)$.   ◇

Example 15.7 If $C = P(x) \vee Q(y)$ and $T = \{a, f(z)\}$, then $\mathcal{I}(C, T) =$
$\{(P(a) \vee Q(a)), (P(a) \vee Q(f(z))), (P(f(z)) \vee Q(a)), (P(f(z)) \vee Q(f(z)))\}$. ◁

A *term set* of a set S of clauses by some Skolem substitution σ is a finite
set of ground terms, defined as follows:

Definition 15.8 Let S be a finite set of clauses, and σ be a Skolem substitution for S. Then the *term set* of S by σ is the set of all terms (including
subterms) occurring in $S\sigma$.   ◇

Example 15.9 The term set of $D = P(f^2(x), y, z) \leftarrow P(y, z, f^2(x))$ by $\sigma = \{x/a, y/b, z/c\}$ is $T = \{a, f(a), f^2(a), b, c\}$. ◁

Consider $C = P(x, y, z) \leftarrow P(z, x, y)$, and D, σ and T as defined in the above example. Then $C \models D$, and also $\mathcal{I}(C, T) \models D\sigma$, since $D\sigma$ is a resolvent of $P(f^2(a), b, c) \leftarrow P(c, f^2(a), b)$ and $P(c, f^2(a), b) \leftarrow P(b, c, f^2(a))$, which are in $\mathcal{I}(C, T)$. As we will show in the next lemma, this holds in general: if $C \models D$ and C is function-free, then we can restrict attention to the ground instances of C instantiated to terms in the term set of D by some σ.

The proof of Lemma 15.10 uses the following idea. Consider a derivation of a clause E from a set Σ of ground clauses. Suppose some of the clauses in Σ contain terms not appearing in E. Then any literals containing these terms in Σ must be resolved away in the derivation. This means that if we replace all the terms in the derivation that are not in E, by some other term t, then the result will be another derivation of E. For example, the left of Figure 15.1 shows a derivation of length 1 of E. The term $f^2(b)$ in the parent clauses does not appear in E. If we replace this term by the constant a, the result is another derivation of E (right of the figure).

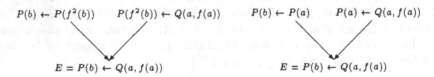

$$P(b) \leftarrow P(f^2(b)) \qquad P(f^2(b)) \leftarrow Q(a, f(a)) \qquad P(b) \leftarrow P(a) \qquad P(a) \leftarrow Q(a, f(a))$$

$$E = P(b) \leftarrow Q(a, f(a)) \qquad\qquad E = P(b) \leftarrow Q(a, f(a))$$

Figure 15.1: Transforming the left derivation yields the right derivation

Lemma 15.10 *Let C be a function-free clause, D be a clause, σ be a Skolem substitution for D with respect to $\{C\}$, and T be the term set of D by σ. Then $C \models D$ iff $\mathcal{I}(C, T) \models D\sigma$.*

Proof

$\Leftarrow$: Suppose $\mathcal{I}(C, T) \models D\sigma$. Since $C \models \mathcal{I}(C, T)$, it follows that $C \models D\sigma$. Now $C \models D$ by Lemma 15.5.

$\Rightarrow$: Suppose $C \models D$. If D is a tautology, then $D\sigma$ is a tautology, so this case is obvious. Suppose D is not a tautology, then $D\sigma$ is not a tautology. Since $C \models D\sigma$, it follows from Theorem 5.9 that there exists a finite set Σ of ground instances of C, such that $\Sigma \models D\sigma$. By the Subsumption Theorem, there exists a derivation from Σ of a clause E, such that $E \succeq D\sigma$. Since Σ is ground, E must also be ground, so we have $E \subseteq D\sigma$. This implies that E only contains terms from T.

Let t be an arbitrary term in T, and let Σ' be obtained from Σ by replacing every term in clauses in Σ which is not in T, by t. Note that since each clause in Σ is a ground instance of the function-free clause C, every clause in Σ' is also a ground instance of C. Now it is easy to see that the same replacement

of terms in the derivation of E from Σ results in a derivation of E from Σ':
(1) each resolution step in the derivation from Σ can also be carried out in
the derivation from Σ', since the same terms in Σ are replaced by the same
terms in Σ', and (2) the terms in Σ that are not in T (and hence are replaced
by t), do not appear in the conclusion E of the derivation.

Since there is a derivation of E from Σ', we have $\Sigma' \models E$, and hence
$\Sigma' \models D\sigma$. Σ' is a set of ground instances of C and all terms in Σ' are terms
in T, so $\Sigma' \subseteq \mathcal{I}(C, T)$. Hence $\mathcal{I}(C, T) \models D\sigma$.   □

Lemma 15.10 cannot be generalized to the case where C contains function
symbols of arity ≥ 1, take $C = P(f(x), y) \leftarrow P(z, x)$ and $D = P(f(a), a) \leftarrow$
$P(a, f(a))$. Then $T = \{a, f(a)\}$ is the term set of D, and we have $C \models D$,
yet it can be seen that $\mathcal{I}(C, T) \not\models D$. The argument used in the previous
lemma does not work here, because different terms in some ground instance
need not relate to different variables. For example, in the ground instance
$P(f^2(a), a) \leftarrow P(a, f(a))$ of C, we cannot just replace $f^2(a)$ by some other
term, for then the resulting clause would not be an instance of C.

On the other hand, Lemma 15.10 can be generalized to a *set* of clauses
instead of a single clause. If Σ is a finite set of function-free clauses, C is an
arbitrary clause, and σ is a Skolem substitution for C with respect to Σ, then
we have that $\Sigma \models C$ iff $\mathcal{I}(\Sigma, T) \models C\sigma$. The proof is almost literally the same
as above.

This result implies that $\Sigma \models C$ is reducible to an implication $\mathcal{I}(\Sigma, T) \models$
$C\sigma$ between ground clauses. Since, by the next lemma, implication between
ground clauses is decidable, it follows that $\Sigma \models C$ is decidable in case Σ is
function-free.

Lemma 15.11 *The problem whether $\Sigma \models C$, where Σ is a finite set of
ground clauses and C is a ground clause, is decidable.*

Proof Let $C = L_1 \lor \ldots \lor L_n$, and $\mathcal{A}$ be the finite set of all ground atoms
occurring in Σ and C. Now:
$\Sigma \models C$ iff (by Proposition 2.37)
$\Sigma \cup \{\neg L_1, \ldots, \neg L_n\}$ is unsatisfiable iff (by Proposition 3.30)
$\Sigma \cup \{\neg L_1, \ldots, \neg L_n\}$ has no Herbrand model iff
no subset of $\mathcal{A}$ is a Herbrand model of $\Sigma \cup \{\neg L_1, \ldots, \neg L_n\}$.
Since $\mathcal{A}$ is finite, the last statement is decidable.   □

Corollary 15.12 *The problem whether $\Sigma \models C$, where Σ is a finite set of
function-free clauses and C is a clause, is decidable.*

The next sequence of lemmas leads to our LGI result.

Lemma 15.13 *Let S be a finite set of non-tautologous clauses, $V = \{x_1, \ldots,$
$x_m\}$ be a set of variables, and let $G = \{C_1, C_2, \ldots\}$ be a (possibly infinite)*

set of generalizations of S under implication. Then the set $G' = \mathcal{I}(C_1, V) \cup \mathcal{I}(C_2, V) \cup \ldots$ is a finite set of clauses.

Proof Let d be the maximal depth of the terms in clauses in S. It follows from Lemma 15.2 that G (and hence also G') cannot contain terms of depth greater than d, nor predicate symbols, function symbols or constants other than those in S. The set of literals which can be constructed from predicate symbols in S, and from terms of depth at most d consisting of function symbols and constants in S and variables in V, is finite. Hence the set of clauses which can be constructed from those literals is also finite. G' is a subset of this set, so G' is a finite set of clauses. $\qquad\square$

Lemma 15.14 *Let C be a function-free clause, D be a clause, and σ be a Skolem substitution for D with respect to $\{C\}$. Suppose $C \models D$, and let $T = \{t_1, \ldots, t_n\}$ be the term set of D by σ, $V = \{x_1, \ldots, x_m\}$ be a set of variables, and $m \geq n$. If E is an LGS of $\mathcal{I}(C, V)$, then $E \models D$.*

Proof Let $\gamma = \{x_1/t_1, \ldots, x_n/t_n, x_{n+1}/t_n, \ldots, x_m/t_n\}$ (it does not matter to which terms the variables $x_{n+1}, \ldots, x_m$ are mapped by γ, as long as they are mapped to terms in T). Suppose $\mathcal{I}(C, V) = \{C\rho_1, \ldots, C\rho_k\}$. Then $\mathcal{I}(C, T) = \{C\rho_1\gamma, \ldots, C\rho_k\gamma\}$. Let E be an LGS of $\mathcal{I}(C, V)$ (note that E must be function-free). Then for every $1 \leq i \leq k$, there are θ_i such that $E\theta_i \subseteq C\rho_i$. This means that $E\theta_i\gamma \subseteq C\rho_i\gamma$ and hence $E\theta_i\gamma \models C\rho_i\gamma$, for every $1 \leq i \leq k$. Therefore $E \models \mathcal{I}(C, T)$.

Since $C \models D$, we know from Lemma 15.10 that $\mathcal{I}(C, T) \models D\sigma$, hence $E \models D\sigma$. Furthermore, since E is an LGS of $\mathcal{I}(C, V)$, all constants in E also appear in C, hence all constants in E must appear in D. Thus σ is also a Skolem substitution for D with respect to $\{E\}$, and we have $E \models D$ by Lemma 15.5. $\qquad\square$

Consider $C = P(x, y, z) \leftarrow P(y, z, x)$ and $D = \leftarrow Q(w)$. Both C and D imply the clause $E = P(x, y, z) \leftarrow P(z, x, y), Q(b)$. Now note that $C \cup D = P(x, y, z) \leftarrow P(y, z, x), Q(w)$ also implies E. This holds for clauses in general:

Lemma 15.15 *Let C, D, and E be clauses such that C and D are standardized apart. If $C \models E$ and $D \models E$, then $C \cup D \models E$.*

Proof Suppose $C \models E$ and $D \models E$, and let M be a model of $C \cup D$. Since C and D are standardized apart, the clause $C \cup D$ is equivalent to the formula $\forall(C) \vee \forall(D)$ (where $\forall(C)$ denotes the universally quantified clause C). This means that M is a model of C or a model of D. Now it follows from $C \models E$ or $D \models E$ that M is also a model of E. Therefore $C \cup D \models E$. $\qquad\square$

Now we can prove the existence of an LGI of any finite set S of clauses which contains at least one non-tautologous and function-free clause. In fact we can prove something stronger, namely that this LGI is a *special* LGI, defined as follows:

Definition 15.16 Let C be a clausal language, and S be a finite subset of C. An LGI C of S in C is called a *special* LGI of S in C, if $C' \succeq C$ for every generalization $C' \in C$ of S under implication. $\diamond$

Note that if D is an LGI of a set containing at least one non-tautologous function-free clause, then by Lemma 15.2 D is itself function-free, because it should imply the function-free clause(s) in S. For instance, $C = P(x, y, z) \leftarrow P(y, z, x), Q(w)$ is an LGI of $D_1 = P(x, y, z) \leftarrow P(y, z, x), Q(f(a))$ and $D_2 = P(x, y, z) \leftarrow P(z, x, y), Q(b)$. Note that this LGI is properly subsumed by the LGS of $\{D_1, D_2\}$, which is $P(x, y, z) \leftarrow P(x', y', z'), Q(w)$. An LGI may sometimes be the empty clause $\square$, for example if $S = \{P(a), Q(a)\}$.

Theorem 15.17 (Existence of special LGI in C) *Let C be a clausal language. If S is a finite set of clauses from C, and S contains at least one non-tautologous function-free clause, then there exists a special LGI of S in C.*

Proof Let $S = \{D_1, \ldots, D_n\}$ be a finite set of clauses from C, such that S contains at least one non-tautologous function-free clause. We can assume without loss of generality that S contains no tautologies. Let σ be a Skolem substitution for S, $T = \{t_1, \ldots, t_m\}$ be the term set of S by σ, $V = \{x_1, \ldots, x_m\}$ be a set of variables, and $G = \{C_1, C_2, \ldots\}$ be the set of all generalizations of S under implication in C. Note that $\square \in G$, so G is not empty. Since each clause in G must imply the function-free clause(s) in S, it follows from Lemma 15.2 that all members of G are function-free. By Lemma 15.13, the set $G' = \mathcal{I}(C_1, V) \cup \mathcal{I}(C_2, V) \cup \ldots$ is a finite set of clauses. Since G' is finite, the set of distinct $\mathcal{I}(C_i, V)$s is also finite. For simplicity, let $\{\mathcal{I}(C_1, V), \ldots, \mathcal{I}(C_k, V)\}$ be the set of all distinct $\mathcal{I}(C_i, V)$s.

Let E_i be an LGS of $\mathcal{I}(C_i, V)$, for every $1 \le i \le k$, such that $E_1, \ldots, E_k$ are standardized apart. For every $1 \le j \le n$, the term set of D_j by σ is some set $\{t_{j_1}, \ldots, t_{j_s}\} \subseteq T$, such that $m \ge j_s$. From Lemma 15.14, we have that $E_i \models D_j$, for every $1 \le i \le k$ and $1 \le j \le n$, hence $E_i \models S$. Now let $F = E_1 \cup \ldots \cup E_k$, then we have $F \models S$ from Lemma 15.15.

To prove that F is a special LGI of S, it remains to show that $C_j \succeq F$, for every $j \ge 1$. For every $j \ge 1$, there is an i ($1 \le i \le k$), such that $\mathcal{I}(C_j, V) = \mathcal{I}(C_i, V)$. So for this i, E_i is an LGS of $\mathcal{I}(C_j, V)$. Since every clause in $\mathcal{I}(C_j, V)$ is an instance of C_j, we have that C_j is itself also a generalization of $\mathcal{I}(C_j, V)$ under subsumption, hence $C_j \succeq E_i$. Then finally $C_j \succeq F$, since $E_i \subseteq F$. $\square$

As a consequence of this result, every finite set S in which *all* clauses are function-free, has an LGI in C.

Corollary 15.18 *Let C be a clausal language. Then for every finite set of function-free clauses $S \subseteq C$, there exists an LGI of S in C.*

Proof Let S be a finite set of function-free clauses in C. If S only contains tautologies, any tautology will be an LGI of S. If S contains some non-tautologous clauses, then by the previous theorem, there is a special LGI of S. ☐

This corollary is not trivial, since even though the number of Herbrand interpretations of a language without function symbols is finite (due to the fact that the number of all possible ground atoms is finite in this case), S may nevertheless be implied by an infinite number of non-equivalent clauses. This may seem like a paradox, since there are only finitely many categories of clauses that can "behave differently" in a *finite* number of finite Herbrand interpretations. Thus it would seem that the number of non-equivalent function-free clauses should also be finite. This is a misunderstanding, since logical implication (and hence also logical equivalence) is defined in terms of *all* interpretations, not just Herbrand interpretations. For instance, define $D_1 = P(a, a)$ and $D_2 = P(b, b)$, $C_n = \{P(x_i, x_j) \mid i \neq j, 1 \leq i, j \leq n\}$. Then we have $C_n \models \{D_1, D_2\}$, $C_n \models C_{n+1}$ and $C_{n+1} \not\models C_n$, for every $n \geq 1$ (see the proof of Proposition 14.32).

The general question concerning the existence of an LGI in clausal languages remains open. We will briefly mention here another attempt to answer this question, using *self-saturated* clauses [MP94b]. A clause is self-saturated if it is subsumed by any clause which logically implies it. A clause D is a *self-saturation* of C, if C and D are logically equivalent and D is self-saturated. Note that if C is a function-free non-tautologous clause, and D is a special LGI of the set $\{C\}$, then D is logically equivalent to C and is subsumed by any clause which logically implies C. Thus every such C has a self-saturation D. Now, if two clauses C_1 and C_2 have self-saturations D_1 and D_2, respectively, then an LGS of D_1 and D_2 is also an LGI of C_1 and C_2. This solves our question concerning the existence of LGIs for clauses which have a self-saturation. However, it is also shown in [MP94b] that there exist clauses which have no self-saturation, so the concept of self-saturation cannot solve our question in general.

Though the general question remains open for clausal languages, we do have the following result, which says that if a set S has a *minimal* generalization under implication (MGI), then this is also a *least* generalization under implication (LGI).

Proposition 15.19 *Let C be a clausal language, and S be a finite subset of C. If $C \in C$ is an MGI of S in C, then C is an LGI of S in C.*

Proof Suppose some $C \in C$ is an MGI of S in C, but not an LGI of S in C. Then $C \models S$, but there also is a $D \in C$, such that $D \models S$ and $D \not\models C$. We can assume C and D are standardized apart. Then by Lemma 15.15, we have $C \cup D \models S$. Since $C \subseteq C \cup D$, we also have $C \models C \cup D$. On the other hand, since $D \models C \cup D$ and $D \not\models C$, we must have $C \cup D \not\models C$. Thus we have $C \models (C \cup D) \models S$, and C and $C \cup D$ are not equivalent. But this contradicts the assumption that C is an MGI of S in $\mathcal{C}$. □

15.2.2 The LGI is Computable

In the previous subsection we proved the *existence* of an LGI in $\mathcal{C}$ of every finite set S of clauses containing at least one non-tautologous function-free clause. In this subsection, we will establish the *computability* of such an LGI. The next algorithm, extracted from the proof of the previous section, computes this LGI of S.

Algorithm 15.1 (LGI Algorithm)
Input: A finite set S of clauses, containing at least one non-tautologous function-free clause.
Output: An LGI of S in $\mathcal{C}$.

1. Remove all tautologies from S, call the remaining set S'.
2. Let m be the number of distinct terms (including subterms) in S', let $V = \{x_1, \ldots, x_m\}$. (Notice that this m is the same number as the number of terms in the term set T used in the proof of Theorem 15.17.)
3. Let G be the (finite) set of all clauses which can be constructed from predicate symbols and constants in S' and variables in V.
4. Let $\{U_1, \ldots, U_n\}$ be the set of all subsets of G.
5. Let H_i be an LGS of U_i, for every $1 \leq i \leq n$ (these H_i can be computed by the LGS Algorithm of Section 14.7).
6. Remove from $\{H_1, \ldots, H_n\}$ all clauses which do not imply S' (since each H_i is function-free, by Corollary 15.12 this implication is decidable), and standardize the remaining clauses $\{H_1, \ldots, H_q\}$ apart.
7. Return the clause $H = H_1 \cup \ldots \cup H_q$.

The correctness of this algorithm follows from the proof of Theorem 15.17. First notice that $H \models S$ by Lemma 15.15. Furthermore, note that all $\mathcal{I}(C_i, V)$s mentioned in the proof of Theorem 15.17 are elements of the set $\{U_1, \ldots, U_n\}$. This means that for every E_i in the set $\{E_1, \ldots, E_k\}$ mentioned in that proof, there is a clause H_j in $\{H_1, \ldots, H_q\}$ such that E_i and H_j are subsume-equivalent. Then it follows that the LGI $F = E_1 \cup \ldots \cup E_k$ of that proof subsumes the clause $H = H_1 \cup \ldots \cup H_q$ that our algorithm returns. On the other hand, F is a special LGI, so F and H must be subsume-equivalent.

Suppose the number of distinct constants in S' is c, and the number of distinct variables in step 2 of the algorithm is m. Furthermore, suppose there are p distinct predicate symbols in S', with respective arities $a_1, \ldots, a_p$. Then the number of distinct atoms that can be formed from these constants, variables and predicate symbols, is $l = \sum_{i=1}^{p} (c + m)^{a_i}$, and the number of distinct literals that can be formed, is $2 \cdot l$. The set G of distinct clauses which can be formed from these literals is the power set of this set of literals, so $|G| = 2^{2 \cdot l}$. Then the set $\{U_1, \ldots, U_n\}$ of all subsets of G contains $2^{|G|} = 2^{2^{2 \cdot l}}$ members.

Thus the algorithm outlined above is not very efficient (to say the least). A more efficient algorithm may exist, but since implication is harder than subsumption and the computation of an LGS is already quite expensive, we should not put our hopes too high. Nevertheless, the existence of the LGI algorithm does establish the theoretical point that the LGI of any finite set of clauses containing at least one non-tautologous function-free clause, is effectively computable.

Theorem 15.20 (Computability of LGI) *Let C be a clausal language. If S is a finite set of clauses from C, and S contains at least one non-tautologous function-free clause, then the LGI of S in C is computable.*

15.3 Greatest Specializations

Now we turn from least generalizations under implication to greatest specializations. Finding least generalizations of sets of clauses is common practice in ILP. On the other hand, the greatest specialization, which is the dual of the least generalization, is used hardly ever. Nevertheless, the GSI of two clauses D_1 and D_2 might be useful. For example, suppose we have one positive example e^+, and two negative examples e_1^- and e_2^-, and suppose that D_1 implies e^+ and e_1^-, while D_2 implies e^+ and e_2^-. Then it might very well be that the GSI of D_1 and D_2 still implies e^+, but is consistent with respect to $\{e_1^-, e_2^-\}$. Thus we could obtain a correct specialization by taking the GSI of D_1 and D_2.

It is obvious from the previous sections that the existence of an LGI of S is quite hard to establish. For clauses which all contain function symbols, the existence of an LGI is still an open question, and even for the case where S contains at least one non-tautologous function-free clause, the proof was far from trivial. However, the existence of a GSI in C is much easier to prove. In fact, a GSI of a finite set S is the same as the GSS of S, namely the union of the clauses in S after these are standardized apart.

To see the reason for this asymmetry, let us take a step back from the clausal framework, and consider full first-order logic for a moment. If ϕ_1 and ϕ_2 are two arbitrary first-order formulas, then it can be easily shown that their least generalization is just $\phi_1 \wedge \phi_2$, and their greatest specialization is just $\phi_1 \vee \phi_2$. See Figure 15.2.

Now suppose ϕ_1 and ϕ_2 are clauses. Then why do we have a problem in finding the LGI of ϕ_1 and ϕ_2? The reason for this is that $\phi_1 \wedge \phi_2$ is not a clause. Instead of using $\phi_1 \wedge \phi_2$, we have to find some least clause which implies both clauses ϕ_1 and ϕ_2. Such a clause appears quite hard to find sometimes.

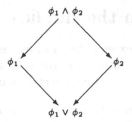

Figure 15.2: Least generalization and greatest specialization in first-order logic

On the other hand, in case of specialization there is no problem. Here we can take $\phi_1 \vee \phi_2$ as GSI, since $\phi_1 \vee \phi_2$ is equivalent to a clause, if we handle the universal quantifiers in front of a clause properly. If ϕ_1 and ϕ_2 are standardized apart, then the formula $\phi_1 \vee \phi_2$ is equivalent to the clause which is the union of ϕ_1 and ϕ_2. This fact was used in the proof of Lemma 15.15.

Suppose $S = \{D_1, \ldots, D_n\}$, and $D'_1, \ldots, D'_n$ are variants of these clauses which are standardized apart. Then clearly $D = D'_1 \cup \ldots \cup D'_n$ is a GSI of S, since it follows from Lemma 15.15 that any specialization of S under implication is implied by D. Thus we have the following result:

Theorem 15.21 (Existence of GSI in C) *Let C be a clausal language. Then for every finite non-empty $S \subseteq C$, there exists a GSI of S in C.*

The previous theorem holds for clauses in general, so in particular also for function-free clauses. Furthermore, Corollary 15.18 guarantees us that in a function-free clausal language, an LGI of every finite S exists. This means that the set of function-free clauses quasi-ordered by logical implication, is in fact a lattice.

Corollary 15.22 *Let C be a function-free clausal language. Then $\langle C, \models \rangle$ is a lattice.*

In case of a Horn language $\mathcal{H}$, we cannot apply the same proof method as in the case of a clausal language, since the union of two Horn clauses need not be a Horn clause itself. In fact, we can show that not every finite set of Horn clauses has a GSI in $\mathcal{H}$. Here we can use the same clauses that we used to show that sets of Horn clauses need not have an LGI in $\mathcal{H}$, this time taking the perspective of specialization instead of generalization.

Again, let $D_1 = P(f^2(x)) \leftarrow P(x)$, $D_2 = P(f^3(x)) \leftarrow P(x)$, $C_1 = P(f(x)) \leftarrow P(x)$, and $C_2 = P(f^2(y)) \leftarrow P(x)$. Then $C_1 \models \{D_1, D_2\}$ and $C_2 \models \{D_1, D_2\}$, and there is no Horn clause D such that $D \models D_1$, $D \models D_2$, $C_1 \models D$ and $C_2 \models D$. Hence there is no GSI of $\{C_1, C_2\}$ in $\mathcal{H}$. Whether any two Horn clauses have a finite complete set of maximal specializations (MSI) under implication in $\mathcal{H}$ is an open question.

15.4 Covers in the Implication Order

In this section, we will extend the negative results of the previous chapter concerning upward and downward covers to the case of implication. This extension is based on the fact that the clauses used there were *non-recursive*.

Definition 15.23 A clause is *recursive* if it contains a positive literal and a negative literal with the same predicate symbol. Otherwise the clause is called *non-recursive*. ◇

Example 15.24 The clauses $P(f(x)) \leftarrow P(x)$ and $\{P(a), Q(x), \neg P(f(y))\}$ are recursive, $\{P(a), \neg Q(x, a)\}$ and $\{P(x, y), P(y, x)\}$ are non-recursive.

Note that not every recursive clause can be resolved with itself, for instance $P(x, a) \leftarrow P(x, b)$. ◁

It can be shown that for non-recursive clauses, subsumption and implication coincide. For instance, if $D = \{P(x_1, x_2), P(x_2, x_1)\}$, then $C \models D$ iff $C \succeq D$. This result follows from the Subsumption Theorem, and the fact that a non-recursive clause cannot be resolved with itself.

Lemma 15.25 *Let C and D be non-recursive clauses. Then $C \models D$ iff $C \succeq D$.*

Proof

$\Leftarrow$: Obvious.

$\Rightarrow$: Suppose $C \models D$. Then by the Subsumption Theorem (Theorem 5.17), there is a clause E such that $C \vdash_r E$ and $E \succeq D$. But since C is non-recursive, the only clause that can be derived from C, is C itself. It follows that $E = C$, and hence $C \succeq D$. □

Let us denote the case where C properly implies D (i.e., $C \models D$ and $D \not\models C$) by $C >_i D$. Then we also have the next lemma:

Lemma 15.26 *Let C and D be non-recursive clauses. Then $C >_i D$ iff $C \succ D$.*

Proof $C >_i D$ iff
$C \models D$ and $D \not\models C$ iff (by the previous lemma)
$C \succeq D$ and $D \not\succeq C$ iff
$C \succ D$. □

Using this result, we can extend Proposition 14.32 to the implication order:

Proposition 15.27 *Let C be a clausal language containing a binary predicate symbol P. Then $C = \{P(x_1, x_1)\}$ has no upward cover in $\langle C, \models \rangle$.*

Proof Suppose D is an upward cover of C in $\langle \mathcal{C}, \models \rangle$. Then $D >_i C$, so it follows from Gottlob's Lemma that D only contains positive literals, hence D is non-recursive. Now by the previous lemma we have $D \succ C$. By Proposition 14.32, D cannot be an upward cover of C in $\langle \mathcal{C}, \succeq \rangle$, so there must be an E such that $D \succ E \succ C$. Because C is non-recursive, E must be non-recursive as well. But then by the previous lemma, we must also have $D >_i E >_i C$, contradicting the assumption that D is an upward cover of C in $\langle \mathcal{C}, \models \rangle$. $\square$

Proposition 14.40 can be extended analogously to the implication order:

Proposition 15.28 *Let $\mathcal{C}$ be a clausal language containing a binary predicate symbol P. Then $C = \{P(x_1, x_2), P(x_2, x_1)\}$ has no finite complete set of downward covers in $\langle \mathcal{C}, \models \rangle$.*

As in the case of subsumption, these results can be translated to the case where $\mathcal{C}$ only contains unary predicate symbols and a binary function symbol f, by replacing every $P(x, y)$ by $Q(f(x, y))$. Also, the negative results of this section can be translated to Horn clauses.

15.5 Summary

This chapter discussed the *implication* order on a clausal language. Implication between (Horn) clauses is undecidable, but using implication as a generality order is more desirable than using subsumption, since it is better able to deal with recursive clauses. The main results on the implication order can be summed up as follows:

- Every finite set of clauses which contains at least one function-free non-tautologous clause, has a computable least generalization (LGI) under implication in $\mathcal{C}$. Every finite set of clauses has a greatest specialization (GSI) under implication in $\mathcal{C}$. As a corollary, if $\mathcal{C}$ is a function-free clausal language, then $\langle \mathcal{C}, \models \rangle$ is a lattice.
- There exist pairs of Horn clauses which do not have an LGI in $\mathcal{H}$. Similarly, there exist pairs of Horn clauses which do not have a GSI in $\mathcal{H}$.
- For general clauses which all contain function symbols, the LGI-question is still open.
- Some clauses, such as $\{P(x_1, x_1)\}$, have no upward covers.
  Some clauses, such as $\{P(x_1, x_2), P(x_2, x_1)\}$, have no finite complete set of downward covers.

Chapter 16

Background Knowledge

16.1 Introduction

The generality orders of the previous two chapters, subsumption and logical implication, were treated as relations between two individual clauses. The background knowledge that figured prominently in our problem setting of Chapter 9 was left out of consideration. In this chapter, we will see how we can incorporate background knowledge into our generality orders.

Why does background knowledge matter? The answer is that combining the examples with what we already know often allows for the construction of a more satisfactory theory than can be glanced from the examples by themselves. To illustrate this, we consider the following two clauses as positive examples (not just ground atoms as examples, this time):[1]

$$D_1 = CuddlyPet(x) \leftarrow Small(x), Fluffy(x), Dog(x)$$
$$D_2 = CuddlyPet(x) \leftarrow Fluffy(x), Cat(x)$$

Given only these clauses, the most obvious way to generalize them is to take their LGS or LGI, which is the rather general clause

$$C = CuddlyPet(x) \leftarrow Fluffy(x)$$

However, suppose we have the following definite program $\mathcal{B}$ which expresses our background knowledge.

$$Pet(x) \leftarrow Cat(x)$$
$$Pet(x) \leftarrow Dog(x)$$
$$Small(x) \leftarrow Cat(x)$$

Given $\mathcal{B}$, we may also use the following clause as generalization:

---

[1] This example and the related Examples 16.2, 16.19, 16.33 are similar to examples given in [Bun88].

$D = CuddlyPet(x) \leftarrow Small(x), Fluffy(x), Pet(x),$

since D *together with* $\mathcal{B}$ implies both examples.[2] Note that without the background knowledge $\mathcal{B}$, our clause D neither subsumes nor implies the examples. If we interpret this example in human terms, the generalization D is much more satisfactory than C. After all, not every fluffy object is a cuddly pet—consider teddy bears. Thus the use of background knowledge allows us to find a better theory.

Given the usefulness of background knowledge, we should find a formalized way to reckon with it in our generality order. In this chapter we will discuss three such ways: Plotkin's *relative subsumption* [Plo71a, Plo71b], *relative implication*, and finally Buntine's *generalized subsumption* [Bun86, Bun88]. Relative subsumption and relative implication apply to arbitrary clauses and the background knowledge may be an arbitary finite set of clauses. Generalized subsumption only applies to definite program clauses and the background knowledge should be a definite program.

Of these three orders, the discussion of generalized subsumption will be the most technical. In order not to put off the reader, we save it for last, discussing relative subsumption and relative implication first. Each of the three orders will be related to some form of deduction. We can use these three forms of deduction to show that generalized subsumption is a weaker quasi-order than relative subsumption, and relative subsumption is in turn a weaker order than relative implication. In other words, if C is more general than D with respect to some definite program $\mathcal{B}$ according to generalized subsumption, it is also more general according to relative subsumption, while the converse need not hold. And similarly, if C is more general than D relative to some set of clauses $\mathcal{B}$ according to relative subsumption, it is also more general according to relative implication, while the converse need not hold. We will show that both relative and generalized subsumption reduce to ordinary subsumption in case of non-tautologous clauses and empty background knowledge. Similarly, with empty background knowledge relative implication is simply logical implication.

Implication relative to background knowledge $\mathcal{B}$ is defined as follows: C logically implies D relative to $\mathcal{B}$ if $\{C\} \cup \mathcal{B} \models D$. The link between relative implication and the normal problem setting of Chapter 9 is obvious: if E^+ is a set of positive examples and C is a least generalization under relative implication (relative to $\mathcal{B}$), then we have $\{C\} \cup \mathcal{B} \models E^+$. Thus such least generalizations may be used to generalize examples while taking into account the background knowledge. The definitions of relative and generalized subsumption are somewhat more complicated, but since each of these orders implies relative implication, we also have $\{C\} \cup \mathcal{B} \models E^+$ if C is a least generalization under relative or generalized subsumption.

---

[2] Actually, it can be shown that this D is a least generalization under generalized subsumption (LGGS) with respect to $\mathcal{B}$ of these two examples. See Example 16.33.

Since empty background knowledge reduces relative and generalized subsumption to ordinary subsumption, and relative implication to ordinary implication, the negative results on covers that we proved in the last two chapters for subsumption and implication, carry over to the three orders of this chapter: some clauses do not have finite complete sets of upward or downward covers in these orders. As to the existence and non-existence of least generalizations or greatest specializations in the three orders, we will only pay attention to least generalizations, since these are used much more often than their dual. In general, whichever of the three orders we use, least generalizations do not always exist in the presence of background knowledge. However, for each of these orders we will prove that certain restrictions on the background knowledge guarantee the existence of a least generalization.

16.2 Relative Subsumption

This section discusses Plotkin's relative subsumption [Plo71a, Plo71b].

16.2.1 Definition and Some Properties

If C is more general than D, under ordinary subsumption, then we have $C\theta \subseteq D$ for some θ. This means that $\forall(C\theta \to D)$ is a tautology: $\models \forall(C\theta \to D)$. We can take background knowledge into account by making $\forall(C\theta \to D)$ relative to the background knowledge. That is, C subsumes D, relative to background knowledge $\mathcal{B}$, if $\mathcal{B} \models \forall(C\theta \to D)$.[3]

Definition 16.1 Let C and D be clauses, and $\mathcal{B}$ be a set of clauses. We say C *subsumes* D *relative to* $\mathcal{B}$, denoted by $C \succeq_\mathcal{B} D$, if there is a substitution θ such that $\mathcal{B} \models \forall(C\theta \to D)$. The $\succeq_\mathcal{B}$-order is called *relative subsumption*, and $\mathcal{B}$ is the *background knowledge* of this order. ◇

In this chapter, both '←' and '→' are used to denote the implication-connective. The former is only used in Horn clauses, the latter everywhere else. Note that $\forall(C\theta \to D)$ will usually not be a clause.

Example 16.2 Let C and D be as follows:

$$C = Small(x) \leftarrow Cat(x)$$
$$D = CuddlyPet(x) \leftarrow Fluffy(x), Cat(x)$$

and let $\mathcal{B}$ consist of the following two clauses:

$$Pet(x) \leftarrow Cat(x)$$
$$CuddlyPet(x) \leftarrow Small(x), Fluffy(x), Pet(x)$$

---

[3]In his PhD thesis, Plotkin also gave an alternative definition of subsumption relative to background knowledge $\mathcal{B}$: $C \succeq_\mathcal{B} D$ iff there is a clause E such that $\mathcal{B} \models \forall(E \leftrightarrow D)$ and $C \succeq E$. He showed this definition to be equivalent to the one we adopt here [Plo71a, p. 49].

C subsumes D relative to $\mathcal{B}$. Informally, this can be seen as follows: suppose for every x it holds that if x is a cat, then x is small (i.e., C is true). Using the first clause of $\mathcal{B}$, we also have that if x is a cat, then x is a pet. Thus if x is a *fluffy* cat, then x is small, fluffy, and a pet, and by the second clause of $\mathcal{B}$, x is a cuddly pet (i.e., D is true).

More formally, we have $C \succeq_\mathcal{B} D$ because $\mathcal{B} \models \forall(C\varepsilon \to D)$.   ◁

Reflexivity and transitivity are easily proved, so relative subsumption is a quasi-order on clauses. Note that each set of clauses $\mathcal{B}$ induces its own quasi-order: the quasi-orders induced by $\mathcal{B} = \{P(a)\}$ and $\mathcal{B} = \{P(a), P(b)\}$ are different. Note also that if D is a tautology, then $C \succeq_\mathcal{B} D$ for any C and $\mathcal{B}$. Furthermore, it is also easy to see that if $C \succeq_\mathcal{B} D$ and $\mathcal{B} \subseteq \mathcal{B}'$, then $C \succeq_{\mathcal{B}'} D$.

We will now show that relative subsumption is stronger than subsumption. Firstly, it is easy to see that subsumption implies relative subsumption. If $C \succeq D$, then $C\theta \subseteq D$, for some θ. But then $\forall(C\theta \to D)$ is a tautology, and $\mathcal{B} \models \forall(C\theta \to D)$ for any $\mathcal{B}$. Hence if $C \succeq D$, then $C \succeq_\mathcal{B} D$.

Now consider propositional atoms P, Q, and R. Let $C = P$, $D = Q$, and $\mathcal{B} = \{Q \leftarrow P\}$. Then $\mathcal{B} \models (C \to D)$, so $C \succeq_\mathcal{B} D$. Since $C \not\succeq D$, we see that relative subsumption does not imply subsumption. This even holds for the case where $\mathcal{B}$ is empty and D is a tautology: if $\mathcal{B} = \emptyset$, $C = Q$, and $D = P \leftarrow P$, then $C \succeq_\mathcal{B} D$, but $C \not\succeq D$. Thus relative subsumption is a strictly stronger quasi-order than ordinary subsumption.

The next proposition establishes a relationship between subsumption and relative subsumption in the case where $\mathcal{B}$ consists of ground literals. We first illustrate with an example. (Recall from Chapter 9 that if $\Sigma = \{C_1, C_2, \ldots\}$ is a set of clauses, then $\overline{\Sigma}$ denotes the set $\{\neg C_1, \neg C_2, \ldots\}$.)

Example 16.3 Let $C = Q(x) \leftarrow P(x)$, $D = Q(a)$, and $\mathcal{B} = \{P(a)\}$. Note that if $\theta = \{x/a\}$, then $\mathcal{B} \models (C\theta \to D)$, so $C \succeq_\mathcal{B} D$. Now suppose we add the negation of the atom in $\mathcal{B}$ to D, obtaining the clause $D' = (D \cup \overline{\mathcal{B}}) = Q(a) \leftarrow P(a)$. Then we have that $C \succeq D'$.   ◁

Proposition 16.4 *Let C and D be non-tautologous clauses, and $\mathcal{B}$ be a finite set of ground literals such that $\mathcal{B} \cap D = \emptyset$. Then $C \succeq_\mathcal{B} D$ iff $C \succeq (D \cup \overline{\mathcal{B}})$.*

Proof

$\Rightarrow$: Suppose $C \succeq_\mathcal{B} D$, so $\mathcal{B} \models \forall(C\theta \to D)$ for some θ. Assume $C\theta \not\subseteq D \cup \overline{\mathcal{B}}$. Then there is an $L \in C\theta$ such that $L \notin D$ and $L \notin \overline{\mathcal{B}}$. Since, furthermore, $\mathcal{B} \cap D = \emptyset$, we can find an interpretation I which makes every literal in $\mathcal{B}$ true (so I is a model of $\mathcal{B}$), and a variable assignment V, such that L (and hence $C\theta$) is true under I and V, while no literal in D is true under I and V. But then $C\theta \to D$ is false under I and V, contradicting $\mathcal{B} \models \forall(C\theta \to D)$. Thus we must have $C\theta \subseteq D \cup \overline{\mathcal{B}}$.

$\Leftarrow$: Suppose $C \succeq (D \cup \overline{\mathcal{B}})$, so $C\theta \subseteq D \cup \overline{\mathcal{B}}$ for some θ. We want to prove $\mathcal{B} \models \forall(C\theta \to D)$. Let M be a model of $\mathcal{B}$, and V be a variable assignment such that $C\theta$ is true under M and V. We need to show that D is also true under M and V. At least one $L \in C\theta$ is true under M and V. Since also $L \in D \cup \overline{B}$ and each literal in $\overline{B}$ is false under M, it follows that $L \in D$, so D is true under M and V. Hence $\mathcal{B} \models \forall(C\theta \to D)$. □

In general, as we have seen, relative subsumption is a stronger quasi-order than subsumption. However, relative subsumption coincides with ordinary subsumption for non-tautologous clauses and empty background knowledge. This is an immediate corollary of the last proposition.

Corollary 16.5 *If C and D are non-tautologous clauses, then $C \succeq_\emptyset D$ iff C subsumes D ($C \succeq D$).*

Each of the three orders that we discuss in this chapter, relative subsumption, relative implication, and generalized subsumption, can be related to some kind of deduction. The relation between relative subsumption and deductions is expressed by the following theorem, due to Plotkin [Plo71a].

Theorem 16.6 *Let C and D be clauses, and $\mathcal{B}$ be a set of clauses. Then $C \succeq_\mathcal{B} D$ iff there exists a deduction of D from $\{C\} \cup \mathcal{B}$ in which C occurs at most once as a leaf.*

Proof

$\Rightarrow$: Suppose $C \succeq_\mathcal{B} D$. If $C \succeq D$, or if D is a tautology, then the theorem is obvious (recall that we included the tautology-case in the definition of a deduction). Suppose that $C \not\succeq D$ and D is not a tautology. There is a θ such that $\mathcal{B} \models \forall(C\theta \to D)$. Let $C = L_1 \vee \ldots \vee L_n$. Note the following equivalences:

$$\forall(C\theta \to D) \Leftrightarrow$$
$$\forall((L_1\theta \vee \ldots \vee L_n\theta) \to D) \Leftrightarrow$$
$$\forall(\neg(L_1\theta \vee \ldots \vee L_n\theta) \vee D) \Leftrightarrow$$
$$\forall((\neg L_1\theta \wedge \ldots \wedge \neg L_n\theta) \vee D) \Leftrightarrow$$
$$\forall((\neg L_1\theta \vee D) \wedge \ldots \wedge (\neg L_n\theta \vee D)) \Leftrightarrow$$
$$\forall(\neg L_1\theta \vee D) \wedge \ldots \wedge \forall(\neg L_n\theta \vee D).$$

Since $\mathcal{B} \models \forall(C\theta \to D)$, we also have $\mathcal{B} \models \forall(\neg L_i\theta \vee D)$, for every $1 \leq i \leq n$. We may assume without loss of generality that there is a j such that $L_i\theta \not\subseteq D$ just in case $1 \leq i \leq j$ (i.e., $L_1\theta \vee \ldots \vee L_j\theta$ is the part of $C\theta$ that does not "overlap" with D). Because $C \not\succeq D$, we must have $j \geq 1$. Since D is not a tautology, the clause $\neg L_i\theta \vee D$ is not a tautology either, for every $1 \leq i \leq j$.

By the Subsumption Theorem, for every i with $1 \leq i \leq j$ there is a derivation from $\mathcal{B}$ of a clause E_i such that $E_i\sigma_i \subseteq \neg L_i\theta \vee D$ for some σ_i. If $\neg L_i\theta \not\subseteq E_i\sigma_i$ for some i, then $E_i\sigma_i \subseteq D$, so then there is a deduction of D from $\mathcal{B}$ itself. Hence the result follows if $\neg L_i\theta \not\subseteq E_i\sigma_i$ for some i.

Now suppose $\neg L_i\theta \in E_i\sigma_i$ for every $1 \leq i \leq j$. Then we can write $E_i\sigma_i = \neg L_i\theta \vee D_i$, where $D_i \subseteq D$. Since $C\theta = L_1\theta \vee \ldots \vee L_n\theta$, there exists an input derivation of the clause $E = L_{j+1}\theta \vee \ldots \vee L_n\theta \vee D_1 \vee \ldots \vee D_j$, with $C\theta$ as top clause and $E_1\sigma_1, \ldots, E_j\sigma_j$ as input clauses. See Figure 16.1 for illustration. Since $L_i\theta \in D$ for $j + 1 \leq i \leq n$ and $D_i \subseteq D$ for $1 \leq i \leq j$, we have $E \subseteq D$.

We can lift the derivation of Figure 16.1 to an input derivation of a clause E' which subsumes D, using C as top clause and $E_1, \ldots, E_j$ as input clauses. Note that C occurs only once as a leaf in this input derivation. Moreover, each E_i is derived from $\mathcal{B}$ alone, so we can construct the required deduction of D from $\{C\} \cup \mathcal{B}$, in which C occurs only once as a leaf.

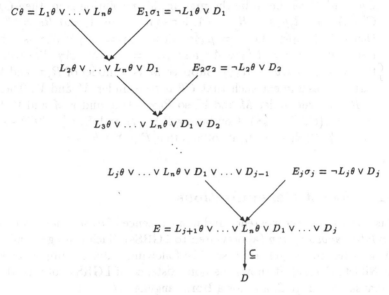

Figure 16.1: An input deduction of D from $C\theta$ and $E_1\sigma_1, \ldots, E_j\sigma_j$

$\Leftarrow$: If D is a tautology, the theorem is obvious, so suppose D is not a tautology. Let $R_1, \ldots, R_n$ be a derivation from $\{C\} \cup \mathcal{B}$ in which C occurs at most once as a leaf, such that R_n subsumes D. If C is not used at all in this derivation, then $\mathcal{B} \models D$, so $C \succeq_{\mathcal{B}} D$ in this case. Suppose C occurs once as a leaf in the derivation. We will prove by induction on n that $C \succeq_{\mathcal{B}} D$.

1. If $n = 1$, then $C \succeq D$, and hence $C \succeq_{\mathcal{B}} D$.
2. Suppose the result holds for $n \leq m$, and $R_1, \ldots, R_{m+1}$ be a derivation from $\{C\} \cup \mathcal{B}$ in which C occurs once as a leaf, such that R_{m+1} subsumes D. Thus C is used exactly once as a parent clause in a resolution step in the tree representing the deduction. Let R_j be the second parent clause, then $\mathcal{B} \models R_j$, because C cannot be used in the derivation of R_j from $\{C\} \cup \mathcal{B}$. Let R_k be the resolvent of C and R_j. If R_k also occurs somewhere else in the tree, then there exists a derivation of R_k from $\mathcal{B}$ alone, since C cannot be used in the derivation of

this second occurrence of R_k as well. But if R_k can be derived without C, we do not need C to derive D. Therefore, if R_k occurs more than once in the tree, then $\mathcal{B} \models D$ and hence $C \succeq_\mathcal{B} D$.

Now we may assume R_k occurs only once in the tree. Remove C and the derivation of R_j (including R_j itself) from the tree. Then we obtain a deduction, of length $\leq m$, of D from $\{R_k\} \cup \mathcal{B}$ in which R_k occurs once as a leaf. By the induction hypothesis, there is a substitution γ such that $\mathcal{B} \models \forall(R_k\gamma \to D)$.

We know that R_k is a resolvent of C and R_j, so there exists a factor $C\mu_1$ of C and a factor $R_j\mu_2$ of R_j, such that R_k is a binary resolvent of $C\mu_1$ and $R_j\mu_2$. Let δ be the mgu in this resolution step, then $C\mu_1\delta = C' \vee A$ and $R_j\mu_2\delta = R'_j \vee \neg A$, for some atom A, and $R_k = C' \vee R'_j$. Define $\theta = \mu_1\delta\gamma$ and $\sigma = \mu_2\delta\gamma$, then $R_k\gamma = C'\gamma \vee R'_j\gamma$ is a binary resolvent of $C\theta = C'\gamma \vee A\gamma$ and $R_j\sigma = R'_j\gamma \vee \neg A\gamma$. We will show that $R_j\sigma \models \forall(C\theta \to R_k\gamma)$. Suppose M is a model of $R_j\sigma$, and V is a variable assignment such that $C\theta$ is true under M and V. Then $C'\gamma$ or $R'_j\gamma$ is true under M and V, so $R_k\gamma$ is true under M and V. Hence $R_j\sigma \models \forall(C\theta \to R_k\gamma)$. Combining $\mathcal{B} \models R_j$ and $R_j\sigma \models \forall(C\theta \to R_k\gamma)$ with $\mathcal{B} \models \forall(R_k\gamma \to D)$, it follows that $\mathcal{B} \models \forall(C\theta \to D)$. $\square$

16.2.2 Least Generalizations

Let us now turn to the existence and non-existence of *least generalizations under relative subsumption* (abbreviated to LGRSs). Such least generalizations need not exist in the general case. The following counterexample is adapted from Niblett [Nib88]. It shows the non-existence of LGRSs both for the case of a clausal language $\mathcal{C}$, and for a Horn language $\mathcal{H}$.

Example 16.7 Let

$$D_1 = Q(a)$$
$$D_2 = Q(b)$$
$$\mathcal{B} = \{P(a,y), P(b,y)\}$$

We will show there is no LGRS of $\{D_1, D_2\}$ relative to $\mathcal{B}$. Consider the following infinite sequence of clauses:

$$C_1 = Q(x) \leftarrow P(x, f(x))$$
$$C_2 = Q(x) \leftarrow P(x, f(x)), P(x, f^2(x))$$
$$C_3 = Q(x) \leftarrow P(x, f(x)), P(x, f^2(x)), P(x, f^3(x))$$
$$\ldots$$

It is easy to see that $C_i \succ_\mathcal{B} C_{i+1}$ for every $i \geq 1$. We also have $C_i \succ_\mathcal{B} D_1$ and $C_i \succ_\mathcal{B} D_2$, for every $i \geq 1$.

Suppose some clause D is an LGRS of $\{D_1, D_2\}$ relative to $\mathcal{B}$, then we should have $C_i \succeq_\mathcal{B} D$, for every $i \geq 1$. Then by Theorem 16.6, for every $i \geq 1$

there exists a deduction of D from $\{C_i\} \cup \mathcal{B}$, in which C_i occurs at most once as a leaf. C_i cannot occur zero times as a leaf, because then a clause from $\mathcal{B}$ would simply subsume D, which is impossible. Thus for every $i \geq 1$, there exists a deduction of D from $\{C_i\} \cup \mathcal{B}$, in which C_i occurs once as a leaf. It cannot be that every C_i subsumes D, for then D would contain an instance of the term $f^i(x)$, for every $i \geq 1$.

Thus for some j, the deduction of D from $\{C_j\} \cup \mathcal{B}$ involves at least one resolution step. Since the members of $\mathcal{B}$ are atoms and C_j only occurs once as a leaf, the parent clauses in the first resolution step must be C_j and a member of $\mathcal{B}$. Suppose this member of $\mathcal{B}$ is $P(a, y)$. Then $P(a, y)$ must be unified with an atom of the form $P(x, f^n(x))$ in the body of C_j. Then the head of the clause C_j is instantiated to $Q(a)$. This head will not be changed anymore in later resolution steps, so D would have $Q(a)$ as head—but then there is no deduction of $D_2 = Q(b)$ from $\{D\} \cup \mathcal{B}$.

Similarly, if the member of $\mathcal{B}$ in the resolution step had been $P(b, y)$ instead of $P(a, y)$, D would have had $Q(b)$ as head, and there would be no deduction of $D_1 = Q(a)$ from $\{D\} \cup \mathcal{B}$. Either way, the assumption that D is an LGRS of $\{D_1, D_2\}$ relative to $\mathcal{B}$ leads to a contradiction.   ◁

Despite this negative result, we can identify a restriction on the background knowledge which guarantees existence (and computability) of an LGRS of any finite set of clauses. This result has been exploited in the GOLEM system, for which see Section 19.6.

Theorem 16.8 (Existence of LGRS in $\mathcal{C}$) *Let $\mathcal{C}$ be a clausal language and $\mathcal{B} \subseteq \mathcal{C}$ be a finite set of ground literals. Then every finite non-empty set $S \subseteq \mathcal{C}$ of clauses has an LGRS in $\mathcal{C}$.*

Proof If a clause D is a tautology or $\mathcal{B} \cap D \neq \emptyset$, then $\mathcal{B} \models D$, hence for any clause C we have $C \succeq_{\mathcal{B}} D$. Remove from S all tautologies and all D for which $\mathcal{B} \cap D \neq \emptyset$, call the remaining set S'. If S' is empty, any tautology is an LGRS of S. If $S' = \{D_1, \ldots, D_n\}$ is non-empty, then it follows easily from Proposition 16.4 that an LGS of $\{(D_1 \cup \overline{\mathcal{B}}), \ldots, (D_n \cup \overline{\mathcal{B}})\}$ in $\mathcal{C}$ is an LGRS of S' in $\mathcal{C}$, and hence also of S. The existence of such an LGS follows from Theorem 14.27.   □

Thus if the background knowledge $\mathcal{B}$ is a finite set of ground literals, then we can construct an LGRS of a set $S = \{D_1, \ldots, D_n\}$ simply by constructing an LGS of $T = \{(D_1 \cup \overline{\mathcal{B}}), \ldots, (D_n \cup \overline{\mathcal{B}})\}$.

Note that if all clauses in S are Horn clauses and each literal in $\mathcal{B}$ is a ground atom, then each $D_i \cup \overline{\mathcal{B}}$ in T is also a Horn clause. In this case, the LGS of T (and hence the LGRS of S) will be a Horn clause as well. If all clauses in S are definite program clauses having the same predicate symbol in their head, this LGS will be a definite program clause as well. Otherwise, this LGS will be a Horn clause without positive literals (i.e., a definite goal). Hence we also have the following result:

Theorem 16.9 (Existence of LGRS in $\mathcal{H}$) *Let $\mathcal{H}$ be a Horn language and $\mathcal{B} \subseteq \mathcal{H}$ be a finite set of ground atoms. Then every finite non-empty set $S \subseteq \mathcal{H}$ of Horn clauses has an LGRS in $\mathcal{H}$.*

16.3 Relative Implication

In this section we discuss the most general quasi-order on clauses: relative implication.

16.3.1 Definition and Some Properties

Relative implication is perhaps the most obvious way to take background knowledge into account. It takes roughly the same form as our problem setting in Chapter 9, and is defined as follows:

Definition 16.10 Let C and D be clauses, and $\mathcal{B}$ be a set of clauses. C *(logically) implies D relative to $\mathcal{B}$*, denoted $C \models_{\mathcal{B}} D$, if $\{C\} \cup \mathcal{B} \models D$. The $\models_{\mathcal{B}}$-order is called *relative implication*, and $\mathcal{B}$ is the *background knowledge* of this order. $\diamond$

Obviously relative implication is reflexive and transitive, so it can serve as a quasi-order on a set of clauses. It is equally obvious that if $C \models D$, then $C \models_{\mathcal{B}} D$. The converse need not hold. Consider $C = P(a) \leftarrow P(b)$, $D = P(a)$, and $\mathcal{B} = \{P(b)\}$: then $C \models_{\mathcal{B}} D$, but $C \not\models D$.

It is important to be precise about the position of the universal quantifiers for C and D when distinguishing between relative subsumption and relative implication. If $C \succeq_{\mathcal{B}} D$, then $\mathcal{B} \models \forall(C\theta \rightarrow D)$ (for some θ). If $C \models_{\mathcal{B}} D$, then $\{C\} \cup \mathcal{B} \models D$, which is equivalent to $\mathcal{B} \models \forall(C) \rightarrow \forall(D)$ by the Deduction Theorem (Theorem 2.36). Relative subsumption implies relative implication, but not conversely:

Example 16.11 Let $\mathcal{B} = \{P(a)\}$, $C = P(f(x)) \leftarrow P(x)$ and $D = P(f^2(a))$. Then $C \models_{\mathcal{B}} D$, because there is a deduction of D from $\{C\} \cup \mathcal{B}$. However, we have $C \not\succeq_{\mathcal{B}} D$, because C has to be used more than once in the deduction of D. $\triangleleft$

Theorem 16.6 characterized relative subsumption by a restricted form of deduction:

$C \succeq_{\mathcal{B}} D$ iff there exists a deduction of D from $\{C\} \cup \mathcal{B}$ in which C occurs at most once as a leaf.

The requirement that C be used at most once means that C cannot be resolved with itself in deductions for relative subsumption. This constraint is lifted for relative implication, as the relation between relative implication and deduction is given by the Subsumption Theorem:

$C \models_\mathcal{B} D$ iff there exists a deduction of D from $\{C\} \cup \mathcal{B}$.

Thus the fact that relative implication is a strictly stronger quasi-order than relative subsumption can also be seen as follows: the restriction on relative subsumption that C be used at most once in a deduction of D (Theorem 16.6), does not hold for relative implication.

16.3.2 Least Generalizations

Here we discuss *least generalizations under relative implication* (LGRIs). Firstly, in case of Horn clauses we have already shown in Section 15.2 that the two definite program clauses $D_1 = P(f^2(x)) \leftarrow P(x)$ and $D_2 = P(f^3(x)) \leftarrow P(x)$ do not have an LGI in $\mathcal{H}$. This negative result carries over to *relative* implication, since ordinary logical implication is just a special case of relative implication.

For general clauses, we have seen in the last chapter that a set S has an LGI if it contains at least one non-tautologous function-free clause. At present, it is not known whether sets of clauses which all contain function symbols always have an LGI. Nevertheless, for *relative* implication, we have a negative result. The next example shows that even if S and $\mathcal{B}$ are both finite sets of function-free clauses, an LGRI of S relative to $\mathcal{B}$ need not exist.

Example 16.12 Consider

$$D_1 = P(a)$$
$$D_2 = P(b)$$
$$\mathcal{B} = \{(P(a) \vee \neg Q(x)), (P(b) \vee \neg Q(x))\}$$

We will show that the set $S = \{D_1, D_2\}$ has no LGRI relative to $\mathcal{B}$ in $\mathcal{C}$.

Suppose D is an LGRI of S relative to $\mathcal{B}$. Note that if D contains the literal $P(a)$, then the Herbrand interpretation which makes $P(a)$ true, and which makes all other ground atoms false, would be a model of $\mathcal{B} \cup \{D\}$ but not of D_2, so then we would have $D \not\models_\mathcal{B} D_2$. Similarly, if D contains $P(b)$ then $D \not\models_\mathcal{B} D_1$. Hence D cannot contain $P(a)$ or $P(b)$.

Now let d be a constant not appearing in D. Let $C = P(x) \vee Q(d)$, then $C \models_\mathcal{B} S$. By the definition of an LGRI, we should have $C \models_\mathcal{B} D$. Then by the Subsumption Theorem, there must be a derivation from $\mathcal{B} \cup \{C\}$ of a clause E, which subsumes D. The set of all clauses which can be derived (in 0 or more resolution steps) from $\mathcal{B} \cup \{C\}$ is $\mathcal{B} \cup \{C\} \cup \{(P(a) \vee P(x)), (P(b) \vee P(x))\}$. But none of these clauses subsumes D, because D does not contain the constant d, nor the literals $P(a)$ or $P(b)$. Hence $C \not\models_\mathcal{B} D$, contradicting the assumption that D is an LGRI of S relative to $\mathcal{B}$ in $\mathcal{C}$. ◁

Thus in general an LGRI of S relative to $\mathcal{B}$ need not exist. But again we can identify a special case in which the existence of an LGRI is guaranteed.

Proposition 16.13 *Let C and D be clauses, and $\mathcal{B}$ be a finite set of function-free ground literals. Then $C \models_\mathcal{B} D$ iff $C \models (D \cup \overline{\mathcal{B}})$.*

Proof

$\Rightarrow$: Suppose $C \models_{\mathcal{B}} D$, i.e., $\{C\} \cup \mathcal{B} \models D$. Let M be a model of C, then we need to show that M is also a model of $D \cup \overline{\mathcal{B}}$. If M is not a model of $\mathcal{B}$, then it is a model of at least one literal in $\overline{\mathcal{B}}$, and hence of the clause $D \cup \overline{\mathcal{B}}$. If, on the other hand, M is a model of $\mathcal{B}$, then it is also a model of D, because $\{C\} \cup \mathcal{B} \models D$. Then M is also a model of $D \cup \overline{\mathcal{B}}$.

$\Leftarrow$: Suppose $C \models (D \cup \overline{\mathcal{B}})$. Let M be a model of $\{C\} \cup \mathcal{B}$, then we need to show M is also a model of D. M is a model of C, and hence of the clause $D \cup \overline{\mathcal{B}}$. But M is also a model of $\mathcal{B}$, and hence not a model of $\overline{\mathcal{B}}$. Therefore M must be a model of D. □

Theorem 16.14 (Existence of LGRI in $\mathcal{C}$) *Let $\mathcal{C}$ be a clausal language and $\mathcal{B} \subseteq \mathcal{C}$ be a finite set of function-free ground literals. If $S \subseteq \mathcal{C}$ is a finite set of clauses, containing at least one D for which $D \cup \overline{\mathcal{B}}$ is non-tautologous and function-free, then S has an LGRI in $\mathcal{C}$.*

Proof Let $S = \{D_1, \ldots, D_n\}$. It follows easily from the previous proposition that an LGI in $\mathcal{C}$ of $T = \{(D_1 \cup \overline{\mathcal{B}}), \ldots, (D_n \cup \overline{\mathcal{B}})\}$ is also an LGRI of S in $\mathcal{C}$. The existence of such an LGI of T follows from Theorem 15.17. □

Note the following special case of this result:

Corollary 16.15 *Let $\mathcal{C}$ be a function-free clausal language and $\mathcal{B} \subseteq \mathcal{C}$ be a finite set of ground literals. If $S \subseteq \mathcal{C}$ is a finite set of clauses, then S has an LGRI in $\mathcal{C}$.*

Proof Let S' be obtained by deleting from S all clauses which are implied by $\mathcal{B}$. If S' is empty, any tautology is an LGRI of S. If $D \in S'$, then $\mathcal{B} \not\models D$, so D cannot contain any of the literals in $\mathcal{B}$. Then $D \cup \overline{\mathcal{B}}$ is non-tautologous and function-free. Hence if S' is non-empty, it has an LGRI in $\mathcal{C}$ by the previous theorem. Clearly, this is also an LGRI of S itself. □

16.4 Generalized Subsumption

In this section we introduce the third quasi-order on clauses with background knowledge, Buntine's generalized subsumption [Bun86, Bun88], and prove some of its properties. It applies only to definite program clauses.

16.4.1 Definition and Some Properties

Suppose we are given some particular definite program $\mathcal{B}$ as background knowledge. Buntine's definition of generalized subsumption can be motivated

as follows: a definite clause C may be said to be more general than another
definite program clause D, if in any situation consistent with what we already
know, C can be used to prove at least as many results as D. Here "a situation
consistent with what we already know" can be formalized as "a Herbrand
model of the background knowledge $\mathcal{B}$." Furthermore "C can be used to prove
at least as many results as D" is formalized as "the set of atoms covered by
C is a superset of the set of atoms covered by D." The notion of 'covering'
(not to be confused with the notion of an upward or downward 'cover' defined
in Chapter 13) is defined below. Recall from earlier chapters that if C is a
definite program clause, then C^+ denotes the head of C, and C^- denotes the
conjunction of the atoms in the body of C.

Definition 16.16 Let C be a definite program clause, A a ground atom,
and I a Herbrand interpretation. We say C *covers* A *under* I if there is a
ground substitution θ for C (i.e., $C\theta$ is ground), such that $C^-\theta$ is true under
I, and $C^+\theta = A$. $\diamond$

Example 16.17 Let $C = P(f(x)) \leftarrow P(x)$ and $A = P(f(a))$. Then C
covers A under $I = \{P(a)\}$, because if $\theta = \{x/a\}$, then $C^-\theta = P(a)$ is true
under I, and $C^+\theta = A$. Note that A itself need not be true under I for the
definition of covering to apply. On the other hand, C does not cover A under
$I = \{P(f(a))\}$, even though A is true under this I.
   $C = P(x)$ covers $A = P(a)$ under any Herbrand interpretation. $\triangleleft$

   Putting the pieces together, generalized subsumption (or g-subsumption)
is defined as follows:

Definition 16.18 Let C and D be definite program clauses and $\mathcal{B}$ be a
definite program. We say C *g-subsumes* D *with respect to* $\mathcal{B}$, denoted by
$C \geq_\mathcal{B} D$, if for every Herbrand model M of $\mathcal{B}$ and every ground atom A such
that D covers A under M, we have that C covers A under M. The $\geq_\mathcal{B}$-order
is called *generalized subsumption*, or *g-subsumption*, and $\mathcal{B}$ is the *background
knowledge* of this order. $\diamond$

Example 16.19 Let $\mathcal{B}$ consist of the following clauses:

$$Pet(x) \leftarrow Cat(x)$$
$$Pet(x) \leftarrow Dog(x)$$
$$Small(x) \leftarrow Cat(x)$$

And suppose

$$C = CuddlyPet(x) \leftarrow Small(x), Pet(x)$$
$$D = CuddlyPet(x) \leftarrow Cat(x)$$

Then we can show that $C \geq_{\mathcal{B}} D$. For suppose M is a Herbrand model of $\mathcal{B}$, and D covers some ground atom $A = CuddlyPet(t)$ under M. Then for $\theta = \{x/t\}$, $D^-\theta = Cat(t)$ is true under M. Since M is a model of $\mathcal{B}$, in particular of the first and third clause of $\mathcal{B}$, $Pet(t)$ and $Small(t)$ must be true under M as well. Then $C^-\theta = Small(t) \wedge Pet(t)$ is true under M, and $C^+\theta = A$, so C also covers A under M. Hence C g-subsumes D with respect to $\mathcal{B}$. Rephrased in natural language: if small pets are cuddly pets, then cats are cuddly pets, since we already know that cats are small pets.   ◁

It is not very difficult to show that subsumption implies g-subsumption. To see this, suppose $C \succeq D$. Then $C\theta \subseteq D$, so $C^+\theta = D^+$ and $C^-\theta \subseteq D^-\theta$ for some θ. If D covers some A under some I, there is a γ such that $D^-\gamma$ is true under I and $D^+\gamma = A$. But then $C^+\theta\gamma = D^+\gamma = A$, and $C^-\theta\gamma \subseteq D^-\gamma$ is true under I, so C covers A under I as well. Hence if $C \succeq D$, then $C \geq_{\mathcal{B}} D$. The converse need not hold: if $\mathcal{B} = \{P(a)\}$, $C = Q(a) \leftarrow P(a)$ and $D = Q(a)$, then $C \geq_{\mathcal{B}} D$ but $C \not\succeq D$.

From the definition it is clear that g-subsumption with respect to some particular definite program $\mathcal{B}$ is reflexive and transitive, so it imposes a quasi-order on the set of definite program clauses. Note that a clause C need not g-subsume every tautology with respect to any $\mathcal{B}$. For instance, consider the empty program $\mathcal{B} = \emptyset$ as background knowledge, $C = P(a)$, and $D = Q(a) \leftarrow Q(a)$. Because $\mathcal{B}$ is empty, any Herbrand interpretation is a model of $\mathcal{B}$ (no members of $\mathcal{B}$ can be false under I, since $\mathcal{B}$ has no members). If we take $I = \{Q(a)\}$, then D covers $Q(a)$ under I, while C does not. So C does not g-subsume the tautology D with respect to the empty program. Finally, note that if $C \geq_{\mathcal{B}} D$, then C and D must have the same predicate symbol in their head.

Buntine himself extended this order on clauses to an order on finite *sets* of clauses (i.e., definite programs), but we will not go into that here.

The next two lemmas, which we illustrate with an example, show the definition of g-subsumption to be equivalent to another formulation, which will be more convenient in later proofs than the definition based on covering. First a notational remark: if D is a definite program clause and σ a substitution, then $D^-\sigma$ is a conjunction of atoms, so we can use $\mathcal{B} \cup D^-\sigma$ to denote the definite program consisting of the clauses in $\mathcal{B}$ and the atoms in $D^-\sigma$.

Example 16.20 Consider

$$C = Q(x, y) \leftarrow P(x), Q(y, x)$$
$$D = Q(a, y) \leftarrow Q(y, a)$$
$$\mathcal{B} = \{P(x)\}$$

then $C \geq_{\mathcal{B}} D$. Let $\sigma = \{y/b\}$ be a Skolem substitution for D. If $\theta = \{x/a, y/b\}$, then $C^+\theta = Q(a, b) = D^+\sigma$, so $D^+\sigma$ is an instance of C^+. Now $\mathcal{B}$ together with $D^-\sigma = Q(b, a)$ logically implies $C^-\theta = P(a) \wedge Q(b, a)$.   ◁

Lemma 16.21 *Let C and D be definite program clauses, $\mathcal{B}$ be a definite program, and σ be a Skolem substitution for D with respect to $\{C\} \cup \mathcal{B}$. Then $C \geq_{\mathcal{B}} D$ iff there exists a ground substitution θ for C, such that $C^+\theta = D^+\sigma$ and $\mathcal{B} \cup D^-\sigma \models C^-\theta$.*

Proof

$\Rightarrow$: Suppose $C \geq_{\mathcal{B}} D$. Let M be the least Herbrand model of $\mathcal{B} \cup D^-\sigma$. The substitution σ is a ground substitution for D, and $D^-\sigma$ is true under M, so D covers $D^+\sigma$ under M. Then C must also cover $D^+\sigma$ under M. Thus there is a ground substitution θ for C, such that $C^+\theta = D^+\sigma$, and $C^-\theta$ is true under M, i.e., $C^-\theta \subseteq M$, so $M \models C^-\theta$. It follows from Theorem 7.16 that $\mathcal{B} \cup D^-\sigma \models M$, hence $\mathcal{B} \cup D^-\sigma \models C^-\theta$.

$\Leftarrow$: Suppose there is a ground substitution θ for C, such that $C^+\theta = D^+\sigma$ and $\mathcal{B} \cup D^-\sigma \models C^-\theta$. Let A be some ground atom and M some Herbrand model of $\mathcal{B}$, such that D covers A under M. To prove that $C \geq_{\mathcal{B}} D$, we need to show that C covers A under M.

Construct a substitution θ' from θ as follows: for every binding $x/a \in \sigma$, replace a in bindings in θ by x. Then we have $C\theta'\sigma = C\theta$, and none of the Skolem constants of σ occurs in θ'. Then $C^+\theta'\sigma = C^+\theta = D^+\sigma$, so $C^+\theta' = D^+$. Since D covers A under M, there is a ground substitution γ for D, such that $D^-\gamma$ is true under M, and $D^+\gamma = A$. This implies $C^+\theta'\gamma = D^+\gamma = A$.

It remains to show that $C^-\theta'\gamma$ is true under M. Because $\mathcal{B} \cup D^-\sigma \models C^-\theta'\sigma$, it follows from the Subsumption Theorem for SLD-resolution that, for every atom B in C^-, there is an SLD-deduction of $B\theta'\sigma$ from $\mathcal{B} \cup D^-\sigma$. We want to turn these into SLD-deductions of $B\theta'\gamma$ from $\mathcal{B} \cup D^-\gamma$, thus proving that $\mathcal{B} \cup D^-\gamma \models C^-\theta'\gamma$. Let $x_1, \ldots, x_n$ be the variables in D^-, $\{x_1/a_1, \ldots, x_n/a_n\} \subseteq \sigma$, and $\{x_1/t_1, \ldots, x_n/t_n\} \subseteq \gamma$. If we replace each Skolem constant a_i in the SLD-deductions by t_i $(1 \leq i \leq n)$, we obtain SLD-deductions of $B\theta'\gamma$ from $\mathcal{B} \cup D^-\gamma$, for every B in C^-. Hence $\mathcal{B} \cup D^-\gamma \models C^-\theta'\gamma$. Since M is a model of $\mathcal{B} \cup D^-\gamma$, it is also a model of $C^-\theta'\gamma$. $\square$

Lemma 16.22 *Let C and D be definite program clauses, $\mathcal{B}$ be a definite program, and σ be a Skolem substitution for D with respect to $\{C\} \cup \mathcal{B}$. Then $C \geq_{\mathcal{B}} D$ iff there exists a substitution θ, such that $C^+\theta = D^+$ and $\mathcal{B} \cup D^-\sigma \models C^-\theta\sigma$, where $C^-\theta\sigma$ is ground.*

Proof By the previous lemma, we have $C \geq_{\mathcal{B}} D$ iff there exists a ground substitution θ' for C, such that $C^+\theta' = D^+\sigma$ and $\mathcal{B} \cup D^-\sigma \models C^-\theta'$. Since σ is a Skolem substitution, we can define a θ such that $C\theta\sigma = C\theta'$ and none of the Skolem constants of σ occurs in θ. Then $C^+\theta = D^+$ and $C^-\theta' = C^-\theta\sigma$, so the result follows. $\square$

The relation between g-subsumption and deductions is given below by Theorem 16.25. First note that a binary resolvent of two clauses is g-subsumed by one of its parent clauses with respect to the other parent clause:

Example 16.23 Consider the following clauses:

$$C = CuddlyPet(x) \leftarrow Cute(x), Cat(x)$$
$$D = CuddlyPet(x) \leftarrow Small(x), Pet(x), Cat(x)$$
$$E = Cute(x) \leftarrow Small(x), Pet(x)$$

Then D is a binary resolvent of C and E, and $C \geq_{\{E\}} D$. ◁

Lemma 16.24 *If D is a binary resolvent of definite program clauses C and E, resolved upon the head of E, then $C \geq_{\{E\}} D$.*

Proof We may assume that C and E are standardized apart. Let $C = B \leftarrow B_1, \ldots, B_s, \ldots, B_n$, where B_s is the atom resolved upon, and μ is the mgu of B_s and E^+ that is used. Then $D = (B \leftarrow B_1, \ldots, B_{s-1}, E^-, B_{s+1}, \ldots, B_n)\mu$. Let M be a Herbrand model of $\{E\}$, and A be a ground atom such that D covers A under M. We need to prove that C covers A under M.

D covers A under M, so there is a ground substitution θ for D, such that $D^+\theta = B\mu\theta = A$, and $D^-\theta = (B_1, \ldots, B_{s-1}, E^-, B_{s+1}, \ldots, B_n)\mu\theta$ is true under M. Let γ be a ground substitution for $B_s\mu\theta$, and define $\theta' = \mu\theta\gamma$. Then $C^+\theta' = B\mu\theta\gamma = A\gamma = A$. Since $D^-\theta$ is ground and true under M, the atoms $(B_1, \ldots, B_{s-1}, B_{s+1}, \ldots, B_n)\theta'$ are ground and true under M. Furthermore, M is a model of E and thus also of $E\theta'$, and $E^-\theta' = E^-\mu\theta\gamma = E^-\mu\theta \subseteq D^-\theta$ is ground and true under M, hence $E^+\theta' = E^+\mu\theta\gamma = B_s\mu\theta\gamma = B_s\theta'$ is ground and true under M. Thus every atom in $C^-\theta'$ is ground and true under M, which means that C covers A under M. □

Theorem 16.25 *Let C and D be definite program clauses and $\mathcal{B}$ be a definite program. Then $C \geq_{\mathcal{B}} D$ iff there exists an SLD-deduction of D, with C as top clause and members of $\mathcal{B}$ as input clauses.*

Proof

$\Rightarrow$: Suppose $C \geq_{\mathcal{B}} D$. Let σ be a Skolem substitution for D with respect to $\{C\} \cup \mathcal{B}$. Then by Lemma 16.22, there is a substitution θ such that $C^+\theta = D^+$, and $\mathcal{B} \cup D^-\sigma \models C^-\theta\sigma$, where $C^-\theta\sigma$ is ground. By Proposition 2.37, $\mathcal{B} \cup D^-\sigma \cup \{\leftarrow C^-\theta\sigma\}$ is unsatisfiable.

By the refutation completeness of SLD-resolution, there is an SLD-refutation of $\mathcal{B} \cup D^-\sigma \cup \{\leftarrow C^-\theta\sigma\}$, with goals $G_0(=\leftarrow C^-\theta\sigma), G_1, \ldots, G_n = \square$, input clauses $E_1, \ldots, E_n$, and mgu's $\theta_1, \ldots, \theta_n$ (here $n = 0$ if C is an atom, and $n \geq 1$ otherwise). Each input clause is either a member of $\mathcal{B}$, or an atom from $D^-\sigma$. By the Switching Lemma, we can assume there is an $i \geq 0$ such that $E_1, \ldots, E_i$ are members of $\mathcal{B}$, and $E_{i+1}, \ldots, E_n$ are the input clauses (atoms) that come from $D^-\sigma$. Note that then $G_i^-\theta_{i+1} \ldots \theta_n \subseteq D^-\sigma$.

For every $0 \leq j \leq n$, define $G_j' = C^+\theta\sigma \leftarrow G_j^-$. That is, add the ground atom $C^+\theta\sigma$ as head to each goal in the refutation. Then $G_0', \ldots, G_i'$ is an SLD-derivation of G_i', with top clause $G_0' = C\theta\sigma$ and input clauses from

$\mathcal{B}$. Furthermore, we have $G'_i\theta_{i+1}\ldots\theta_n = C^+\theta\sigma \leftarrow G^-_i\theta_{i+1}\ldots\theta_n = D^+\sigma \leftarrow G^-_i\theta_{i+1}\ldots\theta_n \subseteq D\sigma$, so G'_i subsumes $D\sigma$. Now by the Lifting Lemma for SLD-resolution (Lemma 7.7), we can find an SLD-derivation of a clause F which subsumes $D\sigma$, with C as top clause and members of $\mathcal{B}$ as input clauses. By Lemma 5.16, F also subsumes D itself, so we have found the required SLD-deduction.

$\Leftarrow$: Suppose $C_0(= C)$, $C_1,\ldots,C_n$ is an SLD-derivation ($n \geq 0$), with C as top clause and members of $\mathcal{B}$ as input clauses, and C_n subsumes D. We will prove by induction on n that $C \geq_\mathcal{B} D$.

1. If $n = 0$, then $C \succeq D$, and hence $C \geq_\mathcal{B} D$.
2. Suppose the result holds for $n \leq m$, and $C_0(= C)$, $C_1,\ldots,C_{m+1}$ be an SLD-derivation, with C as top clause and members of $\mathcal{B}$ as input clauses, and C_{m+1} subsumes D. C_1 is a binary resolvent of C and some $E \in \mathcal{B}$, so we have $C \geq_{\{E\}} C_1$ by Lemma 16.24, and hence also $C \geq_\mathcal{B} C_1$, since $E \in \mathcal{B}$. By the induction hypothesis we have $C_1 \geq_\mathcal{B} D$. Now $C \geq_\mathcal{B} D$ follows from the transitivity of $\geq_\mathcal{B}$.   □

It follows from this that g-subsumption reduces to ordinary subsumption in the presence of empty background knowledge, as was the case for relative subsumption.

Corollary 16.26 *If C and D are definite program clauses, then $C \geq_\emptyset D$ iff $C \succeq D$.*

Finally, let us take a look at the relation between *relative* subsumption and *generalized* subsumption. Comparing the restrictions on deductions stated in Theorems 16.25 and 16.6, the next corollary follows immediately:

Corollary 16.27 *Let C and D be definite program clauses, and $\mathcal{B}$ be a definite program. If $C \geq_\mathcal{B} D$, then $C \succeq_\mathcal{B} D$.*

The converse does not hold, because g-subsumption requires that C and D have the same predicate symbol in their head, while relative subsumption does not (see Example 16.2). Hence Plotkin's relative subsumption is a strictly stronger quasi-order than Buntine's g-subsumption.

16.4.2   Least Generalizations

In this subsection we will investigate the existence and non-existence of *least generalizations under g-subsumption*, which we abbreviate to LGGSs. Example 16.7, which showed that least generalizations need not exist under relative subsumption, may serve as well to show that LGGSs need not exist. We leave the details to the reader.

However, again some important special cases can be identified in which the existence of an LGGS is guaranteed. Buntine himself identified two such cases in which an LGGS of a finite set S (of definite program clauses which all have the same predicate symbol in their respective heads) always exists: (1) if all clauses in S are atoms, and the background knowledge B implies only a finite number of ground atoms (i.e., M_B is finite); and (2) if S and B are all function-free (see Corollaries 7.2 and 7.3 of [Bun88]). We add here a third case, namely (3) if B is ground. Note that case (3) differs from case (1), because B may imply only a finite number of ground examples, and still be non-ground itself. For example, $B = \{P(a), (Q(x) \leftarrow P(x))\}$.

Actually, these three cases are special cases of Theorem 16.29, proved below. Our proof differs slightly from Buntine's. The next lemma is the key to the result. Note that if D is a definite program clause and Σ is a finite set of ground atoms, then $D \cup \overline{\Sigma}$ is also a definite program clause.

Lemma 16.28 *Let C and D be definite program clauses, B a definite program, σ be a Skolem substitution for D with respect to $\{C\} \cup B$, and M be the least Herbrand model of $B \cup D^- \sigma$. Then $C \geq_B D$ iff there is a substitution θ such that $C\theta \subseteq \{D^+\sigma\} \cup \overline{M}$.*

Proof

$\Rightarrow$: Suppose $C \geq_B D$. By Lemma 16.21, there is a ground substitution θ for C, such that $C^+\theta = D^+\sigma$ and $B \cup D^- \sigma \models C^-\theta$. Because M is the least Herbrand model of $B \cup D^- \sigma$, we have $C^-\theta \subseteq M$ from Theorem 7.16. Since also $C^+\theta = D^+\sigma$, we have $C\theta \subseteq \{D^+\sigma\} \cup \overline{M}$.

$\Leftarrow$: Suppose there is a substitution θ such that $C\theta \subseteq \{D^+\sigma\} \cup \overline{M}$. Then $C^+\theta = D^+\sigma$ and $C^-\theta \subseteq M$. This means that we have $M \models C^-\theta$, hence also $B \cup D^- \sigma \models C^-\theta$. Therefore $C \geq_B D$ by Lemma 16.21. $\square$

Note that if the least Herbrand model M of $B \cup D^- \sigma$ is finite, then this lemma becomes: $C \geq_B D$ iff $C \succeq \{D^+\sigma\} \cup \overline{M}$. Thus we have a means to translate g-subsumption to ordinary subsumption.

Theorem 16.29 (Existence of LGGS) *Let $\mathcal{H}$ be a Horn language and B be a definite program. Let $S = \{D_1, \ldots, D_n\} \subseteq \mathcal{H}$ be a finite non-empty set of definite program clauses, such that all D_i have the same predicate symbol in their head. Furthermore, for every $1 \leq i \leq n$, let σ_i be a Skolem substitution for D_i with respect to $B \cup S$, and M_i be the least Herbrand model of $B \cup D_i^- \sigma_i$. If every M_i is finite, then there exists an LGGS of S in $\mathcal{H}$.*

Proof By Theorem 14.27, there exists an LGS in $\mathcal{H}$ of the set of clauses $T = \{(\{D_1^+\sigma_1\} \cup \overline{M_1}), \ldots, (\{D_n^+\sigma_n\} \cup \overline{M_n})\}$. Since each $D_i \in S$ has the same predicate in its head, this LGS of T will be a definite program clause which also has this predicate in its head. Now it follows easily from the previous lemma that this LGS of T in $\mathcal{H}$ is an LGGS of S in $\mathcal{H}$. $\square$

Thus if the least Herbrand models mentioned in the theorem are indeed finite, then we can find an LGGS of a set $\{D_1, \ldots, D_n\}$ simply by constructing an LGS of $\{((\{D_1^+\sigma_1\} \cup \overline{M_1}), \ldots, (\{D_n^+\sigma_n\} \cup \overline{M_n})\}$. The three special cases we mentioned, will be shown to be immediate corollaries of this result.

Firstly, if S is a finite set of atoms, then for each i, $D_i^-\sigma$ will be empty and $M_i = M_{\mathcal{B}}$. If $\mathcal{B}$ implies only a finite number of ground atoms (i.e., if $M_{\mathcal{B}}$ is finite), then the theorem can be applied.

Corollary 16.30 *Let $\mathcal{H}$ be a Horn language and $\mathcal{B}$ be a definite program such that $M_{\mathcal{B}}$ is finite. If S is a finite set of atoms which all have the same predicate symbol, then there exists an LGGS of S in $\mathcal{H}$.*

Secondly, if S and $\mathcal{B}$ are function-free, the set of ground atoms in the Herbrand base $B_{\mathcal{B} \cup S}$ is finite, so the least Herbrand models $M_1, \ldots, M_n$ will be finite as well.

Corollary 16.31 *Let $\mathcal{H}$ be a Horn language and $\mathcal{B}$ be a function-free definite program. If S is a finite set of function-free definite program clauses which all have the same predicate symbol in their head, then there exists an LGGS of S in $\mathcal{H}$.*

Thirdly and finally, if $\mathcal{B}$ is ground, then each M_i will again be finite.

Corollary 16.32 *Let $\mathcal{H}$ be a Horn language and $\mathcal{B}$ be a ground definite program. If S is a finite set of definite program clauses which all have the same predicate symbol in their head, then there exists an LGGS of S in $\mathcal{H}$.*

Example 16.33 Consider the clauses from the introduction:

$$D_1 = CuddlyPet(x) \leftarrow Small(x), Fluffy(x), Dog(x)$$
$$D_2 = CuddlyPet(x) \leftarrow Fluffy(x), Cat(x)$$

And background knowledge $\mathcal{B}$:

$$Pet(x) \leftarrow Cat(x)$$
$$Pet(x) \leftarrow Dog(x)$$
$$Small(x) \leftarrow Cat(x)$$

Let us take $\sigma_1 = \{x/a\}$ and $\sigma_2 = \{x/b\}$ as Skolem substitutions for D_1 and D_2, respectively. Then

$$M_1 = \{Small(a), Fluffy(a), Dog(a), Pet(a)\}$$
$$M_2 = \{Small(b), Fluffy(b), Cat(b), Pet(b)\}$$

The following clause is an LGS of $\{(\{D_1^+\sigma_1\} \cup \overline{M_1}), (\{D_2^+\sigma_2\} \cup \overline{M_2})\}$, and hence also an LGGS of D_1 and D_2:

$$CuddlyPet(x) \leftarrow Small(x), Fluffy(x), Pet(x)$$

$\triangleleft$

Though these existence results are fairly strong, it should be noted that the LGGS obtained from the LGS algorithm may have a huge number of literals. Thus for efficient use of LGGSs, additional constraints may be needed in practice.

16.5 Summary

This chapter discussed three generality orders which are able to take background knowledge into account: Plotkin's *relative subsumption* ($\succeq_B$), *relative implication* ($\models_B$), and finally Buntine's *generalized subsumption* ($\geq_B$). Relative subsumption and relative implication apply to arbitrary clauses and the background knowledge B may be an arbitary finite set of clauses. Generalized subsumption only applies to definite program clauses and the background knowledge should be a definite program. The relations between these three orders and deductions are as follows:

1. $C \succeq_B D$ iff there exists a deduction of D from $\{C\} \cup B$ in which C occurs at most once as a leaf.
2. $C \models_B D$ iff there exists a deduction of D from $\{C\} \cup B$.
3. $C \geq_B D$ iff there exists an SLD-deduction of D, with C as top clause and members of B as input clauses.

We investigated the existence of least generalizations in each of these orders, both in case we are dealing with a Horn language $\mathcal{H}$, and for a general clausal language $\mathcal{C}$. The results are given in the following table, where '+' signifies a positive answer, and '−' means a negative answer. In order to get the total picture, we also include our results on least generalizations under ordinary subsumption and implication from the last two chapters. In case of a '−' for the general case, we include a reference to a theorem describing a special case in which least generalizations are guaranteed to exist. The '?' in the second row indicates that the general question concerning the existence of an LGI for general clauses is still open.

	Horn clauses	General clauses
Subsumption ($\succeq$)	+	+
Implication ($\models$)	−	? (+ Th 15.17)
Relative subsumption ($\succeq_B$)	− (+ Th 16.9)	− (+ Th 16.8)
Relative implication ($\models_B$)	−	− (+ Th 16.14)
Generalized subsumption ($\geq_B$)	− (+ Th 16.29)	undefined

Table 16.1: Existence of least generalizations

Note the trade-off between the strength of the generality order and the existence of least generalizations: in the weakest order (subsumption) least generalizations always exist, while in the strongest order (relative implication) the existence of least generalizations can only be guaranteed in very restricted cases.

Chapter 17

Refinement Operators

17.1 Introduction

In the chapter on Shapiro's model inference technique, we deferred the discussion of refinement operators to this chapter. The reason for this is that refinement operators can be defined for different quasi-ordered sets of clauses. Hence the discussion in this chapter presupposes the investigation of the properties of the various quasi-orders given in the last chapters. In this chapter, we will apply the results of those chapters to the topic of refinement operators.

In Shapiro's sense, a refinement operator is a function which computes a set of specializations of a clause. Specialization is the direction suited for his top-down approach. His kind of refinement operator will therefore be called a *downward* refinement operator. Dually, we might also define operators which compute generalizations of clauses. These can be applied in a bottom-up search, so we will call them *upward* refinement operators.

A "good" downward refinement operator should satisfy certain desirable properties. Ideally, it should compute only a *finite* set of specializations of each clause—otherwise it will be of limited use in practice. This condition is called *locally finiteness*. Furthermore, it should be *complete*: every specialization should be reachable by a finite number of applications of the operator. And finally, it is better only to compute *proper* generalizations of a clause, for otherwise repeated application of the operator might get stuck in a sequence of equivalent clauses, without ever achieving any real specialization. We would also like three analogous conditions to hold for upward refinement operators as well.

We will show in the next section that ideal upward and downward refinement operators exist for the simplest of our quasi-orders: the set of atoms ordered by subsumption. Unfortunately, these ideal conditions cannot all be met at the same time for more complex orders. In Section 17.3, we will prove that ideal refinement operators do not exist for full clausal languages or Horn languages ordered by subsumption or by the stronger orders. This negative result is a concequence of the fact that finite complete sets of covers do not always exist.

In order to define a refinement operator for full clausal languages, we have to drop one of the three properties of idealness. We consider locally finiteness and completeness to be the two most important properties, so we will drop the 'properness'. Accordingly, in Section 17.4 we define locally finite and complete, but *improper* refinement operators for full clausal languages. On the other hand, if we want to retain all three ideal properties, it seems that the only possibility is to restrict the search space. This is done in Section 17.5, where we define ideal refinement operators for clausal languages bounded by a *newsize* restriction. After that, we go into *optimal* refinement operators, and refinement operators for theories (rather than individual clauses) under logical implication.

Refinement operators are used very often in ILP systems, for instance in MIS [Sha81b], SIM [LD90, Lin92], FOIL [Qui90, QC93], CLAUDIEN [DB93], LINUS [LD94], and PROGOL [Mug95]. For reasons of efficiency, those operators are usually less general than the ones we discuss here, and often incomplete. Nevertheless, we feel the complete operators we define here form a good starting point for the construction of practical refinement operators. The material in this chapter is mainly drawn from [LN93, NLT93, LN94a, LN94b, LN97], and is collected in [Laa95].

17.2   Ideal Refinement Operators for Atoms

In this section, we will define the concept of a refinement operator for a quasi-ordered set. As an example, we will then define downward and upward refinement operators which are ideal for the set of atoms.

Definition 17.1 Let $\langle G, \geq \rangle$ be a quasi-ordered set. A *downward refinement operator* for $\langle G, \geq \rangle$ is a function ρ, such that $\rho(C) \subseteq \{D \mid C \geq D\}$, for every $C \in G$.

An *upward refinement operator* for $\langle G, \geq \rangle$ is a function δ, such that $\delta(C) \subseteq \{D \mid D \geq C\}$, for every $C \in G$.   ◇

Usually in this chapter, G will be a clausal language $\mathcal{C}$. In that case, $\rho(C)$ is a set of specializations of a clause C, while $\delta(C)$ is a set of generalizations of C. However, in Section 17.7 we take G to be the set of *finite subsets* of $\mathcal{C}$, and we define an operator which specializes *sets* of clauses.

Several properties of refinement operators are defined as follows:

Definition 17.2 Let $\langle G, \geq \rangle$ be a quasi-ordered set, and ρ be a downward refinement operator for $\langle G, \geq \rangle$.

- The sets of *one-step refinements*, *n-step refinements*, and *refinements* of some $C \in G$ are respectively:

$\rho^1(C) = \rho(C),$
$\rho^n(C) = \{D \mid \text{there is an } E \in \rho^{n-1}(C) \text{ such that } D \in \rho(E)\}, n \geq 2,$
$\rho^*(C) = \rho^1(C) \cup \rho^2(C) \cup \rho^3(C) \ldots.$

- A ρ-*chain* from C to D is a sequence $C = C_0, C_1, \ldots, C_n = D$, such that $C_i \in \rho(C_{i-1})$ for every $1 \leq i \leq n$.

- ρ is *locally finite* if for every $C \in G$, $\rho(C)$ is finite and computable.

- ρ is *complete* if for every $C, D \in G$ such that $C > D$, there is an $E \in \rho^*(C)$ such that $D \approx E$ (i.e., D and E are equivalent in the $\geq$-order).

- ρ is *proper* if for every $C \in G$, $\rho(C) \subseteq \{D \mid C > D\}$.

- ρ is *ideal* if it is locally finite, complete, and proper.

We can define analogous concepts for the dual case of an upward refinement operator δ. $\diamond$

A refinement operator induces a *refinement graph*. This is a directed graph which has the members of G as nodes (here variant clauses in G can be viewed as the same node), and which contains an edge from C to D just in case $D \in \rho(C)$. This refinement graph is the space that is searched for candidates to include in the theory. An ideal refinement operator induces a refinement graph in which only a finite number of edges start from each node (locally finiteness), in which there exists a path of finite length from C to a member of the equivalence class of D whenever $C > D$ (completeness), and which contains no cycles (by properness).

Suppose $\langle G, \geq \rangle$ is a quasi-ordered set of clauses, such that every $C \in G$ has a finite complete set of downward covers. Then a natural approach towards ideal refinement operators, is by defining $\rho(C)$ as such a finite complete set of downward covers of C. As an example, we will show in this section how we can define an ideal downward refinement operator for the set of atoms. In Chapter 13, we have already proved that every atom has a finite complete set of downward covers.

Definition 17.3 Let $\mathcal{A}$ be the set of atoms in a language. The downward refinement operator $\rho_{\mathcal{A}}$ for $\mathcal{A}$ is defined as follows:

1. For every variable z in A and every n-ary function symbol f in the language, let $x_1, \ldots, x_n$ be distinct variables not appearing in A. Let $\rho_{\mathcal{A}}(A)$ contain $A\{z/f(x_1, \ldots, x_n)\}$.
2. For every variable z in A and every constant a in the language, let $\rho_{\mathcal{A}}(A)$ contain $A\{z/a\}$.
3. For every two distinct variables x and z in A, let $\rho_{\mathcal{A}}(A)$ contain $A\{z/x\}$.

$\diamond$

Note that $\rho_{\mathcal{A}}(A)$ may still contain variants. For instance, $\rho_{\mathcal{A}}(P(x,y))$ contains both $P(x,x)$ and $P(y,y)$. Clearly, in a practical application we can ignore any redundant variants.

The three different kinds of atoms in $\rho(A)$ correspond exactly to the three kinds of downward covers that we discussed in Chapter 13. The fact that $\rho_{\mathcal{A}}$ is ideal follows easily from the properties of sets of covers of atoms that were given in that chapter.

Theorem 17.4 *Let $\mathcal{A}$ be the set of atoms in a language containing only a finite number of constants, function symbols, and predicate symbols. Then $\rho_{\mathcal{A}}$ is an ideal downward refinement operator for $\langle \mathcal{A}, \succeq \rangle$.*

Proof By the definition of $\rho_{\mathcal{A}}$, $\rho_{\mathcal{A}}$ is locally finite. The completeness of $\rho_{\mathcal{A}}$ follows from the fact that there exists a finite chain of downward covers between any two atoms $A, B \in \mathcal{A}$ for which $A \succ B$ (Theorem 13.41). Finally, $\rho_{\mathcal{A}}$ is proper since every atom in $\rho(A)$ is a downward cover of A, and hence a proper specialization of A.　　　　　　　　　　　　□

Example 17.5 Suppose we have a language containing one binary predicate G, and two unary functions f and m. Suppose $G(x,y)$ is interpreted as "x is the grandfather of y", $f(x)$ is "the father of x", and $m(x)$ is "the mother of x". Given the positive examples $G(f(m(mary)),mary)$ and $G(f(f(john)),john)$, and the negative examples $G(f(mary),john)$ and $G(m(f(john)),john)$, a good theory would be "x is the grandfather of all those y for which x is the father of the father or mother of y". Or in atoms: $G(f(f(x)),x)$ and $G(f(m(x)),x)$.

Starting from the most general atom $G(x,y)$, we can use our downward refinement operator $\rho_{\mathcal{A}}$ to find a variant of $G(f(f(x)),x)$:

1. $G(f(z),y) \in \rho_{\mathcal{A}}(G(x,y))$
2. $G(f(f(z_1)),y) \in \rho_{\mathcal{A}}(G(f(z),y))$
3. $G(f(f(y)),y) \in \rho_{\mathcal{A}}(G(f(f(z_1)),y))$

Similarly, there is a $\rho_{\mathcal{A}}$-chain from $G(x,y)$ to a variant of $G(f(m(x)),x)$. ◁

Let us now consider the dual case of an *upward* refinement operator for the set of atoms. Since we already know what a complete set of upward covers of an atom is, an operator $\delta_{\mathcal{A}}$ can be defined straightforwardly as follows:

Definition 17.6 Let $\mathcal{A}$ be the set of atoms in a language. The upward refinement operator $\delta_{\mathcal{A}}$ for $\mathcal{A}$ is defined as follows:

1. For every $t = f(x_1,\ldots,x_n)$ in A, for which $x_1,\ldots,x_n$ are distinct variables and each occurrence of some x_i in A is within an occurrence of t, $\delta_{\mathcal{A}}(A)$ contains an atom obtained by replacing all occurrences of t in A by some new variable z not in A.

2. For every constant a in A and every non-empty subset of the set of occurrences of a in A, $\delta_A(A)$ contains an atom obtained by replacing those occurrences of a in A by some new variable z not in A.

3. For every variable x in A and every non-empty proper subset of the set of occurrences of x in A, $\delta_A(A)$ contains an atom obtained by replacing those occurrences of x in A by some new variable z not in A. ◇

Note that in the last item, we cannot replace *all* occurrences of x by a new variable z, for then we would get a variant of A. For instance, $P(z, a, z)$ is a variant of $A = P(x, a, x)$.

As in the case of ρ_A, it easily follows that δ_A is locally finite, complete and proper. We do not even have to presuppose a finite number of constants, function and predicate symbols for this, because when constructing $\delta_A(A)$ we only have to deal with the finite number of symbols in A—there is no need to introduce new constants, functions or predicates.

Theorem 17.7 *Let A be the set of atoms in a language. Then δ_A is an ideal upward refinement operator for $\langle A, \succeq \rangle$.*

17.3 Non-Existence of Ideal Refinement Operators

The previous section defined an ideal refinement operator for the set of atoms ordered by subsumption. In this section, we will show that for the most interesting quasi-orders on a clausal language, ideal refinement operators do not exist.

Lemma 17.8 *Let $\langle G, \geq \rangle$ be a quasi-ordered set. If there exists an ideal downward refinement operator for $\langle G, \geq \rangle$, then every $C \in G$ has a finite complete set of downward covers.*

Proof Suppose ρ is an ideal downward refinement operator for $\langle G, \geq \rangle$, and let $C \in G$. Construct the set dc from $\rho(C)$, as follows:

> $dc := \rho(C)$
> while there are $D, E \in dc$ such that $D \neq E$ and $D \geq E$,
>   do $dc := dc \backslash \{E\}$

Since ρ is ideal, $\rho(C)$ is finite, so the previous construction terminates and yields a finite set dc. By construction we have the following property:

(1) There are no $D, E \in dc$ such that $D \neq E$ and $D \geq E$.

Furthermore, by construction and by the completeness and properness of ρ, we have the following:

(2) For every $E \in G$: if $C > E$ then there is a $D \in dc$ such that $C > D \geq E$.

We will show that every member of dc is a downward cover of C. Suppose some $E \in dc$ is not. Then there is an $F \in G$ such that $C > F > E$, and by (2) there is a D such that $C > D \geq F > E$. But then $D, E \in dc$ with $D > E$, which contradicts (1). Hence dc is a finite set of downward covers of C. Furthermore, by (2) dc is complete.   □

The dual lemma can be proved analogously:

Lemma 17.9 *Let $\langle G, \geq \rangle$ be a quasi-ordered set. If there exists an ideal upward refinement operator for $\langle G, \geq \rangle$, then every $C \in G$ has a finite complete set of upward covers.*

Since we have already proved for the subsumption order and the implication order that there are clauses which do not have a finite complete set of *downward* covers (Propositions 14.40 and 15.28), and clauses that have no finite complete set of *upward* covers (Propositions 14.32 and 15.27), the non-existence of ideal refinement operators for these orders follows immediately.

Corollary 17.10 *Let C be a clausal language containing at least one predicate or function symbol of arity ≥ 2. Then there do not exist ideal downward or ideal upward refinement operators for $\langle C, \succeq \rangle$.*

Corollary 17.11 *Let C be a clausal language containing at least one predicate or function symbol of arity ≥ 2. Then there do not exist ideal downward or ideal upward refinement operators for $\langle C, \models \rangle$.*

These negative results still hold when we replace C by a Horn language $\mathcal{H}$. Of course, they also remain valid when we consider one of the orders with background knowledge of Chapter 16.

However, even in a situation where every clause *does* have a finite complete set of downward covers, defining $\rho(C)$ as a finite complete set of downward covers need not give an ideal downward refinement operator. Consider the infinite chain $C_2 \succ C_3 \succ \ldots \succ C_n \succ \ldots \succ C$ that we used in the proof of Proposition 14.32. Let $G = \{C, C_2, C_3, \ldots\}$. Then the set of all downward covers of C_i in G is $\{C_{i+1}\}$, and the set of downward covers of C is empty. However, due to the infinite length of the chain, C cannot be reached from some C_i by only considering downward covers. So a refinement operator defined as $\rho(C_i) = \{C_{i+1}\}$ is not complete, and hence not ideal. On the other hand, if we define $\rho(C_i) = \{C_{i+1}, C\}$, then ρ is ideal for $\langle G, \succeq \rangle$.

As is often the case, we cannot have it all: finiteness, completeness and properness cannot all be achieved at the same time. Hence in order to define a complete refinement operator, we have to give something up. Either we can drop one of the conditions of locally finiteness, completeness, and properness, or we have to restrict the language. The first approach is pursued in the next section, the second approach in the section after that. The refinement operators in the next sections are defined for general clausal languages, but they can easily be restricted to Horn clauses.

17.4 Complete Operators for Subsumption

Of the three conditions of locally finiteness, completeness and properness, finiteness seems indispensable: an infinite set $\rho(C)$ of refinements of a clause C cannot be handled well, because it would then be impossible to test all members of $\rho(C)$ in finite time. Furthermore, it is obvious that completeness is also a very valuable property, if you want to be able to guarantee that a solution will always be found whenever one exists. Of the three ideal properties, properness seems the least important. Therefore we will drop this requirement, and discuss the case of refinement operators that are locally finite and complete, but *improper*. For subsumption, such refinement operators exist, both for the downward and for the upward case.

17.4.1 Downward

If C subsumes D, then $C\theta \subseteq D$ for some substitution θ. Thus specialization under subsumption can be achieved by applying (elementary) substitutions and adding literals. In fact, when adding literals it is sufficient to add only *most general* literals, since these can always be instantiated by a substitution later on to get the right literals.

Definition 17.12 A literal $P(x_1, \ldots, x_n)$ or $\neg P(x_1, \ldots, x_n)$ is *most general* with respect to a clause C, if $x_1, \ldots, x_n$ are distinct variables not appearing in C. $\diamond$

Example 17.13 If $C = \{P(x, f(x))\}$, $D = \{P(a, f(a)), Q(a, y), \neg P(y, y)\}$, then a variant of D can be constructed from C by the following operations:

1. Add the literal $Q(x_1, x_2)$ (which is most general with respect to C) to C, then we get $\{P(x, f(x)), Q(x_1, x_2)\}$.
2. Add the most general literal $\neg P(y_1, y_2)$, then we obtain $\{P(x, f(x)), Q(x_1, x_2), \neg P(y_1, y_2)\}$.
3. Apply $\theta_1 = \{x/a\}$ to get $\{P(a, f(a)), Q(x_1, x_2), \neg P(y_1, y_2)\}$.
4. Apply $\theta_2 = \{x_1/a\}$ to get $\{P(a, f(a)), Q(a, x_2), \neg P(y_1, y_2)\}$.
5. Apply $\theta_3 = \{y_1/x_2\}$ to get $\{P(a, f(a)), Q(a, x_2), \neg P(x_2, y_2)\}$.
6. Apply $\theta_4 = \{y_2/x_2\}$ to get $\{P(a, f(a)), Q(a, x_2), \neg P(x_2, x_2)\}$, which is a variant of D. $\triangleleft$

This idea is the basis for our complete downward refinement operator. It was first defined by Laird in [Lai88], hence we call it ρ_L.

Definition 17.14 Let $\mathcal{C}$ be a clausal language. The downward refinement operator ρ_L for $\langle \mathcal{C}, \succeq \rangle$ is defined as follows:

1. For every variable z in C and every n-ary function symbol f in the language, let $x_1, \ldots, x_n$ be distinct variables not appearing in C. Let $\rho_L(C)$ contain $C\{z/f(x_1, \ldots, x_n)\}$.

2. For every variable z in C and every constant a in the language, let $\rho_L(C)$ contain $C\{z/a\}$.

3. For every two distinct variables x and z in C, let $\rho_L(C)$ contain $C\{z/x\}$.

4. For every n-ary predicate symbol P in the language, let $x_1,\ldots,x_n$ be distinct variables not appearing in C. Then $\rho_L(C)$ contains both $C \cup \{P(x_1,\ldots,x_n)\}$ and $C \cup \{\neg P(x_1,\ldots,x_n)\}$. $\qquad\qquad \diamondsuit$

Note that the literals $P(x_1,\ldots,x_n)$ and $\neg P(x_1,\ldots,x_n)$ that are added to C by the fourth item in the definition are most general with respect to C. The proof of locally finiteness and completeness is straightforward:

Theorem 17.15 *Let $\mathcal{C}$ be a clausal language, containing only a finite number of constants, function symbols, and predicate symbols. Then ρ_L is a locally finite and complete downward refinement operator for $\langle \mathcal{C}, \succeq \rangle$.*

Proof Locally finiteness follows immediately from the definition of ρ_L and the assumption of only a finite number of constants, function and predicate symbols.

For the completeness, let $C, D \in \mathcal{C}$ such that $C \succ D$. Then there is a substitution θ such that $C\theta \subseteq D$, where θ only acts on variables in C. Consider $D\backslash C\theta = \{M_1,\ldots,M_n\}$ ($n \geq 0$). For every M_i, there is a most general literal L_i, of which M_i is an instance. We can assume that for every $1 \leq i \leq n-1$, the variables in L_{i+1} do not appear in $C \cup \{L_1,\ldots,L_i\}$. Then by the fourth item in the definition of ρ_L we have a finite ρ_L-chain $C, C \cup \{L_1\}, C \cup \{L_1, L_2\},\ldots,C \cup \{L_1,\ldots,L_n\}$.

Furthermore, there is a substitution θ' such that $(C\cup\{L_1,\ldots,L_n\})\theta' = D$, where $\theta \subseteq \theta'$. It is easy to see that there exist elementary substitutions $\theta_1,\ldots,\theta_k$, such that $(C\cup\{L_1,\ldots,L_n\})\theta' = D$ and $(C\cup\{L_1,\ldots,L_n\})\theta_1\ldots\theta_k$ are variants (this is a simple generalization of the same result for atoms). The three kinds of elementary substitutions correspond to the first three items in the definition of ρ_L. Hence there is a finite ρ_L-chain (of length k) from $C \cup \{L_1,\ldots,L_n\}$ to a variant of D, and hence there exists a finite ρ_L-chain from C to a variant of D. $\qquad\qquad \square$

Since we already know that no ideal operators exist for this case, ρ_L cannot be proper. For instance, if $C = \{P(x)\}$ and $D = \{P(x), P(y)\}$, then $D \in \rho_L(C)$ and $C \sim D$. However, this D is needed in a ρ_L-chain from C to $\{P(a), P(b)\}$, as follows: $\{P(x)\}$, $\{P(x), P(y)\}$, $\{P(a), P(y)\}$, $\{P(a), P(b)\}$.

Notice that for every $\square \neq C \in \mathcal{C}$, we have $\square \succ C$, so $\rho_L^*(\square)$ contains a clause which is subsume-equivalent to C. In other words: if we start with the empty clause (as Shapiro's Model Inference Algorithm does), then for every $C \in \mathcal{C}$, a clause C' such that $C \sim C'$ can be reached by means of ρ_L.

17.4.2 Upward

In this subsection, we will define an upward refinement operator δ_u which is the dual of ρ_L. (The 'u' abbreviates 'unreduced', to distinguish the operator of this section from the operator δ_r for reduced clauses in the next section.) At first sight, it appears that inverting the four items in the definition of ρ_L suffices for the definition of δ_u. That is, given the four operations of (1) replacing $f(x_1, \ldots, x_n)$ by a new variable, (2) replacing some occurrences of a constant by a new variable, (3) replacing some (not all) occurrences of a variable by a new variable, and (4) removing a most general literal, we expect to be able to derive from C, after some refinement steps, a clause $E \sim D$ whenever $D \succ C$.

However, it is not quite as simple as that. As the next examples show, it is sometimes necessary to *duplicate literals* before inverting one of the elementary substitutions.

Example 17.16 Let $C = Even(x + x) \leftarrow Even(x)$ and $D = Even(x + y) \leftarrow Even(x), Even(y)$, where '$+$' is a binary function symbol, written in infix notation. Note that $D\{y/x\} = C$. However, we cannot reconstruct D from C simply by replacing some occurrences of x in C by y. The reason for this is that the substitution $\{y/x\}$ has decreased the number of literals in D: it has unified the literals $Even(x)$ and $Even(y)$ in the body of D. Thus in order to reconstruct D from C (i.e., to invert the elementary substitution $\{y/x\}$), we should first duplicate the literal $Even(x)$ in C. Doing this, we get $C' = Even(x + x) \leftarrow Even(x), Even(x)$. Now we can get from C' to D by replacing the 2nd and 4th occurrence of x in C' by y. ◁

Example 17.17 Something similar holds when we want to invert an elementary substitution of the kind $\{x/a\}$. Let $C = Even(a + a) \leftarrow Even(a)$ and $D = Even(x + a) \leftarrow Even(a), Even(x)$. Then $D\{x/a\} = C$. Again, the substitution has decreased the number of literals in D. Thus in order to invert the elementary substitution $\{x/a\}$ correctly, we again should first duplicate literals. Doing this, we get $C' = Even(a + a) \leftarrow Even(a), Even(a)$. Now we can get from C' to D by replacing the 1st and 4th occurrence of a in C' by x. ◁

In our upward refinement operator, $\delta(C)$ should contain a variant of every D for which $D\theta = C$, where θ is an elementary substitution. As can be seen from the above examples, it is sometimes necessary to duplicate literals in order to correctly invert an elementary substitution. Since duplication of literals is not allowed for clauses in set-notation, we will temporarily adopt ordered notation, treating clauses as disjunctions of not necessarily distinct literals. Actually, the particular order of literals in the clause is not important; we only use ordered notation here to enable a clause to contain literals more than once. We use $\vec{C}$ to denote such an ordered clause, and C to denote the set of literals in $\vec{C}$. Thus if $\vec{C} = P(x) \lor P(x) \lor \neg Q(x)$, which may also be written as $\vec{C} = P(x), P(x) \leftarrow Q(x)$, then $C = \{P(x), \neg Q(x)\}$.

Now the problem is: which literals should we duplicate, and how many times should we duplicate them? First, let us consider an elementary substitution of the kind $\theta = \{z/f(x_1, \ldots, x_n)\}$, such that $D\theta = C$. Note that such a substitution cannot unify literals in D, and hence cannot decrease the number of literals, because the variables $x_1, \ldots, x_n$ are required to be *new* variables. Thus to invert a substitution of this kind, we do not need to duplicate any literals. Here it suffices to simply replace all occurrences of $f(x_1, \ldots, x_n)$ in C itself by a new variable z to obtain D.

For the second kind of elementary substitution, $\theta = \{z/a\}$, things are different. As the last two examples showed, it is sometimes necessary to duplicate literals in order to be able to invert a substitution of this kind. Suppose we have the literal $L = P(a, x, a) \in C$. Then D contains literals $L_1, \ldots, L_n$ ($n \geq 1$), which are all mapped to L by this elementary substitution θ. Now the important point is that there is a finite upper bound on n. That is, only a limited number of distinct literals in D can be mapped to L by such an elementary substitution θ. In this particular case, n is at most 4: only the literals $L_1 = P(z, x, z)$, $L_2 = P(z, x, a)$, $L_3 = P(a, x, z)$ and $L_4 = P(a, x, a)$ are such that $L_i\theta = L$. This means that we need 4 copies of L in order to be able to invert any possible substitution $\theta = \{z/a\}$.

More generally, if some literal $L \in C$ contains the constant a k times, then there are 2^k ways in which we can replace some of these k occurrences by z. This means that we need at most 2^k copies of this literal before we apply the inverse substitution: given 2^k copies of L, we can invert the effects of any substitution $\{z/a\}$. Thus, if the literals $L_1, \ldots, L_n \in C$ contain the constant a respectively $k_1, \ldots, k_n$ times, then an ordered clause $\vec{C}$ obtained from C by duplicating L_1 2^{k_1} times, $\ldots$, and duplicating L_n 2^{k_n} times will be sufficient to invert any $\theta = \{z/a\}$ such that $D\theta = C$.

A similar argument holds when we want to invert an elementary substitution of the form $\{z/x\}$. For instance, in Example 17.16 we needed two copies of the literal $Even(x) \in C$. This is in accordance with our upper bound, since the literal contains x once, and $2^1 = 2$.

The following function *dup* computes the required ordered clauses, with the right number of duplications. The first argument of *dup* is the clause (set of literals) which has to be transformed, and the second argument is the term that is to be replaced by a new variable. The function *dup* returns a clause $\vec{C}$ with a sufficient number of duplications of literals.

Definition 17.18 Let $C = \{L_1, \ldots, L_n\}$ be a clause, and t be a term occurring in C. Suppose t occurs k_1 times in L_1, k_2 times in L_2, etc. Then $dup(C, t) = \vec{C}$ is an ordered clause consisting of 2^{k_1} copies of L_1, 2^{k_1} copies of L_2, $\ldots$, 2^{k_n} copies of L_n. $\Diamond$

Note that if some $L \in C$ does not contain the term t, then $\vec{C}$ contains L $2^0 = 1$ times, as it should.

Example 17.19 Let $C = Q(x) \leftarrow P(x, x), P(f(x), a), P(u, v)$. Then we have $dup(C, x) = Q(x), Q(x) \leftarrow P(x, x), P(x, x), P(x, x), P(x, x), P(f(x), a)$, $P(f(x), a), P(u, v)$, and we have $dup(C, a) = Q(x) \leftarrow P(x, x), P(f(x), a)$, $P(f(x), a), P(u, v)$. $\triangleleft$

Using the function *dup* to duplicate literals, we can now define our upward refinement operator δ_u:

Definition 17.20 Let C be a clausal language. The upward refinement operator δ_u for $\langle C, \succeq \rangle$ is defined as follows:

1. For every $t = f(x_1, \ldots, x_n)$ in C, for which all x_i are distinct variables and each occurrence of x_i in C is within an occurrence of t, $\delta_u(C)$ contains the clause obtained by replacing all occurrences of t in C by some new variable z not previously in C.

2. For every constant a in C and every non-empty subset of the set of occurrences of a in $\vec{C} = dup(C, a)$, if $\vec{D}$ is the ordered clause obtained by replacing those occurrences of a in $\vec{C}$ by the new variable z, then $\delta_u(C)$ contains D (D is the set of literals in the ordered clause $\vec{D}$).

3. For every variable x in C and every non-empty proper subset of the set of occurrences of x in $\vec{C} = dup(C, x)$, if $\vec{D}$ is the ordered clause obtained by replacing those occurrences of x in $\vec{C}$ by the new variable z, then $\delta_u(C)$ contains D.

4. If $C = D \cup \{L\}$ and L is a most general literal with respect to D, then $\delta_u(C)$ contains D. ◇

Example 17.21 Let $C = Q(x) \leftarrow P(x,x), P(f(x),a), P(u,v)$. The four items in the definition of $\delta_u(C)$ generate the following:

1. Since x in $f(x)$ also appears outside of occurrences of $f(x)$, this item cannot be applied.

2. $\vec{C} = dup(C, a) = Q(x) \leftarrow P(x,x), P(f(x),a), P(f(x),a), P(u,v)$. The following members of $\delta_u(C)$ can be obtained from this:

   $\vec{D} = Q(x) \leftarrow P(x,x), P(f(x),z), P(f(x),z), P(u,v)$ can be obtained from $\vec{C}$ by replacing both occurrences of a by z, so $D = Q(x) \leftarrow P(x,x), P(f(x),z), P(u,v)$ (which is $\vec{D}$ without duplicate literals) is a member of $\delta_u(C)$.

   $\vec{D} = Q(x) \leftarrow P(x,x), P(f(x),z), P(f(x),a), P(u,v)$ can be obtained from $\vec{C}$ by replacing the first occurrence of a by z, $D = Q(x) \leftarrow P(x,x), P(f(x),z), P(f(x),a), P(u,v)$.

   Note that the latter D can also be obtained from $\vec{C}$ by replacing the *second* occurrence of a by z.

3. $dup(C, x) = Q(x), Q(x) \leftarrow P(x,x), P(x,x), P(x,x), P(x,x), P(f(x),a), P(f(x),a), P(u,v)$. This generates (among others) the following members of $\delta_u(C)$:

   $Q(x) \leftarrow P(x,x), P(x,z), P(z,x), P(z,z), P(f(x),a), P(f(z),a), P(u,v)$.
   $Q(x), Q(z) \leftarrow P(x,z), P(f(x),a), P(u,v)$.

   $dup(C, u)$ and $dup(C, v)$ yield only clauses of $\delta_u(C)$ that are subsume-equivalent to C.

4. Since $\neg P(u, v)$ is most general with respect to $D = Q(x) \leftarrow P(x, x)$, $P(f(x), a)$, we have $D \in \delta_u(C)$.

◁

The proof of locally finiteness and completeness is analogous to the proof of Theorem 17.15.

Theorem 17.22 *Let C be a clausal language. Then δ_u is a locally finite and complete upward refinement operator for $\langle C, \succeq \rangle$.*

We already know that δ_u cannot be proper. For instance, if we let $C = \{P(x), P(y)\}$ and $D = \{P(x)\}$, then $D \in \delta_u(C)$ and $C \sim D$.

17.5 Ideal Operators for Finite Sets

Dropping the condition of properness allows us to define locally finite and complete refinement operators for infinite languages. Alternatively, we could stick to all three requirements of an ideal operator, and restrict the language to a finite set. This approach is discussed in the present section.

In fact, if $\langle G, \geq \rangle$ is a quasi-order, G is finite and $\geq$ is decidable, then there *always* exists an ideal refinement operator for $\langle G, \geq \rangle$. It is easy to show that every $C \in G$ has a finite complete set $dc(C)$ of downward covers, and a finite complete set $uc(C)$ of upward covers in G. These can be found by exhaustively searching the whole quasi-order. If we define $\rho(C) = dc(C)$ and $\delta(C) = uc(C)$, then by definition ρ and δ are locally finite and proper. To show the completeness of ρ, let $C, D \in G$ such that $C > D$. Then either D is a downward cover of C, in which case there is an $E \in \rho(C)$ such that $D \sim E$, or there is an $E \in \rho(C)$ such that $C > E > D$. In the latter case, we can find an $F \in \rho(E)$ such that $C > E > F \geq D$, etc. Since G is finite and ρ is proper, we must eventually find a ρ-chain from C to a member of the equivalence class of D, so ρ is complete, and hence ideal. The idealness of δ is shown similarly.

The fact that there *always* exists an ideal refinement operator for finite sets is mainly of theoretical interest, because in practice it will often be very inefficient to find the sets $dc(C)$ and $uc(C)$ for every $C \in G$. Thus in practice, we usually prefer more constructive—though possibly improper—refinement operators over such very elaborate ideal operators.

In this section we will define ideal downward and upward refinement operators for the set of *reduced* clauses bounded by a size-restriction. These operators take reduced clauses as input, and return sets of reduced clauses. The definitions are constructive, in the sense that they are based on elementary substitutions, as were the operators we saw in earlier sections. However, the operators still involve some subsumption tests. Shapiro defined a downward refinement operator ρ_0 for reduced clauses bounded by *size* in [Sha81b], and included a completeness proof. Unfortunately, this proof contains some errors, and his operator is actually incomplete. For a detailed discussion of this incompleteness, we refer to [LN93] and [Nib93].

Instead of a *size*-bound, we will here use *newsize*. We assume some *newsize*-bound (k, m) is given. The set of all reduced clauses in the language is denoted by $\mathcal{R}$, we use $\mathcal{R}^{newsize}$ to denote the set of reduced clauses bounded by (k, m), and $\mathcal{C}^{newsize}$ for the set of all (possibly non-reduced) clauses bounded by (k, m). The sets $\mathcal{R}^{newsize}$ and $\mathcal{C}^{newsize}$ are finite up to variants, as we showed in Proposition 14.44. This guarantees that ideal downward and upward refinement operators exist for $\mathcal{R}^{newsize}$. The main difficulty for completeness proofs for the particular operators defined below, is to show that all clauses in a refinement chain from some $C \in \mathcal{R}^{newsize}$ to some $D \in \mathcal{R}^{newsize}$ are themselves also members of $\mathcal{R}^{newsize}$.

17.5.1 Downward

Here we will define an ideal downward refinement operator ρ_r for $\mathcal{R}^{newsize}$ (the 'r' subscript abbreviates 'reduced'). One of the main problems in defining an ideal downward refinement operator for reduced clauses, is the fact that addition of more than one literal in one step is sometimes needed to get from one reduced clause to another, as described in the next example.

Example 17.23 Consider the following reduced clauses:

$$C = Q(x) \leftarrow P(x, a)$$
$$D = Q(x) \leftarrow P(x, a), P(y, z), P(z, v)$$

We can prove that there is no E such that $C \succ E \succ D$. Thus for an ideal refinement operator ρ for reduced clauses, we must have $D \in \rho(C)$. However, D contains two more literals than C. This means that a single application of one of the four items in the definition of ρ_L is not sufficient to get us from C to D. ◁

To overcome the problem of this example, we will use non-reduced members of the subsume-equivalence classes of C and D to form a bridge between the reduced clause C and its reduced proper refinements D. For this we make use of the Inverse Reduction Algorithm, which computes the (usually non-reduced) members of the equivalence class of C of at most m literals. Let $eq^m(C)$ denote the set of clauses that the algorithm returns. We assume this set does not contain any variants, which implies that it is finite. The next example shows how these non-reduced clauses can solve the problem of Example 17.23:

Example 17.24 Consider C and D of the previous example. If $m \geq 4$, then we have the clauses $C' = Q(x) \leftarrow P(x, a), P(y, z), P(u, v) \in eq^m(C)$ and $D' = Q(x) \leftarrow P(x, a), P(y, z), P(z, v) \in eq^m(D)$ (in fact, $D' = D$). Since $C'\{u/z\} = D'$ and $C \succ D'$, we can make the reduction of D' (which is D

itself in this example) a member of $\rho(C)$. Thus by applying an elementary substitution to a *non-reduced* member of the equivalence class of C, we can get to D.   ◁

Recall from Chapter 14 that two literals are *compatible* if they have the same predicate symbol and sign, and incompatible otherwise. The fourth item of the definition of ρ_r below adds a most general literal $L = P(x_1, \ldots, x_n)$ or $L = \neg P(x_1, \ldots, x_n)$ to the reduced clause C, which is incompatible with every literal in C. It is easy to see that $D = C \cup \{L\}$ is reduced as well. Furthermore, the next lemma guarantees that C properly subsumes this D.

Lemma 17.25 *Let C be a clause, and L be a most general literal with respect to C. Then $C \succ C \cup \{L\}$ iff L is incompatible with every literal $M \in C$.*

Proof

$\Rightarrow$: Suppose $C \succ C \cup \{L\}$ and L is compatible with some $M \in C$. Let θ be defined on variables in L only, such that $L\theta = M$. Then $(C \cup \{L\})\theta = C$, contradicting $C \cup \{L\} \not\succ C$.

$\Leftarrow$: Suppose L is incompatible with every literal $M \in C$ and $C \not\succ C \cup \{L\}$. Since $C \succeq C \cup \{L\}$ and $C \not\succ C \cup \{L\}$, we have $C \sim C \cup \{L\}$. Then there must be a θ such that $(C \cup \{L\})\theta \subseteq C$. But then $L\theta \in C$, contradicting the assumption that L is incompatible with every $M \in C$.   □

Using the set $eq^m(C)$ for the first three items and incompatible literals for the fourth item, we will now define our ideal downward refinement operator ρ_r.

Definition 17.26 Let (k, m) be a pair of natural numbers, and $\mathcal{R}^{newsize}$ be a language of reduced clauses bounded by (k, m). For a given $C \in \mathcal{R}^{newsize}$, let $\rho_r(C)$ contain all $D \in \mathcal{R}^{newsize}$ that satisfy one of the following conditions:

1. $C \succ D$, and there are $C' \in eq^m(C)$ and $D' \in eq^m(D)$ such that $C'\{z/f(x_1, \ldots, x_n)\} = D'$, where $x_1, \ldots, x_n$ are distinct variables not appearing in C.

2. $C \succ D$, and there are $C' \in eq^m(C)$ and $D' \in eq^m(D)$ such that $C'\{z/a\} = D'$.

3. $C \succ D$, and there are $C' \in eq^m(C)$ and $D' \in eq^m(D)$ such that $C'\{z/x\} = D'$.

4. $|C| < m$, and $x_1, \ldots, x_n$ are distinct variables not appearing in C, $L = (\neg)P(x_1, \ldots, x_n)$ is a most general literal with respect to C that is incompatible with every literal in C, and $D = C \cup \{L\}$.   ◇

Refinement operators as above can easily be adapted for Horn clauses, by restricting $\mathcal{R}^{newsize}$ to the set of reduced Horn clauses bounded by (k, m). In that case, the only D's in the above definition that we need to consider, are Horn clauses.

Example 17.27 Consider the following clauses:

$$C = Q(x) \leftarrow P(x, a)$$
$$D = Q(x) \leftarrow P(x, a), P(y, z), P(z, y)$$

Let $\mathcal{R}^{newsize}$ be bounded by $(3, 4)$, and suppose the language contains only the predicates P and Q, the constant a, and the unary function f. The set $eq^4(C)$ contains, among others, the following clauses:

1. $Q(x) \leftarrow P(x, a)$ (C itself)
2. $Q(x), Q(y) \leftarrow P(x, a), P(y, a)$
3. $Q(x) \leftarrow P(x, a), P(y, z), P(u, v)$

From these respective clauses, we can derive for example the following reduced clauses in $\rho_r(C)$:

1. $Q(f(z)) \leftarrow P(f(z), a)$ (by the first item in the definition)
2. $Q(a) \leftarrow P(a, a)$ (by the second item: $\{y/a\}$ and reduction)
3. $Q(x) \leftarrow P(x, a), P(y, z), P(z, v)$ (by the third item)

From the last of these three clauses, we can then derive D in one further refinement step, so $D \in \rho_r^2(C)$.   ◁

We will first prove the properness of ρ_r, then its locally finiteness, and then its completeness.

Proposition 17.28 ρ_r *is proper for* $\langle \mathcal{R}^{newsize}, \succeq \rangle$.

Proof Let $C \in \mathcal{R}^{newsize}$. If $D \in \rho_r(C)$ is generated by one of the first three items, then by definition $C \succ D$. If D is generated by the fourth item, then $C \succ D$ by the previous Lemma.   □

Locally finiteness is easy to prove. The set of clauses generated by the first three items in the definition of $\rho_r(C)$ is obtained as follows. (1) Construct the set $eq^m(C)$; (2) apply the three kinds of elementary substitutions to all clauses in this set; (3) reduce the resulting clauses; (4) remove from the resulting reduced clauses all those that are not properly subsumed by C or that are not bounded by (k, m). Since $eq^m(C)$ is finite, the number of elementary substitutions is finite. Moreover, reduction is computable and subsumption is decidable, so these 4 instructions can be completed in a finite number of steps. Finally, since the number of predicate symbols that can be used for the fourth item of the definition is finite, $\rho_r(C)$ is finite and computable.

Proposition 17.29 *Given a finite number of constants, function and predicate symbols, ρ_r is locally finite for* $\langle \mathcal{R}^{newsize}, \succeq \rangle$.

For the completeness, we need the following lemmas, the proofs of which are illustrated by some examples.

Lemma 17.30 Let $C, D \in \mathcal{R}^{newsize}$ be reduced clauses such that $C \succ D$, and let $C' \in eq^m(C)$ and $D' \in eq^m(D)$ satisfy $C'\theta = D'$, for some θ. Then there is an $E \in \rho_r(C)$ such that $E \succeq D$.

Proof For simplicity, we identify variant clauses in this proof. Since $C'\theta = D'$, there is a chain of clauses $C' = C_0, C_1, \ldots, C_n = D'$ for which $C_i = C_{i-1}\theta_i$, where θ_i is an elementary substitution as used in the first three items of the definition of ρ_r. Note that these C_i are bounded by (k, m), and are not necessarily reduced. Let C_j be the first C_i for which $C \succ C_i$. Such a C_j exists, since $C \succ D \sim D'$. Let E be a reduction of C_j. We have $C \sim C_{j-1}$, so $C_{j-1} \in eq^m(C)$. Then since $C_{j-1}\theta_i = C_j$ and E is a reduction of C_j, $\rho_r(C)$ contains E. Finally $E \succeq D$, because $E \sim C_j$ and $C_j\theta_{j+1} \ldots \theta_n = D' \sim D$. $\square$

Example 17.31 Let $C = \{P(a, w), P(x, b), P(c, y), P(z, d)\}$ and let $D = \{P(a, b), P(c, b), P(c, d), P(a, d)\}$. If we let $C' = C$, $D' = D$, and $\theta = \{w/b, x/c, y/d, z/a\}$, then $C'\theta = D'$. The substitution θ can be decomposed into the elementary substitutions $\theta_1 = \{w/b\}$, $\theta_2 = \{x/c\}$, $\theta_3 = \{y/d\}$, and $\theta_4 = \{z/a\}$. This gives the following chain of clauses:

$$C' = C_0 = \{P(a, w), P(x, b), P(c, y), P(z, d)\}$$
$$C_1 = C_0\theta_1 = \{P(a, b), P(x, b), P(c, y), P(z, d)\}$$
$$C_2 = C_1\theta_2 = \{P(a, b), P(c, b), P(c, y), P(z, d)\}$$
$$C_3 = C_2\theta_3 = \{P(a, b), P(c, b), P(c, d), P(z, d)\}$$
$$C_4 = C_3\theta_4 = \{P(a, b), P(c, b), P(c, d), P(a, d)\} = D'.$$

C_1 is properly subsumed by C_0, so $\rho_r(C)$ contains the clause $E = \{P(a, b), P(c, y), P(z, d)\}$ (the reduction of C_1), which subsumes D. $\triangleleft$

Lemma 17.32 Let $C, D \in \mathcal{R}^{newsize}$ be reduced clauses such that $C \succ D$ and $C \subset D$. Then there is an $E \in \rho_r(C)$ such that $E \succeq D$.

Proof Let F be a maximal subset of $D \backslash C$, such that $(C \cup F) \sim C$. That is, for every literal $M \in D \backslash (C \cup F)$, we have $C \succ (C \cup F \cup \{M\})$. Let L be a most general literal with respect to $C \cup F$ such that $L\theta = M$ for some $M \in D \backslash (C \cup F)$ and some θ.

If $(C \cup F \cup \{L\}) \not\succ (C \cup F)$, then by Lemma 17.25, L is incompatible with every literal in $(C \cup F)$, so L is incompatible with every literal in C. Hence by the fourth item in the definition of ρ_r, we have $E = (C \cup \{L\}) \in \rho_r(C)$. Furthermore, we have $E \succeq D$ since $E = C \cup \{L\} \succeq C \cup \{M\} \subseteq D$.

Otherwise, $C' = C \cup F \cup \{L\}$ and $D' = C \cup F \cup \{M\}$ satisfy $C' \succ D'$ and $C'\theta = D'$. Then by Lemma 17.30, there is an $E \in \rho_r(C)$ such that $E \succeq D$. $\square$

Example 17.33 Let $C = \{P(x)\}$ and $D = \{P(x), \neg Q(a, x)\}$. The only subset F of $D \backslash C$ such that $(C \cup F) \sim C$, is the empty set. $M = \neg Q(a, x)$ is the only literal in $D\backslash C$, and $L = \neg Q(y, z)$ is a most general literal such that $M\theta = L$, where $\theta = \{y/a, z/x\}$. Now $E = C \cup \{L\}$ is reduced, $E \in \rho_r(C)$, and $E \succeq D$. ◁

Example 17.34 Let $C = \{P(x), \neg Q(x, a)\}$ and $D = \{P(x), \neg Q(x, a), \neg Q(y, z), \neg Q(z, y)\}$. Now $F = \{\neg Q(y, z)\}$ is a maximal subset of $D\backslash C$ such that $(C \cup F) \sim C$. Taking $M = \neg Q(z, y)$, we get $L = \neg Q(u, v)$ as a most general literal with respect to $C \cup F$. If we let $C' = C \cup F \cup \{L\}$, $D' = C \cup F \cup \{M\}$, then $C' \in eq^m(C)$ and $D' \in eq^m(D)$ (assuming $m \geq 4$). Moreover, $C'\theta = D'$ for $\theta = \{u/z, v/y\}$. Hence by Lemma 17.30, there is an $E \in \rho_r(C)$ such that $E \succeq D$, for instance $E = \{P(x), \neg Q(x, a), \neg Q(y, z), \neg Q(z, v)\}$. ◁

Proposition 17.35 ρ_r *is complete for* $\langle \mathcal{R}^{newsize}, \succeq \rangle$.

Proof Let $C, D \in \mathcal{R}^{newsize}$ be reduced clauses such that $C \succ D$. Then there is a θ such that $C\theta \subseteq D$. Let F be a reduction of $C\theta$. Then either $C \succ F$ or $C \sim F$. If $C \succ F$, then C and F satisfy the conditions of Lemma 17.30. If, on the other hand, $C \sim F$, then by Proposition 14.11, F is a variant of C, we have $F \subset D$, and F and D satisfy the conditions of Lemma 17.32.

In either case, there is a $C_1 \in \rho_r(C)$ such that $C \succ C_1 \succeq D$. If $C_1 \sim D$, we have found a ρ_r-chain from C to $C_1 \sim D$. Otherwise, we can again find a $C_2 \in \rho_r(C_1)$ such that $C \succ C_1 \succ C_2 \succeq D$, etc. Since $\mathcal{R}^{newsize}$ is finite up to variants and ρ_r is proper, this chain $C = C_0, C_1, C_2, \ldots$ cannot go on without end. Thus eventually we must find a finite ρ_r-chain $C = C_0, C_1, \ldots, C_n = E$, such that $D \sim E$. □

Corollary 17.36 *Let* (k, m) *be a pair of natural numbers, and* $\mathcal{R}^{newsize}$ *be a language of reduced clauses bounded by* (k, m), *containing only a finite number of constants, function symbols, and predicate symbols. Then* ρ_r *is an ideal downward refinement operator for* $\langle \mathcal{R}^{newsize}, \succeq \rangle$.

The refinement operator ρ_r for $\mathcal{R}^{newsize}$ can easily be changed to an ideal refinement operator ρ_c for $\mathcal{C}^{newsize}$, by defining $\rho_c(C) = \rho_r(D)$, where D is a reduction of C.

17.5.2 Upward

Analogously, we can define an ideal *upward* refinement operator δ_r for a finite quasi-ordered set $\langle \mathcal{R}^{newsize}, \succeq \rangle$. As in the upward refinement operator δ_u, we sometimes have to duplicate literals. But here the ordered clauses obtained after duplication of some literals need at most have m literals, because of the (k, m)-bound. Thus we can use a set $eq^m(\vec{C})$, which contains every ordered clause of at most m literals that is subsume-equivalent to $\vec{C}$. This set can be computed using an algorithm similar to the Inverse Reduction Algorithm. We will just define δ_r here, leaving the proof of idealness to the reader.

Definition 17.37 Let (k, m) be a pair of natural numbers, and $\mathcal{R}^{newsize}$ be a language of reduced clauses bounded by (k, m). For a given $C \in \mathcal{R}^{newsize}$, let $\delta_r(C)$ contain all $D \in \mathcal{R}^{newsize}$ that satisfy one of the following conditions:

1. $D \succ C$, and there are $\vec{C'} \in eq^m(C)$ and $\vec{D'} \in eq^m(D)$ such that $\vec{D'}\{z/f(x_1, \ldots, x_n)\} = \vec{C'}$, where $x_1, \ldots, x_n$ are distinct variables not appearing in $\vec{D'}$.
2. $D \succ C$, and there are $\vec{C'} \in eq^m(C)$ and $\vec{D'} \in eq^m(D)$ such that $\vec{D'}\{z/a\} = \vec{C'}$.
3. $D \succ C$, and there are $\vec{C'} \in eq^m(C)$ and $\vec{D'} \in eq^m(D)$ such that $\vec{D'}\{z/x\} = \vec{C'}$.
4. $C = D \cup \{L\}$ and L is a most general literal with respect to D, incompatible with every literal in D. $\diamond$

17.6 Optimal Refinement Operators

Apart from the concept of an *ideal* refinement operator, one can also define *optimal* refinement operators, which feature a different combination of desirable properties. Optimal refinement operators are studied in [DB93, Gro92, VL93]. In a quasi-ordered set of clauses $\langle G, \geq \rangle$, where G contains a top element $\square$, De Raedt and Bruynooghe [DB93] discuss downward refinement operators ρ satisfying the following properties:

1. For every $C \in G$, $\rho(C)$ is a set of maximal specializations (downward covers, in our terms) of C.
2. $\rho^*(\square) = G$.

Let us call such an operator ρ a *cover*-refinement operator, since it only employs downward covers. By definition, ρ is proper.

Definition 17.38 Let ρ be a cover-refinement operator for a quasi-order $\langle G, \geq \rangle$. ρ is called *optimal* if for every $C, D, E \in G$, $E \in \rho^*(C)$ and $E \in \rho^*(D)$ implies $C \in \rho^*(D)$ or $D \in \rho^*(C)$. $\diamond$

In an optimal cover-refinement operator ρ, there is exactly one ρ-chain from C to D if $C > D$. Translated to the refinement graph, there is exactly one path in the graph from such a C to D. This means that the refinement graph becomes a *tree*, with $\square$ as root. Optimality is clearly desirable for efficiency reasons.

Unfortunately, optimal cover-refinement operators do not exist for most quasi-ordered languages. In fact, cover-refinement operators do not exist at all for most quasi-ordered languages of interest. Since we have already proved in Proposition 14.32 that the clause $C = P(x_1, x_1)$ has no upward covers under subsumption, there is no D for which C is a downward cover. Thus there is no D for which $C \in \rho(D)$, and consequently $C \notin \rho^*(\square)$.

Proposition 17.39 *Let $\mathcal{C}$ be a clausal language containing at least one predicate or function symbol of arity ≥ 2. Then there does not exist a cover-refinement operator for $\langle \mathcal{C}, \succeq \rangle$.*

The same result of course also holds for $\langle \mathcal{C}, \models \rangle$, for the orders with background knowledge from Chapter 16, and for Horn languages $\mathcal{H}$.

17.7 Refinement Operators for Theories

For a clausal language ordered by logical implication, it is much less obvious how we could define a locally finite and complete (but improper) refinement operator than for languages ordered by subsumption. Since the Subsumption Theorem tells us that implication is equivalent to a combination of resolution and subsumption, a first suggestion for the downward case might be to just add the set of self-resolvents of C to $\rho_L(C)$. That is, we could define $\rho_I(C) = \rho_L(C) \cup \{D \mid D$ is a resolvent of C and $C\}$.

However, this approach does not yield a complete refinement operator. For instance, suppose $C = P(f(x)) \leftarrow P(x)$ and $D = P(f^3(x)) \leftarrow P(x)$, then $C \models D$. We have $\rho_I(C) = \rho_L(C) \cup \{P(f^2(x)) \leftarrow P(x)\}$. Unfortunately, the only clauses in $\rho_I(C)$ that imply D, are subsume-equivalent to C. It can be shown that there is no clause $E \in \rho_I^*(C)$ such that $D \Leftrightarrow E$.

The problem here is that in the SLD-derivation of D from C, D is a resolvent of *two* different clauses: $P(f^2(x)) \leftarrow P(x)$, and C itself. Therefore it is rather difficult to define a refinement operator for implication as a function from *a single clause* to a set of clauses.

However, a refinement operator can be defined for arbitrary quasi-ordered sets. For the operators of previous sections, we took this set to consist of individual clauses, ordered by subsumption. But we can also consider the set of all *theories*, ordered by logical implication. In other words, we can take the set G of Definitions 17.1 and 17.2 to consist of finite *sets* of clauses, rather than individual clauses. ρ_I then becomes a function from a theory to a set of theories.

Suppose $\mathcal{S}$ is the set of theories in a clausal language $\mathcal{C}$. The negative result on downward covers from Chapter 15 carries over to $\mathcal{S}$ ordered by implication:

Proposition 17.40 *Let $\mathcal{C}$ be a clausal language containing a binary predicate P, $\mathcal{S}$ be the set of theories in $\mathcal{C}$, and $C = \{P(x_1, x_2), P(x_2, x_1)\}$. Then $\{C\} \in \mathcal{S}$ has no finite complete set of downward covers in $\langle \mathcal{S}, \models \rangle$.*

Proof Suppose $F = \{\Sigma_1, \ldots, \Sigma_n\} \subseteq \mathcal{S}$ is a finite complete set of downward covers of $\{C\}$ in $\langle \mathcal{S}, \models \rangle$. We can assume none of the Σ_i contains any tautologies. Note that since $\{C\} \models \Sigma_i$ and C contains only positive literals, it follows from the Subsumption Theorem that $C \succ D^{pos}$ for every $D \in \Sigma_i$ (here D^{pos} denotes the set of positive literals in D). This means that F would remain a finite complete set of downward covers of $\{C\}$ in $\langle \mathcal{S}, \models \rangle$ if we remove all negative literals from the clauses in the Σ_i's. Thus we can assume each clause in each Σ_i contains only positive literals.

Let Σ be the union of all Σ_i's. We will show that Σ contains a finite complete set of downward covers of C in $\langle \mathcal{C}, \models \rangle$, yielding a contradiction with Proposition 15.28. Firstly, let $D \in \mathcal{C}$ be such that $C \models D$, then we have to show that there is an $E \in \Sigma$ such that $C \models E \models D$. Since $\{C\} \models \{D\}$ and F is a finite complete set of downward covers of $\{C\}$ in $\langle \mathcal{S}, \models \rangle$, there is a $\Sigma_i \in F$ such that $\Sigma_i \models \{D\}$. But since each clause in Σ_i only contains positive literals, this means that some $E \in \Sigma_i$ subsumes D. Hence there is an $E \in \Sigma$ such that $C \models E \models D$. Secondly, for every $D \in \Sigma$ there is an i such that $D \in \Sigma_i$. Hence $C \models D$ because $C \models \Sigma_i$, and $D \not\models C$ because $\Sigma_i \not\models C$. Thus each $D \in \Sigma$ is a proper specialization of C. Then it follows that Σ contains a finite complete set of downward covers of C in $\langle \mathcal{C}, \models \rangle$. But this is not possible. $\qquad\square$

Thus by Lemma 17.8, there is no ideal downward refinement operator for $\langle \mathcal{S}, \models \rangle$. As before, we drop the condition of properness, and we try to construct a locally finite and complete, but improper operator for $\langle \mathcal{S}, \models \rangle$. This operator ρ_I (the 'I' stands for 'implication') employs three operations: (1) add to Σ all resolvents of clauses in Σ; (2) add to Σ some clauses subsumed by a $C_i \in \Sigma$ (using ρ_L); (3) delete a clause from Σ.

Definition 17.41 Let $\mathcal{C}$ be a clausal language, containing only a finite number of constants, function symbols, and predicate symbols. Let $\mathcal{S}$ be the set of finite subsets of $\mathcal{C}$. The downward refinement operator ρ_I for $\langle \mathcal{S}, \models \rangle$ is defined as follows:

1. $(\Sigma \cup \{R \mid R \text{ is a resolvent of } C_1, C_2 \in \Sigma\}) \in \rho_I(\Sigma)$.
2. If $\Sigma = \{C_1, \ldots, C_n\}$, then $(\Sigma \cup \rho_L(C_i)) \in \rho_I(\Sigma)$, for each $1 \leq i \leq n$.
3. If $\Sigma = \{C_1, \ldots, C_n\}$, then $(\Sigma \backslash \{C_i\}) \in \rho_I(\Sigma)$, for each $1 \leq i \leq n$. $\quad\diamond$

Note that every theory in $\rho_I(\Sigma)$ that is specified by one of the first two items in the definition of ρ_I is logically equivalent to Σ. This shows that ρ_I is not proper.

The completeness of ρ_I follows from the Subsumption Theorem, which tells us that logical implication can be implemented by a combination of resolution and subsumption:

Theorem 17.42 *Let $\mathcal{C}$ be a clausal language, containing only a finite number of constants, function symbols, and predicate symbols. Let $\mathcal{S}$ be the set of finite subsets of $\mathcal{C}$. Then ρ_I is a locally finite and complete downward refinement operator for $\langle \mathcal{S}, \models \rangle$.*

Proof Locally finiteness follows from the definition of ρ_I and the locally finiteness of ρ_L.

For the completeness of ρ_I, suppose $\Sigma, \Gamma \in \mathcal{S}$, such that $\Sigma \models \Gamma$ and $\Gamma \not\models \Sigma$. Let $\{C_1, \ldots, C_n\}$ be the set of non-tautologous clauses in Γ. Since $\Sigma \models \Gamma$, we have $\Sigma \models C_i$, for every $1 \leq i \leq n$. C_i is not a tautology, so by the Subsumption Theorem there is a derivation $R_1^i, \ldots, R_{k_i}^i = D_i \ (k_i \geq 1)$ from Σ, where D_i subsumes C_i. Let $k = \max\{k_1, \ldots, k_n\}$. From the first item in the definition of ρ_I, there is a ρ_I-chain $\Sigma_1 = \Sigma, \Sigma_2, \ldots, \Sigma_k$, such that $\Sigma_{j+1} = \Sigma_j \cup \{R \mid R \text{ is a resolvent of } C_1, C_2 \in \Sigma_j\}$, for each $1 \leq j \leq k-1$. Then $\{D_1, \ldots, D_n\} \subseteq \Sigma_k$.

Now since $D_1 \succeq C_1$, it follows from the completeness of ρ_L that by the second item in the definition, there is a ρ_I-chain from Σ_k to a set Δ_1, such that $\Sigma \subseteq \Delta_1$ and there is a $C_1' \in \Delta_1$ which is subsume-equivalent to C_1. By the same reasoning, there is a ρ_I-chain from Δ_1 to a set Δ_2, such that $\Delta_1 \subseteq \Delta_2$ and there is a $C_2' \in \Delta_2$ which is subsume-equivalent to C_2. Repeating this argument a few times, there is a ρ_I-chain from Σ to a set Δ_n, such that $\{C_1', \ldots, C_n'\} \subseteq \Delta_n$, and C_i and C_i' are subsume-equivalent for each $1 \leq i \leq n$.

Now by the third item in the definition of ρ_I, we can remove from Δ_n all clauses except for these C_i'. Thus there is a ρ_I-chain from Σ to a set $\{C_1', \ldots, C_n'\}$, which is logically equivalent to Γ. $\square$

It is instructive to compare ρ_I with the UDS specialization of Chapter 12. In fact, if we restrict $\mathcal{S}$ to the set of definite programs in some language, and we use only *binary* resolvents, then ρ_I is almost the same as UDS specialization. There are two differences. Firstly, the first item in the definition of ρ_I adds all resolvent of clauses in Σ, while UDS specialization would only add the set of all resolvents of some clause C and other members of Σ, resolved upon some atom in the body of C. Secondly, while UDS specialization simply adds a clause that is subsumed by a member of the original set, the second item of ρ_I implements this subsumption stepwisely via ρ_L.

Our downward refinement operator ρ_I combines resolution, subsumption (via ρ_L), and clause deletion. Dually, it may be possible to define an *upward* refinement operator for $\langle \mathcal{S}, \models \rangle$, in terms of *inverse* resolution, *inverse* subsumption (via δ_u), and, if necessary, clause addition. However, as we have seen in Chapter 11, inverse resolution faces many indeterminacies. Therefore we will not pursue definining an upward refinement operator for $\langle \mathcal{S}, \models \rangle$ here.

17.8 Summary

Downward refinement operators compute sets of specializations of a clause, *upward* ones compute sets of generalizations. A refinement operator is *ideal* if it is *locally finite*, *complete*, and *proper*. We defined $\rho_{\mathcal{A}}$ and $\delta_{\mathcal{A}}$, which are ideal downward and upward refinement operators for atoms.

For clausal languages ordered by subsumption or stronger orders, ideal refinement operators do not exist. They can be approximated by dropping the requirement of properness, or by bounding the language. ρ_L and δ_u are locally finite and complete, but improper downward and upward refinement operators for clausal languages ordered by subsumption. Furthermore, ρ_r and δ_r are ideal downward and upward refinement operators for reduced clausal languages ordered by subsumption and bounded by some *newsize*-bound.

(Optimal) cover-refinement operators do not exist for clausal languages ordered by subsumption. For the set of theories ordered by logical implication, we defined the locally finite and complete, but improper downward refinement operator ρ_I.

Chapter 18

PAC Learning

18.1 Introduction

The theory of *learnability* concerns the questions of what *can* or *cannot* be learned, and, in particular, what can be learned *efficiently*. Initial analysis of learnability in machine learning was mainly done in terms of Gold's paradigm of *identification in the limit* [Gol67], which we already saw in Chapter 10. The idea here is that a learning algorithm is given an infinite sequence of examples for some unknown *target* set. Each example is an object x of the domain, together with a label indicating whether or not x is an element of the target set. The learning algorithm reads examples one by one, and after each new example it constructs a theory for the examples read so far. The algorithm is said to *identify the target set in the limit*, if the sequence of theories that it constructs, "converges" to the target set after only a finite number of examples have been read. The major disadvantage of identification in the limit is that, even though you can prove in some cases that there exists an n such that a correct theory will be identified after n examples, you usually do not know what this n is, so you cannot know for sure when you may end the learning.

Nowadays, Valiant's paradigm of *PAC learnability* [Val84] is usually considered to provide a better model of learnability. While identification in the limit is concerned with *exactly* identifying the target in a *finite* number of steps, the aim of PAC learning is to find a good *approximation* to the target in a *small* (polynomially-bounded) number of steps. A PAC algorithm is an algorithm that takes examples concerning some unknown *target concept*, and learns a concept which is *probably approximately correct*. That is, a PAC algorithm will, with high probability, learn a concept which diverges only slightly from the target concept. (The relation between 'concept' and our earlier notion of a 'theory' will be explained below, at the beginning of Section 18.6.)

In this chapter we give an overview of PAC-learnability settings and results relevant for ILP. These learnability results complement the learning
operators of the previous chapters. PAC learnability is concerned with two
major complexity issues: how many *examples* do we need to ensure that we
will probably find an approximately correct concept (*sample complexity*), and
how many *steps* do we need to take to find such a concept (*time complexity*)?
We consider the study of learnability theory to be both highly interesting,
and very important for ILP. Unfortunately, this theory presupposes quite a
lot of other theory, including Turing machines, NP-completeness, statistics,
etc. A fully self-contained treatment of learnability theory would require an
introduction into these topics as well, which would take us far beyond the
scope of the present book. Therefore we have to settle for a much more sketchy
treatment. In particular, we will leave out all proofs of results here, refering
instead to the original papers where those results were reported.

The chapter is organized as follows. In the next section we motivate and
define the standard setting for PAC learning. In Sections 18.3 and 18.4 we
go into sample complexity and time complexity, respectively. Our definitions in Sections 18.2–18.4 follow those of Natarajan [Nat91] quite closely.
Section 18.5 discusses a number of related learning settings. Sections 18.6
and 18.7 are the main sections of this chapter. Here we show how the PAC
setting applies to ILP, and we give an overview of the main results that have
been reported for the normal and nonmonotonic problem settings, respectively.

18.2   PAC Algorithms

Before formally introducing the PAC setting, let us first illustrate and motivate it by means of a metaphorical example. Suppose some biology student
wants to learn from examples to distinguish insects from other animals. That
is, he or she wants to learn the concept of an 'insect' within the domain of
all animals. A teacher gives the student examples: a positive example is an
insect, a negative example is some other animal. The student has to develop
his or her own concept of what an insect is on the basis of these examples.
Now, the student will be said to have learned the concept *approximately correctly*, if, when afterwards tested, he or she classifies only a small percentage
of given test animals incorrectly as insect or non-insect. In other words, his or
her own developed concept should not diverge too far from the real concept
of an 'insect'.

In the interest of fairness, we require that the animals given as examples
during the learning phase, and the animals given afterwards as test, are all
selected *by the same teacher* (or at least by teachers with the same incli-
nations). For suppose the student learns from a teacher with a particular
interest in European insects, whose examples are mainly European animals.
Then it would be somewhat unfair if the animals that were given afterwards

to test the student, were selected by a different teacher having a decisive interest in the very different set of African insects. In other words: the student should be taught and tested by the same teacher.

Let us now formalize this setting:

Definition 18.1 A *domain* X is a set of strings over some finite alphabet Σ. The *length* of some $x \in X$ is the string length of x. $X^{[n]}$ denotes the set of all strings in X of length at most n.

A *concept* f is a subset of X, a *concept class* $\mathcal{F}$ is a set of concepts. An *example* for f is a pair (x, y), where $x \in X$, y is called the *label* of the example, $y = 1$ if $x \in f$ and $y = 0$ otherwise. If $y = 1$ then the example is *positive*, if $y = 0$ it is *negative*.

If f and g are two concepts, then $f \Delta g$ denotes the *symmetric difference* of f and g: $f \Delta g = (f \backslash g) \cup (g \backslash f)$. $\diamond$

In our metaphor, X would be the set of descriptions of all animals, the target concept $f \subseteq X$ would be the set of descriptions of all insects, and the student would develop his or her own concept $g \subseteq X$ on the basis of a number of positive and negative examples (i.e., insects and non-insects). The symmetric difference $f \Delta g$ would be the set of all animals which the student classifies incorrectly: all insects that he or she takes to be non-insects and all non-insects he or she takes to be insects.

For technical reasons, we restrict the examples to those of length at most some number n, so all examples are drawn from $X^{[n]}$. Note that $X^{[n]}$ is a finite set. We assume these examples are given according to some unknown probability distribution $\mathbf{P}$ on $X^{[n]}$, which reflects the particular interests of the teacher. If $S \subseteq X^{[n]}$, we let $\mathbf{P}(S)$ denote the probability that a member of $X^{[n]}$ that is drawn according to $\mathbf{P}$, is a member of S (i.e., $\mathbf{P}(S) = \sum_{s \in S} \mathbf{P}(s)$). Now suppose the student has developed a certain concept g. Then in the test phase, he will misclassify some object $x \in X^{[n]}$ iff $x \in f \Delta g$. Thus we can say that g is *approximately correct* if the probability that such a misclassified object is given during the test phase, is small:

$$\mathbf{P}(f \Delta g) \leq \varepsilon,$$

where $\varepsilon \in (0, 1]$ is called the *error* parameter. For instance, if $\varepsilon = 0.05$, then there is a chance of at most 5% that an arbitrary given test object from $X^{[n]}$ will be classified incorrectly. Note that the set of examples that is given, as well as the evaluation of approximate correctness of the learned concept g, depends on the *same* probability distribution $\mathbf{P}$. This formally reflects the fairness requirement that the student is taught and tested by the same teacher.

After all these preliminaries, we can now define a *PAC algorithm* as an algorithm which, under some unknown distribution $\mathbf{P}$ and target concept f, learns a concept g which is *probably* approximately correct. 'Probably' here means with probability at least $1 - \delta$, where $\delta \in (0, 1]$ is called the *confidence parameter.* For instance, if $\delta = 0.1$ and the algorithm is run an infinite number of times, at least 90% of these runs would output an approximately correct concept. The constants ε, δ, and n are given by the user as input to the algorithm.

Definition 18.2 A learning algorithm L is a *PAC algorithm* for a concept class $\mathcal{F}$ over domain X if

1. L takes as input real numbers $0 < \varepsilon, \delta \leq 1$ and a natural number $n \in \mathbf{N}$, where ε is the *error* parameter, δ is the *confidence* parameter, and n is the *length* parameter.
2. L may call the procedure EXAMPLE, each call of which returns an example for some concept $f \in \mathcal{F}$ according to an arbitrary and unknown probability distribution $\mathbf{P}$ on $X^{[n]}$.
3. For all concepts $f \in \mathcal{F}$ and all probability distributions $\mathbf{P}$ on $X^{[n]}$, L outputs a concept g, such that with probability at least $1-\delta$, $\mathbf{P}(f\Delta g) \leq \varepsilon$.
   $\diamond$

A technicality: a PAC algorithm should be *admissible*, meaning that for any input ε, δ, n, for any sequence of examples that EXAMPLE may return, and for any concept g, the probability that L outputs g should be well defined.

18.3   Sample Complexity

Having a PAC algorithm for a concept class $\mathcal{F}$ is nice, but having an *efficient* PAC algorithm for $\mathcal{F}$ is even nicer. In this section we analyze this efficiency in terms of the *number of examples* the algorithm needs (the *sample complexity*), while in the next section we treat the *number of steps* the algorithm needs to take (*time complexity*).

The sample complexity of a learning algorithm can be seen as a function from its inputs ε, δ, and n, to the maximum number of examples that the algorithm reads when learning an unknown target concept under an unknown probability distribution. Since the examples are drawn according to a probability distribution, different runs of the same algorithm with the same input and the same target concept and distribution may still read different examples. Thus different runs of the same algorithm with the same input may need a different number of examples in order to find a satisfactory concept. Therefore, the sample complexity as defined below relates to the maximum number of examples *over all runs* of the algorithm with the same input.

Definition 18.3 Let L be a learning algorithm for concept class $\mathcal{F}$. The *sample complexity* of L is a function s, with parameters ε, δ and n. It returns the maximum number of calls of EXAMPLE made by L, for all runs of L with inputs ε, δ, n, for all $f \in \mathcal{F}$ and all $\mathbf{P}$ on $X^{[n]}$. If no finite maximum exists, we let $s(\varepsilon, \delta, n) = \infty$.
   $\diamond$

Of course, for the sake of efficiency we want this complexity to be as small as possible. A concept class is usually considered to be efficiently PAC learnable—as far as the required number of examples is concerned—if there is a PAC algorithm for this class for which the sample complexity is bounded from above by a polynomial function in $1/\varepsilon$, $1/\delta$, and n. Of course, even polynomials may grow rather fast (consider n^{100}), but still their growth rate is much more moderate than, for instance, exponential functions.

Definition 18.4 A concept class $\mathcal{F}$ is called *polynomial sample PAC learnable*, if a PAC algorithm exists for f, which has a sample complexity bounded from above by a polynomial in $1/\varepsilon$, $1/\delta$, and n.   ◇

Note that polynomial sample PAC learnability has to do with the *worst case*: if the worst case cannot be bounded by a polynomial, a concept class is not polynomial sample PAC learnable, even though there may be PAC algorithms which take only a small polynomial number of examples on average.[1]

A crucial notion in the study of sample complexity is the dimension named after Vapnik and Chervonenkis [VC71].

Definition 18.5 Let $\mathcal{F}$ be a concept class on domain X. We say that $\mathcal{F}$ *shatters* a set $S \subseteq X$, if $\{f \cap S \mid f \in \mathcal{F}\} = 2^S$, i.e., if for every subset S' of S, there is an $f \in \mathcal{F}$ such that $f \cap S = S'$.   ◇

Note that if $\mathcal{F} \subseteq \mathcal{G}$ and $\mathcal{F}$ shatters S, then $\mathcal{G}$ shatters S as well. Also note that if $T \subseteq S$ and $\mathcal{F}$ shatters S, then $\mathcal{F}$ shatters T as well. In particular, $T = \emptyset$ is shattered by any non-empty $\mathcal{F}$. The Vapnik-Chervonenkis dimension of $\mathcal{F}$ depends on the largest sets that are shattered by $\mathcal{F}$.

Definition 18.6 Let $\mathcal{F}$ be a concept class on domain X. The *Vapnik-Chervonenkis dimension* (VC dimension) of $\mathcal{F}$, denoted by $\mathbf{D}_{VC}(\mathcal{F})$, is the greatest integer d such that there exists a set $S \subseteq X$ with $|S| = d$ that is shattered by $\mathcal{F}$. $\mathbf{D}_{VC}(\mathcal{F}) = \infty$ if no greatest d exists.   ◇

Note that if $\mathcal{F} = 2^S$, then $\mathcal{F}$ shatters S. Thus if $\mathcal{F} = 2^S$ for some finite set S, then $\mathcal{F}$ has $|S|$ as VC dimension.

Example 18.7 Let $X = \{1, 2, 3, 4\}$ and $\mathcal{F} = \{\{1\}, \{2\}, \{3\}, \{4\}, \{1, 2\},$ $\{2, 3\}, \{1, 3, 4\}, \{1, 2, 3, 4\}\}$ be a concept class. Then $\mathcal{F}$ shatters the set $S = \{1, 2\}$, because $\{f \cap S \mid f \in \mathcal{F}\} = \{\emptyset, \{1\}, \{2\}, \{1, 2\}\} = 2^S$. Thus $\mathcal{F}$'s "shattering" of S intuitively means that $\mathcal{F}$ "breaks" S into all possible pieces.

$\mathcal{F}$ also shatters $S' = \{1, 2, 3\}$, because $\{f \cap S' \mid f \in \mathcal{F}\} = \{\emptyset, \{1\}, \{2\},$ $\{3\}, \{1, 2\}, \{2, 3\}, \{1, 3\}, \{1, 2, 3\}\} = 2^S$. $\mathcal{F}$ does not shatter $S'' = \{1, 2, 3, 4\}$, since there is for instance no $f \in \mathcal{F}$ with $f \cap S'' = \{1, 4\}$. In general, there is no set of four or more elements shattered by $\mathcal{F}$, so $\mathbf{D}_{VC}(\mathcal{F}) = |S'| = 3$.   ◁

---

[1]Muggleton and Page's model of *U-learnability* provides a framework which is better suited for *average case* analysis [MP94a]. However, thus far much more research has gone into PAC learning than U-learning.

Some related dimensions are discussed in [Nat91, NP93].

Since we are actually dealing with $X^{[n]}$ rather than with X itself, we need the following definitions, which "project" the VC dimension on $X^{[n]}$.

Definition 18.8 The *projection* of a concept f on $X^{[n]}$ is $f^{[n]} = f \cap X^{[n]}$. The *projection* of a concept class $\mathcal{F}$ on $X^{[n]}$ is $\mathcal{F}^{[n]} = \{f^{[n]} \mid f \in \mathcal{F}\}$.   ◇

Definition 18.9 Let $\mathcal{F}$ be a concept class on domain X. $\mathcal{F}$ is *of polynomial VC dimension* if $\mathbf{D}_{VC}(\mathcal{F}^{[n]})$ is bounded from above by some polynomial in n.   ◇

The following fundamental result, due to [BEHW89], states the relation between polynomial sample PAC learnability and the VC dimension. For a proof we refer to Theorem 2.3 of [Nat91].

Theorem 18.10 *Let $\mathcal{F}$ be a concept class on domain X. Then $\mathcal{F}$ is polynomial sample PAC learnable iff $\mathcal{F}$ is of polynomial VC dimension.*

Thus if we are able to show that some concept class is of polynomial VC dimension, we have thereby shown it to be polynomial sample PAC learnable.

18.4   Time Complexity

In outline, the analysis of *time complexity* is similar to the analysis of sample complexity: the time complexity of a learning algorithm is a function from its inputs to the maximum number of computational steps the algorithm takes on those inputs. Here we assume that the procedure EXAMPLE takes at most some fixed constant number of steps. Again, we are mainly interested in the existence of learning algorithms which have a polynomially-bounded time complexity. (Actually, the work on computationally efficient *learning* algorithms is just a special case of work on efficient algorithms in general, for which see for instance [GJ79, CLR90].)

18.4.1   Representations

Unfortunately, things are somewhat more complicated than in the last section: the "number of examples" that an algorithm needs is unambiguous, but what about the "number of computational steps"? What counts as a computational step? In order to make this notion precise, we have to turn to some precise model of computation, where it is clear what a single step is. Usually Turing machines are used for this.[2] We will not go into details, but will just note here that a Turing machine programmed to learn some concept will often not be able to output the learned concept g itself efficiently,

---

[2]Since Turing machines cannot represent arbitrary real numbers, we have to restrict the parameters δ and ε somewhat, for instance by only allowing them to be the inverses of integers.

for instance because $|g|$ can be very large or even infinite. Therefore, instead of the concept g itself, the Turing machine will have to output some finite representation of g, which we call a *name* of g. Abstractly, a *representation* specifies the relation between concepts and their names:

Definition 18.11 Let $\mathcal{F}$ be a concept class, and Σ a set of symbols. Σ^* denotes the set of all finite strings over Σ. A *representation* of $\mathcal{F}$ is a function $R : \mathcal{F} \to 2^{\Sigma^*}$, where we require that for each $f \in \mathcal{F}$, $R(f) \neq \emptyset$ and for every distinct $f, g \in \mathcal{F}$, $R(f) \cap R(g) = \emptyset$. For each $f \in \mathcal{F}$, $R(f)$ is the set of *names* of f in R.

The *length* of a name $r \in R(f)$ is simply the string length of r, i.e., the number of symbols in r. The *size* of f in R is the length of the shortest name in $R(f)$, denoted by $l_{min}(f, R)$. $\diamond$

The set of symbols Σ that is used here, need not be the same as the alphabet used for the strings in the domain X in Definition 18.1. The requirement that $R(f) \neq \emptyset$ for each $f \in \mathcal{F}$ means that each concept in $\mathcal{F}$ has at least one name, while $R(f) \cap R(g) = \emptyset$ for every distinct f, g means that no two distinct concepts share the same name. Note the difference between the string length of a string $x \in X$ and the size of a concept $f \in \mathcal{F}$ in R: the latter depends on R, the former does not.[3]

The aim of the analysis of time complexity is to be able to bound by a polynomial function the number of steps needed for learning. However, if a learning algorithm provides us with a name of an approximately correct concept in a polynomial number of steps, but we are still not able to decide in polynomial time whether that concept actually contains a given $x \in X$, we would still have a computational problem. Therefore, a representation R should be *polynomially evaluable*: given an $x \in X$ and a name r of a concept f, we should be able to find out, in polynomial time, whether $x \in f$, using r. This is defined as follows.

Definition 18.12 Let R be a representation of a concept class $\mathcal{F}$ over domain X. We say that R is *evaluable* if there exists an algorithm which, for any $f \in \mathcal{F}$, takes any $x \in X$ and any name $r \in R(f)$ as input, and decides in a finite number of steps whether $x \in f$. R is *polynomially evaluable* if there is such an algorithm, which has running time bounded by a polynomial in the lengths of x and r. $\diamond$

In the sequel, whenever we write 'representation' we actually mean a *polynomially evaluable* representation.

---

[3] To give the reader of flavour of what these definitions will be used for: in Section 18.6 we will formalize the normal ILP setting in these terms. Since examples are usually ground atoms, the domain X will consist of all ground atoms in some language, and a concept will be a set of ground atoms. A definite program Π will represent, or be a name of, the concept which equals its least Herbrand model M_Π.

18.4.2 Polynomial Time PAC Learnability

In order to be able to study time complexity, we need to change the definition of a PAC learning algorithm somewhat to incorporate the representation: a PAC algorithm for a concept class $\mathcal{F}$ *in representation* R should output a *name* of a concept g, rather than g itself.

Now time complexity can be defined as follows, where we introduce a new parameter l that bounds the size of the concepts considered:

Definition 18.13 Let L be a learning algorithm for concept class $\mathcal{F}$ in representation R. The *time complexity* of L is a function t, with parameters ε, δ, n, and l. It returns the maximum number of computational steps made by L, for all runs of L with inputs $\varepsilon, \delta, n, l$, for all $f \in \mathcal{F}$ such that $l_{min}(f, R) \leq l$, and all $\mathbf{P}$ on $X^{[n]}$. If no finite maximum exists, we define $t(\varepsilon, \delta, n, l) = \infty$. $\Diamond$

Definition 18.14 A concept class $\mathcal{F}$ is called *polynomial time PAC learnable* in a representation R, if a PAC algorithm exists for f in R, which has a time complexity bounded by a polynomial in $1/\varepsilon$, $1/\delta$, n, and l. $\Diamond$

Let us suppose we have some concept class $\mathcal{F}$ of polynomial VC dimension. Then $\mathcal{F}$ is polynomial sample PAC learnable, so we know we only need a polynomial number of examples. Now to achieve polynomial time PAC learnability, it is sufficient to have an algorithm that finds, in a polynomial number of steps, a concept that is *correct* with respect to these examples. The following definition of correctness is similar in spirit to the one we gave in Chapter 9: a concept is correct if it contains all positive examples and no negative ones.[4]

Definition 18.15 Let g be a concept and S be a set of examples. We say g is *correct* with respect to S, if $x \in g$ for every $(x, 1) \in S$ and $x \notin g$ for every $(x, 0) \in S$. $\Diamond$

An algorithm which returns a name of a concept that is correct with respect to a set of examples S is called a *fitting*, since it finds a concept that "fits" the given examples. As always, we want a fitting to work efficiently. The running time of the fitting should be bounded by a polynomial in two variables. The first is the *length* of S, which we define as the sum of the lengths of the various $x \in X$ that S contains. The second is the size of the shortest correct concept. For this, we will extend the l_{min} notation as follows. If S is a set of examples, then $l_{min}(S, R)$ is the size of the concept $f \in \mathcal{F}$ with smallest size that is correct with respect to S. If no such correct $f \in \mathcal{F}$ exists, then $l_{min}(S, R) = \infty$.

Definition 18.16 An algorithm Q is said to be a *fitting* for a concept class $\mathcal{F}$ in representation R if

---

[4]In the literature on computational learning theory, usually the term 'consistent' is used instead of 'correct'. We use 'correct' here in accordance with our earlier definitions.

1. Q takes as input a set S of examples.
2. If there exists a concept in $\mathcal{F}$ that is correct with respect to S, then Q outputs a name of such a concept.

If Q is a deterministic algorithm such that the number of computational steps of Q is bounded from above by a polynomial in the length of S and $l_{min}(S, R)$, then Q is called a *polynomial time fitting*. $\diamond$

As the next theorem (Theorem 3.1 of [Nat91]) shows, the existence of such a fitting is indeed sufficient for the polynomial time PAC learnability of a concept class of polynomial VC dimension.

Theorem 18.17 *Let $\mathcal{F}$ be a concept class of polynomial VC dimension, and R be a representation of $\mathcal{F}$. If there exists a polynomial time fitting for $\mathcal{F}$ in R, then $\mathcal{F}$ is polynomial time PAC learnable in R.*

Conversely, it is also possible to give a necessary condition for polynomial time PAC learnability in terms of so-called *randomized* polynomial time fittings. We will not go into that here (see Theorem 3.2 of [Nat91]), but just mention that it can be used to establish negative results: if no such fitting for $\mathcal{F}$ in R exists, then $\mathcal{F}$ is not polynomial time PAC learnable in R.

18.5   Some Related Settings

The standard PAC setting of the previous sections may be varied somewhat. In this section, we will mention some alternatives.

18.5.1   Polynomial Time PAC Predictability

In the ordinary PAC setting, a PAC algorithm for a concept class $\mathcal{F}$ reads examples from an unknown target concept f from $\mathcal{F}$, and has to construct a concept g, *also from $\mathcal{F}$*, which is approximately correct. This may lead to a seemingly paradoxical situation: we would expect that learning a superset of $\mathcal{F}$ is at least as hard as learning $\mathcal{F}$ itself, but this need not be the case in the ordinary PAC setting. Namely, it may be that there is no polynomial time PAC algorithm for some concept class $\mathcal{F}$ in some representation R, while for some larger concept class $\mathcal{G} \supset \mathcal{F}$ there *is* such a polynomial time PAC algorithm. The latter algorithm, when given examples for some target concept $f \in \mathcal{F}$, always constructs a name of a probably approximately correct concept $g \in \mathcal{G}$ in polynomial time. Still, $\mathcal{F}$ itself may be hard to learn, because the requirement that the output concept should be a member of $\mathcal{F}$ may be very hard to meet.

We can take this into account by loosening the requirement on g somewhat, and allow it to be a member of a broader concept class $\mathcal{G}$, of which $\mathcal{F}$ is a subset. This gives the learning algorithm more freedom, which may facilitate the learning task. Suppose we have a concept class $\mathcal{F}$, a broader concept class $\mathcal{G} \supseteq \mathcal{F}$, and a representation R of $\mathcal{G}$ (which is of course also a representation of $\mathcal{F}$). Suppose, furthermore, that there exists a learning algorithm L for $\mathcal{F}$ in R, which is just like a PAC algorithm for $\mathcal{F}$ in R, except that it outputs a name of a concept g such that $g \in \mathcal{G}$ but not necessarily $g \in \mathcal{F}$. In this case, we say that $\mathcal{F}$ is *PAC predictable in R in terms of $\mathcal{G}$*. If, furthermore, the time complexity of algorithm L is bounded by a polynomial in $1/\varepsilon$, $1/\delta$, n, and l, we say that $\mathcal{F}$ is *polynomial time* PAC predictable in R in terms of $\mathcal{G}$. If some $\mathcal{G}$ exists such that $\mathcal{F}$ is polynomial time PAC predictable in R in terms of $\mathcal{G}$, we will simply say that $\mathcal{F}$ is polynomial time PAC predictable in R.

Clearly, if some concept class $\mathcal{F}$ is polynomial time PAC learnable in some R, it is also polynomial time PAC predictable in R: simply put $\mathcal{G} = \mathcal{F}$. Hence the setting of polynomial time PAC predictability may be used to establish negative results: if we can prove that some concept class $\mathcal{F}$ is not polynomial time PAC predictable in R in terms of any $\mathcal{G}$, we have thereby also shown that $\mathcal{F}$—as well as any superset of $\mathcal{F}$—is not polynomial time PAC learnable in R. Some results listed below in Section 18.6 actually take this form. The converse need not hold: some classes are polynomial time PAC predictable, but not polynomial time PAC learnable (see Sections 1.4 and 1.5 of [KV94] for an example). Hence polynomial time PAC predictability is strictly weaker than polynomial time PAC learnability.

18.5.2 Membership Queries

We may facilitate the learning task by allowing a PAC algorithm to make use of various kinds of *oracles*. As explained in Chapter 10, an oracle is a device which returns answers to certain questions (*queries*). The most straightforward kind are the *membership* queries. Here the oracle takes some $x \in X$ as input, and returns 'yes' if x is a member of the target concept, and 'no' if not. For the PAC algorithm that uses an oracle, the oracle is like a black box: you pose a question and get an answer, but do not know *how* the oracle constructs it answer. Like the EXAMPLE procedure, oracles are assumed to run in at most some fixed constant number of steps.

If a concept class $\mathcal{F}$ is polynomial time PAC learnable in some R by an algorithm which makes membership queries, we will say that $\mathcal{F}$ is polynomial time PAC learnable in R *with membership queries*. Analogously, we can define PAC predictability with membership queries. Note that if an algorithm makes membership queries, it in a way "creates its own examples." Note also that a polynomial time algorithm can make at most a polynomial number of queries, since each query counts for at least one computational step.

18.5.3 Identification from Equivalence Queries

While polynomial time PAC predictability is strictly weaker than polynomial time PAC learnability, *polynomial time identification from equivalence queries*, introduced by Angluin [Ang87], is strictly stronger. In this setting, we have an oracle which takes a name of a concept g as input, and answers 'yes' if g equals the target concept f, and 'no' otherwise. In case of a 'no', it also returns a randomly chosen *counterexample* $x \in f \Delta g$. There is no need for the oracle to provide the correct label of the counterexample x, because the algorithm can find this out for itself: if $x \in g$ then $x \notin f$, and if $x \notin g$ then $x \in f$. When equivalence queries are available, the requirement that an algorithm outputs a name of an approximately correct concept is replaced by the requirement that the target concept is *identified exactly*: an algorithm that is allowed to make equivalence queries should output a name of the target concept.

Consider a concept class $\mathcal{F}$ and a representation R of $\mathcal{F}$. Let L be an algorithm which uses equivalence queries in order to learn some unknown concept $f \in \mathcal{F}$ under some unknown probability distribution $\mathbf{P}$, and which takes as input an upper bound l on $l_{min}(f, R)$ and an upper bound n on the length of the counterexamples from the oracle. If this algorithm always outputs a name of the target concept, we say $\mathcal{F}$ is *identifiable from equivalence queries* in R. If the running time of the algorithm L is bounded by a polynomial in its inputs l and n, then $\mathcal{F}$ is *polynomial time* identifiable from equivalence queries in R. As in the case of membership queries, an algorithm with a polynomially-bounded running time can make only a polynomially-bounded number of equivalence queries.

It is shown in Section 2.4 of [Ang88] that if a concept class is polynomial time identifiable from equivalence queries in some R, then it is also polynomial time PAC learnable in R. The converse does not hold. Thus, while PAC predictability can be used to establish negative results, identification from equivalence queries may be used for positive results: if we can prove that some concept class $\mathcal{F}$ is polynomial time identifiable from equivalence queries, we have thereby also shown that $\mathcal{F}$, as well as any subset of $\mathcal{F}$, is polynomial time PAC learnable in R.

If polynomial time identification of $\mathcal{F}$ from equivalence queries is done by an algorithm which makes use of equivalence queries as well as membership queries, then we say $\mathcal{F}$ is *polynomial time identifiable from equivalence and membership queries* in R. This implies polynomial time PAC learnability with membership queries.

For an overview of other kinds of queries, we refer to [Ang88].

18.5.4 Learning with Noise

In many learning tasks that involve real-world data, the examples may contain errors (*noise*). There are various ways in which the analysis of noise may be modelled in the theoretical setting for PAC learnability. We will discuss only two kinds of noise here: Valiant's *malicious* noise [Val85], which is also sometimes called *adversarial* noise, and Angluin and Laird's *random classi-*

fication noise [AL88]. For other kinds of noise, see [Lai88, Slo95]. (The way noise may be treated in practice will be further discussed in Section 19.5.)

Firstly, in the malicious noise model, a malicious adversary of the learning algorithm tinkers with the examples: for each example that the learning algorithm reads, there is a fixed, unknown probability $0 \leq \eta$ that the adversary has changed the original, correct example (x, y) to any other (x', y')-pair he chooses. Since y' may not be the correct label for x', the adversary may introduce noise in this way. The adversary is assumed to be omnipotent and omniscient—in particular, he has knowledge of the learning algorithm he is trying to deceive. This means that the learning algorithm should be able to cope even with the worst possible changes in the examples.

Secondly, in the random classification noise model, the EXAMPLE procedure is replaced by a procedure EXAMPLE$^\eta$, and there is a fixed, unknown probability $0 \leq \eta < 0.5$ that the label of an example provided by this procedure is incorrect. For instance, suppose $\eta = 0.1$. If a learning algorithm receives an example (x, y) from EXAMPLE$^\eta$, then there is a probability of 10% that y is incorrect.

In both models, the actual noise rate η is unknown to the learning algorithm. However, an upper bound η_b on the noise rate is given as an additional input parameter to a PAC algorithm, where $0 \leq \eta \leq \eta_b < 0.5$. This η_b is added as a parameter to the time complexity function as well. If there is a PAC algorithm for a concept class $\mathcal{F}$ in some representation R, working in the presence of malicious (resp. random classification) noise, with time complexity bounded by a polynomial in $1/\varepsilon$, $1/\delta$, n, l, and $1/(1 - 2\eta_b)$, then $\mathcal{F}$ is said to be polynomial time PAC learnable in R *with malicious (resp. random classification) noise*.[5] Similarly, we can define PAC predictability with malicious or random classification noise.

18.6   Results in the Normal ILP Setting

Most research in PAC learning has focused on learning various classes of formulas in *propositional* logic. Here the domain X consists of strings of bits (zeros and ones), so a concept is a set of such strings. Each string of length n is an assigment of truth values to the n propositional atoms $p_1, \ldots, p_n$. For instance, the string 101 makes p_1 true, p_2 false, and p_3 true. Thus a string of length n may be seen as an *interpretation* of a propositional language with atoms $p_1, \ldots, p_n$, in the sense of Chapter 1. A propositional formula ϕ containing $p_1, \ldots, p_n$ represents (or is a name of) the concept which consists of all strings of length n that make ϕ true. In other words, ϕ represents the set of its models. For an overview of results in this setting, we refer to [Nat91, AB92, KV94].

---

[5]Kearns' *statistical query method* [Kea93, KV94] provides a way to establish positive learnability results in the presence of random classification noise. Kearns also showed that the assumption that the learning algorithm is given η_b is not necessary.

Below, we will tune the PAC setting to the normal ILP problem setting, which is rather different from the propositional case, and give an overview of the main results that have been obtained here. In Section 18.7, we tune the PAC setting to the *nonmonotonic* ILP problem setting, which may be seen as a generalization of the propositional case.

18.6.1 The Normal ILP Setting in PAC Terms

We will here restrict attention to learning definite programs from positive and negative examples which are ground atoms, labeled with their truth value. Because each example is a ground atom, it is natural to take the set of ground atoms in some language as our domain X. The alphabet Σ used for this is simply the alphabet of the underlying first-order language. Every concept is then a subset of X, i.e., a set of ground atoms, and every concept class is a set of sets of ground atoms.

Now the important thing is to recognise that *definite programs can be used to represent such concepts*: the definite program Π represents its least Herbrand model M_Π. That is, the least Herbrand model M_Π of a definite program Π is a concept, and Π can be seen as a *name* of this concept. Let us call this representation $\mathcal{D}$ (for Definite programs). Here we take the length of a clause to be its string length (including the '$\leftarrow$', ',', '(', and ')' symbols), and the length of a program to be the sum of the lengths of its members. For instance, the length of a program containing $P(a)$ and $P(f(x)) \leftarrow P(x), Q(x)$ is $4 + 17 = 21$. Using this representation, a PAC algorithm takes ground atoms with their truth values as examples, and should return a definite program Π such that Π has a probably approximately correct least Herbrand model: if f is the target concept, then, with probability at least $1 - \delta$, we should have $\mathbf{P}(f \Delta M_\Pi) \leq \varepsilon$. Since distinct programs may have the same least Herbrand model, some concepts will have more than one name in $\mathcal{D}$. On the other hand, however, note that there are also concepts *without* a name in this representation: for some concepts f, there is no Π with $M_\Pi = f$ (see Theorem 9.9). Therefore we can only consider the learnability of concept classes in which each concept is represented by at least one definite program.

One further issue has to be raised: *is $\mathcal{D}$ polynomially evaluable*? Or in other words: can $\Pi \models A$ be decided in polynomial time for arbitrary definite programs Π and ground atoms A? The answer is clearly negative: in general $\Pi \models A$ is not even decidable, let alone decidable in polynomial time. In order to ensure polynomial evaluability, we have to restrict the kinds of programs we use. Most results given below are actually restricted to function-free languages. In the appendix to this chapter, we show implication to be decidable in polynomial time in function-free languages, so $\mathcal{D}$ is polynomially evaluable in this case. For the other kinds of programs mentioned in results below, polynomial evaluability can also be proved. We will leave this to the reader.

One important feature of ILP is the use of background knowledge, which usually forms one of the inputs of the learning task. The ordinary PAC setting does not mention background knowledge, so we have to make an emandation to this setting. Let us assume we have some set $\mathcal{K}$, which contains every definite program that we allow as background knowledge. For instance, $\mathcal{K}$ might contain all finite sets of ground atoms in some language. Now, apart from ε, δ, n, and l, a PAC algorithm for ILP purposes also receives one member $\mathcal{B} \in \mathcal{K}$ as input. $\mathcal{B}$ may not be changed during the run of the algorithm. The algorithm should return a definite program Π such that the concept represented by $\Pi \cup \mathcal{B}$ (i.e., $M_{\Pi \cup \mathcal{B}}$) is probably approximately correct.

Since $\mathcal{B}$ is an additional input to the learning algorithm, it should be reflected in the time complexity. This is done by adding an upper bound b on the length of $\mathcal{B}$ as a fifth parameter to the time complexity function, in addition to the ordinary parameters ε, δ, n, and l that we saw earlier. For polynomial time PAC learnability, we require the time complexity $t(\varepsilon, \delta, n, l, b)$ of the algorithm to be bounded by a polynomial in $1/\varepsilon$, $1/\delta$, n, l, and b. If such an algorithm exists, we will say that $\mathcal{F}$ is polynomial time PAC learnable in $\mathcal{D}$ *with background knowledge from* $\mathcal{K}$. Analogously, we can incorporate the use of background knowledge in PAC predictability, identification from equivalence queries, etc.

One further remark involving background knowledge: many results below concern only single-predicate learning, where there is a single *target* predicate symbol P. In this case, all we need to know about other predicates should already be contained in the input $\mathcal{B}$, only atoms with predicate P are given as examples, and each clause in Π should have P in its head.

In order to avoid too much notation, we will use the following abbreviation (where K_1 and K_2 denote some restrictive property of programs): "definite programs of kind K_1 are polynomial sample/polynomial time PAC learnable with background knowledge of kind K_2" means that the set of concepts representable by a definite program of kind K_1 together with background knowledge of kind K_2 is polynomial sample/polynomial time PAC learnable in representation $\mathcal{D}$, with background knowledge from the set of all programs of kind K_2. Quite a lot of the results we give below are actually restricted to programs of a single clause only. In this case, we say "clauses of kind K_1 are polynomial sample/polynomial time PAC learnable with background knowledge of kind K_2."

With all this notation in place, we are now in a position to give an overview of PAC-learnability results that have been reported for the normal setting. For ease of presentation, we split them into two groups: (1) results on learning non-recursive programs, and (2) results on learning recursive programs. We will only give here the most important results which can be stated without introducing too much additional notation. Other recent overviews may be found in [KD94, CP95]; some further PAC-learnability results, which we do not include below, are given in [Lin92, FP93a, FP93b, Coh93a, Coh93b, Coh94b, Coh95b, Coh95c, Coh95a, Yam95, Dže95b].

18.6.2 Learning Non-recursive Programs

Before we can state the main results for non-recursive clauses and programs, we need to define some restricted kinds of clauses (repeating some notions here that were already defined in earlier chapters).

- A definite program in which each clause has the same predicate symbol P in the head, is called a *definition* of P.

- A *k-literal* definite program clause contains at most k literals in its body. A *k-literal* definite program contains only k-literal clauses.

- A *k-clause* definite program contains at most k clauses.

- A clause or set of clauses is *function-free* if it does not contain function symbols of arity ≥ 1.

- A definite program clause is *non-recursive* if the predicate in its head does not occur in its body. A definite program is *non-recursive* if all its members are non-recursive.

- A clause C is *allowed* if all variables occuring in positive literals in C also occur in negative literals in C. (In ILP, such clauses are also sometimes called *generative, range restricted*, or *connected*.) A set of clauses is *allowed* if all its members are allowed.

- A clause C is *constrained* if all variables occurring in negative literals in C also occur in positive literals in C. A set of clauses is *constrained* if all its members are constrained.

- A *constrained atom* is a constrained non-recursive definite program clause. The predicate symbols in its body are called *constraint predicates*.

- An ordered definite program clause $A \leftarrow B_1, \ldots, B_n$ is *determinate* with respect to a definite program $\mathcal{B}$, if for every $1 \leq i \leq n$ and every substitution θ such that $(A \leftarrow B_1, \ldots, B_{i-1})\theta$ is ground and $\mathcal{B} \models (B_1 \wedge \ldots \wedge B_{i-1})\theta$, there is at most one substitution σ for the variables in $B_i\theta$ such that $B_i\theta\sigma$ is ground and $\mathcal{B} \models B_i\theta\sigma$.

  Suppose $x_1, \ldots, x_n$ are the variables in B_i that already occurred in $(A \leftarrow B_1, \ldots, B_{i-1})\theta$, and $y_1, \ldots, y_m$ are the other variables in B_i. The idea behind determinacy is that $\mathcal{B}$ specifies a partial function from $x_1, \ldots, x_n$ to $y_1, \ldots, y_m$: given ground instantiations of $x_1, \ldots, x_n$, the background knowledge allows at most one ground instantiation of $y_1, \ldots, y_m$.

  For example, suppose we use $F(x, y)$ to denote that y is the father of x, and $G(x, y)$ to denote that y is the grandfather of x. Then the clause $G(x, y) \leftarrow F(x, z), F(z, y)$ is determinate with respect to

$\mathcal{B} = \{F(a,c), F(b,c), F(c,e), F(d,e), F(e,f)\}$. Informally, determinacy follows from the fact that any x has only one father z.

- The *variable-depth* of a variable x in an ordered definite program clause $A \leftarrow B_1, \ldots, B_n$ is defined as follows. If x occurs in A, then its variable-depth is 0. Suppose x first occurs in B_i. If none of the other variables in B_i already occurred in $A \leftarrow B_1, \ldots, B_{i-1}$, then x has variable-depth ∞. Otherwise, the variable-depth of x is 1 plus the variable-depth of the variable in B_i with greatest variable-depth occurring in $A \leftarrow B_1, \ldots, B_{i-1}$. The *variable-depth* of an ordered definite program clause is the largest variable-depth of its variables. Note that such a clause is constrained iff it has variable-depth 0.

  If a definite program clause is determinate with respect to some definite program $\mathcal{B}$, its variable-depth is at most i and the arity of its predicate symbols is at most j, then it is called *ij-determinate* with respect to $\mathcal{B}$.[6] A definite program is ij-determinate with respect to $\mathcal{B}$ if all its members are.

  The clause from the last item has variable-depth 1 (because of z), so this clause is $(1,2)$-determinate with respect to $\mathcal{B}$.

- Let C be a definite program clause. A term t in some literal $L \in C$ is *linked* with linking-chain of length 0, if t occurs in C^+, and is linked with linking-chain of length $d+1$, if some other term in L is linked with linking-chain of length d. The *link-depth* of a term t in some $L \in C$ is the length of the shortest linking-chain of t. A literal $L \in C$ is linked if at least one of the terms it contains is linked. C itself is linked if each literal $L \in C$ is linked.

  For example, the clause $P(x) \leftarrow Q(x,y,z), Q(x,y,w)$ is linked. The term x has link-depth 0, while y, z, and w have link-depth 1. Note that w is linked with two linking-chains: one of length 1 (via x) and one of length 2 (via y and x). Also note that the variable-depth of w is 2. The clause $P(x) \leftarrow Q(x,y), P(z)$ is not linked, because z is not linked.

- If a definite program clause is not determinate with respect to some definite program $\mathcal{B}$, the link-depth of its terms is at most i, and the arity of its predicate symbols is at most j, then the clause is called *ij-nondeterminate* with respect to $\mathcal{B}$.

  For instance, $P(x) \leftarrow Q(x,y,z), Q(x,y,w)$ is $(1,3)$-nondeterminate with respect to $\mathcal{B} = \{Q(a,b,b), Q(a,b,c)\}$.

- A definite program $\mathcal{B}$ is *efficient* if the set of computed answers for $\mathcal{B} \cup \{\leftarrow A\}$, for arbitrary atoms A, can be computed by an algorithm

---

[6]Various non-equivalent definitions of ij-determinacy have appeared in the literature. The one we give here is slightly different from the original definition given in [MF92], but the details are not important for our purposes.

with running time polynomial in the length of A. In the appendix of this chapter, it is shown that any function-free definite program is efficient.

- A definite program $\mathcal{B}$ is *ffga* if it consists of function-free ground atoms.

- Consider an ffga definite program $\mathcal{B}$, in which all atoms have the same binary predicate symbol R. We can take $R(a,b) \in \mathcal{B}$ as denoting an edge from a to b. If $\mathcal{B}$ represents a set of trees with edges directed towards the roots, it is called a *forest*. If $\mathcal{B}$ represents a disjoint union of directed cycles, it is called *cyclical*.

  For example, $\mathcal{B} = \{R(a,c), R(b,c), R(c,d)\} \cup \{R(e,f), R(f,g)\}$ is a forest (with two trees, respectively having d and g as root), and $\mathcal{B} = \{R(a,b), R(b,c), R(c,a)\} \cup \{R(d,e), R(e,d)\}$ is cyclical (with two cycles).

In terms of these restrictions, we have the results listed below. For results involving ij-determinacy, k-literal clauses or k-clause programs, etc., we assume some fixed i, j, and k are given. Furthermore, instead of "ij-(non)determinate with respect to the background knowledge" we will simply write ij-(non)determinate. Many results given below presuppose a fixed upper bound on the arities of predicate symbols. Note, however, that such a bound (for instance the j in ij-determinacy), together with a restriction to function-free clauses, implies a fixed upper bound on the length of the examples, rendering the length parameter n irrelevant. Therefore, some of the more recent results do not presuppose a bound on the arity of predicate symbols, but let this vary with the length parameter.

- Constrained atoms are polynomial time PAC learnable with efficient background knowledge which uses only constraint predicates [PF92, Theorem 7].

- Finite sets of atoms are polynomial time identifiable from equivalence and membership queries [AIS97, Theorem 13]. (Background knowledge is not considered here.)

- k-literal constrained function-free non-recursive definitions of the target predicate are polynomial time PAC learnable with efficient background knowledge [DMR93, Theorem 2]. This also holds with $\eta < 0.5$ random classification noise [Dže95a, Theorem 4] and with a "small" amount of malicious noise [Dže95b, Theorem 3.5].

- k-literal function-free non-recursive definitions of the target predicate are polynomial time PAC learnable with ffga background knowledge [Coh93b, Theorem 8]. This also holds with $\eta < 0.5$ random classification noise [Dže95a, Theorem 4].

- k-clause ij-determinate function-free non-recursive definitions of the target predicate are polynomial time PAC predictable with efficient background knowledge [Dže95b, Theorem 3.4]. This also holds with $\eta < 0.5$ random classification noise [Dže95a, Theorem 4].

  In [DMR92, Theorem 2], the same class had earlier been shown to be polynomial time PAC learnable under simple distributions. In the "simple distributions" setting, examples are drawn according to the so-called *universal* distribution. See [LV91] for details.

- If the widely assumed $RP \neq PSPACE$ conjecture[7] is true, then determinate linked function-free non-recursive definite program clauses are not polynomial time PAC learnable with ffga background knowledge [Kie93, Corollary 15].

  If the widely assumed $RP \neq NP$ conjecture is true, then $(1,2)$-nondeterminate function-free non-recursive definite program clauses are not polynomial time PAC learnable with ffga background knowledge [Kie93, Corollary 19].

- Function-free non-recursive definite program clauses with the target predicate in the head and only atoms with binary predicate symbol R in the body, are polynomial time PAC learnable with forest background knowledge [HT96, Theorem 21]. This also holds with $\eta < 0.5$ random classification noise [HST96, Theorem 4].

  The same clauses are polynomial time PAC learnable with cyclical background knowledge if we use a non-standard representation [HT96, Section 7.2].

18.6.3 Learning Recursive Programs

Here we will give an overview of PAC-learnability results for programs involving recursion. Quite a lot of these results are negative, because learning recursive clauses is in general more difficult than learning non-recursive ones. In addition to the concepts of the last subsection, we also need the following:

- Let C be an ordered definite program clause with predicate symbol P in its head. An atom in C^- with predicate P is called *recursive*. C is *linearly recursive* if it contains exactly one recursive atom, and *k-ary recursive* if it contains k such atoms. A recursive atom A in C^- is *closed* if each variable it contains already occurs in the literals to the left of A. C is *closed* if all its recursive atoms are closed.

---

[7]Very briefly and informally, the complexity classes mentioned here are the following: P is the class of problems solvable in polynomial time by a deterministic algorithm; RP is the class of problems solvable in polynomial time by a randomized algorithm; NP is the class of solvable problems for which the correctness of a solution can be verified in polynomial time by a deterministic algorithm; $PSPACE$ is the class of problems solvable by a deterministic algorithm using a polynomially-bounded amount of storage space. See [HU79, GJ79, CLR90] for more details.

- A definite program clause C is *term-related* if it is an atom, or if any term occuring in C^- also occurs (possibly within another term) in C^+. A definite program is *term-related* if all its members are. Note that a term-related clause is constrained.

Before we can state the main PAC-learnability results involving recursive clauses, two additional kinds of queries have to be mentioned. These are not applicable in the general PAC setting, but are useful in this particular ILP formalization. The first concerns *existential queries*. Here we have an oracle that takes a (possibly non-ground) atom A as input, and returns all ground instances of A which are members of the target concept. The use of such an oracle presupposes that any A has only a finite number of ground instances which are members of the target concept. Existential queries can be seen as a generalization of membership queries.

The second kind are the *basecase queries* [Coh95b]. Here the target concept is represented by a particular definite program Π containing two kinds of clauses, recursive and non-recursive ones. The oracle takes a ground atom A as input, and returns whether A is a member of the concept represented by the non-recursive clauses of the target program Π together with the background knowledge $\mathcal{B}$ (this concept is of course a subset of the target concept).

- k-clause ij-determinate function-free definitions of the target predicate are polynomial time PAC learnable under simple distributions with existential and membership queries about the target predicate, and with efficient background knowledge [DMR92, Theorem 3].

- k-clause l-literal term-related definite programs are polynomial sample PAC learnable [NP94, Theorem 3]. (Background knowledge is not considered here.)

- Closed k-ary recursive ij-determinate function-free definite program clauses are polynomial time identifiable from equivalence queries with ffga background knowledge [Coh95b, Theorem 7]. (Cohen's use of ij-determinateness involves so-called *mode declarations*. This is slightly different from the definition we gave above. Furthermore, his treatment of examples is somewhat more general than ours. For the details, we refer to his paper.)

  Definite programs consisting of two ij-determinate function-free clauses of which the first is closed k-ary recursive and the second is non-recursive, are polynomial time identifiable from equivalence and base-case queries with ffga background knowledge [Coh95b, Proposition 9]. For $k = 1$, the latter result also holds with $\eta < 0.5$ random classification noise [HST96, Theorem 7].

- Under certain plausible cryptographic assumptions (similar to the $P \neq NP$ assumption), definite programs consisting of an arbitrary finite number of closed linearly recursive ij-determinate function-free clauses are not polynomial time PAC predictable with ffga background knowledge [Coh95c, Theorem 2].

Under the same assumptions, and if the arity of the target predicate is at least 3 and $i \geq 3$, ij-determinate function-free definite program clauses containing an arbitrary number of closed recursive atoms are not polynomial time PAC predictable with ffga background knowledge [Coh95c, Theorem 3].

18.7 Results in the Nonmonotonic Setting

The PAC formalization of the nonmonotonic ILP setting is somewhat different from the normal setting, but is a generalization of the setting for learning propositional formulas with which we started the previous section. Let us consider a function-free clausal language C with only a finite number of ground atoms. Then any Herbrand interpretation of C is finite, and there are only finitely many distinct Herbrand interpretations of C. Let the domain X be a set of such Herbrand interpretations. Since a concept is a subset of the domain, a concept is a finite set of Herbrand interpretations.

We use the following representation: a theory (finite set of clauses) T represents the set of its models in X. That is, T is a name of $\{I \in X \mid I$ is a model of $T\}$. Let us see if this representation is polynomially evaluable. Consider a function-free theory T and a Herbrand interpretation $I \in X$. Then we need to be able to determine whether T is true under I in time polynomial in the lengths of T and I. T is true under I iff all ground instances of clauses in T are true under I. The number of such ground instances is easily seen to be bounded by a polynomial (analogous to step 1 of the appendix). Furthermore, a ground clause is true under I iff at least one of its literals is true under I, which obviously can be decided in polynomial time. In sum, our representation is polynomially evaluable.

Furthermore, it can be proved that in this representation, any set $\mathcal{I} \subseteq X$ of Herbrand interpretations has a name. That is, for any set $\mathcal{I} \subseteq X$, there exists a theory T such that $\mathcal{I}$ is the set of Herbrand models of T. Given a Herbrand interpretation $I \in X$, we define ϕ_I to be a conjunction of ground literals, with the following property: $A \in \phi_I$ iff $A \in I$, and $\neg A \in \phi_I$ iff $A \notin I$. Then it is easy to see that the set of Herbrand models of ϕ_I is exactly $\{I\}$. For instance, if $P(a), P(b), P(c)$ are the only ground atoms in C, and $I = \{P(a), P(c)\}$, then $\phi_I = (P(a) \wedge \neg P(b) \wedge P(c))$. Clearly, I is the only Herbrand model of ϕ_I. Now suppose $\mathcal{I} = \{I_1, \ldots, I_n\} \subseteq X$ is a set of Herbrand interpretations. We define $\psi_{\mathcal{I}} = \phi_{I_1} \vee \ldots \vee \phi_{I_n}$. Note that I is a Herbrand model of $\psi_{\mathcal{I}}$ iff $I \in \mathcal{I}$. Thus $\mathcal{I}$ is exactly the set of Herbrand models of $\psi_{\mathcal{I}}$. By the construction in the proof of Theorem 3.8, we can find a conjunction (or set) T of ground clauses which is logically equivalent to $\psi_{\mathcal{I}}$.

Since $\mathcal{I}$ is exactly the set of Herbrand models of T, the theory T is a name of $\mathcal{I}$ in our representation.

The main result in this setting is:

- A *jk-clausal theory* is a set of allowed clauses such that each clause contains at most k literals, and the length of each literal is at most j. Function-free jk-clausal theories are polynomial time PAC learnable in the nonmonotonic setting [DD94, Theorem 9].

  This result remains valid with a "small" amount of malicious noise, and with $\eta < 0.5$ random classification noise [Dže95a, Theorems 2 and 3, respectively].

18.8 Summary

A *concept* is a subset of a domain X, and a *concept class* is a set of concepts. A *PAC algorithm* takes examples for an unknown *target concept*, drawn according to an unknown probability distribution, and learns, with tunably high probability, a tunably good approximation of the target concept. A concept class $\mathcal{F}$ is *polynomial sample PAC learnable* if a PAC algorithm exists for $\mathcal{F}$ that uses only a polynomially-bounded number of examples, and is *polynomial time PAC learnable* if the algorithm uses only a polynomially-bounded number of steps. In the latter case, the algorithm should output a *name* of the learned concept in some polynomially evaluable *representation*. Polynomial time *PAC predictability* is weaker than polynomial time PAC learnability, while polynomial time *identification from equivalence queries* is stronger. When *noise* is involved, the examples may sometimes be incorrect.

In the *normal* ILP problem setting, a concept is a set of ground atoms, and our aim is to find a definite program whose least Herbrand model probably approximates the target concept. In the *nonmonotonic* setting, concepts are sets of Herbrand interpretations, and our aim is to find a theory whose set of Herbrand models probably approximates the target concept. We gave overviews of the main results reported for both settings.

18.A   A Polynomial Time Decision Procedure

In this appendix, we will show that there is an algorithm which, when given an arbitrary function-free definite program Π and an arbitrary function-free ground atom A, decides whether $\Pi \models A$ in time polynomial in the length $l(\Pi)$ of Π and the length $l(A)$ of A. We do not claim that the method outlined below is the most efficient there is, but merely give it in order to establish polynomial time decidability.

The construction is divided in two steps. First we show that $\Pi \models A$ iff $\Pi_g \models A$, where Π_g is a set of ground instances of clauses from Π, and the length $l(\Pi_g)$ of Π is bounded by a polynomial in $l(\Pi)$ and $l(A)$; then we show that $\Pi_g \models A$ can be decided in time polynomial in $l(\Pi_g)$. Together these steps enable us to decide $\Pi \models A$ in time polynomial in $l(\Pi)$ and $l(A)$.

Step 1: Reduction to ground case

Let Π be a function-free definite program and A be a function-free ground atom. Recall from Chapter 15 that if Σ is a set of clauses and T is a set of ground terms, then $\mathcal{I}(\Sigma, T)$ denotes the set of all ground instances of clauses in Σ, instantiated with terms from T. Let T be the set of constants occurring in A, and define $\Pi_g = \mathcal{I}(\Pi, T)$.

Let us see how many clauses Π_g contains. If a clause contains v distinct variables, it has $v \cdot |T| < v \cdot l(A)$ ground instances over T. Furthermore, $|\Pi| \leq l(\Pi)$ and each clause in Π contains less than $l(\Pi)$ distinct variables. Hence the total number of ground clauses in Π_g is bounded by a polynomial in $l(\Pi)$ and $l(A)$. Since the length of each clause in Π_g is at most $l(\Pi)$, it follows that the length $l(\Pi_g)$ of Π_g is bounded by a polynomial in $l(\Pi)$ and $l(A)$.

From the remarks following the proof of Lemma 15.10, we have $\Pi \models A$ iff $\Pi_g \models A$. Thus if we can decide $\Pi_g \models A$ in polynomial time, we are done.

Step 2: Deciding the ground case

Here we will show that given a ground definite program Π and a ground atom A, it can be decided in time polynomial in $l(\Pi)$ whether $\Pi \models A$. $\Pi \models A$ iff $A \in M_\Pi$ (Theorem 7.16), so it will be sufficient to construct the least Herbrand model M_Π in polynomial time, since $A \in M_\Pi$ can clearly be decided in polynomial time. We will show that the following algorithm does just that.

Algorithm 18.1 (Algorithm for constructing M_Π)
Input: A ground definite program Π.
Output: The least Herbrand model M_Π.

   1. Set $M = \emptyset$ and $\Pi' = \Pi$.

2. If there is a $C \in \Pi'$ such that $C^- \subseteq M$,
   then set $M = M \cup \{C^+\}$ and $\Pi' = \Pi'\backslash\{C\}$,
   else output M and stop.
3. Goto 2.

We will informally show that the running time of this algorithm is bounded by a polynomial in $l(\Pi)$. Each execution of step 2 adds one atom to M and deletes one clause from Π'. Hence step 2 can only be executed $|\Pi| \leq l(\Pi)$ times and we have $|M| \leq |\Pi| \leq l(\Pi)$ at each step. Each execution of step 2 has to examine at most $|\Pi'| \leq |\Pi| \leq l(\Pi)$ clauses C. Furthermore, for a given $C \in \Pi$ and M we have $|C| \leq l(\Pi)$ and $|M| \leq l(\Pi)$, so the number of steps required to test whether $C^- \subseteq M$ is bounded by a polynomial in $l(\Pi)$. It follows that the algorithm works in polynomial time.

It remains to show that the algorithm does indeed construct M_Π when given Π as input:

Proposition 18.18 *Let Π be a ground definite program, and M be the set that the previous algorithm outputs when given Π as input. Then $M = M_\Pi$.*

Proof It is easy to see that if $A \in M$, then $\Pi \models A$. Hence $M \subseteq M_\Pi$. To show that also $M_\Pi \subseteq M$, suppose some $A \in M_\Pi$, so $\Pi \models A$. Since Π is ground and A is a ground atom, it follows from the Subsumption Theorem for SLD-resolution that there is an SLD-derivation of A from Π, of some length n (i.e., involving n resolution steps). We will prove $A \in M$ by induction on n.

1. If $n = 0$, then $A \in \Pi$, and step 2 of the algorithm will clearly add A to M before it terminates.
2. Suppose the statement holds for $n \leq m$, and consider an SLD-derivation of A from Π of length $m + 1$, with top clause $A \leftarrow B_1, \ldots, B_k$. Then for each $1 \leq i \leq k$, there is an SLD-derivation of length $\leq m$ of B_i from Π, hence $B_i \in M$ by the induction hypothesis. This means that after a finite number of executions of step 2 of the algorithm, we have $C^- \subseteq M$. Therefore step 2 of the algorithm must also add A to M before termination. □

Chapter 19

Further Topics

19.1 Introduction

Those of our readers who were already well acquainted with ILP before reading this book will no doubt have noticed that we have thus far more or less ignored some topics that are considered very important in the ILP community. These include some theoretical issues such as predicate invention, but in particular more practical topics such as implementation and application of ILP, efficiency, language restrictions (language bias), and noise handling. In this book, we have concentrated on the fundamental concepts needed to understand ILP, rather than on *every* topic of interest to ILP. This chapter is to discuss a number of further topics. Due to restrictions of time and space, the discussion will be much more informal and sketchy than before (except for some proofs in the appendix). Our aim here is to provide the reader with a "map" of some of these subfields of ILP: to outline the main problems and results, and to give pointers to the relevant literature.

Like logic programming, ILP can be seen as a branch of formal logic. As such, it is worthy of investigation for its own sake. On the other hand, ILP also has roots in the much more practical and application-oriented community of machine learning. For many people in machine learning, the real test of some learning technique lies in its practical success: implement it and see how well it works on particular learning problems.

When one tries to implement some of the ILP techniques that we introduced before, such as inverse resolution, unfolding, least generalizations, or refinement operators, a number of problems immediately come up. In particular, the search space is usually enormous, which makes a complete search very inefficient. Furthermore, testing whether a theory is correct is usually undecidable or very inefficient as well. This is borne out both by results from formal learnability theory, and by practical experience from actual implementations. In the previous chapters we have been more concerned with

completeness than with efficiency, but the problem of intractable search is a
very serious one.

In order to make search more tractable, one can use *heuristics*, which we
will not discuss in any detail in this book, or put restrictions on the language
used, thereby reducing the number of possible theories. Such *language bias*
is discussed in Section 19.2. On the other hand, the language sometimes also
needs to be extended with new predicate symbols if a good theory cannot be
found in the existing language. This problem of *predicate invention* will be
treated in Section 19.3. The method of *flattening*, discussed in Section 19.4,
allows us to make a theory function-free, transferring the function symbols
to new predicates in the background knowledge. Apart from these language-
related issues, a further topic of interest is *imperfect data*: the examples for
real-world learning tasks often contain errors or inaccuracies. How we can deal
with this will be briefly discussed in Section 19.5. In Section 19.6 we describe
some of the main implemented ILP systems and mention a few areas in which
they have been applied. Finally, Section 19.7 identifies some topics that we
do not treat at all, but which should not go unmentioned because of their
potential relevance to ILP.

19.2   Language Bias

As we stated in the introduction, the search space of clauses that may be
included in the theory is usually enormous. More often than not, complete
search is out of the question. Furthermore, testing whether a theory is correct
with respect to the examples is undecidable in "full" clausal languages, and
computationally highly expensive in decidable cases such as function-free
clausal languages. In order to make search and testing tractable, we need
bias. Following [NRA+96], we distinguish three kinds of bias:

1. *Language bias* specifies and restricts the set of clauses or theories that
   are permitted.

2. *Search bias* concerns the way the system searches through this set of
   permitted clauses or theories.

3. *Validation bias* determines when the learned theory is acceptable, so
   when the learning process may stop.

It should be noted that for each of these three kinds, the appropriate bias
is rather application-dependent. We will here only discuss language bias in
some more detail. Some restrictions that may, individually or in combination,
be put on the language are given below:

- Restrict to definite or normal program clauses instead of general clauses
  (this restriction is very common).
- Restrict to function-free clauses.

- Restrict to non-recursive clauses.
- Put an upper bound on the number of clauses in the theory.
- Put an upper bound on the depth, or the number of literals or variables in a clause.
- Use only *allowed* clauses (as defined in Chapter 8), where every variable in a positive literal should also occur in a negative literal. In ILP, such clauses are also sometimes called *generative*, *range restricted*, and *connected*.
- Use only *constrained* clauses, where every variable in a negative literal should also occur in a positive literal.
- Use only clauses which are *ij-determinate* with respect to the background knowledge (as Defined in Chapter 18).

Note that certain combinations of these biases imply polynomial time PAC learnability. The effects of some of these biases are experimentally evaluated in [NRA+96].

Of course, the simplest form of language bias is just an explicit list of all clauses permitted in the theory. *Clause Sets* [BG96a] provide a useful shorthand notation for writing down such a (finite) list. A somewhat more general approach is to specify the language bias by giving a *grammar* of the permitted clauses, as done in [Coh94a, DD95].

Clearly, there is a trade-off between the tractability of search, which is improved by a small search space, and the availibility of a correct theory, which is improved by a large search space. Hence it may sometimes be that a particular bias is too restrictive: it rules out all correct theories. In this case, we need to change our bias, by using a more liberal language bias and/or a more complete—and correspondingly less efficient—search strategy than before.

The former, a *language bias shift*, may be achieved either by weakening one or more of the restrictions on the theory, or by including new predicates in the language. Repeatedly shifting the language bias leads to a sequence of languages: first start with a simple language L_1, and try to find a correct theory in this language; if this is not possible, try again with a richer language L_2, and so on. This approach was used in CLINT [DR92].

19.3 Predicate Invention

In this section, we discuss *predicate invention*: the automatic introduction of new predicate symbols in the language.

We can roughly distinguish two different uses for predicate invention. The first of these is relevant to logic programming as a whole, not just to ILP. Here predicate invention is used for transforming or restructuring a program, for instance in order to make it more readable, or to make deduction more efficient. Applications of such restructuring in the ILP literature may be found in [Fla93, Som95, Rie96a, Rie96b].

Example 19.1 Consider the following normal program Π (adapted from [Sta96b]):

$$Chimp(x) \leftarrow Brown(x), Hairy(x), Biped(x), \neg Winged(x)$$
$$Gorilla(x) \leftarrow Black(x), Hairy(x), Biped(x), \neg Winged(x)$$
$$Human(x) \leftarrow \neg Hairy(x), Biped(x), \neg Winged(x)$$

Using the new predicate symbol *Primate*, this may be rewritten to the following, more readable program Π':

$$Chimp(x) \leftarrow Brown(x), Hairy(x), Primate(x)$$
$$Gorilla(x) \leftarrow Black(x), Hairy(x), Primate(x)$$
$$Human(x) \leftarrow \neg Hairy(x), Primate(x)$$
$$Primate(x) \leftarrow Biped(x), \neg Winged(x)$$

$\triangleleft$

Note that the reformulation in the above example is actually a generalization step: $\Pi' \models \Pi$, but $\Pi \not\models \Pi'$. This generalization step may be seen as an application of inverse resolution, since the three clauses of Π are resolvents of the fourth clause of Π' with the first three clauses of Π', respectively. However, this generalization is merely an accidental by-product of the restructuring, not its aim.

The second use of predicate invention is more specific for ILP, and hence more directly relevant to us. Here predicate invention is necessary in order to be able to formulate a correct theory. Of course, if E^+ is finite and there are no further restrictions on the theory, then E^+ will be a correct theory. However, things change when we use additional restrictions, such as putting a maximum on the number of clauses in a theory, or when we use an enumeration with infinitely many examples. Let us suppose no correct theory exists using only the predicate symbols in the background knowledge and examples. Then in the initial language, the learning task is unsolvable. Now it might very well be that adding one or more new predicate symbols to the language makes it possible to construct a correct theory. This is illustrated by the next example.

Example 19.2 Suppose we start with a language containing only predicate P, unary function f, and constant a, empty background knowledge, and the following positive and negative examples:

$$E^+ = \{P(f^{4k}(a)) \mid k = 0, 1, 2, \ldots\} \cup \{P(f^{5k}(a)) \mid k = 0, 1, 2, \ldots\}$$
$$E^- = \text{all other ground atoms.}$$

We want to induce a definite program that is correct with respect to these examples. Unfortunately, it can be shown that there is no such program using only the symbols P, f, and a. In particular, the following program does not work, because apart from the positive examples, it also implies $P(f^9(a))$, $P(f^{13}(a))$, etc.

$$P(f^4(x)) \leftarrow P(x)$$
$$P(f^5(x)) \leftarrow P(x)$$
$$P(a).$$

Intuitively, the clause for the $4k$-example "interferes" with the clause for the $5k$-examples, because they have to use the same predicate symbol P.

However, if we extend the language with two new predicate symbols Q and R, then we can find the following correct program:

$$Q(a)$$
$$Q(f^4(x)) \leftarrow Q(x)$$
$$R(a)$$
$$R(f^5(x)) \leftarrow R(x)$$
$$P(x) \leftarrow Q(x)$$
$$P(x) \leftarrow R(x)$$

Informally, we use the Q-predicate to generate the $4k$-examples, and the R-predicate for the $5k$-examples. Thus predicate invention is sometimes needed in order to be able to construct a correct theory. ◁

Clearly, in order to know whether predicate invention is required, we first need to find out whether a correct theory exists using only the initial language bias. This is called the *language bias shift problem*. Unfortunately, this problem is often undecidable, because the undecidability of logical implication carries over to the undecidability of the correctness of theories.

A second problem concerns the *utility* of predicate invention. In some cases, where we have already found out that a correct theory does not exist in the initial language, it can be shown that adding any finite number of new predicates to the language will not make a correct theory available. This is for instance the case in function-free Horn languages (see Theorem 6 of [Sta94]). In this situation, predicate invention is useless as a bias shift operation. Stahl [Sta96b] gives an overview of the (un)decidability of the language bias shift problem and the utility of predicate invention in various restricted languages.

Once we have established the need for an application of predicate invention, new problems come up. In the first place, what should be the *arity* of the new predicate be? Secondly, in which way should the new predicate be used in the theory? Clearly, many different choices are possible, and we need systematic ways to explore those choices.

The previous chapters contained only one explicit reference to a particular operator for predicate invention, namely the W-operator for inverse resolution. However, it should be noted that downward refinement operators may also invent new predicates. For example, the fourth item in the definition of $\rho_L(C)$ in Section 17.4 adds a most general literal $(\neg)P(x_1, \ldots, x_n)$ to C, and there is no reason why P could not be a new predicate, not occurring in the examples or background knowledge. At the start of refinement, we might reserve one or two new predicates, and the refinement operator will automatically generate clauses containing those new predicates.

For more on predicate invention in ILP, we refer the interested reader to Stahl's overview paper [Sta96b] and the references therein; for a comparison of the efficiency of the two kinds of language bias shift (weakening restrictions versus predicate invention), see [Sta95].

19.4 Flattening

Introducing new predicate symbols is also sometimes used in *flattening*. This is a method to make a theory function-free, by replacing every n-ary function symbol f in the theory by a new predicate symbol P_f, of arity $n + 1$, and transferring the occurrence of f itself to the background knowledge. This technique was introduced in the ILP context by Rouveirol [RP89, Rou92, Rou94] (though similar ideas had already been used in other fields). Restricting to function-free theories can simplify the search for a correct theory. For instance, if we use the refinement operator ρ_L to search for a correct theory which is known in advance to be function-free, we can simplify ρ_L by omitting $\{z/f(x_1, \ldots, x_n)\}$ substitutions. On the other hand, since the function symbols are only moved elsewhere (from the theory to the background knowledge), one might argue that flattening only relocates the difficulties introduced by function symbols, instead of solving them. Despite this, flattening is invoked quite often in ILP practice: some implemented systems only work with function-free theories and examples, and use flattening to make clauses function-free.

How does flattening work? We will first illustrate the idea by means of a simple example, and then give a general algorithm. Suppose we want to make the following clause function-free:

$$C = P(f(x)) \leftarrow P(x).$$

Then we have to get rid of the term $f(x)$ in the head of C. We can do this by replacing $f(x)$ by a new variable y, but then the connection between the terms in the head and the body of C is lost. In order to preserve this connection, we introduce a new binary predicate symbol P_f, and add $P_f(x, y)$ to the body of the clause. Thus we obtain the function-free clause

$$Flat(C) = P(y) \leftarrow P(x), P_f(x, y).$$

Informally, $P_f(x, y)$ means that y is the image of x under the function f. In order to formalize this, we define a new clause $P_f(x, f(x))$ to constrain the interpretation of P_f, which we add to the background knowledge.

In general, flattening may involve replacing different function symbols, as well as different occurrences of the same function symbol. The following algorithm flattens a clause C, yielding a function-free clause $Flat(C)$. The atoms that define the new predicates together form the set $FlatDefs(C)$, which may be added to the background knowledge. We restrict attention to flattening definite program clauses, but the generalization of the idea to arbitrary clauses is straightforward.

Algorithm 19.1 (Flattening Algorithm)
Input: A definite program clause C.
Output: A function-free definite program clause $Flat(C)$ and a set of atoms $FlatDefs(C)$.

1. Set $C' = C$ and $Defs = \emptyset$.
2. While C' is not function-free, do
   1. Let $t = f(t_1, \ldots, t_n)$ be a term occurring in C', such that each t_i is either a variable or a constant $(n \geq 1)$.
   2. Replace all occurrences of t in C' by a new variable y.
   3. Add $P_f(t_1, \ldots, t_n, y)$ to the body of C'.
   4. If an atom of the form $P_f(x_1, \ldots, x_n, f(x_1, \ldots, x_n))$ is not yet a member of $Defs$, then add this atom to $Defs$.
3. Return $Flat(C) = C'$ and $FlatDefs(C) = Defs$.

Note that the above algorithm is non-deterministic, since different choices for t may be possible in the first step of the while-loop. However, it can easily be shown that these choices do not influence the output of the algorithm: no matter which of the possible t we choose in each step, the returned clause $Flat(C)$ will be the same up to variants.

Example 19.3 Consider the application of the algorithm to the clause $C = P(g(f(x), y)) \leftarrow Q(f(x), f(y))$.

1. First we remove $f(x)$, using a new variable z, yielding:
   $C' = P(g(z, y)) \leftarrow Q(z, f(y)), P_f(x, z)$.
   $Defs = \{P_f(x, f(x))\}$.
2. Then we remove $f(y)$, using a new variable u:
   $C' = P(g(z, y)) \leftarrow Q(z, u), P_f(x, z), P_f(y, u)$.
   $Defs = \{P_f(x, f(x))\}$.
3. Finally we remove $g(z, y)$, using v, and obtaining:
   $Flat(C) = P(v) \leftarrow Q(z, u), P_f(x, z), P_f(y, u), P_g(z, y, v)$.
   $FlatDefs(C) = \{P_f(x, f(x)), P_g(x, y, g(x, y))\}$. ◁

Several different variants on this scheme are possible, and our version of flattening differs somewhat from Rouveirol's [Rou94]. Rouveirol flattens away the constants as well, replacing them by new unary predicate symbols. Thus from the clause $C = P(a)$, we would then obtain $Flat(C) = P(x) \leftarrow P_a(x)$ and $FlatDefs(C) = \{P_a(a)\}$. Furthermore, instead of adding the atom $P_f(x_1, \ldots, x_n, f(x_1, \ldots, x_n))$ to $FlatDefs(C)$, her version adds the formula $\forall(P_f(x_1, \ldots, x_n, x) \leftrightarrow x = f(x_1, \ldots, x_n))$. The use of the equality predicate '=' introduces the additional need for an equality theory, which our version of flattening does not require.

The above algorithm works on a single clause C, but we can easily flatten a definite program $\Pi = \{C_1, \ldots, C_n\}$ by defining

$Flat(\Pi) = \{Flat(C_1), \ldots, Flat(C_n)\}.$

$FlatDefs(\Pi) = FlatDefs(C_1) \cup \ldots \cup FlatDefs(C_n).$

Note that in the example we gave before stating the algorithm, resolving $Flat(C) = P(y) \leftarrow P(x), P_f(x, y)$ with $P_f(x, f(x))$ gives us back the original clause $C = P(f(x)) \leftarrow P(x)$. This holds in general: there exists an SLD-derivation of (a variant of) a clause C using $Flat(C)$ as top clause and members of $FlatDefs(C)$ as input clauses. This process of resolving $Flat(C)$ with atoms from $FlatDefs(C)$ to obtain the original C may be called "un-flattening".

In the appendix to this chapter, we prove the following two results:

- Let C and D be definite program clauses, not containing any of the P_f predicate symbols. Then $C \succeq D$ iff $Flat(C) \succeq Flat(D)$.
- Let Π be a definite program and C be a definite program clause, such that Π and C do not contain any of the P_f predicate symbols. Then $\Pi \models C$ iff $Flat(\Pi) \cup FlatDefs(\Pi) \models Flat(C)$.

These results show that flattening preserves some important properties of the original clauses.

19.5   Imperfect Data

Thus far, we have simply assumed that the data we are given (examples and background knowledge) are *correct*. This assumption was shared by many of the earlier ILP systems. However, in large real-world applications, one often has to deal with sets of examples or background knowledge that contain some inaccuracies or other flaws, which might for instance be caused by inaccurate measurements. This section briefly discusses how to deal with such imperfect data. Following [LD94, LDB96], we distinguish four kinds:

1. Random errors (*noise*) in (a) the examples or (b) the background knowl-edge.

2. A too sparse set of examples, from which it is hard to find regularities.

3. Imperfect background knowledge, (a) containing irrelevant clauses or predicates, or (b) lacking some useful clauses or predicates.

4. Missing argument values in some of the examples.

Regarding the fourth kind of imperfect data, to some extent it is possible to induce the missing values in an argument place in some examples from other examples that do have values for those arguments. For instance, suppose we have $A = P(a, ?)$ as a positive example, where the term at the second argument place is unknown. If the majority of other instances of $P(x, y)$ in E^+ have b at the second argument place, we may replace A by $P(a, b)$.

In the remainder of this section, we will restrict attention to 1(a), noise in the examples. (For more on handling imperfect data, see the overview paper by Lavrač, Džeroski, and Bratko [LDB96], and the references therein.) The problem of noisy examples is that they thwart regularities that would have been present if the examples had been non-noisy. For example, suppose some regularity expressed by $P(x) \leftarrow Q(x), R(x)$ holds true in the domain we are working in. However, for some reason we are given $Q(a), R(a) \in E^+$ and $P(a) \in E^-$, where $P(a)$ is noisy. Because of this noise, the clause $P(x) \leftarrow Q(x), R(x)$ is contradicted by the examples, and we cannot induce it. As this example illustrates, noisy examples often create exceptions to general regularities. The presence of such "illegal" exceptions has two adverse effects: (1) the "true" general regularities cannot be induced from the examples, and (2) in order to imply many "irregular" positive examples, the theory will probably have to contain many very specific clauses, tailored to particular examples, and not very useful in general. In other words, noise often causes us to "overfit" the positive examples, which very much decreases the predictive power of the theory.

One crude and straightforward way to solve this, is to weaken the requirement of 100% correctness with respect to the examples. That is, we may allow a few negative examples to be implied by the theory and background knowledge, and a few positive examples not to be implied. More sophisticatedly, several statistical and information theoretical measures have been developed. These can be incorporated in search heuristics and/or stopping criteria, in order to deal with noise *during* the search for a correct theory. For an overview of these measures, we refer to Part III of [LD94].

There are also ways to detect and eliminate the noisy examples right at the beginning, *before* the actual search for a theory starts, and then to conduct the search for a correct theory using a purified, noise-free set of examples [GL96]. One advantage of this approach is its independence of the actual search method used, thus allowing for a modular construction of a system: the noise elimination method and the search method may be developed separately.

From a theoretical perspective, the implementation of this approach based on Rissanen's *minimum description length* (MDL [Ris78], which is strongly linked to so-called *Kolmogorov complexity* [LV97]), is very interesting. If Σ is a set of clauses, then the MDL of Σ is the length of the shortest description of Σ in some optimal encoding scheme. Now, because noisy examples thwart regularities, removing a noisy example from E^+ or E^- will often allow for the construction of a correct theory that is simpler than the simplest theory that is correct with respect to E^+ and E^-. Thus if we have some way of computing the MDL of the simplest correct theory for given sets of examples, then we can identify an example e as noisy, in case this MDL is significantly lowered by removing e from the examples. In this way, we have a heuristic to detect—and afterwards eliminate—noisy examples. Unfortunately, the actual MDL of the simplest correct theory is usually not computable, so in order to be able to apply this method in practice, we need to approximate it in some way. An overview of some approximations may be found in [Sta96a].[1]

19.6   Implementation and Application

Below we describe, more or less chronologically, the basic features of some of the best known implemented ILP systems. No doubt this section of our book will be outdated within a few years, since new systems come up all the time. Nevertheless, there are two good reasons for discussing some implementations here. Firstly, these systems provide examples of the way that the results of the previous chapters can be used in practice. We want to emphasise that the results we presented in this book are not just theory, but are the actual building blocks of practical and useful learning programs. Secondly, ILP papers often mention these systems as related work, without explaining how they work. We hope the short descriptions below help the reader to understand those papers better.

Mis Since we have devoted quite a lot of attention to Shapiro's work in Chapter 10, we can be brief about his top-down, interactive, incremental multiple-predicate learner Model Inference System Mis [Sha81b, Sha83]: it is an implementation of the Model Inference Algorithm, restricted to Horn clauses.

Cigol Muggleton and Buntine's Cigol [MB88] is a bottom-up, interactive, incremental multiple-predicate learner. Given a positive example that is not implied by the theory, the system uses inverse resolution to construct definite program clauses which enable the positive example to be deduced, while remaining consistent with respect to the negative examples. It uses the W-operator for predicate invention. The search through the possible inverse resolution steps is guided by a heuristic based on data compression, while an oracle—the user—is asked whether induced clauses are true (in the interpretation intended by the user), and how invented predicates should be named.

Other systems based on some form of inverse resolution include Marvin [SB86] and Itou [Rou92].

Foil Quinlan's Foil [Qui90, QC93, CQ93, CQ94] is a top-down, non-interactive, batch single-predicate learner, which upgrades his earlier decision tree learner Id3 [Qui86]. It learns function-free normal programs using the *covering approach* of the AQ system [Mic83], which means that the

---

[1] Actually, MDL can also be used to compare the "simplicity" of various theories, or the extent to which those theories "compress" (represent more economically) the examples When faced with the choice between several correct theories, it is usually good advice to choose the simplest or most compressive theory. See, e.g. [MB94, Sta96a].

clauses of the theory are learned one by one. Each new clause C that the system constructs should be such that C, together with the current theory (i.e., the clauses already constructed earlier) and the background knowledge implies some positive examples that are not implied without C, while C together with the positive examples and the background knowledge implies no negative examples. It adds this clause to the current theory and removes the derived positive examples from the set of examples. It then constructs another clause, adds it to the current theory, and so on, until all positive examples can be derived. Each clause of the theory is constructed starting from the head $P(x_1, \ldots, x_n)$ (where P is the predicate to be learned), which is then specialized by means of a downward refinement operator that adds new literals to the body of the clause. The search through the refinement graph (i.e., the selection of literals that will be added) is guided by an information gain heuristic.

Golem Muggleton and Feng's GOLEM [MF92] is a bottom-up, non-interactive, batch single-predicate learner, which employs least generalizations under relative subsumption (LGRS). Given an allowed definite program Π as background knowledge, it first constructs M_h, which is the set of all ground atoms that can be deduced from Π with at most h resolution steps. It generalizes positive examples (ground atoms) $e_1, \ldots, e_n$ by taking their LGRS relative to M_h, which is the LGS of $\{(e_1 \leftarrow M_h), \ldots, (e_n \leftarrow M_h)\}$ (see Chapter 16). Because this LGS may have up to $1 + |M_h|^n$ literals, GOLEM only uses the largest subclause of this LGS which is ij-determinate with respect to M_h (h, i, and j are constants provided by the user). This subclause can be shown to have a polynomially-bounded number of literals. Since the induced clauses must be consistent with respect to E^-, it is usually not possible to construct a single LGRS for all positive examples, so different subsets of E^+ need to be generalized to different clauses.

Linus The non-interactive batch single-predicate learner LINUS [LDG91, LD94] transforms ILP problems to an attribute-value representation, consisting of a number of objects that have certain values for certain attributes. The transformed learning problem is then solved by an attribute-value learner, for example ASSISTANT [CKB87], which uses decision trees, or CN2 [CN89, CB91], which uses a kind of downward refinement operator to learn appropriate if-then rules. The solution induced by such a system is then translated back to a set of clauses. Handling of noise and real-valued parameters is also done by these attribute-value learners. The possible theories that LINUS induces are constrained, non-recursive function-free normal programs.

Clint The interactive and incremental multiple-predicate learner CLINT [DB92, DR92] combines many different features. It starts with an initial knowledge base KB (a definite program), which is adjusted to the examples that are given. If a negative example is implied, the Backtracing Algorithm is invoked to find a clause responsible for this, which is then deleted. If a positive example is not implied, CLINT first tries an abductive procedure. If this fails, it tries to find a new definite program clause in a simple language L_1 such that addition of the new clause would make KB correct. If such a clause cannot be found in L_1, the system tries again in a more expressive language L_2, and so on. CLINT is one of the few systems able to deal with a set IT of *integrity constraints*. Such a constraint is a clause expressing some relationship that should hold, such as $Male(x) \lor Female(x) \lor \neg Human(x)$ (every human being is male or female) or $\neg Male(x) \lor \neg Female(x)$ (nothing is both male and female). The union of KB and IT should be consistent. Finally, CLINT is able use a multi-valued logic in order to handle negation better.

Mobal This is an integrated knowledge acquisition environment, consisting of several parts [MWKE93]. One of these is the top-down, non-interactive, batch multiple-predicate learner RDT [KW92]. It learns function-free normal programs, using a set of ground literals as background knowledge (if the background knowledge is a normal program, this is replaced by a set of ground literals as in GOLEM). The language bias is specified by a set of *rule schemas*. A rule schema is a "clause" with predicate-variables instead of ordinary predicate symbols. Only clauses that can be obtained by instantiating the predicate-variables in one of the given rule schemas to ordinary predicate symbols may be used in the theory. The search space is further restricted by partitioning the set of available predicates in (not necessarily disjoint) sets. Each set is a node in a tree, the so-called *predicate topology*, which describes dependency-relations among the predicates. The predicates in the body of clause should either be in the same node as, or in a child of the node that contains the predicate in the head of the clause. As a simple example, suppose $\Phi(x) \leftarrow \Psi(x)$ is a given rule schema, where Φ and Ψ are predicate-variables. Now any clause obtained by substituting predicate symbols P and Q for Φ and Ψ, respectively, is permitted for the theory, provided P and Q are in the same node of the predicate topology or Q is in a child of the node of P. The resulting search space is then searched in a top-down fashion.

Claudien The clausal discovery engine CLAUDIEN is a top-down, non-interactive batch learner [DB93]. It operates in the nonmonotonic setting, where each example is a Herbrand interpretation, using only positive examples. The system starts with the empty clause $\Box$, and uses a downward refinement operator to find the most general clauses true in each of the positive examples. Of the systems listed in this section,

CLAUDIEN is the only one that induces full, rather than definite or normal program clauses.

Spectre Boström and Idestam-Almquist's SPECTRE [BI94, Bos95a] is a top-down, non-interactive, batch single-predicate learner, which specializes an overly general definite program using type 1 unfolding and clause deletion. If A is a negative example such that there is an SLD-refutation of the theory Π and $\leftarrow A$ (i.e., $\Pi \models A$), then the first input clause in the derivation is unfolded and deleted; the literal on which to unfold is selected by an information gain heuristic, similar to the one FOIL uses. SPECTRE II [Bos95b] overcomes some difficulties of SPECTRE concerning recursive clauses, and enables multiple-predicate learning.

Other systems that use unfolding are IMPUT [AGB96], which selects the clause that will be unfolded using a version of the Backtracing Algorithm, and JIGSAW [AB95].

Progol Muggleton's PROGOL [Mug95] is a top-down, non-interactive batch multiple-predicate learner. It learns clauses one by one, using an A*-like heuristic algorithm to search top-down through a refinement graph. It restricts attention to clauses that subsume some *bottom clause*, which is constructed on the basis of the examples and background knowledge.[2]

Of the many other existing systems, let us just mention CRUSTACEAN [ALLM94a, ALLM94b], which can induce small recursive programs, and TRACY [BG94, BG96b, BG96a], which is based on exhaustive search of a finite Clause Set provided by the user.

We end this section by mentioning some of the most prominent real-world domains in which the above-mentioned systems—as well as many others— have been applied. How should we judge or evaluate a theory induced from real-world examples? The most common method is to split the given sets of examples in two parts: the *training* set and the *test* set. The theory is then learned from the first group of examples, and tested on the second. The main outcome of this test is the *accuracy* of the theory, the percentage of the examples from the test set that were classified correctly as true or false by the theory (and background knowledge). The higher this accuracy, the more confidence we have in the theory. Apart from such a "mechanical" evaluation, one can also ask domain experts (e.g., biologists, doctors) whether they understand and accept the induced theory.

Thus far, the most successful real-world applications of ILP have been in the field of biology. Particularly the work on *molecular* biology is really a showcase for the potential power of ILP. GOLEM has been used to learn rules that can predict the 3-dimensional shape (*secondary structure*) of a protein from its amino acid sequence (*primary structure*) [KS90, MKS92], and to

---

[2]However, Yamamoto [Yam96] has noted some difficulties here.

learn regularities in the relationship between chemical structure and activity [KMLS92, KSS95]. PROGOL has also been used for predicting structure-activity relationships, including the *mutagenicity* of molecular compounds, which is a cause of cancer [SMKS94, KMSS96, MSP96, SK96, SMSK96]. The results obtained by these systems are particularly impressive in that they were understandable for human biologists and were sufficiently novel to be published in the scientific literature on molecular biology. Other biological applications of ILP include classifying the quality of river water [DDRW94] (using GOLEM and CLAUDIEN).

Apart from biology, some other areas of application are finite element mesh design, which is concerned with partitioning an object into a finite number of elements in order to be able to do some computation on it [DM92, DBJ94]; the modeling and control of dynamical systems [BMV92, UB94]; medical diagnosis [LDPK93, MODS96]; natural language processing [Coh96, MC95, Moo96]; and software engineering [BG96a]. Further information on applications of ILP may be found in a number of recent overview papers [BK94, BD95, BM95, DB96].

19.7   What Has Not Been Covered

Inevitably, there remain some topics that are important for ILP, and yet have not been covered in this book. To make the reader aware of some of these, we end this book with the following list:

- In the introduction to this chapter, we mentioned that search could be made more tractable by means of heuristics or by means of language bias. We have not devoted any attention to search heuristics, because these are often rather application-dependent.

- The possible instantiations of an atom are often restricted by prescribing a *type* for each argument place in the predicate. Each object in the domain then has its own type, and can only be inserted in argument places for which the same type has been prescribed. For instance, if we want to use $OwnsPet(x, y)$ to denote that person x owns animal y as a pet, then we may only substitute terms of type 'human being' for x, and terms of type 'animal' for y. This reduces the number of possible ground instances of atoms.

- Handling numbers and (in)equalities, and doing arithmetical computations is quite cumbersome in clausal logic, because each number has to be represented by a unique ground term. We might for instance represent the natural numbers by 0, $s(0)$, $s^2(0)$, etc., but definite programs that compute addition or multiplication for numbers in this representation are rather inefficient. Handling *real* (or, at least, non-integer) numbers proves to be even more difficult within the boundaries of logic.

Usually, extra-logical means are needed to handle numbers and numerical computations efficiently. Only recently has the ILP community begun to incorporate ways of handling numbers into its systems. (Some work on this may be found in Part III of [Dže95b].)

- In connection with the problem of handling numbers, *constraint logic programming* (CLP) [JM94] deserves to be mentioned. CLP is a recent extension of logic programming in which a clause is augmented by a set of (often numerical) *constraints*, that have to be solved by a constraint solver. This enables CLP to handle numbers and arithmetic in an efficient way, thereby correcting one of the deficiencies of "plain" logic programming.

  As yet, not much attention has gone into combining ILP and CLP, the only exception we know of is [SR96]. Another way to remedy the weaknesses of ILP regarding numbers and arithmetic is to combine ILP with learning techniques better suited for handling numbers, such as instance-based learning [EW96].

- Except for Chapter 18, we have made virtually no use of *statistics* in this book. Still, statistics—particularly Bayes' Theorem—may sometimes be very useful in theoretical analysis. For statistical work on ILP, we refer to Section 6 of [MD94], and [Mug94, Mug96a]. Related to this are so-called *stochastic* definite programs [Mug96b], which work probabilistically.

19.8 Summary

In this chapter we briefly covered some topics that had been touched on only marginally in earlier chapters. Firstly, in order to make the search for a correct theory and the testing of correctness tractable, we have to impose some constraints (*language bias*) on the set of clauses which may be included in the theory. On the other hand, the extension of the language with new predicate symbols (*predicate invention*) is also sometimes required. *Flattening* allows us to make a theory function-free, transferring the function symbols to new predicates. Furthermore, practical applications of ILP often have to cope with *imperfect data*, particularly random errors in the examples (*noise*). We indicated some ways to deal with this. Finally, we gave an overview of some of the most prominent implemented systems.

19.A   Results for Flattening

In this appendix we prove some results about flattening. Here we use P_f to refer to the new predicate symbol introduced by flattening to replace the function symbol f. Firstly, we will show that flattening "preserves" the subsumption relation. The following lemma can be illustrated with an example.

Example 19.4 Suppose $C = P(f(x), f(y))$ and $D = P(f(a), f(a))$, then $C\theta \subseteq D$ for $\theta = \{x/a, y/a\}$. Flattening D yields $Flat(D) = P(z, z) \leftarrow P_f(a, z)$. Now we no longer have $C \succeq Flat(D)$, since $f(x)$ and $f(y)$ in C, which were mapped to $f(a)$ by θ, cannot be mapped to z. However, suppose we "flatten away" the terms $f(x)$ and $f(y)$ in C as well, replacing $f(x)$ by u and $f(y)$ by v. Then we obtain $Flat(C) = P(u, v) \leftarrow P_f(x, u), P_f(y, v)$, and we have $Flat(C)\theta' \subseteq Flat(D)$ for $\theta' = \{x/a, y/a, u/z, v/z\}$.   ◁

Lemma 19.5 *Let C and D be definite program clauses. If $C \succeq D$, then $Flat(C) \succeq Flat(D)$.*

Proof Suppose $C \succeq D$. Let θ be such that $C\theta \subseteq D$, and let e be the number of executions of the while-loop that the Flattening Algorithm uses to flatten D (note that e equals the number of new P_f-atoms in the body of $Flat(D)$). The proof will be by induction on e.

1. If $e = 0$, then D is function-free and $Flat(D) = D$. By Gottlob's Lemma (Lemma 15.2), C must be function-free as well, so $Flat(C) = C$ and the result follows.

2. Suppose the lemma holds for $e \leq m$, and the algorithm needs $m + 1$ executions of its while-loop to flatten D. Let $t = f(t_1, \ldots, t_n)$ be the term in D that is flattened in the first execution of the while-loop, and D' be the clause obtained after this first execution. Then D' contains the atom $P_f(t_1, \ldots, t_n, y)$ in its body.

   We assume without loss of generality that C does not contain the variable y, and θ only acts on variables in C. We will adjust C to C', and θ to θ', in such a way that we have $C'\theta' \subseteq D'$. Let $\{s_1, \ldots, s_k\}$ be the set of distinct terms occurring in C for which $s_i\theta = t$. For $i = 1, \ldots, k$, successively adjust C and θ in the following way. If s_i is a variable, then replace the binding s_i/t in θ by s_i/y. If $s_i = f(r_1, \ldots, r_n)$, in which case the r_j are variables or constants, then replace all occurrences of s_i in C by a new variable y_i, add $P_f(r_1, \ldots, r_n, y_i)$ to the body of C (note that this is actually one application of the while-loop of the flattening algorithm), and add the binding y_i/y to θ. Call the clause resulting from these k adjustments C'. Finally, replace all occurrences of t in bindings in (the adjusted version of) θ by y, and call the resulting substitution θ'.

   Now it can be seen that $C'\theta' \subseteq D'$, so we have $C' \succeq D'$. The Flattening Algorithm needs only m executions of its while loop in order to flatten

D', so from the induction hypothesis we have $Flat(C') \succeq Flat(D')$. Because C' has been obtained from C by several applications of the while-loop of the Flattening Algorithm, $Flat(C)$ and $Flat(C')$ must be variants. Since also $Flat(D) = Flat(D')$, the result follows.   □

The exact converse to this lemma does not hold. For instance, let C be some clause which is not function-free, and $D = Flat(C)$. Then we have $Flat(C) \succeq Flat(C) = D = Flat(D)$, yet clearly $C \not\succeq D$ by Gottlob's Lemma. We do, however, have the following:

Lemma 19.6 *Let C and D be definite program clauses, not containing any of the P_f predicate symbols. If $Flat(C) \succeq Flat(D)$, then $C \succeq D$.*

Proof Suppose $Flat(C)\theta \subseteq Flat(D)$, for some θ. If D is function-free, then by Gottlob's Lemma C must be function-free as well, hence $C = Flat(C)$ and $D = Flat(D)$, and the lemma holds. If D is not function-free, we will stepwisely "unflatten" $Flat(C)$ and $Flat(D)$, preserving the subsumption relation in each step.

Let $A = P_f(t_1, \ldots, t_n, y)$ be the last atom added to the body of D in the application of the Flattening Algorithm to D, and $A_1 = P_f(s_{1,1}, \ldots, s_{n,1}, y_1)$, $\ldots, A_k = P_f(s_{1,k}, \ldots, s_{n,k}, y_k)$ be the $k \geq 0$ atoms in $Flat(C)$ which are mapped to A by θ. Note that $y_i\theta = y$ and $s_{j,i}\theta = t_j$ is a constant or variable, for every $1 \leq i \leq k$ and $1 \leq j \leq n$. Change $Flat(D)$ to D' in the following way: replace all occurrences of y in $Flat(D)$ by $t = f(t_1, \ldots, t_n)$, and remove A from the body of D (this amounts to undoing one flattening step). Change $Flat(C)$ to C' in the following way: for every $i = 1, \ldots, k$, replace all occurrences of y_i by $f(s_{i,1}, \ldots, s_{i,n})$, and remove A_i from the body of $Flat(C)$ (this amounts to undoing k flattening steps). Change θ to θ' by replacing every occurrence of y in bindings in θ by t, and by removing all bindings x/s from θ for which x does not occur in C'. Note that since θ maps every literal in $Flat(C)$ to a literal in $Flat(D)$, we must have that θ' maps every literal in C' to a literal in D', hence $C'\theta' \subseteq D'$.

If we apply this unflattening step to C' and D' a number of times, we end up with C and D themselves, and we have $C \succeq D$.   □

Combining the last two lemmas:

Corollary 19.7 *Let C and D be definite program clauses, not containing any of the P_f predicate symbols. Then $C \succeq D$ iff $Flat(C) \succeq Flat(D)$.*

Now that we have shown that flattening preserves the subsumption relation, we will continue to show that it also preserves the implication relation, if we take into account the atoms in $FlatDefs$. Firstly, since resolving a flattened clause $Flat(C)$ with atoms from $FlatDefs(C)$ gives us back the original clause C, we immediately have the following result:

Theorem 19.8 *If* Π *is a definite program, then* $Flat(\Pi) \cup FlatDefs(\Pi) \models$ Π.

The converse of this theorem does not hold. For example, Π does not imply the atoms in $FlatDefs(\Pi)$. We do have the following results.

Lemma 19.9 *Let* Π *be a definite program and* C *be a definite program clause, such that* Π *and* C *do not contain any of the* P_f *predicate symbols. If* $Flat(\Pi) \vdash_{sr} Flat(C)$, *then* $\Pi \vdash_{sr} C$.

Proof Suppose there is an SLD-derivation of $Flat(C)$ from $Flat(\Pi)$, with top clause $Flat(C_1)$ and input clauses $Flat(C_2), \ldots, Flat(C_n)$. Let k_i be the number of new atoms (each having P_f as predicate symbol, for some f) added to the body of C_i when $Flat(C_i)$ was obtained ($1 \leq i \leq n$). Note that each of these atoms must occur in $Flat(C)$, since none of them could have been resolved away. Thus $Flat(C)$ contains $k = k_1 + \ldots + k_n$ new atoms with P_f predicate symbols.

There exists an SLD-derivation of C from $Flat(C)$ and k input clauses (atoms) from $FlatDefs(C)$. Adding this derivation "under" the derivation we already had, we obtain an SLD-derivation of C from $Flat(\Pi)$ and $FlatDefs(\Pi)$, with top clause $Flat(C_1)$, and input clauses $Flat(C_2), \ldots,$ $Flat(C_n)$, followed by k input clauses from $FlatDefs(\Pi)$.

Similar to the Switching Lemma, we can move the k input clauses from $FlatDefs(\Pi)$ "upward" in the derivation, such that each (top or input) clause $Flat(C_i)$ in the derivation is followed by k_i input clauses from $FlatDefs(\Pi)$, which exactly resolve away the k_i P_f-atoms introduced in the center clauses by $Flat(C_i)$. Now, leaving some details to the reader, each combination of $Flat(C_i)$ and k_i atoms from $FlatDefs(\Pi)$ may be replaced by C_i itself. This yields an SLD-derivation of C from Π, with top clause C_1 and input clauses $C_2, \ldots, C_n$. Thus we have $\Pi \vdash_{sr} C$. □

Combining the previous lemma with the result about subsumption:

Theorem 19.10 *Let* Π *be a definite program and* C *be a definite program clause, such that* Π *and* C *do not contain any of the* P_f *predicate symbols. If* $Flat(\Pi) \models Flat(C)$, *then* $\Pi \models C$.

Proof Suppose $Flat(\Pi) \models Flat(C)$. If $Flat(C)$ is a tautology, then C is a tautology and the lemma holds. Suppose C is not a tautology. Then by the Subsumption Theorem for SLD-resolution, there exists a function-free clause D such that $Flat(\Pi) \vdash_{sr} D$ and $D \succeq Flat(C)$. Note that there must be a clause D', not containing any P_f predicate symbol, such that $D = Flat(D')$ (i.e., D' is the "unflattened" version of D). Then by the previous lemma, we have $\Pi \vdash_{sr} D'$. From Lemma 19.6 it follows that $D' \succeq C$. Hence $\Pi \models C$ □

In particular, if C and D do not contain any of the P_f predicate symbols, and $Flat(C) \models Flat(D)$, then $C \models D$.

Together, Theorems 19.8 and 19.10 give us the following result, which shows that flattening in a certain sense "preserves" the logical consequences of the original theory Π.

Theorem 19.11 *Let Π be a definite program and C be a definite program clause, such that Π and C do not contain any of the P_f predicate symbols. Then $\Pi \models C$ iff $Flat(\Pi) \cup FlatDefs(\Pi) \models Flat(C)$.*

List of Symbols

Sets

$\in$	element
$\subseteq$	subset
$\subset$	proper subset
$\supseteq$	superset
$\supset$	proper superset
$\cup$	union
$\cap$	intersection
$\setminus$	set difference
Δ	symmetric difference
$\emptyset$	empty set
$|S|$	cardinality of set S
2^S	power set (set of all subsets) of set S
$S \times T$	Cartesian product of sets S and T
S^n	n-fold Cartesian product of set S
$\mathbf{N}$	the set of natural numbers
$\mathbf{Q}$	the set of rational numbers
$\mathbf{R}$	the set of real numbers

Logic

$\wedge$	conjunction (and)
$\vee$	disjunction (or)
$\neg$	negation
$\rightarrow$	implication
$\leftarrow$	implication (in program clauses)
$\leftrightarrow$	equivalence
$\forall$	universal quantifier
$\exists$	existential quantifier
T	true
F	false

$\models$	logical implication
$\Leftrightarrow$	logical equivalence
ε	empty substitution
$\overline{S}$	set of negations of formulas in set S
M_Π	least Herbrand model of definite program Π
F_Π	SLD finite failure set of definite program Π
$comp(\Pi)$	completion of normal program Π
$\vdash_r$	(unconstrained) derivation
$\vdash_d$	(unconstrained) deduction
$\vdash_{lr}$	linear derivation
$\vdash_{ld}$	linear deduction
$\vdash_{ir}$	input derivation
$\vdash_{id}$	input deduction
$\vdash_{sr}$	SLD-derivation
$\vdash_{sd}$	SLD-deduction
$\vdash_{snf}$	SLDNF-resolution
$\mathcal{R}$	computation rule

Languages and quasi-orders

$\mathcal{A}$	set of all atoms in a language
$\mathcal{H}$	Horn language
$\mathcal{C}$	clausal language
$\mathcal{C}^{newsize}$	$\mathcal{C}$ bounded by $newsize$
$\mathcal{C}_h$	hypothesis language in model inference
$\mathcal{C}_o$	observational language in model inference
$\mathcal{C}_o^I$	part of $\mathcal{C}_o$ that is true under interpretation I
$\mathcal{R}$	set of all reduced clauses in $\mathcal{C}$
$\mathcal{R}^{newsize}$	$\mathcal{R}$ bounded by $newsize$
$\mathcal{S}$	set of all theories from $\mathcal{C}$
C^{pos}	clause consisting of all positive literals in clause C
C^{neg}	clause consisting of all negative literals in clause C
C^+	head of program clause C
C^-	body of program clause C
$\top$	top element in lattice
$\bot$	bottom element in lattice
$\square$	empty clause
$\geq$	arbitrary quasi-order
$\langle S, \geq \rangle$	set S quasi-ordered by $\geq$
$A \sqcap B$	greatest lower bound of $\{A, B\}$
$A \sqcup B$	least upper bound of $\{A, B\}$
$\succeq$	subsumption
$\approx$	equivalence relation induced by quasi-order (for atoms: variants)
$\sim$	subsume-equivalence

$\succeq_a$	atomic order
$\mathcal{B}$	background knowledge
$\succeq_\mathcal{B}$	relative subsumption
$\models_\mathcal{B}$	relative implication
$\geq_\mathcal{B}$	generalized subsumption

Refinement operators

$\rho_\mathcal{A}$	downward refinement operator for atoms
ρ_L	downward refinement operator under subsumption
ρ_r	downward refinement operator for reduced clauses
ρ_I	downward refinement operator under implication
$\delta_\mathcal{A}$	upward refinement operator for atoms
δ_u	upward refinement operator under subsumption
δ_r	upward refinement operator for reduced clauses

PAC learning

Σ^*	set of all finite strings over alphabet Σ
$X^{[n]}$	set of all strings of length at most n in domain X
$\mathcal{F}$	concept class
$f^{[n]}$	projection of concept f on $X^{[n]}$
$\mathcal{F}^{[n]}$	projection of concept class $\mathcal{F}$ on $X^{[n]}$
$\mathbf{P}$	probability distribution
$\mathbf{D}_{VC}$	Vapnik-Chervonenkis dimension
δ	confidence parameter
ε	error parameter
η	rate of malicious or random classification noise
η_b	upper bound on η
$l_{min}(f, R)$	size (shortest name) of concept f in representation R

Bibliography

[AB92]   M. Anthony and N. Biggs. *Computational Learning Theory.* Cambridge University Press, Cambridge, UK, 1992.

[AB94]   K. R. Apt and R. Bol. Logic programming and negation: A survey. *Journal of Logic Programming*, 19/20:9–71, 1994.

[AB95]   H. Adé and H. Boström. JIGSAW: Puzzling together RUTH and SPECTRE. In [LW95], pages 263–266.

[AD94]   K. R. Apt and K. Doets. A new definition of SLDNF-resolution. *Journal of Logic Programming*, 18(2):177–190, 1994.

[AE82]   K. R. Apt and M. H. van Emden. Contributions to the theory of logic programming. *Journal of the ACM*, 29(3):841–862, 1982.

[AGB96]   Z. Alexin, T. Gyimóthy, and H. Boström. Integrating algorithmic debugging and unfolding transformation in an interactive learner. In [Wah96], pages 403–407.

[AIS97]   H. Arimura, H. Ishizaka, and T. Shinohara. Learning unions of tree patterns using queries. *Theoretical Computer Science*, 1997. Forthcoming.

[AISO94]   H. Arimura, H. Ishizaka, T. Shinohara, and S. Otsuki. A generalization of the least general generalization. *Machine Intelligence*, 13:59–85, 1994.

[AL88]   D. Angluin and P. Laird. Learning from noisy examples. *Machine Learning*, 2(4):343–370, 1988.

[ALLM94a] D. W. Aha, S. Lapointe, C. X. Ling, and S. Matwin. Inverting implication with small training sets. In [BD94], pages 31–48.

[ALLM94b] D. W. Aha, S. Lapointe, C. X. Ling, and S. Matwin. Learning relations with randomly selected small training sets. In W. Cohen and H. Hirsh, editors, *Proceedings of the 11th International Conference on Machine Learning (ICML-94)*, pages 12–18. Morgan Kaufmann, San Mateo, CA, 1994.

[Ang87]   D. Angluin. Learning regular sets from queries and counterex-
            amples. *Information and Computation*, 75(2):87–106, 1987.

[Ang88]   D. Angluin. Queries and concept learning. *Machine Learning*,
            2(4):319–342, 1988.

[Apt90]   K. R. Apt. Logic programming. In J. van Leeuwen, editor,
            Handbook of Theoretical Computer Science, Volume B, pages
            493–574. Elsevier, Amsterdam, 1990.

[Apt97]   K. R. Apt. *From Logic Programming to Prolog*. Prentice-Hall,
            1997.

[Ari60]   Aristotle. *Posterior Analytics*. Harvard University Press, Cam-
            bridge, MA, 1960. Edited and translated by Hugh Tredennick.

[AS83]   D. Angluin and C. H. Smith. Inductive inference: Theory and
            methods. *Computing Surveys*, 15:237–269, 1983.

[ASY92]   S. Arikawa, T. Shinohara, and A. Yamamoto. Learning elemen-
            tary formal systems. *Theoretical Computer Science*, 95:97–113,
            1992.

[AT95]   K. R. Apt and F. Teusink. Comparing negation in logic pro-
            gramming and in Prolog. In K. R. Apt and F. Turini, editors,
            Meta-Logics and Logic Programming, pages 111–133. MIT Press,
            Cambridge, MA, 1995.

[Bac94]   F. Bacon. *Novum Organum*. Open Court, Chicago, IL, 1994.
            Edited and translated by P. Urbach and J. Gibson. First pub-
            lished in 1620.

[Baj93]   R. Bajcsy, editor. *Proceedings of the 13th International Joint
            Conference on Artificial Intelligence (IJCAI-93)*. Morgan Kauf-
            mann, San Mateo, CA, 1993.

[Ban64]   R. B. Banerji. A language for the description of concepts. *Gen-
            eral Systems*, 9:135–141, 1964.

[Ban87]   R. B. Banerji. A discussion of a report by Ehud Shapiro. *Com-
            putational Intelligence*, 3:295–303, 1987.

[BB75]   L. Blum and M. Blum. Towards a mathematical theory of in-
            ductive inference. *Information and Control*, 28:125–155, 1975.

[BD94]   F. Bergadano and L. De Raedt, editors. *Proceedings of the 7th
            European Conference on Machine Learning (ECML-94)*, Vol.
            784 of *Lecture Notes in Artificial Intelligence*. Springer-Verlag,
            Berlin, 1994.

[BD95]   I. Bratko and S. Džeroski. Engineering applications of inductive
            logic programming. *New Generation Computing*, 13:313–333,
            1995.

[BEHW89]   A. Blumer, A. Ehrenfeucht, D. Haussler, and M. Warmuth.
            Learnability and the Vapnik-Chervonenkis dimension. *Journal
            of the ACM*, 36(4):929–965, 1989.

[Bez90]   M. Bezem. Completeness of resolution revisited. *Theoretical
            Computer Science*, 74:227–237, 1990.

[BG93]   F. Bergadano and D. Gunetti. Basing top-down methods on
            inverse resolution. In [Tor93], pages 190–201.

[BG94]   F. Bergadano and D. Gunetti. Learning clauses by tracing
            derivations. In [Wro94], pages 11–29.

[BG96a]   F. Bergadano and D. Gunetti. *Inductive Logic Programming:
            From Machine Learning to Software Engineering*. MIT Press,
            Cambridge, MA, 1996.

[BG96b]   F. Bergadano and D. Gunetti. Learning logic programs with
            negation as failure. In [DR96], pages 107–123.

[BGA56]   J. S. Bruner, J. J. Goodnow, and G. A. Austin. *A Study of
            Thinking*. Wiley, New York, 1956.

[BGS91]   F. Bergadano, A. Giordana, and L. Saitta. *Machine Learning:
            An Integrated Framework and its Applications*. Ellis Horwood,
            New York, 1991.

[BI94]   H. Boström and P. Idestam-Almquist. Specialization of logic
            programs by pruning SLD-trees. In [Wro94], pages 31–48.

[BJ89]   G. S. Boolos and R. C. Jeffrey. *Computability and Logic*. Cam-
            bridge University Press, Cambridge, UK, third edition, 1989.

[BK94]   I. Bratko and R. D. King. Applications of inductive logic pro-
            gramming. *SIGART Bulletin*, 5(1):43–49, 1994.

[BM92]   M. Bain and S. Muggleton. Non-monotonic learning. In
            [Mug92a], pages 145–153.

[BM95]   I. Bratko and S. Muggleton. Applications of inductive logic pro-
            gramming. *Communications of the ACM*, 38(11):65–70, 1995.

[BMV92]   I. Bratko, S. Muggleton, and A. Varšek. Learning qualitative
            models of dynamic systems. In [Mug92a], pages 437–452.

[Boo58]   G. Boole. *An Investigation of the Laws of Thought on which are Founded the Mathematical Theories of Logic and Probabilities.* Dover, New York, 1958. First published in 1854.

[Bos95a]   H. Boström. Covering vs. divide-and-conquer for top-down induction of logic programs. In *Proceedings of the 14th International Joint Conference on Artificial Intelligence (IJCAI-95)*, pages 1194–1200. Morgan Kaufmann, San Mateo, CA, 1995.

[Bos95b]   H. Boström. Specialization of recursive predicates. In [LW95], pages 92–106.

[Bra90]   I. Bratko. *Prolog Programming for Artificial Intelligence.* Addison Wesley, Wokingham, second edition, 1990.

[Bra93]   P. B. Brazdil, editor. *Proceedings of the 6th European Conference on Machine Learning (ECML-93)*, Vol. 667 of *Lecture Notes in Artificial Intelligence*. Springer-Verlag, Berlin, 1993.

[Bun86]   W. Buntine. Generalized subsumption. In *Proceedings of the 7th European Conference on Artificial Intelligence (ECAI-86)*. Brighton, 1986.

[Bun88]   W. Buntine. Generalized subsumption and its applications to induction and redundancy. *Artificial Intelligence*, 36(2):149–176, 1988.

[Car50]   R. Carnap. *Logical Foundations of Probability.* Routledge & Kegan Paul, London, 1950.

[Car52]   R. Carnap. *The Continuum of Inductive Methods.* The University of Chicago Press, Chicago, IL, 1952.

[CB91]   P. Clark and R. Boswell. Rule induction with CN2: Some recent improvements. In [Kod91], pages 151–163.

[Chu36]   A. Church. A note on the Entscheidungsproblem. *Journal of Symbolic Logic*, 1(1):40–41, 1936. Correction, ibidem (3), pages 101–102.

[CKB87]   B. Cestnik, I. Kononenko, and I. Bratko. ASSISTANT 86: A knowledge elicitation tool for sophisticated users. In I. Bratko and N. Lavrač, editors, *Progress in Machine Learning*, pages 31–45. Sigma Press, Wilmslow, UK, 1987.

[CL73]   C. L. Chang and R. C. T. Lee. *Symbolic Logic and Mechanical Theorem Proving.* Academic Press, San Diego, CA, 1973.

[Cla78]   K. L. Clark. Negation as failure. In [GM78], pages 293–322.

[Cla79]   K. L. Clark. Predicate logic as a computational formalism. Research Report DOC 79/59, Department of Computing, Imperial College, London, 1979.

[CLR90]   T. Cormen, C. Leiserson, and R. Rivest. *Introduction to Algorithms*. MIT Press, Cambridge, MA, 1990.

[CM87]   W. F. Clocksin and C. S. Mellish. *Programming in Prolog*. Springer-Verlag, Berlin, third edition, 1987.

[CN89]   P. Clark and T. Niblett. The CN2 induction algorithm. *Machine Learning*, 3(4):261–283, 1989.

[Coh93a]   W. W. Cohen. Cryptographic limitations on learning one-clause logic programs. In *Proceedings of the 10th National Conference on Artificial Intelligence*. 1993.

[Coh93b]   W. W. Cohen. Learnability of restricted logic programs. In [Mug93], pages 41–71.

[Coh94a]   W. W. Cohen. Grammatically biased learning: Learning logic programs using an explicit antecedent description language. *Artificial Intelligence*, 68:303–366, 1994.

[Coh94b]   W. W. Cohen. Pac-learning nondeterminate clauses. In *Proceedings of the 11th National Conference on Artificial Intelligence*. 1994.

[Coh95a]   W. W. Cohen. Pac-learning non-recursive Prolog clauses. *Artificial Intelligence*, 79(1):1–38, 1995.

[Coh95b]   W. W. Cohen. Pac-learning recursive logic programs: Efficient algorithms. *Journal of Artificial Intelligence Research*, 2:501–539, 1995.

[Coh95c]   W. W. Cohen. Pac-learning recursive logic programs: Negative results. *Journal of Artificial Intelligence Research*, 2:541–573, 1995.

[Coh96]   W. W. Cohen. Learning to classify English text with ILP methods. In [DR96], pages 124–143.

[CP95]   W. W. Cohen and C. D. Page. Polynomial learnability and inductive logic programming: Methods and results. *New Generation Computing*, 13:369–410, 1995.

[CQ93]   R. M. Cameron-Jones and J. R. Quinlan. Avoiding pitfalls when learning recursive theories. In [Baj93], pages 1050–1055.

[CQ94] R. M. Cameron-Jones and J. R. Quinlan. Efficient top-down induction of logic programs. *SIGART Bulletin*, 5(1):33–42, 1994.

[DB92] L. De Raedt and M. Bruynooghe. An overview of the interactive concept-learner and theory revisor CLINT. In [Mug92a], pages 163–191.

[DB93] L. De Raedt and M. Bruynooghe. A theory of clausal discovery. In [Baj93], pages 1058–1063.

[DB96] S. Džeroski and I. Bratko. Applications of inductive logic programming. In [DR96], pages 65–81.

[DBJ94] B. Dolšak, I. Bratko, and A. Jezernik. Finite-element mesh design: An engineering domain for ILP application. In [Wro94], pages 305–320.

[DD94] L. De Raedt and S. Džeroski. First order jk-clausal theories are PAC-learnable. *Artificial Intelligence*, 70:375–392, 1994.

[DD95] L. Dehaspe and L. De Raedt. A declarative language bias for concept learning and knowledge discovery engines. Report CW 214, Computer Science Department, Katholieke Universiteit Leuven, 1995.

[DDRW94] S. Džeroski, L. Dehaspe, B. Ruck, and W. Walley. Classification of river water quality data using machine learning. In *Proceedings of the 5th International Conference on the Development and Application of Computer Techniques to Environmental Studies, Vol. I: Pollution Modeling*, pages 129–137. Computational Mechanics Publications, Southampton, 1994.

[DK96] Y. Dimopoulos and A. Kakas. Abduction and inductive learning. In [DR96], pages 144–171.

[DM92] B. Dolšak and S. Muggleton. The application of inductive logic programming to finite-element mesh design. In [Mug92a], pages 453–472.

[DMR92] S. Džeroski, S. Muggleton, and S. Russell. PAC-learnability of determinate logic programs. In *Proceedings of the 5th Annual ACM Workshop on Computational Learning Theory (COLT-92)*, pages 128–135. ACM Press, Baltimore, MD, 1992.

[DMR93] S. Džeroski, S. Muggleton, and S. Russell. Learnability of constrained logic programs. In [Bra93], pages 342–347.

[Doe94] K. Doets. *From Logic to Logic Programming*. MIT Press, Cambridge, MA, 1994.

[DR92]   L. De Raedt. *Interactive Theory Revision: An Inductive Logic Programming Approach.* Academic Press, London, 1992.

[DR95]   L. De Raedt, editor. *Proceedings of the 5th International Workshop on Inductive Logic Programming (ILP-95).* Katholieke Universiteit Leuven, 1995.

[DR96]   L. De Raedt, editor. *Advances in Inductive Logic Programming.* IOS Press, Amsterdam, 1996.

[Dže95a]   S. Džeroski. Learning first-order clausal theories in the presence of noise. In *Proceedings of the 5th Scandinavian Conference on Artificial Intelligence*, pages 51–60. IOS Press, Amsterdam, 1995.

[Dže95b]   S. Džeroski. *Numerical Constraints and Learnability in Inductive Logic Programming.* PhD thesis, Faculty of electrical engineering and computer science, University of Ljubljana, Slovenia, 1995.

[Ede85]   E. Eder. Properties of substitutions and unifications. *Journal of Symbolic Computation*, 1:31–46, 1985.

[EW96]   W. Emde and D. Wettschereck. Relational instance-based learning. In L. Saitta, editor, *Proceedings of the 13th International Conference on Machine Learning (ICML-96)*, pages 122–130. Morgan Kaufmann, San Mateo, CA, 1996.

[Fla92]   P. A. Flach. A framework for inductive logic programming. In [Mug92a], pages 193–211.

[Fla93]   P. A. Flach. Predicate invention in inductive data engineering. In [Bra93], pages 83–94.

[Fla94]   P. A. Flach. Inductive logic programming and philosophy of science. In [Wro94], pages 71–84.

[Fla95]   P. A. Flach. *Conjectures: An Inquiry Concerning the Logic of Induction.* PhD thesis, Tilburg University, 1995.

[FP93a]   M. Frazier and C. D. Page. Learnability in inductive logic programming: Some basic results and techniques. In *Proceedings of the 10th National Conference on Artificial Intelligence.* 1993.

[FP93b]   M. Frazier and C. D. Page. Learnability of recursive, nondeterminate theories: Some basic results and techniques. In [Mug93], pages 103–126.

[Fre79]   G. Frege. *Begriffsschrift, eine der arithmetischen nachgebildete Formelsprache des reinen Denkens.* Halle, 1879. English translation in [Hei77].

[GF93]   G. Gottlob and C. G. Fermüller. Removing redundancy from a clause. *Artificial Intelligence*, 61(2):263–289, 1993.

[GJ79]   M. R. Garey and D. S. Johnson. *Computers and Intractability: A Guide to the Theory of NP-Completeness*. Freeman, New York, 1979.

[GL96]   D. Gamberger and N. Lavrač. Noise detection and elimination applied to noise handling in a KRK chess endgame. In [Sto96], pages 59–75.

[GM78]   H. Gallaire and J. Minker, editors. *Logic and Data Bases*. Plenum Press, New York, 1978.

[GN87]   M. R. Genesereth and N. J. Nilsson. *Logical Foundations of Artificial Intelligence*. Morgan Kaufmann, Palo Alto, CA, 1987.

[Gol67]   E. M. Gold. Language identification in the limit. *Information and Control*, 10:447–474, 1967.

[Goo83]   N. Goodman. *Fact, Fiction, and Forecast*. Harvard University Press, Cambridge, MA, fourth edition, 1983.

[Got87]   G. Gottlob. Subsumption and implication. *Information Processing Letters*, 24(2):109–111, 1987.

[Gro92]   M. Grobelnik. Markus: An optimized model inference system. In C. Rouveirol, editor, *Proceedings of the ECAI Workshop on Logical Approaches to Machine Learning*. Wiley, Chichester, 1992.

[Hei77]   J. van Heijenoort, editor. *From Frege to Gödel: A Source Book in Mathematical Logic, 1879–1931*. Harvard University Press, Cambridge, MA, 1977.

[Hel89]   N. Helft. Induction as nonmonotonic inference. In R. J. Brachman, H. J. Levesque, and R. Reiter, editors, *Proceedings of the 1st International Conference on Principles of Knowledge Representation and Reasoning*, pages 149–156. Morgan Kaufmann, San Mateo, CA, 1989.

[Hem45a]   C. G. Hempel. Studies in the logic of confirmation (part I). *Mind*, 54(213):1–26, 1945.

[Hem45b]   C. G. Hempel. Studies in the logic of confirmation (part II). *Mind*, 54(214):97–121, 1945.

[Hem66]   C. G. Hempel. *Philosophy of Natural Science*. Prentice-Hall, Englewood Cliffs, NJ, 1966.

[Hil74]   R. Hill. LUSH-resolution and its completeness. DCL Memo 78, Department of Artificial Intelligence, University of Edinburgh, 1974.

[HS91]   D. Hume and C. Sammut. Using inverse resolution to learn relations from experiments. In L. A. Birnbaum and G. C. Collins, editors, *Proceedings of the 8th International Workshop on Machine Learning*, pages 412–416. Morgan Kaufmann, San Mateo, CA, 1991.

[HST96]   T. Horváth, R. H. Sloan, and G. Turán. Learning logic programs with random classification noise. In [Sto96], pages 97–118.

[HT96]   T. Horváth and G. Turán. Learning logic programs with structured background knowledge. In [DR96], pages 172–191.

[HU79]   J. E. Hopcroft and J. D. Ullman. *Introduction to Automata Theory, Languages, and Computation*. Addison Wesley, Reading, MA, 1979.

[Hum56]   D. Hume. *An Enquiry Concerning Human Understanding*. Gateway edition, Chicago, IL, 1956. First published in 1748.

[Hum61]   D. Hume. *A Treatise of Human Nature*. Dolphin Books. Doubleday, 1961. First published in 1739–1740.

[HW93]   P. Hanschke and J. Würtz. Satisfiability of the smallest binary program. *Information Processing Letters*, 45(5):237–241, 1993.

[Ide92]   P. Idestam-Almquist. Learning missing clauses by inverse resolution. In *Proceedings of the International Conference on Generation Computer Systems*. Ohmsha, Tokyo, 1992.

[Ide93a]   P. Idestam-Almquist. *Generalization of Clauses*. PhD thesis, Stockholm University, 1993.

[Ide93b]   P. Idestam-Almquist. Generalization under implication by using or-introduction. In [Bra93], pages 56–64.

[Ide93c]   P. Idestam-Almquist. Generalization under implication: Expansion of clauses for indirect roots. In *Proceedings of the 4th Scandinavian Conference on Artificial Intelligence*. IOS Press, Amsterdam, 1993.

[Ide95]   P. Idestam-Almquist. Generalization of clauses under implication. *Journal of Artificial Intelligence Research*, 3:467–489, 1995.

[Ino92]   K. Inoue. Linear resolution for consequence finding. *Artificial Intelligence*, 56:301–353, 1992.

[Jev74]   W. S. Jevons. *The Principles of Science: A Treatise.* Macmillan, London, 1874.

[JLL83]   J. Jaffar, J-L. Lassez, and J. W. Lloyd. Completeness of the negation as failure rule. In A. Bundy, editor, *Proceedings of the 8th International Joint Conference on Artificial Intelligence (IJCAI-83)*, pages 500–506. Morgan Kaufmann, Los Altos, CA, 1983.

[JM94]   J. Jaffar and M. J. Maher. Constraint logic programming: A survey. *Journal of Logic Programming*, 19/20:503–581, 1994.

[KD94]   J-U. Kietz and S. Džeroski. Inductive logic programming and learnability. *SIGART Bulletin*, 5(1):22–32, 1994.

[Kea93]   M. J. Kearns. Efficient noise-tolerant learning from statistical queries. In *Proceedings of the 25th ACM Symposium on the Theory of Computing*, pages 392–401. ACM Press, New York, 1993.

[Kie93]   J-U. Kietz. Some lower bounds for the computational complexity of inductive logic programming. In [Bra93], pages 115–123.

[KK71]   R. Kowalski and D. Kuehner. Linear resolution with selection function. *Artificial Intelligence*, 2:227–260, 1971.

[KKT93]   A. C. Kakas, R. A. Kowalski, and F. Toni. Abductive logic programming. *Journal of Logic and Computation*, 2(6):719–770, 1993.

[KL94]   J-U. Kietz and M. Lübbe. An efficient subsumption algorithm for inductive logic programming. In [Wro94], pages 97–105.

[KMLS92]   R. D. King, S. Muggleton, R. A. Lewis, and M. J. E. Sternberg. Drug design by machine learning: The use of inductive logic programming to model the structure-activity relationship of trimethoprim analogues binding to dihydrofolate reductase. In *Proceedings of the National Academy of Sciences*, Vol. 89(23), pages 11322–11326. 1992.

[KMSS96]   R. D. King, S. Muggleton, A. Srinivasan, and M. J. E. Sternberg. Structure-activity relationships derived by machine learning: The use of atoms and their bond connectivities to predict mutagenicity by inductive logic programming. In *Proceedings of the National Academy of Sciences*, Vol. 93, pages 438–442. 1996.

[Kod91]   Y. Kodratoff, editor. *Proceedings of the 6th European Working Sessions on Learning (EWSL-91)*, Vol. 482 of *Lecture Notes in Artificial Intelligence*. Springer-Verlag, Berlin, 1991.

[Kom82]   H. J. Komorowski. Partial evaluation as a means for inferencing data structures in an applicative language: A theory and implementation in case of Prolog. In *Proceedings of the 9th ACM Symposium on Principles of Programming Languages*, pages 255–267. ACM Press, New York, 1982.

[Kow70]   R. A. Kowalski. The case for using equality axioms in automatic demonstration. In [Lau70], pages 112–127.

[Kow74]   R. A. Kowalski. Predicate logic as a programming language. *Information Processing*, 74:569–574, 1974.

[Kow79]   R. A. Kowalski. *Logic for Problem Solving*. North-Holland, New York, 1979.

[KS90]   R. D. King and M. J. E. Sternberg. Machine learning approach for the prediction of protein secondary structure. *Journal of Molecular Biology*, 216:441–457, 1990.

[KSS95]   R. D. King, A. Srinivasan, and M. J. E. Sternberg. Relating chemical activity to structure: An examination of ILP successes. *New Generation Computing*, 13:411–434, 1995.

[KV94]   M. J. Kearns and U. V. Vazirani. *An Introduction to Computational Learning Theory*. MIT Press, Cambridge, MA, 1994.

[KW92]   J-U. Kietz and S. Wrobel. Controlling the complexity of learning in logic through syntactic and task-oriented models. In [Mug92a], pages 335–359.

[Laa95]   P. R. J. van der Laag. *An Analysis of Refinement Operators in Inductive Logic Programming*. PhD thesis, Erasmus University Rotterdam, 1995.

[Lai88]   P. D. Laird. *Learning from Good and Bad Data*. Kluwer Academic Publishers, Boston, MA, 1988.

[Lau70]   M. Laudet, editor. *Proceedings of the IRIA Symposium on Automatic Demonstration, Versailles, France, 1968*, Vol. 125 of *Lecture Notes in Mathematics*. Springer-Verlag, Berlin, 1970.

[LD90]   C. Ling and M. Dawes. SIM the inverse of Shapiro's MIS. Technical Report 263, University of Western Ontario, 1990.

[LD94]   N. Lavrač and S. Džeroski. *Inductive Logic Programming: Techniques and Applications*. Ellis Horwood, New York, 1994.

[LDB96]   N. Lavrač, S. Džeroski, and I. Bratko. Handling imperfect data in inductive logic programming. In [DR96], pages 48–64.

[LDG91]   N. Lavrač, S. Džeroski, and M. Grobelnik. Learning non-recursive definitions of relations with LINUS. In [Kod91], pages 265–281.

[LDPK93]   N. Lavrač, S. Džeroski, V. Pirnat, and V. Križman. The utility of background knowledge in learning medical diagnostic rules. *Applied Artificial Intelligence*, 7:273–293, 1993.

[Lee67]   R. C. T. Lee. *A Completeness Theorem and a Computer Program for Finding Theorems Derivable from Given Axioms*. PhD thesis, University of California, Berkeley, 1967.

[Lin92]   C. X. Ling. Logic program synthesis from good examples. In [Mug92a], pages 113–129.

[Llo87]   J. W. Lloyd. *Foundations of Logic Programming*. Springer-Verlag, Berlin, second edition, 1987.

[LMM88]   J-L. Lassez, M. J. Maher, and K. Marriot. Unification revisited. In J. Minker, editor, *Foundations of Deductive Databases and Logic Programming*, pages 587–625. Morgan Kaufmann, Los Altos, CA, 1988.

[LN92]   C. X. Ling and M. A. Narayan. A critical comparison of various methods based on inverse resolution. In [Mug92a], pages 131–143.

[LN93]   P. van der Laag and S-H. Nienhuys-Cheng. Subsumption and refinement in model inference. In [Bra93], pages 95–114.

[LN94a]   P. van der Laag and S-H. Nienhuys-Cheng. Existence and nonexistence of complete refinement operators. In [BD94], pages 307–322.

[LN94b]   P. van der Laag and S-H. Nienhuys-Cheng. A note on ideal refinement operators in inductive logic programming. In [Wro94], pages 247–262.

[LN97]   P. van der Laag and S-H. Nienhuys-Cheng. Completeness and properness of refinement operators in inductive logic programming. *Journal of Logic Programming*, 1997. Forthcoming.

[Lov70]   D. W. Loveland. A linear format for resolution. In [Lau70], pages 147–162.

[Lov78]   D. W. Loveland. *Automated Theorem Proving: A Logical Basis*. North-Holland, New York, 1978.

[LP91]   J-L. Lassez and G. Plotkin, editors. *Computational Logic*. MIT Press, Cambridge, MA, 1991.

[Luc70]   D. Luckham. Refinements in resolution theory. In [Lau70], pages 163–190.

[LV91]   M. Li and P. M. B. Vitányi. A theory of learning simple concepts under simple distributions. *SIAM Journal of Computing*, 20(5):915–935, 1991.

[LV97]   M. Li and P. M. B. Vitányi. *An Introduction to Kolmogorov Complexity and its Applications*. Springer-Verlag, Berlin, second edition, 1997.

[LW95]   N. Lavrač and S. Wrobel, editors. *Proceedings of the 8th European Conference on Machine Learning (ECML-95)*, Vol. 912 of *Lecture Notes in Artificial Intelligence*. Springer-Verlag, Berlin, 1995.

[MB88]   S. Muggleton and W. Buntine. Machine invention of first-order predicates by inverting resolution. In J. Laird, editor, *Proceedings of the 5th International Conference on Machine Learning (ICML-88)*, pages 339–352. Morgan Kaufmann, San Mateo, CA, 1988.

[MC95]   R. J. Mooney and M. E. Califf. Induction of first-order decision lists: Results on learning the past tense of English verbs. *Journal of Artificial Intelligence Research*, 3:1–24, 1995.

[MD94]   S. Muggleton and L. De Raedt. Inductive logic programming: Theory and methods. *Journal of Logic Programming*, 19/20:629–679, 1994.

[Men87]   E. Mendelson. *Introduction to Mathematical Logic*. Wadsworth & Brooks, Belmont, CA, third edition, 1987.

[MF92]   S. Muggleton and C. Feng. Efficient induction of logic programs. In [Mug92a], pages 281–298.

[Mic83]   R. S. Michalski. A theory and methodology of inductive learning. In R. S. Michalski, J. G. Carbonell, and T. M. Mitchell, editors, *Machine Learning: An Artificial Intelligence Approach*, Vol. 1, pages 83–134. Morgan Kaufmann, Palo Alto, CA, 1983.

[Mil58]   J. S. Mill. *A System of Logic, Ratiocinative and Inductive*. Harper, New York, 1858.

[Min68]   M. L. Minsky, editor. *Semantic Information Processing*. MIT Press, Cambridge, MA, 1968.

[Mit82]   T. M. Mitchell. Generalization as search. *Artificial Intelligence*, 18:203–226, 1982.

[MKS92]   S. Muggleton, R. D. King, and M. J. E. Sternberg. Protein sec-
           ondary structure prediction using logic-based machine learning.
           Protein Engineering, 5:647–658, 1992.

[MM82]   A. Martelli and U. Montanari. An efficient unification algo-
           rithm. *ACM Transactions on Programming Languages and Sys-
           tems*, 4(2):258–282, 1982.

[MODS96]   F. Mizoguchi, H. Ohwada, M. Daidoji, and S. Shirato. Learning
           rules that classify ocular fundus images for glaucoma diagnosis.
           In [Sto96], pages 191–204.

[Moo96]   R. J. Mooney. Inductive logic programming for natural language
           processing. In [Sto96], pages 205–224.

[Mor89]   K. Morik, editor. *Proceedings of the 4th European Working Ses-
           sions on Learning (EWSL-89)*. Pitman, London, 1989.

[MP92]   J. Marcinkowski and L. Pacholski. Undecidability of the Horn-
           clause implication problem. In *Proceedings of the 33rd Annual
           IEEE Symposium on Foundations of Computer Science*, pages
           354–362. Pittsburgh, PA, 1992.

[MP94a]   S. Muggleton and C. D. Page. A learnability model for universal
           representations. In [Wro94], pages 139–160.

[MP94b]   S. Muggleton and C. D. Page. Self-saturation of definite clauses.
           In [Wro94], pages 161–174.

[MR72]   E. Minicozzi and R. Reiter. A note on linear resolution strategies
           in consequence-finding. *Artificial Intelligence*, 3:175–180, 1972.

[MSP96]   S. Muggleton, A. Srinivasan, and D. Page. An initial experiment
           into stereochemistry-based drug design using ILP. In [Sto96],
           pages 245–261.

[Mug87]   S. Muggleton. Duce, an oracle based approach to constructive
           induction. In J. McDermott, editor, *Proceedings of the 10th In-
           ternational Joint Conference on Artificial Intelligence (IJCAI-
           87)*, pages 287–292. Morgan Kaufmann, Los Altos, CA, 1987.

[Mug90]   S. Muggleton. Inductive logic programming. In S. Arikawa,
           S. Goto, S. Ohsuga, and T. Yokomori, editors, *Proceedings of
           the 1st International Workshop on Algorithmic Learning Theory
           (ALT-90)*, pages 42–62. Ohmsha, Tokyo, 1990.

[Mug91a]   S. Muggleton. Inductive logic programming. *New Generation
           Computing*, 8(4):295–318, 1991.

[Mug91b]   S. Muggleton. Inverting the resolution principle. *Machine Intelligence*, 12, 1991.

[Mug91c]   S. Muggleton, editor. *Proceedings of the 1st International Workshop on Inductive Logic Programming (ILP-91)*. Viana de Castelo, Portugal, 1991.

[Mug92a]   S. Muggleton, editor. *Inductive Logic Programming*, Vol. 38 of *APIC Series*. Academic Press, London, 1992.

[Mug92b]   S. Muggleton. Inductive logic programming. In [Mug92a], pages 3–27.

[Mug92c]   S. Muggleton. Inverting implication. In S. Muggleton and K. Furukawa, editors, *Proceedings of the 2nd International Workshop on Inductive Logic Programming (ILP-92)*. Tokyo, 1992. ICOT Research Center. ICOT Technical Memorandum TM–1182.

[Mug93]   S. Muggleton, editor. *Proceedings of the 3rd International Workshop on Inductive Logic Programming (ILP-93)*. Ljubljana, 1993. Jožef Stefan Institute. Technical Report IJS–DP–6706.

[Mug94]   S. Muggleton. Bayesian inductive logic programming. In M. Warmuth, editor, *Proceedings of the 7th Annual ACM Conference on Computational Learning Theory (COLT-94)*, pages 3–11. ACM Press, 1994.

[Mug95]   S. Muggleton. Inverse entailment and Progol. *New Generation Computing*, 13:245–286, 1995.

[Mug96a]   S. Muggleton. Learning from positive data. In [Sto96], pages 225–244.

[Mug96b]   S. Muggleton. Stochastic logic programs. In [DR96], pages 254–264.

[MWKE93]   K. Morik, S. Wrobel, J-U. Kietz, and W. Emde. *Knowledge Acquisition and Machine Learning: Theory, Methods and Applications*. Academic Press, London, 1993.

[Nat91]   B. K. Natarajan. *Machine Learning: A Theoretical Approach*. Morgan Kaufmann, San Mateo, CA, 1991.

[NF91]   S-H. Nienhuys-Cheng and P. Flach. Consistent term mappings, term partitions and inverse resolution. In [Kod91], pages 361–374.

[Nib88]   T. Niblett. A study of generalisation in logic programs. In
            D. Sleeman, editor, *Proceedings of the 3rd European Working
            Sessions on Learning (EWSL-88)*, pages 131–138. Pitman, Lon-
            don, 1988.

[Nib93]   T. Niblett. A note on refinement operators. In [Bra93], pages
            329–335.

[NLT93]   S-H. Nienhuys-Cheng, P. van der Laag, and L. van der Torre.
            Constructing refinement operators by deconstructing logical im-
            plication. In [Tor93], pages 178–189.

[NP93]   S-H. Nienhuys-Cheng and M. Polman. Complexity dimensions
            and learnability. In [Bra93], pages 348–353.

[NP94]   S-H. Nienhuys-Cheng and M. Polman. Sample PAC-learnability
            in model inference. In [BD94], pages 217–230.

[NRA⁺96]   C. Nédellec, C. Rouveirol, H. Adé, F. Bergadano, and
            B. Tausend. Declarative bias in ILP. In [DR96], pages 82–103.

[NW95]   S-H. Nienhuys-Cheng and R. de Wolf. The equivalence of the
            subsumption theorem and the refutation-completeness for un-
            constrained resolution. In K. Kanchanasut and J-J. Lévy, ed-
            itors, *Proceedings of the Asean Computer Science Conference
            (ACSC-95)*, Vol. 1023 of *Lecture Notes in Computer Science*,
            pages 269–285. Springer-Verlag, Berlin, 1995.

[NW96a]   S-H. Nienhuys-Cheng and R. de Wolf. A complete method for
            program specialization based on unfolding. In [Wah96], pages
            438–442.

[NW96b]   S-H. Nienhuys-Cheng and R. de Wolf. Least generalizations and
            greatest specializations of sets of clauses. *Journal of Artificial
            Intelligence Research*, 4:341–363, 1996.

[NW96c]   S-H. Nienhuys-Cheng and R. de Wolf. Least generalizations un-
            der implication. In [Sto96], pages 262–275.

[NW96d]   S-H. Nienhuys-Cheng and R. de Wolf. The subsumption theorem
            in inductive logic programming: Facts and fallacies. In [DR96],
            pages 265–276.

[Pei58]   C. S. Peirce. *Collected Papers*. Harvard University Press, Cam-
            bridge, MA, 1958. Edited by C. Harstshorne and P. Weiss. Vol-
            umes I–VII.

[PF92]   C. D. Page and A. M. Frisch. Generalization and learnability.
            A study of constrained atoms. In [Mug92a], pages 29–61.

BIBLIOGRAPHY 385

[Plo70]   G. D. Plotkin. A note on inductive generalization. *Machine Intelligence*, 5:153–163, 1970.

[Plo71a]   G. D. Plotkin. *Automatic Methods of Inductive Inference*. PhD thesis, Edinburgh University, 1971.

[Plo71b]   G. D. Plotkin. A further note on inductive generalization. *Machine Intelligence*, 6:101–124, 1971.

[Pop59]   K. R. Popper. *The Logic of Scientific Discovery*. Hutchinson, London, 1959.

[PP94]   A. Pettorossi and M. Proietti. Transformation of logic programs: Foundations and techniques. *Journal of Logic Programming*, 19/20:261–320, 1994.

[PW78]   M. S. Paterson and M. N. Wegman. Linear unification. *Journal of Computer and Systems Sciences*, 16(2):158–167, 1978.

[QC93]   J. R. Quinlan and R. M. Cameron-Jones. Foil: A midterm report. In [Bra93], pages 3–20.

[Qui86]   J. R. Quinlan. Induction of decision trees. *Machine Learning*, 1(1):81–106, 1986.

[Qui90]   J. R. Quinlan. Learning logical definitions from relations. *Machine Learning*, 5(3):239–266, 1990.

[Qui93]   J. R. Quinlan. *C4.5: Programs for Machine Learning*. Morgan Kaufmann, San Mateo, CA, 1993.

[Rei49]   H. Reichenbach. *The Theory of Probability*. University of California Press, Berkeley, 1949.

[Rei78]   R. Reiter. On closed world data bases. In [GM78], pages 55–76.

[Rey70]   J. C. Reynolds. Transformational systems and the algebraic structure of atomic formulas. *Machine Intelligence*, 5:135–151, 1970.

[Rie96a]   A. Rieger. MP: An efficient method for calculating the minimum Herbrand model of chain datalog programs. In [Wah96], pages 385–389.

[Rie96b]   A. Rieger. Restructuring chain datalog programs. In [Sto96], pages 292–311.

[Ris78]   J. Rissanen. Modeling by shortest data description. *Automatica*, 14:465 471 1978.

[RN95]   S. J. Russell and P. Norvig. *Artificial Intelligence: A Modern Approach.* Prentice-Hall, Englewood Cliffs, NJ, 1995.

[Rob65]   J. A. Robinson. A machine oriented logic based on the resolution principle. *Journal of the ACM*, 12(1):23–41, 1965.

[Rou92]   C. Rouveirol. Extensions of inversion of resolution applied to theory completion. In [Mug92a], pages 63–92.

[Rou94]   C. Rouveirol. Flattening and saturation: Two representation changes for generalization. *Machine Learning*, 14:219–232, 1994.

[RP89]   C. Rouveirol and J-F. Puget. A simple and general solution for inverting resolution. In [Mor89], pages 201–210.

[RP90]   C. Rouveirol and J-F. Puget. Beyond inversion of resolution. In B. Porter and R. Mooney, editors, *Proceedings of the 7th International Conference on Machine Learning (ICML-90)*, pages 122–130. Morgan Kaufmann, San Mateo, CA, 1990.

[Rus48]   B. Russell. *Human Knowledge: It's Scope and Limits.* George Allen and Unwin, London, 1948.

[Rus80]   B. Russell. *The Problems of Philosophy.* Oxford University Press, Oxford, 1980. First published in 1912.

[SA93]   T. Sato and S. Akiba. Inductive resolution. In K. P. Jantke et al., editors, *Proceedings of the 4th International Workshop on Algorithmic Learning Theory (ALT-93)*, Vol. 744 of *Lecture Notes in Artificial Intelligence*, pages 101–110. Springer-Verlag, Berlin, 1993.

[SADB92]   G. Sablon, H. Adé, L. De Raedt, and M. Bruynooghe. Some thoughts on inverse resolution. In [Mug92a], pages 409–422.

[Sam81]   C. A. Sammut. *Learning Concepts by Performing Experiments.* PhD thesis, University of New South Wales, 1981.

[Sam93]   C. A. Sammut. The origins of inductive logic programming: A prehistoric tale. In [Mug93], pages 127–147.

[SB86]   C. A. Sammut and R. B. Banerji. Learning concepts by asking questions. In R. S. Michalski, J. G. Carbonell, and T. M. Mitchell, editors, *Machine Learning: An Artificial Intelligence Approach*, Vol. 2, pages 167–192. Morgan Kaufmann, Los Altos, CA, 1986.

[SCL69]   J. R. Slagle, C. L. Chang, and R. C. T. Lee. Completeness the-
            orems for semantic resolution in consequence-finding. In D. E.
            Walker and L. M. Norton, editors, *Proceedings of the 1st Inter-
            national Joint Conference on Artificial Intelligence (IJCAI-69)*,
            pages 281–285. Morgan Kaufmann, Los Altos, CA, 1969.

[Sha81a]   E. Y. Shapiro. An algorithm that infers theories from facts.
            In A. Drinan, editor, *Proceedings of the 7th International Joint
            Conference on Artificial Intelligence (IJCAI-81)*, pages 446–451.
            Morgan Kaufmann, Los Altos, CA, 1981.

[Sha81b]   E. Y. Shapiro. Inductive inference of theories from facts. Re-
            search Report 192, Yale University, 1981. Reprinted in [LP91],
            pages 199–254.

[Sha83]   E. Y. Shapiro. *Algorithmic Program Debugging*. MIT Press,
            Cambridge, MA, 1983.

[She94]   J. C. Shepherdson. The role of standardising apart in logic pro-
            gramming. *Theoretical Computer Science*, 129:143–166, 1994.

[SK96]   A. Srinivasan and R. D. King. Feature construction with in-
            ductive logic programming: A study of quantitative predictions
            of biological activity aided by structural attributes. In [Sto96],
            pages 352–367.

[Sla67]   J. R. Slagle. Automatic theorem proving with renamable and
            semantic resolution. *Journal of the ACM*, 14(4):687–697, 1967.

[Slo95]   R. H. Sloan. Four types of noise in PAC learning. *Information
            Processing Letters*, 54:157–162, 1995.

[SMB94]   A. Srinivasan, S. Muggleton, and M. Bain. The justification
            of logical theories based on data compression. *Machine Intelli-
            gence*, 13:87–123, 1994.

[SMKS94]   A. Srinivasan, S. Muggleton, R. D. King, and M. J. E. Sternberg.
            Mutagenesis: ILP experiments in a non-determinate biological
            domain. In [Wro94], pages 217–232.

[SMSK96]   A. Srinivasan, S. Muggleton, M. J. E. Sternberg, and R. D. King.
            Theories for mutagenicity: A study in first-order and feature-
            based induction. *Artificial Intelligence*, 85:277–300, 1996.

[Som95]   E. Sommer. FENDER: An approach to theory restructuring. In
            [LW95], pages 356–359.

[SR96]   M. Sebag and C. Rouveirol. Constraint inductive logic program-
            ming. In [DR96], pages 277–294.

[SS88]   M. Schmidt-Schauss. Implication of clauses is undecidable. *Theoretical Computer Science*, 59:287–296, 1988.

[SS94]   L. Sterling and E. Shapiro. *The Art of Prolog: Advanced Programming Techniques*. MIT Press, Cambridge, MA, second edition, 1994.

[Stä90]   R. F. Stärk. A direct proof for the completeness of SLD-resolution. In E. Börger, H. Kleine Büning, and M. M. Richter, editors, *Computer Science Logic 89*, Vol. 440 of *Lecture Notes in Computer Science*, pages 382–383. Springer-Verlag, Berlin, 1990.

[Sta94]   I. Stahl. On the utility of predicate invention in inductive logic programming. In [BD94], pages 272–286.

[Sta95]   I. Stahl. The efficiency of predicate invention in ILP. In [DR95], pages 231–246.

[Sta96a]   I. Stahl. Compression measures in ILP. In [DR96], pages 295–307.

[Sta96b]   I. Stahl. Predicate invention in inductive logic programming. In [DR96], pages 34–47.

[Sto96]   Stockholm University/Royal Institute of Technology, Department of Computer and Systems Sciences. *Proceedings of the 6th International Workshop on Inductive Logic Programming (ILP-96)*, Report Series No. 96–019. 1996.

[Tar36]   A. Tarski. Der Wahrheitsbegriff in den formalisierten Sprachen. *Studia Philosophica*, pages 261–405, 1936. English translation in [Tar56].

[Tar56]   A. Tarski. *Logic, Semantics, Metamathematics. Papers from 1923 to 1938*. Oxford University Press, New York, 1956.

[Tay93]   K. Taylor. Inverse resolution of normal clauses. In [Mug93], pages 165–177.

[Tor93]   P. Torasso, editor. *Proceedings of the 3rd Conference of the Italian Association for Artificial Intelligence (AI*IA-93)*, Vol. 728 of *Lecture Notes in Artificial Intelligence*. Springer-Verlag, Berlin, 1993.

[TS84]   H. Tamaki and T. Sato. Unfold/fold transformation of logic programs. In S-Å. Tärnlund, editor, *Proceedings of the 2nd International Logic Programming Conference*, pages 127–138. Uppsala University, Uppsala, 1984.

[Tur36]   A. M. Turing. On computable numbers, with an application to the Entscheidungproblem. In *Proceedings of the London Mathematical Society*, Vol. 42, pages 230–265. 1936. Correction, ibidem (vol. 43), pages 544–546.

[UB94]   T. Urbančič and I. Bratko. Reconstructing human skill with machine learning. In A. G. Cohn, editor, *Proceedings of the 11th European Conference on Artificial Intelligence (ECAI-94)*, pages 498–502. Wiley, Chichester, 1994.

[UM82]   P. Utgoff and T. M. Mitchell. Acquisition of appropriate bias for inductive concept learning. In *Proceedings of the National Conference on Artificial Intelligence*, pages 414–417. Morgan Kaufmann, Los Altos, CA, 1982.

[Val84]   L. G. Valiant. A theory of the learnable. *Communications of the ACM*, 27(11):1134–1142, 1984.

[Val85]   L. G. Valiant. Learning disjunctions of conjunctions. In *Proceedings of the 9th International Joint Conference on Artificial Intelligence (IJCAI-85)*, pages 560–566. Morgan Kaufmann, 1985.

[VC71]   V. N. Vapnik and A. Y. Chervonenkis. On the uniform convergence of relative frequencies of events to their probabilities. *Theory of Probability and its Applications*, 16(2):264–280, 1971.

[Ver75]   S. Vere. Induction of concepts in the predicate calculus. In *Proceedings of the 4th International Joint Conference on Artificial Intelligence (IJCAI-75)*, pages 351–356. Morgan Kaufmann, Los Altos, CA, 1975.

[Ver77]   S. Vere. Induction of relational productions in the presence of background information. In *Proceedings of the 5th International Joint Conference on Artificial Intelligence (IJCAI-77)*. Morgan Kaufmann, Los Altos, CA, 1977.

[VL93]   W. Van Laer. Inductief afleiden van logische regels. Master's thesis, Katholieke Universiteit Leuven, 1993. In Dutch.

[Wah96]   W. Wahlster, editor. *Proceedings of the 12th European Conference on Artificial Intelligence (ECAI-96)*. Wiley, Chichester, 1996.

[Wir89]   R. Wirth. Completing logic programs by inverse resolution. In [Mor89], pages 239–250.

[WR27]   A. N. Whitehead and B. Russell. *Principia Mathematica*. Cambridge University Press, Cambridge, UK, 1927. First published in 1910–1913.

[Wro93]   S. Wrobel. On the proper definition of minimality in specialization and theory revision. In [Bra93], pages 65–82.

[Wro94]   S. Wrobel, editor. *Proceedings of the 4th International Workshop on Inductive Logic Programming (ILP-94)*, Vol. 237 of *GMD-Studien*. Bad Honnef/Bonn, 1994. Gesellschaft für Mathematik und Datenverarbeitung.

[Yam95]   A. Yamamoto. Learning logic programs using definite equality theories as background knowledge. *IEICE Transactions on Information & Systems*, E78-D(5):539–544, 1995.

[Yam96]   A. Yamamoto. Improving theories for inductive logic programming systems with ground reduced programs. Forschungsbericht AIDA-96-19, Technische Hochschule Darmstadt, 1996.

Author Index

Subject Index

Lecture Notes in Artificial Intelligence (LNAI)

Lecture Notes in Computer Science